INDUSTRIAL RELATIONS

INDUSTRIAL RELATIONS

THEORY AND PRACTICE

Second Edition

EDITED BY
PAUL EDWARDS

Blackwell
Publishing

350 Main Street, Malden, MA 02148-5020, USA
108 Cowley Road, Oxford OX4 1JF, UK
550 Swanston Street, Carlton, Victoria 3053, Australia

First edition published 1995
Reprinted 1996 (twice), 1998, 1999, 2001
Second edition published 2003
Reprinted 2004

Library of Congress Cataloging-in-Publication Data

Industrial relations : theory and practice / edited by Paul Edwards. —
2nd ed.
    p. cm.
Includes bibliographical references and index.
    ISBN 0–631–22257–X (hbk : alk. paper)—ISBN 0–631–22258–8 (pbk :
alk. paper)
    1. Industrial relations—Great Britain. I. Edwards, P. K. (Paul K.)
    HD8391 .I478 2003
    331′.0941—dc21

                  2002009533

A catalogue record for this title is available from the British Library.

Set in 10/12pt Meridien
by Graphicraft Ltd, Hong Kong
Printed and bound in the United Kingdom
by MPG Books, Bodmin, Cornwall

For further information on
Blackwell Publishing, visit our website:
http://www.blackwellpublishing.com

CONTENTS

FIGURES AND TABLES

Figures

Tables

COMMON ABBREVIATIONS

ACAS	Advisory, Conciliation and Arbitration Service
CAC	Central Arbitration Committee
CBI	Confederation of British Industry
DE	Department of Employment
DfES	Department for Education and Skills (formerly the Department for Education and Employment)
DoH	Department of Health
Donovan Commission	Royal Commission on Trade Unions and Employers' Associations, chaired by Lord Donovan, 1965–8
DTI	Department of Trade and Industry
ECJ	European Court of Justice
EWC	European Works Councils
HRM	Human resource management
HSC	Health and Safety Commission
IIP	Investors in People
ILO	International Labour Organization
NBPI	National Board for Prices and Incomes
NEDC	National Economic Development Council
NES	New Earnings Survey
NHS	National Health Service
NMW	National Minimum Wage
NVQ	National Vocational Qualification
SME	Small and Medium-Sized Enterprises
SNB	Special Negotiating Body
TUC	Trades Union Congress
WERS	Workplace Employment Relations Survey (1998)

CONTRIBUTORS

Stephen Bach is Senior Lecturer at the Management Centre, King's College, London.

William Brown is the Master of Darwin College and Professor of Industrial Relations at Cambridge University. He is a member of the Council of ACAS and of the Low Pay Commission and Chair of the Disputes Committee for Fire Brigades.

Trevor Colling is Senior Research Fellow, Department of Human Resource Management, de Montfort University, and an Associate Fellow of the Industrial Relations Research Unit, University of Warwick.

Colin Crouch is Chairman of the Department of Social and Political Sciences and Professor of Sociology at the European University Institute, Florence. He is External Scientific Member of the Max Planck Institute for Social Research, Cologne.

Linda Dickens is Professor of Industrial Relations in the Industrial Relations Research Unit at Warwick Business School, University of Warwick. She is an ACAS mediator and arbitrator, a Deputy Chair of the Central Arbitration Committee, and an editor of the *British Journal of Industrial Relations*.

Paul Edwards is Professor of Industrial Relations at Warwick Business School, University of Warwick. He is a former Director of the Industrial Relations Research Unit and former editor of *Work, Employment and Society*.

Anthony Ferner is Professor of International Human Resource Management in the Department of HRM, Leicester Business School, de Montfort University, and an Associate Fellow of the Industrial Relations Research Unit, University of Warwick.

John F. Geary is Lecturer in Industrial Relations at the Michael Smurfit Graduate School of Business, University College Dublin and an Associate Fellow of the

Industrial Relations Research Unit, University of Warwick. He was Jean Monnet Fellow at the European University Institute, Florence (2001–2).

Mark Hall is Principal Research Fellow in the Industrial Relations Research Unit at the Warwick Business School, University of Warwick. He co-edits the *European Works Councils Bulletin* and manages the UK input to the European Industrial Relations Observatory.

Richard Hyman is Professor of Industrial Relations at the London School of Economics and editor of the *European Journal of Industrial Relations.*

Ewart Keep is Deputy Director of the ESRC Centre for Skills, Knowledge and Organizational Performance in Warwick Business School, University of Warwick.

Ian Kessler is Fellow in Human Resource Management at Templeton College and Lecturer in Management Studies at the Said Business School, University of Oxford.

Sonia Liff is a Reader in Industrial Relations and Organizational Behaviour in the Industrial Relations Research Unit at Warwick Business School, University of Warwick. She is an associate editor of the journal *Gender, Work and Organization.*

Paul Marginson is Professor of Industrial Relations at Warwick Business School, University of Warwick, and Director of the Industrial Relations Research Unit.

Peter Nolan is the Montague Burton Professor of Industrial Relations, University of Leeds, and Director of the ESRC Future of Work Programme.

Kathy O'Donnell is Senior Lecturer in Economics, University of Leeds.

John Purcell is Professor of Human Resource Management at the University of Bath. He is editor of the *Human Resource Management Journal* and a Deputy Chairman of the Central Arbitration Committee.

Helen Rainbird is Professor of Industrial Relations at University College Northampton and an Associate Fellow of the Industrial Relations Research Unit, University of Warwick.

Jill Rubery is Professor of Comparative Employment Systems at the Manchester School of Management, University of Manchester Institute of Science and Technology. She is a member of the ACAS Board of Arbitrators.

Richard Scase is Professor of Sociology at the University of Kent at Canterbury and a member of the editorial boards of the *International Small Business Journal* and the *International Journal of Human Resource Management.*

Keith Sisson is Emeritus Professor of Industrial Relations at the University of Warwick. He is a former Director of the Industrial Relations Research Unit and was founding editor of the *Human Resource Management Journal.*

Gary Slater is Lecturer in Economics, Nottingham Trent University.

Michael Terry is Professor of Industrial Relations in the Industrial Relations Research Unit at Warwick Business School, University of Warwick.

Jeremy Waddington is Reader in International Human Resource Management at the Manchester School of Management, University of Manchester Institute of Science and Technology, and is a Project Co-ordinator for the European Trade Union Institute, Brussels. He is on the editorial board of *Transfer*.

Janet Walsh is Reader in Human Resource Management, School of Management, Royal Holloway, University of London.

David Winchester is former Senior Lecturer in the Industrial Relations Research Unit at Warwick Business School, University of Warwick and is a Visiting Lecturer at the University of the West of England.

PREFACE

This is the second edition of a book published in 1995, which was itself the descendant of the volume *Industrial Relations in Britain*, edited by George Bain and published in 1983. The present volume aims to continue the style of its predecessors, notably, in the words of the preface to the 1995 edition, through 'comprehensiveness and an authoritative blend of description and analysis'. Much of the structure of the book has been retained, though every chapter has been updated and revised, in some cases very extensively so that the text is in effect wholly new. The main changes to the book since 1995 are as follows. First, the effects of international developments are stronger than they were in 1995. The implications for the development of industrial relations in the UK run through many chapters, and there is one wholly new chapter, on multinationals and industrial relations innovation. Second, the 'individualization' of employment relations has been a developing theme. It is considered in several revised chapters, and there is a new chapter on the management of the 'individualized' employment relationship. Related to the new contours of industrial relations, there is no longer a need for a separate chapter on strikes and collective industrial action, which are covered in chapter 9. Third, 'outcomes' for managements and workers of industrial relations arrangements have been receiving increased attention. The former chapter on industrial relations and productivity has accordingly been rewritten, and placed at the end, drawing together the implications of many of the foregoing chapters. A brief set of concluding comments aims to highlight current issues and possible lines of development.

The substantially rewritten chapter 1 tries to analyse the changing nature of industrial relations as a field of enquiry and to spell out its links to terms such as human resource management. There is no need to repeat that discussion here, though it is worth highlighting that, as indicated by the quality of the main journals, the growing membership and activity of the British Universities Industrial Relations Association, and the number of important research books on employment relations which have appeared in the past five years, the subject is in a strong condition.

Like its predecessors, this is largely a Warwick-based volume. Since 1995, four contributors (Stephen Bach, Anthony Ferner, Richard Hyman and Jeremy Waddington) have moved from Warwick to senior positions elsewhere. I am very grateful for their continued involvement in this book. I am indeed indebted to all the contributors. Producing this book has taken much longer than its predecessor, which is a reflection of the growing demands on academic time. The contributors have, however, avoided the temptation to take short cuts, and have written substantial scholarly essays.

Two other changes of personnel deserve special mention. First, David Winchester retired, officially at least, in 2001 after eight years at the London School of Economics and then 23 years at Warwick. A text such as this is an appropriate place to mark David's contribution to the teaching of industrial relations. He is marked above all by his enormous interest in and dedication to students. He has inspired generations of them through his care and commitment. In this spirit, he provided some particularly helpful comments on chapter 1 of this book.

Second, Keith Sisson retired in 1998 from his position as director of the Industrial Relations Research Unit. He led IRRU for 13 years with a clear vision, a fundamental commitment to scholarly integrity, and a dedication to bringing the best out of his colleagues. I am delighted that he continues to play an active part in IRRU's continuing programme of research and teaching (which included some helpful suggestions on the concluding comments of this book).

Paul Edwards

1

THE EMPLOYMENT RELATIONSHIP AND THE FIELD OF INDUSTRIAL RELATIONS

PAUL EDWARDS

The term 'industrial relations' (IR) came into common use in Britain and North America during the 1920s. It has been joined by personnel management (PM) and, since the 1980s, human resource management (HRM). All three denote a practical activity (the management of people) and an area of academic enquiry. Texts in all three fields commonly take as their starting point the corporate assertion that 'people are our most important asset': if this is indeed so, there is little further need to justify a text. Yet we need first to explain what lies behind this apparent axiom. It is then important to highlight some of the key current issues about the conduct of work in modern Britain. We can then consider how IR as an academic approach addresses these issues and the distinction between it and the other two fields of enquiry. Finally, the structure of the book is explained.

First, some basic explanation. 'Industry' is sometimes equated with manufacturing, as in contrasts between industry and services. 'Industrial relations' has in principle never been so restricted. In practice, however, attention until recently often focused on certain parts of the economy. These in fact embraced more than manufacturing to include the public sector for example, but there was neglect of small firms and large parts of the private service sector. Whether or not there were good reasons for this neglect (and the case is at least arguable), the situation has changed, and recent research has addressed growing areas of the economy such as call centres. To avoid confusion some writers prefer the term 'employment relations', and if we were starting from scratch this might be the best label; yet the term 'industrial relations' has become sufficiently embedded that it is retained here to cover relations between manager and worker in all spheres of economic activity. The focus is employment: all forms of economic activity in which an employee works under the authority of an employer and receives a wage in return for his or her labour. Industrial relations thus excludes domestic labour and also the self-employed and professionals who work on their own account: the contractual relations between a self-employed plumber and his customers are not 'industrial relations', but the relations between a plumbing firm and its employees are. In the UK self-employment comprises about 12 per cent of people in employment (see table 1.1, below). The bulk of the working population is thus in an employment relationship, with the great majority of them, of course, being employees rather than employers.

Some writers define IR no more exactly than the study of all forms of the employment relationship. This is not sufficiently precise to distinguish it from the economics or sociology of work. More importantly, there are some distinct emphases in an IR approach which give it a specific value in explaining the world of work. These emphases are discussed below. There has been much debate over the years as to whether the emphases and analytical preferences of IR make it a discipline, as distinct from a field of study. The view taken in this chapter (which is not necessarily shared by other chapters) is that IR is a field of study and not a distinct discipline. Indeed, one of its strengths is its willingness to draw from different disciplines so that people who specialize in the field have developed an analytical approach which is more than the sum total of the application of individual disciplines. Even if this view is accepted, there are competing views as to the strengths and weaknesses of the approach, and whether it has responded adequately to the changing nature of work. Some of these issues are addressed below.

Why is paid employment important? It is important *to the employee* most obviously as a source of income. Note that it is not the case that work outside employment is an easy alternative: at one time, it was argued by some that a combination of unemployment, self-provisioning and work in the informal economy provided an alternative to the formal economy, but research found that such work tends to be additional rather than an alternative to formal employment. Work is also important to the employee as a means of identity. 'What do you do for a living?' is a standard query to locate a new acquaintance. And what goes on within the employment relationship is crucial, not only in terms of the pay that is earned but also the conditions under which it is earned: the degree of autonomy the employee is granted, the safety of the work environment, the opportunity for training and development, and so on.

For the employer the work relationship is crucial in two different senses. First, it is commonly argued that capital and technologies are increasingly readily available, so that a firm's competitive position depends on the skills and knowledge of its workers. Some analytical grounding for this argument comes from the resource-based view of the firm which developed from debates on strategic management. This view sees the firm as a bundle of assets and argues that it is the configuration of these assets, rather than positioning in relation to an external market, which is central to competitive advantage (Wernerfeld 1984; see further chapter 7). Not surprisingly, HRM and IR writers have latched on to this idea, arguing that 'distinctive human resources' are the core resource (Cappelli and Crocker-Hefter 1996). Second, and fundamentally, these 'human resources'

Table 1.1   Employment, unemployment and earnings, UK

Population by employment status (thousands)

	Total	Economically active	In employment	Unemployed (ILO definition)	Economically inactive
Males aged 16–64					
1990	18,312	16,175	15,027	1,148	2,136
2000	19,020	16,034	15,049	984	2,987
Females aged 16–59					
1990	16,706	11,912	11,122	790	4,794
2000	17,292	12,534	11,916	618	4,758

Distribution of employed population (thousands)

	Employees		Self-employed	
	Full-time	Part-time	Full-time	Part-time
All males				
1992	10,971	658	2,260	182
2000	11,917	1,064	2,029	272
All females				
1992	5,963	4,491	420	366
2000	6,489	5,032	427	423

Percentage of age group in employment in 2000

	Age 18–24	25–34	35–49	50–64 (M) / 50–59 (F)	65+ (M) / 60+ (F)
Males	71.3	88.9	88.5	68.8	7.6
Females	64.1	71.7	74.9	63.9	8.2

Percentage of all unemployed who were out of work > 12 months in 2000, by age (ILO definitions)

	Age 18–24	25–49	50+
Males	20.4	39.3	46.2
Females	10.3	21.2	31.6

Hourly earnings in £ (all full-time employees) and prices

	Earnings			RPI
	All	Male	Female	(1987 = 100)
1990	6.37	6.88	5.31	126.1
2000	10.32	11.00	9.02	170.3

Figures are for spring each year and seasonally adjusted. Earnings data are derived from the New Earnings Survey.

Source: *Labour Market Trends* (March 2001).

are different from other resources because they cannot be separated from the people in whom they exist. The employment relationship is about organizing human resources in the light of the productive aims of the firm but also the aims of employees. It is necessarily open-ended, uncertain, and, as argued below, a blend of inherently *contradictory* principles concerning control and consent.

Finally, paid employment is important *to society* for what it expects in terms of 'inputs' and produces as 'outputs'. Inputs include how much labour is demanded (with obvious implications if demand is less than supply, resulting in unemployment) and what types of labour are sought (influencing, for example, the kinds of skills which 'society' provides through the education system). If employment is structured on gender lines, this will have major consequences for the domestic division of labour and the roles of men and women in society; the traditional image of the male breadwinner applied not only to paid employment but also had implications for the ability of women to engage in politics, the arts, and sport. 'Outputs' include not only goods and services but also structures of advantage and disadvantage. These are properly called structures because they are established features of society which are hard to change, for example differences of pay between occupations and between men and women.

Issues in the Regulation of Work

If work is important, how many people are in an employment relationship and how many are not, and what has been happening to work relationships? The exercise in box 1.1 may be helpful.

Alongside such trends have been developments in the management of work which are analysed in detail in this book. They include a decline in traditional ways in which people represent their views to their employers (termed 'indirect' or 'representational' participation), which in Britain means through a trade union. Associated with a decline of unions has been a reduction in the percentage of employees who are covered by collective bargaining. Collective bargaining is a key focus in IR (the term having been coined by two of the UK founders of the subject, Sidney and Beatrice Webb, at the end of the nineteenth century). It means the negotiation of pay and other conditions of employment between an employer (or a group of employers) and a trade union acting for its members (see chapter 8). There has also been a growth in 'direct' participation, that is involvement not through a representative structure but through work-based activity; examples are problem-solving groups and teamworking (see chapters 7 and 13). The legal framework has also changed rapidly, as discussed in chapters 5 and 6. Some of these developments reflect developments within Britain itself, some stem from Europe, some from the specific influence of multinational companies, and some from broader trends in the world economy.

These developments in the management of work are highly important in themselves, in shaping how much autonomy workers have in their work and their ability to shape key decisions that affect them. But what goes on within IR can have substantial effects on wider aspects of society. To take but one example,

Box 1.1   Labour market participation, pay, and inequality

Consider the population of working age. Official statistics distinguish between the economically active and the inactive. The former group is then divided into those currently employed and the unemployed. The employed can be divided according to status (employee or self-employed), whether the work is full- or part-time, and so on. Table 1.1 provides some basic figures on these categories, together with information on unemployment and earnings. Table 1.2 gives abbreviated data on the distribution of employment by sector. What are the main patterns that can be observed? It may also be useful to consider what such terms as 'economically active' mean and how statistics on such things as unemployment and earnings are compiled.

There are several important features of work in Britain which need to be borne in mind in considering the implications of the figures. Details and further discussion can be found in Gregg and Wadsworth (1999).

- The number of 'economically inactive' people of working age has risen, particularly among the over-fifties. Early retirement is a common means for firms to shed labour. What might this say about the nature of jobs?
- Work has polarized across households: there are more families where all the adults work, and more where no one is in paid employment. What might this say about links between work and home? Regional differences in employment and unemployment rates are also substantial, as a glance at the relevant figures in *Labour Market Trends* will show. For example, in January 2001 unemployment (based on those claiming unemployment benefit, not the ILO definition used in table 1.1) was 6.6 per cent in the region of highest unemployment in the UK, the north-east of England, but within that region rates for localities ranged from 3.4 to 12.3 per cent. In the lowest unemployment region, the south-east, the average rate was 1.9 per cent, with localities varying between 0.5 and 7.4 per cent.
- If we look at households where someone is in work, the number of hours per week devoted to work has risen since about 1980. Work effort intensified over the same period, at first in manufacturing and then in services (Green 2001). Why might this be, and what does it say about workers' experience of work?
- Men's employment rates have fallen while women's have risen. But this latter rise is largely restricted to women with working partners; there is no change for single women or lone parents. The gender pay gap has narrowed, but it remains substantial, and has in fact widened for women working part-time. Why?
- Wage inequality has risen (as it has in other countries, though generally more slowly) to reach levels higher than during most of the twentieth century. Why?

chapter 8 shows that the decline of unions and collective bargaining explains some of the rise in wage inequality; as mentioned below, moreover, it appears that international differences in IR structures help to explain the size of the gender pay gap. It might be helpful to pause to consider what mechanisms might explain such links between processes and outcomes, and which of the other features in the bullet points in box 1.1 could be the result of trends in the handling of IR. IR thus has important implications for life beyond its own terrain.

What are the pressing current issues in employment? Three examples are given, partly for their substantive importance, but also to signal the critical view of them which is developing within IR.

Table 1.2   Distribution of employees by sector, UK (thousands)

	1990	2000
Mining, quarrying, electricity, gas and water	406	204
'Engineering'	1,544	1,258
All other manufacturing	3,334	2,705
All services	16,643	18,597
Wholesale and retail trade, repairs	3,741	4,126
Hotels and restaurants	1,207	1,395
Financial intermediation	1,055	992
Renting, research, computers etc	2,410	3,207
Health and social work	2,311	2,541

'Engineering' = machinery, electrical equipment plus transportation equipment.
Source: Summarized from data in *Labour Market Trends* (March 2001), which contains a more detailed breakdown.

The first concerns so-called 'high-commitment' or 'high-involvement' work systems. These are discussed in detail in chapter 13, but essentially embrace systems such as teamworking and are often linked to new managerial techniques such as Business Process Re-engineering. Some research in the UK and the US finds that these systems 'work' in that they produce improvements in efficiency and (though the evidence is much more controversial here) can be associated with benefits for workers too (see chapter 19). Yet it is also found that they exist only rarely; perhaps 2 per cent of UK workplaces conform to the high-commitment model. This situation is often seen as a paradox.

There is some value in posing the matter this way, but there are now some reasonably well-established resolutions of the paradox as posed. As will be seen in chapters 7 and 13 in particular, the benefits depend on certain conditions and they operate best only in the long term whereas their costs are significant and immediate. The structure of British firms tends to mean that the conditions are hard to secure and that the short-term considerations outweigh the long-run ones. Moreover, what is meant by 'working' requires more exploration: working in what ways and for whom? Other modes of organizing work, notably those based on low skills and low wages, can equally work for employers in producing acceptable profits; and, some commentators would argue, they are well suited to the British context (see chapter 15). And high-commitment systems will have their own tensions: they are a way of managing the contradictions of control and consent, not escaping from them.

A second pressing issue is the international context. Some writers deploy concepts such as globalization to capture new international competitive pressures. They are better seen as convenient labels rather than developed concepts, for issues immediately arise as to the novelty of the developments identified and what identifiable social forces are actually causing them. In the field of work, three interrelated forces are international competition, the role of multinational companies (MNCs), and European integration. Under the first, the British economy has become increasingly open, as indicated by a growth in imports and exports as a proportion of GDP and the use of explicit wage and cost comparisons by companies in the making of investment decisions (see chapters 3 and 7). A well-known UK example is the decision in early 2000 of the German firm BMW to sell the Rover car company, which it had acquired in 1994, blaming the value of the pound in relation to the euro and the difficulty of restructuring the Rover operations to attain satisfactory productivity levels. That the UK is not alone is illustrated by the case of Renault in Belgium, which in February 1997 announced without warning the closure of its Vilvoorde plant with the loss of 3,000 jobs.

This example also points to one role of the MNC. But, as discussed in chapter 4, there are other roles, notably the importing of forms of work organization, and it is often US MNCs which are in the lead here. Finally, European integration has effects through the impact of European labour law on Britain and through the wider processes of economic and monetary union (EMU). Under the first, European directives have had clear effects on matters as varied as the regulation of working time, consultation over redundancies and European Works Councils (requiring that certain large MNCs establish such councils for the purposes of information and consultation about their European operations). Under the second, unit wage costs are increasingly subject to comparison across Europe, while the implications spread outside the traded goods sector. Thus government finances are shaped by pressures on interest rates and the public sector borrowing requirement, which in turn has implications for the control of costs, including pay, in the public sector.

One aspect of internationalization which has recently come to the fore is whether British industrial relations are being Europeanized or Americanized.

- Europeanization means either or both of: the influence of European-level developments in Britain (either directly, for example the application of directives, or indirectly, for example where monetary union brings pressure for convergence in IR practice); and the development of a common model across Europe. Such a model often embraces ideas of 'social partnership'. As discussed in chapters 7, 9 and 10, these ideas are often imprecise and contested, but at their core is the notion of a common agenda between representatives of capital and labour.
- Americanization embraces the continuing decline of unions and the assertion of a market-driven model.

The former process is perhaps the more obvious in the light of European integration and the promulgation of a European social model claiming to combine flexibility with security and to promote employee participation without threatening efficiency (see Bach and Sisson 2000: 35). As Bach and Sisson stress, however, such a model is a prescription for what might be rather than an account of what exists, and several aspects of it are under challenge from international cost pressures. At the same time, the rapid growth of the American economy during the 1990s and the European interest in its ability to generate jobs indicate that the American model of weak trade unions and extensive flexibility is equally influential. It is not of course the case that these models are tightly integrated packages or that one can simply choose between them. Different features can be combined in different ways.

A third set of issues concerns 'outcomes' of a pattern of IR. The most discussed outcome, touched on above, is economic performance. Chapter 19 discusses the linkages between IR arrangements and performance. But other outcomes include the level and pattern of pay. As indicated above, one of the outstanding features of the British economy has been the rise in income inequality since 1980. A closely connected form of outcome is the pattern of gender inequality, as indexed by pay differentials and the degree to which women gain access to the most desirable occupations (see chapter 16). It has been shown across many advanced industrialized countries that various measures of equality and well-being, including the size of the pay gap between men and women and the degree of pay inequality between the top and bottom of the income distribution, are affected by the extent of collective bargaining (e.g. Whitehouse and Zetlin 1999). Given that collective bargaining has been in long-term decline in the UK, key issues are whether this decline is likely to be reversed, and if not what other arrangements might be put in place and what implications they have for economic welfare.

Analysing the Employment Relationship

Components of industrial relations

What has IR to say about how we might analyse such issues? The employment relationship has two parts, market relations and managerial relations (Flanders 1974). The former is the more obvious. It covers the price of labour, which embraces not only the basic wage but also hours of work, holidays and pension rights. In this respect, labour is like any other commodity, with a price which represents the total cost of enjoying its use. Yet labour differs from all other commodities in that it is enjoyed in use *and* is embodied in people. A machine in a factory is also enjoyed in use and for what it can produce. Yet how it is used is solely up to its owner. The 'owner' of labour, the employer, has to persuade the worker, that is, the person in whom the labour is embodied, to work. Managerial relations are the relationships that define how this process takes place: market relations set a price for a set number of hours of work, and managerial relations determine how much work is performed in that time, at what specific task or tasks, who has the right to define the tasks and change a particular mix of tasks and what penalties will be deployed for any failure to meet these obligations. A standard text thus defines IR as the 'study of the rules governing employment' (Clegg 1979: 1). The importance of this definition is developed below.

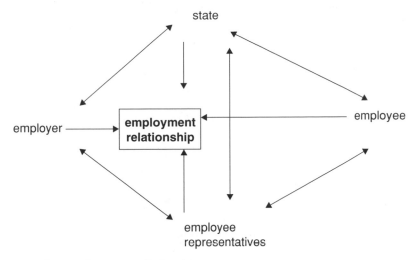

Figure 1.1   The employment relationship

The employment relationship is by definition a relationship between an employee and an employer. As shown in figure 1.1, this direct relationship may be mediated by the two other key institutions to IR, the trade union (or more rarely a non-union collectivity representing employees) and the state. A trade union in its most basic role represents a group of workers in a specified part of their relations with a single employer. A union's role can be measured in terms of density, extent, mobilization and scope.

- Density is the proportion of an identified constituency who are members of a union.
- The extent of a union's activity refers to the range of the constituency: a union can represent a small group of employees in one locality, or all the employees in an occupation, or all the employees of a given employer, or extend beyond an occupation or an employer.
- Mobilization – the degree to which unions identify common interests among their members, persuade the members as to what the interests are, and organize in pursuit of the interests – is important because, most obviously in countries such as France, a union may be capable of mobilizing more employees than its nominal members. By the same token, members will not necessarily follow a union's policy. Unions face issues of how far they represent members and of aggregating membership interests into a common policy.
- Scope is the degree to which the various aspects of the employment relationship are within the purview of the union: it may bargain only over wages and hours, or cover also working conditions, or extend further to issues including training, the classification of jobs and the system of workplace discipline.

Unions engage with employees through efforts to organize them and through mobilization around sets of demands. They engage with employers by taking part in collective bargaining. They may also engage with the state, for example in making demands for legislation or in engaging in more lasting forms of accommodation (such as 'corporatism' in the Nordic countries or a series of 'Accords' in Australia).

The state influences the employment relationship directly through laws on wages (e.g. minimum wages), working conditions (e.g. on hours of work) and many other issues, and through its role as the employer of public sector workers (see chapter 11). It also has a series of indirect influences. It has relationships with unions, either through laws on union government, or through bilateral arrangements (e.g. the UK 'social contract' of the 1970s in which unions promised to moderate wage demands in return for tax concessions), or through trilateral relationships also involving employers (corporatism). In addition to corporatism, the state may have bilateral relations with employers (e.g. various periods of incomes policy in France) and also shape employers' conduct through legally mandated collective bargaining. Finally, the state can play a critical role in the character of market and managerial relations. In Anglo-Saxon countries, the two have not been distinguished, and a collective agreement may cover seniority rules and discipline as well as wages and conditions. The sharpest contrast is Germany, where unions handle wages and conditions and have the right to strike on these matters but where legally mandated works councils deal with a range of other issues, including work organization and staffing and disciplinary questions, but do not have the right to strike. Many other countries have collective structures in addition to trade unions. As discussed in chapter 6, the issue of legally underpinned rights of information and consultation has emerged in the UK, and is likely to grow in significance.

Conflict, power and frames of reference

An understanding of the nature of workplace rules can be developed by considering three perspectives on rules, usually termed 'frames of reference'. The origin of the debate on frames of reference was a distinction made by Fox (1966) between unitary and pluralist approaches.

- The *unitary view* is that there is an identity of interest between employer and employee. Any conflict that may occur is then seen as 'the result of misunderstanding or mischief; in other words, as pathological' (Crouch 1982: 18). This view underlay much taken-for-granted managerial thinking about everyone in an enterprise having shared goals, and also underpinned several academic approaches, notably the 'human relations' tradition (see Rose 1988). Unitarism was often used as a straw man representing old-fashioned and unrealistic ideas, but surveys found that many managers continued to believe in a harmony of interest, and, as should already be clear, a resurgence of managerial self-confidence and a reassertion of market individualism underpinned a revival of unitarism from the 1980s. During the 1990s, HRM often implied that management was the sole or at least key authority. HRM practice is likely to have a strong unitary aspect, as reflected in the finding of the

1998 Workplace Employee Relations Survey that 72 per cent of workplace managers responsible for personnel matters prefer to consult directly with employees rather than with trade unions (Cully et al. 1999: 88). Managers without these responsibilities are likely to be even more strongly 'unitarist'.

- *Pluralists* see conflict as inevitable because, to cite Clegg (1979: 1), various organizations participate in determining the rules of employment. These have their own bases of authority, and 'whenever there are separate sources of authority there is the risk of conflict'. Pluralism underlay the views of the Donovan Commission, which was established in 1965 to analyse the increasingly conflictual state of industrial relations and whose analysis encapsulated some basic assumptions, notably the reassertion of the value of voluntarism. Pluralism was particularly salient in the approach of management: instead of a unitary denial that there was any rational basis for conflict, managers should recognize the inevitability of disputes and seek means to regulate them. In Flanders's (1970: 172) oft-quoted dictum, 'the paradox, whose truth managements have found it so difficult to accept, is that they can only regain control by sharing it'.

- A third, *radical*, approach developed as a critique, or in the significant case of Fox (1974) an auto-critique, of pluralism (see also Hyman 1978; Edwards 1998). Pluralists assumed, first, that reform could be in the interests of all, thus neglecting major differences of interest between workers and managers, and, second, that institutional tinkering could meet the goals of a reformist management, thus failing to acknowledge that 'disorder' ran much deeper than a weakness of institutions.

Much of the academic debate on these approaches treated them as mutually exclusive and incommensurable. Each approach also bore the mark of its origins: unitarism in human relations traditions, pluralism in organized collective bargaining, and radicalism in shop-floor discontent that seemed immune to all attempts at institutionalization. Yet it would be as wrong to write off radicalism on the grounds of the apparent disappearance of this discontent as it was to see unitarism as simply naive and outdated. A biography of radicalism's key influence, Karl Marx, notes that an investment banker told *New Yorker* magazine in 1997 that 'Marx's approach is the best way to look at capitalism' (Wheen 1999: 5). Each approach has some strengths, though an appropriately explicated radical view is in my view analytically the best means to understand the nature of the employment relationship (Edwards 1998).

Consider the unitary view. To assume that all conflict is pathological is plainly an unsatisfactory view of organizational life. Yet the view made two key points. First, surveys have found that managers, and indeed many workers, tend to see their firms in unitary terms; for example, when asked whether a firm is like a football team or whether employers and workers are on opposite sides, workers often choose the former. The first UK study to ask this question found that 67 per cent of a sample of manual workers agreed with the statement that 'teamwork means success and is to everyone's advantage' (Goldthorpe et al. 1968: 73). Similarly, overt disputation is relatively rare.

Second, at the analytical level there are areas of shared interest: if workers and managers were totally opposed to each other, workplace relations would simply break down. Consider some deeper analysis of the football team analogy. In reviewing the team analogy, Ramsay (1975) noted, first, that Goldthorpe et al. did not equate teamwork with harmony but rather 'interdependence' of management and worker: teamwork was likely to mean pragmatic acceptance of the need for co-operation and not a completely shared vision with management. Second, when workers have been asked whether teamwork specifically describes their own situation, the proportion saying that it does declines. Third, in his own work Ramsay asked workers whether they agreed with the team view 'because people have to work together to get things done' or because 'managers and men [sic] have the same interests in everything that matters'; respondents split about six to one in favour of the former. Pragmatic acceptance of current conditions and not ideological agreement with management was predominant. As this book shows, such results continue to have resonance, in particular in relation to HRM and commitment (see chapters 13 and 14).

As for the pluralist and radical views, there may at one time have been clear distinctions. Differences certainly remain, but the debate has moved on. British pluralism proved to be flexible. Clegg (1979) responded to radicalism in a measured way, arguing that pluralism could embrace many of the radicals' points and that for many practical purposes there was nothing to choose between the perspectives. This contrasts with the situation in the United States where conventional writers (Kochan 1982) simply dismissed the radical critique (Hyman 1982). Though this difference is hard to explain, one reason is surely the openness of British pluralism (see Edwards 1995). In particular, the stress on the inevitability of conflict at the point of production was compatible with a pluralist view. In his pluralist phase Fox (1966: 14) had noted that 'co-operation needs to be engineered'; that is, securing workers' consent is an active and uncertain process. Flanders (1964: 243–4) had earlier drawn on the important work of Baldamus (1961) to argue that bargaining was a continuous and uncertain process. This is not to say that pluralism and radicalism are identical, but there has been constructive debate, out of which the approach developed below has emerged.

Finally, note the word 'power' in the heading of this sub-section. An alleged failing of IR texts is their lack of attention to this concept (Kelly 1998: 9–12). It is true that explicit discussion is often absent. Authors of the classic texts, such as Clegg, might well have replied that power and conflict are the very stuff of industrial relations, for the negotiation of rules necessarily entails power and influence, and hence that separate discussion was redundant. They might also have said that it was the place of disciplines such as political science to debate the concept, and that IR could use the results. There are of course problems with such a neat division of labour, but it has a point. IR *is* a field of study, and cannot debate the fundamentals of concepts developed in politics, sociology, economics, and psychology. Yet it does have an underlying view of power which might be summarized in propositions such as the following.

- Power is a capacity to pursue one's own interests, and it can be activated through individual or collective means.
- Power involves the capacity to oppose the actions of others (reactive power) and to pursue one's own objectives (proactive power). For example, in the UK, trade unions are often seen as having had reactive power but as lacking the means to pursue a proactive agenda.
- As in other areas of social life, power is embedded in continuing relationships, and establishing 'interests' is never easy. For example, if a management proposes a new payment scheme, workers may favour it on the grounds that it is 'fairer' than a previous scheme and that it offers the prospect of increased earnings, but have doubts as to the chance that the promise will be realized and perhaps also fear managerial good intentions (e.g. does the scheme foreshadow a move towards individual merit pay, or job losses or . . . ?)
- Power resources can shift over time (most obviously the declining power of trade unions since 1980).
- Resources are not fixed 'things' but are also developed through use. For example, it is often found that new forms of work organization 'fail' for lack of managerial commitment (i.e. the resources were not in fact deployed effectively) or because the initiatives run counter to other activities (i.e. employment relations have many aspects, and the power to impose a new work organization may run counter to the need to retain employee consent).
- Power resides in organizational routines and assumptions as well as in overt actions. Managements may exert power over workers by shaping expectations, but workers also have resources which they can mobilize, so that power relations are necessarily fluid and uncertain.

Such themes run through this book, and the reader may find it helpful to bear them in mind. Many IR studies, of which the work of Armstrong et al. (1981) still stands out, also clearly deploy analyses of power. They use concepts discussed further below which refine the above bullet points.

Rules, power and the negotiation of order

It is useful to begin with the nature of rules. Rules do not have to be clearly enunciated, and many of the most important ones are not. A long series of shop-floor studies (summarized in Edwards 1988, 2000) has revealed that expectations about how work is to be performed often arise from informal understandings. For example, a worker new to an establishment may discover that a supervisor permits workers to leave early at the end of a shift. She may then learn that this concession is granted only when work is slack or when a strict manager is absent, and that it is not wise to advertise it too widely. She may even find that this local understanding counts for nothing if managers decide to enforce the formal rules. Whether or not managers in fact enforce the formal rules and how they do so will depend on a variety of factors. These include:

- *The procedures of the firm.* If it has a system of warnings and appeals, it may issue a warning for a first offence, but in the absence of such disciplinary procedures it may act in a more sudden and less predictable way.
- *The presence of a union.* Can a representative make out a case for clemency on the grounds of the inexperience of the worker concerned or that the relevant practice had become taken for granted?
- *The role of the law.* If a worker is dismissed for a breach of a rule, can it be shown that the dismissal was fair in the circumstances?

This example shows that 'the rules' are many and varied, that different types of rule may apply to any given situation, and that rules have to be interpreted in action for them to have any practical meaning. The status of a rule also varies. A loose understanding may indicate normally accepted practice. But it may have little force. When understandings attain rather more acceptance and legitimacy they may be termed *custom and practice* rules. As the classic study of the subject (Brown 1973) shows, managements may unwittingly allow one-off concessions to grow into established expectations. Where workers have the power to insist that the expectations are honoured, a custom and practice rule is born. A later study showed that managers, too, generate custom and practice rules (Armstrong and Goodman 1979). In one case, a written rule in a collective agreement requiring that workers be given notice if they were to be laid off was successfully ignored by managers who pointed out that workers who stood on their rights would be entitled to only their low basic rate of pay, whereas if they went home early they could 'get a lift with the housework'. Managers here used power to persuade workers where their own interests lay.

Finally, why does not custom and practice continue to grow by a process of accretion? One important answer is that managements crack down on activities which get out of hand. They may do so on a piecemeal basis (for example in much of the UK car industry during the 1950s, when managements would attack shop-floor leaders when immediate conditions allowed, but without rooting out the challenge and in fact helping further to embed it: Jefferys 1988) or as part of a general campaign. Examples of such campaigns became familiar from the 1980s as managements reasserted their authority and rooted out formerly tolerated practices. The point is particularly significant in Britain. The lack of legal enforceability of collective agreements, combined with the preferences among managements and unions for informality, means that settling issues through unwritten understandings has played a particularly large part in the way in which the rules of employment are generated and sustained.

Why is the making of rules so difficult? A key reason is that the employment contract is indeterminate. In a commercial contract, a product or service is supplied for a price. In the labour contract, the worker sells an ability to work, which is translated into actual labour only during the course of the working day. Expectations about standards of performance have to be built up during the process of production. A rule is a complex social institution, not just a few sentences in a rule book. It can comprise beliefs, ideologies and taken-for-granted assumptions as well as formal provisions of rights and obligations. As noted above, the actual operation of legal rights in the workplace depends on the power, knowledge and organization of the parties as well as on the statute book.

Perspectives on rules

These points remain as valid today as they were when workplace custom and practice was relatively well established. The current concept of the 'psychological contract' tries to capture the idea of explicit and implicit expectations among employees about what their work will deliver. The concrete functioning of informal negotiation has changed, but the analytical principles remain important, as seen, for example, in explanations of why changing IR institutions proves harder than might seem at first sight (see e.g. chapters 7, 11 and 12). Three levels of analysis may be distinguished.

The first level concerns *the immediate balance of co-operation and conflict*. Radicals and labour process writers, for example, allegedly saw everything in terms of conflict and managerial efforts to control workers more completely. Yet no serious discussion would deny that there can be shared interests (for example, workers may develop new abilities when advanced technology is introduced, as well as benefit from the employment security of working for a successful firm), while also recognizing potential lines of tension (the technology may place new demands on workers and reduce the scope for informal control of the pacing and timing of work effort). The point is not whether employers and workers have interests that are shared or that conflict. It is how these dimensions of the employment relationship are organized: how far does new technology, for example, promote both the shared interest of working for an advanced company and possibly conflicting interests around the work practices that it may entail?

Second, *the broader policies underlying workplace relations* received attention. To continue with the example of new technology, what does it mean to say that it entails certain work practices? Are these determined by the technology or, as many writers began to argue, the product of managerial choice? Although at the level of the individual workplace certain developments may seem inevitable, seen more broadly they may themselves reflect choice. There are two aspects of analysis here.

- The first considered the various approaches to labour regulation that managers might pursue, with the concept of managerial strategy being intensively debated. From a relatively orthodox IR position, Purcell and Sisson (1983) identified a set of 'styles'. The way in which analysis was developing is illustrated by their inclusion of two styles which lay outside the usual IR focus on collective bargaining. These styles were an authoritarian non-union approach and a 'sophisticated paternalist' style, the latter generally involving a refusal to recognize unions and the intensive fostering of a sense of commitment to the company. Seen in retrospect, these styles foreshadowed what were later seen as two leading patterns of the management of labour, respectively, cost minimization and 'high-commitment' policies.

From a labour process approach, Friedman (1977) introduced the distinction between the strategies of responsible autonomy and direct control. These strategies can be seen as underlying the more concrete styles identified by Purcell and Sisson. For Friedman, managements faced the problem of securing workers' co-operation while controlling them so that they would continue to accept the authority of management and to work as directed. The two strategies represented approaches based on one or the other approach to the problem. Though Friedman sometimes presented the strategies as polar opposites, it is preferable to see them as elements which can be combined in various ways. Thus an employer may introduce quality circles to try to release workers' creativity while also asserting 'direct control' over issues such as absenteeism and time-keeping.

The analytical task is to show how the various strands of labour management are connected. For example, a major theme to emerge in Britain concerned the lack of deliberate linkages and the absence of a coherent approach implied by the term 'strategy'. A theoretical perspective on this was provided by Hyman (1987), who argued that, because firms pursue the *contradictory* objectives of consent and control and because, moreover, they are operating in an unpredictable external environment, strategies must be routes to partial failure. That is, a strategy is not a neat package producing clear outcomes but necessarily contains several competing elements and has to be constantly reinterpreted as new results emerge and as the world changes. Management, in short, is not only a continuous, active and uncertain process but also necessarily involves the balancing of forces which are pushing in opposing directions.

- The second aspect of analysis concerned the environment of labour management policies. The links between the regulation of labour and business structure and strategy received considerable attention. How far are different approaches to labour the product of different product market circumstances? For example, does a competitive situation promote certain approaches and retard others? Attention was also directed not at variations between firms but at the overall environment in which they operated. How far is the labour policy of British firms shaped by the macroeconomic circumstances of the country and by generic features of its operation, notably the education and training of the workforce?

The third level of analysis concerns *the fundamental nature of the employment relationship*. Many texts note that conflict and co-operation are both important, but they tend to stop at this point. This raises the question of whether conflict is any more than an occasional accident and whether it is more basic than co-operation. The key point about the indeterminacy of the labour contract and strategies of labour control is that managers and workers are locked into a relationship that is contradictory and antagonistic. It is contradictory not in the sense of logical incompatibility but because managements have to pursue the objectives of control and releasing creativity, both of which are inherent in the relationship with workers and which call for different approaches. The relationship is antagonistic because managerial strategies are about the deployment of workers' labour power in ways which permit the generation of a surplus. Workers are the only people who produce a surplus in the production process but, unlike the independent artisan, they do not determine how their labour power is deployed to meet the objective.

There is thus a relation of 'structured antagonism' between employer and worker (Edwards 1986). This term is used to stress that the antagonism is built into the basis of the relationship, even though on a day-to-day level co-operation is also important. It is important to distinguish this idea from the more usual one of a conflict of interest. The latter has the problem of implying that the real or fundamental interests of capital and labour are opposed, and hence that any form of participation scheme is simply a new way of bending workers to capital's demands. The fact that workers have several interests confounds this idea. A structured antagonism is a basic aspect of the employment relationship which shapes how day-to-day relations are handled but is not something which feeds directly into the interests of the parties. Firms have to find ways to continue to extract a surplus, and if they do not then both they and their workers will suffer. Balancing the needs of controlling workers and securing commitment rests ultimately on ensuring that a surplus continues to be generated. It may well be in workers' interests that it is indeed generated, but this should not disguise the fact that they are exploited.

The contemporary significance is simply that much workplace change is presented as though it cuts through old relations of conflict to promote total unity. Yet any unity has to be actively created, and it cannot be total because of the structural conditions in which employers and workers find themselves.

Methods of enquiry

What methods have been used to pursue this agenda? A feature of many older texts, and indeed some more recent ones, is the detailed account of institutions and of how bargaining is carried out. There is little self-conscious discussion of methodology or of exactly how information is gathered. This reflects the way in which they are written: they draw on their authors' personal knowledge of the operation of procedures, which is generally backed up by statistics on wages or strikes and the results of official inquiries. Over the past two decades, analysis has become less institutionally focused and more conscious of the nature of the research base. Two developments stand out.

First, a series of surveys has been conducted. The best known are the three Workplace Industrial Relations Surveys (WIRS) of 1980, 1984 and 1990 and their successor of 1998, now called the Workplace Employment Relations Survey (WERS). These are based on large samples which are representative of the great majority of workplaces in Great Britain; each survey has involved interviews with the manager responsible for IR and where relevant an employee representative, and in 1998 there was also a survey of employees. The surveys not only provide a mass of information about institutional arrangements such as the structure of the personnel function and the extent and coverage of collective bargaining. They also contain important information on working practices such as the extent of systems of communication and involvement and the use of teamwork. The survey design has included a panel element which has been crucial in distinguishing two possible sources of change. For example, coverage of collective bargaining in 1998 was much lower than it was in 1980. This could be due to one of three sorts of change:

- *changes within continuing establishments*, that is, a reduced propensity to engage in collective bargaining;
- *structural changes*, whereby sectors where bargaining is most common consti-tute a declining proportion of the population of establishments; and
- changes due to *'births and deaths'*, so that even within a given sector newly established workplaces are less likely to engage in collective bargaining, an effect which may be further distinguished according to whether the 'births' differ from the 'deaths', or from deaths and also continuing establishments.

Such differences are considered throughout this volume, but two contrasting findings may be highlighted now to illustrate the potentially different dynamics (Millward et al. 2000: 105, 190):

- Change in the *presence of trade unions* in the workplace has reflected the third influence: continuing workplaces were stable in the presence of unions between 1990 and 1998, but newly established workplaces were much less likely to have a union presence.
- By contrast, there was a *shift away from multi-employer collective bargaining* even among continuing workplaces, so that in this respect the first influence was operating: the same managements were changing their policies.

Second, case-study work has explored the processes underlying the patterns described by surveys. Case studies have developed in three main ways. First, their theoretical orientation has developed in the light of interests in the labour process and management strategy. Second, though it is sometimes said that the rise of HRM led to a neglect of the worker's point of view, in fact many studies (e.g. those discussed in chapters 13 and 18) have addressed the effects of change on workers, thus developing the point that the rules of employment are not just about the activities of managements and trade unions. Third, some researchers have used case studies in more than one location, in order to explore variations in behaviour and thus deepen the explanations offered. IR research combines survey and case-study methods, as well as using established methods such as analysis of official statistics. The following chapters draw on these methods in varying degrees and where relevant they highlight gaps in knowledge as well as differences in interpretation.

Contract and status

Work relationships in the UK, and indeed in most advanced industrial econo-mies, have, then, seen many confusing and apparently contradictory trends. One device to understand these trends is the distinction between contract and status (Streeck 1987). 'Contract' refers to a relationship based on the principles of 'hire and fire' and individual responsibility. It is thus related to the more obvious idea of a relationship based on pure market principles, but is also broader in recognizing that specific and detailed obligations can be provided through organizational rules and not the market. For example, many organizations use systems of performance appraisal which are defined by the organizations' rules rather than a market in any exact sense of the term. 'Status' covers longer-term relationships and the treatment of the employee as an investment rather than a cost; for current purposes, we may include the provision of means for employees to participate in decision-making. A purely contractual relationship will give no space for such 'voice' and will treat employees simply as hired help, whereas in a more lasting relationship members of an organization may be expected to engage in its key choices. There are two reasons, which run through many debates on the employment relationship. The first relates to efficiency: giving workers a say may improve organizational functioning in some way. The second relates to equity: employees investing in a long-term relationship have rights which need to be respected.

Europeanization would imply an emphasis on status while Americanization implies more stress on contract. Some trends in the direction of contract and status are more securely documented than others, as this book aims to show. For the present, we simply note the following.

Trends towards contract would include:

1   A rise in the use of temporary and agency workers. The increase is, however, from a low base, and quite small proportions of the workforce are involved.
2   An increased reliance on the measurement of performance and the tying of reward to this measurement. Performance measurement is certainly extensive, but direct links to reward are highly variable, and many appraisal schemes are very standardized rather than offering a strictly individual market exchange between each worker and the employer.
3   A decline in the role and influence of trade unions, which were traditionally the only real means for UK employees to express their voice collectively (works councils – representative structures not based on trade unions but instead being elected by all employees of a firm – on the continental European model being largely absent). Trade union membership fell rapidly during the 1980s and 1990s, with little replacement by other representative structures; hence the widespread concern about a 'representation gap'.
4   Insecurity in the sense of (a) an increased objective chance of job loss and (b) an increased *perception* that job prospects are uncertain. There is evidence of insecurity. One measure is job tenure where, as noted above, there have been contrasting trends for men and women. Staying in a job can, however, represent insecurity because of fear that another job will not be found. Other aspects of insecurity include career insecurity: a concern that a predictable, or at least manageable, progression of jobs is not possible. Heery and Salmon (2000) argue that the combination of increased risks of unemployment, a

rise in temporary and casual work, a reduction in legal protections, and a rise in employee perceptions of an uncertain future together point to a growth of insecurity, though they also note that there will be important differences between sections of the workforce.

In relation to status, trends in employee voice running counter to that just mentioned include an increase in the use of *direct* rather than representative participation, for example the use of teamworking and problem-solving groups. Status would also be reflected in other practices associated with human resource management, such as improved communication with employees, a move towards 'single status' (that is, treating all employees the same in terms of such things as working hours, sick pay and pensions, in place of long-entrenched distinctions between non-manual and manual workers), and the use of profit-related pay and share-ownership schemes. There is evidence of growing use of many of these measures, though it is also well established that the adoption of them in so-called bundles of high-involvement practices remains very rare.

Streeck's summary of moves towards contract and status is given in table 1.3, which also indicates where the matters are pursued in this book. This listing anticipated several developments, notably around teamwork and shifts away from collective bargaining, which have become more salient since 1987. A particularly foresightful point was the highlighting of 'the possible contradictions inherent in a *simultaneous pursuit of restored contract and extended status*' and the fact that employers will 'find it exceedingly hard to formulate a consistent strategic approach to building a more flexible system' of employment relations (Streeck 1987: 295, emphasis added; see further chapter 7 on the different dimensions of flexibility). As discussed below, contract and status are not poles on a continuum but separate dimensions which can vary independently.

Table 1.3 Two routes to organizational flexibility

	Return to contract	*Extension of status*	*Chapter*
Employment status of workers	Temporary	Permanent	3
Numerical flexibility	Hire and fire	Flexible working time	7, 14
Functional flexibility	Hire and fire	Self-regulated job rotation	13, 14
Work organization	Taylorist	Teamwork	13, 14
Qualifications sought	Narrow	Broad	15
Wage determination	Industrial engineering	Payment by ability	8, 12
Management style	Unilateral prerogative	Consultation, participation	7, 9, 10, 12

Source: Abbreviated from Streeck (1987: 294).

One recent research study illustrates the problems of developing consistent employment relations strategies. Grimshaw et al. (2001) draw on studies of four organizations to demonstrate shifts away from structured approaches associated with well-ordered internal labour markets (systems with clear promotion ladders and established pay structures). They argue that they have been replaced with a contradictory mix of policies. As an earlier study (Marginson et al. 1994) put it, employer policies were increasingly 'eclectic'. The implication is that we are seeing complex efforts to use aspects of contract and status rather than a coherent shift from one form of employment relationship to another. Several strands run through this book's efforts to make sense of these developments.

- First, contract and status can obviously both exist if they apply to different groups of workers. For example, temporary workers may be subject to contractual relations while permanent ones enjoy status. There is also some evidence of a *polarization* of experience, for example rising skill levels in some but not all occupations, so that contract and status receive different emphases in different jobs.
- Second, they often coexist in the same workplace, for example where employees work in teams but are also subject to closer performance measurement. Figure 1.2 attempts to make this point more analytically.
  Note first the dimensions. If we classified status and contract according to their presence or absence, we would have one area of the diagram where neither was being used. It probably makes more sense to think in terms of how developed and explicit the adoption of one dimension or the other is. The conventional cases are in the bottom right and top left. The first of these is a traditional 'hire and fire' employment relationship, but note that for contract to be developed this will need to entail formal and explicit managerial rules specifying the terms of the contract and the consequences of a breach. High status and low contract is associated with what is now termed 'soft HRM', meaning an emphasis on training, career development and 'empowerment', but it would also characterize much more traditional paternalist

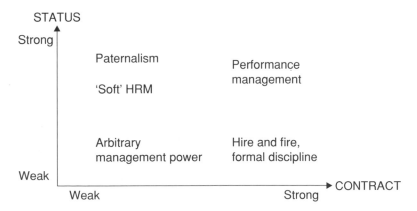

Figure 1.2 Status and contract

relationships based on unwritten understandings and diffuse obligations. Now, research literature on both these situations finds that in practice there is often a hard edge to the relevant relationships. The point is not to say that, empirically, situations lacking hard and coercive elements are at all likely. It is to establish that there can be situations where there are *tendencies* in this direction, and to indicate a *benchmark* against which actual practice can be measured.

The case in the top right is of particular interest. It identifies cases where status and contract are both emphasized, notably through such practices as performance management, where employees may have a degree of autonomy and even 'empowerment' but are also held to account against explicit, hard performance standards. Finally, the reverse position is also important: status is not important, and contract is weak in that there are no formal and explicit rules: the employment relationship is weakly institutionalized. For long periods before the arrival of trade unions, this model applied to large parts of the workforce. Trade union and legal and other pressures have moved many employers away from the extremes of this, but the model still characterizes some employers and it also captures a tendency that can be found widely, for example the desire to 'get rid of problem staff' quickly and the consequent tendency to ignore formal procedures.

Chapters 7 and 12 focus specifically on employer strategies. Chapter 14 illustrates such themes through case studies of two organizations which might be expected to have clear strategies but which in practice combine different ways of managing labour in complex ways. Eclecticism remains a central feature of how the tensions of the employment relationship are handled.

- Third, it is impossible to add up different dimensions to produce a simple overall balance sheet. For example, the decline of unions has entailed a significant reduction in the extent to which many key issues of pay and working conditions are subject to any serious discussion with employees or their representatives. It is not possible to say that this is 'balanced' by any growth in direct participation, for the dimensions are different.
- Fourth, what benchmark is used in assessing the state of industrial relations? One is an alleged past of powerful trade unions and perennial strikes, as represented in the continuing use of the image of the 'winter of discontent' (a period of industrial militancy in 1978–9, the label apparently being introduced, so the IR academic W. E. J. McCarthy has discovered, by an inspired sub-editor on the *Sun*). Yet trade unions covered at their peak only half the workforce; strikes were concentrated in a very narrow sector of the economy and even there were quite rare; and, as in any conflict, militancy takes two sides, so that to jump from the existence of many strikes to the presumption that the 'cause' was militant and irresponsible unions was a common but plainly faulty leap of logic. Another model uses heady labels such as 'employee empowerment', the 'skills revolution' and the 'learning society'. As this book will show, there has been change in relevant areas, but there remains a large gap between the rhetoric of these terms and the reality of the limited extent and depth of change. IR research has a strong sense of history (see chapters

2 and 14), and thus helps to counteract the many claims that work is fundamentally different from its shape in 'the past'.

The Changing Character of Industrial Relations

The above description reflects IR scholarship going back many years. It treats
IR as a process largely confined to a nation-state and has thus required amendment in the light of supra-national regulation and 'globalization'. There have
also been challenges to the intellectual integrity of IR as a field of study. They
arise from the emergence of HRM (which offers a different way of looking at
established themes in the management of labour) and some broader analyses
(which suggest that these themes need to placed in a wider context).

Industrial relations systems and globalization

As noted above, writers on industrial relations systems have tended to present
these systems as self-contained. Influences and borrowings were recognized,
for example the role of the British in shaping the German post-war 'system', the
American influence on Japanese post-war reconstruction, and direct borrowings
by the British Conservative government of 1970–4 of aspects of American industrial relations. Yet such events were seen as unusual and often unsuccessful.
In the attention to nationally bounded 'systems' IR writers were far from alone.
Indeed, it was well after Dunlop (1958) popularized the idea in IR that in the
study of management more generally the concept of the national business system
(that is, a distinctive and connected set of institutions of corporate governance)
emerged (e.g. Lane 1989).

Given their emphasis on uncertainty and the management of compromises,
IR writers might have been more open than they were to challenges to the idea
of national systems. In the event, however, it has taken real-world events to
undermine the idea. Three may be highlighted. First, several countries experienced a wave of Japanese direct investment which, though small in absolute
terms (see chapter 4), was seen as significant in importing new ideas. The term
'Japanization' was coined in 1986 (Turnbull 1986). The new ideas included close
attention to detail, a focus on the quality of goods and services, and continuous
improvement. Second, European legislation had an increasingly direct impact
across the European Union. During the 1990s directives on such issues as
working time and European Works Councils applied in the UK, and in addition
matters as diverse as pension payments and procedures for consultation about
redundancy were subject to European legal decision. Third, the concept of
globalization attained increasing prominence. Its precise meaning is disputed, as
is the extent of the development which it characterizes, but the essential idea is
that economic activity takes on a global character, so that national systems lose
their distinctiveness and are increasingly influenced by international forces. Some
writers identify a 'hollowing out' of the nation-state, meaning that its influence
is weakened through the simultaneous rise of global regulation as in the World

Trade Organization, European monetary union, and the international transfer of models of work organization by multinationals (see chapter 4).

Some of the more popular ideas about globalization are 'historicist', simply identifying a trend and projecting it forward as well as, characteristically, portraying the present as a complete break with the past and seeing the trend as an asocial and inevitable development (e.g. Ohmae 1995) that is the identification of a trend and its projection into the future. (Note in passing the irony that historicism was seen originally, and most famously by the philosopher Popper (1957; see also Goldthorpe 1971), as a besetting failing of Marxism, and yet it is now dedicated anti-Marxists who fall into the trap). Three key problems here are:

- the failure to specify the causal processes underlying an observed trend, which is simply projected into the future;
- the assumption that a trend in some parts of the economy will become general: it may be that portfolio careers can be identified where they did not exist, but they may reflect very specific circumstances;
- the neglect of countervailing tendencies.

These ideas are essentially positive about the effects of globalization. Others use the same method to portray an international 'race to the bottom' wherein capital seeks the cheapest site of production and thus undermines legal protections to employees elsewhere. Such ideas have been popular since at least the 1970s when the New International Division of Labour thesis made this argument. Yet it was soon shown that the great bulk of world trade remained within the developed economies and that multinational companies generally retained strong bases in their countries of origin (see Hirst and Thompson 1996).

More serious analysis speaks of competing models of capitalism and their intersection: globalization is not a force of nature but an actively managed process (Coates 2000). For present purposes, we do not need to debate the theory of globalization, but may simply note some implications for IR in the UK. First, it is reasonably clear that the economy has been increasingly exposed to competitive pressures (whether these are labelled global or international is not important). Examples from the car industry were given above. Second, it does not follow that the coercive comparisons practised by large firms will necessarily lead directly to a shift towards countries with the lowest unit costs: there are many reasons to produce in particular markets, and many considerations in location decisions. Third, the UK has benefits as a production location, including relatively low wage costs by the standards of some European countries and, it is often argued, labour laws which place few restrictions on redundancies and restructuring. Fourth, issues of 'best practice' in the organization of work are likely to have an increased salience, as are the links between IR and economic performance. Fifth, however, many parts of the economy remain relatively free from direct international competition. Finally, there is little evidence of one dominant route to the management of employment relations. Different models remain in competition, and as this book shows American and European pressures can both be discerned in the British context.

Industrial relations and human resource management

The contrast between IR on the one hand and PM and HRM on the other may be specified with the help of figure 1.2. The contrast with PM is conventionally made in terms of the collective focus of IR and the individual focus of PM. There is a degree of truth in this, with IR having a strong emphasis on an organized relationship between managements and trade unions and with collective bargaining between them being both an empirical focus and a key analytical category. PM and HRM have given more attention to such 'individual' issues as recruitment and training. Until the 1980s, there was a tacit division of labour between IR and PM which was sometimes mirrored on the ground, with a firm's industrial relations manager (often a man) dealing with collective bargaining and trade unions while a female personnel or welfare officer handled health and safety, pensions, and the works canteen. This situation was thrown into question by two developments: a decline in the coverage of collective bargaining plus an even steeper decline in one of the staples of IR, organized industrial conflict, and a rise in HRM which claimed to offer an integrated approach to the management of labour, in which IR was only a small part.

Expressions of HRM imperialism are, however, misplaced. Whether the rules of employment are established collectively between an employer and its employees acting in concert, or individually, is evidently a major empirical question, but IR is perfectly capable of dealing with both. And HRM has some major limitations of its own. Its starting point is how managers can organize their 'human resources', which leads to two distinct issues.

First, it takes the managerial perspective as its reference point: it asks, not how employment is organized, but what managers can do to manage their employees. Employees are resources to be controlled and deployed, not equal parties to a relationship. Consider for example the features of HRM listed in table 1.4 that were identified by Storey (1992: 35) and are widely reproduced in HRM books. The approach is explicitly unitarist in its perspective, and it also seeks a move from collective to individualized relations with workers. It is true that researchers in the field are not necessarily committed to such a view. HRM

Table 1.4 HRM and the management of labour

	Personnel and IR	*HRM*
Nature of relations	Pluralist	Unitarist
Conflict	Institutionalized	De-emphasized
Labour management	Collective bargaining contracts	Towards individual contracts
Thrust of relations with stewards*	Regularized through facilities and training	Marginalized

* i.e. shop stewards: elected trade union workplace representatives (see chapter 10 for details).
Source: Abbreviated from Storey (1992: 35).

Table 1.5   Managerial approaches to labour management

	Strategic	*Non-strategic*
People as resource	HRM	Personnel
People as cost	Not HRM?	Traditional management

Source: Redman and Wilkinson (2001: 11). By permission of Pearson Education.

is far from being a settled approach, and indeed one recent text starts by stress-ing its 'diversity' (Beardwell and Holden 1997). It is also true that many texts do not assume any simply harmony of interest between employer and employee; one even goes so far as to say that it adopts an 'industrial relations approach' (Bach and Sisson 2000: 8). Yet such analytical views are consciously aimed at correcting a mismatch between the 'rhetoric' of harmony and the 'reality' of conflicting interests. And the critique is needed because the field starts from a managerial problematic even when it is not directly managerialist. An IR approach starts from a different position. In the words of a leading US authority, IR 'starts from an assumption that an enduring conflict of interests exists between workers and employers' (Kochan 1998: 37), though as argued above this is not in fact an assumption but a demonstrable characteristic.

Second, as an analytical approach HRM tends to assume what it sets out to prove. Another recent book usefully brings out the point. Redman and Wilkinson (2001: 11) argue that people can be seen as a resource or a cost and that manag-erial approaches can be strategic or non-strategic, which generates table 1.5. HRM describes only one cell in the matrix and, as will be seen throughout this book, one which applies to only a minority of organizations. To be clear, it is not being argued that students of HRM are unaware of such points; indeed, the more analytical books provide a balanced and critical appraisal. But they draw, explicitly or implicitly, on IR writings to make sense of the terrain. For example the remarks quoted above by Bratton and Gold (1999: 28) on 'tensions and contradictions' of HR strategies draw directly on IR analyses.

Third, HRM gives little direct attention to the role of the state in the regulation of labour. It is more interested in policy within the enterprise and not the dynamic interplay between the state, employers, unions and employees.

To see recent developments in the UK as a secular shift from a collective and conflict-based system to one based on individualism and consent is to commit several sorts of error. First, collective bargaining was never ubiquitous: at their peak unions covered only half the workforce, and organized overt conflict was the exception rather than the norm (see chapter 10). Second, the undoubted decline in institutional industrial relations (declining union membership, many fewer strikes, reduced union influence at national level) leaves open the issue of what has replaced it. As later chapters in this book show, a reasonable pic-ture is one of variation and fragmentation, with only a minority of employers embracing anything like the full suite of HRM practices, and with many others relying on traditional approaches to labour based on cost minimization.

Underlying these empirical issues are two theoretical problems. The first is common in efforts to analyse contemporary developments, for example claims that 'employability' and 'portfolio careers' are replacing traditional bureaucratic career structures. They often fall into the error of historicism, In the IR sphere, the trend may be the decline of collectivism, but it would be rash to suppose that this will continue without limit or that it cannot be counteracted by forces moving in the opposite direction.

The second theoretical issue turns on the conceptualization of the employment relationship. IR research has been predicated on the assumption that the relationship is one of conflict, power and inequality. The core of IR is that it sees the employment relationship as based on a structured antagonism, with any unity and co-operation being built on uncertain foundations and with the creation of consent being inherently partial and uncertain.

An irony here is that proponents of new techniques such as business process re-engineering recognize in passing that co-operation indeed has to be engineered. Consider the following from an HRM text:

> management's actions often have unintended consequences. Thus, for example, the[re is a] paradox contained in the prescriptive advice to managers which encourages leaders to 'gain control by giving it up' (Champy 1996). . . . [This paradox] suggests that because of persistent and fundamental continuities in the post-industrial labour process, there is no such thing as the 'right' human resource strategy, system or technique and that, whatever systems are adopted, they will have to be regularly modified or replaced as their internal tensions and contradictions appear. (Bratton and Gold 1999: 28)

The irony is the rediscovery of Flanders's language discussed above without reference to it, yet with the underlying unitarist assumption that re-engineering is a process managed from the top in the interests of all. The idea that there are legitimate competing sources of authority seems alien, as does Flanders's discussion of the tendency of managers to rely on their right of command and their failure seriously to engage with employees (see discussion of contract and status below). Business process re-engineers could read the conclusion of Flanders's account of an earlier effort at re-engineering with profit (Flanders 1964).

Challenges to IR as a domain

It was argued above that British pluralism responded constructively to some challenges, notably the radical view of the negotiation of order on the shop floor. It has arguably been less open to other challenges. Three may be highlighted.

- *Worker interests.* According to Kelly (1998), IR retains a descriptive approach, its research agenda is unduly driven by employers, and, as noted above, it lacks a proper theory of power. As a result, 'we don't know', for example, 'precisely why and how union power declined or by how much in the 1980s' (1998: 23). The answer is mobilization theory and in turn 'the fulcrum of the model is *interests* and the ways in which people (particularly members of subordinate groups) come to define them. To what extent do they believe their interests to be similar to, different from, or opposed to, those of the ruling group?' (Kelly 1998: 25, emphasis original). Other concepts address the degree to which a group organizes around given interests, mobilizes against other groups, and has the opportunity to pursue its interests. This theory has, says Kelly (1998: 126–9) three advantages over 'rival approaches':

– instead of starting from the employer's need for co-operation and to secure work performance, it starts from injustice and exploitation;
– it does not depend on a simple distinction between individualism and collectivism, but distinguishes interest definition, organization, mobilization, and so on, treating 'as problematic what previous industrial relations researchers often took for granted, namely the awareness by workers of a set of common interests opposed to those of the employer';
– it helps address key issues such as how employees define interests in particular ways.

• *Gender.* Traditional IR, according to Wajcman (2000), took the male worker as the norm and saw women as marginal or of secondary interest. More fundamentally, it was not just that women as a group were neglected despite their substantial and growing place in the workforce. The gendered processes underlying much of the substance of IR were also neglected. The very institutions of IR are not gender-neutral. For example, payment systems contain gendered assumptions in how they define and measure the attributes of jobs, so that jobs typically performed by women will be rated differently from male jobs. Collective bargaining was not well attuned to the representation of equality agendas (Colling and Dickens 1998). Men's work is also gendered, for example in the ways in which managers tend to recruit people in their own image, and an informal 'men's club' atmosphere creates expectations as to acceptable styles of behaviour.
• *Work and society.* Ackers (2002) criticizes IR for its focus on relations in the workplace, to the neglect of links with the family and other spheres, and for the absence of an explicit ethical dimension. He offers 'neo-pluralism' as the means to develop a critical analysis of management practice and an understanding of the normative aspects of the regulation of employment.

These views are plainly very different. Kelly focuses virtually exclusively on the traditional terrain of worker–manager relations and has been criticized explicitly by Ackers (2002) for the emphasis on economistic workplace militancy. His text would not be viewed, I believe, as gender-sensitive. Kelly offers a deepening of the agenda, that is a consideration of fundamental conflicts between workers and managers, rather than a broadening. Wajcman and Ackers aim to view the terrain in new ways and to link it to other aspects of society.

These issues are raised here partly to stress that texts such as this have been found wanting in the ways specified, and to invite the reader to consider the value of the criticisms during study of this book. It is not, however, wholly satisfactory to leave evaluation up to the reader, and some initial comments on the three views are thus offered here.

First, and in opposition to Kelly, in the identification of a field of study, a focus on employee interests is as unsatisfactory as one on those of employers. IR examines job regulation, but this is scarcely to adopt an employer's agenda (whereas HRM arguably does adopt such an agenda). Second, Ackers reasonably points to the need to link IR to other aspects of society, which is not a new call and which raises the question of how broadly a field is defined. The key issue is how far it makes sense to analyse a particular theme while leaving others to one side. For example, the institutions of collective bargaining are shaped by managerial policy elsewhere in the firm, and their operation in practice will depend on the negotiation of rules informally. In the same way, it can be argued that changes in the family, for example, may influence IR without necessarily needing analysis in their own right. The danger of broadening an approach is of course that it loses all coherence. A useful model was introduced by Emmett and Morgan (1982; for further discussion see Edwards 1986: 280). In their analysis of workplace ethnographies, they liken the walls of a workplace to a 'semi-permeable membrane', which filters influences from outside and also shapes how processes within the workplace affect relations elsewhere. If the membrane were wholly permeable, then Ackers might well be right, though it might also follow that IR was simply the working out in the workplace of forces determined elsewhere, which would make the subject of rather trivial importance. But, as we have seen, and as for example studies of pay determination show (see chapter 8), processes of negotiation develop their own logic and dynamic. IR is of course influenced by other forces, and as a developing field it needs to pay attention to new ones, but it can be reasonably bounded as a field with its own issues.

Third, Kelly's arguments for mobilization are wholly consistent with the approach of this book. To the extent that he directs attention to issues which may have been relatively neglected, he helps to re-emphasize some key themes. But, in many ways like this book, he retains a relatively orthodox view as to what IR is about.

Fourth, it is true that institutions and processes are not gender-neutral (and also true that there are important lines of division other than gender). Yet this does not mean that everything about them is so suffused with gender that they cannot be discussed without gender being included at every turn. More precisely, we can identify at least four situations. Some institutions directly entail gender issues, for example equal opportunities policy and practice. Others are likely to have less direct but still obvious gender implications, for example pay structures which are based on estimates of the value of certain skills (and which have been found to reward some (male) skills more than others). Others need have no gender implications even though in practice they do so. For example, there is nothing inherent in trade union election procedures which excludes women and ethnic minorities, but the fact that unions have historically been male-dominated, together with their tendency to reproduce the gender assumptions of society at large, has tended to produce marked gender differences in access to positions of power. Finally, some institutions, for example those of corporatism, are relatively distant from gender divisions. It is thus reasonable to continue to address some institutions and processes without necessarily drawing out the gender implications.

The reader may well wish to use these four categories to assess how well this book reflects gender issues. For example, under the second and third categories, how clearly are the gender implications drawn out? In doing so, some benchmarks may be helpful. The point of Wajcman's critique is that IR research has given insufficient attention to gender issues; this text necessarily reflects that research and cannot be expected to go far beyond it. It is also open to the reader to consider the implications of particular themes. For example, this book's analysis of managerial strategies discusses such things as 'flexibility', and plainly there can be gender assumptions built into this notion. The analysis does not necessarily need to spell out the gender implications at every turn, and the key issue is whether the tools of analysis can be deployed to address them. IR research is arguably reasonably well equipped to do this. Finally on this point, however, IR structures and institutions have many implications, for class, ethnic inequality, and many other things. It is not reasonable to expect an IR book to deal with them all, and nor should it: the argument here is that these structures and institutions deserve attention in their own terms, and they can be analysed accordingly. Links with gender and other processes should not be neglected, but, to put the point bluntly, these links are only one part of a story which can be told without making them the central theme.

Fifth, in relation to theory, some brief comments and references to social theory may be made, for those readers with a particular concern on this score. It is true that IR has always had a strong pragmatic bent, as is illustrated by the saying (attributed to different members of the 'Oxford school' of reformist, pluralist scholars associated with the Donovan Report) that 'an ounce of fact is worth a ton of theory'. It is also always useful to ask what we do not know and to question existing assumptions. Yet it would be wrong to infer that IR has failed to explain key issues within its domain. First, there are specific issues within the core domain of IR, such as the decline in union membership and in the role of union workplace representatives. Many such matters have been extensively debated, and there is arguably a reasonable set of explanations. Second, there are more complex issues, such as the effects of new work organization on employees. Plainly, one needs to distinguish different types of worker and different types of effect, and we are dealing with some effects such as perceptions of autonomy which are more complex than, say, the number of people belonging to trade unions. Yet research has pursued an agenda which is *progressive* in the sense that the topic under discussion is understood better (e.g. the balance between autonomy and responsibility) and the causes of different patterns are analysed. In like manner, the links between IR and various outcomes for workers and firms have been detailed.

IR is less explicit about its theory than are the core disciplines of social science. Scepticism about the ability of a single discipline to explain complex phenomena has been a key strength. Perhaps the most extensively debated example is pay, with IR research over many years showing that economists' theories of pay fail to explain important regularities, notably different rates of pay for apparently similar work (see Rubery 1997). It is true that an empiricist stress on 'the facts' has sometimes interfered with the development of alternative explanations. Yet if the effort is made the theoretical contribution of IR should not be too hard to find. At the very least, we can say that IR is consistent with those modern social theories which stress the connected nature of social phenomena, which refuse to privilege structure or action, and which argue that the 'causal powers' of certain forces are not invariate but depend on their context (see e.g. Sayer 2000 for explication of one pertinent approach to these matters).

Approach and Plan of this Book

Texts on industrial relations reflect the analytical developments discussed above. The traditional method was to concentrate on the main institutions and trends, with any explanation being inductive. More recent books pursue theoretical debates on management strategy and the labour process with rather little empirical information being provided. This book tries to steer a course between these extremes. While describing the key trends in British industrial relations, the book is analytical: each chapter provides a strong argument, and issues such as the coherence of efforts to reform industrial relations and the potential different routes of development run through many of the chapters.

Chapter authors are experts in their fields, and they do not necessarily share their interpretations. But one reading of the central themes of the book is as follows.

• First, there has been massive change over about the last 20 years, with a decline in the extent of collective bargaining, in trade union membership, and in strike activity. In addition, over the period since 1971, the involvement of the law has increased dramatically. New forms of work organization have emerged. The drivers here include tensions within the British mode of managing the employment relationship (see especially chapters 2 and 5), pressures of globalization and the restructuring of labour markets (chapter 3) and the introduction of work organization practices via multinationals (chapter 4).

• Second, this does not mean that industrial relations have moved from one model to another. A traditional model would be one of extensive collective bargaining and joint regulation. But such a model was always far from universal, failing to touch many workers in services and small firms, for example (see chapters 17 and 18). Various alternative models can be identified, of which some illustrations are listed in table 1.6; they are discussed fully in chapters 7, 12 and 13 in particular). It should already be apparent from the discussion of contract and status above that no single model fits all situations. For example, collective bargaining has been reduced but not eliminated so

Table 1.6   Models of the emerging employment relationship

Model	Key features
Free market (a)	Individual contracts replace collective bargaining, focus on direct relations between worker and employer, efficient market solutions, conflict largely eliminated
Free market (b)	Individualization, but managerial domination, management by fear and work intensification, conflict suppressed not eliminated
HRM	High skills and commitment, direct communication with workforce, managerially led agenda
Unitarist social partnership	Similar to HRM, plus systems for employee consultation, agenda still managerially led
Pluralist social partnership	As above, but more independent voice for workers organized as a collectivity (in practice in a trade union)

Source: Redman and Wilkinson (2001: 11).

that the free market models do not fit all cases. More importantly, as shown in chapters 12 and 14, individualism was evident in the past while some contemporary aspects of it display remarkable standardization: the fundamental message of chapter 12 is that the individual and collective methods of managing employment are bound to coexist, albeit in different combinations at different times. Similarly, some elements of the HRM and partnership models can be discerned, but systems of managing employment evolve relatively slowly and, crucially, actuality on the ground may suggest less change than appearances from company philosophy suggest. Chapters 7 and 8 review the evidence in detail, but the theme of limited practical change runs through many others, notably on training (chapter 15) and gender equality (chapter 16).

• Third, one way to think about the balance between models is to use the contrast mentioned above between Americanization and Europeanization. As chapters 5 and 6, for example, show, the emphasis in the period 1979–97 was strongly on the former, but since 1997 elements of it remain, notably in the government's concern to be 'business-friendly', while Europeanization has proceeded unevenly and sometimes through drift rather than deliberate choice.

• Fourth, the outcomes of industrial relations change are variable and uncertain. There are two kinds of outcome which need to be distinguished.

  – The first relates to the functioning of the IR system and the parties to it. Does it deliver reasonable wages, the ability to participate actively in one's work, adequate training, and fairness between workers? There have been some improvements, for example in training and the development of

equal opportunities agendas, but as the relevant chapters show performance has been patchy and it remains some way away from a benchmark of
multi-skilled workers enjoying freedom of opportunity. Chapter 17 under-
lines continuing pay inequality. In addition, chapter 6 shows that the legal
framework leaves several issues of fairness unresolved, while chapters 9
and 10 point to the limited progress of social partnership agendas.

- – The second set of outcomes relates to the economic performance of firms
  and the economy as a whole. As chapter 19 shows, this area is particularly controversial. But it is clear that any view that 'bad IR' in the past
  was the cause of bad performance was inadequate. What is more plausible is that some aspects of the IR system, notably fragmented and competing wage demands, could exacerbate tendencies in other parts of the
  economy towards inflation. A fundamental lesson from the past is that IR
  was part of a much wider picture, so that 'good' and 'bad' IR were as
  much a consequence as a cause of the activities of firms. That is, successful firms could invest in appropriate ways to manage their workers (not
  that they necessarily did so). Those who seek 'effects' of IR arrangements
  on outcomes such as productivity need to bear this point in mind, for
  many studies reveal correlation and not causation, and there is growing
  evidence that the necessary mechanisms between an IR practice and an
  outcome are absent, weak, or contingent on specific contextual factors.

The remaining chapters in the book fall into four main groups. They have not
been categorized into separate parts, however, since themes overlap. The first
group (chapters 2–5) covers the historical, economic, international, and political
context of industrial relations. Chapter 5 also acts as a bridge to the second
group (chapters 6–10) that deals with the standard actors in regulating employment, namely, the state through labour law, management, and trade unions.
Chapter 9 is also a convenient place to deal with data on strikes. Chapter 10
deals not just with the institutions of unions at workplace level but also with
non-union employee representation and processes of representation, and thus
leads into the third group.

This set of chapters (11–18) examines some of the key processes of industrial
relations. The logic behind three of them is worth highlighting. Chapter 11 deals
with the public sector because the conduct of industrial relations has traditionally been distinctive and the conduct of collective bargaining, for example, remains
different from the private sector patterns discussed in chapter 8. Chapter 12 examines theory and evidence around individualism and collectivism in industrial
relations; it places some of the themes of chapters 6–10 in a theoretical context.
Chapter 18 gives particular attention to small firms, for collective management–
union relations have always been rare here, and yet 'industrial relations' is
still practised; the chapter addresses the nature of this process. Finally, chapter
19 examines the issue of 'outcomes' and thus acts to draw the threads of the
volume together.

The book can be read sequentially, and chapters 2 and 3 form a necessary
introduction to the rest of the book. But some readers may prefer to move on

then to the main structures of industrial relations (chapters 6–11). Alternatively, those interested in the nature of work from the point of view of employees may prefer to focus on chapters 10 and 13–18. Additionally, chapter 12 provides an overview of pertinent themes here, and may be read as an introduction to those chapters, as a complement to chapter 7, or as a link between the present chapter and chapter 7 onwards. Readers particularly interested in the role of law in industrial relations may wish to read chapter 16 and to some extent chapter 17 alongside chapter 6. Those who seek overviews of the state of employment relations from the points of view of sociology and politics may wish to start with chapters 2, 5 and 14, followed by chapter 18.

References

Ackers, P. 2002: Reframing employment relations: the case for neo-pluralism, *Industrial Relations Journal*, 33 (1), 2–19.

Armstrong, P. J., and Goodman, J. F. B. 1979: Managerial and supervisory custom and practice, *Industrial Relations Journal*, 10 (3), 12–24.

Armstrong, P. J., Goodman, J. F. B. and Hyman, J. 1981: *Ideology and Shopfloor Industrial Relations*. London: Croom Helm.

Bach, S., and Sisson, K. 2000: Personnel management in perspective. In S. Bach and K. Sisson (eds), *Personnel Management*, 3rd edn. Oxford: Blackwell.

Baldamus, W. 1961: *Efficiency and Effort*. London: Tavistock.

Beardwell, I., and Holden, L. (eds) 1997: *Human Resource Management: A Contemporary Perspective*, 2nd edn. London: Financial Times/Pitman.

Bratton, J., and Gold, J. 1999: *Human Resource Management*. Basingstoke: Macmillan.

Brown, W. 1973: *Piecework Bargaining*. London: Heinemann.

Cappelli, P., and Crocker-Hefter, A. 1996: Distinctive human resources are firms' core competencies, *Organizational Dynamics*, 25 (1), 7–22.

Champy, J. 1996: *Reengineering Management*. New York: Harper.

Clegg, H. A. 1979: *The Changing System of Industrial Relations in Great Britain*. Oxford: Blackwell.

Coates, D. 2000: *Models of Capitalism*. Cambridge: Polity.

Colling, T., and Dickens, L. 1998: Selling the case for gender equality: deregulation and equality bargaining, *British Journal of Industrial Relations*, 36 (3), 389–411.

Crouch, C. 1982: *Trade Unions*. London: Fontana.

Cully, M., Woodland, S., O'Reilly, A. and Dix, G. 1999: *Britain at Work*. London: Routledge.

Dunlop, J. T. 1958: *Industrial Relations Systems*. New York: Holt.

Edwards, P. K. 1986: *Conflict at Work*. Oxford: Blackwell.

Edwards, P. K. 1988: Patterns of conflict and accommodation. In D. Gallie (ed.), *Employment in Britain*. Oxford: Blackwell.

Edwards, P. K. 1995: From industrial relations to the employment relationship, *Relations Industrielles*, 50 (1), 39–65.

Edwards, P. K. 1998: Alan Fox. In M. Warner (ed.), *The Handbook of Management Thinking*. London: International Thomson.

Edwards, P. K. 2000: Discipline: towards trust and self-discipline? In S. Bach and K. Sisson (eds), *Personnel Management*, 3rd edn. Oxford: Blackwell.

Emmett, I., and Morgan, D. H. J. 1982: Max Gluckman and the Manchester shopfloor ethnographies. In R. Frankenberg (ed.), *Custom and Conflict in British Society*. Manchester: Manchester University Press.

Flanders, A. 1964: *The Fawley Productivity Agreements*. London: Faber & Faber.

Flanders, A. 1970: *Management and Unions*. London: Faber & Faber.

Flanders, A. 1974: The tradition of voluntarism, *British Journal of Industrial Relations*, 12 (3), 352–70.

Fox, A. 1966: *Industrial Sociology and Industrial Relations*. London: HMSO.

Fox, A. 1974: *Beyond Contract*. London: Faber & Faber.

Friedman, A. L. 1977: *Industry and Labour*. London: Macmillan.

Goldthorpe, J. H. 1971: Theories of industrial society, *Archives européennes de sociologie*, 12 (2), 263–88.

Goldthorpe, J. H., Lockwood, D., Bechhofer, F. and Platt, J. 1968: *The Affluent Worker: Industrial Attitudes and Behaviour*. Cambridge: Cambridge University Press.

Green, F. 2001: It's been a hard day's night: the concentration and intensification of work in late twentieth century Britain, *British Journal of Industrial Relations*, 39 (1), 53–80.

Gregg, P., and Wadsworth, J. (eds) 1999: *The State of Working Britain*. Manchester: Manchester University Press.

Grimshaw, D., Ward, K. G., Rubery, J. and Beynon, H. 2001: Organisations and the transformation of the internal labour market in the UK, *Work, Employment and Society*, 15 (1), 25–54.

Heery, E., and Salmon, J. 2000: The insecurity thesis. In E. Heery and J. Salmon (eds), *The Insecure Workforce*. London: Routledge.

Hirst, P., and Thompson, G. 1996: *Globalization in Question*. Cambridge: Polity.

Hyman, R. 1978: Pluralism, procedural consensus and collective bargaining, *British Journal of Industrial Relations*, 16 (1), 16–40. Repr. in R. Hyman, *The Political Economy of Industrial Relations*. Basingstoke: Macmillan.

Hyman, R. 1982: Contribution to review symposium on Collective Bargaining and Industrial Relations, *Industrial Relations*, 21 (1), 73–122.

Hyman, R. 1987: Strategy or structure, *Work, Employment and Society*, 1 (1), 25–56.

Jefferys, S. 1988: The changing face of conflict. In M. Terry and P. Edwards (eds), *Shopfloor Politics and Job Controls*. Oxford: Blackwell.

Kelly, J. 1998: *Rethinking Industrial Relations*. London: Routledge.

Kochan, T. A. 1982: Contribution to review symposium on Collective Bargaining and Industrial Relations, *Industrial Relations*, 21 (1), 73–122.

Kochan, T. A. 1998: What is distinctive about industrial relations research? In K. Whitfield and G. Strauss (eds), *Researching the World of Work*. Ithaca: ILR Press.

Lane, C. 1989: *Management and Labour in Europe*. Aldershot: Edward Elgar.

Marginson, P., Olsen, R. and Tailby, S. 1994: *The Eclecticism of Managerial Policy towards Labour Regulation: Three Case Studies*. Warwick Papers in Industrial Relations, 47. Coventry: IRRU, University of Warwick.

Millward, N., Bryson, A. and Forth, J. 2000: *All Change at Work?* London: Routledge.

Ohmae, K. 1995: *The End of the Nation State*. New York: HarperCollins.

Popper, K. R. 1957: *The Poverty of Historicism*. London: Routledge.

Purcell, J., and Sisson, K. 1983: Strategies and practice in the management of industrial relations. In G. S. Bain (ed.), *Industrial Relations in Britain*. Oxford: Blackwell.

Ramsay, H. 1975: Research note: firms and football teams, *British Journal of Industrial Relations*, 13 (3), 396–400.

Redman, T., and Wilkinson, A. (eds) 2001: *Contemporary Human Resource Management*. London: Financial Times/Prentice Hall.

Rose, M. 1988: *Industrial Behaviour*. Harmondsworth: Penguin.

Rubery, J. 1997: Wages and the labour market, *British Journal of Industrial Relations*, 35 (3), 337–62.

Sayer, A. 2000: *Realism and Social Science*. London: Sage.

Storey, J. 1992: *Developments in the Management of Human Resources*. Oxford: Blackwell.

Streeck, W. 1987: The uncertainties of management in the management of uncertainty, *Work, Employment and Society*, 1 (3), 281–308.

Turnbull, P. J. 1986: The 'Japanisation' of production and industrial relations at Lucas Electrical', *Industrial Relations Journal*, 17 (3), 193–206.

Wajcman, J. 2000: Feminism facing industrial relations in Britain, *British Journal of Industrial Relations*, 38 (2), 183–202.

Wernerfeld, B. 1984: A resource-based view of the firm, *Strategic Management Journal*, 5 (2), 171–80.

Wheen, F. 1999: *Karl Marx*. London: Fourth Estate.

Whitehouse, G., and Zetlin, D. 1999: Globalization and the pursuit of pay equity. In P. Edwards and T. Elger (eds), *The Global Economy, National States and the Regulation of Labour*. London: Mansell.

2

THE HISTORICAL EVOLUTION OF BRITISH INDUSTRIAL RELATIONS

RICHARD HYMAN

Until recently, any text on British industrial relations would emphasize at the outset the importance of history. At the end of the nineteenth century, Sidney and Beatrice Webb (1894) commenced their analysis of trade unionism with a classic narrative which traced unions' development from the seventeenth century; most of their successors displayed similar concerns. The first forerunner of the present book, *The System of Industrial Relations in Great Britain* (Flanders and Clegg 1954), opened with a chapter by an eminent social historian. The members of the 'Oxford school' who led the consolidation of industrial relations as an academic subject in the 1960s were as accomplished in the study of the past as of the present.

At the time, the reasons for an historical focus seemed self-evident. Most of the institutions of British industrial relations had evolved incrementally over decades or even centuries – most obviously trade unions, described by one writer (Turner 1962: 14) as 'historical deposits and repositories of history'. As in so many areas of British public affairs, appeals to precedent and tradition figured prominently in the conduct of industrial relations. Union representatives at workplace level conventionally employed the rhetoric of 'custom and practice' – meaning informal rules, conventional arrangements, or merely behaviour which had become tolerated over time – in order to justify their own claims or resist those of management (Brown 1972). The fact that institutions and practices had seemingly persisted for so long was often regarded as a decisive argument against change.

Most academic writers, until 20 years ago, emphasized the strength of inertia in British industrial relations. They insisted that the functioning of institutions is shaped by the inheritance of beliefs and relationships which frame their context. There were no simple panaceas for the perceived problems of industrial relations: German works councils, Swedish centralized bargaining or American legalism might be effective on their home ground, but could not readily be transplanted into so different a cultural setting. Change could not be achieved – or only at immense cost – if it was imposed 'against the historical grain' (Fox 1985: pp. xii–xiii). The experience of the 1971 Industrial Relations Act – a fiasco in its attempts to erect novel regulations and procedures – seemed to offer solid confirmation (Weekes et al. 1975).

Writing in the year 2000, the historical inheritance must evidently be reappraised. The Conservative government in office from 1979 to 1997 presided over the most radical changes in British industrial relations since the Industrial Revolution. The Labour government which replaced it declared an equal commitment to reform and transformation. Have the constraints of history finally been dissolved?

The authors who follow will provide evidence on which to base an answer to this question. This chapter, meanwhile, has two purposes: to outline the historical background to the developments of the 1980s and 1990s and to highlight a number of important long-term continuities relevant to any assessment of recent experience. The discussion will cover in turn the role of the state, of employers and of trade unions, exploring how each contributed to the evolution of a system of industrial relations so different from those in almost every other country. A key contention is that the popular view of trade unions as the primary cause of Britain's economic weakness – the assumption which underlay the initiatives of the Conservatives – was misconceived. The character and practices of British unions were very largely shaped by national political traditions and by the structure and priorities of employers. The adversarial nature of British industrial relations reflected distinctive features of society which were evident long before the rise of trade unionism and which remain apparent despite the recent weakening of union membership and influence. Whether adversarialism has finally been displaced by partnership remains a moot question.

The State in Industrial Relations: The Tradition of Voluntarism

In the early formative period of British industrial relations, governments and the law were serious obstacles to the growth of collective regulation of employment. This was reflected not only in the oppressive content of statute law (most notably the Combination Acts of 1799 and 1800, partially repealed a quarter of a century later), but more fundamentally in the individualist free-market presuppositions of the common law. The latter underwrote the rights of property, and as a corollary the sanctity of individual contracts. Attempts by workers to organize collectively, to submit joint demands to their employers, or to unite in strike action all fell foul of the prohibition of 'restraint of trade'; those committing such acts risked conviction on the serious charge of conspiracy. While there is debate about how rigorously and systematically the legal restrictions were enforced, there exists a lengthy record of fines, imprisonment and even penal deportation suffered by nineteenth-century trade unionists.

The method by which trade unions and collective bargaining were eventually legalized was not, as in many countries, by establishing a positive right to organize, to negotiate and to strike, but by defining an area of industrial relations 'immunities' where the effect of the common law was inhibited. As Wedderburn has emphasized (1980: 69), 'in strict juridical terms, there does not exist in Britain any "right" to organise or any "right" to strike'. The key legislative initiatives – the Trade Union Act 1871, the Conspiracy and Protection of Property Act 1875 and the Trade Disputes Act 1906 – were designed to remove the specifically legal obstacles to collective action. But while workers were thus free to organize collectively, the employer was equally free to dismiss a worker for joining a union; while unions were entitled to bargain collectively, employers were equally at liberty to refuse to negotiate; and while a union could lawfully call a strike 'in contemplation or furtherance of a trade dispute', striking workers were in breach of their contracts of employment and might therefore be dismissed (or even sued individually for damages). This was in marked contrast to many other national labour law regimes, which obliged employers to respect workers' right to unionize, to bargain 'in good faith' with representative unions, and to impose no penalty (beyond withholding pay) on those participating legally in a strike.

Why British trade unions, for the most part, found so ambiguous a framework of rights acceptable is discussed in more detail below. Two particular consequences deserve emphasis at this point. The first, particularly important in the context of strike law, is that a relatively technical redefinition of the scope of trade union immunities (whether by new enactment or by judicial creativity) could substantially alter the boundaries of legitimate action. The second, more diffuse, is that the interrelationships of workers, employers and unions became treated in public policy as a largely private arena of social behaviour. Moreover, the traditional disjuncture between industrial relations and the law has meant that the very notion of a collective contract, of central importance in many other nations, does not exist in Britain: collective agreements have always been 'binding in honour only', of legal relevance only to the extent that their terms might be explicitly or implicitly incorporated into the individual employment contracts of those covered. Likewise, trade unions have not traditionally possessed the status of agents of their members.

It is plausible to explain the tradition of legal 'abstentionism' by reference to distant history. Successful resistance to royal power in the seventeenth century involved the assertion of the rights of the individual against the state. This in turn encouraged the entrenchment of market individualism as the dominant principle of the British political economy, an ideology which both underwrote the rights of property and gave legitimacy to notions of plebeian independence (Fox 1985). The outcome was a society in which consciousness of class distinction and division was particularly acute, but in which opposing interests were normally reconciled through compromise and accommodation. This was the matrix in which industrial relations evolved: marked by an adversarial tradition in which it was natural to speak of the 'two sides' of industry (the Continental vocabulary of 'social partners' was, at least until very recently, almost incomprehensible in English), yet which generated 'rules of the game' facilitating voluntary agreement. Workers, unions and employers (who typically behaved pragmatically once unions gained too much support to be easily repressed or excluded) drew on dispositions inherited from the past in order to regulate their mutual relationships.

The absence of statutory regulation, a condition known as voluntarism or collective laissez faire (see chapter 6), was long celebrated as an index of maturity and sophistication. Collective laissez faire is perhaps the most precise term; it was coined by the legal scholar Otto Kahn-Freund in 1959 to describe the preference for abstention, a reliance on collective bargaining and 'the free play of collective forces in society', shared by state, employers and unions (McCarthy 1992: 6). The Royal Commission on Labour in 1894 concluded its lengthy deliberations by insisting that strong organizations of workers and employers, and voluntary agreement between the two parties, offered the most stable and desirable basis for regulating employment. For almost a century thereafter, a major policy commitment of governments of every political complexion was to encourage the institutions and processes of collective self-regulation. In the hubristic words of the Ministry of Labour in 1934, collective bargaining

> has, for many years, been recognised in this country as the method best adapted to the needs of industry and to the demands of the national character . . . [It] has discharged its important functions, on the whole, so smoothly and efficiently and withal so unobtrusively, that the extent of its influence is apt to be, if not altogether overlooked, at least underestimated. (quoted in Hawes 2000: 3)

This is not to say that the law and the state had no direct impact on industrial relations. As Flanders (1974) has demonstrated, even fervent supporters of voluntarism tended to apply the principle selectively. But while legislation on individual employment conditions has always been part of the British system, the rights provided have in general been far weaker than in most other European countries (making the more ironical the passionate commitment to deregulation of Conservative governments in the 1980s and 1990s, to a significant extent shared by their Labour successor). Traditionally, most individual employment law covered either segments of the labour market not adequately regulated by collective bargaining, or issues (such as health and safety) with a clear-cut public interest. More systematic legal regulation which could be found in many other national jurisdictions – minimum wages, maximum working hours, protection against dismissal – was considered undesirable by most of those who shaped British developments.

When governments assumed an industrial relations role, this was most often restricted to providing assistance to collective bargainers. The Labour Department set up within the Board of Trade in 1893 was designed primarily to provide statistical information, the better to inform the decisions of employers and unions. This essentially advisory and auxiliary status was sustained after the creation of a separate Ministry of Labour in 1917. A touchstone was the question of intervention in industrial disputes. An Act of 1898 established a governmental conciliation service (since 1974 institutionally separated within the Advisory Conciliation and Arbitration Service, ACAS); but its role depended totally on the readiness of the conflicting parties to accept its mediation, and even voluntary conciliation was offered only when any company- or industry-specific procedures for dispute resolution had been exhausted. In major conflicts, governments might appoint a court of inquiry, but without power to arbitrate. More radical intervention was possible under the Emergency Powers Act 1920; but even in the case of 'national emergencies' a government could not – as in some other countries – impose a 'cooling-off' period, order strikers back to work, or impose a settlement.

Finally, the treatment of public employees is noteworthy. At the end of the nineteenth century the government accepted the principle that the conditions of its own employees should not be inferior to those established by collective bargaining for analogous workers in the private sector. Until the Whitley Reports in 1917, public sector unions faced serious problems in gaining recognition and establishing negotiating procedures; but thereafter the legitimacy of union organization was confirmed, and was indeed explicitly underwritten in the nationalization legislation which extended the scope of the public sector after 1945. The period after the Second World War also saw the elaboration of the principle of 'fair comparisons' between pay and working conditions in public and private sectors, with institutionalized arrangements ensuring that the terms of agreements in the latter were transferred to analogous workers in the former. Although (with very minor exceptions) the right of public employees to strike has never been subject to special restrictions, such arrangements helped sustain relative industrial peace. In general, then, the government as employer tended to follow 'good practice' in the private sector; only in recent times has it embraced a more active and initiating role.

Employers: The Tradition of Unscientific Management

Karl Marx saw the nineteenth-century British employer as progenitor of 'modern industry', a form of production in which the worker was subjected to the new organizational disciplines of the factory system, with a detailed subdivision of tasks and sophisticated technology eliminating all traditional skills. This view was consistent with the arguments of many contemporary British commentators on the 'industrial revolution'; and certainly there was evidence to support such a perspective. Many of the new factory entrepreneurs imposed the 'barrack-like discipline' of which Marx wrote; some of the leading coal-owners were notorious for their autocratic treatment of labour; the railways were managed on military lines, and so on.

Nevertheless, such contexts were not the main influence on the development of industrial relations. The rise of British industry was not primarily based on large-scale factory production; the slogan 'workshop of the world' reflected the reality of a multiplicity of small-scale producers. The metal-working trades which figured so prominently in the success of Victorian capitalism manufactured an immense variety of commodities, often tailored to the specific requirements of individual customers. Vertical integration was low; complex products were often the outcome of a lengthy chain of supplier–contractor relationships (a feature which was later to distinguish the British motor industry from most of its foreign competitors).

In short, the very notion of an industrial revolution is misleading. Technological innovation was intermittent and uneven: new machinery was often expensive, unreliable and inflexible (Samuel 1977). To cope with fluctuating and diversified product markets, employers in much of British industry relied heavily on the expertise and versatility of a labour force whose skills pre-dated capitalist manufacturing (Littler 1982). Some firms might possess a formal hierarchy of managers, supervisors and chargehands, but more commonly the employer depended on the largely autonomous self-regulation of work teams, sustained either by systems of payment by results (the 'internal sub-contract') or by workers' acceptance of the obligation to perform 'a fair day's work'. A classic instance is the case of cotton-spinning: the introduction of the 'self-acting' mule in the first half of the century was regarded by Marx (and other contemporaries) as a means of enforcing unqualified managerial control, but mule-spinning soon became established as a craft-type occupation exercising a high degree of autonomous job control (Lazonick 1990).

The system of 'unscientific management' was attractive to small employers in uncertain markets, and also to many larger producers. The costs of supervisory and technical staff – and of fixed capital – could be kept to a minimum, their functions performed by a skilled manual workforce which could be hired and fired with scant notice. 'Craft control', as Lazonick (1990: 113) has argued, 'was consistent with, and perhaps even fundamental to, British industrial success.' However, only some industries, notably engineering and printing, had clear craft traditions involving the control of the work process by craft workers and associated controls of entry to the trade. Others had similar practices, though without any craft control in the strict sense, cotton being the key example. Many others, notably new mass production and chemicals sectors, had no such traditions (Glucksmann 1990). There are thus two key qualifications to Lazonick's account. First, the role of crafts in engineering did not prevent all change: work was indeed rationalized. But the process was limited and uneven, and was dependent on traditional ideas of management. Second, in other sectors the failure to rationalize was due not to any externally imposed craft rules but to employers' own preferences. To experiment with alternative systems of work organization and labour control could be rationally viewed as an unnecessary risk for companies which were already achieving acceptable levels of profit.

It is only relatively recently that this system became widely regarded as a source of stagnation and an explanation of eventual competitive decline, in the face of economic rivals with far more elaborate managerial systems and far more sophisticated methods of organization and control. In a global economy where strategic innovation came to count for more than pragmatic adaptation, the traditional strengths of British industrial organization increasingly came to be regarded as weaknesses. Very often, labour was made the scapegoat for the newly perceived deficiencies. Workers' natural response to labour market insecurity was to regard change suspiciously, to protect inherited job territories, and hence to defend traditional demarcations in the organization of work. In the twentieth century such job controls were commonly denounced as 'restrictive practices', as employee-imposed constraints on managerial initiative. It is, however, far more appropriate to regard them as the heritage of a traditional relationship between management and labour, in which decisions on product range, marketing, technology and corporate structure all helped shape employers' approaches to the organization of work (Hyman and Elger 1981; Elbaum and Lazonick 1986). In this sense, any transformation of the management–labour relations from which employers had historically benefited required much more far-reaching changes within management itself: one reason for the problematic nature of the rationalization processes attempted in recent decades.

This traditional basis of the management of work within the enterprise had important implications for the evolution of industrial relations in its conventional sense. Employers were anxious to assert the right to unfettered control over their own capital. This was the meaning of the term 'laissez faire': the historic demand of the new entrepreneurial class for the removal of pre-capitalist state restrictions on economic activity. Most employers had no desire – and saw no need – for government intervention in the nineteenth-century labour market. 'Collective laissez faire' thus suited their perceived self-interest. By the same token, many employers considered trade union organization a challenge to their right to dispose of their own property without interference; hence the long record of conflict over the right to union membership. But, as the Victorian era proceeded, employers became increasingly reconciled to the existence of unionism, and some indeed came to appreciate collective regulation of the labour market as a means of taking wage costs out of competition.

Most employers were reluctant, however, to concede a formal role for trade union representation within their own establishments; the characteristic means to 'neutralize the workplace from trade union activity' (Sisson 1987: 13) was to agree to meet union representatives only in the context of multi-employer collective bargaining. Such collective regulation developed initially at district level, but after the turn of the century also nationally, primarily over rates of pay. What most employers continued to resist was collective bargaining over questions of work organization, a subject which fell squarely within the protected territory of 'managerial prerogatives'. Employers and their associations were prepared to go to the lengths of enforcing protracted lock-outs in response to trade union challenges, real or imagined, to their 'right to manage'. 'The Federated Employers, while disavowing any intention of interfering with the proper functions of the Trade Unions, will admit no interference with the management of their businesses': with this formula began the terms of settlement imposed by the engineering companies at the end of the lock-out of 1897–8. Yet the elusive boundary between management rights and trade union functions was in practice untenable, not least because – as already argued – employers so often lacked both the will and the competence to 'manage their businesses' without at least the tacit agreement of their workforce (whether unionized or not).

The familiar managerial dilemma of sustaining control while retaining consent was resolved in Britain – in the absence of the formal machinery of employee workplace representation which emerged in most Continental countries – by covert and ad hoc accommodation (Tolliday and Zeitlin 1991). There is a direct historical linkage from the social regulation of the Victorian workplace to the pattern described by the Donovan Commission (1968: 12) as 'two systems of industrial relations. The one is the formal system embodied in the official institutions. The other is the informal system created by the actual behaviour of trade unions and employers' associations, of managers, shop stewards and workers.' While employers refused to undertake formal and co-ordinated negotiation with trade unions over issues which trespassed on their 'right to manage', in reality the day-to-day exigencies of production in most unionized environments required a constant process of give and take between first-line supervisors, individual workers and their workplace union representatives. Shop-floor bargaining, as Flanders argued (1970: 169), was 'largely informal, largely fragmented and largely autonomous'. Employers traditionally preferred matters this way, in the fond belief that concessions not explicitly admitted could more readily be withdrawn if circumstances altered. The uncertain progress of voluntary industrial relations 'reform' from the 1960s onwards showed that even informal social arrangements could acquire the resilience of officially consecrated institutions. This helps explain the more traumatic and conflictual implementation of change from the 1970s onwards.

Trade Unions: The Tradition of Free Collective Bargaining

British trade unions originated as local societies of skilled workers (and were regarded by some historians as direct successors of the medieval craft guilds). In many cases their functions were only marginally related to industrial relations as the term is usually understood: the typical craft association operated as a social club, a local labour exchange, and an insurance society (providing 'friendly benefits' in the case of death, injury, unemployment, or loss of tools). In terms of regulating employment conditions, their usual concern was to ensure that masters respected customary rates of pay, job demarcations and ratios of apprentices to adult workers. If price levels and technologies remained stable, and employers (whose own roots were often within the craft tradition) observed the proprieties, there was no occasion for collective bargaining. Indeed the Webbs – who coined the term 'collective bargaining' at the end of the nineteenth century – referred to the practice of the early craft societies as 'the method of mutual insurance': workers would simply refuse employment with masters who flouted the standard conditions of the trade, and would be supported by union funds until they found acceptable work elsewhere. The corollary of this method – unilateral regulation, as Flanders later called it – was that the need for formal organizational structures was minimal. The early unions operated on the basis of what the Webbs termed 'primitive democracy', with lay officers who often served only for a limited period of time, and with policy decisions based on collective discussion by the whole membership.

Craft unions were forced to adapt over time as technologies altered, employers grew larger and more assertive, improved transport widened labour markets, and sharp occupational segmentations became blurred. From the middle of the nineteenth century, local societies began to form national amalgamations; after the turn of the century, unions of cognate trades began to merge; subsequently, most craft unions opened their membership to include non-craft occupations. Increased size and scope, and the development of formal collective bargaining, led to the growth of more elaborate organizational structures and the creation of a hierarchy of full-time officials. Nevertheless, the process of bureaucratization was relatively limited: there were few officers per member, lay representatives and officials retained important functions, and the traditions of rank-and-file democracy remained powerful.

The coverage of trade unionism extended progressively from the 1860s, as phases of successful recruitment spread to new sectors and occupations. Stable unionism became established in the large-scale Victorian industries with no significant basis in craft production: mining, textiles, railways. Two waves of expansion around the turn of the century – in 1888–90 and 1910–20 – laid the basis for the giant modern general unions. The unionization of public sector and white-collar workers – to a large extent within separate organizations – followed thereafter. Lacking the craft societies' traditional unilateral control within specialist labour markets, these newer unions were from the outset concerned to develop collective bargaining relationships with employers. In many cases they were also more centralized and authoritarian – one writer (Turner 1962) described them as 'popular bossdoms'. Yet non-craft unions often modelled their governance on the craft societies, and incorporated their own traditions of decentralized initiative. The Transport and General Workers' Union (TGWU), for example, was established in 1921 following a series of amalgamations involving a hundred or more separate organizations, notably dockers' unions in individual ports with a strong commitment to local democracy.

The long historical evolution of British trade unionism explains three distinctive features which deserve emphasis. They are: structural complexity and fragmentation; an ambiguous orientation to political action; and the potent moral value attached to the principle of 'free collective bargaining'.

Britain is notable for its number of competing trade unions. In the 1890s, when official statistics were first compiled, there were well over 1,000, with an average membership of little over 1,000. As discussed in chapter 9, only since the Second World War has the number fallen rapidly, largely through amalgamation; but over 200 still survive. The great majority of unions have always been tiny, with a handful of large organizations accounting for the bulk of trade union membership (for several decades, the largest dozen have contained over 60 per cent of aggregate membership). The formation by merger of a small group of numerically dominant unions, while in some respects reducing structural complexity, has in other respects intensified it. In the early decades of the twentieth century the familiar distinction between craft, industrial and general unionism had some foundation in reality, but amalgamation has increasingly made multi-industry and multi-occupational unionism the norm; most workers could in principle join any of a number of cross-cutting organizations.

It is common to stress that Britain is one of the few countries in which a single central confederation exists, encompassing the great majority of unionized workers (even though only a minority of unions). This contrasts with the situation in most other nations, where rival confederations embrace opposing political or ideological principles, or where manual, white-collar and professional unions are affiliated to separate central bodies. The monopoly position of the Trades Union Congress (TUC) is indeed distinctive in this respect. No less significant, however, are its limited role and status. Founded in 1868 as an annual 'parliament of labour', it was not until the 1920s that the TUC acquired its own organizational apparatus. Affiliated unions have always been parsimonious in the resources which they vote to the central body, and even more restrictive in the powers that they are willing to cede to it. In the twentieth century it came to act as an adjudicator in organizational disputes between member unions; a channel of communication with government, and with its counterpart on the employers' side, the Confederation of British Industry (CBI); and a 'think tank' for trade unions collectively. But the majority of influential unions have been consistently reluctant to allow it to launch policy initiatives on their behalf, to intervene in collective bargaining, or to engage in 'neo-corporatist' centralized negotiations on Continental lines which might result in commitments on behalf of the movement as a whole (see chapter 5).

The latter reservation reflects a more general ambivalence towards politics and the law. One important reason why British unions accepted a system of labour law based on immunities rather than positive rights was their experience of the incomprehension and hostility of judges and the courts: the anti-collectivist bias of the legal system was such that even seemingly supportive legislation might be construed to their detriment. Laissez faire was in this respect as resonant a slogan for trade unionists as for early British capitalists. There was also a powerful opinion that what the law bestowed, the law could take away, and that rights and benefits guaranteed by legislation would deter workers from unionizing. For this very reason, many union leaders were critical of the 1909 legislation establishing Trade Boards (later Wages Councils) to prescribe minimum pay in badly organized sectors; as discussed in chapter 18, hostility towards legislative 'interference' in wage determination continued to the 1980s.

As late as 1966 the TUC, in its evidence to the Donovan Commission, articulated the traditional suspicion of legal regulation:

> no state, however benevolent, can perform the function of trade unions in enabling workpeople themselves to decide how their interests can best be safeguarded. It is where trade unions are not competent, and recognise that they are not competent, to perform a function, that they welcome the state playing a role in at least enforcing minimum standards, but in Britain this role is recognised as the second best alternative.

The preferred alternative was the consolidation of unions' own bargaining strength in order to negotiate acceptable standards with employers through 'free collective bargaining'. A good example is the question of the regulation of working time. Towards the end of the nineteenth century a legally enforced eight-hour day was a prominent demand of many socialists. The objective was endorsed by many 'new unionists' organizing lower-skilled workers whose bargaining power was uncertain. It was fervently opposed by more established union leaders, who insisted that legislation would conflict with bargaining autonomy. Although the TUC was persuaded to declare in principle for the statutory regulation of hours, in practice the views of the advocates of piecemeal collective bargaining prevailed. In certain industries – notably coalmining – unions campaigned successfully for the statutory regulation of working time, but the comprehensive enforcement of maximum hours was never seriously pursued.

In more recent times, the commitment to 'free collective bargaining' had two important implications. The first was a generally hostile attitude to government attempts to control the level of pay settlements (a theme considered further below). The second was a widespread suspicion of forms of employee participation in management decision-making which have long been institutionalized in many other European countries. The recommendations of the Bullock Committee, in 1977, for legislation to introduce worker representatives on company boards, was as strongly opposed by some trade unionists as by employer organizations (Elliott 1978). 'There is an essential need to preserve trade union independence', one union leader had written at an earlier stage of the industrial democracy debate. 'The unions must not be directly involved in controlling industry' (Scanlon 1968: 7).

There is an apparent paradox in the political stance of British trade unions. They have always been strongly committed to the autonomy of their negotiations on behalf of their specific membership constituencies, but have also long employed the language of socialist class politics, regarding the Labour Party as a partner in an integrated labour movement. But rhetoric and practice – declamatory appeals to a general working-class interest, day-to-day preoccupation with the bread-and-butter concerns of much narrower sectoral and occupational groups – have traditionally diverged. For British unions, unlike those elsewhere in Europe, the state was not a major focus of concern once the basic legal framework of the 1870s had been achieved; the democratization of the franchise, an issue which encouraged unions elsewhere to politically oriented militancy, was achieved incrementally and relatively consensually over many decades; British socialism was non-existent in the key mid-Victorian years when union organization was consolidated.

Superficially, the end of the nineteenth century brought a new alignment between trade unionism and socialist politics. But whereas in much of Europe modern union organization emerged as an offshoot of social democracy, in Britain the relationship was reversed. In the 1890s, the aggressive stance of some leading employers, together with a series of hostile judicial decisions, persuaded many orthodox trade unionists of the need for a more active political strategy. The outcome was the foundation in 1900 of what would soon become the Labour Party; but this stemmed from a decision within the TUC that the representation of workers' interests in parliament should be 'hived off' to a separate (and, it was initially assumed, subsidiary) body, allowing the unions to concentrate on their primary function in collective bargaining.

The relationship between party and unions has been described as a 'contentious alliance' (Minkin 1991). For most of the twentieth century, however, a relatively consensual demarcation of functions existed. Most major unions were affiliated to the Labour Party (though the TUC itself was not), contributed the bulk of its funds and held the majority of votes at its conference; but they rarely attempted to interfere with the autonomy of the parliamentary leadership in determining general party policy. Conversely, the party traditionally refrained from taking policy initiatives which impinged on the trade union role in regulating employment matters through collective bargaining. The more recent strains in the relationship largely reflected the growing artificiality of any demarcation between the spheres of 'politics' and 'industrial relations'. It was the same erosion of traditional boundaries which put the whole traditional system of industrial relations in Britain under increasing stress.

Pressures for Change

The doctrine of laissez faire prescribed and presupposed a clear separation between the economy and the state. Governments should protect the integrity of contracts, and sustain whatever force was needed to guarantee the security of British capital at home and overseas, but had no other role in the marketplace. As has been seen, the traditional institutions of industrial relations were cast within the mould of these assumptions.

Developments in the twentieth century made 'collective laissez faire' increasingly anomalous. Two world wars, and high levels of peacetime military expenditure, gave the state a central economic role. Keynesian notions of macroeconomic management, encouraged by the experience of crisis and mass unemployment between the wars, established economic policy as a legitimate concern of government. The nationalization of specific industrial sectors, and the growth of public services, made the state an increasingly important employer (directly or indirectly responsible for almost a third of the labour force by the late 1970s).

In this changed context three key issues – inflation, public expenditure and productivity – made industrial relations increasingly a focus of political attention. Post-war governments of both parties were committed to the goal of full employment, but were concerned that workers' increased labour market strength would result in inflationary wage movements. Already during the Second World War this was perceived as a potential problem, and there were calls for government regulation of wages; but the Ministry of Labour (headed during the coalition government by Ernest Bevin, leader of the TGWU) insisted on sustaining the principle of 'voluntaryism' (Bullock 1967), relying on the self-restraint of union negotiators together with temporary provision for compulsory arbitration in the case of disputes. Faced with a serious economic crisis, the post-war Labour government in 1948 introduced a policy of wage restraint which received the backing of the TUC and had no compulsory legal foundations. After a Conservative government attempted to influence pay determination in the early 1960s, its Labour successor elected in 1964 made a prices and incomes policy central to its economic strategy. Initially voluntary, the policy was given statutory backing in 1966, despite objections from the TUC. New governments elected in 1970 and in 1974 first abandoned their predecessors' incomes policies, then introduced their own measures of wage restraint when faced with severe economic difficulties.

In the main, governments in their intermittent pursuit of wage restraint policies attempted to avoid too frontal a challenge to 'free collective bargaining'. Labour governments in particular were anxious to win trade union co-operation, and in 1964 attempted to institutionalize this by creating the National Board for Prices and Incomes (NBPI) with trade union (and employer) members. The TUC was likewise represented on the National Economic Development Council (created by the Conservatives in 1962), having acquired over previous decades the right to appoint nominees on a multiplicity of less important quasi-governmental bodies. As discussed in chapter 5, however, Continental-style tripartite macroeconomic bargaining was only superficially imitated in Britain. Firstly, the TUC lacked control over its affiliates, as did most individual unions over their local negotiators; formal agreement to a pay norm gave no guarantee that it would be respected in practice. Secondly, the voluntarist tradition still shaped union attitudes. The majority, in 1964, were prepared to endorse what Labour leaders called the 'planned growth of incomes'; wage restraint was quite a different matter, from time to time tolerated rather than approved when a Labour government faced overwhelming economic difficulties. The proactive agreement on a set of demands which might be bargained against collective union self-regulation in pay negotiations – what in other countries is often known as 'political exchange' – has never been feasible in Britain.

Government concern with the general level of pay settlements became even stronger in the case of public employees. The principle that the state should follow the trends in collective bargaining in the private sector (the principle often known as 'fair comparisons') came under growing strain as public employment and expenditure expanded, and as pressures for fiscal economy mounted. Most exercises in incomes policy were regarded by public sector unions – usually correctly – as bearing particularly rigorously on their own members, since the government could exert more direct influence over their negotiations. After 1970, controls over public expenditure levels also impinged directly on the resources available for pay increases. The dual impact of these constraints was to make public employment – for the most part traditionally a haven of peaceful industrial relations – into a major arena of conflict.

Preoccupations with productivity crystallized a variety of criticisms which were regularly voiced in the post-war decades, and which identified the declining competitiveness of British industry with the established industrial relations arrangements. Three themes were prominent in a catalogue of complaints: strikes, trade union power and restrictive practices.

Traditionally, all main parties to industrial relations assumed that conflict between employers and workers was inevitable from time to time, but could best be contained by allowing the two sides to reach their own settlements rather than attempting to impose peace from outside. This argument, regarded as self-evident by industrial relations pluralists, was one of the conclusions of the 1894 Royal Commission: strong organization on both sides of industry might occasionally give rise to major confrontations, but in the long run it would bring

more regular and peaceable relationships. This view was at least partially vindic-
ated by subsequent experience: apart from periods of great social and economic
turbulence – notably the years around the First World War, which began with
the 'labour unrest' of 1910–13 and culminated in the 1926 General Strike –
industrial conflict in Britain was relatively contained, in terms both of the volume
of strike activity and of its usually low-key nature. The decades around the
Second World War were indeed notable for the complete absence of official
industry-wide stoppages.

The development of 'two systems' of industrial relations was, however,
particularly marked in the case of strikes. In the period when national trade
unions virtually abandoned the strike weapon, the number of small, local, usually 'unofficial' disputes increased considerably. The process began in the 1930s
as unemployment declined, trade union membership increased, and workplace
bargaining by shop stewards became more common, and was only partially
inhibited by wartime conditions. Much of the early growth of strike activity was
in coalmining (mainly involving disputes about piece rates and working conditions); but from the end of the 1950s, strike-proneness in manufacturing industry increased rapidly; the total number of officially recorded strikes reached
almost 4,000 in 1970 (see chapter 9; Hyman 1989).

The most common reaction to these trends – particularly from Conservative
politicians and the press – held workers and trade unions exclusively responsible. The system of legal immunities meant, it was argued, that trade unions
were 'above the law'. The prevalence of the closed shop – an agreement or
practice that only union members would be employed at a particular workplace
– was held to give unions unjustifiable power over individual workers. Many
alleged that 'politically motivated' union leaders or shop stewards were able to
apply this power to sinister ends. Industrial militancy, it was suggested, was
sabotaging British economic performance and thus explained the deteriorating
position in world markets.

Such arguments were a major reason for the appointment in 1965 of the
Donovan Royal Commission. Its analysis, however, differed considerably from
more strident opinions: British industrial relations were indeed marked by 'anarchy
and disorder', but this stemmed primarily from institutional deficiencies for which
all parties shared responsibility. Employers had failed, or refused, to maintain
the collective solidarity necessary to make industry-wide agreements effective;
but in the main they had been equally unwilling or unable to admit the reality
of shop-floor collective bargaining and to plan and co-ordinate this. Unions for
their part were too weak rather than too strong, doing little to advise or assist,
let alone control, their workplace representatives. Shop-floor bargainers were
often 'striving to bring some order into a chaotic situation'; but the unco-ordinated
and opportunistic manner in which decisions on pay and conditions, hiring and
firing, and the organization of work were taken led inevitably to conflict.

The Donovan Report also addressed the issue of 'restrictive practices'. The
popular argument was that workers or their unions gratuitously enforced a
variety of archaic or artificial restrictions which prevented employers from introducing new technologies, reorganizing work more efficiently, or increasing the

pace of production. The Donovan view was that the sources of poor productivity were more complex. Sheer managerial incompetence was one cause. More generally, workers often responded rationally to situational imperatives which were not of their making. Job protection was inevitably a powerful motive when employment was insecure. Those whose basic rates of pay were low had every incentive to spin out the work so as to increase their earnings through overtime (a distinctive feature of much manual employment in Britain, which has remained highly resistant to change to the present day for reasons including managerial reliance on the ease and simplicity of overtime: see Arrowsmith and Sisson 2000: 303). Co-operation in productivity improvements could be expected only if workers had reason to believe that these would work to their benefit rather than their disadvantage, and only management could provide such guarantees – as had been offered in the case of some much commended 'productivity agreements' in the 1960s, notably at Esso's Fawley refinery (Flanders 1964).

The 1970s: The Failure of Reform?

The Donovan recommendations placed the responsibility firmly upon management to develop a system of industrial relations more attuned to the realities of work and employment in the 1960s. At the same time, government itself should take a more active role in encouraging reform. The NBPI was already giving systematic attention in its reports to productivity questions. Following the Donovan recommendations, a permanent Commission on Industrial Relations was also established. These initiatives helped accelerate an already apparent trend by many companies to reorganize their handling of industrial relations, drawing up more systematic negotiation and disputes procedures, formalizing the status of shop stewards, introducing new arrangements for discipline and dismissals, rationalizing payment systems, and harmonizing employment conditions in different establishments.

One body of opinion within the Donovan Commission had doubted whether a purely voluntary reform strategy would prove adequate, and the report was widely criticized on this score. The Labour government which had appointed the commission proposed legislation in 1969 which, while largely consistent with the Donovan recommendations, included more coercive elements; but faced with the resistance of most trade unions and many of its own backbenchers it retreated (Jenkins 1970). The Conservative government elected in 1970 was committed to a far more interventionist approach. Its Industrial Relations Act 1971 imposed elaborate regulations on trade unions (whose internal procedures had hitherto been scarcely affected by the law), severely restricted strike immunities, and made unions liable to heavy penalties if judged responsible for a variety of 'unfair industrial practices'.

The 1971 Act was a failure, for reasons including determined union opposition, significant employer doubts about using its powers, and the fact that it introduced untried mechanisms at one blow and was thus felt to be out of step with established approaches; on this last score, the Conservative governments of the 1980s learnt the lesson by introducing union reforms on a 'step by step' basis using existing legal structures. But the legalism which the Act introduced was to persist. As well as its obviously anti-union elements the Act had established a new concept of unfair dismissal and provided (limited) legal remedies. A procedure for unions to claim recognition from employers was also created. The legislation of the 1974 Labour government (Trade Union and Labour Relations Act 1974, Employment Protection Act 1975) sustained and extended these rights largely because the TUC, virtually without debate, had changed its views considerably from the strict 'voluntarist' line which it had expounded to the Donovan Commission. Together with other pieces of legislation enacted in the 1960s and 1970s (notably those concerning sex and race discrimination), and in the context of the external jurisdiction stemming from accession to the European Community in 1973, the traditional idea of 'legal abstentionism' no longer matched reality.

On other counts, the attractions of 'free collective bargaining' were waning by the 1970s. Many critics of Donovan had argued that the commission had overestimated the possibility of consensual change. Shop-floor workers may not have been the prime authors of the 'informal system' of decentralized workplace negotiation, but to an important extent those with sufficient collective strength were its beneficiaries, able to combine a high degree of job control with opportunities to raise earnings regularly through piecework bargaining. With levels of unemployment rising through much of the 1970s, the incentive to resist rationalization measures (often involving job cuts) was increased. If some companies did succeed in introducing reform by agreement, others faced resistance. Confronted by rapidly intensifying competitive pressures, employers – including a growing number of multinationals accustomed to very different overseas industrial relations institutions – were in many cases losing patience.

Within unions themselves there were also more critics than in the past of 'free collective bargaining'. In particular, the influence of feminism within some unions brought growing awareness that collective bargaining had traditionally been oriented to a white, male workforce employed full-time in relatively secure occupations. This was the population in which union organization was strongest and among which the coverage of collective bargaining was most extensive; and the whole agenda of union–employer negotiations, it was argued, was oriented to their particular interests. There were calls for an agenda which met the problems and wishes of the growing proportion of the labour force that did not fit the traditional stereotypes, and for types of action going beyond the exclusive reliance on collective bargaining.

Such arguments had particular resonance in public sector unions, with a high proportion of female, part-time, low-paid members, and without the 'industrial muscle' of many traditional sections of unionized workers. Here too, though, there were pockets of workers with greater capacity to take disruptive collective action, and feelings of grievance reduced customary inhibitions against militancy. The Donovan analysis of the deficiencies of British industrial relations and the consequential proposals for reform had focused almost exclusively on private industry. The pressures already provoking public sector conflict were ignored;

but they were to become increasingly obvious – as already noted – in the 1970s, culminating at the end of the decade in the so-called 'winter of discontent'.

The Transformation of British Industrial Relations: Still the European Exception?

This chapter has surveyed the emergence, the long and seemingly robust consolidation, and the eventual erosion of a system of industrial relations which differed radically from other national models. British exceptionalism rested on the interlocking and mutually reinforcing features of (relative) state abstention, unscientific management, and business unionism. The stability of the system depended, above all else, on the international viability of the British economy. Its character was set in the golden age of British capitalism. Competitiveness was already under threat by the end of the nineteenth century; but victory in two world wars provided interludes of temporary respite. By the 1970s, however, the evidence of sustained relative decline was undeniable; and this is one reason why, by the time of the fateful general election of 1979, defenders of the existing system of industrial relations were far fewer than a decade earlier. Yet there was little consensus on what might replace it. Had voluntary reform proved inadequate because a more fundamental shift in the balance of power between employers on the one hand, unions and workers on the other, was essential? Or was the problem more deep-rooted, in a structure of relationships profoundly resistant to change?

The government elected in 1979 had no doubts on this score. Shortly before the election, one of its leading figures issued a pamphlet entitled *Solving the Union Problem is the Key to Britain's Economic Recovery*, and this slogan encapsulated the strategic thrust of its industrial relations policies. The tradition of voluntarism was consigned to the dustbin of history with a succession of major pieces of legislation between 1980 and 1993. Their primary aim was to narrow many of the traditional trade union immunities and eliminate others: the closed shop was outlawed, the scope for lawful industrial action was drastically reduced, the internal affairs of unions became subject to detailed regulation, individual members acquired new rights against their unions even as their rights against employers were reduced. The support in public policy for the principle of collective bargaining was abandoned, and most of the tripartite institutions established over previous decades were eliminated.

There were other major breaks with tradition. The commitment expressed by all previous post-war governments to the priority of full employment was rejected: unemployment was the consequence of irresponsible collective bargaining or of misguided government interference with the market, or both. The public sector and the institutions of Whitleyism were regarded as market-distorting monopoly arrangements which fostered trade union power; hence a series of initiatives to cut the sector down to size (through privatization and compulsory competitive tendering) and to restrict and decentralize collective bargaining. The scope of individual employment protections (such as unfair dismissals legislation), already narrow by Continental European standards, was further limited. The underlying logic was to empower managements, in both private and public sectors, by restoring their 'prerogatives' (Purcell 1991) while at the same time intensifying the pressure for them to compete or go under.

It would be wrong to suggest that there was a clear and consistent industrial relations strategy underlying the eighteen years of Conservative government. Initiatives were incremental and often seemingly opportunistic. Evaluating their impact is not straightforward. As detailed in chapters 8 and 9, these years saw a marked decline in union membership, in numbers of strikes and in the coverage of collective bargaining. What is debatable is how much of this is attributable to the new political and legislative regime, how much to high unemployment, how much to changes in the occupational and sectoral structure, and how much to management responses to a tougher competitive environment which was developing world-wide. As far as the effect on the 'British problem' in industrial relations is concerned, different assessments are again possible. Some have argued that the 'shock therapy' of the Thatcher and Major governments impelled a paradigm shift from adversarialism to management–employee co-operation, resulting in a marked improvement in economic performance; others that the sharp swing in the balance of power reinforced the management 'short-termism' which was the deeper-seated source of Britain's economic woes, encouraging primarily cost-cutting responses to competitive pressures and evoking a sullen compliance from employees. The evidence is sufficiently ambiguous to permit diametrically opposed conclusions.

Also ambiguous was the approach of the Labour government elected in May 1997. First, it is notable that the economic environment of industrial relations remained largely unaltered. Labour maintained the monetary regime adopted by the Conservatives, including its tight public expenditure limits, and indeed increased the autonomy of the Bank of England in setting interest rates. Against the background of the appreciation of the pound in relation to currencies of competitor economies, this intensified the recessionary pressures already generated by global economic trends.

Like the Conservatives, Labour strongly emphasized the need for labour market 'flexibility'. This commitment – together with an evident desire to maintain the goodwill of business interests and the employers' organizations – made it resistant to most proposals for new employment rights and to most aspects of the social agenda developed by the European Commission. The government placed considerable emphasis on 'employability' and, influenced in part by American 'workfare' programmes, launched a 'new deal' aimed at transferring the long-term unemployed (in particular, those aged 18–24) from the unemployment register into education and training or into jobs, including subsidized work in the voluntary sector at pay only a little above benefit levels.

In the sphere of industrial relations more narrowly defined there was considerable continuity with the previous government but also some shifts in policy. As discussed in chapter 6, Labour ended the UK 'opt-out' from the social protocol agreed at Maastricht. In consequence the working time directive was incorporated into British law, a significant change, since average working time in Britain is the highest in the whole European Union (EU). Equally notably, the European Works Council directive was also transposed, though the government has been one of the strongest opponents of the draft EU directive on information and consultation in national-level companies. Other directives given effect include those on part-time employment and parental leave. However, in general the government adopted a 'minimalist' approach to implementing EU law, indeed in some cases arguably failing to meet its requirements.

In addition, the government implemented the Labour Party's commitment to introduce a national minimum wage, appointing a Low Pay Commission to oversee the process. The rate recommended by the commission, initially £3.60 an hour, was well below trade union demands but nevertheless expected to entail pay increases for 2 million workers (see chapter 17). This enlargement of employee rights may be seen as the most significant break with the approach of the Conservatives.

Thirdly, the 1999 Employment Relations Act introduced procedures for compulsory trade union recognition. These were far more restrictive than had been hoped by the trade unions: recognition requires majority support in an employee ballot, but in addition 40 per cent of all employees covered must vote in favour (a rule which would disqualify most members of the British parliament). According to the WERS 1998 survey, in only 1 per cent of all British workplaces do unions lack recognition despite having majority membership.

Other continuities may be noted. The separate Employment Department, broken up by the Conservatives, was not re-established. The 1980–93 legislation regulating and restricting unions was not altered significantly, and limitations on strike action remain virtually unchanged. Even the statutory requirement for ACAS to promote collective bargaining – uncontentious when adopted in 1975, but abolished in 1983 – was not to be restored on the grounds that ACAS should not be 'seen to be biased by statute'.

The new government thus brought some important changes but against a background of underlying continuity. British industrial relations remain confused and confusing. It remains possible to argue that Britain has two systems of industrial relations, but in a different sense from that intended by Donovan. There remains a declining but substantial sector in which trade union organization is still relatively intact and employment is still regulated by collective bargaining – though its agenda and substantive outcomes may be very different from in the past. The second system – though this term is perhaps hardly appropriate – allows management almost unrestricted autonomy in defining terms and conditions of employment. The weight of evidence – discussed in detail in the chapters that follow – suggests that the outcomes are rarely benign.

Is the UK any longer the European exception in its approach to industrial relations? Again, different answers are possible. In introducing Labour's programme of industrial relations legislation, Prime Minister Blair proudly declared (1998: 3) that 'even after the changes we propose, Britain will have the most lightly regulated labour market of any leading economy in the world'. Nevertheless, membership of the EU has led incrementally to the implantation of 'alien' forms of regulation. This process has been reinforced to some extent by the reversal of the Maastricht 'opt-out' – although by 'opting in' the Labour government strengthened its ability to resist the many initiatives of which it disapproved. The decline in union membership, and reduction in strike activity, which are part of the transformation of industrial relations have also occurred (though to varying degrees) in many other European countries. Some would argue that such trends reflect an underlying international shift from a 'Fordist' industrial regime marked by large-scale, standardized production to a more variegated 'post-Fordist' model less conducive to collective regulation of employment relations. It should be noted, however, that Britain is exceptional in that falling union membership has been linked to a sharp decline in the coverage of collective agreements; in most of Europe, a range of 'extension practices' ensure that even workplaces not covered by union organization are nevertheless affected by the agreements negotiated at sectoral level (Traxler 1998). Nevertheless, there is evidence that in different ways the effectiveness of such mechanisms is weakening in much of Europe. If this is so, some regard the highly decentralized British system as the norm towards which the rest of Europe may be moving. In a process of 'converging divergences' (Katz and Darbishire 2000), it is argued that most national industrial relations systems are becoming increasingly internally diversified (by sector and by company), while at this disaggregated level there are increasing cross-national similarities. If this is true, the weakening of historically inherited industrial relations institutions is a process by no means peculiar to Britain.

References

Arrowsmith, J., and Sisson, K. 2000: Managing working time. In S. Bach and K. Sisson (eds), *Personnel Management*, 3rd edn. Oxford: Blackwell.

Blair, T. 1998: Foreword, *Fair Deal at Work*, pp. 3–4. London: HMSO, Cm 3968.

Brown, W. A. 1972: A consideration of 'custom and practice', *British Journal of Industrial Relations*, 10 (1), 42–61.

Bullock, A. 1967: *Life and Times of Ernest Bevin*, volume 2, *Minister of Labour*. London: Heinemann.

Donovan Commission 1968: Royal Commission on Trade Unions and Employers' Associations, *Report*. London: HMSO.

Elbaum, B., and Lazonick, W. (eds) 1986: *The Decline of the British Economy*. Oxford: Clarendon Press.

Elliott, J. 1978: *Conflict or Cooperation?* London: Kogan Page.

Flanders, A. 1964: *The Fawley Productivity Agreements*. London: Faber & Faber.

Flanders, A. 1970: *Management and Unions*. London: Faber & Faber.

Flanders, A. 1974: The Tradition of Voluntarism. *British Journal of Industrial Relations*, 12 (3), 352–70.

Flanders, A., and Clegg, H. A. (eds) 1954: *The System of Industrial Relations in Great Britain*. Oxford: Blackwell.

Fox, A. 1985: *History and Heritage*. London: Allen & Unwin.

Glucksmann, M. 1990: *Women Assemble*. London: Routledge.

Hyman, R. 1989: *Strikes*, 4th edn. Basingstoke: Macmillan.

Hyman, R., and Elger, T. 1981: Job controls, the employers' offensive and alternative strategies, *Capital and Class*, 15, 115–49.

Jenkins, P. 1970: *The Battle of Downing Street*. London: Charles Knight.

Katz, H. C., and Darbishire, O. 2000: *Converging Divergences: Worldwide Changes in Employment Systems*. Ithaca: ILR Press.

Lazonick, W. 1990: *Competitive Advantage on the Shop Floor*. Cambridge, Mass.: Harvard University Press.

Littler, C. 1982: *The Development of the Labour Process in Capitalist Societies*. London: Heinemann.

McCarthy, W. E. J. 1992: The rise and fall of collective laissez faire. In McCarthy (ed.), *Legal Intervention in Industrial Relations*. Oxford: Blackwell.

Minkin, L. 1991: *The Contentious Alliance: Trade Unions and the Labour Party*. Edinburgh: Edinburgh University Press.

Purcell, J. 1991: The rediscovery of the management prerogative, *Oxford Review of Economic Policy*, 7 (1), 33–43.

Samuel, R. 1977: The workshop of the world: steam power and hand technology in mid-Victorian Britain, *History Workshop*, 3, 6–72.

Scanlon, H. 1968: *The Way Forward for Workers' Control*. Nottingham: Institute for Workers' Control.

Sisson, K. 1987: *The Management of Collective Bargaining*. Oxford: Blackwell.

Tolliday, S., and Zeitlin, J. (eds) 1991: *The Power to Manage? Employers and Industrial Relations in Comparative Historical Perspective*. London: Routledge.

Towers, B. 1999: Editorial: 'The most lightly regulated labour market . . .': the UK's third statutory recognition procedure, *Industrial Relations Journal*, 30 (1), 82–95.

Traxler, F. 1998: Collective bargaining in the OECD: developments, preconditions and effects, *European Journal of Industrial Relations*, 4 (2), 207–26.

Turner, H. A. 1962: *Trade Union Growth, Structure and* Policy. London: Allen & Unwin.

Webb, S., and Webb, B. 1894: *History of Trade Unionism*. London: Longman.

Wedderburn, K. W. 1980: *The Worker and the Law*. Harmondsworth: Penguin.

Weekes, B. C., Mellish, M., Dickens, L. and Lloyd, J. 1975: *Industrial Relations and the Limits of the Law*. Oxford: Blackwell.

3

THE LABOUR MARKET: HISTORY, STRUCTURE AND PROSPECTS

PETER NOLAN AND GARY SLATER

Labour markets, countless studies report, are changing fast. The 'stable career' and 'job for life' – key historical reference points in contemporary debates – are expected to assume a diminishing role in the employment patterns of the twenty-first century. With renewed efforts by employers to achieve greater 'flexibility' in the rhythms, places and patterns of work, labour markets are set to become more dynamic, fluid and heterogeneous. Visionaries anticipate a proliferation of portfolio workers, fixed term contracts, and a higher incidence of part-time working and sabbaticals as individuals strive for a better work–life balance. Self-employment, currently accounting for one in ten British workers, is also expected to rise steeply as the emerging 'new economy' spurs the growing ranks of relatively privileged, mobile, and time-sovereign entrepreneurs.

By contrast, the large public and private sector organizations that shaped the employment experience of millions of workers in the past are said to be in retreat. Their once dominant position will be eclipsed by new networks of autonomous business, technical and professional 'e-lancers'. Linked to deeper structural developments, these predicted shifts in employment and labour markets are commonly connected to the dynamic forces of globalization, the wider application of new information and communication technologies (ICTs), and the international restructuring that has de-industrialized many Western economies.

This chapter critically examines these claims about the labour markets of the future with reference to past and present developments in Britain. The analysis, drawing upon comparative data from the leading OECD countries, is elaborated in four parts. The first reviews some of the more influential accounts of the future of work. The second highlights key developments in Britain's labour markets and the third places these developments in historical and international context. The final section evaluates the contention that the 'old' economy, and its associated labour markets and industrial relations, is fast giving way to a new knowledge-intensive and conflict-free economic paradigm.

Work Futures

Globalization and ICTs are widely cited as the key contemporary levers of change in work and employment relations, but their apparent effects in reshaping the labour markets of the twenty-first century do not command a consensus. Some analysts conjure a haunting spectre of disappearing employment opportunities in the traditional sectors of the economy, and point to growing insecurities, widening social divisions and mass unemployment. Others acknowledge that contemporary changes in work systems may prompt significant changes in employment patterns in the future, but also anticipate important continuities in, for example, the service sector that accounts for the vast majority of paid jobs in the advanced economies.

Bridges (1995) and Rifkin (1995) were among the first to point to the 'stable career' and 'job for life' as key casualties of the emerging information age. Focusing on the effects of the business re-engineering processes that allegedly gripped US corporations in the 1990s, Bridges's accent is on the growth of insecurity and the rise of the portfolio career. Rifkin's vision is more apocalyptic. 'The industrial worker', he argues, 'is being phased out of the industrial process . . . While the unskilled and semi-skilled continue to be cut by the introduction of new information and communication technologies, other positions within the hierarchies are also being threatened with extinction. No group is being harder hit than management' (Rifkin 1995: 9, 101).

From a European perspective, Beck (2000) advances an equally pessimistic prognosis. Drawing parallels between the more informal, casual and precarious labour markets of the Brazilian economy and contemporary developments in western Europe, Beck alleges that 'highly skilled and well paid full-time employment is on its way out'. In the West, 'the work society is coming to an end, as more and more people are ousted by smart technologies. Rising unemployment can no longer be explained in terms of cyclical economic crises; it is due rather to the successes of technologically advanced capitalism'. Projecting forward, but with very little elaboration of the relevant social dynamics for change, Beck argues for a new 'political society' in which housework, family work, club work and voluntary work should take priority over the paid work society.

Leadbeater (2000), in contrast, is optimistic about the prospects for working life in the twenty-first century. Echoing earlier accounts (e.g. Reich 1993; Hamel and Prahalad 1996), he argues that the wider application of 'smart' technologies and the forces of globalization are inducing the emergence of a knowledge-driven economy centred on the exploitation of intangible assets. The 'real wealth creating economy is de-materialising'. 'The private and public sectors are increasingly using the same sorts of intangible assets – people, knowledge, ideas, information – to generate intangible outputs, services and know how.' The consolidation of the new economy will, according to Leadbeater, 'have far reaching consequences for the way we work, and for how organizations are managed and owned'. The hierarchical structures and internal labour markets that characterized large private and public sector organizations are being supplanted in the new economy by networks of independent, small-scale companies based on cellular, self-managed teams. 'Networks are sets of relationships between independent producers . . . and the basic unit of competitiveness and growth within the modern economy.' Teams of entrepreneurs, designers and technicians, working collaboratively on a project-by project basis, 'are the modern versions of clans, fiefs and guilds' (Leadbeater 2000: 126).

With no shortage of anecdotes and rich metaphors to support their competing claims, writers on the future of work have succeeded in attracting the attention of leading policymakers while eschewing basic theoretical and methodological questions. What are the critical moments, dimensions and causal factors in the transformation of work? How can we establish whether work and employment relations are subject to incremental or intermittent paradigm shifts, and what are the relevant concepts and empirical evidence to guide the study of these complex questions? A striking feature of the contributions cited above is the almost complete absence of any grounded theory or systematic data.

Rifkin and Bridges, for example, signal the collapse of the wage labour system that has underpinned market capitalism for at least the past 200 years, yet provide no explanation for this quiet revolution. There are references to the upheavals and dynamic effects of ICTs, globalization and business restructuring, but almost no attempt to unravel the complex connections. Nor do they explore alternative hypotheses or reconnect with the history of work, which records countless episodes of radical change as well as significant continuities. Viewed historically, and reversing the arrow of causality, globalization and the drive to reduce labour costs in production through the wider application of ICTs could be more plausibly interpreted as the concomitants of accelerated and expanded capital accumulation rather than its demise.

Leadbeater's vision, also dismissive of the durability of established employment patterns, is scarcely less controversial. His description of work relations under the new economy recalls earlier predictions that the once dominant Fordist command and control systems of management are a major impediment to competitive success in the more flexible and global markets that characterize contemporary economic transactions. Trade unions and other allegedly rigid institutions must adapt or die, for there is no place in the new economy for traditional, adversarial industrial relations. With networks supplanting hierarchical modes of business organization, long-standing conflicts between worker and boss will become a distant memory. Future economic prosperity will be driven by the expanding production of knowledge and intangible assets, and the steady erosion of traditional manufacturing and heavy industry.

Engaging with such broad apocalyptic visions of the future of work is not straightforward, as so many of the claims advanced are abstract and conjectural. There is also the problem that the writers commonly project a future that is constructed upon a limited view of the past. The stock reference point is the period of economic renewal that took root in the advanced economies in the 1950s. With men dominating the paid workforce, employment was predominantly full-time, permanent and located in expanding private and public sector organizations. The giant factories in engineering, pharmaceuticals and steel – for some a leitmotif of paid work in this period – enforced a rigid separation between home and work, manual and mental labour. Elements of this description have some basis in evidence, but fail to do full justice to the diverse patterns of employment, labour market segments, and work routines of the past.

Changing Contours of British Labour Markets

Interpreting the scale and scope of contemporary labour market changes poses similar if not greater difficulties. How can we differentiate secular shifts from cyclical movements, and what role should we assign to agency and politics in the construction of labour market dynamics? As noted, a tendency of much recent writing is to postulate universal or dominant trends, as a consequence of radical shifts in technology or globalization, but the changes taking place in labour markets and work patterns are typically more piecemeal, uneven and contradictory. To be sure, claims that employment is becoming more insecure, unstable, and casualized have resonance for many people, but nevertheless must be reconciled with contradictory findings that show for the UK, for example, that permanent jobs and a measure of stability remain salient features of the contemporary labour market. The discussion that follows highlights some of the key developments in the structure of employment, occupations, institutionalized (internal) labour markets, unemployment and inactivity.

Employment restructuring

The key aggregate developments in employment structure include a decisive shift in broad sectoral terms away from agriculture and primary and manufacturing industries towards services. Manual employment, still accounting for approximately 10.5 million employees, has been eclipsed by non-manual occupations. Part-time work has expanded at the expense of full-time employment, and female participation rates have increased significantly, such that women presently constitute half of the paid labour force.

Figure 3.1 describes the broad sectoral changes in employment since the late 1970s. Agricultural employment has remained constant at around 1 per cent, having declined steadily over previous decades. Employment in construction and the former public utilities (gas, water and mining) dipped after the privatization programme of the 1980s, yet by far the most marked changes are in manufacturing and services. The falling share of manufacturing employment (the process of de-industrialization) is common to most advanced economies, but the magnitude of decline in Britain has been especially pronounced, at over 50 per cent since 1960. By contrast, service sector employment has been growing, in absolute numbers and as a share of total civilian employment, since the mid-1950s.

These wider shifts, particularly the continuing growth of the so-called service economy, provide the context for the more specific changes in the organization of work and employment that have formed the empirical backdrop to the

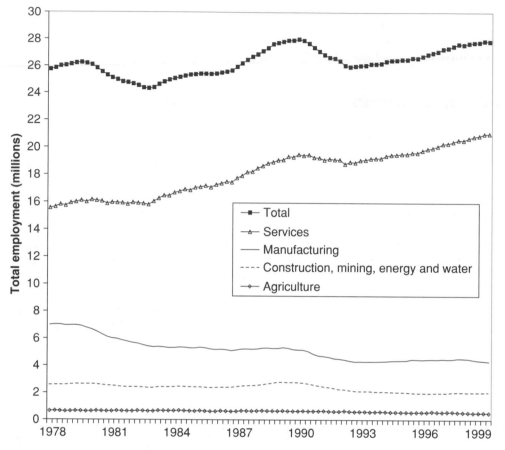

Figure 3.1   Workforce jobs by industry, UK 1978–1999

Source: *Labour Market Trends*, various issues.

Note: Quarterly data on total employment (i.e. employees in employment, self-employed and employers).

contemporary debate on work futures. The changing balance between 'standard' and 'non-standard' employment has been of central concern. Standard employment refers to full-time dependent jobs, non-standard to part-time, temporary and self-employed workers. The trends in non standard employment are depicted in figure 3.2.

Figure 3.2 shows that temporary employment at the end of the 1990s accounted for approximately 7 per cent of all jobs. It exhibited little growth in the 1980s, rose rapidly in the early 1990s, and tailed off in the latter part of the decade, but these aggregate data conceal radical shifts in particular sectors. Most striking is the expansion of short, fixed-term contracts in the public services, particularly in health and education, which began in the early 1980s and accounted for over two-fifths of all temporary employment at the end of the

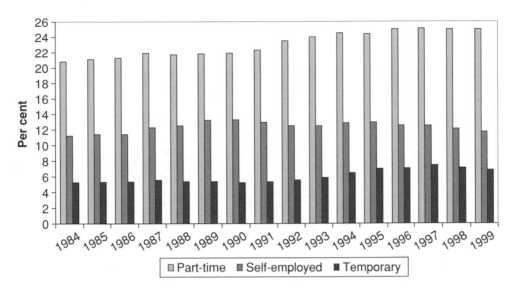

Figure 3.2   Part-time, temporary and self-employment, UK 1984–1999

Source: Labour Force Survey, Spring 2001.

Note: Figures for temporary employment are expressed as a proportion of employees. Part-time and self-employment are defined as a proportion of total employment.

1990s. In the private sector, temporary working increased in most sectors after the early 1980s (Casey et al. 1997), although often from a low base, and for the first time took root in industries, such as banking and finance, previously associated with stable employment and 'jobs for life'.

Making sense of the determinants and significance of temporary employment is far from straightforward. Does it reflect shifts on the side of labour supply or demand side factors associated with employers' preferences? The available data do not permit a decisive answer to this complex question, but the most recent research findings reveal that temporary workers in the UK report lower levels of job satisfaction, receive less work-related training, and are less well-paid than their counterparts in permanent employment (Booth et al. 2000). From a comparative perspective, moreover, it is clear that there is enormous variation in the incidence of temporary work in Europe. Table 3.1 reveals that between the mid-1980s and 1998 temporary working grew rapidly in Spain, Finland and France, declined in Denmark and Greece, and remained more or less constant in Belgium and the UK. A plausible interpretation is that specific national institutional arrangements (e.g. regulations that discriminate against non-permanent employees), rather than any possible global forces, have shaped employers' preferences for temporary rather than permanent employment.

In the UK, self-employment grew most rapidly during the early 1980s recession. Numbers rose sharply from just over 7 per cent of total employment in 1979 to around 11 per cent in 1984, and continued a slow rise for the remainder

Table 3.1   Temporary employment across Europe (% temporary employees)

	1985	1990	1998
Spain	15.6	29.8	32.9
Finland	10.5	11.5	17.7
Portugal	14.4	18.3	17.3
France	4.7	10.5	13.9
Greece	21.1	16.5	13.0
Sweden	11.9	10.0	12.9
Germany	10.0	10.5	12.3
Netherlands	7.5	7.6	12.7
Denmark	12.3	10.8	10.1
Italy	4.8	5.2	8.6
Ireland	7.3	8.5	*9.2
UK	7.0	5.2	7.1
Belgium	6.9	5.3	7.8

*1996
Source: OECD (1999a).

of that decade. The recovery in the share of self-employment following the 1990s recession has not been sustained, with absolute and relative falls since 1997, particularly in the construction sector, which has traditionally had a high incidence of such employment. The predictions of a step rise in self-employment under the new economy may yet be fulfilled, but the available evidence reveals little support for such claims at the present time.

By far the most striking trend in UK employment is the long-standing growth of part-time employment. In 1971, one in six employees worked part-time. By 1999, with approximately 6.5 million part-timers, this ratio had risen to one in four. In 1979 there were 18.5 million full-time employees in the UK, but in 1999 the total had shrunk by over 2 million. The contraction in full-time jobs has been most keenly felt by male workers in manual occupations, notably in manufacturing, and in the coal, shipbuilding, steel and dock industries which have been decimated since the late 1960s under the twin pressures of international restructuring and government rationalization and privatization policies.

The continuing expansion of part-time employment, sustained since 1979 by the net creation of 4.5 million jobs in services, has affected both private and public sectors. In one in four private sector workplaces more than half the workforce now work part-time; for the public sector the figure is closer to one in three (Cully et al. 1999: 33). At industry level the share of part-time employment is particularly high in the private sector in wholesale and retail (47%), and hotels and catering (47%), whereas in the public services it features prominently in community services (36%), health (44%) and education (40%). Overwhelmingly filled by women, these jobs are much more likely to be poorly paid, low-skilled and unstable (Cully et al. 1999; Stewart 1999). Around half of part-time employees occupy 'small' jobs involving less than 16 working hours, and almost 1 million work as few as eight paid hours per week (see chapter 16). Trends in temporary work and self-employment do not, therefore, suggest radical shifts in the nature of jobs. Part-time work has risen, but this is at least as much concerned with patterns of 'poor' work as with portfolio careers.

Occupational changes

With a record of continuous employment growth since 1992, the UK provides a good test of the contention that paid employment is moving decisively away from low-value production and service activities towards new knowledge-intensive sectors engaged in the production of 'intangible assets' (e.g. Reich 1993; Leadbeater 2000; Scase 2000). Labour Force Survey data permit an assessment of the degree to which new patterns of employment are displacing more established occupations.

Table 3.2 traces movements in the relative shares of the main occupational categories in the 1990s. Divided into three broad groups – professional 'white-collar', 'traditional services' and 'manual manufacturing and construction workers' – it shows, in line with the dominant futurology, that higher-level professionals, managers and technical workers have increased their share of total employment in the 1990s by nearly 3 percentage points. The share of traditional services has remained constant, reflecting the considerable expansion of services in the UK described above, and the share of traditional manual workers in manufacturing and construction has declined from 25 to 22 per cent. Nevertheless

Table 3.2 Occupational change in the 1990s (employees and self-employed, including second jobs, UK)

	1992	1999	Absolute change	Compound growth 1992–9
	%	%	(000s)	%
'White-collar' (managers, professionals, associate professionals)	34.6	37.2	1,518	2.2
'Traditional' services (clerical and secretarial, personal and protective, sales, postal, cleaning)	40.0	40.7	1,109	1.5
Craft, operative and labouring (manual manufacturing and construction workers)	25.4	22.2	–319	–0.7
Total employment (000s)	26,174	28,483	2,308	1.2

Source: Labour Force Survey.

to draw from these aggregate figures the conclusion that the 'old' economy is in retreat and that future employment patterns will be driven by the rate of expansion of the new economy would be misleading for the following reasons.

First, as Warhurst and Thompson (1998: 3) point out, 'official classifications of the occupational structure focus upon the form of jobs rather than the content of labour'. The corollary is that survey data are open to competing interpretations which may only be resolved by undertaking more detailed studies of specific labour processes. What, for example, is the nature of professional work in legal, medical and educational institutions and how is it experienced by the workers involved?

Second, the growing share of managerial and professional employment may reflect in part nationally specific definitions. Managers of shops are classified as 'sales' workers in the US, but are treated as 'managers' in the UK. Germany and Japan include only senior managers, whereas the UK classification includes many managerial and administrative jobs that elsewhere would be defined as 'clerical' occupations (Robinson 1997).

Third, a significant proportion of the increasing share of managerial and professional workers is associated with developments in the public sector. There have been large absolute increases in 'new' sectors such as computer system managers (62,000), software engineers (109,000) and computer programmers (92,000). But these increases are eclipsed by the expansion of public sector professional groups in education, health and welfare, that account for two in five (approximately 520,000) of the total increase in higher 'white-collar' employees. The development of professional management cadres in fields such as schools and hospitals points to a reorganization of activities rather than to a rise in the number of professional jobs, as implied by writers alleging a radical transformation of work.

Closer scrutiny (at the three-digit level) shows that, in terms of absolute employment growth between 1992 and 1999, the fastest-growing occupations have been in four long-established services (sales assistants, data input clerks, storekeepers, and receptionists); state-dominated education and health services; and the caring occupations (care assistants, welfare and community workers, nursery nurses). In short, employment growth has been concentrated in occupations that could scarcely be judged new, still less the fulcrum of the new economy. Looking back on this debate about the balance between the old and new economy, scholars of the future may well see the irony that the fastest-growing occupation in the UK in the 1990s was hairdressing.

Internal and external labour markets

The limitations of perspectives counterposing the fluid, flexible and diverse employment patterns of the present (and future) with the supposedly stable, rigid and relatively homogeneous labour markets of the past have been referred to above. The rich history of the sometimes radical, sometimes incremental shifts in the arrangements governing the recruitment, allocation and utilization of labour power in the UK defies such simplistic accounts. A key element in this history is the shifting boundaries between external and internal labour markets.

In the external labour market the forces of supply and demand dictate the allocation of labour power between sectors, industries and firms. In the internal labour market the utilization of labour power is governed by management hierarchies, rules and conventions. Internalization, according to Williamson, provides employers 'with access to a distinctive inventory of incentive and control techniques'. The key issue for management is to organize jobs 'in a way that best promotes cooperative adaptations to changing market and technological conditions' (Williamson 1975: 69).

If that is the theory, the reality has proved to be more complicated. Internalization strategies, notwithstanding Williamson's clear endorsement, have been the subject of struggle, major reversals and ambiguity. Their history in Britain illustrates the point graphically. Slow to emerge, the semblance of primitive internal labour markets began to spread intermittently in the 1960s (see also chapter 7). At this time, the vast majority of employees worked full-time, were trade union members, and settled their pay and conditions through collective bargaining. Often employed in large, multi-establishment enterprises, these workers had variously gained rights to training, overtime working, annual pay increases, and a measure of autonomy within the labour process. Conditions differed within and between industries of course, but for thousands of skilled and semi-skilled workers the 1960s and 1970s were years of significant material advance (see Bélanger and Evans 1988; Lyddon 1994).

Characterized by contemporary observers as a period of developing chaos in the workplace, this period is perhaps better seen in retrospect as a time of formative change. In many organizations the arrangements governing access to jobs, work allocation, remuneration and promotion were in the process of being reordered and systematized through the elaboration of enterprise-specific job, pay and promotion structures, so-called internal labour markets. The changes were often negotiated, sometimes imposed by management, but whatever their immediate source the elaboration of more formal rules and procedures at workplace level entailed a redefinition of the boundaries between the organization and the external labour market.

The research literature on the origins, incidence and significance of internal labour markets highlights these contradictory pressures. American writers have tended to emphasize the dominant and strategic role of management, arguing that such systems were spearheaded by firms such as IBM and Kodak in the early decades of the twentieth century in order to forestall the spread of unionism (Jacoby 1984). In Britain, they were firmly embedded in areas of the public sector such as the civil service and post office before 1945, but elsewhere their presence and effects have been patchy. One possible explanation for this uneven pattern of development is the persistence of craft union practices, which helped sustain patterns of intra-occupational mobility between firms. Another is the lack of strategic management in many parts of British industry (see chapter 2).

Evidence for the 1960s confirms this picture of tentative and piecemeal advances in the scope and coherence of internal structures. In finance, chemicals and oil-refining, where large international firms dominated production and service provision, 'strategies of internalization' were very much in evidence 'especially during the first three decades of post-war full employment' (Gospel 1992: 165). Elsewhere the process of change was more protracted. A major study of engineering firms in Glasgow and the west Midlands, spanning the period 1959–66, thus highlighted the continuing salience of management prerogative in matters of recruitment, work allocation and promotion, while concluding that the 'internal labour markets in the plants studied, and in the engineering industry generally, [had] not . . . reached a very advanced and formal stage of development' (Mackay et al. 1971: 321).

Efforts by management to systematize and formalize the arrangements governing the deployment and remuneration of labour power intensified in the 1970s, however, particularly in medium-sized and large manufacturing establishments where work study methods, job evaluation and single-employer bargaining, either at company or establishment level, became the norm. The impact of these and related innovations was probably most visible in the arena of pay determination. In engineering, for example, a local labour market study of the pay movements of 55,000 employees between 1970 and 1980 found that an individual's pay was affected more by place of work than occupational grade (Nolan and Brown 1983). Revealing significant and enduring intra-occupational pay differentials, the study reported that employers saw benefits in preserving a stable internal wage structure, often with trade union support, in the face of shifting conditions in the external labour market.

While it remains an open question as to whether these practices served to dilute or enhance management prerogative, it is clear that many employers had come to regard internalization as a form of 'best' practice: so much so indeed that by the mid-1980s, according to one study, half the employed workforce was covered by an internal labour market of one sort or another (Siebert and Addison 1991). Yet no sooner had the principles of internalization become established than the tide turned again. The compelling equation which linked internal labour markets with increased employee commitment and greater production and transactions cost efficiency came under siege from new-right theorists committed to the law of contract, deregulation and employment flexibility. Their arguments did not take root immediately, nor did they necessarily inform the practice of all, or even the most important, employers. But neither can they be dismissed as having been inconsequential.

Arguably the most potent challenge to internalization came from government. Its policies, directly and indirectly, served to promote fragmentation and casualization in the privatized industries, in the remaining nationalized industries, and in the resource-constrained local authorities and the health and education services. In the civil service, once a major source of secure lifetime employment, the unified structures that governed pay, mobility and progression were supplanted by a conglomeration of separate agencies (see chapter 11). As personnel policy has been delegated to individual units, pay and grading structures have become increasingly differentiated. Together with further 'market testing' of activities and the increasing use of temporary and casual appointment accompanying these changes, promotion ladders within and between the various parts of the civil service have been curtailed.

Beyond the public sector, employees in banking – an industry also associated with stable, long-term and company-specific jobs – experienced successive waves of redundancy and the substitution of part-time and fixed-term contracts for permanent career posts. New technologies have been harnessed by employers to divide, centralize and routinize many business functions and rupture internal lines of promotion. Positions that once served as staging posts in a career have thus become jobs in their own right. Often physically separated from the branches in factory-like processing centres, these jobs offer few opportunities for advancement and have greatly expanded the use of on-call, zero-hours contract workers to cover absences and busy periods.

While the civil service and banking sectors provide clear examples of employers retreating from established employment practices, it would be misleading to suggest that the disintegration and compression of internal job structures have been all-embracing trends. Countervailing pressures, for example developing labour market shortages in key occupations and the soaring costs of negotiating contracts with freelance staff, alerted employers in some industries to the potential hazards of unlimited dependency on the external labour market. Television and broadcasting is a particularly illuminating case.

Described by Mrs Thatcher in the mid-1980s as 'the last bastion of [trade union] restrictive practices', the television and broadcasting industry was targeted for radical reform and restructuring. The 1990 Broadcasting Act, reflecting earlier recommendations by the Peacock Committee, introduced a competitive auction of the ITV regional franchises and a binding requirement on all broadcasters to purchase at least 25 per cent of programming hours from independent producers. The stated intention was to improve production efficiency, sharpen competition and check producer power, but the consequences for skill formation, employment relations and staff morale were destabilizing and contradictory.

Survey evidence reveals that the expansion of independent production failed to deliver the cost savings, quality improvements, and enhanced flexibilities in production anticipated by the architects of the 1990 Act (Saundry and Nolan 1998). The enforced fragmentation of the industry, dictated by the imposed 25 per cent quota, meant that key staff in production were lost from the established integrated producer-broadcasters. Some turned to freelance work, others left the industry. The growth of freelance labour, which increased steeply after 1989 from 39 per cent to 60 per cent in 1996, contributed to a sharp deterioration in the skills base of the industry. In the independent sector, 63 per cent of respondents said that they did not provide training opportunities for new employees. Half of the ITV companies and the BBC reported significant skill shortages, and stated that the provision of training for freelancers was inadequate (Nolan et al. 1997).

Nor was the greater use of freelance and contract labour linked to improvements in costs and labour efficiency; indeed a majority of employers (58%) reported that freelance employment created an added administrative burden and cost. Two-thirds of employers also indicated that the wider use of freelance labour and fixed-term contracts was having a negative effect on morale and motivation (Saundry and Nolan 1998).

By the mid-1990s, the mounting difficulties faced by employers in securing an adequately trained and motivated workforce prompted a partial reversal of tactics. Deepening skill shortages, and significant structural developments (notably the proliferation of channels and the increasing demand for programming) allowed key workers with a strong track record to exploit their market power. In the BBC, where it had become commonplace to employ staff on temporary contracts, concerted efforts were made to improve job security for existing staff and persuade freelancers to return to permanent contracts. With similar developments in the ITV companies, the radical shift in employment practices that followed the Broadcasting Act had begun to turn full circle. The contradictions of employment instability and the challenges that employers faced in dealing with market vicissitudes had begun to remake the case for internalization. (For further discussion of the management of an 'individualized' workforce, see chapter 14.)

Flexibility and segmentation

Issues of flexibility and labour market segmentation have been at the centre of recent controversies about the performance of the labour market. Here the focus is on broader macro developments. Did the radical reforms introduced by successive Conservative governments during the 1980s and 1990s succeed in increasing flexibility, labour mobility and access to paid employment? The erosion of trade union power and the other measures intended to deregulate labour markets were judged essential to secure the gains in performance that had eluded governments in the 1960s and 1970s (Evans et al. 1992). Orthodox economic theory provides unqualified support for policies that rid markets of institutional rigidities, and many leading economists endorsed the measures that were enacted. Did they succeed?

Comparing developments during the recovery from the 1990s recession with those of a decade earlier allows an assessment to be made of labour market performance before and after the 1980s reforms. The recorded changes in the level of unemployment appear to support the advocates of measures to enhance labour market flexibility. The lag between output recovery and falling claimant unemployment shortened considerably to six months from five years, while employment also began to grow much sooner (increasing after one year, rather than three). But a closer examination of the trends reveals a rather less impressive record and three areas of particular concern.

Firstly, the recovery of employment in response to economic changes was weaker in the 1990s than the 1980s. The growth rates achieved were half those of the 1980s, despite only marginally lower output growth. Secondly, as noted above, employment growth in the 1990s was dominated by part-time and temporary jobs, especially in the early years of recovery. Thirdly, there was a significant rise in the 1990s in the number of people who would otherwise have been unemployed withdrawing from the labour market altogether. Morgan (1996) thus noted that over one-quarter of the improvement in the unemployment record was due to rising rates of economic inactivity among the working-age population in the 1990s.

Higher rates of inactivity of the population of working age contributed to the earlier fall in unemployment and have had a continuing bearing on the levels and rates of unemployment in recent years. Previously, economic inactivity followed the economic cycle, falling as output and employment expanded. This pattern has now been broken, with inactivity rates as high in 1999 as in 1993 when unemployment peaked. Indeed, had inactivity followed previous trends and fallen by the same proportion in the 1990s as in the 1980s calculations show that by 1999 the rate of unemployment on the ILO measure would have stood at 9 per cent of the workforce (2.6 million), rather than the recorded 6.1 per cent (1.7 million). What explains this rise in the number of people withdrawing from the labour market?

Disaggregation of the trends reveals a strong gender dimension. Female participation has continued to increase, but rapidly rising rates of inactivity among men of working age are driving the aggregate trends. In the mid-1970s there were 400,000 men outside the labour force, but currently the figure is over 2 million (Dickens et al. 2000). According to Gregg and Wadsworth (1999) inactivity has risen across all age groups, and retirement still only accounts for one-quarter of male inactivity in the 50–64 age class. Although this proportion has been on the increase, Disney (1999) argues that there has been a clear demand shift against older workers. Firms, in short, are increasingly using early retirement as a means to shed unwanted labour.

The dominant reason for rising rates of inactivity is the increasing incidence of long-term sickness among men. By 1996 the number of people of working age claiming sickness-related benefits had risen to almost 2.5 million (Beatty et al. 1997). Much of the growth occurred in the early 1990s, when the numbers claiming invalidity benefit alone increased by 50 per cent, and the rises were geographically concentrated. Rowthorn (2000) shows that non-employment rates for men aged 25 to 64 are highest in the old industrial regions, such as Merseyside, South Yorkshire, and Tyne and Wear, reaching around 30 per cent by the late 1990s.

These patterns reflect the erosion of the UK's industrial base in the 1980s, and the failure of the service sector to provide alternative employment in the areas most in need. The long-term downward multiplier effects set in train by industrial decline cast doubt on the efficacy of the supply-side-oriented policy of labour market flexibility in restoring employment opportunities. The trends outlined challenge 'the complacent view that Britain's economic performance has been a shining success, that our country is now an advertisement for the virtues of de-regulation and labour market flexibility' (Rowthorn 2000: 163). The next section places the recent performance of the UK labour market in historical and international context.

Britain and the International Division of Labour

Patterns of international trade and divisions of labour within and between nation-states were traditionally thought to reflect the operation of the 'law of comparative advantage'. Each country or region, on this view, would specialize in the production

Table 3.3 Inward and outward foreign direct investment (FDI) 1998 (stock in $billions)

	Inward FDI		Outward FDI		
	Stock	% of world total	Stock	% of world total	Outward/ inward
USA	875	21	994	24	1.1
Japan	30	1	296	7	9.8
France	179	4	242	6	1.4
Germany	229	6	390	9	1.7
UK	327	8	499	12	1.5
EU	1,486	36	1,956	48	1.3

Source: United Nations (1999).

of those goods and services in which it had a cost advantage, as determined by its endowments of factor inputs (natural resources, land, labour and capital).

But the realities of trade and capital flows suggest that the determinants of the international division of labour are more complex. A growing proportion of world trade takes place between advanced economies with similar factor endowments, and between the subsidiaries of multinational corporations (MNCs), developments which are incompatible with the traditional, static approach. Indeed a crucial distinguishing feature of the contemporary capitalist economy is the extent to which production itself has been 'set free' from specific national and regional resource constraints. The growth of world trade, international portfolio investments, and the growing significance of MNCs are thus three interconnected aspects of the internationalization of capital, a process in which Britain has been a prime mover.

As a home for MNCs which invest abroad, Britain is second only to the United States. The relevant figures are set out in table 3.3. It shows, on the one hand, that the ratio of the stock of outward to inward investment, at 1.5 for the UK, is not out of line with the rest of Europe. On the other hand, in terms of magnitude, the UK alone accounts for a quarter of Europe's total stock of outward direct investment.

British-based MNCs, to an extent which differentiates them from their German, American and Japanese counterparts, have preferred to source international markets from production facilities located abroad. Before the 1980s outward investment was concentrated in manufacturing, especially in low-tech industries such as textiles, food, drink and tobacco, but in more recent years growing investment in services (banking, finance and insurance) and the extractive industries (oil and gas) have cut back the share of manufacturing to a third.

Inward investment in the three decades after 1945 was dominated by US MNCs (see chapter 4). Their investments were concentrated in manufacturing, particularly technology-intensive sectors such as chemicals, mechanical and instrument engineering, and electrical and electronic engineering. But for several reasons this pattern has begun to change: aggregate US foreign direct investment has declined; US direct investment in services has grown at the expense of manufacturing; and Britain's status as the preferred location within Europe for US technology-intensive (and other) affiliates has been eroded. The evidence points to a significant reorganization of US MNCs in Europe, with Germany in particular emerging as the favoured site for capital, technology and skill-intensive production. Such trends have been reinforced by newer sources of inward direct investment, for example from Japanese MNCs, which have also favoured financial and commercial services (Roy 2001).

Assessments of the impact of MNCs on the British economy have yielded conflicting results. Dunning (1985) claims they have had a positive 'transformative' effect. Capital has been directed to efficient production locations overseas, while 'foreign multinationals have generally benefited the UK's industrial restructuring in as much as they . . . tend to favour growth sectors which are skill and technology intensive'. Other researchers, for example Fine and Harris (1985), argue that the presence of MNCs in Britain has been neither positive nor benign.

Focusing on the 'feedback' effects of outward investment, for example technology transfers and the formation of backward linkages in the production chain, Fine and Harris note that direct investment from Britain was until recently heavily skewed towards low-technology, low-skill 'colonial' production, which thrived on low wages and exploitative conditions. Such activities did have important feedback effects, but of a wholly negative kind, in that they served 'to direct the British economy towards more labour intensive low-wage production' (1985: 112).

Britain emerged from the Second World War as the leading industrial nation in Europe, yet by the early 1960s was manifestly underperforming across a range of critical indicators. The symptoms of relative weakness were most apparent in manufacturing, and were such that the focus of analysis and debate shifted in the mid-1970s from the problems of relative to absolute decline, to the haunting spectre of 'de-industrialization' (Singh 1976; Blackaby 1979).

The decline of manufacturing employment is not a uniquely British phenomenon. Table 3.4 describes the changing share of manufacturing employment since 1960 and shows the halving of employment in the UK. Britain's peculiar trajectory has been characterized by some writers as a process of 'negative' de-industrialization. According to Rowthorn and Wells (1987), 'a dynamic manufacturing sector may be shedding labour, yet at the same time, contributing to the creation of employment in the economy as steady increases in industrial production lay the material foundation for a prosperous and expanding service sector'. This is the case of 'positive' de-industrialization. But Britain's experience has been different: manufacturing output and employment changes have been conditioned by internal weaknesses (lack of investment and competitiveness) and by adverse shifts in the pattern of demand. On the one hand, the pattern of domestic demand has shifted in favour of commodities produced overseas; on the other hand, as table 3.5 shows, manufacturers located in Britain have experienced increasing difficulties in maintaining their share of international

Table 3.4   Employment in manufacturing as a percentage of civilian employment, 1960–1997

						Percentage change in share		
	1960	*1974*	*1980*	*1990*	*1997*	*1980–90*	*1990–7*	*1960–97*
USA	26.4	24.2	22.1	18.0	16.1	−19	−11	−39
Japan	21.3	27.2	24.7	24.1	22.0	−2	−9	+3
France	27.3	28.3	25.8	21.0	18.4	−19	−12	−33
Germany[a]	34.3	35.8	33.9	31.6	24.0	−7	−24	−30
UK	38.4	34.6	30.2	22.3	18.6	−26	−17	−52

[a] Data refer to West Germany pre-1991, Germany thereafter.
Source: OECD (1991, 1999b).

Table 3.5   Shares of world trade in manufactures (%), 1960–1998

	1960	*1970*	*1979*	*1990*	*1998*
USA	21.6	18.6	16.0	16.0	13.9
Japan	6.9	11.7	13.7	15.9	9.4
France	9.6	8.7	10.5	9.7	10.2
Germany	19.3	19.8	20.9	20.2	18.2
UK	16.5	10.8	9.1	8.6	7.9

Source: Crafts (1991); OECD (1999c).

markets. Britain became a net importer of manufactures for the first time in its history in 1983, and by 1998 has seen its share slump to under 8 per cent of the total. Part of the explanation for this adverse development is to be found in the structure of industry located in Britain.

Table 3.6 describes the technology content of British manufacturing output, dividing the latter into three main categories: high-, medium- and low-tech. The data show that only one-fifth of total output is in the high-tech range. Industry case studies suggest that firms in Britain have been importing higher-value added products, while exporting goods with a lower-value added content; this is true not only for the 'high-tech' sector but across the spectrum. Recent evidence for the relatively 'low-tech' food-processing industry, for example, shows that when international productivity comparisons are adjusted for product quality, Britain's relative position, particularly with respect to Germany, is far worse than is suggested by the crude comparative data on output per employee hour (Mason et al. 1994; see further chapter 15).

As early as the 1960s, Britain had become a centre for relatively cheap labour. This is revealed by the data in table 3.7 on total hourly labour costs, which are

Table 3.6 Technology and production shares in UK manufacturing output, 1971–1997

	1971	1979	1980	1986	1990	1997	Increase (% pa)		
							1971–9	1980–6	1990–7
High-tech	11.9	11.4	12.5	16.0	17.0	19.0	−0.5	4.2	1.7
Mid-tech	29.2	30.8	29.2	29.9	31.0	30.5	0.7	0.6	−0.2
Low-tech	58.9	57.8	58.3	53.8	52.2	50.0	−0.2	−1.3	−0.6

Source: Buxton and Clokie (1992) for 1971–86; 1990–7 estimated from OECD Industrial Structure Statistics, various years, on the same basis.

Table 3.7 Hourly labour costs in manufacturing, 1960–2000

	1960	1970	1980	1987	1990	2000
USA	296	250	131	149	118	125
Japan	30	57	73	119	101	139
France	94	105	118	136	122	104
Germany[a]	98	144	162	187	173	151
UK	100	100	100	100	100	100

[a] Data refer to former West Germany.
Costs are for production workers, compared at current exchange rates. Index, UK = 100.
Sources: Figures for 1960 and 1970: Ray (1972); other years: Bureau of Labor Statistics (2001).

derived by summing total hourly earnings and social charges (national insurance, holiday and sick pay). It places the UK well down the international league table. After the Second World War Britain was a relatively high-wage economy, but by 1970 only Japan had lower labour costs than Britain. Since then the gap has narrowed between Britain and the USA but not with France, Japan and Germany.

The relatively low cost of labour in Britain is one issue, but how productively is that labour utilized? Productivity, it should be stressed, is notoriously difficult to measure, and comparisons across time, different industries and national frontiers are fraught with difficulties (see chapter 19). Nevertheless the evidence – whatever its shortcomings – does reveal a substantial and enduring shortfall in productivity levels in Britain as compared to the United States, Japan and the leading west European countries.

The differential with the United States opened up early in the twentieth century, and, while the extent of the gap varies significantly across industries, it is estimated to be as high as 100 per cent in some cases (Crafts and Broadberry, 1990). The gap with workers in Europe developed much later, in the 1950s and

Table 3.8 Relative labour productivity levels in manufacturing (GDP per hour worked)

	1950	1960	1970	1980	1987	1990	2000
USA	248	218	196	190	172	158	181
Japan	28	43	85	124	116	128	128
France	88	109	140	167	146	145	168
Germany	71	126	153	180	142	138	159
UK	100	100	100	100	100	100	100
Sweden	109	120	170	187	151	142	172

Source: 1987–2000 figures from Groningen Growth and Development Centre. Other years from same source, reproduced in Scarpetta et al. (2000).

1960s, as other countries achieved much higher productivity growth rates following the reconstruction of their industries after 1945. By the 1970s, as table 3.8 reveals, this pattern had become entrenched.

A decade of poor, often negative, annual rates of productivity growth in the 1970s was followed by more rapid advances in the 1980s. The apparent improvement was widely attributed to the Thatcher governments' policies, and was thought to be indicative of a new, sustainable high-growth trajectory (e.g. Crafts 1988). Compared with the record of the 1970s, there was an improvement, but the argument about government policies is unconvincing: productivity increases for the economy as a whole, including services and primary industries, were quite modest, rising annually by only 2.3 per cent between 1979 and 1988, which was broadly in line with international experience. The gains in the 1980s were insufficient to close the gap with other leading economies. As table 3.8 indicates, the position has if anything deteriorated in the 1990s.

The result, as far as cost competitiveness is concerned, is to leave industries in Britain at a substantial disadvantage. Unit labour costs – total labour costs divided by the productivity of labour – are relatively high despite Britain's low labour costs. Nor is the problem limited to manufacturing. Evidence adduced by O'Mahony et al. (1998) for services, which compares the relative performance in 1993 of distribution, hotels and catering, transport and communication and financial and business services, reveals substantial productivity differentials between the UK and the US (38%), the UK and Germany (34%) and the UK and France (36%). The implications for future patterns of employment are discussed below.

Labour Markets of the Twenty-First Century

The British economy's insertion into the international division of labour has been associated with the development and consolidation of particular weaknesses. A long-standing and seemingly unbreakable record of low productivity (see chapter 19) has coincided in many industries with a history of low relative wages and inferior skill-formation systems. There is evidence, moreover, that patterns of inward and outward capital flows have skewed production towards relatively low-skill, low-value-added products and services. It is arguable that these long-established characteristics are being reflected and reproduced in contemporary employment patterns by the expansion of relatively routine and poorly paid jobs in the service economy.

Reference to the service rather than the new economy arguably better encapsulates the reality of the changes in British employment in the final years of the twentieth century. Too much emphasis on the growth of independent entrepreneurs at the expense of the dependent workforce misses the point. With nearly eight in ten workers employed in services, the critical issue is the shifting balance between high-, mid- and low-skilled occupations. The historical and contemporary evidence points to considerable barriers to the construction of a vibrant, technologically advanced and knowledge-intensive workforce in the UK.

Is there compelling evidence to support claims that the labour markets and employment patterns of the future will be radically different from those of the past? The data reviewed above point to significant shifts and important lines of continuity. The proportion of the workforce engaged in the professions and in scientific and technical occupations has increased in the last decade from 34 to 37 per cent. But over the same period the total number of manual workers has been remarkably stable at around 10.5 million, or 40 per cent of total employment. It is perhaps telling that the fastest-growing manual occupation since 1992 is housekeepers, at 368 per cent. Add to this figure other traditional services, for example clerical and secretarial work, and the size of the 'traditional' labour force soars to 17 million. The fastest-growing occupations include software engineers and management and business consultants, but also shelf-fillers, nursery nurses, and prison officers.

The dangers of developing a stylized account of the changing world of work by appealing to simple dualisms, such as the old (industrial) and new (knowledge-intensive) economies, are transparent. Complexity, unevenness, contradictions and the important continuities in the social structure and relations of employment are crowded out by images of universal paradigm shifts. Popular with policymakers, such terms at best obscure, at worst impede the dissemination of the detailed studies that are able to illuminate the changes and challenges of labour markets and employment in the future. If the concept of the new economy was solely deployed to signal incremental changes in occupational structure and the growing salience of 'knowledge' workers it would be relatively benign; low on content, but, like many other categories used to describe different periods of capitalism (e.g. the railway age), pretty harmless. But it is more than that. Advocates typically invest the concept with both analytical and prescriptive significance.

Linked to the rise of more democratic forms of work organization, the new economy is identified with a fresh pattern of work relations free from long-standing hierarchical and conflictual employment relations. Some accounts conjure a world in which there are no workers and bosses, merely transactors.

Dissolving the wage-labour system, and consigning large bureaucratic corporations to the historical waste-bin, the pundits evoke images of an economy in which the institutions that shaped the organization of work and workers' lives in the twentieth century are simply abolished. There is, moreover, a strong anti-productionist slant to the argument. As noted, the labour markets of the future will allegedly be shaped by the transactions between 'intangible inputs' (knowledge, ideas and information), but the evidence reveals a different reality.

On the one hand, manufacturing remains essential to provide the means of production for the new knowledge industries. On the other hand, as revealed by the United States – for many the blueprint of the knowledge economy – the uncomfortable truth is that nearly half of employment in high-tech industries is concentrated in just five industries: computer services, motor vehicles, engineering, electronic components, and management and public relations services. Of the 29 high-tech industries identified, 25 were in the traditional manufacturing sector.

The new economy may yet surface and succeed in transforming the future world of work, but the present structure of employment points to the emergence of an 'hourglass' economy. At the top end of the jobs hierarchy there has been an increased proliferation of highly paid jobs, whose incumbents enjoy substantial discretion over the hours, places and patterns of their working time. But, in Britain, their fortunes have merely served to fuel the growth of low-paid, routine and unskilled employment in occupations that would have been pre-eminent fifty years ago.

References

Beatty, C., Fothergill, S., Gore, T. and Herrington, A. 1997: *The Real Level of Unemployment.* Sheffield: Centre for Regional Economic and Social Research, Sheffield Hallam University.

Beck, U. 2000: *The Brave New World of Work.* Cambridge: Polity.

Bélanger, J., and Evans, S. 1988: Job controls and shop steward leadership among semi-skilled engineering workers. In M. Terry and P. K. Edwards (eds), *Shopfloor Politics and Job Controls: The Post-War Engineering Industry.* Oxford: Blackwell.

Blackaby, F. (ed.) 1979: *De-industrialisation.* London: Heinemann.

Booth, A. L., Francesconi, M. and Frank, J. 2000: Temporary jobs: who gets them, what are they worth and do they lead anywhere? Institute for Labour Research, Discussion Paper no. 00–57, University of Essex.

Bridges, M. 1995: *Job Shift: How to Prosper in a Workplace Without Jobs.* London: Nicolas Brealey.

Bureau of Labor Statistics 2001: *International Comparison of Hourly Compensation Costs for Production Workers in Manufacturing, 1975–2000.* Washington: US Department of Labor.

Buxton, T., and Clokie, S. 1992: Technology and structural change. In P. Dunne and C. Driver (eds), *Structural Change and Economic Growth.* Cambridge: Cambridge University Press.

Casey, B., Metcalf, H. and Millward, N. 1997: *Employers' Use of Flexible Labour.* London: Policy Studies Institute.

Crafts, N. 1988: The assessment: British economic growth over the long run, *Oxford Review of Economic Policy*, 4 (1), i–xxi.

Crafts, N. 1991: Reversing relative economic decline? The 1980s in historical perspective, *Oxford Review of Economic Policy*, 7 (3), 81–98.

Crafts, N., and Broadberry, S. 1990: Explaining Anglo-American productivity differences in the mid-twentieth century, *Oxford Review of Economics and Statistics*, 52 (4), 375–402.

Cully, M., Woodland, S., O'Reilly, A. and Dix, G. 1999: *Britain at Work*. London: Routledge.

Dickens, R., Gregg, P. and Wadsworth, J. 2000: New Labour and the labour market, *Oxford Review of Economic Policy*, 16 (1), 95–113.

Disney, R. 1999: Why have older men stopped working? In P. Gregg and J. Wadsworth (eds), *The State of Working Britain*. Manchester: Manchester University Press.

Dunning, J. 1985: Multinational enterprise and industrial restructuring in the UK, *Lloyds Bank Review*, October, 1–19.

Evans, S., Ewing, K. and Nolan, P. 1992: Industrial relations and the British economy in the 1990s: Mrs Thatcher's legacy, *Journal of Management Studies*, 29 (5), 571–89.

Fine, B., and Harris, L. 1985: *The Peculiarities of the British Economy*. London: Lawrence & Wishart.

Gospel, H. 1992: *Markets, Firms and the Management of Labour in Modern Britain*. Cambridge: Cambridge University Press.

Gregg, P., and Wadsworth, J. 1999: Economic inactivity. In P. Gregg and J. Wadsworth (eds), *The State of Working Britain*. Manchester: Manchester University Press.

Hamel, G., and Prahalad, C. K. 1996: Competing in the new economy: managing out of bounds, *Strategic Management Journal*, 17 (2), 237–42.

Jacoby, S. 1984: *Employing Bureaucracy: Managers, Unions and the Transformation of Work in American Industry, 1900–1945*. New York: Columbia University Press.

Leadbeater, C. 2000: *Living on Thin Air: The New Economy*. London: Viking.

Lyddon, D. 1994: The car industry: 1945–1979. Mimeo, Centre for Industrial Relations, University of Keele.

Mackay, D., Boddy, D., Brack, J., Diack, J. and Jones, N. 1971: *Labour Markets under Different Employment Conditions*. London: Allen & Unwin.

Mason, G., van Ark, B. and Wagner, K. 1994: Productivity, product quality and workforce skills: food processing in four European countries, *National Institute Economic Review*, 147, 62–83.

Morgan, J. 1996: What do comparisons of the last two economic recoveries tell us about the UK labour market? *National Institute Economic Review*, 156, 80–92.

Nolan, P., and Brown, W. 1983: Competition and workplace wage determination, *Oxford Bulletin of Economics and Statistics*, 45 (3), 269–87.

Nolan, P., Saundry, R. and Sawyer, M. 1997: Choppy waves on air and sea, *New Economy*, May, 167–72.

OECD (Organization for Economic Co-operation and Development) 1991: *Historical Statistics 1960–1990*. Paris: OECD.

OECD 1999a: *Employment Outlook*. Paris: OECD

OECD 1999b: *Labour Force Statistics 1978–1998*. Paris: OECD.

OECD 1999c: *Foreign Trade Statistics*. Paris: OECD.

O'Mahony, M., Oulton, N. and Vass, J. 1998: Market services: productivity benchmarks for the UK, *Oxford Bulletin of Economics and Statistics*, 60 (4), 529–51.

Ray, G. 1972: Labour costs and international competitiveness, *National Institute Economic Review*, 61, 53–8.

Reich, R. 1993: *The Work of Nations*. London: Simon & Schuster.

Rifkin, J. 1995: *The End of Work: The Decline of the Global Labour Force and the Dawn of the Post-Market Era.* New York: G. P. Putnams Sons.

Robinson, P. 1997: *Labour Market Studies: United Kingdom.* Luxembourg: Office for Official Publications of the European Communities.

Rowthorn, R. 2000: Kalecki centenary lecture: the political economy of full employment in modern Britain, *Oxford Bulletin of Economics and Statistics*, 62 (2), 139–73.

Rowthorn, R., and Wells, J. 1987: *Deindustrialization and Foreign Trade.* Cambridge: Cambridge University Press.

Roy, A. 2001: The European internationalisation of Japan's service THCs: a study of the financial sector in the UK. University of Leeds, unpublished Ph.D.

Saundry, R., and Nolan, P. 1998: Regulatory change and performance in TV production, *Media, Culture and Society*, 20 (3), 409–26.

Scarpetta, S., Bassanoni, A., Pilat, D. and Schreyer, P. 2000: Economic growth in the OECD area: recent trends at the aggregate and sectoral level. OECD Economics Department Working Paper No. 248.

Scase, R. 2000: *Britain in 2010: The New Business Landscape.* Norwich: Capstone.

Siebert, W., and Addison, J. 1991: Internal labour markets: causes and consequences, *Oxford Review of Economic Policy*, 7 (1), 76–92.

Singh, A. 1976: UK industry and the world economy: a case of de-industrialisation, *Cambridge Journal of Economics*, 1 (2), 113–36.

Stewart, M. 1999: Low pay in Britain. In P. Gregg and J. Wadsworth (eds), *The State of Working Britain.* Manchester: Manchester University Press.

United Nations 1999: *World Investment Report.* New York: UN.

Warhurst, C., and Thompson, P. 1998: Hands, hearts and minds. In P. Thompson and C. Warhurst (eds), *Workplaces of the Future*, London: Macmillan.

Williamson, O. 1975: *Market and Hierarchies.* London: Sage.

4

FOREIGN MULTINATIONALS AND INDUSTRIAL RELATIONS INNOVATION IN BRITAIN

ANTHONY FERNER

Britain has long been one of the most open economies in the developed world. Its level of both inward and outward foreign direct investment (FDI) as a percentage of GDP is the highest of any major developed economy. As a result, it has been peculiarly open to the influences of other national business systems. The scale of FDI in Britain has encouraged a long-standing interest in its impact on British patterns of industrial relations and employment practices. From the 1980s, the deregulation of the economy and growing concern about the bases of Britain's national competitiveness within the global economy have refocused interest on the potential transfer of practices from other business systems and on the contribution they might make to institutional renewal and innovation in Britain. At the same time, thorough deregulation, the minor role of statutory regulation of collective relations compared with Continental European business systems, and the undermining of the position of trade unions and of workplace representative arrangements in the past 20 years may be seen as providing foreign companies with fertile ground for industrial relations experimentation.

This chapter considers the influence of foreign companies on industrial relations and work practices in Britain. The following section provides an overview of the development and current pattern of foreign ownership in British industry. The bulk of the chapter then examines the role of MNCs as industrial relations innovators. In recent years, debate has centred on the contentious question of 'Japanization'. One reason has been the explicit emphasis by policymakers on the lessons to be learnt from the Japanese in areas such as work organization and HRM. This debate is examined in some detail. But the innovation issue goes considerably wider than the impact of Japanese transplants, and the influence of US and other MNCs is also considered. The conclusion reviews the argument by examining the complex interplay between the British environment and the features transferred to Britain by foreign MNCs, leading to a process of partial innovation and adaptation.

The Evolution of Foreign Direct Investment in Britain

The pattern of FDI

Foreign direct investment in British manufacturing has a long history. The evolution of FDI can be considered in terms of successive phases or waves of investment (Dunning 1998; Fraser 1999; Jones 1996). Singer set up a sewing-machine plant in Scotland as early as 1867; within a decade it had become a major exporter. American subsidiaries became influential in the early development of branches of activity such as electrical equipment, telecommunications equipment and, subsequently, in the motor industry. US investment increased rapidly from the 1920s, and particularly in the post-war period, across a wide front ranging from engineering to consumer products, food processing, and chemicals and pharmaceuticals (Dunning 1998: ch. 1). American investment was the earliest, and the most strongly established, attracted by easy access, a common language, and the presence in the UK of a supportive infrastructure of American banks and business services. But Continental European companies – Siemens, SKF, Philips and Nestlé among them – were early arrivals, all in Britain by the early years of the century.

Since the Second World War, American capital has continued to predominate. However, waves of French, German, and, famously from the 1970s, Japanese investment have diluted the American presence. The first Japanese manufacturing subsidiary was established by YKK in Runcorn as late as 1972, to be followed by Sony in Wales in 1973, NSK Bearings in Peterlee in 1974, and Toshiba in Plymouth in 1977. One of the biggest investments was made by Nissan. Its Sunderland car plant, opened in 1984, employed over 4,000 in 1998. Honda and Toyota also arrived in the 1980s. German companies, whose long history of operating in Britain had been disrupted by two world wars, began to arrive in force from the 1970s and 1980s, with a heavy flow of investment in sectors such as chemicals, motor vehicle components (in some cases prompted by the arrival of Japanese customers in the UK), and service industries such as retail and media; French companies too began a notable process of internationalization in the 1970s and 1980s (Mtar 2001; Sally 1995).

The growth of overall investment has been driven by a number of factors. From the mid-1970s, government policy has tended to support the influx of foreign capital, which was regarded as a source of innovation, employment, improved productivity and the reform of new labour practices and industrial relations. The decline of traditional industries such as coal, steel and shipbuilding gave added impetus to the search for foreign investment, and state incentives were used to attract inward capital flows to declining regions in particular. Accession to the European Economic Community in 1974 initiated the process of market unification that attracted market-serving investment to Europe, allowing MNCs to establish a single base for their European manufacturing operations, and encouraging them to restructure their organizations on pan-European lines. The Conservatives' programme of deregulation was seen as creating the conditions in which a large proportion of that investment would flow into Britain (e.g. Fraser 1999). Deregulation of product markets, notably financial services in the 1980s, removed constraints on international flows of investment (Stopford and Turner 1985: 242–6). The wholesale privatization of state enterprises and the ending of their monopolies opened up previously closed areas of activity such as telecommunications, water, and electricity supply to foreign ownership. As important, the programme of labour market deregulation, together with its hacking away at the bases of trade union power, contributed in the view of supporters to the 'the kind of labour flexibility of the 1990s that set the UK apart from European competitors', helped reduce industrial conflict to a fraction of the EU average and fostered a 'new spirit of industrial partnership', providing an attractive environment for foreign capital (Fraser 1999: 9). This was complemented by sharp reductions in personal (and corporate) taxation that had by the early 1990s helped give Britain the lowest total labour costs of all the major European countries.

These developments have consolidated Britain's status as the location of choice of foreign investment. Between 1990 and 1996, Britain received cumulative foreign direct investment of $140 bn. (the third highest in the world after USA and China), and in 1998 recorded a record inflow of £38 bn. (ONS 1999). In that year, it was the site of 8 per cent of the world's total stock of inward investment and 23 per cent of all inward FDI in the EU (UNCTAD 1998). Britain has consistently hosted the highest level of FDI as a proportion of GDP of any major economy: inward investment in 1997 equalled 2.88 per cent of GDP, compared with 1.66 per cent in France and 1.16 per cent in the USA (Germany actually had negative inward investment in that year) (OECD 1999). Forty-four per cent of all Japanese FDI flows to the EU between 1951 and 1998 went to the UK (Fraser 1999: 13). Similarly, Britain was the preferential destination for US investment (Dunning 1998: appendix 3; *US Survey of Current Business*). In 1996 FDI in British manufacturing accounted for 19 per cent of manufacturing employment, 28 per cent of net output, and around 50 per cent of gross exports (Fraser 1999: 12).

The sectoral distribution of FDI within manufacturing has remained reasonably stable; in 1968 the food, chemicals, electrical and mechanical engineering, and transport equipment industries were the dominant targets of investors, together accounting for 78 per cent of foreign investment in UK manufacturing; in 1990 the same industries accounted for 71 per cent (Dunning 1998: 296). (Japanese manufacturing investment has of course been overwhelmingly concentrated in two sectors: electrical engineering and transport equipment.) As can be seen from table 4.1, manufacturing employment is largely concentrated in chemicals, machinery, electrical equipment and motor vehicles. However, there have been major changes in the distribution between manufacturing and other activities, especially services. In the 1950s and 1960s, for example, over 60 per cent of US FDI was in manufacturing; by 1995 the figure had dropped to under a quarter as services such as finance, banking and insurance, and business services have grown in weight (Dunning 1998: 290). For FDI as a whole, the proportion of manufacturing was 31 per cent in 1998 (ONS 2000). Financial services,

Table 4.1   Employment in foreign-owned manufacturing enterprises by industry, 1995

SIC	Industry	Employment (000s)	% of total
15–16	food, beverages and tobacco	67.8	9.4
17–19	textiles, clothing and footwear	18.8	2.6
20–1	pulp and paper; wood products	31.3	4.4
22	publishing, printing	24.4	3.4
23	refined petroleum products	5.9	0.8
24	chemicals and chemical products	87.6	12.2
25	rubber and plastic products	39.8	5.5
26	other non-metallic mineral products	15.4	2.1
27	basic metals	22.2	3.1
28	metal products	32.6	4.5
29	machinery	81.5	11.3
30	office machinery and computers	24.6	3.4
31	electrical machinery and apparatus	33.3	4.6
32	radio, television and communication equipment	48.6	6.8
33	medical, precision and optical instruments	20.9	2.9
34	motor vehicles	122.3	17.0
35	other transport equipment	26.3	3.7
36–7	other manufacturing	15.1	2.1
	TOTAL	718.4	99.8

Source: Calculated from figures in ONS (1983, 1995).

business services, utilities, and transport and communications were major areas of growth.

Attracted by regional grants, much foreign capital has flowed into less developed areas of the country. In 1995 the south-east still accounted for 26 per cent of manufacturing employment by foreign MNCs (ONS 1997). But its position was in decline. And foreign manufacturing companies were more than proportionately located in less prosperous regions such as the north-east and especially Wales, and Scotland, relative to the presence in those regions of manufacturing generally (Dunning 1998: 311).

In terms of country of origin, the USA continues, as noted above, to be the predominant source of FDI. In 1998 the USA still accounted for almost half of total FDI in the UK (see table 4.2). Although its weight was considerably below the peak values of the 1960s and 1970s (US companies accounted for as much as 87 per cent of foreign-owned manufacturing employment in 1973 – see Dunning 1998: 295), the USA continued to dwarf other foreign investors. Table 4.3 shows employment in foreign-owned companies in manufacturing, by country

Table 4.2 Foreign direct investment in UK manufacturing by country of origin, 1965–98 (%)

	USA	Western Europe	Japan
1965	68.0	18.3	0.0
1971	66.9	23.2	0.0
1978	66.8	26.5	0.0
1981	67.0	23.3	0.4
1984	64.2	25.5	0.7
1987	61.2	24.3	1.5
1990	55.6	27.5	1.7
1992	46.5	30.2	3.2
1994	46.4	34.0	4.0
1995	44.7	32.0	2.5
1998	49.2	36.6	3.6

Source: ONS (1999); Dunning (1998: 291).

of origin for 1995. Some 718,000 were employed in foreign subsidiaries in manufacturing (compared with a peak of almost one million in 1979); of these, 323,000 were in US-owned companies, 45 per cent of the total and four times the number in the next most important foreign owner, Germany, with 78,000. In 1997, total employment in US subsidiaries, including non-manufacturing, amounted to close on 1 million (*US Survey of Current Business*).[1] However, as Table 4.3 shows, in the period 1983–95, the contribution of Japanese, French and German, but also Dutch, Swedish and Swiss companies, grew significantly.

Inward investment has tended to be concentrated in the hands of a relatively small number of companies. In 1981 the 100 largest foreign firms were responsible for around 60 per cent of total investment, while the 37 largest non-bank investors (by sales) employed 410,000 people in 1983, half of them in six firms (Stopford and Turner 1985: 135). At the end of the 1990s, over 18,000 foreign firms were operating in Britain, more than 500 of which had 1,000 or more employees.

Pay, productivity and employment

Macro-level statistics show that foreign companies tend to have higher productivity and pay higher wages than indigenous firms (Dunning 1998: 295; Stopford and Turner 1985: 139, 144). US firms, for example, have consistently paid wages between 10 and 20 per cent higher per head than industry averages. Japanese companies paid rather less than average compensation throughout the 1980s, but in the early 1990s their wage rates started to move ahead of industry as a whole. The foreign capital effect on wages is particularly noticeable in industries such as mechanical engineering, motor vehicles and parts, and rubber and plastics.

Table 4.3 Employment in foreign-owned enterprises in UK manufacturing by country of origin, 1983 and 1995

	No. of enterprises	% total foreign enterprises	Employment (000s)		% total foreign employment	
	1995	1995	1983	1995	1983	1995
All enterprises in UK	170,227			4,184.2		
Total foreign companies	2,397	100.0	736.0	718.4	100.0	100.0
France	151	6.3	31.3	51.4	3.8	7.2
Germany	256	10.7	24.0	78.4	3.3	10.9
Netherlands	161	6.7	36.6	38.8	4.1	5.4
Sweden	127	5.3	17.1	23.6	2.3	3.3
Switzerland	153	6.4	38.7	43.1	5.3	6.0
USA	873	36.4	459.5	323.1	62.4	45.0
Canada	118	4.9		36.4		5.1
Japan	138	5.8	3.7	51.7	0.1	7.2
Rest of world	420	17.5	125.1	71.9	18.7	10.0

Source: Calculated from figures in ONS (1983, 1995).

Foreign firms' productivity in terms of net output per head was 25 per cent higher in manufacturing, and in some industries, notably food, drink and tobacco, considerably higher still. However, such data need to be treated with caution since they ignore differences in market segment, size and date of establishment of firm. Stopford and Turner (1985: 144) conclude judiciously that there 'is some evidence that when more detailed comparisons are made, the foreigners follow local wage practices, perhaps paying a slight premium in some sectors'. On productivity, the evidence tends to suggest that subsidiaries perform better than local firms but worse than home-country operations of the same company (Stopford and Turner 1985: 144).

Foreign firms' record on employment is also mixed. Overall, foreign-controlled manufacturing employment has fallen sharply (see table 4.3), but Stopford and Turner (1985: 183–7) argue that the decline in MNC employment in the early 1980s was much less precipitate than the decline in UK MNCs or UK domestic companies. A more recent, detailed analysis by Richard Harris for the Department of Trade and Industry (DTI) compared 1,800 foreign-owned plants acquired in between 1987 and 1992 with similar UK-owned plants. He too found that the acquired companies reduced employment considerably less than did UK manufacturing as a whole, and at the same time improved productivity and real wages compared with UK firms (unpublished research reported in Fraser 1999: 26–8).

One of the claims regularly made by policymakers was that the loose regulation of the British labour market and industrial relations, and the labour flexibility that this permitted, provided a major attraction for foreign capital and hence was a source of employment creation. On the face of it, the above figures are consistent with this claim, in that the gap between employment creation and destruction in foreign MNCs has been less than in British firms. However, there are two counter-arguments. First, there is considerable evidence (summarized in Ferner 1998) that labour relations factors are only one element in companies' location decisions. Industrial relations 'climate' is rarely a primary motivation for these decisions, and labour costs are complicated by such factors as skill composition of the labour force and the capital intensity of local production. In terms of serving the wider European market as a whole, Britain's failure to join the euro zone is of greater potential importance than labour costs; several foreign investors – notably Japanese car manufacturers – have been vociferous in complaining about the detrimental impact of this on the performance of their operations in Britain.

Second, although deregulation may attract foreign capital to Britain in the first place, it may also facilitate relocation of production away from Britain if the context changes. This 'easy come, easy go' nature of British deregulation contrasts with other European countries, where institutional constraints make the cost of divestment in terms, for example, of processes of consultation with the workforce and redundancy payments, much higher than in the UK. The relocation issue was brought into sharp focus in 2000 by BMW's divestment of Rover and the announcements by Ford and General Motors of the end of vehicle-making at Dagenham and Vauxhall Luton respectively; the end of the 1990s had witnessed the closure of Siemens' and Fujitsu's major semi-conductor plants in the north-east, the former shortly after it had opened. The BMW case is likely to reinforce the suspicion that German and other MNCs from relatively regulated national systems may exploit the ease of redundancy in Britain to load the burden of international corporate readjustment onto their British subsidiaries while maintaining traditional employment stability in their home operations (see Ferner and Varul 1999).

Despite Britain's apparent attractions as a site for investment, the lack of constraints on foreign capital may become more significant as a result of structural developments in the international economy. One factor is the consolidation of the euro zone; the relocation of foreign capital from Britain to Continental Europe is likely to increase if Britain fails to join the euro in the medium term. Another factor is the growing integration of production internationally, combined with the increasing sophistication of management tools for comparing performance across operating units internationally, which raises question marks over the commitment of foreign companies to the UK.

MNCs as Industrial Relations Innovators

One of the most important themes concerning foreign MNCs is whether they adapt to local practices, or import innovative IR practices which may subsequently diffuse into the local environment. This issue is increasingly pertinent as the impact of globalization raises questions about the competitiveness of national systems in the world economy. Multinationals are not the only conduit for foreign IR innovations: management consultants, business associations and governmental initiatives may all be important channels for the dissemination of practices from other business systems. But multinationals are probably the single most important mechanism through which practices are diffused from one national business system to another. For this reason, policymakers have been exercised by the question of whether foreign MNCs 'import' into Britain employment practices that raise the quality and performance of British industry.

The notion of 'innovation' is fraught. In the minds of policymakers, it has tended to carry positive connotations of progress, higher productivity and more 'harmonious' employment relations. Yet the positive nature of innovations is often a matter for debate. In extreme cases, foreign MNCs have introduced harsh anti-union policies and acrimonious industrial relations. The strong-arm tactics of the American textile manufacturer Roberts in the 1960s, in which a year-long strike was precipitated by the dismissal of union members and their replacement by non-union labour, led one commentator to remark that the underlying problem was:

> simply a matter of ignorance by the company concerned of the practices, the traditions, the matters regarded as of importance in the United Kingdom, and an assumption that methods hallowed by tradition and supplemented by law in the United States must be right wherever they are exported. (Silkin 1970, quoted in Blanpain 1977: 121)

Similar, though more complex, issues surround the question of 'innovations' by Japanese companies which, as will be seen below, have been seen by many observers as retrograde in important respects, despite their connotations of best practice and efficiency.

But do MNCs act as innovators, or do they merely adapt to local practices? As Marginson and Sisson (1994) argue, there are grounds for expecting MNCs increasingly to import their own company-specific employment practices, rather than to adapt to the host country. First, MNCs possess ever more sophisticated 'information-processing capacities', allowing them to monitor routinely a wide range of performance indicators such as unit labour costs, numbers employed, and productivity (see also Marginson et al. 1995). Second, the international integration of production and marketing, particularly in sectors such as motor vehicles, has encouraged the creation of international business divisions and strategic business units, 'responsible for the production, distribution and market-ing of particular products and services across territories' (Marginson and Sisson 24–5). This has created the 'strategic potential to establish a pan-European approach to employee and industrial relations management' (1994: 25), an ap-proach encouraged by the completion of the single European market in the early 1990s. It also provides a mechanism for disseminating employment and work organization practices across borders in the form of 'coercive comparisons' (Mueller and Purcell 1992) whereby superior performance and practice in one plant can be used to lever change in comparable plants in other countries.[2] In short, there are structural factors leading MNCs away from traditional 'multi-domestic' strategies (Porter 1990) of serving distinct national markets through largely autonomous territorial subsidiaries.

The other side of the equation is that the deregulation of the British environment has in many ways made it easier for foreign MNCs wishing to import new practices to do so, relatively untrammelled by institutional constraints on management prerogative in the host economy, particularly in the industrial relations arena. For example, Bélanger, Edwards and Wright (1999) show how, in the 'permissive' UK context, the British subsidiary of a Canadian metal company was able to introduce a more developed form of teamworking than the Canadian plant: the absence of detailed rules on job classifications and labour assignment embodied in legally enforceable collective agreements, together with the relative ease of redundancy, made change easier to accomplish in Britain. Indeed, the British environment may provide a test bed where MNCs from more institutionally constrained parent economies, such as France or Germany, may develop new approaches to industrial relations and human resource management which they can then 'reverse diffuse' (Edwards and Ferner 2000) to their operations at home.

One indication that MNCs act as IR innovators would be the existence of markedly different employment practices in foreign firms compared with indigenous British firms. The evidence on this is very mixed. Many surveys have shown only muted differences in industrial relations behaviour of foreign and national firms. An analysis of 1980 WIRS data (Buckley and Enderwick 1983) showed relatively few differences in the two groups. Foreign companies more strongly favoured single employer bargaining, had a more decentralized (plant- or company-based) approach to bargaining, were more likely to refuse to negotiate on areas such as labour utilization, had a more specialized and professional approach to IR, and tended to use rewards based on merit and performance rather than seniority. Significantly, they were also twice as likely as domestic firms to have no union members among manual workers (1983: 35–7). Overall, though, Stopford and Turner (1985: 146) describe the differences as 'marginal in the extreme'.

This picture has been repeated in successive WIRS/WERS surveys (e.g. Millward et al. 1992; Millward 1994; Guest and Hoque 1996; detailed analysis from the 1998 survey is still awaited). The 1990 WIRS survey, for example, showed that foreign- and UK-owned workplaces had similar degrees of multi-unionism once workplace size was taken into account, and differences were relatively few. Guest and Hoque (1996) found that US- and UK-owned plants differed little from each other. There *are* differences. In 1990, for example, foreign firms were more likely than indigenous establishments to have non-union representatives, to consult with higher-level managers during pay negotiations, to have specialist IR or personnel managers, to use job evaluation, and to have at least some staff on incentive pay; they were less likely to engage in multi-employer bargaining, to have joint consultative committees, or to employ lower-paid workers (Guest and Hoque 1996: 57–8; Millward et al. 1992: 83, 164, 227, 235, 245, 261). The Company-Level Industrial Relations Survey showed that foreign firms spent more on training and used more methods of employee communication, and that their personnel functions exerted greater influence over strategic decisions (Marginson et al. 1995). But the absence of far-reaching differences is notable.

The failure of surveys to reveal striking differences is hard to interpret. It may mean, as Stopford and Turner suggest (1985: 147), that the 'story is one of the foreign multinationals successfully adapting to local practices, but being especially alert to spot occasions when reforms could be successfully introduced'. This interpretation is supported by numerous studies showing that employment and IR issues in subsidiaries are much less subject to the direct influence of parent headquarters than are financial, production or marketing decisions (e.g. Young et al. 1985).

However, the absence of difference does not necessarily imply that foreign MNCs are adapters rather than innovators: it may mean, for example, that any innovative practices have already diffused to indigenous companies. An example is the decline of multi-employer bargaining. With earlier WIRS surveys showing that foreign firms had a much lower propensity to engage in such bargaining than national firms, Millward et al. (1992: 227) argue that it is 'difficult to dismiss the suggestion that the increase in overseas-owned firms [over the period] played a part in the decline in multi-employer bargaining'. It may also be that differences in practices are too subtle to be captured easily by survey methods. IR practices such as 'teamworking' or 'quality circles' are open to huge variation in aspects such as purpose, frequency, context, and practical operation; similar levels of teamworking may hide major differences in practice; and similar rates of non-unionism may be associated with a wide variety of human resource strategies in national and foreign firms (cf. Geary and Roche 2001). Moreover, there is likely to be differentiation between foreign-owned plants. Studies of Japanese MNCs in the US have clearly shown that some innovate but that a large number of smaller firms tend to adapt to the local environment (Milkman 1991). It is likely that innovation is driven by the minority, with a large number of less innovative firms leading surveys to reveal few overall differences from UK firms.

A wide variety of other studies strongly suggest that foreign companies' behaviour is different, and in many respects a force for innovation within the British IR system. One aspect is the variation in innovatory behaviour among foreign firms of different national origin, reflecting the wide differences in economic organization and institutional regulation found in national business systems (Ferner 1997). As Edwards and Ferner (2000) have argued, systematic innovation in host economies is more likely to be found in MNCs originating in business systems that are regarded as dominant within the global economy. This is because companies will wish to transfer to hosts those practices that have served as a source of international competitive advantage for the parent business system. (By contrast, MNCs from national business systems providing fewer sources of international comparative advantage are less likely to transfer practices and more likely to adapt to host environments.)

The focus of much literature has been on the role of Japanese transplants as innovators. The interest in these companies has been out of all proportion to their weight among foreign MNCs in the UK: in 1995 they employed just over 50,000, on a par with French MNCs, significantly less than German ones, and a fraction of the US subsidiaries in Britain. As Elger and Smith (1994: 49) comment, the symbolic significance of Japanese investment in British has been enormous: 'From "After Japan" onwards, claims about Japanese manufacturing and lean production have become central to the rhetoric and negotiating positions of senior managers in non-Japanese firms, as they have sought to recast established working patterns and bargaining arrangements.' In earlier decades, US MNCs were cast in much the same light for their innovatory approach to industrial relations (Enderwick 1985: 115–19; Flanders 1964). In the following sub-sections, the influence of US and of Japanese MNCs on British industrial relations patterns are considered in turn.

American MNCs and industrial relations innovation

Given their predominant weight among foreign investors in the British economy, the attention paid to the role of US MNCs in industrial relations has been relatively muted compared to that devoted to Japanese companies. There are, however, grounds for arguing that their influence on the British scene has been profound for much of the past century and particularly in the post-war period. Though in recent decades the emphasis has been on the international competitiveness of the Japanese production model, for many decades prior to that the American Taylorist paradigm was being widely diffused through the operations of US companies abroad (e.g. Kogut 1991). The Ford Motor Company began assembling cars at Trafford Park, Manchester from 1911: 'from the very beginning, use was made of the semi-automatic principle of large-scale production as adopted by the parent plant' (Dunning 1998: 19). By 1913, Ford's system for producing low-priced standardized cars had made it the largest UK producer. It was to be followed by a stream of American manufacturers using standardized mass production methods, both in capital-intensive sectors using continuous production technology (such as chemicals, oil-refining, rubber), and in sectors producing for the growing mass consumption markets for durable and semi-durable consumer products (see also Chandler 1990; Jones 1995: ch. 4).

Second, American MNCs imported to Britain the organizational forms and management methods that had emerged to help companies service large-scale mass markets in the USA. They brought to Britain and to other European countries the multi-divisional organizational form with its associated management control mechanisms such as financial planning and budgeting, as well as the division of management functions into distinct and highly professionalized specialisms such as production, finance, and personnel (Dunning 1998: ch. 9; Chandler 1990). Even in the 1950s, they possessed the managerial techniques to impose systematic cross-frontier comparisons on their subsidiaries. For example, the Esso Fawley refinery's poor showing on Standard Oil's new international system for the statistical comparison of labour utilization helped create the pressure that was to lead to the 1960 'Blue Book' productivity deal (Flanders 1964: 65–6). The importing of formal American management systems was promoted by the relatively high degree of centralization in US MNCs in a range of management functions, including personnel, compared with other foreign MNCs. Young et al. (1985), for example, in their survey of over 150 foreign subsidiaries, found that the Americans were more likely to establish financial targets and more central-ized on employment and personnel decisions (see also Kujawa 1979: 4–5).

Third, there is considerable evidence that US MNCs have consistently been IR innovators in Britain, and that their innovations in areas such as pay systems and bargaining structure and strategy have subsequently been absorbed into the host system, one reason why differences with British companies sometimes appear muted in surveys. Companies such as Ford and General Motors long insisted on hourly-based pay instead of the often chaotic piecework systems used by British-owned firms, and Chrysler (which took over the British Rootes Group in the 1960s) was a pioneer in the shift from piecework to measured day work (Clegg 1979: 146; Blanpain 1977: 122). In the bargaining arena, the desire to maintain managerial control over labour issues induced companies such as Ford, Kodak, Heinz and Esso Petroleum to eschew employers' associations and to develop company-based IR policies (Gennard and Steuer 1971: 152–3; Roberts 1972). In this they were the precursors of the trend away from multi-employer bargaining in the UK. They also innovated in the use of multi-year agreements, productivity bargaining and concession bargaining (in which workforces traded pay freezes or cuts against employment safeguards) (Enderwick 1985: 115–17). The Fawley Blue Book agreement was the earliest and most famous example of the innovatory productivity bargaining brought to Britain by MNCs such as Esso (and also Mobil) from the early 1960s, and which addressed questions such as rigid inter-craft demarcations and routine overtime working (Flanders 1964). Towards the mid-1960s, British companies began to adopt similar agreements (Gennard and Steuer 1971: 157).

Dunning's 1950s survey of more than 200 US subsidiaries (Dunning 1998: 194–201) shows that such developments have a long history in the UK. Sixty per cent of his sample adopted the same pay principles – and in a significant number of cases, the same detailed pay policies – as the US parent, while 40 per cent adapted to the local environment. Many firms adopted a policy of paying above the market rate to attract and retain good employees. Innovations in-cluded the use of job evaluation and work study, and the introduction of bonus and merit systems in companies such as Black & Decker, Monsanto, Vauxhall, Edison and Mars (1998: 197). Dunning's conclusion in 1958 was that 'many American-financed firms are recognized as being amongst the most progressive and enlightened of employers, both for their willingness to adopt the latest wage and incentive systems, and for their belief that a workforce well paid, properly trained and regularly consulted pays dividends in the long run through improved personnel efficiency and reduced labour turnover' (1998: 201). As more recent surveys show, American companies continue to be distinctive in their use of merit pay and job evaluation (e.g. Guest and Hoque 1996).

Innovation has not been confined to pay and bargaining. Dunning (1998: 196–201) also noted that US subsidiaries were in the vanguard in introducing high-quality social amenities, non-contributory pension schemes, and even a measure of job or pay security. As early as 1947, Thomas Hedley (a wholly owned acquisition of Procter & Gamble) guaranteed permanent employment to hourly-paid workers with two years' service; Heinz guaranteed 4,000 hourly-paid workers a minimum weekly wage for a year in advance. More recently, American companies have led in the use of 'sophisticated' HRM in arenas such as 'diversity' policy, performance and competency appraisal, evaluation of work-force attitudes through regular surveys, formalized management development systems, and so on.

A final and controversial area of innovation in the British context has been relations with unions. Observers have repeatedly noted the reluctance of US companies to recognize unions and in many cases their active hostility to unions and unionism (Gennard and Steuer 1971; ILO 1976: 3–9). Ford, for example, under the influence of Detroit, did not recognize unions in its British operations until official pressure compelled it to do so during the Second World War (Roberts 1972: 120). As Shearer (1967) pointed out, this attitude had much to do with the historical background of union recognition in the USA, where companies tended to avoid recognizing unions until compelled to do so by the election process under the 1935 Wagner Act. This contrasted with the less 'systematic' non-unionism of indigenous British firms (Jefferys 1988; also chapter 2 above) and was characteristic of larger as well as smaller US companies.

American MNCs are likewise distinguished in their non-unionism from other foreign firms in Britain. Some (e.g. Guest and Hoque 1996: 63) have concluded that, while US firms are less likely than equivalent UK firms to recognize unions, they are no different from other foreign firms. But case studies suggest a deeper underlying distinction. Ferner and Varul (1999) found that non-unionism in German MNCs in Britain reflected a pragmatic devolution of recognition issues by the German parent to the British subsidiary. Companies such as IBM, Hewlett Packard, McDonald's and many others have, by contrast, been well known for their deep-seated ideological or philosophical commitment to non-unionism, and this orientation has been transferred to their overseas subsidiaries (e.g. Roberts 1972: 124–5; Royle 2000), whether through formal or informal policy directives, or through a more diffuse culture which permeates management thinking in the subsidiaries.[3]

Beaumont and Townley (1985) found that non-unionism in American firms was linked (in contrast to UK non-union firms) to the adoption of other innov-ative workplace policies such as problem-solving groups, for example quality circles, in-house training, autonomous work groups and joint health and safety committees. This they relate to the home-country strategies of non-union US companies based on 'union substitution' through careful employee recruitment and selection; wage levels equal to or better than those of comparable union-ized firms, with performance appraisal and reward for merit; high investment in training; mechanisms of employee communication and informal participation; and the fostering of organizational commitment and loyalty. An earlier study similarly showed that foreign (largely US) firms 'attempted to check demands for unionism by the payment of relatively higher wages and the provision of good fringe benefits' (Gennard and Steuer 1971: 154).

More generally, the combination in US MNCs of anti-union sentiment (even in unionized companies) and 'sophisticated' HRM reflects the long-term dynamic interaction between the unionized and non-union sectors of American business depicted by Jacoby (1997). A typically American phenomenon has been the segment of large non-union firms with aspirations to provide a unitarist form of 'industrial community' for employees through the adoption of 'enlightened' personnel policies such as relative employment security, social amenities and high rewards. The way in which this sector has defined itself in relation to the union sector may be seen as the motor for much of the innovative IR and HR policies subsequently exported to British subsidiaries (see Ferner 2000). An important question is how far changes in the American business system – notably the rise of international competitive challenges, and profound changes in corporate governance (see especially O'Sullivan 2000) – are undermining the structural basis of sophisticated non-unionism as a strategy of US MNCs at home and abroad.

In any event, case studies such as Royle's work (2000) on McDonald's suggest that non- or anti-union approaches do not inevitably go hand in hand with the more sophisticated forms of personnel management of the major electronics or pharmaceutical companies. One of the key determinants appears to be the nature of product and labour markets; in labour-intensive, relatively low-skilled sectors such as the fast-food industry, a policy of high commitment, high skills, a developed internal labour market and stable employment is unlikely to be viable.

'Japanization'

The Conservative governments of the 1980s energetically wooed Japanese capital, on the explicit grounds that it would bring with it Japanese management techniques and act as a catalyst for reforming employment relations in the motor industry and elsewhere (Dohse 1987: 138). Over the past two decades, the influence of Japanese companies in the UK has been profound, although not always as clear-cut as policymakers would have liked. An extensive and by now familiar academic debate has raged for much of the period, although many of the issues remain contentious (see further chapter 13, on the impact on working practices).[4] To what have extent Japanese transplants brought with them new methods and approaches, particularly those associated with the 'Toyota production system' based on 'lean production' and high-commitment employment policies? How far have these innovations influenced indigenous firms and existing approaches to the management of labour? How homogeneous are practices among different Japanese transplants? Are imported practices modified to bring them in line with the British environment? How do British workforces and their representatives respond to the influx of Japanese capital?

It has been frequently pointed out that those elements of a Japanese model that were deeply rooted in a particular set of domestic institutional arrangements, such as seniority-based pay structures and lifetime employment, were not brought to the UK at all. Nonetheless, there is some degree of consensus that Japanese companies have brought with them a distinctive mode of managing labour. This comprises, on the one hand, the use of innovative methods of work organization, including continuous improvement of quality, flexibility of work-ing methods, and work organization based around notions of teamworking, and, on the other, high-commitment employment policies emphasizing employee com-munication and involvement, relative job security, and 'harmonious' workplace relations. In many cases, Japanese subsidiaries have looked to recruit 'green' workers (Elger and Smith 1994b) in labour markets isolated from industrial and, particularly, unionized traditions, often locating in areas of high unemployment such as South Wales, the north-east of England and the newer industrial areas of the West Midlands, such as Telford. Intensive induction and training are used to inculcate corporate values and approaches in the workforce. In traditionally unionized areas, such as South Wales, the potential impact of unionism is con-strained through single-union deals (IRS 1993: 13; Bassett 1987); elsewhere, non-unionism tends to be the norm, although some studies (e.g. Wood 1996) have found no difference between Japanese and other firms in the propensity to recognize unions. For some, notably Oliver and Wilkinson (1992), the dissemina-tion of Japanese methods through the presence of transplants in Britain has begun to bring about a profound change in the basis of Britain's international competitive advantage, reshaping workplace relations and working practices.

Part of the significance of the influx of Japanese methods is that they have reportedly been disseminated to other companies, notably through relations with suppliers. A survey in the mid-1990s of UK, US and other European motor components companies (IRS 1995) suggested that there had been a wide diffu-sion of methods associated with Japanese-style lean production, reflecting the arrival in Britain in the 1980s of the three Japanese car firms, Honda, Nissan and Toyota. Most of these suppliers were introducing typical Japanese work practices such as JIT, total quality, teamworking, and cellular production (that is, based on stand-alone units responsible for their own quality and performance), al-though other practices such as multi-skilling were relatively rare. As a result of these innovations, some have pointed to a growing convergence of Japanese and other firms on Japanese-style employment practices (IRS 1993; Oliver and Wilkinson 1992). The evidence is complex. An IRS report (1993) suggests that there were significant differences in what was meant by particular practices in different firms. 'Team briefings' in British firms, for example, tended to be infre-quently held and to focus on the pronouncements 'from on high' of senior executives; while Japanese-style team 'meetings' were generally held at the beginning or end of each shift (a point also emphasized by Wood, 1996: 519–20), and were often forums for taking decisions on issues such as training, performance, quality improvement, and covering absences (IRS 1993: 10).

Wood's comparison (1996) of 'high-commitment management' practices in Japanese and non-Japanese manufacturing plants in Britain found significant differences. In particular, Japanese plants were much more likely to use most of the high-commitment practices (such as teamworking, quality circles, training, team briefings, flexibility of tasks, no compulsory redundancy, formal assess-ment of production workers, career ladders for all, single status), and on average deployed a significantly higher number of such practices than their non-Japanese counterparts, taking account of sector and technology. A number of these findings were confirmed by Guest and Hoque's study (1996: 64, 71) of the effect of nationality of ownership in greenfield establishments. Moreover, Wood found that Japanese companies tended to be distinctive in the way in which they used high-commitment practices; for example, the concept of 'team' rather than that of 'job' was the basic organizing principle for the Japanese plant, and Japanese no-redundancy policies entailed a commitment to long-term stable employment rather than merely avoiding compulsory redundancy as in non-Japanese plants (1996: 520). Nor was there any indication that non-Japanese firms were converging on a Japanese pattern over time.

There have been doubts as to how deeply these innovative Japanese practices have taken root even in Japanese subsidiaries in Britain. A survey of Japanese subsidiaries in UK manufacturing in the early 1990s showed that by no means all Japanese subsidiaries adopted quality, flexibility and teamworking (IRS 1993). This is confirmed by detailed case studies; for instance, the study by Taylor et al. (1994) of a Japanese electronics firm showed that elements of Japanese practice claimed to be present, such as JIT, did not operate in reality. Overall, the picture is one of considerable heterogeneity, between firms and between the two main sectors of electronics and the motor industry.

Researchers have also tended to argue that the diffusion of Japanese practices to the wider environment has been 'wide but shallow' (Smith and Elger 1997: 289). Turnbull and Delbridge (1994: 351) describe it as reactive, 'ad hoc, pragmatic and opportunistic responses by employers to the socio-economic conditions created by the New Right in the 1980s and 1990s, rather than a strategic response to, or attempts to emulate, Japanese best practice'. Abo (1994) and others have used the term 'hybridization' to describe the process of partial adoption and adaptation of country-of-origin approaches. Elger and Smith (1994b: 50) argue that the unevenness of adoption of Japanese practices reflected the fact that they were used opportunistically to pursue long-standing management goals, particularly securing greater control over worker effort on the shop floor by reshaping formal relations with unions and informal relations with workgroups.

The resulting 'hybrid policy repertoires' (Smith and Elger 1997) based on the partially digested adoption of Japanese practices both in Japanese subsidiaries and in other companies have led to considerable tensions in workplace relations. A number of researchers have pointed to a reality at odds with the idealized notion of efficient and innovative work organization coupled with a committed workforce. Detailed case studies (e.g. Delbridge 1998; Garrahan and Stewart 1992; Mair 1998; Wilkinson et al. 1995) have painted a picture of a strict and regimented industrial discipline characterized by direct surveillance; line speed up and an obsessive concern for cycle times; low worker initiative and autonomy; a bias towards routinized machine-minding jobs; limited variety of tasks; and limited workforce involvement. Direct managerial control is replaced or supplemented by a more insidious discipline based on peer pressure and social control, leading to a high degree of self-exploitation.

Overall, one may conclude that Japanese transplants have had a major impact on industrial relations in Britain, but one that is more complex and ambiguous than the proponents of 'Japanization' would argue. They have introduced new forms of work organization and employment practices, and stand out from non-Japanese firms in the bundles of practices they employ; but the incidence of Japanese elements is patchy, and those that are adopted are modified to fit in with aspects of the British institutional environment. Finally, the Japanization debate has had a high ideological content. Policymakers and advocates of the Japanese contribution (e.g. Wickens 1987) have trumpeted the innovations Japanese transplants have brought, but others have pointed to the sometimes detrimental impact on the working lives of employees.

The 'mediating' influence of the British context on industrial relations innovation

The debates around Japanization point to wider issues of cross-national dissemination and the way in which the host environment 'mediates' the transmission and adoption of innovative practices. This issue goes wider than the case of Japanese MNCs. In the 1950s, Dunning (1998: 103–5) was observing that American forms of work organization had to be adapted to the British environment, particularly at the height of the Taylorist production model, since this was predicated on the specialized machinery and intense division of labour that the American market made possible but that were not viable in Britain. Researchers have continued to note the effects of the British environment in mediating the precise form that innovations have taken, whether those introduced by Japanese MNCs or others. Scarbrough and Terry (1998: 234), for example, argue that a 'creative process of adaptation' to lean production has taken place in non-Japanese car manufacturers in Britain, influenced by the wider UK institutional context, but also by 'company and plant-level path dependencies', that is by such factors as past labour process and work organization practices, and by the continuing presence of influential trade unions. The six-country study of ABB's power transformer division conducted by Bélanger and colleagues (Bélanger, Berggren et al. 1999; Martin and Beaumont 1999) likewise showed how the particular dynamic of management–union relations in the company's Scottish plant influenced the way in which international initiatives on work organization were implemented in practice.

Morris et al. (1998), in their study of the supervisor's role in Japanese subsidiaries in Britain, point to the role of British arrangements for vocational education and training. They argue that the British context makes it unrealistic to expect UK supervisors to carry out the same range of functions as their Japanese correlates (e.g. they are less heavily involved in kaizen), but that nonetheless they were assuming a far greater role in dealing with quality issues than would generally have been the case in UK manufacturing plants. In other words, dissemination is mediated by key institutional features such as the nature of vocational education institutions and their interaction with labour markets.

The Morris et al. study hints at the way in which the UK environment can impose constraints on the adoption of foreign practices despite its much-vaunted freedom from regulation and from rigid industrial relations institutions. A concrete example is provided by Dickmann (1999) in his study of HRM in German subsidiaries in Britain and Spain. He argues that the deregulated UK environment provided poor terrain to which to disseminate the German 'dual' system of vocational training, since the lack of institutional regulation permitted free-riding (in the form of 'poaching' of trained staff by non-training companies) and thus made the costs of the system unviable. This does not mean that a serious emphasis on training is absent in German MNCs, merely that it assumes forms more appropriate for the British context. This is true, too, of the relatively consensual, co-operative, long-termist approach to employment relations characteristic of firms in the German business system and embodied in institutions such as the works council. Surveys (e.g. Guest and Hoque 1996) find little evidence that German institutions are transferred to UK subsidiaries, but more detailed case studies (Ferner and Varul 1999) suggest that, even in subsidiaries where unions were not recognized for bargaining, a more intangible co-operative ethos was transferred and informed management decision-making in areas such as redundancy and employee participation. This is confirmed in Tueselmann's survey comparison between German subsidiaries in Britain and British-owned firms (2000). This finds evidence of a German co-operative culture in the tendency of German firms to adopt a collective orientation to employment relations; the 'Bleak House' approach (Sisson 1993), characterized by the absence of both comprehensive individual and collective employee voice mechanisms, is markedly less common in German than in British companies. Moreover, Tueselmann suggests that, although the UK may provide a test bed for innovative practices to be 'exported' back to Germany, such practices comprise a mix of collective and individual HR elements, rather than the substitution of the former by the latter.

Writers on Japanese companies in Britain (Oliver and Wilkinson 1992) have pointed to the way in which functional equivalents may be found within the British system to the characteristics of the domestic Japanese system: for example, location in areas of high unemployment and manufacturing desolation have created the possibility for Japanese MNCs to recruit and retain workforces capable of implementing a Japanese style of work organization, while the decline of unions in manufacturing has provided fertile grounds for either non-unionism or the 'beauty contests' between unions for the right to sign single union agreements, creating a functional analogue of Japanese-style company unions (Elger and Smith 1994b: 47–8).

A corollary of the 'host country' effect is that ostensibly common international employment policies in MNCs may be implemented in significantly different ways in different host environments. One example is the implementation of teamworking in the British and Spanish subsidiaries of General Motors studied by Ortiz (1998). He found that union resistance was greater in Britain since teamworking undermined the position of shop stewards in the workplace, whereas the Spanish unions were more acquiescent since teamworking gave them a foothold in work organization matters that had previously been within management's sole jurisdiction.

Conclusion

British industrial relations have been unusually open to influences from other business systems. The UK's status as home and host to a high level of multinational activity has been a major element in this. In the last two or three decades, the growth in cross-border operations of firms has intensified, bringing a broader range of companies and of other national influences into Britain. At the same time, the deregulation of swaths of economic life, including labour markets and industrial relations, has increased the 'permeability' of the British system; that is, it has removed some of the institutional impediments to the absorption of outside influences. Flexibility of markets and loose institutional regulation have been the watchwords of successive governments since the late 1970s.

As a result, there has been a constant flow of innovation in British industrial relations across a wide range of issues and areas, including work organization, human resource policy, pay systems, collective relations, and workforce participation. The spotlight in the UK has been on Japanese influence, but American companies have arguably been even more influential, and over a far longer period. MNCs of other nationalities, notably the Germans, have also had an impact that is at times subtle, and in general less pervasive than American or Japanese firms. The influence of Japanese and American MNCs reflects the fact that they are transmitting the practices that have been sources of competitive advantage of their home business systems, the two dominant economies of the post-war period. Japan's superiority was rooted in innovations in the organization of production, supplanting America's early leadership role in this regard. America's early development of 'organizational capabilities' (Chandler 1990) for managing mass markets over extended geographical areas allowed them to internationalize early and to build new capabilities – for example, in the management of human resources across borders – that have continued to be a source of advantage emulated by other countries. MNCs from other parent business systems are as likely to use British subsidiaries as a deregulated test bed for innovations that they can subsequently rediffuse to their domestic operations (or to engage in 'coercive comparisons' with domestic workforces).

However, the extent of foreign influence does not mean that British industrial relations have become some strange amalgam of Japanese and American styles. Innovations, it was argued, have been widely adapted to the peculiarities of the local business system: the nature of labour markets, institutions of vocational training, the organization of management functions and so on. Moreover, there may well be resistances within the host country to the transmission of practices that undermine existing power relations – as Ortiz's study (1998) of British unions' response to teamworking in General Motors shows. Likewise, Dunning notes that in workforce resistance to the introduction by US MNCs of merit pay and 'targets' in the 1950s in some cases led to the withdrawal of imported pay policies (p. 196). The collective capacity of British workforces to resist innovation has undoubtedly declined as a result of the weakening of the unions. But some of the detailed studies cited above of innovative work environments in

Japanese and other foreign companies suggest that more passive forms of resistance continue to occur, resulting in modifications to the way in which policies are implemented (see further chapter 13). Resistance may also come from managers themselves, concerned at the disruption to career opportunities or to existing relations between management functions implied by the introduction of innovative approaches in foreign MNCs (e.g. Broad 1994).

The implication of these considerations is that innovations rarely function in precisely the same manner in the British environment as they did in their system of origin. In short, a process of 'hybridization' (Abo 1994) or 'transmutation' of practices (Ferner and Varul 2000) takes place. As a result, even though international borrowings have a transformative effect on the British system and on industrial relations practices, this does not necessarily entail an international convergence of practices. More plausibly, we are witnessing a process of 'change without convergence' (Kester 1991, cited in Westney 1999), influenced by the distinctive historical features of the British industrial relations model.

A final theme is whether innovation by foreign MNCs has, in the context of a flexible deregulated industrial relations system, encouraged the degradation of IR/HR strategies. Has the lack of controls encouraged the driving out of 'good' IR practices and a move towards lowest-common-denominator 'Bleak House' strategies in which companies fail to invest either in collective relationships or effective individual bases of employee relationships? At present there is insufficient evidence from a wide enough range of sectors and of MNCs of different national origin to provide a definitive answer. Although the research cited above provides little evidence of 'low-road' employment relations strategies, more research will be needed on a range of sectors. Particularly in services, in which MNCs are becoming increasingly prominent as a result of privatization and deregulation, market conditions may be more conducive to low-road strategies aimed at short-term minimization of labour costs. That said, as shown in chapters 17 and 18, the true low road of low pay and managerial domination remains the preserve of small, usually UK-owned, firms in highly competitive sectors.

As for the future, the growing international integration of production activities and product markets in an ever-widening range of industries, together with the increasing technical sophistication of international systems for comparing across operations in different countries, are likely to consolidate the international diffusion of industrial relations practices.

Notes

I would like to thank Paul Edwards for his very helpful editorial suggestions.
1 By comparison with the 977,000 in US subsidiaries in the UK, there were 484,000 in France, 627,000 in Germany and 942,000 in Canada.
2 It should be added that the use of such comparisons is hardly a new phenomenon among MNCs. See Kujawa 1979: 7–9; also Flanders 1964: 65–9 on the use of inter-plant performance comparisons in Standard Oil as a factor leading to the Blue Book productivity agreements in Esso Fawley.

3 Early findings from current case studies being conducted as part of an ESRC-funded research project on employment relations in US MNCs in Britain, Germany, Ireland and Spain have tended to confirm this picture of companies having a pervasive global predisposition to avoid unions where feasible to do so.

4 From a voluminous literature, see e.g. Bassett 1987; Delbridge 1998; Garrahan and Stewart 1992; IRS 1995; Morris et al. 1998; Oliver and Wilkinson 1992; Elger and Smith 1994a; Wood 1996.

References

Abo, T. 1994: *Hybrid Factory: The Japanese Production System in the United States*. Oxford: Oxford University Press.

Bassett, P. 1987: *Strike Free: New Industrial Relations in Britain*. London: Macmillan.

Beaumont, P., and Townley, B. 1985: Non-union American plants in Britain, *Relations Industrielles*, 40 (4), 810–25.

Bélanger, J., Berggren, C., Björkman, T. and Köhler, C. (eds) 1999: *Being Local Worldwide: ABB and the Challenge of Global Management*. Ithaca: ILR Press.

Bélanger, J., Edwards, P. and Wright, M. 1999: 'Best practice' and the diffusion of human resource innovation in the multinational company: a test case, *Human Resource Management Journal*, 9 (3), 53–70.

Blanpain, R. 1977: Multinationals' impact on host country industrial relations. In R. Banks and J. Stieber (eds), *Multinationals, Unions, and Labor in Industrialized Countries*. Ithaca: Cornell.

Broad, G. 1994: The managerial limits to Japanization: a manufacturing case study. *Human Resource Management Journal*, 4 (3), 52–69.

Buckley, P., and Enderwick, P. 1983: *The Industrial Relations Practices of Foreign-Owned Firms in Britain*. London: Macmillan.

Chandler, A. 1990: *Scale and Scope: The Dynamics of Industrial Capitalism*. Cambridge, Mass.: Belknap Press.

Clegg, H. A. 1979: *The Changing System of Industrial Relations in Great Britain*. Oxford: Blackwell.

Delbridge, R. 1998: *Life on the Line in Contemporary Manufacturing*. Oxford: Oxford University Press.

Dickmann, M. 1999: Balancing global, parent and local influences: international human resource management of German multinational companies. Unpublished Ph.D. thesis, London: Birkbeck College.

Dohse, K. 1987: Innovations in collective bargaining through the multinationalization of Japanese auto companies: the cases of NUMMI (USA) and Nissan (UK). In M. Trevor (ed.), *The Internationalization of Japanese Business: European and Japanese Perspectives*. Frankfurt am Main and Boulder, Colo.: Campus/Westview.

Dunning, J. 1998 (1958): *American Investment in British Manufacturing*, revised edn. London: Routledge.

Edwards, T., and Ferner, A. 2000: Multinationals, reverse diffusion and national business systems. Paper presented to Conference on Multinationals and the Management of the Workplace, Wayne State University, Detroit, April.

Elger, T., and Smith, C. (eds) 1994a: *Global Japanization?* London: Routledge.

Elger, T., and Smith, C. 1994b: Global Japanization? Convergence and competition in the organization of the labour process. In Elger and Smith (eds), *Global Japanization?* London: Routledge.

Enderwick, P. 1985: *Multinational Business and Labour.* London: Croom Helm.

Ferner, A. 1997: Country of origin effects and human resource management in multinational companies, *Human Resource Management Journal,* 7 (1), 19–37.

Ferner, A. 1998: Multinationals, 'relocation', and employment in Europe. In J. Gual (ed.), *Job Creation: The Role of Labour Market Institutions.* London: Edward Elgar.

Ferner, A. 2000: The embeddedness of US multinational companies in the US business system: implications for HR/IR. De Montfort University Business School Occasional Paper No. 61.

Ferner, A., and Varul, M. 1999: *The German Way: German Multinationals and Human Resource Management.* London: Anglo-German Foundation.

Ferner, A., and Varul, M. 2000: 'Vanguard' subsidiaries and the diffusion of new practices: a case study of German multinationals, *British Journal of Industrial Relations,* 38 (1), 115–40.

Flanders, A. 1964; *The Fawley Productivity Agreements: A Case Study of Management and Collective Bargaining.* London: Faber & Faber.

Fraser, A. 1999: Case study: inward investment in the UK, Conference on Industrial Globalisation in the Twenty-First Century: Impact and Consequences for Asia and Korea. East–West Center, Seoul, August.

Garrahan, P., and Stewart, P. 1992: *The Nissan Enigma: Flexibility at Work in the Local Economy.* London: Cassell.

Geary, J., and Roche, B. 2001: Multinationals and human resource practices in Ireland: a rejection of the 'New Conformance Thesis', *International Journal of Human Resource Management,* 12 (1), 109–27.

Gennard, J., and Steuer, M. 1971: The industrial relations of foreign-owned subsidiaries in the United Kingdom, *British Journal of Industrial Relations,* 9 (2), 143–59.

Guest, D., and Hoque, K. 1996: National ownership and HR practices in UK greenfield sites, *Human Resource Management Journal,* 6 (4), 50–74.

ILO (International Labour Organization) 1976: *Multinationals in Western Europe: The Industrial Relations Experience.* Geneva: ILO.

IRS (Industrial Relations Services) 1993: The impact of Japanese firms on working and employment practices in British manufacturing industry, *IRS Employment Trends,* 540, 4–16.

IRS 1995: Lean suppliers to lean producers, *IRS Employment Trends,* 583, 3–16.

Jacoby, S. 1997: *Modern Manors: Welfare Capitalism since the New Deal.* Princeton: Princeton University Press.

Jefferys, S. 1988: The changing face of conflict: shopfloor organization at Longbridge, 1939–80. In M. Terry and P. Edwards (eds), *Shopfloor Politics and Job Controls.* Oxford: Blackwell.

Jones, G. 1996: *The Evolution of International Business: An Introduction.* London: Routledge.

Kogut, B. 1991: Country capabilities and the permeability of borders, *Strategic Management Journal,* 12 (1), 33–47.

Kujawa, D. 1979: The labour relations of the United States multinationals abroad: comparative and prospective views, *Labour and Society,* 4 (1), 1–25.

Mair, A. 1998: Internationalization at Honda: transfer and adaptation of management systems, *Employee Relations,* 20 (3), 285–302.

Marginson, P., Armstrong, P., Edwards, P. and Purcell, J. 1995: Extending beyond borders: multinational companies and the international management of labour, *International Journal of Human Resource Management,* 6 (3), 702–19.

Marginson, P., and Sisson, K. 1994: The structure of transnational capital in Europe: the emerging Euro-company and its implications for industrial relations. In R. Hyman and A. Ferner (eds), *New Frontiers in European Industrial Relations.* Oxford: Blackwell.

Martin, G., and Beaumont, P. 1999: ABB in Scotland: managing tensions between trans-national strategy, market decline, and customer focus. In J. Bélanger, C. Berggren, T. Björkman and C. Köhler (eds), *Being Local Worldwide: ABB and the Challenge of Global Management*. Ithaca: ILR Press.

Milkman, R. 1991: *Japan's California Factories: Labor Relations and Economic Globalization*. Los Angeles: University of California Press.

Millward, N. 1994: *The New Industrial Relations?* London: Policy Studies Institute.

Millward, N., Stevens, M., Smart, D. and Hawes, W. 1992: *Workplace Industrial Relations in Transition: The ED/ESRC/PSI/ACAS Surveys*. Aldershot: Dartmouth.

Morris, J., Lowe, J. and Wilkinson, B. 1998: 'Front-end reflections': supervisory systems in the UK's Japanese transplants and in 'Japanized' companies, *Employee Relations*, 20 (3), 248–61.

Mtar, M. 2001: HRM in French multinationals. Unpublished doctoral thesis, Warwick Business School, University of Warwick.

Mueller, F. 1996: National stakeholders in the global contest for corporate investment, *European Journal of Industrial Relations*, 2 (3), 345–68.

Mueller, F., and Purcell, J. 1992: The Europeanisation of manufacturing and the decentralisation of bargaining: multinational management strategies in the European automobile industry, *International Journal of Human Resource Management*, 3 (1), 15–34.

OECD (Organization for Economic Co-operation and Development) 1999: *OECD in Figures. 1999*. Paris: OECD.

Oliver, N., and Wilkinson, B. 1992: *The Japanisation of British Industry*. Oxford: Blackwell.

ONS (Office for National Statistics) 1983: *Manufacturing: Production and Construction Inquiries – Summary Volume*. PA1002. London: ONS.

ONS 1995: *Manufacturing: Production and Construction Inquiries – Summary Volume*. PA1002. London: ONS.

ONS 1997: *Manufacturing: Production and Construction Inquiries – Summary Volume*. PA1002. London: ONS.

ONS 1999: *Overseas Direct Investment 1998*. London: ONS.

ONS 2000: *Economy: Overseas Direct Investment*. MA4. London: ONS.

Ortiz, L. 1998; Unions' response to teamwork: differences at national and workplace level, *Industrial Relations Journal*, 29 (1), 42–57.

O'Sullivan, M. 2000: *Contests for Corporate Control: Corporate Governance and Economic Performance in the United States and Germany*. Oxford: Oxford University Press.

Porter, M. 1990: *The Competitive Advantage of Nations*. Basingstoke: Macmillan.

Roberts, B. 1972: Factors influencing the organisation and style of management and their effect on the pattern of industrial relations in multi-national corporations. In H. Günter (ed.), *Transnational Industrial Relations*. London: Macmillan.

Royle, T. (ed.) 2000: *Working for McDonald's in Europe*. London: Routledge.

Sally, R. 1995: *States and Firms: Multinational Enterprises in Institutional Competition*. London: Routledge.

Scarbrough, H., and Terry, M. 1998: Forget Japan: the very British response to lean production, *Employee Relations*, 20 (3), 224–36.

Shearer, J. 1967: Industrial relations of American corporations abroad. In S. Barkin et al. (eds), *International Labour*. New York: Harper & Row.

Silkin, S. 1970: American investment and European cultures: conflict and cooperation. In A. Kamin (ed.), *Western European Labor and the American Corporation*. Washington: Bureau of National Affairs.

Sisson, K. 1993: In Search of HRM? *British Journal of Industrial Relations*, 31 (2), 201–10.

Smith, C., and Elger, T. 1997: International competition, inward investment and the restructuring of European work and industrial relations, *European Journal of Industrial Relations*, 3 (3), 279–304.

Stopford, J., and Dunning, J. 1983: *Multinationals: Company Performance and Global Trends.* London: Macmillan.

Stopford, J., and Turner, L. 1985: *Britain and the Multinationals.* Chichester: John Wiley.

Taylor, B., Elger, T. and Fairbrother, P. 1994: Transplants and emulators: the fate of the Japanese model in British electronics. In Elger and Smith (eds), *Global Japanization?* London: Routledge.

Traxler, F., and Woitech, B. 2000: Transnational investment and national labour market regimes, *European Journal of Industrial Relations*, 6 (2), 147–60.

Tueselmann, H.-J. 2000: Employee relations of German multinationals in the UK: nationality of ownership, Anglo-Saxonisation and the future of the German approach. Unpublished paper, Manchester Metropolitan University.

Turnbull, P., and Delbridge, R. 1994: Making sense of Japanisation: a review of the British experience, *International Journal of Employment Studies*, 2 (2), 343–64.

UNCTAD (United National Conference on Trade and Development) 1998: *World Investment Report.* New York: United Nations.

US Survey of Current Business, June 2000, 80 (6), D-59.

Westney, D. 1999: Organisational evolution of the multinational enterprise: an organisational sociological perspective, *Management International Review*, 39 (2), 55–72.

Wickens, P. 1987: *The Road to Nissan: Flexibility, Quality, Teamwork.* Basingstoke: Macmillan.

Wilkinson, B., Morris, J. and Munday, M. 1995: The iron fist in the velvet glove: management and organization in Japanese manufacturing transplants in Wales, *Journal of Management Studies*, 32 (6), 819–30.

Wood, S. 1996: How different are human resource practices in Japanese 'transplants' in the United Kingdom? *Industrial Relations*, 35 (4), 511–25.

Young, S., Hood, N. and Hamill, J. 1985: *Decision-making in Foreign-Owned Multinational Subsidiaries in the United Kingdom.* Multinational Enterprises Programme, Working Paper 35. Geneva: ILO.

5

THE STATE: ECONOMIC MANAGEMENT AND INCOMES POLICY

COLIN CROUCH

The United Kingdom differs from virtually all other western and several central European polities in the low political profile occupied by organized actors in industrial relations, especially on the labour side. As noted in chapter 2, a weak co-ordination of interests is a long-standing feature, but during the past 20 years it has intensified. This Americanization of British developments has ironically taken place during the major part of the period in which the country has been a member of the European Community and Union. We are here concerned only with the British case, but it is useful to set changes taking place in that country within the varied set of changes occurring elsewhere. This is especially so if we want to understand the extent and limitations of British exceptionalism within Europe, for at a deeper level of economic policy the UK has been more of a front runner than an outlier.

British changes can initially be interpreted in terms of the neo-liberal ideology of both the Conservative governments which held office from 1979 to 1997 and their Labour successors. This ideology implies avoidance of entanglements between government and organizations that are, at least in part, devoted to interfering with pure market forces. Behind this development stand major changes in power relations within the global economy, which have affected virtually all countries. There are further, however, some local British peculiarities resulting from the dilemmas and contradictions of British industrial relations in the preceding period.

While neo-liberalism has been an ideology particularly strongly associated with the UK and the USA, which partly explains their growing similarity, it has also been powerful in societies throughout the rest of the world, which have been affected by economic globalization whatever the political ideologies of their governments. This overall convergence is transformed into a number of partial divergences mainly by the fact that many governments have a strong need to maintain a system of political exchange. As well as the threat of union militancy if they took a different course, there are also benefits of such a system, including union co-operation in altering existing institutions (e.g. the reform of the *scala mobile* in Italy: Regalia and Regini 1998); reform of Dutch labour regulations (Visser and Hemerijck 1997) and the sharing of unpopular decisions (Ferner and Hyman 1998a: p. xxi). Where 'social partnership' exists, a neo-liberal agenda may be contained. This is the case in most of western and central Europe, Australasia and, in a different way, Japan. Explaining British (and US) exceptionalism is therefore a matter of accounting for the relatively undiluted implementation of neo-liberal policy in this area.

To some extent the changes in the UK can be explained through changes in industrial relations law, as discussed in chapter 6, and in the government's role as an employer (see chapter 11). But there have also been important developments in general economic management, which will be our concern here.

Analysing Industrial Relations Systems

Elsewhere (Crouch 1994) I have proposed a classification of industrial relations systems of the kind summarized in figure 5.1. This embodies the following assumptions. First, the most important variables are (1) the strength of organized labour; and (2) the extent to which both labour and capital have organizations with central co-ordinating capacity. Labour strength (which can be measured by union membership and legal and bargained rights) is an important determinant of the extent to which workers are able to express their interests, and of whether employers need to come to terms with that strength. Such organized strength is not the sole means by which workers express their interests; as discussed in chapter 13, at the level of the firm informal methods are also significant. As noted in chapter 2, the failure to regulate the 'informal system' was a long-standing feature of the British case. It was the inability of labour to

| | | Co-ordinating capacity of capital and labour | |
		Low	High
Strength of organized labour	**High**	I Unstable collective bargaining	IV Tense neo-corporatism
		II Stable collective bargaining	V Stable neo-corporatism
	Low	III Ineffective labour organization	VI Stable neo-corporatism through social promotion

Figure 5.1   Forms of high-level industrial relations systems

articulate such dispersed influence which was a key weakness in its co-ordinating capacity.

Second, it is assumed that the organization of labour presents a problem to a market economy, as in the simplest case workers use their organizations to seek better wages and conditions than the market makes possible. In a pure market economy the consequences of this will be unemployment for the workers concerned. In a Keynesian economy, where government has the avoidance of unemployment as a policy priority, it will take fiscal and monetary measures to avoid this occurring. If the unemployment is being partly caused by labour market pressure through organization, the consequence will be inflation. Labour markets are never perfect. There is no unique market-clearing wage rate, since firms set pay according to a wide range of influences (see chapter 7). Links between wage inflation and unemployment are far from direct. It remains true, however, that wage pressure is a problem for any capitalist economy; the links are indirect and variable, but still present.

Third, where organizations of both capital and labour have some kind of central co-ordinating capacity, they may become aware of these likely inflationary consequences, perceive them as problems, and have the capacity to take action to moderate their own behaviour. A centralized organization that represents a high proportion of a given workforce cannot easily ignore the consequences of its actions, as these are large enough to be perceptible, and the organization knows it has the capacity to do something about them. Where there is no co-ordinating capacity, a mass of small-scale groups is each able to claim that its own particular actions have no measurable effect, and no one is in a position to do anything about the cumulative effect.

Following this logic, figure 5.1 shows that where co-ordinating capacity is weak, the only form of regular interaction possible is collective bargaining; at low levels of labour strength this can be a stable model (II), but as labour's strength grows its bargaining power will cause macroeconomic problems which the system lacks the capacity to accommodate, rendering it unstable (I). At the extreme of labour weakness, workers may not be able to insist on any interaction at all (III).

When labour and capital possess capacity for both strategy and articulation they are likely to develop neo-corporatist structures (IV and V). By 'articulation' is meant a systematic linkage between the levels of an organization (in the case of unions, for example, between national leaderships and the shop floor). These make it possible to contain workers' strength at higher levels of labour's organizational power than under weakly co-ordinated systems, though there will still be tension as this rises in level IV.

The only other point that requires to be demonstrated is the possibility of co-ordinative ability by weak labour movements (VI). According to most theories, including that outlined so far above, labour acquires a co-ordinating capacity only as it develops organized power. The exception occurs in societies where, for some exogenous reason, the state (or possibly employers) needs to give organized labour a place of recognition that its industrial strength does not strictly 'deserve'. This is not a model that is relevant to the UK. It is however relevant at

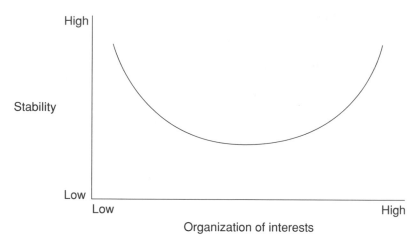

Figure 5.2   Organization of interests and economic outcomes

the level of the European Commission within the EU. The Commission seeks to build relations with groups in Europe other than the national governments, in order to reduce its dependence on those governments, both by talking directly to national and more local organizations and by constructing organizations at the European level. It therefore has an interest in both developing its own relations with existing trade unions and employers' associations, and establishing a European tier of these bodies. It does this irrespective of the power that these might wield.

Implicit in this model is a curvilinear relationship between stability (measured by inflation, industrial conflict, etc.) and degree of organization of the labour market, as shown in figure 5.2. Co-ordinating capacity and union strength have been presented as independent variables in figure 5.1, but it is possible to see them combining in a complex way to form a single indicator of organization in the sense of departure from a pure market. The more that workers are able to organize, the more there is such a departure; but, given that an essential feature of the market is an absence of co-ordination, then the possession of co-ordinating capacity by unions and employers' associations is also a departure. The polar opposite cases are therefore: a pure labour market in which workers have no organizations at all, and hence no co-ordinating capacity; and a highly organized system in which a central organization has authority on behalf of the mass of employed persons. Under these circumstances, there will be stability either where organization is very weak (because workers cannot disrupt effectively) or where there is central co-ordinating capacity. In between these poles, where there is uneven organization, or powerful organization with poor co-ordination, there is likely to be a higher level of disruption.

There is some support for such a curvilinear relationship within economic theory. Olson (1982) argued that, when interest organizations interfered with the market to achieve gains for their members, they generally did so by externalizing on to the general public the costs of such gains. However, where organizations were so encompassing in their membership and centralized in their decision-making structure that they included within them a large proportion of that public, a significant part of the cost would be internalized. This would lead the organization to avoid behaviour of this kind. Empirical evidence was provided by Calmfors and Driffill (1988), who plotted increases in wage costs against indices of corporatism or the co-ordinating power of organizations for a sample of countries, and found a curvilinear relationship (see also Iversen 1999). An example of encompassingness is a national union in an industry heavily dependent on exports; it is likely to be wary of raising the costs of products to the advantage of foreign competitors and is thus likely to participate in wage moderation (Crouch 1993; Wallerstein 1990).

More recent research qualifies this argument. Traxler et al. (2001: 237) show that the Calmfors and Driffill measure is inaccurate in its categorization of some countries and that it conflates the centralization of bargaining with the degree of co-ordination. Their own empirical work offers only very limited support for a curvilinear relationship, and suggests instead that it is the particular form of co-ordination which is crucial. This leads us to the analysis of co-ordination in the UK case.

The UK Case

The UK has usually been a country with highly unco-ordinated labour market organizations, for historical reasons discussed in chapter 2 (see also Crouch 1993). Given that, especially during the decades of full employment and Keynesian demand management from the Second World War onwards, it also had strong trade unions, British industrial relations tended to move towards position I in figure 5.1, an unstable one. The response of governments was usually to seek more co-ordination of the labour market, in other words to move to position V, stable neo-corporatism. Although there were occasional successes, periods of successful co-ordination proved to be brief. As Keynesian demand management became increasingly incapable of coping with the inflationary tendencies of the world economy during the 1970s, the instability induced by relapses to position I became increasingly severe. In 1979 the election of a Conservative government committed to a neo-liberal economic strategy finally brought an end to attempts to co-ordinate the labour market. Henceforth policy would be directed at regaining stability by weakening the power of organized labour, in other words moving towards positions II or III. In practice, this meant a combination of the two, with collective bargaining being hard to dismantle where it existed; provided only a few sectors had collective bargaining, the externalities they produced could be absorbed.

Most of the following discussion will be occupied with a discussion of how this shift has been managed in detail. First, however, it is important to place the apparently abrupt change from the pursuit of position V to that of position III in a wider perspective of the British polity and economy. The British political legacy of the mid-twentieth century had two components. The first comprised a mix of several items. First was the country's past as the first industrial nation, with a heavy inheritance of manufacturing industry that had become inflexible. Second was the pattern of compromise and give and take in industrial relations between employers and unions, combined with the generally decentralized, non-strategic pattern of organization of collective laissez faire discussed in chapter 2. Third, the country had also developed, after 1945, a strong welfare state, which in its way fitted into the country's general record of expansive, benign institutions and care for the public interest, conceived in a non-strategic way. This side of the British legacy was relaxed, even incoherent. Nothing united the different components in a way that might make possible a national strategy, since the only thing that really brought them together was their incapacity for strategy. The general mix has become known in a vague way as the post-war consensus, but it was not a real consensus in the sense of a true agreement, oriented to widely discussed, chosen goals. Rather, it was the kind of consensus that arises when various groups put the avoidance of struggle beyond the search for agreement. This was not a context that would make for stability at the high-co-ordination pole; but neither would it produce the attack on labour's rights and capacities implied by a switch to the opposite approach.

Two areas of employment were favoured by and favoured this first model, though for different reasons: manufacturing and the public services. Employers and workers alike in manufacturing benefited from the stable product markets afforded by Keynesian demand management, and needed to take advantage of the general climate of compromise and consensus to reduce the high level of conflict embedded in the employment relationship in many sectors. In the public services, employees and their managers benefited from the high level of service provision and public spending implied by the welfare state, Keynesian policies, and the general context of social consensus. Significantly, these two sectors were those in which trade unions and organized industrial relations developed most powerfully.

The second component, which was internally far more coherent, also had its heart in the unforced character of the British Industrial Revolution, not in its legacy of old manufacturing industry; rather in the idea of laissez-faire capitalism. The acme of this side of British life was the City of London and its associated financial sector. This was only marginally associated with the long-term investment decisions and responsibilities for maintaining a stable workforce associated with manufacturing, but was based on the model of a set of highly flexible markets geared to very rapid changes and short-term calculations. This model informed British company law, with its emphasis on shareholding, short-term bank lending and dividend calculations, where the hostile takeover was an accepted part of business life and prevented managers from undertaking long-term investments that might push the real assets of a company above its quoted value. There was a further hostility, or at least indifference, to industrial interests in the role of the pound sterling and its over-valuation, and in the City's international orientation (Coates 2000). This second model also implied hostility to the large economic role for government envisaged by the first model. It tended therefore to oppose the expansion of public services, the employees of which had incomes financed through taxation, partly levied on the business sector. There was therefore little to connect this second model to the interests of organized labour in either of its strongholds of manufacturing and the public services. It is this lack of connection which is critical. There is now a substantial revisionist school, arguing that, in Owen's (1999: 406) words, the British financial system 'should be struck off the list of factors contributing to British industrial decline'. Yet this school tends to treat the supply of capital by the system in isolation from other factors. The characteristics of the financial system, in combination with the structure of relationships between management and labour, helped to make any efforts at rationalization more difficult than they would otherwise have been.

For many years after the Second World War the two Britains coexisted. This was possible because both models shared a lack of interest in long-term strategy: the former because it had no capacity for it, the second because it had no need for it. This coincidence of interest was expressed in the particular form of British Keynesianism. The Treasury manipulated a few central policy instruments to sustain demand and therefore employment (favouring the interests associated with the first Britain), but having done that left the economy alone to be run by virtually free market forces (the second Britain). If the second Britain had no particular interest in industrial relations, it did not interfere with their conduct according to the laws of the first Britain, which in any case accounted for so much employment.

The inflationary crises of the 1970s and the decline of manufacturing eroded both the credibility of Keynesian demand management and the power of the manual working class. Meanwhile, the more general changes in the economy loosely covered by the idea of 'globalization' were rendering the central co-ordination model more difficult to achieve. A series of innovations in information technology was making it possible for financial capital to move around the world at considerable speed while remaining under the complete control of its owners. The same technologies also made possible effective managerial control over manufacturing and other operations across great distances. This new potential flexibility of capital was restrained only by various national regulations of capital movements. Lobbying by financial interests to secure a deregulation of these controls was successful in almost all parts of the world. As this process developed during the 1980s and particularly the 1990s, capital came to enjoy a power imparted by a freedom of movement which could in no way be matched by workforces or governments. Capital holders can now choose locations for investment across the globe which most favour their interests over others, which usually implied low taxes (and therefore low public spending), and weak labour rights. Stock exchanges acquired a new importance in company finance, since, in contrast with other forms such as long-term bank loans, they could rapidly bring together very large investment sums. The deregulation of capital markets made possible a vast extension of risk-sharing through the growth of such mechanisms as futures and derivatives markets and levered buy-outs. The maximization of shareholder value acquired a priority in managerial thinking at the expense of other potential stakeholders in firms, including of course employees.

This extreme model of deregulated global capitalism is not always realized in practice. Certain kinds of manufacturing and business services require extensive social infrastructure and highly skilled labour. They often also have extensive sunk costs, which means that investment cannot so easily be moved around the world. A full analysis of the impact of the changes therefore requires careful attention to the situation faced by various sectors of the economy. We cannot attempt such an analysis here, though we shall see several of its consequences in the subsequent discussion.

In the advanced world, two countries were in a particularly strong position to benefit from these developments: the UK and the USA. Both had strongly developed stock markets. Two potential problems for the new model – strong trade unions and welfare states – were already being weakened in the USA, and were vulnerable to the new political coalitions of the 1980s in the UK. As by far the most powerful country in the world and the home of the world's largest corporations, the USA and its firms would also stand to gain from a growth of competition which would favour the possessors of large assets. The USA was also the national base of the information technology companies which provided the technical infrastructure needed by the new system. Particularly after the collapse of the Soviet Union in 1989, which made it unnecessary any longer for the US government to underwrite social democracy in various parts of the world in order to rebut the challenge of communism, the US state lent its support to all moves to deregulate the world's economies. International economic organizations largely dominated by the USA, such as the International Monetary Fund, the Organization for Economic Co-operation and Development, and to some extent the World Bank, threw their weight behind the campaign to reduce the role of institutions which interfered with free markets: public spending, state ownership of resources, labour and other forms of social regulation, and organized industrial relations. A US model of corporate governance, favouring the shareholder model, was also imposed on many countries in the world (Coates 2000).

The UK could not gain as strongly as the USA from these changes, as it lacked the latter's political and economic weight, but it shared many of the institutions being promoted by the new model. Particularly important, the new model clearly and decisively favoured what I have called the second Britain, precisely at the moment when the forces around the first Britain were breaking up. The financial markets, which during the Keynesian period had sustained themselves in a lucrative but marginal corner of the economy, now moved to centre stage, both economically and politically. At the same time, as discussed in chapter 7, an increasing number of firms were seeking company autonomy in planning their human resource management, and wanted interference from neither an external trade union nor even an employers' association. The company, not the industrial branch, was increasingly becoming the important unit. And of course both manufacturing and public services, the two sectors which were the cornerstones of trade unionism, were both marginalized by the priorities of the new economy.

Economic policies associated with free markets and minimal government economic activity secured increased support of a kind not experienced since the earlier part of the twentieth century. Keynesian and other social consensus policies having become associated with rigidities and blockages, there was a widespread welcome among policymakers of all parties for an approach which might create new spaces for action and loosen inflationary rigidities. Meanwhile, at a more purely political level, the Labour Party had split in the early 1980s. For the whole decade the party of organized labour ceased to be a serious political force. The Conservative Party was enabled by this context to make the difficult transition from being a party of the Keynesian consensus to being one representing the new forces of mobile financial capitalism without suffering electoral vulnerability.

Further, as the years passed, so successive governments felt confident that they could take risks with social stability. This is an important socio-political point, often forgotten by industrial relations analysts, especially in the UK, where social order is taken for granted. In a number of advanced industrial countries there is often concern among governing elites to ensure that social stability will not be threatened by social groups feeling alienated from and therefore hostile to the socio-political order. This may be because of recent past histories of civic unrest or of dissident regional groups (as in Belgium, France, Italy and Spain), or general anxieties about a longer past (as in Austria, Germany and Japan), or the recency of establishing a stable democratic order (Spain, or the new countries of eastern Europe) (Ferner and Hyman 1998b). In these situations even governments that are essentially hostile to the aspirations of organized labour nevertheless retain for it a role of national consultation and respectability. Britain, as a country with a long history of social stability, is among those in which these issues have low priority. During the 1980s they faded even further, as the traditional issue of ensuring that the working class was nationally integrated, which had dogged earlier Conservative governments, became a thing of the past.

A final element placing the UK in the vanguard of the neo-liberal era where industrial relations are concerned relates to the role of unions in aspects of welfare policy, particularly unemployment, sickness and retirement pensions insurance. In most western European countries trade unions (and employers' associations) have since the late nineteenth century been involved in the management of these schemes, though through a diversity of forms. Initially this had also been true of Britain, until during the 1920s the unions relinquished their role. The extent of the unemployment crisis of that period made it difficult for them to meet their own financial obligations to the schemes, and they decided instead to support a purely state-controlled system. Today, in virtually every European country, difficult decisions are being made about the future form and funding of these schemes. In almost all countries reform and change are possible only if the unions can be persuaded to support the reforms; only in the UK are they entirely outside this policy frame. This imposes on all governments except the British one a requirement to sustain good relations with union organizations.

All these changes placed the UK in a special position within the EU. Many of the other countries within the latter had governments representing social interests that wanted to gain from the new model, or at least which saw adopting it as the only way to thrive in a US-dominated global economy. However, none had the UK's capacity unambiguously to embrace it. In many cases the system of corporate governance and finance differed strongly from the stock-exchange model. In some cases there were doubts about social stability, or at least a need to involve unions in social pacts for pensions or other welfare reform. Therefore, while these governments sought to imitate, and often imitated, British policy in many areas of neo-liberal reform, they balked at the move towards dismantling tripartite industrial relations.

It was noted above that the European Commission itself is an example of an authority which pursues a form of neo-corporatist industrial relations in order to resolve problems of its own weakness. The fact that industrial relations actors at the European level are themselves extremely weak intensifies rather than weakens this strategy. The Commission and the social partners exchange legitimacy by expressing a willingness to deal with each other, and in that way acquire a kind of strength, which can sometimes be converted into real strength. This strategy, which was pursued particularly in the late 1980s when the president of the Commission was Jacques Delors, a Catholic social democrat, further isolated the UK government from the EU. On the other hand, it had the opposite consequences for British trade unions, the majority of which had hitherto been highly sceptical of all things European. As detailed in chapter 9, they now saw tripartism and certain forms of labour regulation being encouraged in Brussels while they were being dismantled in London. 'Delors is our shepherd', remarked the general secretary of the TUC after the Commission president had addressed Congress in 1987.

Over subsequent years the Delors vision of a new social compromise, joining a participative, tripartite social Europe to the market-oriented thrust of other areas of the Commission's work, was to fade. However, the different stances of the different actors on the British scene did not subsequently change. However neo-liberal European policy was subsequently to become, Conservatives strengthened their hostility to European integration, while unions remained loyal to it. Employers, on the other hand, were cross-pressured to the point of immobility. On one side they approved of the neo-liberal turn, and welcomed this within both British and European policy. On another side, many of them increasingly identified their interests with those of the globalized financial sector and therefore a US-rather than an EU-oriented position for the UK. On a further side, others, particularly those in manufacturing, saw more chance of policies to assist their sector emanating from Brussels than from London. Fortunately for them all, European employers in general gradually moved into a position of resisting the growth of a Europe-level tripartism. A policy of quietism on the question of European industrial relations provided a useful lowest common denominator.

The Details of British Policy

What were the detailed contents of the policies of the neo-liberal turn as they affected industrial relations? We concentrate on the overall contribution of general economic management to the 'weakening and localizing' strategy towards trade unions (discussed in more detail in chapters 8, 9 and 15). This has primarily taken four forms:

- replacing demand management with action on the supply side to create employment;
- encouraging the dismantling of collective bargaining, especially at levels above the individual firm;
- ceasing to encourage the pursuit of 'good' industrial relations;
- gradually abolishing all tripartite mechanisms for addressing economic questions.

Supply-side labour policies

Demoting the full-employment commitment by prioritizing the conquest of inflation was an initial *sine qua non* for cutting free from dependence on central co-ordination, as the above analysis implies. Once it was possible for the commitment to be dropped, monetary policy could be less accommodating to wage-push inflation. When this had been achieved, and labour markets deregulated, it paradoxically became possible for neo-liberals to prioritize job creation as a policy goal, and to cast union resistance as a commitment to inflexibility which hindered the reduction of unemployment. Once demand management would no longer be used to create employment, this latter could only come through the lowering of wages and other employment costs and restrictions on employment, increasing demand for labour by reducing the direct and indirect cost of its supply. This was coupled with changes in the system of unemployment compensation and advice services for the unemployed which made it more difficult for people to register as unemployed without demonstrating a willingness either to take any work offered to them or to attend training courses. Some of the latter policies are described in more detail below, where consideration is given to the fate of tripartite manpower policy.

For many years the collapse of employment caused by the abandonment of demand management and the exacerbated decline of manufacturing outweighed any positive consequences that might flow from the new supply-side policies. However, by the mid-1990s the policy began to bear some fruit. Employment began to expand in the service industries, particularly among women and concentrated mainly in part-time jobs. The strongest growth was in relatively low-skilled jobs in the distributive sector (shops) and office administration, but there was also expansion in financial services and some high-tech areas. Employment in manufacturing continued to decline, and that in public services was static. Changes in employment therefore reduced the most strongly unionized sectors and advanced those where unions were weakest.

The shift was initially engineered by what was originally experienced as a policy disaster: a major decline in the level of sterling, in particular in relation to the German mark, the requirement to leave the European Exchange Rate Mechanism in 1991, and consequent exclusion of the UK from the construction of a single European currency. The countries involved in that process were required, by the neo-liberal terms of the treaty initiating the move (a double irony) to pursue heavily deflationary economic policies for a number of years. This produced considerable unemployment, which was exacerbated in the German case by the over-valuation of the mark in the context of currency instability and by the costs of German unification. The UK was freed from these constraints and could pursue a more expansionary strategy. For the first time since 1979, British unemployment levels began to decline, while those in other western European countries rose.

This situation also enabled the Conservative Party to resolve its earlier ambiguities over European monetary union. Manufacturing interests tended to support monetary union, as a means of ensuring stability in terms of trade with the country's main trading partners. The interests of the City of London, however, were mainly in favour of the UK remaining outside the regulatory framework of the European Central Bank and becoming an unregulated offshore island of the new currency. This was another clash between the two Britains analysed above. As with virtually all other areas of policy, the advantage now lay decisively with the second, City-oriented interpretation of the national interest. This also fitted well with the preference of those associated with the second Britain and more generally with the neo-liberal project to stress the UK's alliance with the USA rather than the EU. It was also a gift to the Conservatives' potentially contradictory policy mix of simultaneously pursuing an extension of globalization and an isolationist nationalism. If attention could be concentrated on opposing European integration, it did not matter whether those rallying round that cause did so for globalizing or xenophobic reasons. And the British model was now associated with post-Keynesian employment growth.

The main policy stance was continued by the 1997 Labour government. As part of its distancing of the UK from the so-called social Europe project, the Conservative government had refused to sign the Social Protocol to the Treaty of Maastricht, under which workers' rights at the European level could in principle be introduced (see chapter 6). Labour accepted the Social Protocol, which was subsequently incorporated fully into the Treaty of Amsterdam. However, it then proceeded to adopt a minimal approach to directives issued under the treaty, such as the Working Time Directive. Acceptance of the protocol had more to do with the new government's initial strategy of avoiding a continuation of the Conservatives' isolationist policy within Europe.

By 2000 the relationship of the UK economy to that of the EU had reversed direction considerably. The single currency was launched, and during its first two years weakened in relation to the US dollar and sterling. The value of the pound rose. This reduced the relative prices of goods from the single-currency area and increased those of British ones. Employment in UK manufacturing declined again. Particularly salient in terms of labour market policy was the decision of two large motor-manufacturing firms, BMW and Ford, to scale down operations in the UK in favour of plants in Germany – the country often depicted negatively in relation to the UK's much-praised deregulated labour markets. However, the further decline in manufacturing only advanced further the shift from what I have called here the first Britain to the second one.

Dismantling inter-company collective bargaining

An essential part of a strategy to move away from neo-corporatist forms of stability in the labour market towards neo-liberal ones is the dismemberment of structured collective bargaining. Conservative governments pursued several strategies consistent with this shift. Within the public services they encouraged the disbanding of national pay settlements and the use of comparisons between public- and private-sector pay to determine the scope for rises in the latter (see chapter 11). In the economy at large they encouraged a breakdown of institutional arrangements in general (Purcell 1993), and specifically discouraged the use of comparability in mechanisms for conciliation and arbitration. In 1982 the UK formally denounced its earlier adherence to Convention 94 of the International Labour Organization that commits signatory governments to observing parity with terms and conditions in the private sector in their role as a public employer (Davies and Freedland 1993: 540–1). Between 1986 and 1993 government first reduced the powers of and then abolished the Wages Councils that for most of the twentieth century had maintained minimum standards in designated low-paid industries (see chapter 17). Introduction of the minimum wage by the Labour government marked an important change from this aspect of the policy, though in other respects Labour did nothing to reduce the trend towards fragmentation.

Several other causes apart from government policy came together to produce the collapse of inter-firm bargaining. First, the strains of maintaining national structures, or even (in large corporations) company structures, of pay when local labour markets were becoming so divergent were often unsupportable. Despite the arguments above concerning the damaging effects of wide regional pay disparities, if regional fortunes begin to diverge widely workers in poorer regions stand a chance of employment only if their relative wages are reduced. Pressures to do this broke several industry-wide agreements.

Second, new managerial doctrines of the promotion of company culture and the pursuit of human resource management led companies to want to depart from inter-firm arrangements and stamp their own identity on their payment systems. Third, large companies with complex internal bureaucracies were increasingly trying to resolve their problems of inflexibility by granting local plant or divisional managers limited autonomy over pay and conditions. Managers might be given a cash budget and a set of basic rules, and told to resolve their labour market problems how they liked within that frame. This could lead to considerable divergence in practice; it certainly created a disincentive for firms to co-operate in inter-firm agreements.

But fragmented bargaining systems have often been associated with strong inflationary pressures. For much of the period under review unemployment was sufficiently high to offset this potential pressure. However, in the end the UK economy became one of relatively low unemployment. In any case, the strong regional imbalances of British economic development meant that even when unemployment was high overall, it was low in parts of the south-east and in sectors requiring trained labour. How was inflation combated?

One explanation of the wage militancy of the late 1960s had been that workers were seeking to restore through wage increases real income that they had lost through the rapidly rising rates of income taxation during that period (Jackson et al. 1972). An important limb of economic strategy during the 1980s and 1990s was to reduce levels of taxation in general and of direct taxation in particular. The motives for this were of course by no means limited to questions of industrial relations. Governments believed that public expenditure should decline in relation to private; this requires reductions in both public expenditure and taxation. They also believed that during the post-war decades inequalities had been too much reduced. Since direct taxation has been a source of income redistribution, it was logical to reduce it, especially for higher incomes. Frequent tax cuts may therefore have alleviated wages pressure.

However, the overall conclusion must be that, paradoxically, low inflation has not been a particular achievement of the neo-liberal years. Although inflation rates have generally been lower than during the 1970s, this has been true everywhere in the advanced world, and UK inflation has continued to be among the highest in western Europe. Particularly in south-east England, where economic dynamism was heavily concentrated, UK wage rises have continued to outpace improvements in the level of productivity. To some extent increasing labour costs in growth sectors was offset by the rise in low-wage employment elsewhere. As noted above, a model of free collective bargaining with weak unions produces, not a general weakness of wage interests, but a very patchy result, with some points of strong wage growth and others of weakness.

There is debate among economists whether disaggregating pay determination to local levels is likely to create employment in poorer areas by reducing wage costs there, or whether the consequent reduction in overall income in an area which follows from such a policy might worsen the local economy. If wages rise consistently more slowly in poor districts, consumption declines, local shops and other services decline, and unemployment rises. Meanwhile, inflation takes place in the prosperous areas. Labour cannot respond easily to market signals by relocating, as the movement of people across regions of the country is cumbersome and disruptive. In fact, what has happened in the UK is that labour has left the declining areas in Scotland, the north and parts of the Midlands and south-west and moved to the south-east, further exacerbating the uneven economic development of the country.

Political preference, regional divergence, managerial strategies, and the almost unmanageable changes happening in the economy therefore combined to weaken the role of organizations and further push moves to resolve British stability crises towards the left-hand pole of the curve in figure 5.2.

The fate of 'good' industrial relations

For many years British governments maintained a concept of 'good industrial relations', which they claimed to follow in their own conduct as employers and which they imparted to other employers through the practices of national conciliation and mediation agencies and in the general stance of the Ministry of

Labour and its successor, the Department of Employment (DE). This approach was prominent during the Second World War, when firms could only acquire government contracts for war equipment if they recognized unions and followed other 'progressive' employment policies. At the other end of the pre-1979 period, similar concepts were embodied in the *Industrial Relations Code of Practice* of the Conservative government of 1970–4 (Department of Employment 1972), even though this was within the context of an overall approach to industrial relations considered by the unions to be hostile to them.

The central labour market aim of the 1979–97 Conservative governments was a certain kind of flexibility. This meant reducing as much as possible all restrictions on the deployment of labour, whether from unions, employers' organizations or protective legislation giving workers rights either at work or against its loss. In all this, as in the law reforms, government's central aim was to restore the initiative to employers (as opposed to either unions or the government itself). In so doing, it was concerned to ensure that employers' freedom was strongly structured by market incentives. Governments also encouraged temporary and part-time contracts, a low level of established rights, and avoidance of stipulated minimum standards. This can be traced from the denunciation of ILO Resolution 94 to the refusal to sign the Social Protocol to the Treaty of Maastricht. In 1993, in a symbolically important move, the statutory duty of the Advisory, Conciliation and Arbitration Service was altered so that a particular requirement to 'encourage the extension of collective bargaining' was removed.

The Labour government of 1997 departed from this new model in a number of ways. It introduced a legal right to trade union recognition as well as the minimum wage and European social protocol already discussed. Yet pay comparability and other explicit aspects of the government's role as a 'good employer' were not reinstated.

Under the Conservatives there was no longer a government concept of 'good' industrial relations; no expressed preference for union recognition, or for the provision of stable conditions of employment. Under Labour there was a partial return to the classical model, but still within the general framework of encouraging the flexibility of labour to employers' requirements.

The abandonment of tripartism

As part of the same logic, government gradually abandoned most elements of tripartite co-operation and ceased to encourage any bipartite co-operation among unions and employers. This happened partly at the political level (Middlemas 1991). Conservative ministers rarely saw union leaders, and early in the 1980s the government announced that it was ending the previous principle of twentieth-century government whereby trade union figures were often members of government inquiries, committees, commissions, and so forth. (The aim of this earlier practice had been to ensure some kind of voice for representatives of working people in a system otherwise dominated by business, the professions and politicians.) Henceforth, it was announced, unions would be involved in public business only where matters concerning them as organizations were concerned. Unions' contact with government, especially contact through meetings and personal visits, has declined steadily since 1979 (Middlemas 1991; Marsh 1992).

Apart from these ad hoc developments, at the outset of the 1980s there were four main channels for tripartism: the National Economic Development Council (NEDC), the Manpower Services Commission (MSC), the Advisory, Conciliation and Arbitration Service (ACAS) and the Health and Safety Commission (HSC). The NEDC, a tripartite deliberative body for trying to seek consensus on the main outlines of British economic development, had been established in 1961 and survived several changes of government before being abolished in the late 1980s.

The MSC had been established in 1973 by a Conservative government to give new impetus to training and employment services. It formed part of a general policy move of that time, overlapping a Labour and a Conservative government, to take the central functions of the DE – 'manpower' policy (training and employment services), conciliation services, and occupational health and safety – and place them under tripartite control. This resulted in the formation of the MSC, ACAS and the HSC respectively. The aim was to involve employers' and workers' organizations more deeply in the administration of labour market and industrial relations issues. It was a highly corporatist concept, based on Swedish models. Representatives of government, the CBI and the TUC or their affiliates participated in these bodies. Initially its role expanded under the post-1979 Conservative government, and at one point it seemed to rival the Department of Education in its activism throughout education policy. However, increasingly ministers used MSC training schemes to reduce the wages of young workers (Davies and Freedland 1993: 541–5, 601–6; Marsh 1992: 125–34). Union representatives became increasingly dissatisfied. In 1987 government reduced the role of unions within the Commission, and in 1989 abolished it entirely.

It was replaced by a Training Agency without union representation. Within another two years this had also been abolished and an unco-ordinated national network of local Training and Enterprise Councils (Local Enterprise Councils in Scotland) established in its place. These were to be run by boards of local business leaders, chosen as individuals and not as representatives, able to co-opt a small number of local trade union leaders and local education authority chiefs or head teachers – all serving as individuals, not as representatives – if they so chose. The link between training and employment policy and industrial relations organizations was completely severed. Policy changed again under the Labour government, which recentralized training policy to the level of appointed regional arms of government. These were again employer-dominated, but unions were restored to a formal, if minority, role (see further chapter 15).

ACAS was established in 1974 as part of the same wave of corporatist thinking as informed the establishment of the MSC, though as Davies and Freedland point out (1993: 409), it was also an attempt at rescuing the old 'voluntarist' model of industrial relations from government attempts to impose ideas of incomes policy on its own mediating institutions. Though, as noted above, it has lost a considerable number of functions, it has been the great survivor of these corporatist bodies, and its role has in some ways grown, notably in the huge rise in the number of cases of individual employment rights which it now handles (Towers and Brown 2000). The role of ACAS has evolved. As Brown and Towers (2000: p. x) put it, the change in role has not been despite the decline in collectivism but because of it: the retreat from collective bargaining left ACAS as the only route for conciliation and advice. ACAS is no longer part of a specifically corporatist set of institutions. The HSC, another corporatist creation of the early 1970s, also continues and has been largely uncontroversial.

With the minor exception of the regional agencies, the 1997 Labour government made virtually no changes to this policy of gradually disappearing tripartism. In some respects this is surprising. Many of the neo-liberal policies of British Conservatives have been widely imitated in Continental Europe, but there has always been one major difference: governments have sought to sustain or build tripartite consensus over their policy changes. In some cases (as in the Netherlands and on occasion in Italy) this has involved major substantive exercises in national agreements on policy change. Elsewhere the process has been more symbolic, but nonetheless important for the general profile of national policy. The UK is unique within western (and central) Europe in entirely lacking any policies of this kind. Although the Labour government departed from Conservative policy on a number of key points, such as union recognition and the minimum wage, on this central plank it has continued the UK's isolation from the European mainstream. The answer probably lies in the point made earlier: given the complete absence of any formal role for British unions in the management of the welfare state, and British governments' general confidence that they can manage unaided any problems of social order, British unions have simply lost any claim to be of wide social importance. They retained such a possibility during the 1960s and 1970s, when they seemed potentially capable of assisting in the search for the collective good of labour market restraint, but were proved incapable of fulfilling that role. They can therefore make little claim to be anything more than special interest lobbies for particular parts of the workforce. This role entirely suits the neo-liberal conception of the place of interest groups. An essentially neo-liberal Labour government therefore has no incentive to treat them in any other way.

Conclusions

The combined effects of all these strategies has been to move Britain sharply towards the left-hand pole of figure 5.2, with some limited withdrawal from this line after the change of government in 1997. The results have been ambiguous. Inflation has certainly been reduced, and so have industrial disputes – though it is not clear whether either has been reduced in a comparative context, the whole period of the 1980s and early 1990s having been years of lower inflation and lower strikes than the 1970s. There is also evidence of improved working practices and productivity, and very considerable success in employment growth.

On the negative side one can list several items. First, as we have seen, the counter-inflationary strategy has remained fragile. In particular the laissez-faire approach to regional labour markets, which is itself central to the general strategy, creates regional imbalances and skill shortages that create inflation at early stages of recoveries.

Second, because the counter-inflation strategy embodies its own weaknesses, there has been excessive reliance on holding down pay (perhaps by reducing numbers of employees) in the public sector as a means of support for the strategy. Not only does this weaken morale among public employees, but as more and more of the public sector is privatized it leaves a rather small tail trying to wag the dog, especially as most privatized corporations remain monopolies or oligopolies.

Third, the manufacturing base continues to erode. The UK now depends heavily on the possibility of pursuing economic strength through services alone.

Finally, the erosion of the institutional base, which is fundamental to the leftward shift along the figure 5.2 curve, may have wider implications. It diminishes the capacity of the British economy to make more general use of co-operative and co-ordinating institutions, not only between business and labour but even within business. This occurs because, for example, as supra-company bargaining declines, so employers' associations decline, and so does the capacity of business interests to engage in any collective-goods provision, apart from lobbying for their own interests. This may diminish business co-operation leading to enhanced performance in occupational training, research and development, joint export promotion, and other issues in a manner common in some other economies. As noted above, the British experiment has been followed by other European countries at several points. The aspect which has not been followed is the rejection of tripartism or social partnership. This is, however, the main area where there has been continuity between Conservative and Labour governments, but the one where the success of the UK model has been most dubious.

References

Brown, W., and Towers, B. 2000: Introduction: ACAS's first quarter century. In Towers and Brown (eds), *Employment Relations in Britain: 25 Years of the Advisory, Conciliation and Arbitration Service*. Oxford: Blackwell.

Calmfors, L., and Driffill, J. 1988: Bargaining structure, corporatism and economic performance, *Economic Policy*, 6 (1), 13–61.

Coates, D. 2000: *Models of Capitalism: Growth and Stagnation in the Modern Era*. Cambridge: Polity.

Crouch, C. 1993: *Industrial Relations and European State Traditions*. Oxford: Clarendon Press.

Crouch, C. 1994: Beyond corporatism: the impact of company strategy. In R. Hyman and A. Ferner (eds), *New Frontiers in European Industrial Relations*. Oxford: Blackwell.

Davies, P., and Freedland, M. 1993: *Labour Legislation and Public Policy*. Oxford: Clarendon Press.

Department of Employment 1972: *Industrial Relations Code of Practice*. London: HMSO.

Ferner, A., and Hyman, R. 1998a: Introduction: Towards European Industrial Relations? In Ferner and Hyman (eds), *Changing Industrial Relations in Europe*. Oxford: Blackwell.

Ferner, A., and Hyman, R. (eds) 1998b: *Changing Industrial Relations in Europe*. Oxford: Blackwell.

Iversen, T. 1999: *Contested Economic Institutions*. Cambridge: Cambridge University Press.

Jackson, D., Turner, H. A. and Wilkinson, F. 1972: *Do Trade Unions Cause Inflation?* Cambridge: Cambridge University Press.

Marsh, D. 1992: *The New Politics of British Trade Unionism*. Basingstoke: Macmillan.

Middlemas, K. 1991: *Power, Competition and the State*, volume 3, *The End of the Postwar Era*. Basingstoke: Macmillan.

Olson, M. 1982: *The Rise and Decline of Nations*. New Haven: Yale University Press.

Owen, G. 1999: *From Empire to Europe*. London: HarperCollins.

Purcell, J. 1993: The end of institutional industrial relations, *Political Quarterly*, 64 (1), 6–23.

Regalia, I., and Regini, M. 1998: Italy. In Ferner and Hyman (eds), *Changing Industrial Relations in Europe*. Oxford: Blackwell.

Towers, B., and Brown, W. (eds) 2000: *Employment Relations in Britain: 25 Years of the Advisory, Conciliation and Arbitration Service*. Oxford: Blackwell.

Traxler, F., Blaschke, S. and Kittel, B. 2001: *National Labour Relations in Internationalized Markets*. Oxford: Oxford University Press.

Visser, J., and Hemerijck, A. 1997: *A Dutch 'Miracle'*. Amsterdam: Amsterdam University Press.

Wallerstein, M. 1990: Centralized bargaining and w age restraint, *American Journal of Political Science*, 43 (4), 649–80.

6

LABOUR LAW AND INDUSTRIAL RELATIONS: A NEW SETTLEMENT?

LINDA DICKENS AND MARK HALL

This chapter describes the current framework of labour law and analyses its nature and rationale in the light of major changes to the 'voluntarist' system introduced by Conservative governments in the period 1979–97 and by Labour governments since 1997. We chart the demise of the voluntary system and the increasing juridification of industrial relations in Britain. Voluntarism may remain a touchstone at the level of rhetoric, but it has ceased to be the keystone of British industrial relations.

The Labour government elected in May 1997 and re-elected in June 2001 introduced significant changes in the legislative framework for industrial relations in the UK, changing not merely the detail but the nature of legal regulation of the employment relationship. An example of this is the legal regulation of pay and working time which represents a major development in British industrial relations, reflecting the domestic agenda (legal regulation of pay) and implementation of European law (on working time). But there are important continuities as well as breaks with the previous Conservative legislation, notably in restrictive regulation of industrial action. There are tensions and ambiguities within the legislative package which the Labour government presented as an industrial relations 'settlement'. These arise from differing policy preferences, a desire to balance contrasting domestic pressures (including employer concerns about regulatory burdens), and the need to manage these contrasting pressures in the light of EU requirements. The Labour government adopted an attitude towards EU social policy different from that of its Conservative predecessor, and we show how, as a result, this increasing supra-national influence is shaping British labour law so that the current position cannot be seen as final.

Voluntarism and the Growth of Legal Intervention

The period up to the 1960s

In Britain, for most of the twentieth century, the regulation of the employment relationship by means of collective bargaining between employers and unions (and, where absent, by employers acting unilaterally) was far more important than legal regulation through Acts of Parliament. As discussed in chapter 2, 'voluntarism' (or, more precisely, 'collective laissez-faire': McCarthy 1992), as this approach is termed, was supported by both sides of industry. Unions saw the main role of legislation as preventing hostile intervention by the courts in industrial disputes. Employers were keen to avoid legislation that constrained their freedom to manage.

Voluntarism did not simply equate to a minimal role for legal regulation permitting the free play of collective forces; it also encompassed the extension and support of social regulation through collective bargaining. Nor did it imply the complete absence of statutory intervention. Legislation was necessary in the late nineteenth and early twentieth centuries to legalize trade union activity, notably to provide 'immunity' in order for unions to organize industrial action during disputes with employers, which would otherwise be unlawful under common (judge-made) law and to encourage and support voluntary collective bargaining. A number of *auxiliary* measures were introduced (e.g. the provision of conciliation and arbitration machinery), and *regulatory* measures were enacted governing the terms and conditions of employment for certain groups, notably those not covered by collective bargaining. These gap-filling measures included legally binding minimum wage rates set by wages councils in sectors where collective bargaining was underdeveloped, and the statutory regulation of the working hours of women and young workers. There were also health and safety laws covering various occupations and industries. Moreover, the voluntary system of industrial relations was temporarily replaced by special measures during both world wars, and legislation passed in the wake of the 1926 general strike and repealed in 1946 introduced restrictions on union activity which clearly fell outside the tradition of voluntarism.

Nevertheless, compared with other industrialized countries, the crucial and distinguishing characteristic of British employment law from 1870 to the 1960s was its limited role. In 1954 a leading academic lawyer commented:

> There is, perhaps, no major country in the world in which the law has played a less significant role in the shaping of industrial relations than in Great Britain and in which today the law and legal profession have less to do with labour relations. (Kahn-Freund 1954: 44)

The 1960s and 1970s

The 1950s proved to be the heyday of voluntarism. By the end of the decade greater legal intervention was increasingly advocated to achieve a range of labour market and industrial relations objectives. Early signs of a shift to greater legal regulation included the Contracts of Employment Act 1963, which introduced minimum periods of notice of termination of employment and written particulars of terms and conditions of employment, and the Redundancy Payments Act 1965, which provided for compensation to be paid to workers losing their jobs for economic reasons. The Donovan Commission, established in 1965 in response to growing pressure for the greater legal regulation of industrial relations, particularly strikes, argued against 'destroying the British tradition of keeping industrial relations out of the courts' (Royal Commission on Trade Unions and Employers' Associations 1968: 47). Controversially, however, both the Labour government's 1969 White Paper *In Place of Strife* and the subsequent Conservative government's Industrial Relations Act 1971 accorded a central role to legal intervention in the reform of industrial relations. The 1971 Act, in particular, represented an ambitious attempt at the comprehensive legal regulation of industrial relations. However, despite giving rise to a number of confrontations between unions and the courts, the legislation was little used and had little impact on day-to-day industrial relations in most workplaces before its repeal in 1974 (Weekes et al. 1975). Only its statutory protections against unfair dismissal, originally proposed by the Donovan Commission, were re-enacted.

The remainder of the 1970s saw a return to a modified, supplemented form of voluntarism under the Labour governments of 1974–9. The 1971 Act's abandonment of the traditional system of immunities for industrial action was reversed and various auxiliary measures to support collective bargaining were enacted, including a statutory procedure whereby a union refused recognition for collective bargaining by an employer could seek determination of the issue. A mass of piecemeal legislation in the health and safety area gave way to a more comprehensive system following the Health and Safety at Work Act 1974, which emphasized self-regulation within a framework of state inspection and enforcement, and the associated Regulations (1977) provided for union safety representatives. Anti-discrimination legislation was enacted covering sex and race, and Equality Commissions were established. The Employment Protection Act 1975 restructured much of the institutional framework of the industrial relations and employment law system, providing a statutory basis for the activities of the Advisory, Conciliation and Arbitration Service (ACAS), which took over dispute settlement functions from the government, and establishing the Central Arbitration Committee (CAC) to carry out statutory functions, including generalizing collectively agreed terms of employment. It also introduced important new individual employment rights and strengthened others. The previous gap-filling role of the law gave way to a more 'universal' approach. Davies and Freedland (1984: 347) argue that the Employment Protection Act 1975 'accomplished the crucial transition from a statutory floor of rights concerned primarily with the termination of employment to [one] concerned with the content of the employment relationship'.

1979–1997

Although the 1970s therefore saw an increase in the *extent* of legal regulation, social regulation through voluntary collective bargaining was supported and the legislation was seen as compatible with voluntarism. It was the *nature* of the employment law reforms introduced by Conservative governments between 1979 and 1997 which constituted a decisive shift away from voluntarism. The long-standing public policy view that joint regulation of the employment relationship through collective bargaining was the best method of conducting industrial relations was no longer accepted. Law was used to curb union strength and to restrict and reduce social regulation, but not to replace it with legal regulation. The scope of individual legal rights was curtailed, employer freedom of action enhanced and union autonomy reduced.

The Conservative governments in the 1980s and 1990s made extensive use of the law with the aim of radically redressing the balance between employers and trade unions, between individual liberty and collective interests and between managerial prerogative and employee rights – in each case tilting the balance towards the first. The legislative agenda was strongly influenced by the government's neo-liberal economic and social objectives, with law being seen as a key instrument facilitating labour market restructuring. Anti-unionism also provided a political resource for the Conservative Party in general elections. The major elements of the Conservatives' employment law programme were the legal restriction of industrial action; the eradication of the closed shop (compulsory union membership); the regulation of internal union government; the dismantling of statutory support for collective bargaining (including the recognition procedure); removing statutory floors to wages; and the curtailment of individual employment rights.

This deregulation of the labour market conflicted with the approach being taken at European level. As a member of the European Community (later Union) the UK government is required to conform to EC requirements. Particularly from the 1980s on, legal intervention in the employment relationship has reflected not only national concerns but also this increased supra-national influence. European legal instruments (usually legally binding Directives) were used as a way of addressing disparities between levels and costs of employment protection legislation in different member states, and as part of the social dimension of the single European market. The growing significance of EU employment law developments in shaping or constraining the domestic legislative agenda will be seen at various points in the discussion which follows.

Key aspects of the industrial relations agenda pursued by the Conservative governments of the 1980s and 1990s – especially the restriction of the freedom to take industrial action and the statutory regulation of trade union government – were unaffected by EU requirements (although they breached other, non-enforceable, international standards). But the need to conform to EU law limited the extent to which they were able to pursue their deregulatory ambitions. In a succession of instances, the government was forced – by EU directives and rulings of the European Court of Justice (ECJ) – to take legislative steps it would rather have avoided. Examples include the Transfer of Undertakings Directive of 1977, which the government transposed into national law in 1981 with a self-confessed 'remarkable lack of enthusiasm' (Davies and Freedland 1993: 577) and developments in equal pay and sex discrimination legislation in the 1980s which reflected EC influence as domestic law failed to keep pace with the ECJ's progressive development of Community law (Davies 1992: 343), for example the concept of equal pay for work or equal value.

The mismatch that clearly existed between the Conservatives' domestic labour market policies and the EU social agenda reflected different regulatory traditions. The legal regulation of employment has been embedded more deeply in most Continental European countries than it has in Britain, and legal requirements, for example to consult over redundancies, have been translated into practice through such bodies as statutory works councils, which have been absent in Britain. But it also reflected a clash between competing philosophies of liberalism and collectivism in labour market regulation, that is, whether government intervention, regulation and corporatist-style arrangements promote or detract from efficiency, employment creation and growth (see chapter 5). As a result, the Conservatives attempted to extricate the UK from the EU social policy framework. In 1989 the UK government refused to sign the Community Charter of the Fundamental Social Rights of Workers (the 'social charter'). More significantly, in 1991 it negotiated an 'opt-out' from the proposed 'Social Chapter' of the Maastricht Treaty on European Union, fearing that it would further erode the UK's ability to block legislation it opposed (Hall 1994). Nevertheless, EU measures originating before the UK's 'opt-out' continued to have an impact on the domestic labour law agenda.

Post-1997

By the time a Labour government was returned to office in 1997, the debate had switched from whether the law should play a role in British industrial relations to what role it should play (Dickens and Hall 1995: 294). The Labour Party accepted large parts of the Conservatives' legislation, notably restrictions on industrial action and the control of internal union affairs, while in other areas such as minimum wages both the party and the TUC had come to believe in legal intervention.

The Labour government has not sought to reverse its Conservative predecessors' reforms of the law on industrial action. Indeed, retention of the existing laws on strikes was strongly emphasized by the party's 1997 election manifesto and was seen as central to the 'business-friendly' credentials of the 'New Labour' project. Accordingly, with some relatively minor exceptions, the restrictions imposed on industrial action, picketing and ballots remain in place, as do the provisions on internal trade union government. However, as Wedderburn (1998: 254) has noted, the Labour government's White Paper *Fairness at Work* (DTI 1998) was 'the first major government document since 1981 to recognize and promote instruments of collective industrial relations'. A key proposal in the White Paper, enacted in the Employment Relations Act (ERA) 1999, was a statutory procedure for gaining trade union recognition. The emphasis on the desirability of a flexible labour market remains but, in contrast to its predecessor, the Labour government declares that it is seeking to balance employers' flexibility with minimum standards of 'fairness at work'. This change of emphasis and the reversal of the UK opt-out from the EU Social Chapter have resulted in significant legislative development.

In signing up to the Maastricht Social Chapter the Labour government demonstrated an attitude radically different from that of its predecessor, and significant aspects of the current legislative framework flow from this decision. The regulation of working time, the reform of employee consultation procedures, improved rights for non-standard workers, and the introduction of statutory rights to parental leave are among the EU-driven developments in British employment law which stand alongside Labour's major 'home-grown' policies of the national minimum wage and trade union recognition.

The following sections look in more detail at the current legal framework, discussing the measures enacted since 1997 against a consideration of what preceded them. We first explore the rationale, nature and impact of individual employment rights and then turn to collective rights (relating to union organization, collective bargaining and representation, and industrial action). This presentational distinction does not seek to deny the interplay between these areas of law; indeed, in the concluding section to this chapter we argue that it is important that collective and individual legal rights are seen as complementary and interconnected.

Individual Rights: Managerial Prerogative and Worker Protection

Rationale for action

A 1986 White Paper asked why it is 'necessary to depart from the basic principle that terms and conditions of employment are matters to be determined by the employer and the employees concerned (where appropriate through their representatives) in the light of their own individual circumstances' (DE 1986: para. 7.2). The essential answer to this question is that statutory regulation that constrains the freedom of the contracting parties is justified because it counteracts the inequality of bargaining power which is inherent in the employment relationship. The individual employee's position is one of subordination, though the asymmetry in power is clothed 'by that indispensable figment of the legal mind known as the contract of employment' (Kahn-Freund 1983: 18).

As we have noted, under the voluntarist system collective bargaining was seen as the primary method of addressing this inequality, and the regulatory function of law was limited. In the 1960s and 1970s, however, there was a marked increase in the extent to which the law sought to restrict managerial prerogative in handling the employment relationship, particularly in the areas of recruitment (through discrimination law) and job termination. Importantly, however, the redundancy payments and unfair dismissal legislation was also seen as a means of promoting efficient management and reducing industrial conflict (Anderman 1986: 433; Dickens et al. 1985).

In a marked change of approach, Conservative governments from 1979 to 1997 aimed to reduce or remove workers' statutory employment rights in order, it was argued, to promote employment and enhance the flexibility seen as crucial to competitive success (e.g. DE 1989). There was a shift towards an increasingly 'contractualist' approach which, in the writings of the 'new right', treated freedom of contract as if it were a social fact rather than a conceptual apparatus of the law. Protection of workers imposes costs on employers which, it was argued, worked to the disadvantage of job creation. The Conservatives also thought that downward pressure on wages would stimulate employment; therefore, measures (whether in labour law or social security) which acted to provide a floor to wages were seen as undesirable. Thus, for example, long-established (although never universal) minimum-wage-fixing machinery (the Wages Council system) was first restricted and then abolished.

Overall, however, the Conservatives' deregulation programme was fairly limited. In a comparative European context, the employment relationship in the UK, even after the increased statutory intervention of the 1970s, was still relatively unregulated by law. Thus there was little to deregulate. Furthermore, in practice the protection afforded by statutory rights was limited, and employee rights could be seen to serve managerial (and state) interests in underpinning (rather than challenging) managerial prerogative and promoting 'orderly' industrial relations (Dickens 1994). At the same time, while committed to deregulation, the Conservatives had to retain and even enhance employee rights in some areas to meet its European Community obligations, notably in equal pay and sex discrimination, although in each case it adopted a minimalist response, often coupled with deregulatory measures (Deakin 1990).

At the end of the Conservatives' period of deregulation, therefore, the framework of individual employment rights remained largely intact, although in some cases their substantive content was weakened. But – importantly – coverage of these rights was substantially reduced. For example, the service qualification required for many employment protection rights was increased from six months to two years, depriving many of protection. Labour Force Survey data for 1988 indicated that after various legislative changes some 55 per cent of part-time workers and 29 per cent of full-time workers were excluded from unfair dismissal and other employment protections because of the hours and length of service qualifications (Hakim 1989; Disney and Szyszczak 1989). Deregulation removed certain legal protections from those least likely to be in unions, particularly those in atypical or 'peripheral' employment. Unorganized employment became unregulated employment. Also, through changes to substantive law and enforcement procedures, it was made harder for those who were covered by the legislation to pursue their legal rights and to succeed, and the available remedies deteriorated.

As noted, partly as a result of a different attitude to Europe, and partly through the Labour government's own legislative initiatives, the importance of legislation as a source of employment rights in Britain has increased significantly since the 1997 election. Whereas the Conservatives promoted flexibility at the expense of security, there is now an attempt to develop a 'flexible labour market under-pinned by fair, minimum standards'. The Labour government is prepared to articulate rationales for legal intervention in this area based on notions of social justice and fairness.

But there is a continuing concern not to overburden employers (e.g. DTI 1998: para 1.13). This meant that the extent of the shift towards worker protec-tion under the 1997–2001 Labour government was less than originally heralded in pre-election declarations and in early formulations of legislative proposals and regulations. A decision not to remove the ceiling on compensation for those unfairly dismissed from their jobs (proposed in the White Paper) but instead to raise the limit, for example, was made 'in the light of employer concerns expressed during the consultation period about ill-founded claims, burdens on business and employment prospects'. Similarly Simpson (1999b: 172) notes that the regulations relating to the newly introduced National Minimum Wage (NMW) were diluted, for example, widening the categories of those who could be paid at a rate less than the minimum.

Finally, in terms of rationales for legal intervention, it is worth noting that some rights (notably maternity and parental leave rights) are presented in the legislation as 'family-friendly measures' rather than as individual rights at work as such. This links them to a different policy debate, concerning family policy and work/life balance rather than labour relations, with which New Labour may feel more comfortable (Simpson 1998). This arguably also serves to make overt employer resistance more difficult, not least since such measures are presented as helping parents 'balance the needs of their work and their children so that they may contribute fully to the competitiveness and productivity of the modern economy' (DTI press release, 22 June 2000).

Individual employment rights: nature and scope

When the Labour government was elected in 1997, statutory rights included the following:

- minimum period of notice of termination
- statement of principal terms and conditions of the contract of employment and of discipline and dismissal procedures
- right to receive an itemized pay statement
- right to a statement of reason for dismissal
- right not to be unfairly dismissed
- right not to be unfairly discriminated against on grounds of race, sex, or disability
- right to maternity pay and the right to return to work after leave for childbirth
- right to time off for various public and trade union duties and for antenatal care
- right to equal pay and other contractual terms as between men and women

- right to receive severance payment in the event of redundancy
- rights relating to trade union membership and non-membership and protection for union activity
- preservation of acquired rights on the transfer of undertakings.

Since 1997, a range of new rights and protections have been enacted, notably:

- right to National Minimum Wage
- 'whistle-blower' (public interest) protection
- right to be accompanied in grievance and disciplinary hearings (an individual right with clear collective implications, see below)
- working time protection
- right to urgent family leave
- right to parental leave
- part-time workers' right to equal treatment
- protection for fixed-term contract workers.

The last five items implemented European directives, the last two of which resulted from framework agreements reached between the European-level social partners.

Some new rights and increased protections for workers were contained in the ERA 1999, but it was the implementation of the EU Working Time Directive in October 1998 and the introduction of the NMW with effect from April 1999 which marked the most significant development in the legislative framework of UK industrial relations, constituting the general regulation of pay and working time through basic universal minimum standards.

Historically, in keeping with the voluntarist tradition, there was no general legal regulation of working time in the UK. Moreover, through the 1980s and 1990s, in line with their policy of deregulating the labour market, successive Conservative governments repealed legislation which protected the working hours of women and young workers and enabled statutory wages councils to regulate working hours and paid holidays (Hall and Sisson 1997). It also challenged the legal basis of the EU Working Time Directive. This challenge was rejected by the ECJ in 1996 and now, as a result of the Working Time Regulations 1998, there is for the first time in the UK a comprehensive statutory framework regulating a broad range of working time issues, including a 48-hour limit on average weekly working hours, minimum daily rest periods, rest breaks, restrictions on night- and shift-work and the provision of paid annual leave (see Hall et al. 1998). However, following the directive, the working time standards specified in the legislation are subject to a complex set of exceptions and 'derogations'. More generally, the flexible application of some of the regulations' standards is possible via collective agreements with trade unions or, where there is no recognized trade union, by 'workforce agreements', i.e. agreements negotiated by elected employee representatives. Crucially, the regulations also provide that individual employees can voluntarily opt out of the 48-hour limit on average weekly working hours.

Whereas the Working Time Regulations implement an EU directive, the NMW is part of the government's domestic agenda, and in the view of one commentator (Simpson 1999a: 1) is arguably 'the most radical and far reaching reform of employment rights made by the 1997 Labour government'. Legislation had been used in the past to protect particularly vulnerable workers against abusive practices by employers relating to the amount of pay (Wages Councils, Fair Wage Resolutions) and to regulate deductions from pay and methods of payment (Truck Acts), and legislation concerning gender pay equality was enacted in the 1970s. But the NMW has brought in the principle of a universal floor for pay (for details see chapter 17; Simpson 2001).

In addition to enacting additional rights for workers vis-à-vis their employers, the Labour government has reversed the narrowing of the coverage of existing protections which occurred under its Conservative predecessors and has improved the remedies. The service qualification period which applies for a number of rights was reduced to one year, and clauses in fixed-term contracts whereby people could be asked to waive their right to claim unfair dismissal are no longer allowed. Further, in an important recognition of the diverse (and at times disguised) nature of subordinate labour, and the changing nature of the UK labour market, there is provision for bringing workers who may not be classified as 'employees' within the scope of employment protections. Legislation, for example on working time, increasingly refers to 'workers' and not 'employees'. Workers, for example homeworkers, are, according to one study, people who 'do not have a contract of employment, but who nevertheless contract to supply their own personal services to the employer and who, to some degree, are economically dependent on the employer's business' (Burchell et al. 1999: 1); the study estimates that about 5 per cent of the workforce may fall into this category.

The remedies for unfair dismissal were improved by raising the maximum compensation limit from £12,500 to £50,000 and index-linking it. There is no maximum limit for compensation in discrimination cases; the maximum in sex discrimination cases was removed in 1993 to comply with European law, and in race discrimination cases in 1994.

Some 'family-friendly' employment rights pre-date the current Labour government. Maternity leave and pay provisions have been in place since 1975 and a right to time off for antenatal care was introduced in 1980. The more recent reforms have been driven largely by the EU. New statutory entitlements to parental leave and time off work for family emergencies, required by EU Parental Leave Directive, were introduced by the Maternity and Parental Leave Regulations 1999 and the ERA 1999. The regulations also improved existing maternity leave arrangements. Further legislation is expected in this area. The Labour Party's manifesto for the 2001 election contained commitments to lengthen the period for which maternity leave is paid, to increase statutory maternity pay, and introduce paid paternity leave for fathers. A Work and Parents Taskforce has been set up to examine ways of giving working parents of young children the legal right to request flexible working hours.

Improvements have been made in the area of disability discrimination through increasing the scope of the 1995 legislation to cover smaller firms, and establishing a Disability Rights Commission on the same footing as the existing equality commissions (Equal Opportunities Commission and Commission for Racial Equality). The Labour government moved away from a pre-1997 election promise to introduce age discrimination legislation, however, favouring a non-binding code of practice instead (although as noted later, legislation will be required under a recent EU directive). The Race Relations Act has been amended to place a duty on specified public bodies to promote race equality in undertaking their functions, which may include ethnic monitoring (*EOR* 2001), but no other significant changes have been made in the framework of UK sex and race discrimination law despite long-recognized inadequacies (Hepple et al. 2000) and reform suggestions from the equality commissions (e.g. EOC 1998; see chapter 16).

Enforcement of rights

There is no general labour inspectorate in Britain for monitoring and enforcing legal protections. An (under-resourced) inspectorate operates in the area of health and safety, and the equality commissions have a (relatively infrequently used) investigative and enforcement role. The NMW Act provides for two routes: administrative enforcement through Inland Revenue officers (rather than a dedicated agency) and by way of individual complaint. For the most part, although legal regulation of the employment relationship has increased, the individualized, private law model characteristic of the UK leaves individual workers to enforce their legal rights against employers. The legislation does not provide any enforcement role for trade unions, although of course they can play an important role in practice, not only in helping members bring individual cases, but also in seeking to translate statute and case law into changed employment practice and in building upon basic legal standards via collective bargaining (an activity limited, of course, to companies where unions are recognized).

The main route for individuals seeking to enforce their statutory rights is an application to an employment tribunal (ET). ETs are independent judicial bodies, comprising a legally qualified chair and two lay members. ACAS provides conciliation in an attempt to settle cases without the need for a hearing. Tribunal hearings take place in locations throughout the country. Legal representation is not required, and no legal aid is available. Appeal from the ETs is made to another specialist tripartite body (the Employment Appeal Tribunal) and then (on points of law only) to the ordinary courts.

Claims to tribunals have trebled since 1990, reaching record levels during 2000–1 with 130,408 tribunal applications referred to ACAS for conciliation. Explanations for the increase can be found in the expansion of jurisdictions and the widening coverage of protection (Dickens 2000), as well as conditions in the economy (Knight and Latreille 2000: 534) and the changing structure of employment towards small, non-unionized, service sector employers most likely to generate tribunal claims (Cully et al. 1999). Despite the increase, it is estimated that only some 15–25 per cent of disputes which involve a breach of legal rights go to tribunals (DTI 2001) and it is still only a minority of employers who face such claims each year. WERS 1998 data reveal that 13 per cent of workplaces had at least one tribunal application lodged against them in the preceding year; 71 per cent of workplaces had had no tribunal claims made against them in the previous five years (Cully et al. 1999: 128–9).

Only a minority of claims (about one-quarter) are heard by a tribunal. Most are settled through conciliation by ACAS, acting under its statutory duty, or are otherwise withdrawn, settled privately, or abandoned. Applicants succeed in just under half of all the heard cases, although success rates vary by jurisdiction, being particularly low in the discrimination jurisdictions and high in redundancy payments claims. Implementation of a recent EU directive adjusting the burden of proof in sex discrimination cases may lead to improved success rates. About one-third of unfair dismissal applications (the largest jurisdiction by caseload) succeeded at tribunal in 1998/9. Compensation is the normal remedy. The statute's primary remedy of reinstatement is sought only by a minority of applicants and is very rarely awarded by tribunals (less than 1 per cent of cases), who are sensitive to employer arguments concerning potential problems if they had to take someone back into a job from which they had been dismissed. The median compensation award for 1998/9 was £2,388, similar to the previous two years (*Labour Market Trends* 1999). In discrimination cases the median award was £5,000 for race discrimination and £4,044 in sex discrimination cases, both showing an increase over previous years.

A new optional route for determining some statutory employment rights disputes has been introduced. Initially proposed by the Conservative government at a time when the tribunal system appeared to be unable to cope effectively with increasing caseloads and required increased funding, the idea was adopted by the Labour government, and the scheme, devised by ACAS, as required by the Employment Rights (Dispute Resolution) Act 1998, came into operation in May 2001. This 'arbitration alternative' is supported by both the CBI and TUC as a way of tackling undue legalism and the failure of the tribunals to live up to their original remit to provide an accessible and informal way of resolving individual employment disputes. In unfair dismissal cases the parties can agree to go before a single arbitrator rather than an employment tribunal to have the case decided. Entry is via an agreement ending the right to go to a tribunal hearing. As in the ETs, reinstatement, re-engagement, and compensation are the available remedies if the dismissal decision is not upheld. Unlike in the ETs, however, the hearing is in private and the award confidential to the parties, and there is no appeal on point of law: the arbitrator's award is final and binding.

Impact of individual rights

Employees have benefited from the enactment of individual employment rights in that many seek and gain redress at employment tribunals in circumstances where previously none would have been available. A positive summary of impact would encompass the following. Arbitrary 'hire and fire' approaches to discipline have been curbed;, and 'due process' and corrective procedures instituted. Those losing their jobs through no fault of their own may be compensated. Pay structures have been revised and de-sexed with the use and threat of equal pay actions providing a lever to reform, and the gender pay gap has narrowed. Discrimination legislation has curbed the most overt discriminatory practices, especially in recruitment; it has indicated how less overt, taken-for-granted practices can be discriminatory, and it has encouraged the development of equal opportunity policies. Maternity rights facilitate mothers' interaction with the labour market, and parental rights may provide a stimulus to reconsider the current, gendered distribution of paid and unpaid work.

These positive achievements must be seen in perspective, however. As we have just seen, although litigation is increasing, individuals make relatively limited use of their legal rights to challenge employers, and do so generally with minority success and with limited redress for those who are successful. Broader examination indicates little impact (direct or indirect) of the legislation in terms, for example, of enhanced employee job security or greater equality of opportunity in employment. The unfair dismissal law does not go very far in challenging managerial prerogative and has afforded only limited protection to employees. The redundancy legislation was only ever intended to compensate for job loss, not to prevent it, and in practice many of those made redundant do not qualify for statutory payment. Any talk of enhanced job security or 'job property rights' here is misplaced. As the dismissal law was applied by the tribunals it became clear that the job security interests of workers were recognized, but only so far as they were consistent with managerial objectives (Forrest 1980: 379; Dickens et al. 1985: 106).

Achievements of the discrimination and equal pay legislation appear slight when placed in the context of evidence of continuing discrimination and the continued pay and labour market disadvantage of women, ethnic minorities and other social groups, discussed in chapters 16 and 17. What law may achieve here is necessarily limited, but there are considerable weaknesses in the legal provisions, procedures and enforcement mechanisms, and in the assumptions underlying the legislation, which restrict its potential impact (Dickens 1992; Hepple et al. 2000).

There is evidence that individual statutory rights have provided a floor for collectively bargained improvements (though there are also indications that the 'floor' may form a 'ceiling', with employer provision restricted to that required by legislation). For those outside the union-organized sectors, however, there is no bargaining to improve on the floor, nor any union to ensure the floor is actually provided. Employee statutory rights do not appear to have prevented employers from pursuing the competitive strategies they wished to adopt. In as much as compensation for job loss facilitates the smooth handling of redundancies and restructuring, they may have even been of assistance (Turnbull and Wass 1997). Certainly, despite the legal protections afforded to their workers, employers retained sufficient scope in the 1980s to pursue quantitative and qualitative flexibility in labour utilization and to introduce technological and other change (Napier 1992; Dickens 1994).

The impact of the legislation on employers has not been to weaken their control over hiring and firing (indeed it has served to legitimate it) but, rather, has tended to foster improvements in managerial efficiency in the handling of job terminations, and the development of 'good employment practice' or more professional personnel policies. This was seen, for example, in greater care being taken over recruitment, and in the development and reform of disciplinary rules and procedures (which remain managerially determined), with consequent restrictions on the freedom of action of lower-level management and enhanced importance, at least initially, of the personnel function (Dickens et al. 1985: 264–5). Similar impacts can be attributed to the discrimination legislation (Hitner et al. 1982; chapter 16).

The extent to which statutory rights deliver gains for workers will be affected by the degree to which workers are able to avail themselves of such rights. Looked at narrowly, this means the ease of enforcing rights via the available mechanisms. But, more broadly, it relates to the context within which rights operate. For example, fiscal, welfare and social policies in the 1980s which reinforced women's domestic role and underpinned inequalities in the home served to undermine rights to equality at work without any deregulatory change to the equality legislation. A right to return after maternity leave is only a formal right for women with no access to childcare. New Labour has begun to address elements of this context, with, for example, a national childcare strategy.

Just as the impact of the Conservatives' deregulation had a particular (negative) impact on women, so too (positively) has Labour's re-regulation. A 'woman's take' on the rights in the ERA (and not only those relating to maternity and parental rights) is fairly positive. The extended coverage and nature of the individual employment rights enacted since 1997 is particularly beneficial to women, who constitute over 80 per cent of part-time workers and form the majority of those in temporary jobs. Women are more likely than men to have short service in their current job and are also less likely to work in unionized sectors. Similarly, although the NMW was set at a low level, overall some 2 million low-paid workers gained, two-thirds of them women. The NMW affects one in 12 employees; one in three is a homeworker, one in five a part-timer, one in eight an ethnic minority worker (Bain 1999).

Collective Rights: Collective Bargaining, Employee Representation, and Industrial Action

The process of 're-regulation' by the Labour government is not simply a question of enacting additional individual employment rights. The major target of deregulation under the Conservative governments between 1979 and 1997 was the social regulation of employment and industrial relations provided through collective organization and bargaining. As we have seen, auxiliary measures to support and encourage collective bargaining were also dismantled. Whether or not to engage in collective bargaining became a matter of employer choice, regardless of levels of union membership or support. Increasingly employers took advantage of this freedom of choice to manage without unions. De-recognition of unions became more common, particularly from the mid-1980s (Gall and McKay 1999; Claydon 1996); unions experienced difficulty in expanding into new or traditionally under-organized areas (Cully et al. 1999: 296) and privatization and compulsory contracting out of public sector services under-mined long-established public sector bargaining relationships (see chapters 8, 9 and 11). In the name of promoting 'partnership', the Labour government intro-duced important new statutory provisions affecting collective bargaining, employee representation, and information and consultation, while largely retaining its predecessors' legislation restricting industrial action and regulating unions' inter-nal procedures.

Statutory trade union recognition

The ERA 1999 fulfilled one of Labour's major electoral commitments by provid-ing a statutory procedure through which a union can seek an enforceable award from an independent body (the Central Arbitration Committee) that an em-ployer recognizes it for collective bargaining. Statutory recognition is in respect of pay, hours and holidays, and there is a requirement for the employer to inform the union about training plans. The recognition procedure clearly demar-cated the New Labour government's approach from that of its predecessors. In its detail, however, the procedure falls short of the statutory assistance the unions had hoped for, and in its final form it incorporates most of what the employers lobbied for rather than union demands (Wood and Godard 1999).

Firms with fewer than 21 workers are excluded, and a union (or more than one union acting jointly) needs a threshold membership of 10 per cent of its proposed bargaining unit (the workers for whom it wishes to bargain), plus the majority of workers likely to support it, in order to have its application accepted by the CAC. The application will not be accepted where there is already a recognition agreement applying to workers in the proposed bargaining unit, even if this agreement is with a union which is not independent of the employer or does not cover pay. The CAC determines the appropriate bargaining unit where this is not agreed between the employer and union, paying particular regard to the need for it to be 'compatible with effective management' and avoiding fragmentation. The CAC can declare the union recognized without a ballot if more than 50 per cent of the workers in the bargaining unit are mem-bers of the union, but it will not do this if it considers a ballot would be in the interests of good industrial relations, or where there is evidence that employees do not want the union to conduct collective bargaining on their behalf. Where the CAC calls for a ballot recognition will be granted if a majority of those voting, and at least 40 per cent of the workers in the bargaining unit, vote in favour. This majoritarian principle contrasts with the 1970s approach, which was more concerned with whether there was sufficient support to sustain collect-ive bargaining, acknowledging the 'virtuous circle' effect, whereby union mem-bership increases following employer recognition.

Following a declaration of recognition the parties are required to agree a method of bargaining and, if they do not, the CAC will impose a procedure which is legally binding unless the parties agree otherwise. Where one party does not abide by the procedure the other may apply to the courts for an order that that the party act as required (specific performance). Failure to abide by an order for specific performance could (in theory) lead to quasi-criminal sanctions for contempt of court, although the circumstances in which a court would order this remedy and its willingness to do so in this area are uncertain (Hepple 2000). The enforcement approach has been criticized for bringing unnecessary legalism into a statutory procedure which has sought to avoid this (Hepple 2000: 157–8). Various observers argue that a better approach to enforcement would have been to have arbitration on substantive terms and conditions as the sanction for non-compliance, with the Canadian system of first contract arbitration providing one apparently successful model (Wood and Godard 1999; Simpson 2000; McCarthy 1999: 44–51). The limitations of such an approach in practice, however, were evident in the British 1970s procedure (Dickens and Bain 1986: 91–2).

By the time of the CAC's first annual report (2001) no case had reached the stage where the enforcement mechanism had been tested, few cases having reached the stage at which a method might be imposed. That few cases have gone through the whole procedure largely reflects its relative newness (it started in June 2000), but also the emphasis throughout the procedure on facilitating agreement between the parties. A number of applications were withdrawn at different stages of the statutory procedure after voluntary agreement was reached.

The CAC deals with cases through tripartite panels: the chair or one of the deputy chairs sits with a member with employer experience and another with experience of unions. Although operating as a judicial tribunal, the CAC places much emphasis on the industrial relations expertise of its members in exercising its statutory discretion in decision-making and in devising workable procedures. The ERA procedure avoids a number of the difficulties which gave rise to intervention by the courts through judicial review in the 1970s (Dickens 1987: 124–9), but there remains scope for challenges to be made (Simpson 2000: 219). However, an early judicial review challenge before the Scottish courts was unsuccessful, with the court upholding the CAC decision, confirming its status as an 'experienced industrial jury' entitled to reach its own decision as to what would be in the interests of good industrial relations (IDS 2001).

Impact of the procedure

It is too early to assess the operation of the CAC and the direct impact of the statutory procedure. Unions have approached the new statutory procedure cautiously, bringing forward cases where they felt secure in the level of membership. Generally employers in the early cases were prepared to recognize the union once they realized that this was legally required if the majority of their employees were in favour of it. As time passes applications in more problematic cases are likely, where membership levels may be lower at the time of application and employers more hostile to collective bargaining in principle.

Experience suggests that it is prudent not to expect too much from direct use of the statutory procedure in terms of overall extension of collective bargaining. But previous experience also indicates that there may be important indirect and symbolic effects. The removal of statutory support for recognition by the incoming 1979 Conservative government came at a time when the previous statutory recognition procedure had almost run aground (Dickens and Bain 1986: 93), and its direct achievements in terms of the numbers to whom collective bargaining was extended (65,000) appear relatively modest. The symbolic function of that legislative change, however, may have been as important as the change itself, helping foster an anti-collectivist culture.

By the same token, the enactment of the statutory procedure serves to reinforce the social and political legitimacy of trade unions, and the symbolic and indirect effects of the procedure may be more substantial than those gained by its actual use. Certainly the early cases involved relatively small organizations and small groups of employees. Sixty per cent of the companies concerned in applications in the first year had fewer than 200 employees and 54 per cent of applications were for bargaining units of fewer than 100. Nine per cent of applications involved a bargaining unit of more than 500 workers (CAC 2001). However, there was early indication of an indirect impact in terms of a change of policy of a number of employers towards union recognition once it became clear that the New Labour government would enact a statutory procedure; new recognition agreements started outnumbering instances of de-recognition (Gall and McKay 1999). Agreements continue to be reached in the shadow of law now the procedure is in operation (ACAS 2001). This is a measure of the success of the procedure, which was always intended to be a last resort, with primacy accorded to the achievement of voluntary agreements (TUC/CBI 1997).

The procedure may assist in the growth of enterprise- or plant-level collective bargaining; it does not offer any prospect of a return to more centralized (sectoral- or national-level) collective bargaining, nor does it provide for any generalization of collectively agreed terms and conditions of employment. In terms of growth in union membership it should be noted also that a statutory award of recognition does not impose a requirement on anyone to join the recognized union, nor does it preclude workers in the bargaining unit from entering into individual contractual arrangements with the employer. The Labour government has made only a limited change to the ability of employers to offer inducements to employees to enter into individualized contracts.

A right to representation

British legislation protects freedom of association (the right of an individual to join or not to join a trade union), and this was strengthened by the ERA, which banned employer blacklists of union activists. But the law provides no right to trade unions to organize. Where the statutory recognition procedure is used and the CAC orders a ballot, the union has a right of access to employees to seek support, but this right does not apply outside these circumstances. However the ERA 1999 introduced a statutory right for workers to be accompanied by a trade union official or fellow worker at workplace disciplinary and grievance hearings. This individual employment right is also potentially significant in collective industrial relations terms.

Union officials now have the right to attend disciplinary and grievance hearings where invited to do so by workers (not necessarily members) even where no union is recognized by the employer for collective bargaining. This applies irrespective of firm size and so covers those with fewer than 21 employees outside the statutory recognition procedure. The new statutory provisions fall short of providing a fully fledged 'right to representation', as they limit the extent to which the accompanying person can intervene in the proceedings (and do not actually require employers to introduce discipline and grievance procedures). Nevertheless, unions hope – and some employers fear – that in workplaces where unions are not recognized, the operation of the new right may boost unions' organizing efforts by enabling them to gain access to the workplace and demonstrate the value of their role in supporting workers with problems (Hall 2000).

Statutory information and consultation provisions

The statutory regulation of employee representation is not confined to union recognition provisions. On certain issues, UK law, reflecting EU requirements, obliges employers to inform and consult employee representatives whether or not unions are recognized. Originally, the UK's legislation confined the right to be consulted to representatives of trade unions recognized by the employers concerned, and provided no mechanism for consulting employee representatives in the absence of union recognition. In 1994 the ECJ ruled that this approach did not adequately implement the relevant EU directives on impending redundancies and transfers of undertakings. Consequently, in 1995 the then Conservative government introduced regulations requiring consultation on these issues either with representatives of recognized unions or with other representatives elected by employees.

These regulations, however, were strongly criticized by trade unions and labour lawyers on the grounds that, since the choice of which type of representatives to consult lay with the employer, employers who recognized unions had the option of 'bypassing' existing union machinery and consulting elected employee representatives instead. Further regulations introduced by the Labour government in 1999 addressed this bypassing problem by providing that, where an employer recognizes an independent trade union in respect of employees affected by the proposed redundancies/transfer, consultation must take place with representatives of that union. Consultation may take place exclusively with other (existing or specially elected) representatives only in the absence of a recognized union.

In public policy terms, the reforms introduced by the 1995 regulations and refined by those of 1999 are of considerable significance. Traditionally, recognized unions have constituted the 'single channel' through which collective statutory employment rights have been applied (see also chapter 10). However, this policy was effectively overturned by the ECJ. For the first time – and specifically for the purposes of consultation over redundancies and transfers – the UK introduced supplementary, statutory employee representation mechanisms to fill the increasingly wide gaps left by reliance on employer recognition of trade unions (Hall and Edwards 1999).

Other issue-specific employee representation mechanisms have followed. The ECJ ruling also prompted the introduction of the Health and Safety (Consultation with Employees) Regulations 1996. These 'top up' earlier regulations by requiring employers to consult employees who are not covered by safety representatives appointed by recognized unions. However, the 1996 regulations give employers the discretion to consult employees directly or through elected representatives (James and Walters 1997). The Working Time Regulations 1998 make provision for the (voluntary) conclusion of 'workforce agreements' regulating working time issues with elected employee representatives in respect of groups of employees not covered by collective bargaining (Hall et al. 1998). This is intended to offer employers without union recognition arrangements covering their workforce the same flexibility in the application of the regulations as that available through traditional collective agreements with trade unions. The concept of workforce agreements has also been extended to the issue of parental leave: the Maternity and Parental Leave Regulations 1999 include provision for derogation from a model parental leave scheme by means of collective or workforce agreements, provided the resulting company-specific scheme meets certain minimum standards and forms part of employees' contracts of employment. These developments represent further steps in the piecemeal process of providing for issue-specific, statutory employee representation mechanisms in the absence of representation via recognized unions.

One consequence of the Labour government reversing its predecessor's 'opt-out' from the Maastricht Social Chapter was the eventual implementation of the requirements of the 1994 European Works Councils (EWCs) directive in the UK through the Transnational Information and Consultation of Employees Regulations 1999. These represent a further landmark in the 'Europeanization' of UK labour law (Carley and Hall 2000). Not only do they bring the UK within the Europe-wide legal framework for EWCs, but they also accentuate certain trends already evident in UK labour law in response to EU legislation. The regulations clearly represent a significant further extension of the range of issues on which employees have statutory rights to information and consultation, encompassing key business, employment and restructuring issues – though of course the new rights will apply on a transnational basis and are confined to 'Community-scale' undertakings or groups (i.e. larger companies operating in at least two member states of the European Economic Area). The regulations also introduce – again on a transnational basis – a further instance of 'bargaining in the shadow of the law', i.e. enabling negotiated provisions to replace statutory norms which are otherwise applicable.

Most strikingly, the regulations provide for the creation of a statutory standing works-council-type employee representation body for the first time ever in the UK, albeit on a transnational basis. However, in the context of the universal approach to employee information and consultation rights embodied by the directive, the UK government has again had to resort to introducing a further issue-specific employee representation mechanism into UK law, adding to the already burgeoning range of examples discussed above. Rather than being a mechanism which applies only to groups of workers without union representation, a ballot will be required, notwithstanding the existing trade union structures within the enterprise's UK operations, for selecting UK members of special negotiating bodies (SNBs) where there is no group-wide consultative committee, and for selecting UK members of statutory EWCs where not all UK employees already have representatives. In most other countries covered by the directive, SNB and statutory EWC representatives are drawn from existing workplace or company-level representation structures, guaranteeing at least some degree of articulation between national and transnational levels of representation. In the UK, however, the balloting mechanism has the potential to produce SNB negotiators or representatives on statutory EWCs who have no direct connection with domestic trade union or other existing representative structures.

The latest development in this area is the draft directive on consultation and information arrangements in companies at national level. It remains to be seen whether this draft EU directive on national information and consultation rules, on which the EU Council of Ministers agreed a 'common position' in June 2001, will provide the basis for a move towards comprehensive works-council-type employee representation structures in the UK which could not only mesh effectively with European-level representation arrangements but also supersede the current disparate range of issue-specific employee representation mechanisms in UK law. What is clear is that by 2005 the UK will have to legislate for substantially enhanced information and consultation rights for employees – a development with highly significant implications for UK industrial relations in an area which until now has been largely unregulated by the law, and one which will take the UK further away from its voluntarist traditions.

The legal developments in information and consultation could potentially have a great impact on workplace industrial relations in Britain. Although the extent and nature of their impact remains uncertain and contested (contrast, for example, Hyman 1996 and Kelly 1996; see also McCarthy 2000), it is undoubtedly the case that, as Terry (chapter 10) notes, the terrain of workplace unionism will increasingly be contoured by legal rights and statutory structures, posing particular challenges for unions and management at workplace level.

The legal regulation of industrial disputes

The freedom to take industrial action has traditionally been seen as offering the prospect of some kind of countervailing social power for employees via effective trade unionism, recognizing the disparity between the bargaining position of individual employees and that of their employer. In Britain, there is no *right* to strike as such. Instead, the freedom to take industrial action has been conferred by granting trade unions, their officials and representatives statutory protections or 'immunities' from common law liabilities which would otherwise make their action unlawful. Without these, the organizers of industrial action would be liable for civil wrongs (torts), including that of inducing breach of employment contracts, and would thus be exposed to injunctions and damages claims. The system of immunities was developed in the late nineteenth and early twentieth centuries, culminating in the Trade Disputes Act 1906, and remains the cornerstone of the contemporary statutory framework for industrial action – having been briefly displaced in favour of (highly circumscribed) positive rights under the Industrial Relations Act 1971.

One problem with relying on immunities is that their effectiveness has at various points been undermined by the development by the courts of new common law liabilities, outflanking the scope of the existing statutory protections. Judgments of this kind led to the Trade Disputes Act 1965, introduced to restore the intended effect of the 1906 legislation. Similarly, the Trade Union and Labour Relations (Amendment) Act 1976 was introduced to widen the scope of the statutory immunities in response to judicial creativity during the second half of the 1960s. Moreover, the language and legal form of the immunities enabled politicians and commentators on the political right increasingly to characterize them as 'unique privileges' which put trade unions 'above the law – terminology designed to create an impression of unwarranted legal status' (Fredman 1992: 26) – despite the immunities being the functional equivalent of the positive right to strike enjoyed by workers in other countries. Such arguments provided the basis for successive changes to the law introduced by the Conservative governments of the 1980s and 1990s to narrow the scope and application of the immunities and thus tighten the legal restrictions on industrial action. By the end of the era of Conservative government the freedom to strike still existed in the UK, but 'a host of cumulative, interlocked limitations ensure it is more circumscribed than at any time since 1906' (McIlroy 1999: 523).

The current position can be summarized as follows. Trade unions organizing industrial action have immunity from liability for inducing or threatening to induce breach of a contract or interference with its performance where they are acting 'in contemplation or furtherance of a trade dispute' (i.e. a dispute between workers and their employer which relates wholly or mainly to a range of issues including pay and conditions, dismissal, allocation of work, discipline, negotiating rights and machinery, etc.). Immunity for unions is dependent on gaining majority support in a postal ballot of the members concerned and giving due notice to the employer of the ballot and the commencement of industrial action. Immunity does not apply to 'secondary' industrial action (i.e. by workers whose employer is not party to the dispute) or to picketing other than at the pickets' own workplace. Government codes of practice on picketing and balloting procedures contain further 'practical guidance' which can be – and on occasion has been (Davies and Freedland 1993: 461) – taken into account in relevant court proceedings. The provisions of the codes are in places more restrictive than the legislation they purport to amplify, as in the case of the 'six picket maximum', which is widely thought to be a statutory requirement but in fact is guidance in the code of practice on picketing.

It is open to employers or any party to a contract broken or interfered with by unlawful industrial action to take legal action against the union or individual organizers concerned. The range of potential litigants in cases of unlawful industrial action was widened in the late 1980s and the early 1990s to include union members and citizens deprived of goods and services. Legal action normally takes the form of seeking an injunction (court order) requiring named organizations and individuals to cease organizing unlawful industrial action. Unions are liable for unlawful action they have authorized or endorsed, including unofficial action if not 'repudiated'. Non-compliance with an injunction is a contempt of court and could lead to the imposition of fines and the sequestration of union assets. An injunction is technically an interim measure prior to the full trial of an action for damages, but normally the employer's aim is to stop industrial action rather than obtain damages.

The Labour government has reduced the scope for the lawful dismissal of employees involved in industrial action. The ERA 1999 makes it unfair to dismiss an employee for taking part in lawfully organized industrial action unless the action lasts for more than eight weeks and the employer has taken reasonable procedural steps to resolve the dispute. As previously, it remains unfair to dismiss some of those taking lawful industrial action but not others at the same establishment (though selective re-engagement is permitted after three months). Since 1990, those dismissed in the course of unofficial industrial action may not claim unfair dismissal.

The effects of this restrictive legal framework for industrial action can be seen in a number of developments. During the 1980s, particularly after the Employment Act 1982 exposed unions to damages claims for unlawful industrial action and the Trade Union Act 1984 made strike ballots a legal requirement, a rise in the level of legal action by employers against unions was observed, though this appears to have been temporary, declining again once unions learnt to live with the new legal constraints. Although legal action by employers had a profound impact in several key disputes during the 1980s in terms of weakening the position of the unions involved (Dickens and Hall 1995: 283; McIlroy 1999), litigation during disputes remains wholly exceptional – even if legal action is reported to be threatened by employers more frequently (Dunn and Metcalf 1996: 85).

The legal changes prompted the overhaul of union procedures for handling industrial action. Despite initial attempts to pursue a policy of non-co-operation with the 1980 and 1982 Employment Acts (Dickens and Hall 1995: 285), unions tended to become more cautious in the tactics they adopted during disputes and to strengthen central union control over how and when industrial action was called and who should be empowered to authorize it. In particular, the use of strike ballots rapidly became the norm.

In terms of the implications for collective bargaining, it is widely perceived that the use of ballots has often helped strengthen the union's negotiating position (Elgar and Simpson 1993). The outcome of the great majority of strike ballots is a vote in favour of industrial action, but in most cases this leads to the settlement of the dispute without a strike occurring, suggesting that balloting is now part of the negotiation process in many organizations.

However, the extent to which the legislation introduced over the 1980s and 1990s has been a factor in the current, historically low levels of industrial action in the UK is difficult to assess (see chapter 9). Some econometric studies have suggested a correlation between restrictive legislation and a fall in the level of industrial action (Dunn and Metcalf 1996: 86–7). But other social, economic and political factors are clearly likely to have been influential. The safest conclusion is that the legal changes were part of a much wider range of developments affecting strike activity. It is unlikely that the specific legal reforms had a direct effect on the number of strikes, but they certainly symbolized a determination to act against what was perceived as the inappropriate use of industrial power, and the numerous legal restrictions made the use of industrial action a more considered move than it had been in the 1970s.

The legal regulation of internal union affairs

A key element of the traditional 'voluntarist' framework of British industrial relations was the limited statutory regulation of internal trade union affairs. In Kahn-Freund's words (1983: 274), it had, 'on the whole, been common ground that in [the] dilemma between imposing standards of democracy and protecting union autonomy the law must come down on the side of autonomy'. With the exception of the statutory requirements governing the administration of unions' political funds and union amalgamations, unions were generally free to devise their own rules and procedures without statutory regulation (although at times the common law intruded, as in the miners' strike 1984/5). The position, however, was radically altered by the Conservative governments of the 1980s and 1990s through a series of measures regulating unions' internal affairs which reflected a highly individualistic conception of the rights and obligations associated with trade union membership (McKendrick 1988: 141). The main focus of these was to require the use of secret ballots by unions in internal elections and before taking industrial action. The stated rationales for this policy concerned both its internal and external impacts (Auerbach 1990: 118). The basic internal justification for intervention was to make unions more democratic and responsive to the wishes of their members. This in turn was expected to have important external effects: more representative (and, implicit in the Conservatives' analysis, more moderate) union leaderships, and the use of strike ballots, were expected to help restrain industrial action.

Unions are required to hold five-yearly ballots for election of union executive committees, presidents and general secretaries. As already noted above, industrial action not preceded by an independently scrutinized postal ballot is unlawful, and union members have the statutory right to seek court orders to restrain non-balloted industrial action. Unions' political funds, which are necessary to finance party political affiliation and political campaigning activities, are subject to ten-yearly review ballots. Although trade unions opposed the introduction of this legislation, the balloting practices it required rapidly became accepted as a fact of union life. The electoral systems of many unions were transformed by the legal requirements, but in few cases has the political complexion of the union leadership undergone significant change as a result. Similarly, against initial expectations, union political funds have in every case been maintained despite the balloting requirements.

The law also provides individual union members with a range of statutory rights enforceable against their union, among them the right not to be unjustifiably disciplined, including for refusing to take part in industrial action. A Commissioner for the Rights of Trade Union Members was established in 1988 to assist members in legal action against unions, including cases alleging breach of union rules, but little use was made of this institution. It was abolished by the ERA 1999 with its main responsibilities being subsumed into the remit of the Certification Officer with the aim of boosting the Certification Officer's role as an alternative to the courts for dealing with such issues.

Conclusion: Juridification, Compromises and Europeanization

After a period of relative stability between the Trades Disputes Act 1906 and the 1960s, British employment law underwent a series of rapid and far-reaching changes which moved it away from the traditional pattern of voluntarism. Although differing legal strategies have been pursued by Labour and Conservative governments, both furthered the trend towards the legal regulation of industrial relations and juridification of the employment relationship, whereby management policy is shaped by law and legal norms and values permeate industrial relations practice.

In the name of labour market flexibility, the Conservative governments of the 1980s and 1990s engineered a pronounced shift in policy towards the restriction of trade union activity and deregulation in the areas of individual employment rights and collective bargaining. The 'deregulatory' measures, however, did little in practice to stem the juridification of industrial relations. The basic system of individual employment rights, developed over the 1960s and 1970s, remained largely intact and the extensive use of legislation to restrict industrial action and regulate trade union activity meant that the law came to have an increasing impact on the conduct of industrial disputes. Nevertheless, and in contrast to other European countries, at the time of the 1997 election, central elements of British industrial relations remained to a very large extent outside the scope of statutory regulation. Crucially, the determination of employees' pay and other terms and conditions and institutional relations between employers and trade unions or other employee representatives were regulated, if at all, through voluntary agreements.

This situation has been changed by key aspects of the Labour government's employment law programme – principally, the legislation introduced on the national minimum wage, working time, and information, consultation and negotiation. These measures not only represented a marked change in policy but they also push further the juridification of industrial relations, extending legal regulatory norms into areas of the employment relationship which previously had been largely a matter for voluntary determination.

Labour came into office with a carefully balanced package of measures, defined as much, if not more so, by the need to reassure the business community and to distance New Labour in the voters' minds from the 'bad old days' of industrial relations in the 1960s and 1970s, as by the need to respond to at least some elements of the trade unions' agenda. Although, as we have seen, there are clear breaks with past Conservative policy, at the same time the party leadership made it clear that their underlying analysis of the importance of labour market flexibility did not differ fundamentally from that of the previous government, and key elements of the 1980s industrial relations legislation were to be kept in place. Some argue that the result is greater continuity than change (e.g. Smith and Morton 2001).

It is perhaps inevitable that in seeking to depart from some aspects of what has gone before, while simultaneously seeking to retain and modify others, tensions and seeming contradictions will emerge. Pressures on government from within (employers effectively arguing for the status quo, and trade unions pushing for change) and pressures from without, notably arising from UK membership of the EU, also led to a series of compromises. One observer notes that the Labour government seems to be engaged in a balancing act 'seeking to relocate labour law in relation to EC employment law and its own more than slightly North American impulses' (Freedland 1999: 200; see also Marquand 1998 cited in Undy 1999: 316).

These tensions and contradictory pressures can be seen in both the individual and collective areas of law discussed above. Compromises have been struck between managerial freedom and worker protection, and in the area of collective rights and representation. While outright governmental opposition to the EU social agenda has ceased, generous use has been made of exceptions and derogations and, as we have seen, not all EU developments have been welcomed by the Labour government. The compromises struck can be seen as largely pragmatic and practical-political rather than as guided by a clear unifying ideology, or some worked-through 'third way' between voluntarism and Conservative neo-liberalism (Undy 1999).

Striking a balance: managerial freedom and worker protection

There are differing views over the correct balance to be struck between employer freedom and managerial prerogative on the one hand, and protections for workers on the other. As we have seen, the Labour government elected in 1997 made an assessment different from that of its neo-liberal predecessor in its attempt to balance the interests of social justice, the need to curb abusive employer behaviour and the provision of minimum standards on the one hand with, on the other, the desire to be 'business-friendly' and not be seen to be burdening employers and jeopardizing entrepreneurship, growth and competitiveness.

One way of approaching this apparent balancing act is to see social justice as contributing to economic success and competitiveness rather than running counter to it, and thus to make the case for labour standards as an input into enhancing competitiveness rather than simply a cost of production (Deakin and Wilkinson 1994). Although it has suggested that 'fair treatment of individuals enhances commitment and competitiveness' (DTI 1998: para 3.1), the government has not sought to justify worker protection as a productive factor per se, and the view that employee protections are costs to be minimized has not been completely displaced.

As we have noted, ministers have been willing to respond to employer contentions about the adverse effects which it is alleged that increased worker protection will have, despite the lack of sound empirical support for such views (see Dickens and Hall 1995: 272 and McCarthy 1992: 60 for a review of the evidence). Major new rights for workers have always been greeted with dire predictions about adverse consequences for the economy and for workers themselves (usually diminished employment opportunities), but these have not been realized in practice. The introduction in the 1970s of the requirement for women to receive pay equal to that of men is a case in point. Many of the fears raised then (and not realized) were echoed in the opposition to the introduction of the NMW and have likewise proved to be unfounded (see chapter 17).

The Labour government has been sensitive to employers' concerns, attempting to quantify the burdens or adverse impacts which any particular proposed piece of legislation would impose and thus respond appropriately. It has also attempted in some areas, notably the NMW and the statutory recognition procedure, to formulate legislation through involving representatives of employers and employees at macro level, working together to produce what are considered to be workable (or at least acceptable) measures (Brown 2000).

Although acknowledging that employment rights introduced since 1997 have had relatively little impact on most firms (CBI 2000), employers have increasingly complained that regulation is adversely affecting economic performance, arguing that the growing regulatory burden on business is imposing higher employment costs on employers, constraints on flexibility in labour use and excessive administration. In response the government has pledged to reduce the regulatory burden on businesses. This has involved a commitment to 'light touch' regulation; and recently an indication that 'soft law' such as codes of practice and good practice exemplars might be used instead of 'hard' regulation through legislation (Hewitt 2001). There is a responsiveness to employer lobbying in the framing of legislation, with minimalist implementation of EU directives, as well as specific deregulatory moves. Among these are amendments to the Working Time Regulations to reduce the record-keeping requirements on employers where employees 'opt out' of the statutory 48-hour limit on the average working week. In certain cases, however, 'business-friendly' concessions in implementing directives have had to be revisited following successful union challenges, on the grounds that they do not comply with EU law (i.e. the Working Time Regulations' 13-week qualifying period for paid annual leave, and the Maternity and Parental Leave Regulations' restriction of the right to parental leave to parents of children born on or after 15 December 1999).

In the area of equality, the government has not accepted proposals for strengthening the law, for example a recommendation by the Equal Opportunities Commission's Task Force on Equal Pay for the introduction of mandatory employer pay reviews (*EOR* 2001). It has moved a little, but not far, from its predecessor's 'privatized', market-driven approach to equality, which rests on employers being persuaded to take voluntary equality action on the basis of self-interested business arguments, with the legal emphasis on complaints by 'victims' rather than action by power holders (Dickens 1999). A different approach is being developed at European level, however (Fredman 2001), and it remains to be seen whether this is adopted in Britain when legislating to implement the recent EU anti-discrimination framework directive. This covers age, sexual orientation, and religion and belief as well as those areas currently subject to anti-discrimination legislation in Britain. Rather than instituting a move away from the 'victim complains' approach, however, the focus currently in Britain is on trying to simplify and speed up the process of complaint and rights enforcement.

The rise in tribunal applications, indicated earlier, has prompted concern, particularly on the part of employers, that there is a growth in a 'compensation culture' and frivolous cases. Although, as noted, other explanations for the rise in applications can be found, this concern prompted the government in July 2001 to amend tribunal procedures to deter and penalize the pursuit of unreasonable cases. These build on earlier measures introduced by previous Conservative governments, which were aimed at deterring and weeding out weak cases but which risk deterring applicants more generally. Following the 2001 general election, the government initiated a broader review of mechanisms for resolving individual employment grievances with the objective of encouraging the resolution of problems within the workplace without recourse to litigation. At the same time it proposed erecting greater financial barriers for applicants (DTI 2001).

The rise in applications to ETs coincides with the decline in collective bargaining coverage in the UK economy. The 1998 WERS survey noted that the rate of claims from firms with 25 employees or more had been increasing at approximately the same rate as the increase in the number of such firms with no union recognition agreement. The obvious inference is that workplace employee representation arrangements encourage internal solutions to individual employment rights disputes. Thus it could be argued that the statutory union recognition procedure and UK implementation of the EU information and consultation directive seem likely to make a more fundamental contribution to stemming the rising tide of tribunal applications than will erecting barriers to pursuing cases. That this important connection between the collective and individual areas of labour law is not being made at policy level may reflect the way in which collective rights are often seen as being about 'rights for trade unions', rather than a way of providing substantive rights and protections to workers, and perhaps also reflects the fact that there is some ambiguity in Labour's attitude towards collective labour rights and EU-driven forms of employee representation at the workplace.

Collective rights and representation

The white paper *Fairness at Work* (*FAW*) revealed an apparent reluctance to privilege collective bargaining over more individualized methods of conducting industrial relations, and the Labour government only recently ended its consistent opposition to the EU directive requiring national-level companies to establish consultation and information bodies. In *FAW* the government acknowledged that collective representation can give employees an effective voice, and be a force for fair treatment, but stressed the importance of voluntary choices. It argued that 'mutually agreed arrangements for representation, *whether involving trade unions or not*, are the best ways for employers and employees to move forward' (para 4.10, emphasis added).

In a similar way, as we have noted, the possibility for employers to obtain flexibility in moving away from the basic legal standards (as for example in the Working Time and Parental Leave Regulations) is afforded not only to those reaching agreement with trade unions, but also to non-union 'workforce agreements' and even (in respect of the 48-hour week) 'agreements' reached with individual employees. The intention of the EU Working Time Directive to promote 'agreement between the two sides of industry' becomes diluted in the UK context.

There is no longer the hostility to collective bargaining which characterized its predecessor in government, but there has been no sign from New Labour of a general commitment to the democratic case for trade unionism and collective bargaining (Smith and Morton 2001). What emerges instead is an acknowledgement that unions may demonstrate to employers and employees that they can 'add value'. Although it may be ambivalent about support for collective bargaining, *FAW* reveals that enterprise-based partnership 'between employers and their employees' is seen as a route to competitive success. Such partnership does not appear to require the presence of trade unions, however. Where trade unions are present, workplace partnership envisages a more co-operative and less confrontational relationship (see chapter 10). Inasmuch as partnership is a symptom of a weakened trade union movement (Brown 2000: 307), its promotion fits with the retention of restrictive industrial action legislation, and Wood (2000) argues that what might be seen as weaknesses in the statutory recognition procedure can be understood in terms of a desire to promote partnership approaches.

The term partnership echoes European terminology, but the Labour government has been reluctant to adopt a European model of social partnership. There has been some partnership-type engagement over the detail of controversial legislation, as indicated above, but no introduction of representative structures with mechanisms for employee voice at workplace and strategic levels of the kind found elsewhere in Europe. We described earlier the UK government's ad hoc approach to addressing the representation gap in non-union workplaces in order to implement European requirements for employer consultation with worker representatives over a growing range of issues, and noted its initial opposition to the proposed EU directive on national information and consultation rules.

The British and Irish governments resisted the directive for as long as possible on the grounds that Continental European systems of formalized, representative employee consultation are not appropriate to the 'voluntarist' Anglo-Saxon traditions of industrial relations. As this and other statements indicate, voluntarism remains a touchstone, if no longer the keystone, for British industrial relations. The term, however, has undergone subtle shifts in meaning, and for some means 'leaving it to employers', or simply 'no legal regulation'; the other aspect – allowing the free play of collective forces and supporting collective bargaining – fades from view.

A final settlement?

In his foreword to *FAW*, Prime Minister Tony Blair stated that the legislation to implement the White Paper – the ERA 1999 – would 'draw a line under the issue of industrial relations law', and represent 'an industrial relations settlement for this Parliament'. The party's manifesto for the 2001 election proposed few further labour law reforms of major significance. But, as the discussion above indicates, it is clear that the labour law 'settlement' claimed by the government is unlikely to be final, not least as the continuing influence of EU-level social policy developments will inevitably mean a more substantial agenda for reform.

Although important, to date the impact of EU legislation has been limited to certain issues. This is codified in the 'Social Chapter' of the EU treaty which identifies a range of subjects on which directives are subject to qualified majority vote by the Council and 'co-decision with the European Parliament (among them working conditions, information and consultation, and sex equality), and others in which directives require unanimous Council voting (including social security, workers' rights on termination of employment and collective represent-ation, including co-determination). Certain key issues are specifically excluded from the field of Community action, that is, pay, the right of association, the right to strike and the right to impose lock-outs. For some commentators, devel-opments such as the adoption of the EU charter of fundamental social rights in 2000 raise the prospect of more extensive EU influence in key areas such as strikes and collective bargaining in the future. The scope for this to happen may depend on the outcome of continued inter-governmental discussion of the status of the charter. The UK government, encouraged by the CBI, has been seeking to ensure that charter does not become legally binding by incorporation into the EU treaties, and that it is declaratory only. However, whatever uncertainties remain about the precise status of the charter, its provisions may still be influ-ential on the ECJ's approach to relevant cases and contribute more generally to the broadening of the EU's social policy agenda and its continuing impact on labour law and industrial relations in Britain.

References

ACAS (Advisory, Conciliation and Arbitration Service) 2001: *Annual Report 2000–2001*. London: ACAS.

Anderman, S. 1986: Unfair dismissals and redundancy. In R. Lewis (ed.), *Labour Law in Britain*. Oxford: Blackwell.

Auerbach, S. 1990: *Legislating for Conflict*. Oxford: Clarendon Press.

Bain, G. S. 1999: The national minimum wage: further reflections, *Employee Relations*, 21 (1), 15–25.

Brown, W. 2000: Putting partnership into practice in Britain, *British Journal of Industrial Relations*, 38 (2), 299–316.

Burchell, B., Deakin, S. and Honey, S. 1999: *The Employment Status of Individuals in Non-standard Employment*. Employment Relations Research Series 6, London: DTI. Available at <www.dti.gov.uk/er/emar>.

Carley, M., and Hall, M. 2000: The implementation of the European Works Councils Directive, *Industrial Law Journal*, 29 (2), 103–24.

CAC (Central Arbitration Committee) 2001: *Annual Report 2000/01*. London: CAC.

CBI (Confederation of British Industry) 2000: *Cutting through Red Tape*. London: CBI.

Claydon, T. 1996: Union derecognition: a re-examination. In I. Beardwell (ed.), *Contemporary Industrial Relations*. Oxford: Oxford University Press.

Cully, M., Woodland, S. O'Reilly, A. and Dix, G. 1999: *Britain at Work as Depicted by the 1998 Workplace Employee Relations Survey*. London: Routledge.

Davics, P. 1992: The emergence of European labour law. In W. McCarthy (ed.), *Legal Intervention in Industrial Relations*. Oxford: Blackwell.

Davies, P., and Freedland, M. 1984: *Labour Law: Text and Materials*. 2nd edn. London: Weidenfeld & Nicolson.

Davies, P., and Freedland, M. 1993: *Labour Legislation and Public Policy*. Oxford: Clarendon Press.

DE (Department of Employment) 1986: *Building Businesses . . . Not Barriers*. London: HMSO.

DE 1989: *Removing Barriers to Employment*. London: HMSO.

Deakin, S. 1990: Equality under a market order: the Employment Act 1989. *Industrial Law Journal*, 19 (1), 1–19.

Deakin, S., and Wilkinson, F. 1994: Rights vs. efficiency? The economic case for transnational labour standards, *Industrial Law Journal*, 23 (3), 289–310.

Dickens, L. 1983: The Advisory, Conciliation and Arbitration Service: regulation and voluntarism in industrial relations. In R. Baldwin and C. McCrudden (eds), *Regulation and Public Law*. London: Weidenfeld & Nicolson.

Dickens, L. 1987: Advisory Conciliation and Arbitration Service: regulation and voluntarism in industrial relations. In R. Baldwin and C. McCrudden (eds), *Regulation and Public Law*. London: Weidenfeld & Nicolson.

Dickens, L. 1992: Anti-discrimination legislation: exploring and explaining the impact on women's employment. In W. McCarthy (ed.), *Legal Intervention in Industrial Relations*. Oxford: Blackwell.

Dickens, L. 1994: Deregulation and employment rights in Great Britain. In R. Rogowski and T. Wilthagen (eds), *Reflexive Labour Law*. Deventer: Kluwer.

Dickens, L. 1999: Beyond the business case: a three pronged approach to equality action, *Human Resource Management Journal*, 9 (1), 9–19.

Dickens, L. 2000: Doing more with less: ACAS and individual conciliation. In B. Towers and W. Brown (eds), *Employment Relations in Britain. 25 Years of the Advisory Conciliation and Arbitration Service*. Oxford: Blackwell.

Dickens, L., and Bain, G. 1986: A duty to bargain? Union recognition and information disclosure. In R. Lewis (ed.), *Labour Law in Britain*. Oxford: Blackwell.

Dickens, L., and Hall, M. 1995: The state, labour law and industrial relations. In P. Edwards (ed.), *Industrial Relations: Theory and Practice in Britain*. Oxford: Blackwell.

Dickens, L., Weekes, B., Jones, M. and Hart, M. 1985: *Dismissed: A Study of Unfair Dismissal and the Industrial Tribunal System*. Oxford: Blackwell.

Disney, R., and Szyszczak, E. 1989: Part-time work: a reply to Catherine Hakim, *Industrial Law Journal*, 18 (4), 223–9.

DTI (Department of Trade and Industry) 1998: *Fairness at Work*. Cm 2968. London: HMSO.

DTI 2001: *Routes to Resolution: Improving Dispute Resolution in Britain*. London: HMSO.

Dunn, S., and Metcalf, D. 1996: Trade union law since 1979. In I. Beardwell (ed.), *Contemporary Industrial Relations*. Oxford: Oxford University Press.

Elgar, J., and Simpson, B. 1993: *Union Negotiators, Industrial Action and the Law*. Mimeo. London School of Economics.

EOC (Equal Opportunities Commission) 1990: *Equal Pay for Men and Women: Strengthening the Acts*. Manchester: EOC.

EOC 1998: *Equality in the 21st Century: A New Approach* Manchester: EOC.

EOR 2001: Compulsory pay reviews proposed by task force, *Equal Opportunities Review*, 96 (March/April), 36–43.

Forrest, H. 1980: Political values in individual employment law. *Modern Law Review*, 43, (4), 361–80.

Fredman, S. 1992: The new right: labour law and ideology in the Thatcher years, *Oxford Journal of Legal Studies*, 12 (1), 24–44.

Fredman, S. 2001: Equality: a new generation? *Industrial Law Journal*, 30 (2), 145–68.

Freedland, M. 1999: Labour law beyond the horizon, *Industrial Law Journal*, 28 (2), 197–200.

Freeman, R., and Pelletier, J. 1990: The impact of industrial relations legislation on British union density. *British Journal of Industrial Relations*, 28 (2), 141–64.

Gall, G., and McKay, S. 1999: Developments in union recognition and derecognition in Britain, 1994–1998, *British Journal of Industrial Relations*, 37 (4), 601–14.

Hakim, C. 1989: Employment rights: a comparison of full-time and part-time employees. *Industrial Law Journal*, 18 (2), 69–83.

Hall, M. 1994: Industrial relations and the social dimension of European integration: before and after Maastricht. In R. Hyman and A. Ferner (eds), *New Frontiers in European Industrial Relations*. Oxford: Blackwell.

Hall, M. 2000: 'New right for workers to be accompanied at disciplinary and grievance hearings', *EIRObserver*, 6'00, 13–14. <www.eiro.eurofound.eu.int>

Hall, M., and Edwards, P. 1999: 'Reforming the statutory redundancy consultation procedure', *Industrial Law Journal*, 28 (4), 299–319.

Hall, M., Lister R. and Sisson, K. 1998: *The New Law on Working Time: Managing the Implications of the 1998 Working Time Regulations*. London and Coventry: IRS and IRRU.

Hall, M., and Sisson, K. 1997: *Time for Change? Coming to Terms with the EU Working Time Directive*. London and Coventry: IRS and IRRU.

Hepple, B. 2000: Supporting collective bargaining: some comparative reflections. In B. Towers and W. Brown (eds), *Employment Relations in Britain. 25 Years of the Advisory Conciliation and Arbitration Service*. Oxford: Blackwell.

Hepple, B., Coussey, M. and Choudbury, T. 2000: *Equality: A New Framework*. University of Cambridge Centre of Public Law and Judge Institute of Management Studies.

Hewitt, P. 2001: Business and society: roles and responsibilities. Speech to Guardian/Observer Conference, 9 July.

Hitner, T. et al. 1982: *Racial Minority Employment: Equal Opportunity Employment Policy and Practices*. Department of Employment Research Paper 35. London: HMSO.

Hyman, R. 1996: Is there a case for statutory works councils in Britain? In A. McColgan (ed.), *The Future of Labour Law*. London: Cassell.

IDS 2001: Statutory trade union recognition, *IDS Briefing*, 692 (September), 3–5.

James, P., and Walters, D. 1997: Non-union rights of involvement: the case of health and safety at work, *Industrial Law Journal*, 26 (1), 35–50.

Kahn-Freund, O. 1954: Legal framework. In A. Flanders and H. A. Clegg (eds), *The System of Industrial Relations in Great Britain*. Oxford: Blackwell.

Kahn-Freund, O. 1983: *Labour and the Law*. 3rd edn, ed. P. L. Davies and M. Freedland. London: Stevens.

Kelly, J. 1996: Works councils: union advance or marginalisation? In A.McColgan (ed.), *The Future of Labour Law*. London: Cassell.

Knight, K., and Latreille, P. 2000: Discipline, dismissals and complaints to employment tribunals, *British Journal of Industrial Relations*, 38 (4), 533–55.

Labour Market Trends 1999: Employment tribunal and Employment Appeal Tribunal statistics 1997–98 and 1998–99, *Labour Market Trends*, September, 493–7.

Marquand, D. 1998: 'The Blair paradox', *Prospect*, May.

McCarthy, W. (Lord) 1992: The rise and fall of collective laissez faire. In W. McCarthy (ed.), *Legal Intervention in Industrial Relations*. Oxford: Blackwell.

McCarthy, W. (Lord) 1999: *Fairness at Work and Trade Union Recognition: Past Comparisons and Future Problems*. London: Institute of Employment Rights.

McCarthy, W. (Lord) 2000: Representative consultations with specified employees: or the future of rung two. In H. Collins, P. Davies and R. Rideout (eds), *Legal Regulation of the Employment Relation*. Deventer: Kluwer.

McIlroy, J. 1999: Unfinished business: the reform of strike legislation in Britain, *Employee Relations*, 21 (6), 521–39.

McKendrick, E. 1988: The rights of trade union members: Part 1 of the Employment Act 1988, *Industrial Law Journal*, 17 (3), 141–61.

Napier, B. 1992: Computerisation and employment rights, *Industrial Law Journal*, 21 (1), 1–14.

Royal Commission on Trade Unions and Employers' Associations 1968: Report. Cmnd 3623. London: HMSO.

Simpson, B. 1998: Fairness at work, *Industrial Law Journal*, 27 (3), 245–53.

Simpson, B. 1999a: A milestone in the legal regulation of pay: the National Minimum Wage Act 1998, *Industrial Law Journal*, 28 (1), 1–32.

Simpson, B. 1999b: Implementing the National Minimum Wage: the 1999 regulations, *Industrial Law Journal*, 28 (2), 171–82.

Simpson, B. 2000: Trade union recognition and the law: a new approach, *Industrial Law Journal*, 29 (3), 193–222.

Simpson, B. 2001: *Building on the National Minimum Wage*. London: Institute of Employment Rights.

Smith, P., and Morton, G. 2001: New Labour's reform of Britain's employment law: the devil is not only in the detail but in the values and policy too, *British Journal of Industrial Relations*, 39 (1), 119–38.

TUC/CBI 1997: *Statutory Trade Union Recognition: Joint Statement by TUC and CBI*. London: TUC/CBI.

Turnbull, P., and Wass, V. 1997: Job insecurity and labour market lemons: the (mis)management of redundancy in steel-making, coal mines and port transport, *Journal of Management Studies*, 34 (1), 27–51.

Undy, R. 1999: New Labour's 'industrial relations settlement': the third way? Annual review article, *British Journal of Industrial Relations*, 37 (2), 315–36.

Wedderburn, K. W. (Lord) 1998: A British duty to bargain: a footnote on the end-game, *Industrial Law Journal*, 27 (3), 253.

Weekes B., Mellish. M., Dickens, L. and Lloyd, J. 1975: *Industrial Relations and the Limits of Law.* Oxford: Blackwell.

Wood, S. 2000: Learning through ACAS: the case of statutory recognition. In B. Towers and W. Brown (eds), *Employment Relations in Britain. 25 Years of the Advisory Conciliation and Arbitration Service,* Oxford: Blackwell.

Wood, S., and Godard, J. 1999: The statutory union recognition procedure in the employment relations bill: a comparative analysis, *British Journal of Industrial Relations,* 37 (2), 203–44.

7
MANAGEMENT: SYSTEMS, STRUCTURES AND STRATEGY

KEITH SISSON AND PAUL MARGINSON

In recent years there has been a dramatic change in the treatment of management in the industrial relations literature. Until the 1980s most commentators paid no more than perfunctory attention to it. This reflected the view that, compared to trade unions and the state, management was a relatively unproblematic, if not necessarily unimportant, industrial relations actor: it seemed to have settled for a particular way of doing things and to be more concerned with maintaining the status quo than with changing it. Since the beginning of the 1980s, instead of responding to government and trade unions, management has been taking more initiatives, leading some commentators to suggest that it is now the critical actor in industrial relations.

This chapter is concerned with some of the key issues to have emerged as a result of the increasing activity of, and growing attention paid to, management in industrial relations. The first is management's role in industrial relations. Three main models of how it is conceived are identified and considered: *the systems actor*, *the strategic actor* and *the agent of capital*. The second issue is the nature and extent of the changes in management's approach. Here particular attention is paid to the influential concepts of the flexible organization, 'high-commitment management' and 'partnership' before going on to consider the realities of management industrial relations decision-making. The third issue is the variety of management industrial relations practice and how sense can be made of it. Here the focus is on the influence of such variables as occupation, sector, size, ownership, along with the associated business strategies, structures and styles of organizations. The final section looks at some of the major industrial relations challenges British management is likely to face in the foreseeable future.

Three Models of Management's Role

A systems actor

The first, and dominant, model of management's role is firmly rooted within the industrial relations tradition. It is most clearly expressed in Dunlop's (1958) *Industrial Relations Systems*. Management is seen as only one of a number of actors working within a system of institutions, processes and rules which, in turn, are shaped by technology and markets. Other actors in the system, notably the state and trade unions, are seen as equally, if not more, important in shaping the development of the system. It is the policies and approaches of the state and trade unions, for example, which are seen as largely shaping the structure of collective bargaining. Management reacts to the pressures that come from the other two and have to work with the constraints that the subsequent compromises entail. For the most part, however, they do not do this under duress. The assumption is that management shares the same interests – or 'ideology' in Dunlop's word – of the state and trade unions in having a relatively stable framework of the 'rule of law' within which it can get on with the job of managing its affairs as efficiently as possible.

Although it wields considerable influence, this model focuses on relations with trade unions rather than the management of the employment relationship more generally. It also treats industrial relations as a self-contained world in isolation from wider strategic objectives. The role of management in industrial relations thus tends to be accorded less attention than it deserves. Even its motivation for working within the industrial relations 'system' had not been properly explored. For example, employers in many countries have used multi-employer bargaining to help to neutralize the workplace from trade union activity, yet the active managerial role in doing so and the links with the wider objective of maintaining the stability of the employment relationship have begun to be appreciated only recently (Sisson 1987; Gospel 1992).

A different and more recent version of the systems model, which acknowledges the influence of differing production and organizational systems, is that of Maurice and his colleagues (1986). Especially important in this so-called 'societal approach' is the complex process of interaction between the parties, which is shaped by the pattern of industrialization. Thus, for example, the different approaches of management in France and Germany towards training are explained in terms of the occupational stratification within workplaces in the two countries as well as the different status accorded to education as opposed to training in the wider society. In France there is a greater reliance on non-manual employees, and education carries the higher status, whereas in Germany there is a higher proportion of manual employees and the qualifications from training are held in high regard.

The implication, that management's behaviour cannot simply be explained in terms of technology or markets, but only understood in terms of management's specific institutional and historical experience, is especially important. In the case of the UK, two sets of features in the complex of institutions, processes and rules making up the national industrial relations system go a long way in helping us to understand management's behaviour:

- the tradition of 'voluntarism' discussed in chapter 2, which has shaped virtually every area of UK employment relations and which means that the legal framework of rights and obligations (individual and collective) is much less influential than in most other countries; and
- a highly decentralized and diverse structure of collective bargaining, deeply embedded in procedural rather than substantive rules, which means that, save for a few exceptions, the UK no longer possesses the detailed multi-employer agreements that supplement and extend the legislative framework in most other EU member countries.

Alongside this, there is a widely held view that the approach of UK management in industrial relations has been influenced strongly by the Anglo-Saxon system of corporate governance which has an orientation to short-term results (see, for example, Coates 2000; Sisson 1989; Keep and Mayhew 1998). The most important features may be summarized as follows:

- a privileged position for shareholders and an overwhelming emphasis on shareholder value as the key business driver as opposed to the interests of other stakeholders;
- a high concentration of institutional share ownership by investment trusts and pension funds which encourages a focus on short-term profitability, rather than long-term market share or added value, as the key index of business performance;
- relative ease of take-over, which not only reinforces the pressure on short-term profitability to maintain share price, but also encourages expansion by acquisition and merger rather than by internal growth;
- a premium on 'financial engineering' as the core organizational competence, and the domination of financial management over other functions.

The result, it has been argued, is an approach which treats employees as liabilities and a cost to be minimized, rather than as assets and a resource to be nurtured and developed (Marginson and Sisson 1994). This stands in contrast to the Continental European 'insider' systems of corporate governance, with their emphasis on rights for stakeholders (including employees) other than shareholders; less developed stock markets; concentrations of inter-corporate and family ownership stakes; and constraints on hostile take-over. The result is an approach by management which places greater emphasis on long-term performance, and where employees are more likely to be treated as resources than liabilities.

Like Dunlop's systems model, however, the 'societal' approach has considerable problems in accounting for change, and in particular change that is driven by management. This helps to explain why both variants of the model have attracted particular criticism in Britain and the USA. The 'system' of industrial relations is less institutionalized and/or centralized than it is in many Continental European countries and, throughout the 1980s and early 1990s, the pace of management-driven change appears to have been much greater.

A strategic actor

The second model has largely developed out of the first, although it has also been influenced by the wider recognition accorded to the importance of strategy and strategic choice in social behaviour (Mintzberg et al. 1998). Rather than being regarded as members of an interlocking system working to its own internal logic, the parties to industrial relations – management, trade unions and governments – are seen as 'agents' who shape the environment in which they operate and who are also influenced by forces from outside industrial relations itself. By implication, the environment does not determine behaviour; the parties – above all, the management of the large companies so important in shaping the framework of industrial relations – have some discretion or choice in deciding what courses of action or strategies to follow.

The most explicit use of the strategic choice approach is to be found in the work of Kochan and his colleagues in the USA (1986) where it is almost elevated to the status of a theory (see also Poole 1986). Management is seen as a *strategic actor* in two particular senses: its actions are held to be critical not only in determining the main changes taking place in industrial relations, but also in the choice of business strategy to be pursued. Thus US management, faced with intensifying international competition, was said to be confronted with the choice of pursuing a strategy of either quality or low cost. Both routes involved making radical changes in existing industrial relations arrangements and, in particular, in the provisions for collective bargaining of the 'New Deal' system dating back to the 1930s.

Although the approach's focus on the purposive behaviour of the parties, rather than on the outcome of some form of autonomous system working to its own logic, has been a positive step, critics argue that it makes a number of highly questionable assumptions. One is that strategy formulation is a straightforward process. To the contrary, as business theorists increasingly recognize, strategy is a most problematic concept (see, for example, the review in Whittington 1993). At best, strategies, understood as a sense of a direction, emerge as a result of a series of decisions made by people at many levels in the organization; they involve continual reassessments and readjustments of position. Depending on the particular ways in which management runs the organization, strategies, in the sense of a set of medium- and long-term plans, may not emerge at all; there may simply be a series of vague statements or a few key financial ratios. In the circumstances, it may not be feasible to expect the detailed integration of personnel policies and practices implied in the prescription of Kochan and his colleagues, let alone the fundamental shift in attitudes and behaviours entailed, for example, in managing a change in culture or task participation.

A second, crucial, assumption is that managers have the degree of choice with which they are credited. Clearly, managers, especially those who run large private sector companies, have enormous resources at their disposal and a significant measure of control over large numbers of employees. Yet, the evidence suggests, they still may not be willing or able to shape their environment in ways that may seem logical to the analyst. Pressure to deliver short-term profits, for example, may militate against making the investments necessary for a quality strategy. The key point that many proponents of the strategic choice model neglect is that choices are not made in a vacuum. The notion of strategic choice implies, at the very least, circumstances over which even chief executives do not have total control. As the systems actor model reminds us, the structures within which this choice is exercised are profoundly important: they can support or hinder the development of particular approaches.

An agent of capital

The third model comes from outside the industrial relations tradition. It appears in both neo-classical economics and radical theories of capitalist production (see Gospel and Palmer 1993: 37). Whereas in the first case the implications tend to be implicit, in the second they are usually very explicit. Basically, this model sees management as an agent that is obliged by the 'laws' of the market to treat the workforce as a factor of production. As with the other factors of production, management must have primary regard to its costs. This does not necessarily mean that management will always be driven to minimize wages; the main concern, as will be explained below, is with unit labour costs (that is, labour cost per unit of production). The model does nonetheless imply that the efficiency with which human resources are used will be of overriding concern. It is therefore extended to 'not-for-profit' organizations such as publicly owned services and voluntary organizations, even though ownership relations are very different from the typical capitalist enterprise with its shareholders.

There have also been significant developments in recent years which have gone a long way to dealing with what was the main weakness of the model, namely its difficulty in dealing with the diversity of management behaviour allowing for similar technology and markets. Thus, efficiency wage theorists (see chapter 8) have recognized that management may pay higher wages than competitors, as Henry Ford did in the USA in 1914, or provide superior welfare conditions, as Quaker families did at the turn of the century in Britain, in order to generate higher productivity. Likewise proponents of the 'new institutional economics' have recognized that many of the industrial relations arrangements that their neo-classical colleagues have seen as impediments to the 'proper' working of the labour market, such as systems of job evaluation, lifelong employment, procedures for consultation and negotiation, and compulsory training provisions, can bring significant benefits in terms of economic efficiency (Lazear 1995; Williamson 1985).

For their part, writers in the radical tradition have recognized that management has to find ways and means of legitimating its authority in the eyes of the workforce in order to get them to do the job that it wants. This is why management is usually willing to introduce a 'rule of law': the policies, practices and procedures of selection, training and development, appraisal, pay systems and pay structures, which supplement or replace the direct control by individual managers and the technical controls of machines and processes of operations. This is also why, rather than deciding the 'rule of law' unilaterally, management has been prepared to give workers or their representatives a say in making and administering it in the form of collective bargaining.

There has also been a differentiation between management approaches in which the primary emphasis is on securing effort from the workforce through detailed supervision and strict discipline, what Friedman (1977) terms a regime of 'direct control', and those which emphasize management's need to release the creativity of the workforce and elicit productivity through yielding a measure of discretion to employees over the organization and performance of work, or a regime of 'responsible autonomy'. By implication, however, a regime of 'responsible autonomy' is contingent on a particular set of market circumstances: it is not an end in itself.

Thus this model of management has sought to explain many of the recent initiatives being undertaken by management in terms of a reassertion of control. According to Burawoy (1985), many of the developments associated with HRM involve new and much subtler forms of indirect control based on appraisal and performance measurement. Moreover, the retreat from bureaucracy is not as altruistic as it is often presented: many of the bureaucratic controls developed in the wake of 'Fordism' and 'Taylorism', says Burawoy (1985: 263), had 'established constraints on the deployment of capital, whether by tying wages to profits or by creating internal labour markets, collective bargaining and grievance machinery which hamstrung management's domination of the workplace'. Such constraints are no longer acceptable under conditions of increasing global competition, which explains why management is supporting the deregulation of the labour market and rolling back the influence of trade unions.

Conclusions

Each of the models offers valuable insights, but is not sufficient in itself. The complexity of the issues that have to be taken into account in understanding management's role is considerable. Management is a critical actor and efficiency is fundamental to its actions. Institutions contribute to and shape this search for efficiency, however. Management and managers cannot be abstracted from the wider contexts in which they operate. These, as the next sections point out, are extremely diverse. The result is that management practice is also characterized by great complexity and variety. Nonetheless, a framework in terms of the context of existing relationships and their constraints on behaviour (systems model), the range of choices open and the uncertainties of strategy formulations (strategic choice) and pressures to contain costs and raise efficiency ('agent of capital' view) helps to order some of the complexity of empirical developments.

Recipes and Realities

In recent years, a bewildering array of new concepts and practices has emerged, reflecting views about what management is doing or should be doing to improve its performance in managing employees. The context has been set by intensifying competition brought about by developments such as trade liberalization (e.g. the European Single Market and World Trade Agreements), the emergence of a world market for capital, the growth in the number and significance of multinational companies (MNCs) discussed in chapter 4, the deregulation and privatization of many publicly owned corporations and the widespread diffusion of information technology. In this environment, it is argued, management is adopting or needs to adopt structures and processes that make it possible to continuously improve the products and services available to the customer. Supposedly new organizational forms have been canvassed, emphasizing 'federal', 'network', 'cluster', 'horizontal' and 'virtual' structures. Meanwhile, management has been encouraged to think in terms of 'business process re-engineering' (BPR), 'total quality management' (TQM), 'lean production', 'agile production' and not just 'human resource management' (HRM), but 'high-commitment' or 'high-involvement' management (HCM or HIM).

Figure 7.1 tries to capture the prima facie logic underlying the various types of restructuring advocated within conventional organizational boundaries. On the horizontal axes are the dimension of centralized to decentralized (at the top) and the size dimension (at the bottom). On the vertical axes are the dimensions from 'directive' to 'autonomous' (on the left) and from 'fat' to 'lean' (on the right).

For illustrative purposes, a selection of different organizational arrangements is shown. At the bottom left, the bureaucratic form is located to suggest a centralized, directive mode. Ascending the ladder and moving rightwards, one

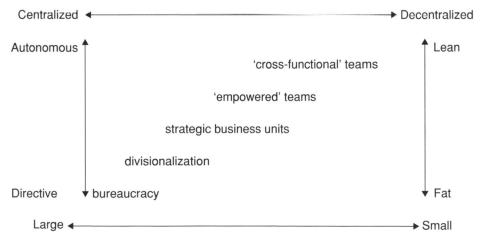

Figure 7.1   Restructuring within conventional organizational boundaries
Source: Based on Mabey et al. (1998: 235).

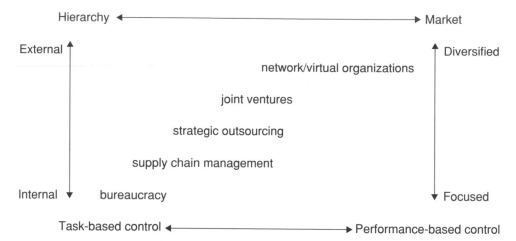

Figure 7.2   Restructuring beyond conventional organizational boundaries
Source: Based on Mabey et al. (1998: 236).

progressively moves to divisionalized arrangements, strategic business units (SBUs), autonomous empowered teams associated with new production arrangements such as cellular manufacturing and flexible manufacturing systems and cross-functional teams resulting for example from the integration of product design and development with manufacturing.

Figure 7.2 focuses on the developments beyond the confines of conventional organizational boundaries leading to the so-called 'extended organization' (Colling 2000). Again, there are four dimensions. The first, running along the top of the figure, illustrates the continuum from hierarchical relations at one end to open market relations at the other. The second dimension, located at the bottom of the figure, depicts the continuum between task-based control and performance-based control. The third dimension, located on the left-hand vertical axis, shows the spectrum from internal to external relationships. The fourth, on the right-hand side of the figure, relates to the complexity of the organization's activities and ranges from the relatively straightforward, or 'focused', to the relatively complex, or 'diversified'. In this case, starting at the bottom left of the figure, the bureaucratic form of organization can be seen as characterized by an emphasis on internal relationships, a hierarchical command structure and a mainly task-based set of control criteria. Progressing up the ladder, supply chain management/process engineering, strategic outsourcing, joint ventures, and networks are shown to represent, and result from, varying degrees of shift along each of the dimensions.

In general, as chapter 13 argues in detail, movement upwards and to the right in both figures represents a shift from the control of production and the performance of work away from direct mechanisms emanating from a single corporate centre towards indirect, devolved and networked forms of control. Accompanying these changes, management has been encouraged to take a much more strategic approach to managing human resources. There are many definitions of 'human resource management' and the term continues to be surrounded by controversy (Bach and Sisson 2000: 11–16). As well as a greater emphasis on planning than in other approaches, most embrace a number of common elements:

- the assumption of responsibility by senior line management, reflecting the view that people are a strategic resource for achieving competitive advantage;
- a stress on the coherence of personnel policies and their integration with business planning more generally;
- a proactive rather than reactive approach;
- a shift in emphasis from management–trade union relations to management–employee relations;
- a stress on the commitment and the exercise of initiative on the part of employees, with managers assuming the role of 'enabler' or 'facilitator'.

Further, in circumstances where organizations are unionized and collective agreements are well established, movement towards the upper-right-hand areas of figures 7.1 and 7.2 is likely to require that management address the collective interests of employees and introduce changes in co-operation with their representatives. It is in this context that the adoption of 'partnership' arrangements between management and trade unions has increasingly been advocated as a means of securing organizational change by simultaneously reworking the basis for collective relations between management and employees and the trade unions which represent them.

Our task in the remainder of this section is to consider the impact of these new organizational concepts on the organization of work, working practices and industrial relations. Three main areas are selected for attention: the 'flexible organization', 'high-commitment management' and 'partnership'. The first involves movement towards the autonomous and decentralized ends of the vertical and horizontal axes, respectively, in figure 7.1 and a shift away from the internal and the hierarchical poles in figure 7.2. High-commitment management is, in the eyes of many commentators, associated with movement towards autonomous and lean forms of work organization in figure 7.1 and an emphasis on performance- rather than task-based control in figure 7.2. 'Partnership' does not map onto either of the two figures, because they neglect the collective aspects of work relations as discussed further in chapter 12.

The flexible organization

The issue of workforce flexibility has been central to both the scientific and the policy debate. A key distinction is between external and internal forms of flexibility. A study across 10 European countries (European Foundation 1999: 4) found that the essential features of the two approaches were:

- *External flexibility* is the ability of the organization to adjust the volume of work undertaken, and therefore the amount of labour engaged, to meet peaks and troughs in demand through the use of external contractors and/or workers. It can involve the use of outsourcing, subcontracting, self-employment and the engagement of temporary agency workers. It also covers the employment of temporary workers.

* *Internal flexibility* is the ability to adjust to fluctuations in demand, and to deploy labour to best effect, through forms of task and temporal flexibility within the organization. In terms of task flexibility it involves job rotation, delegation of responsibility and the use of teams, together with an emphasis on continuing training to enable employees to acquire new skills and competencies. Temporal flexibility is obtained via flexible working time arrangements for full-time workers, such as annualized hours and use of working time corridors, and through part-time working arrangements.

Earlier work, encapsulated in the influential 'flexible firm' model proposed by Atkinson (Atkinson 1984; Atkinson and Meager 1986), drew a distinction between 'numerical' and 'functional' forms of flexibility. Essentially, the model involved seeing the workforce in terms of a 'core' and 'periphery'. The core is made up of a numerically stable group of employees responsible for the organization's critical firm-specific activities who work in a functionally (or task-) flexible manner. The periphery comprises numerically flexible groups of workers with part-time and/or temporary contracts, along with the employees of subcontractors, whose activities are not critical to the organization. Under conditions of increased market demand, the periphery expands; under reverse conditions, the periphery contracts. The core workforce by contrast is shielded from market fluctuations.

The crucial conceptual difference between the two approaches is in the labelling of activities, and therefore the workforce concerned, as either 'core' or 'periphery'. Early critics of the 'flexible firm' model underlined, for instance, the extent to which 'core' activities in organizations in the service sector were undertaken by part-time workers (Pollert 1988). Moreover, the extent to which such workers were numerically flexible, in the sense of being subject to repeated changes in working hours, was also questioned. More recently, Ackroyd and Procter (1998), demonstrate how in the manufacturing sector both 'numerical' (or 'external') and 'functional' (or 'internal') forms of flexibility intrude into core activities. Analysing the 1998 WERS, Cully et al. (1999: 35–8) show how far the use of temporary contracts and agency workers has extended into the core, but find that with the exception of subcontracting, the use of external forms of flexibility is negatively correlated with the use of internal forms, suggesting that organizations are tending to emphasize one or other approach, but not both.

In terms of take-up of external forms of flexibility, there has certainly been growth in the different forms of so-called atypical or non-standard forms of employment. Self-employment increased from 8 per cent of the workforce in the mid-1980s to 13 per cent ten years later, at which level it has remained. The proportion of the workforce on temporary contracts remained at 5 per cent until

1990, but has grown to 7 per cent since. This is reflected in a leap in the proportion of workplaces engaging employees on fixed-term contracts of less than 12 months' duration, up from 22 per cent in 1990 to 35 per cent in 1998 (Millward et al. 2000: 47). A greater proportion of workplaces are using temporary agency workers than 20 years ago: 28 per cent in 1998 as compared with 20 per cent in 1980 (Millward et al. 2000: 47). Meadows (1999: 5) reports that around 1 million workers are on agency placements at any one time, representing 4 per cent of the workforce. There has also been growth in outsourcing. Subcontracting of at least one activity to another organization, already widespread in 1990 at 72 per cent (Millward et al. 1992: 340) had become practically universal by the end of the decade, being reported by 91 per cent of workplaces in 1998 (Cully et al. 1999: 35). Colling's (2000: 74–6) detailed analysis suggests an increase in the proportion of workplaces putting out activities such as cleaning, security, transport and maintenance. Less clear, however, is whether things have gone beyond these essentially ancillary services to mainstream activities.

Turning to internal forms of flexibility, most obvious is the growth in part-time work. The proportion of the workforce working part-time grew from 21 to 26 per cent during the 1980s, but has plateaued at this level thereafter. Most striking during the 1990s has been the increase in the number of workplaces where 50 per cent or more of the workforce are part-time, which doubled to 27 per cent of all workplaces comparing 1990 with 1998 (Millward et al. 2000: 44). Other forms of working-time flexibility are much less in evidence. Indeed, the Labour Force Survey suggests fewer than one in four people had any flexible working arrangements – the numbers with annual hours arrangements, for example, being less than 5 per cent (Labour Market Trends 1997).

There is also mixed evidence for the practices that have come to be associated with task or functional flexibility. As discussed in chapter 13, in the case of teamwork, the proportion of workplaces with some type of teamwork is substantial, but numbers fall sharply when more advanced approaches are considered. Likewise, chapter 15 points to continuing issues over the extent and quality of training. In short, flexibility is widely evident, but its use can, as Legge (2000) points out, be associated with cost-cutting in line with the views of the 'agent of capital' approach, while firms' mixed approaches to flexibility suggest that 'strategic choice' in this area has been highly variable and contingent.

High-commitment management

As well as seeking the greater adaptability associated with internal flexibility from their workforces, organizations are increasingly said to be adopting practices aimed at eliciting their active commitment. The emphasis on securing the commitment of individual employees, which is at the heart of many of the recipes of HRM, has both intellectual and pragmatic roots. Intellectually, the main source is the 'neo-human relations' school, which goes back to the work of Herzberg (1966) and McGregor (1960). In McGregor's formulation, which has become almost the staple diet of management courses, two contrasting styles or approaches are presented: Theory X and Theory Y. Most managers start from Theory X, the scientific management approach, which holds that individuals are motivated simply by financial self-interest and have to be controlled and directed. The problem is that this brings about resentment and resistance and so is self-defeating. Much more preferable is Theory Y, which holds that individuals have higher growth needs, including independence, responsibility and recognition of their contribution. Management should design jobs that are as interesting and meaningful as possible and promote individuals' involvement and participation, and they will respond with their creativity as well as hard work and energy.

Although the thinking has a long history, it is the severe economic pressures confronting most industrialized countries in recent years that lie behind the present interest. Especially relevant is the emergence of the so-called 'resource-based' view of the organization. This argues that organizations comprise unique bundles of assets and that access to these, plus the ability to make effective use of them, provides the essential source of a firm's competitive advantage (Barney 1991; Grant 1991, 1995; Hamel and Prahalad 1994). Developed economies, it is argued, cannot hope to compete solely in terms of cost with competitors in eastern Europe and the Far East, let alone the Third World. Instead, the emphasis needs to be on quality products and services. Not only will these satisfy the growing demand for more specialized niche goods, but, more fundamentally, they make it possible to build on employees' long-standing demands for more challenging and rewarding jobs and exploit their higher education and skills to contribute to the process of continuous improvement. In the words of the European Commission's Green Paper,

> It is about the scope for improving employment and competitiveness through a better organization of work at the workplace, based on high skill, high trust and high quality. It is about the will and ability of management and workers to take initiatives, to improve the quality of goods and services, to make innovations and to develop the production process and consumer relations. (CEC 1997: 2)

A further reason why some organizations have become attracted to the ideas is that they can no longer afford the costly managerial hierarchies required to control 'subordinates'. For example, Overell (1998) describes the situation confronting British Steel (now Corus). Output levels had improved nearly five times since 1977 with substantial and regular job losses, yet still the pressure to do better had mounted, fuelled by the substantial rise in the pound in 1997 and 1998, which threatened to price the company out of many markets. The cornerstone of the survival strategy is delayering and teamwork. Already in many units, 15 levels have been cut back to one with managers themselves being absorbed into teams.

The approach has come to be associated with a number of mutually reinforcing practices. Legge (2000: 59), drawing on a range of authors (Guest 1997; Huselid 1995; MacDuffie 1995; Purcell 1999; Whitfield and Poole 1997; Wood and Albanese 1995; Wood 1996), suggests the following:

- 'trainability' and commitment as key criteria in employee recruitment, selection and promotion;
- extensive use of systems of communication;
- teamworking with flexible job design;
- emphasis on training and learning;
- involvement in operational decision-making with responsibility;
- performance appraisal with tight links to contingent rewards, including promotion;
- job security/no compulsory redundancies.

A growing literature has sought to identify the extent to which such practices are being deployed in 'bundles' (see e.g. Wood 1995; Wood and de Menezes 1998; Ichniowski et al. 1996). Also at issue is whether the high-commitment management model is a universal panacea, as suggested by Walton (1985) and endorsed by Huselid (1995) and Wood (1995), widely applicable in response to the changing competitive circumstances faced by all organizations in the industrialized economies, or whether it is contingent on business strategy, operational strategy (including technology, production organization and management organization) and, reflecting the resource view, the resources at the disposal of the organization (Purcell 1999). Under the first view, which has been predominant, high-commitment management becomes a 'best practice' model. In Purcell's words,

> if high commitment management is universally applicable, only two substantial problems remain to be tackled. First is the need to identify components of HCM. . . . The second problem is one of diffusion. If HRM is 'the most important' area to focus on if managers want to improve organizational performance . . . why do so many firms fail to do so? (1999: 27)

By contrast, under the second view it equates to a 'best fit' approach only applicable in certain types of organization. And there will be other routes to successful organizational performance, which do not involve the HCM bundle of practices. This is underlined by Wood and de Menezes's (1998) finding that organizational performance in 'high' HCM workplaces was no better than that in 'low' HCM workplaces. In a further twist, Ramsay et al. (2000) show from WERS 1998 that the putative mechanism from HCM through employee commitment to outcomes is at best weak, and they suggest (in line with the above critique of strategic choice models) that a key reason may be that managements lack the skills actually to make HCM work.

An authoritative indication of the diffusion of practices associated with HCM is provided in the 1998 WERS report (see table 7.1). Evidently, even the individual practices are far from universal in UK workplaces. Even in the 'best case' in the first column, where there is a personnel specialist and an integrated employee development plan, only six of the 15 practices are practised in a majority of workplaces. Barely half of these workplaces (51 per cent) had single-status arrangements between manual and non-manual employees. In the 'worst case'

Table 7.1 Management practices, by presence of personnel specialist and integrated employee development plan

	% of workplaces			
	Personnel specialist and integrated employee development plan	*Personnel specialist only*	*No personnel specialist or integrated employee development plan*	*All workplaces*
Largest occupational group has:				
Temporary agency workers	19	18	14	18
Employees on fixed-term contracts	38	32	12	28
Personality tests	17	10	5	11
Performance tests	42	34	17	35
Formal off-the-job training for most employees	51	30	18	36
Profit-related pay*	24	14	5	15
Employee share-ownership scheme*	12	10	1	6
Regular appraisals	69	61	31	58
Fully autonomous or semi-autonomous teams	44	33	14	34
Single status for managers and other employees	51	42	22	40
Guaranteed job security	20	14	1	13
Workplace has:				
Formal disciplinary and grievance procedure	97	95	64	88
Group-based team briefings with feedback	65	52	48	59
Most non-managerial employees participate in problem-solving groups	20	11	6	15
Two or more family friendly practices or special leave schemes	59	45	15	41

Based on all workplaces with 25 or more employees.
Figures are weighted and based on responses from between 1,835 and 1,889 managers.
*Profit-related pay and employee share-ownership schemes are based on responses from 1,287 and 1,291 private sector managers respectively.
Source: Cully et al. (1999: table 4.12 (p. 81)). By permission of Routledge.

in the third column, where there is no personnel specialist and no integrated employee development plan, only one of the 15 practices is to be found in a majority of workplaces. Needless to say, this one, a formal disciplinary and grievance procedure, is hardly the epitome of a 'high-commitment management' practice.

Perhaps even more telling, though, are the figures from the First Findings of WERS (Cully et al. 1998: 11) for the total number of practices being used in each workplace. Only one in seven (14 per cent) of workplaces had half or more of the practices. The overall picture is not very different from that emerging from Wood and de Menezes's (1998) more robust, multivariate, analysis of the earlier 1990 survey, which found 11 per cent of workplaces to be 'high' users of a bundle of seven HCM practices. Details of the combination, or 'bundling', of practices in 1998 are also illuminating. Training, teamworking and supervisor training appear to go together, as do individual performance pay, profit-sharing and share ownership. Yet single status is associated with the first cluster but not the second, suggesting that direct participation and financial participation are seen as alternatives rather than complementary, as might have been expected. If, in Peters's (1987: 302–3) uncompromising words, 'the only possible implementers' of a strategy of quality production are 'committed, flexible, multi-skilled, constantly re-trained people, joined together in self-managed teams', many organizations in the UK clearly have a very long way to go. If, however, this is not the strategic objective of large parts of UK enterprise, and if, moreover, organizations do not have the resources to pursue such a strategy of quality production, then the 'best fit' approach would find the relatively low diffusion of HCM unsurprising. Chapter 13 reviews in detail the effects of HCM systems on employees, and chapter 19 the performance implications.

Partnership?

Although some organizations in the UK claiming to be partnership companies, such as Motorola and Unipart, do not recognize trade unions, partnership agreements, along with the wider notion of partnership, have come to imply something like internal flexibility and elements of the high-commitment management model combined with collective employee representation or 'voice'. The TUC (1999: 13) draws on the earlier work of the Involvement and Participation Association (IPA 1992) in identifying six key principles that it believes should underpin the model:

- a shared commitment to the success of the enterprise, including support for flexibility and the replacement of adversarial relations;
- a recognition that interests of the partners may legitimately differ;
- employment security, including measures to improve the employability of staff as well as limit the use of compulsory redundancy;
- a focus on the quality of working life;
- a commitment to transparency, including a real sharing of 'hard, unvarnished information', an openness to discussing plans for the future, genuine

consultation and a preparedness to listen to the business case for alternative
strategies;

• adding value – the 'hallmark of an effective partnership is that it taps into
  sources of commitment and/or resources that were not accessed by previous
  arrangements'.

As the earlier discussion suggested, the essence of partnership is management's acceptance that, in situations where employees are highly organized,
they are unlikely to achieve a commitment to improvement unless their collective interests are recognized. Three main sources for the partnership idea can
be identified. One is the USA in the form of the 'mutual gains' or 'productivity coalition' approach promoted by Kochan and his colleagues (Kochan et al.
1986; Kochan and Osterman 1994). A second is Continental Europe. 'Social
partnership', in the sense of national-level relations, had long been a feature
of a number of EU member countries. In the wake of the completion of the
single European market with Economic and Monetary Union (EMU), the European Commission has sought to promote it at every level. It is seen not only
as way of responding to demands for developing social policy, but also of dealing
with the expected restructuring and bringing about much-needed modernization
of work organization as a means to competitive success (see e.g. CEC 1997,
1998).

  The third source is the UK itself, where trade union debates over 'new
realism' in the mid-1980s led to the proposal that they should develop a joint
approach with employers 'to create the conditions for economic success and
social cohesion in the 1990s' (Edmonds and Tuffin 1990). Out of this came a
joint statement of intent, *Towards Industrial Partnership* (IPA 1992), signed by
leading management and trade union representatives in membership of the
Involvement and Participation Association, which in turn was the catalyst for
the negotiation of so-called 'partnership' agreements by a number of companies.

  'Partnership' agreements in the UK differ considerably in their details, reflect-
ing the involvement of companies as diverse as Blue Circle (IRS 1997), BGT
(British Gas call centres) (IRS 1998b), Hyder Utilities (formerly Welsh Water)
(IRS 1998c), Legal and General (IRS 1998a), Littlewoods (Terry 1999), Rover
(IRS 1992), Tesco (Allen 1998) and United Distillers (Marks et al. 1998). Some
idea of their contents and the time-scale that can be involved appears in the
following summary of the first phase of the pioneering Hyder agreement in 1990
(Thomas and Wallis 1998: 162):

• replacement of the traditional annual pay negotiations by an objective formula (embracing the November RPI percentage; links with the local labour
  market undertaken by an independent organization (Cardiff Business School);
  and a profit-related component);
• a new single-table representative council supported by joint 'issue' groups;
• new working time arrangements involving greater flexibility, a form of annual
  hours arrangements and a reduction in the working week for 'manual' and
  'craft' employees;

- the harmonization of the working conditions, policies and procedures of all employees;
- the introduction of monthly pay through credit transfer for all employees;
- a commitment to introduce a new pay structure;
- a range of measures to improve productivity through greater flexibility;
- a no compulsory redundancy policy.

For the moment, 'partnership' agreements remain very much a minority movement. Indeed, critical aspects of the partnership agenda are as yet far from a widespread practice: while single-table bargaining is practised in three-fifths of workplaces which recognize two or more unions, and single-status arrangements are found in 41 per cent of workplaces, the low incidence of flexible working time arrangements has already been noted and, crucially, only 14 per cent of workplaces guaranteed job security or had a no compulsory redundancy policy (Cully et al. 1999: 74, 79, 94). On this last, securing a trade-off between employee acceptance of greater adaptability and flexibility and management commitment to employment security frequently only appears possible within a partnership framework (Hall and Marginson 1999).

The significance of partnership for British industrial relations is difficult to assess, in light of its novelty and the imprecision with which the term is often used. Further analysis can be found in chapters 9 and 10. For the present we would note, first, that the number of agreements reflecting partnership in any exact sense remains very small. Second, even where partnership is practised, it may be undercut by changes within the company. The experience of Blue Circle, one of the pioneer group of companies, is illustrative: management abandoned its partnership approach following acquisition by an international competitor in 2001. Third, the wider adoption and stability of partnership arrangements depends on the political context. The new Labour government, for all its commitment to the language of partnership, has proved markedly reluctant to legislate for the universal right to employee voice. An EU directive on employee information and consultation at national level could shift the political context. But it is unlikely to take effect in the UK before 2005, and in any event will not entail strong rights to consultation based on a requirement to reach agreement with the workforce. It will thus not directly underpin partnership, though it could act as a catalyst. Until then at least, management and unions will be left to make their own decisions.

The reality of management decision-making

The assumption that management is capable of selecting its approach from a range of options lies at the heart of many of the recipes and prescriptions for improving the management of industrial relations. Yet it sits very uneasily with a context in which business considerations are impacting ever more sharply on industrial relations practice and the institutional context serves to emphasize short-run returns.

Thus, most commentators have considerably underestimated the problems in modernizing employee management. This is above all true of the typical brownfield operations. It is not just a question of the considerable time and resources that are involved, although these are fundamental. A major problem, as Pil and MacDuffie's (1996) review of the literature on innovation reminds us, is that there are costs associated with unlearning old practices and introducing new ones. In the circumstances, there is a strong temptation for managers to prefer the incremental path to change, i.e. to try one or two elements and assess their impact before going further. The problem is that this means forgoing the benefits of the integration associated with 'bundles' of complementary practices. It is not perhaps surprising, therefore, that individual practices are often tried and dropped because they do not appear to 'work'.

Many of the prescriptions put forward also serve only to highlight the contradictory tensions involved in managing the employment relationship. The 'core-periphery' model, for example, appears to make intuitive sense and yet the introduction of such an obvious status divide patently runs counter to the precepts of teamworking, high-commitment management and partnership. Similarly, the 'lean production' model expects workers to engage in their own work intensification, while annual hours arrangements suppose a measure of trust that very often appears to be beyond the parties. 'Outsourcing', in Storey's (1998: 41) words, 'may "hollow out" the organization, threatening any aspirations towards organizational learning, corporate culture and shared vision'.

There are also important limits to the much-vaunted flexibility that management needs or can cope with. Managers need at the very least a measure of certainty, for example, about attendance, starting and finishing times, working-time patterns and the competences to perform particular skills. All of these assume high levels of workforce discipline and control. This point emerges most forcibly from Clark's (1995) detailed study of the Italian-owned Pirelli plant at Aberdare in South Wales. Specifically, Clark (1993: 128) found that 'under conditions that were highly favourable to full flexibility – contractual requirement, high level of automation, greenfield site – it has been neither required nor used'. He gives five reasons why management sought limited rather than full flexibility, which are profoundly important in helping to develop a more realistic perspective on the potential of many of the new working arrangements:

- *the 'horses for courses' principle*: many employees were more suited to, and interested in, certain tasks than others;
- *specialist knowledge*: there were significant advantages in employees being specialized and 'knowing what their job is';
- *'ownership'*: employees given responsibility for a particular area were more likely to be committed to the achievement of high-quality work;
- *training*: there was a substantial requirement for on-the-job training of new recruits requiring existing employees to be fully up to date with their particular process;
- *skill retention*: employees could not use skills adequately if they were not given the regular opportunity to practise them.

As Legge's (2000) and Colling's (2000) reviews of the literature dealing with the incidence of changes associated with the 'lean organization' and 'extended organization' respectively confirm, context is also fundamentally important. For example, Ackroyd and Procter's (1998) analysis of the largest 200 British-owned firms (size measured by capitalization) suggests that a particular form of lean organization has emerged in the UK, reflecting the origins and development of companies and the wider context in which they operate. The typical British manufacturing firm, they point out, has grown through merger and acquisition, comprising a large number of decentralized production facilities producing a very wide range of 'cash cow' goods for retail in mature markets. These are firms that favoured tight control of financial performance from the centre, with a good deal of operational freedom allowed to plant management. Against this background, the form of lean organization that has emerged shows little signs of high levels of investment in advanced technology or of multi-skilling or of 'high-commitment' HRM practices associated, for example, with the Japanese model. Rather, as noted earlier, employees do not enjoy privileged status or high employment security, but have to compete with subcontracted labour and alternative suppliers. Flexibility is achieved by teams of semi-skilled workers performing a range of specific tasks and given some on-the-job training. As Legge (2000: 63) puts it,

> For low-cost producers, particularly operating in mature markets, investment in training, intensive communications and guarantees of job security may be seen as both unnecessary and undesirable. If behavioural compliance is sufficient, why go to the expense of trying to secure additional commitment?

In the case of the 'extended organization', Colling (2000: 72) shows that the type of relationship that has emerged in the UK both within and between organizations subject to subcontracting has been profoundly shaped by the regulatory context and the dynamics of business services markets. These have tended to 'perpetuate arm's-length contractual relationships', considerably complicating the management of industrial relations.

More generally, as Bach and Sisson (2000: 28–9) argue, the sheer pace and extent of the change in business portfolios that has been encouraged has been a further consideration in many organizations. Not only has it produced massive insecurity on the part of managers and employees alike; it has also made it very difficult to develop the consistency in approach that is necessary to create the long-term relationships of the 'high-commitment management' or 'partnership' models. Personnel managers, who have been urged to add a strategic dimension to their operating role, have found themselves spending most of their time handling redundancies rather than fulfilling the dreams of the HRM agenda. In Hunt's words (2000), 'cuts in staff have placed it [the personnel function] in the role of decapitator rather than resource developer'. Even many 'blue chip' organizations are littered with half-finished initiatives that had to be interrupted because of take-over or merger or change of business direction or divestment (Storey et al. 1997).

Variations on a Theme

Our attention now turns to the variety of management's industrial relations practice. Managements differ not only in their approach to trade unions but also in the ways in which they recruit, develop, motivate and reward employees. Such variety is not quite as random as it appears, however. Much management practice differs in predictable ways according to several key variables. Especially important are sector, occupation, size and ownership of the organization, together with the business strategies, structures and styles management pursues. Chapter 12 examines this issue further by developing a typology of management styles.

Sector

In the light of the decline in multi-employer bargaining in the UK, there has been a tendency to ignore the significance of the sector in discussions of the management of industrial relations. Yet, as Arrowsmith and Sisson (1999) have argued, there continues to be a large degree of common practice even where the formal emphasis is local, as in engineering and retail. Moreover, when change does occur, it tends to be fairly widely followed throughout the sector. Even in localized bargaining structures, when it comes to change, managers tend to move like ships in a convoy.

The reason is that workplaces in any given sector tend to share a number of fundamental characteristics whether or not they have sector-level bargaining. First of these are the *structural boundaries provided by markets, technology and labour.* Although there is enormous variety in markets and technology within sectors, there are a number of significant features which workplaces share in each case. These include:

- labour market composition, union organization and skills;
- common changes in the organization of work, often promoted by shared technologies facilitating 'just in time' in engineering or print, or integrated scanning and labour scheduling in retail;
- pressure to extend operating hours to make better use of capital;
- tighter deadlines and variable demand associated with increased competition;
- deregulation of store opening hours and the need for part-time labour in retailing;
- sectoral concentration and 'leadership'.

In each of the four sectors studied, Arrowsmith and Sisson found that management was often subject to a set of constraints and common pressures promoting a degree of convergence in pay and working time arrangements. Of course, these did not necessarily preclude managerial choice. They nonetheless encouraged very similar outcomes, especially when taken into account with other considerations discussed below.

The second set of factors relates to issues of *legitimacy, uncertainty* and *durability* in existing arrangements. The tried and tested nature of existing arrangements invests them with a high degree of legitimacy in the eyes of both managers and employees. This particularly applies if these arrangements appear to be widely practised in other workplaces with which the actors are most familiar, i.e. within the sector.

Third is the significance of *shared information sources*. Information plays a critical role in helping to explain many of the common features of pay and working time arrangements in every sector. It takes on a special significance, however, where the settlement process is as highly decentralized as it has become in engineering and retail. In the absence of a national framework, information offers an alternative set of benchmarks which individual managements can use to help decide the appropriateness of their arrangements.

Many of the most fundamental changes in the management of industrial relations also reflect shifts in the industrial structure of the workforce in the UK and, in particular, the ongoing shift from manufacturing to services. One is the decline in joint regulation by collective bargaining discussed in chapter 8. Another is the growth in part-time work and in the different forms of so-called atypical or non-standard forms of employment discussed in chapter 3.

Occupation

These structural shifts have also had profound effects on the occupational structure of the workforce: coalminers and agricultural workers have all but disappeared while the ranks of the personal service and care workforce have burgeoned. More people are employed in 'personal and protective services' (3 million) than as 'plant and machine operators' (2.6 million). While developments in the *horizontal, across industry structure* are being driven by industrial change, those in the *vertical, hierarchical structure* of occupations reflect additional dynamics.

Occupation is a critical reference point. There are long-standing differences in many of the terms and conditions between so-called 'blue-collar' and 'white-collar' jobs, reflecting the very different disciplinary regimes under which they worked. At the risk of over-simplification, this took the form of 'management through control' in the case of 'manual workers' and 'management through commitment' in the case of their 'white-collar' counterparts (Edwards 2000: 318–19). Typically, 'blue-collar' workers were subject to a tight regime of discipline, including clocking on and off, with little flexibility of working time arrangements. Very often they were paid by results. Holidays and pension arrangements were inferior to those of their 'white-collar' colleagues, as were provisions for employment security. 'Blue-collar' workers, for example, were usually paid weekly and could be laid off at short notice. 'White-collar' workers, by contrast, were paid monthly salaries with annual increments based on length of service and it was very rare for them to be laid off (Price and Price 1994).

It is widely accepted that much of this divide has disappeared in recent years, as the boundaries between supervisory, craft and operative jobs in industry have become increasingly blurred, with decision-making responsibility delegated downwards in a wide range of organizations. Meanwhile, significant elements of traditional white-collar work have become routinized, as in banking or sales, where there is greater management control over working time and an emphasis on individual performance pay. There has been a tendency towards the harmonization of conditions in many areas as management finds an interest in promoting a common identity. Even so, in many cases the status divide would appear to persist: as noted earlier, the 1998 WERS found that less than half of workplaces accorded single status to all their non-managerial employees (Cully et al. 1999: 74), and other surveys report continuing differences in the experience of redundancy, levels of training and job autonomy (Gallie et al. 1998).

Elsewhere, the boundaries of the status divide have been redrawn and its features continue in the different treatment accorded to 'managers' and the 'managed'. Significantly, for example, the focus of many of the 1998 WERS questions is implicit recognition of this: managers are expected to be subject to individual performance pay, appraisal, a special status and security, whereas for other employees it is more of an open question. Managers are typically covered by individual contracts rather than by collective agreements. Managers receive development, whereas the 'managed' are trained. Careers continue to be an important form of motivation for 'managers', even if there is controversy about the future (Newell 2000). The target of HRM, it can be argued, is often 'managers' rather than employees in general (Legge 2000).

A major consideration here is the changing occupational structure of the workforce discussed in chapter 3. Not surprisingly, the typical employee is no longer a blue-collar worker in manufacturing. Indeed, such occupations represent a dwindling minority as manufacturing shrinks. The largest single groups are 'management and administrators' (4.3 million) followed by 'clerical' (4.1 million). The two groups of 'professional' and 'professional and technical' amount to 5.5 million, whereas 'craft and related' accounts for 3.4 million.

Size

A further consequence of the shift from manufacturing to services is a decline in the size of workplaces. In contrast to workplace size, the size of the organizations of which workplaces are part has declined only slightly over the years since 1980 (Millward et al. 2000: 31): decline in large manufacturing organizations has been offset by the growth of large private service organizations. As successive WIRS have clearly demonstrated, the size of workplace is positively related to a wide range of industrial relations phenomena. These include whether or not the workplace has a specialist personnel manager, belongs to an employer's organization, recognizes trade unions, uses a wide range of involvement and participation methods, practises job evaluation, and has profit-sharing. For example, in 1998 larger workplaces (employing 500 or more) were around twice as likely as those employing fewer than 50 to have non-managerial employees involved in problem-solving groups, suggestion schemes and attitude surveys (Cully et al. 1999: 68). Moreover, also underlining the importance of the size of the organization of which workplaces are a part (Marginson 1984), stand-alone workplaces are much less likely to have these practices than those that belong to larger organizations.

The reduction in the size of workplaces in the UK is also a key factor in many of the changes taking place in management industrial relations practice. Much of the decline in trade union membership and the scope of collective bargaining, for example, reflects closure and redundancy in the larger workplaces in manufacturing.

Size is important in management industrial relations practice because, other things being equal, the larger the organization, the more complex the management task (see further chapter 18). The more complex the management task, the greater the need for rules and procedures to achieve consistency of behaviour on the part of individual managers. The greater the need for rules and procedures, the greater the need to have the legitimacy of workers and their representatives. Significantly, a recognition of the importance of size of organization in industrial relations is one of the considerations in the adoption of more devolved forms of management structures, such as strategic business units discussed below.

Ownership

Until recently, as chapter 11 describes in more detail, public ownership was also a significant factor in management practice. This is because, at a peak in the early 1980s, some 7 million people, or more than one-quarter of the working population, were employed in the public sector. As in the case of size, it was possible to list a range of industrial relations phenomena strongly associated with public ownership. These included the recognition of trade unions, which was virtually universal, including managers up to director level, and the structure of collective bargaining, which was extremely centralized. Especially important was the widespread acceptance that the public sector should be the 'good' or 'model' employer whose management should set standards for others to follow. Though this situation is disappearing, strong elements remain. Many aspects of practice in, for example, local authorities and the health service, including pensions and grading structures, reflect this. But increasing diversity of practice is evident: there have been considerable differences in approach to compulsory competitive tendering between Labour and Conservative-controlled local authorities, which reflect contrasting commitments to the principle of the 'good employer' (Colling 1993).

A second major difference is between British and overseas-owned companies. This is important because not only is Britain the 'home' of a large number of international companies (see chapter 4), but also 'host' to an equally large number of foreign-owned companies, such as Ford, IBM, Nestlé, and Nissan. Using a survey of 176 large companies with 1,000 or more employees, Marginson et al. found that, although there was little difference in approach to trade unions and collective bargaining, there were significant differences in a range of other aspects.

Overseas-owned companies were distinctive in their approaches to employee development, communication and involvement. As compared with UK-owned companies, they tended to have relatively high levels of expenditure on employee training; employed a wider range of methods of employee communication; were more likely to use upwards and two-way forms of communication; were more likely to provide information on investment plans to employees; and were less likely to utilise forms of financial participation. Overseas-owned companies were also distinctive in their policies towards managerial employees. Overseas-owned multinationals were more likely to move managerial staff between countries, to use a common job grading scheme for senior managers (such as Hay-MSL) across their world-wide operations and to have a separate head office department responsible for the training and development of managers in their subsidiaries overseas, than were UK-owned multinationals. (Marginson et al. 1993: 13–14)

Furthermore, overseas-owned companies accorded personnel a higher profile in their management structures. Thus they were twice as likely as their British-owned counterparts to have a personnel director on the main board in Britain. They were also more likely to have a corporate personnel policy committee comprised of senior managers from a range of functions and to hold meetings of personnel managers from different locations. The overall conclusion was that the influence of the personnel function over budgetary and strategic decisions was greater in overseas-owned than in British-owned enterprises.

There has yet to be a detailed investigation of the wider significance of ownership for policies and practices arising from the 1998 WERS. Its findings nonetheless suggest that the contrast between UK and foreign-owned organizations will be as 'striking' as Millward et al. (1992: 33) found when analysing the 1990 WIRS. Thus, in 1998 foreign-owned workplaces (51 per cent) were almost twice as likely to employ a personnel specialist as UK-owned ones (27 per cent). The personnel specialists in foreign-owned workplaces were also much more likely to include 'human resources' in their titles. Human resource managers accounted for nearly two-thirds of personnel specialists in foreign-owned workplaces (64 per cent) compared with around a quarter (26 per cent) in UK-owned ones. Inasmuch as the further analysis by Hoque and Noon (1999) shows a positive relationship between the use of the 'human resources' title and the adoption of a more strategic approach as measured by a greater emphasis on employee development in the strategic plan and greater personnel specialist involvement in its drawing up, it is highly likely that foreign-owned organizations will also be found to have had a more strategic approach than their UK ones.

Strategies, structures and styles

Although the bulk of organizations are small, Britain has a very significant number of large companies accounting for a substantial share of private sector employment. In the case of these large organizations, three significant axes of differentiation with important implications for people management are diversification, divisionalization and strategic style.

- *Diversification* concerns whether companies are involved in related activities, and the associated degree of integration between different activities, or in unrelated activities, or whether they are spatially diversified but undertake the same kind of activity in many different locations.
- *Divisionalization* relates to internal structure, which can be primarily territorial (i.e. segmented according to regions or districts) or business-based (i.e. segmented into product or service divisions).
- *Strategic style* concerns the level at which strategic business decisions are taken (business unit, division, national subsidiary or corporate headquarters), the role of corporate headquarters in business development (planning, reviewing, monitoring) and the degree to which it stresses 'numbers-driven' rather than 'issue-driven' planning (Goold and Campbell 1987).

Marginson et al. (1995) show that to a considerable extent these three axes overlap. Divisionalized structures are found in virtually all large companies, but their nature differs according to diversification strategy. Where organizations are spatially diversified, undertaking the same activity in many different locations, the basis of divisional units tends to be territorial and their autonomy relatively constrained. Otherwise divisionalization is on a basis of different lines of business, with greater restraints on business division autonomy in the case of diversification into related businesses as compared to that into unrelated businesses, which is the case of the conglomerates. In terms of strategic style, a 'numbers-driven' or 'financial control' style is more likely to be found among companies diversified into unrelated businesses, whereas a 'strategic planning' style, characterized by longer-run approaches in terms of market position and share, is more likely to be found among the spatial diversifiers or related diversifiers.

Differences along these three axes generate differences in the extent to which companies are centralized or decentralized in their overall management approach, with consequent implications for their industrial relations policies. For example, where there is a high degree of integration in production or service provision, as in the case of automobile manufacturers, management will tend towards a centralized approach. A centralized approach is also likely where the organization is carrying out the same activity in different locations, because of gains to be made in standardized operating procedures and/or common purchasing. Here the main clearing banks and multiple retailers would be examples. A decentralized approach is more likely where different kinds of business activity, which are not closely related, are being undertaken in different locations. The extreme case would be that of the diversified conglomerate or industrial holding company such as Tomkins, which covers automotive components, heating, ventilating and air-conditioning equipment, plumbing products and security systems.

Variations in the size of corporate personnel function, for example, are only partially accounted for by the employment size of companies (Marginson et al. 1993: 5). The largest corporate personnel functions tend to be found among single-business enterprises and strategic planners, whereas conglomerates and financial controllers tend to have small numbers of specialist staff or no corporate function at all. Similarly it is no coincidence that it is the single-business enterprises, such as the automobile manufacturers, clearing banks and multiple retailers, which have multi-establishment bargaining or pay determination, whereas it is the conglomerates which are more likely to have decentralized arrangements (see chapter 8).

The 1998 WERS results confirm, however, that the appearance of devolution in multi-establishment organizations does not necessarily equate to delegation of real decision-making authority. The existence of organization-wide policies on operational matters such as recruitment, performance appraisal, training, pay systems and pay and conditions of employment was widespread, as was the need for workplace managers to follow them. For many of these issues, a majority of workplace managers had to follow policies set at a higher level in the organization. A summary measure of autonomy suggested that this was especially likely to be the case where there was a personnel specialist at higher level. The overall conclusion of Cully et al. (1999: 59) is that 'the broad picture is . . . one of relatively well-developed structures for the management of employees, with control largely retained by personnel departments in the centre of the organization'.

Also clear is that the degree of control exercised from the centre seems to have grown in the 1990s, reflecting the restructuring described above. Indeed, the WERS team talks of 'unequivocal evidence' of this happening. In both 1990 and 1998, respondents belonging to larger organizations were asked how decisions were made on three issues: the appointment of a senior manager, the recognition or de-recognition of a trade union and the use of any financial or budgetary surplus. In each case, the proportions of workplace respondents saying that they were able to make such decisions declined over the period: from 39 per cent to 24 per cent for the appointment of a senior manager; from 31 per cent to 23 per cent for union recognition or de-recognition; and from 34 per cent to 14 per cent for the use of financial surpluses.

Conclusions

Management industrial relations practice in Britain is characterized by immense variety. In the absence of a detailed framework of multi-employer agreements or legal regulations, this reflects the fact that British managers have had considerable scope to exercise choice in what they do. Such practice is not entirely random, however. Much of it can be related to specific structural features. Of the many involved, it has been argued, sector, occupation, size, ownership, and the business strategies, structures and styles of the organization are especially important in shaping, but not determining, practice. The headquarters of large multiple organizations have the capacity to exert influence from the centre in personnel matters and they choose to do so to a considerable extent.

Challenges Ahead?

Looking to the future, there are signs that British management is likely to face a number of major challenges to the way it conducts industrial relations. There is a growing consensus, in the USA (Cappelli et al. 1997: 226) as well as in Europe (CEC 1997), about the major challenge facing management for the foreseeable future, even if there is no easy answer. Management has to reconcile two seemingly conflicting requirements, reflecting the intensifying competition and/or pressure on scarce resources (Herriot et al. 1998). It has to cut costs to the bone and yet at the same time promote the security, autonomy and teamwork necessary for innovation into new markets, products and services. The European Commission's Green Paper (CEC 1997: 5) puts it nicely in suggesting that the policy challenges could be 'summarised in one question: how to reconcile security for workers with the flexibility which firms need'.

Crucially, the international terrain on which management is looking to reconcile these seemingly conflicting requirements is continually shifting. For certain types of business activity, the scope for management to exercise the 'exit' option of relocation to parts of the globe offering plentiful supplies of relatively cheap, disciplined, but educated and trained labour – and hence to achieve a resolution of these pressures which avoids the kind of reconciliation embodied in so-called 'pacts for employment and competitiveness' (Sisson and Artiles 2000) – has widened over the past decade or so. Within Europe, the fall of the Berlin Wall has opened up new production possibilities, especially in central Europe. Beyond Europe, activities as diverse as automotive component manufacture, software development and airline ticketing are moving towards south and east Asia, notably India and China. Even among the advanced industrialized economies, the emergence of the transatlantic mega-merger, such as BP Amoco or Lucas-Varity (subsequently taken over by TRW), indicates that the degrees of manoeuvre for the management of international companies in deciding what to produce where is multiplying further.

Closer to home, the introduction of the third and critical stage of EMU at the beginning of 1999 (the setting up of the European Central Bank with responsibility for EU-wide monetary policy and the timetable for the introduction of a single currency) is likely to be especially important. Regardless of its decision on the adoption of the euro, the UK is unlikely to escape the significant pressure for restructuring that the greater transparency of prices and costs, coupled with the development of a single capital market, will generate. Indeed, there are strong grounds for suggesting that the pressure in the UK is likely to be greater than in most other countries because of the presence of a large number of MNCs, one of the loosest sets of arrangements governing site closure, and the relatively low levels of productivity (Sisson et al. 1999).

Also clear is that, with the UK's signature of the 'Social Chapter' and its incorporation into the Treaty of Amsterdam in 1997, the future direction of the European social dimension is also likely to have a profound effect on employment relations in the UK. As the previous chapter suggests, it is difficult to escape the conclusion that, whatever else happens, the European connection signals the end of the 'voluntarism' characterizing UK employment relations for a century. Significant, too, is that much of the recent legislation provides for information and consultation through employee representatives, from trade unions and/or some form of works council, reflecting the importance attached by our EU partners to both representative (i.e. collective) and direct (i.e. individual) participation. As well as the specific arrangements for European-level information and consultation in MNCs required under the European Works Council Directive, there are general provisions in such areas as collective redundancies and transfers of undertakings, health and safety, and working time. The European Commission is also proposing that there should be a universal right to information and consultation in national-level undertakings with more than 50 employees. UK management, it seems, is going to have to get used to the idea of managing individually *and* collectively.

References

Ackroyd, S., and Procter, S. 1998: British manufacturing organization and workplace industrial relations: some attributes of the new flexible firm, *British Journal of Industrial Relations*, 36 (2), 163–83.

Allen, M. 1998: All-inclusive, *People Management*, 11 June.

Arrowsmith, J., and Sisson, K. 1999: Pay and working time: towards organization based arrangements? *British Journal of Industrial Relations*, 37 (1), 51–75.

Atkinson, J. 1984: Manpower strategies for flexible organizations, *Personnel Management*, August, 28–31.

Atkinson, J., and Meager, N. 1986: Is flexibility just a flash in the pan? *Personnel Management*, September, 3–6.

Bach, S., and Sisson, K. 2000: Personnel management in perspective. In S. Bach and K. Sisson (eds), *Personnel Management: A Comprehensive Guide to Theory and Practice*. Oxford: Blackwell.

Barney, J. 1991: Firm resources and sustained competitive advantage, *Journal of Management*, 17 (1), 99–120.

Burawoy, M. 1985: *The Politics of Production: Factory Regimes under Capitalism and Socialism*. London: Verso.

Cappelli, P., Katz, H. and Osterman, P. 1997: *The New Deal at Work*. Boston: Harvard Business School Press.

CEC (Commission for the European Communities) 1989: *Comparative Study on Rules Governing Working Conditions in the Member States*. SEC (89) 1137. Luxembourg: Office for the Official Publications of the European Communities.

CEC 1997: *Partnership for a New Organization of Work* (Green Paper). Bulletin of the European Union. Supplement 4/97. Luxembourg: Office for the Official Publications of the European Communities.

CEC 1998: *Managing Change: Final Report of the High Level Group on Economic and Social Implications of Industrial Change*. Luxembourg: Office for the Official Publications of the European Communities.

Clark, J. 1993: Full flexibility and self-supervision in an automated factory. In J. Clark (ed.), *Human Resource Management and Technical Change*. London: Sage.

Clark, J. 1995: *Managing Innovation and Change*. London: Sage.

Claydon, T. 1998: Problematizing partnership: the prospects for a co-operative bargaining agenda. In P. Sparrow and M. Marchington (eds), *Human Resource Management: The New Agenda*. London: Financial Times/Pitman.

Coates, D. 2000: *Models of Capitalism: Growth and Stagnation in the Modern Era*. Cambridge: Polity.

Colling, T. 1993: Contracting public services: the management of compulsory competitive tendering in two county councils, *Human Resource Management Journal*, 3 (4), 1–15.

Colling, T. 2000: Personnel management in the extended organization. In S. Bach and K. Sisson (eds), *Personnel Management: A Comprehensive Guide to Theory and Practice*. Oxford: Blackwell.

Cully, M., O'Reilly, A., Millward, N., Forth, J., Woodland, S., Dix, G. and Bryson, A. 1998: *The 1998 Workplace Employee Relations Survey: First Findings*. London: DTI.

Cully, M., Woodland, S., O'Reilly, A. and Dix, G. 1999: *Britain at Work*. London: Routledge.

Daniel, W. W., and Millward, N. 1983: *Workplace Industrial Relations in Britain*. London: Heinemann.

Dunlop, J. T. 1958: *Industrial Relations Systems*. New York: Holt.

Edmonds, J., and Tuffin, A. 1990: *A New Agenda*. London: GMB/UCW.

Edwards, P. K. 2000: Discipline: towards trust and self-discipline? In S. Bach and K. Sisson (eds), *Personnel Management: A Comprehensive Guide to Theory and Practice*. Oxford: Blackwell.

European Foundation for the Improvement of Living and Working Conditions 1997: *New Forms of Work Organization: Can Europe Realise its Potential? Results of a Survey of Direct Employee Participation in Europe*. Luxembourg: Office for the Official Publications of the European Communities.

European Foundation for the Improvement of Living and Working Conditions 1999: *Employment through Flexibility: Squaring the Circle? Findings from the EPOC Survey*. Luxembourg: Office for the Official Publications of the European Communities.

Friedman, A. L. 1977: *Industry and Labour: Class Struggle at Work and Monopoly Capitalism*. London: Macmillan.

Gallie, D., White, M., Cheng, Y. and Tomlinson, M. 1998: *Restructuring the Employment Relationship*. Oxford: Oxford University Press.

Goold, M., and Campbell, A. 1987: *Strategies and Styles: The Role of the Centre in Managing Diversified Corporations*. Oxford: Blackwell.

Gospel, H. 1992: *Markets, Firms and the Management of Labour in Modern Britain*. Cambridge: Cambridge University Press.

Gospel, H., and Palmer, G. 1993: *British Industrial Relations*. 2nd edn. London: Routledge.

Grant, R. M. 1991: The resource-based theory of competitive advantage: implications for strategy formulation, *California Management Review*, 33 (3), 114–35.

Grant, R. M. 1995: *Contemporary Strategy Analysis*. Oxford: Blackwell.

Guest, D. 1997: Human resource management and performance: a review and research agenda, *International Journal of Human Resource Management*, 8 (3), 264–76.

Hall, M., and Marginson, P. 1999: *Collective Bargaining on Employment and Competitiveness: Report on the UK*. Report prepared for the European Foundation for the Improvement of Living and Working Conditions. Coventry: Industrial Relations Research Unit, University of Warwick.

Hamel, G., and Prahalahad, P. K. 1994: *Competing for the Future*. Boston, Mass.: Harvard Business School Press.

Herriot, P., Hirsch, W. and Reily, P. 1998: *Trust and Transitions: Managing the Employment Relationship*. Chichester: Wiley.

Herzberg, F. 1966: *Work and the Nature of Man*. Cleveland, Ohio: World Publishing.

Hoque, K., and Noon, M. 1999: Counting angels: the personnel/human resource function in the UK: Evidence from the 1998 Workplace Employee Relations Survey. Paper for the British Universities' Industrial Relations Association conference, de Montfort University, July.

Hunt, J. 2000: Human resources: untapped resources, *Financial Times*, 25 February.

Hunter, L. C., and MacInnes, J. 1991: *Employers' Labour Use Strategies: Case Studies*. Employment Research Paper No. 87. Sheffield: Employment Department.

Huselid, M. 1995: The impact of human resource management practices on turnover, productivity and corporate financial performance, *Academy of Management Journal*, 38 (3), 635–72.

Ichniowski, C., Kochan, T. A., Levin, D., Olson, C. and Strauss, G. 1996: What works at work: overview and assessment, *Industrial Relations*, 35 (3), 299–333.

IPA (Involvement and Participation Association) 1992: *Towards Industrial Partnership: A New Approach to Relationships at Work*. London: IPA.

IPA 1997: *Towards Industrial Partnership: New Ways of Working in British Companies*. London: IPA.

IPA 1998: *The Partnership Company*. London: IPA.

IPD (Institute of Personnel and Development) 1997a: *The People Management Implications of Leaner Ways of Working*. Issues in People Management 15. London: IPD.

IPD 1997b: *Impact of People Management on Business Performance*. Issues in People Management 22. London: IPD.

IPD 1999: *Training and Development in Britain, 1999*. London: IPD.

IRS (Industrial Relations Services) 1992: Rover's 'New Deal', *Employment Trends*, 514, 12–15.

IRS 1997: Cementing a new partnership at Blue Circle, *Employment Trends*, 638, August, 11–16.

IRS 1998a: Partnership in practice at Legal and General, *Employment Trends*, 650, 12–15.

IRS 1998b: BGT partners new deal, *Pay and Benefits Bulletin*, 453 (August), 5–8.

IRS 1998c: Hyder maintains long-term partnership, *Employment Trends*, 662 (August), 12–16.

IRS 1999: United we stand, *Employment Trends*, 682 (June), 6–11.

Keep, E., and Mayhew, K. 1998: Was Ratner right? Product market and competitive strategies and their links with skills and knowledge, *Employment Policy Institute Economic Report*, 12 (3), 1–14.

Kochan, T. A., Katz, H. C. and McKersie, R. B. 1986: *The Transformation of American Industrial Relations*. New York: Basic Books.

Kochan, T. A., and Osterman, P. 1994: *The Mutual Gains Enterprise: Forging a Winning Partnership among Labor, Management and Government*. Boston: Harvard Business School Press.

Labour Market Trends 1997: Labour Force Survey Help-Line 105, 12 (December), LFS61–4.

Lazear, E. 1995: *Personnel Economics*. Cambridge, Mass.: MIT Press.

Legge, K. 2000: Personnel management in the 'lean organization'. In S. Bach and K. Sisson (eds), *Personnel Management: A Comprehensive Guide to Theory and Practice*. Oxford: Blackwell.

Mabey, C., Salaman, G. and Storey, J. 1998: *Human Resource Management: A Strategic Introduction*. Oxford: Blackwell.

Marchington, M. 1998: Partnership in context: towards a European model? In P. Sparrow and M. Marchington (eds), *Human Resource Management: The New Agenda*. London: Financial Times/Pitman.

Marginson, P. 1984: The distinctive effects of plant and company size on workplace industrial relations, *British Journal of Industrial Relations*, 22 (1), 1–14.

Marginson, P., Armstrong, P., Edwards, P. and Purcell, J., with Hubbard, N. 1993: *The Control of Industrial Relations in Large Companies*. Warwick Papers in Industrial Relations, 45. Coventry: Industrial Relations Research Unit, University of Warwick.

Marginson, P., Edwards, P., Armstrong, P. and Purcell, J. 1995: Strategy, structure and control in the changing corporation: a survey-based investigation, *Human Resource Management Journal*, 5 (2), 3–27.

Marginson, P., Edwards, P., Martin, R., Purcell, J. and Sisson, K. 1988: *Beyond the Workplace: Managing Industrial Relations in Multi-Establishment Enterprises*. Oxford: Blackwell.

Marginson, P., and Sisson, K. 1994: The structure of transnational capital in Europe. In R. Hyman and A. Ferner (eds), *New Frontiers of European Industrial Relations*. Oxford: Blackwell

Marks, A., Findlay, P., Hine, J., McKinlay, A. and Thompson, P. 1998: The politics of partnership? *British Journal of Industrial Relations*, 36 (2), 209–26.

Maurice, M., Sellier, F. and Silvestre, J.-J. 1986: *The Social Foundations of Industrial Power: A Comparison of France and Germany*. Cambridge, Mass.: MIT Press.

MacDuffie, J. P. 1995: Human resource bundles and manufacturing performance, *Industrial and Labor Relations Review*, 48 (2), 197–221.

McGregor, D. C. 1960: *The Human Side of the Enterprise*. New York: McGraw-Hill.

Meadows, P. 1999. The flexible labour market: implications for pension provision. Paper prepared for the National Association of Pension Funds.

Millward, N. 1994: *The New Industrial Relations*. London: Routledge.

Millward, N., Forth, J. and Bryson, A. 2000: *All Change at Work*. London: Routledge.

Millward, N., Stevens, M., Smart, D. and Hawes, W. 1992: *Workplace Industrial Relations in Transition*. Aldershot: Dartmouth.

Mintzberg, H. 1978: Patterns in strategy formation, *Management Science*, 24 (9), 934–48.

Mintzberg, H., Quinn, J. and Gosh, S. 1998: *The Strategy Process*. London: Prentice Hall.

Newell, H. 2000: Managing careers. In S. Bach and K. Sisson (eds), *Personnel Management: A Comprehensive Guide to Theory and Practice*. Oxford: Blackwell.

Overell, S. 1998: Delayering to fire steel profits drive, *People Management*, 25 June, 12.

Peters, T. J. 1987: *Thriving on Chaos: Handbook for a Management Revolution*. London: Macmillan.

Pil, F. K., and MacDuffie, J. P. 1996: The adoption of high-involvement work practices, *Industrial Relations*, 35 (3), 423–55.

Pollert, A. 1988: The 'flexible firm': fixation or fact? *Work, Employment and Society*, 2 (3), 281–316.

Poole, M. 1986: *Industrial Relations: Origins and Patterns of National Diversity*. London: Routledge.

Price, L., and Price, R. 1994: Change and continuity in the status divide. In K. Sisson (ed.), *Personnel Management: A Comprehensive Guide to Theory and Practice in Britain*. Oxford: Blackwell.

Purcell, J. 1999: Best practice and best fit: chimera or cul-de-sac? *Human Resource Management Journal*, 9 (3), 26–41.

Ramsay, H., Scholarios, D. and Harley, B. 2000: Employees and high performance work systems: testing inside the black box, *British Journal of Industrial Relations*, 38 (4), 501–32.

Sisson, K. 1987: *The Management of Collective Bargaining: An International Comparison*. Oxford: Blackwell.

Sisson, K. 1989: Personnel management in perspective. In K. Sisson (ed.), *Personnel Management in Britain*. Oxford: Blackwell.

Sisson, K., Arrowsmith, J., Gilman, M. and Hall, M. 1999: *A Preliminary Review of the Industrial Relations Implications of Economic and Monetary Union.* Warwick Papers in Industrial Relations, 62. Coventry: Industrial Relations Research Unit, University of Warwick.

Sisson, K., and Artiles, A. M. 2000: *Handling Restructuring: A Study of Collective Agreements Dealing with Employment and Competitiveness.* Luxembourg: Office for the Official Publications of the European Communities.

Storey, J. 1998: *Managing Organizational Structuring and Restructuring,* unit 4, *Managing Human Resources.* Buckingham: Open University Press.

Storey, J., Edwards, P. and Sisson, K. 1997: *Managers in the Making: Careers, Development and Control in Corporate Britain and Japan.* London: Sage.

Tailby, S., and Winchester, D. 2000: Management and trade unions: towards social partnership? In S. Bach and K. Sisson (eds), *Personnel Management: A Comprehensive Guide to Theory and Practice.* Oxford: Blackwell.

Terry, M. 1999: Assessing the significance of partnership agreements, *EIROnline,* July. Available at <www.eiro.eurofound.eu.int>.

Thomas, T., and Wallis, B. 1998: Dwr Cymru/Welsh Water: A case study in partnership. In P. Sparrow and M. Marchington (eds), *Human Resource Management: The New Agenda.* London: Financial Times/Pitman Publishing.

TUC (Trades Union Congress) 1997: *Partners for Progress.* London: TUC.

TUC 1999: *Partners for Progress: New Unionism in the Workplace.* London: TUC.

Walton, R. E. 1985: From control to commitment in the workplace, *Harvard Business Review,* 53 (2), 77–84.

Whitfield, K., and Poole, M. 1997: Organizing employment for high performance, *Organization Studies,* 18 (5), 745–63.

Whittington, R. 1993: *What is Strategy?* London: Routledge.

Williamson, O. E. 1985: *The Economic Institutions of Capitalism: Firms, Markets, Relational Contracting.* New York: Free Press.

Wood, S. 1995: The four pillars of HRM: are they connected? *Human Resource Management Journal,* 5 (5), 48–58.

Wood, S. 1996: High commitment management and payment systems, *Journal of Management Studies,* 33 (1), 53–78.

Wood, S., and Albanese, M. T. 1995: Can we speak of high commitment management on the shop floor? *Journal of Management Studies,* 32 (2), 215–47.

Wood, S., and de Menezes, L. 1998: High commitment management in the UK: evidence from the WIRS and EMSPS, *Human Relations,* 51 (4), 485–515.

8

THE MANAGEMENT OF PAY AS THE INFLUENCE OF COLLECTIVE BARGAINING DIMINISHES

WILLIAM BROWN, PAUL MARGINSON AND
JANET WALSH

The payment of labour is a core element of the employment relationship, and it is the most conspicuous focus of labour's collective concern. This chapter discusses the strategies adopted by employers in fixing pay in Britain. These strategies have undergone fundamental changes in recent years as the influence of trade unions has diminished, and as competitive pressures have increased and become more international. But pay is also the price of labour, and as such is subject to market forces encompassing far wider terrains than those of any single employer. How far do these forces constrain the employer's discretion?

This chapter starts by looking at how much discretion individual employers have over pay. Because conventional economic theory implicitly denies that employers have any distinct role, we look at economic explanations for the substantial pay differences that are actually to be found between similar firms. We then develop a richer explanation by drawing attention to the uses of pay manifest in the differing ways in which employers try to secure productive effort from their workforces. For much of the last century their discretion was greatly modified by trade unions. But in recent years the consequent institutions of collective bargaining have seen substantial decline and change. We discuss the implications of this for employer pay strategies, and also the ways in which these strategies are increasingly transcending national frontiers. The chapter concludes with discussion of the implications of diminishing trade union influence for the distribution of pay.

The Dispersion of Pay

A fundamental question when considering how much discretion employers have over their employees' pay is why it is, in practice, that workers who are performing similar jobs for different employers in the same labour market are typically paid at different rates. The starting point for the orthodox economic analysis of pay is the work of Hicks (1932) in his application of marginalist economic theory to the labour market. Wages, he argued, are determined by the interaction of the forces of labour supply and labour demand in a competitive labour market with the result that, at the equilibrium wage for a particular occupational group, no firm will wish to hire any more workers. Moreover, because the equilibrium wage is assumed to be equivalent to the contribution to revenue of the last (or marginal) worker employed in each firm, the competitive process by which such a wage is determined serves also to secure an efficient allocation of labour between different firms. Consequently, within a given labour market, wage differentials between firms for a given type of labour will not be sustainable for long. Any firm paying above the competitive wage will make a loss and will eventually be driven out of business. Any firm paying below the competitive wage will find itself unable to recruit and retain its workforce.

An important departure from this competitive model of wage determination arises from the effect of trade unions. Hicks portrayed unions as monopoly suppliers of labour able to raise wages above the competitive level. In an otherwise competitive economy the consequence of unions' effect on wage levels will be that employment will contract in the unionized sector, and the displaced workers will eventually find employment in non-union firms which will lower their wage offers in the face of excess labour supply. There is the implication that, in aggregate, output and income will fall because the allocative efficiency of the competitive labour market has been impaired. But introducing the effects of unionism does not, by itself, assist an explanation of inter-employer wage differences.

The question of inter-firm wage dispersion is important because, contrary to the expectations implied by the competitive model of wage determination, empirical studies have repeatedly found that this pay dispersion is substantial and sustained. Within the same local labour market – that is, where there are no spatial barriers to labour mobility – it is normal to find a range of earnings across firms for workers in similar occupational categories at a given point in time. The magnitude of these inter-plant pay differentials is substantial. Similarly substantial pay dispersion is apparent in different economies, despite their having very different wage-fixing institutions. A comparison of the labour markets of Chicago, Coventry and Adelaide found the inter-plant coefficient of variation of standard earnings of, for example, fork-lift truck drivers to be, respectively, 15, 13 and 11 per cent (Brown et al. 1980).

Additional evidence of the distinctive role played by the firm in pay determination comes from studies, not of pay levels, but of pay changes. The pay rises achieved by individual workers in a given year in the same labour market are commonly more in line with pay rises received by other occupations within the same firm than with those received by other individuals in the same occupation in other firms (Nolan and Brown 1983). In this British study of highly unionized workers, pay rises appeared to be determined more by the competitive circumstances confronting employers in their product market than by those confronting workers as individuals in their local occupational labour market. Evidence from a more industrially diverse Australian sample suggested that this dominance of firm-specific effects was a feature of manufacturing industry rather than of industries with more fluid labour markets such as building or retailing. Within manufacturing it was particularly strong for larger firms in more monopolistic industries (Brown et al. 1984).

Another firm-related finding that has eluded straightforward market-related explanation is the consistent relationship between firm size and pay levels. There is evidence from several countries that the average earnings of workers in particular occupation categories tend to increase with the size of establishment and, in the case of multi-plant enterprises, with the size of the parent company (Weiss and Landau 1984; Thomson and Sanjines 1990). The sources of these size effects are likely to be connected with other size-dependent aspects of labour management (Marginson 1984). Findings of this sort led the authors of the early American studies to question the competitive model of wage determination. Lester (1952) concluded that wage setting in local labour markets was characterized by a substantial 'range of indeterminacy' within which employers could select a stable point consistent with their chosen style of labour management, largely untroubled by short-term fluctuations in the labour market. This range of indeterminacy has been estimated to be of the order of 20 per cent of average earnings in one British study (Blanchflower et al. 1990).

Evidence on inter-firm wage dispersion draws attention to the extent to which employers may deliberately seek to shelter their workforces from the effects of the external labour market. An example is the creation of so-called 'internal labour market' structures. These are coherent wage and career structures internal to the firm by means of which employers use organizational rather than market relationships to motivate labour. They are characterized by ports of entry at lower job grades, by on-the-job training, by internal promotion, and by seniority systems in which pay and job security are related to length of service (Doeringer and Piore 1971). Later we shall consider how the circumstances of internal labour markets are changing.

Economic Explanations of Pay Dispersion

Economists have responded to the challenge posed by the findings on pay dispersion with several different approaches (Groshen 1991). Three of these approaches remain within the orthodox framework of competitive equilibrium. One approach suggests that labour may be 'sorted by ability' so that differences in earnings reflect different productive capacities of workers, either innate or acquired. But while such considerations may account for earnings differentials between individual workers, they do not thereby explain differences between firms. Even controlling for the fact that different firms may employ workers with different productive capacities leaves an important element of the inter-firm wage differential unexplained (Abowd et al. 1999). Another approach seeks to explain wage dispersion by the absence of perfect information to workers about job opportunities so that their job search is costly. Hence workers may take a job at a wage rate less than that prevailing elsewhere, thereby giving rise to a range of wages for similar jobs at any one time. But, again, random variations in search behaviour or wage offers cannot account for the persistence of inter-firm pay differentials.

An approach that does imply firm-specific effects is that there may be 'compensating differentials' of non-wage factors. It starts with the observation that the wages that are paid do not fully reflect employees' net compensation because they leave out a range of other factors that affect the return to employment. Positive factors include such things as fringe benefits and good working conditions, whereas negative factors cover dirty or dangerous working conditions and unsociable hours. This theory suggests that, once these compensating differentials have been taken into account, returns to employment should be similar across all firms in the labour market. Unfortunately for the theory, however, evidence from a variety of studies finds that wages tend to be positively, not negatively, correlated with the provision of fringe benefits and good working conditions (Mackay et al., 1971; Freeman, 1989). Firms that pay relatively well also tend to provide relatively good non-pay conditions.

These approaches to pay dispersion do not explain why particular employers might choose to pitch their wage offers higher or lower in the range of indeterminacy than others. They are cast as passive recipients of labour market conditions. This weakness is addressed by three approaches that have attracted considerable attention in recent years: 'monopsony' models, 'insider-outsider' models and 'efficiency wage' models.

Monopsony models of the labour market address the question of how some firms are able to pay at levels below the competitive rate without losing their workforce to competitors. In the simplest case this arises where a single employer is a monopoly purchaser of a given type of labour within a local labour market. Workers find it costly to go elsewhere to find work, hence the employer is able to exercise 'monopsony' power in the labour market, and to pay less than the competitive rate. Even if firms are unable to attract sufficient numbers of workers at such rates of pay, they may nonetheless choose to operate with a permanent stock of vacancies because this represents a lower cost option than that of raising the pay rate to attract additional workers. One important implication is that a statutory minimum wage may actually result in an increase in employment, because it forces monopsony employers to raise their wage rates and thereby fill existing vacancies (Card and Krueger 1995; Stewart 2001). Further work has underlined the extent to which many labour markets could be subject to 'dynamic monopsony' (Card and Krueger 1995), because of the difficulties workers face in gaining accurate information about alternative jobs and the costs incurred in leaving one job and starting another. Chapter 17 discusses the limitations of this view.

The central presupposition of 'insider-outsider' models is that firms enjoy a degree of product market power, and hence possess the ability to extract an economic rent from consumers over and above the costs of producing goods and services. Workers can obtain a share of this rent if they are able to deploy bargaining power. Such power is said to derive either from the possession of firm-specific skills (which are therefore costly for the firm to replace) or from union organization (which enables workers to exercise monopoly power over the supply of labour). Wages are consequently determined by two sets of influences: 'outsider', reflecting the interaction of supply and demand in the labour market, and 'insider', reflecting the relative bargaining power of the employer and workers within the firm. Providing the forces shaping the 'insider' influences can be shown to be firm-specific, then an explanation can be developed of the employer effect on wages (Lindbeck and Snower 1986; Carruth and Oswald 1989).

Empirical evidence provides some support for 'insider-outsider' models expressed in terms of worker bargaining power. Analysis of the 1984 Workplace Industrial Relations Survey (Blanchflower et al. 1990), for example, found, first, that the presence of a pre-entry closed shop is associated with relatively high manual earnings and, second, that the ability of skilled workers to extract a rent appears to be less dependent on trade union organization than is the case for semi-skilled or unskilled workers. But how far the sources of 'insider' bargaining power might depend upon union organization rather than upon employer circumstances was questioned by Stewart (1990). He was able to demonstrate that, providing firms possess a degree of product market power, semi-skilled workers in non-union plants are as likely to benefit from a wage mark-up above competitive levels as their counterparts in unionized plants.

This suggests that it may be fruitful to consider Slichter's notion of the firm's 'ability to pay' (Slichter 1950). According to this, those firms that possess a degree of product market power are more likely to pay above competitive wage levels because of their 'super-normal' profits. Given the usual economic assumption of profit maximization, however, conventional theory does not explain why employers should choose to pay over the competitive rate, unless coerced by union pressure. The sixth approach offers an explanation.

'Efficiency wage' theories share the central proposition that workers' productivity will, in part, be determined by the level of wages (Akerlof 1984; Akerlof and Yellen 1986). The payment of a wage in excess of competitive levels can, by eliciting extra productivity from workers, result in increments to output from which the revenue offsets the extra wage costs incurred. From this perspective, pay is an important element in securing productive efficiency – that is, the maximization of outputs from labour effort – as distinct from allocative efficiency. Various sources of this increased productivity have been suggested. They include the coercive pressure on workers who would face an increased cost of job loss where their jobs are paid above market levels; the motivational effects stemming from greater worker commitment to high-paying employers; the savings in direct supervision costs associated with increased trust between employer and employee; and the savings associated with reduced labour turnover.

The pay-off between higher pay and increased productivity that is implied by efficiency wage theories suggests that a competitive market might tolerate a spread of inter-firm differences in pay levels, as a result of either deliberate or random choices by employers. Empirical tests of efficiency wage theory are so far inconclusive (Groshen 1991). They will remain so until the factors underlying the decisions of employers to position themselves differently in terms of the pay-productivity pay-off can be specified more clearly. Despite this, there is considerable value in the central proposition that pay should be seen to play a part not only as a market price for labour, but also as a means by which managements can elicit productive effort from their workforce.

The Employer's Role in Pay Determination

The discussion so far has described how economists' conceptions of pay have shifted, somewhat uncertainly, to focus increasingly on the distinctive role played by the firm as the employer of labour. Starting from the undeniable fact of substantial inter-firm pay dispersion, so unsatisfactory for an orthodox labour market theory, attention has moved to consider the pay-fixing behaviour of firms when they possess a degree of product market power, when they bargain with trade unions, and when they can use pay to elicit productivity (Rubery, 1997). This admission that the employer may have a distinctive role in pay determination is, however, only a starting point. Before discussing the many aspects of the role it is necessary to establish four important empirical points about the competitive constraints under which labour is managed and paid.

The first is that, in a world of imperfect competition, the influences of the product market are in contest with those of the labour market in determining pay, and employers have to mediate between them. There are thus tensions between the *productive* and the *allocative* properties of pay. So long as employers have to recruit and retain labour they cannot wholly free themselves from the influences of the external labour market. If pay for a particular skill falls too far out of line with the external market, labour turnover may rise. But, in the context of an internal labour market, raising the pay of one group may have disruptive effects on established differentials with other groups in the firm's workforce. While such disruption may have costly consequences in terms of morale or strike action, it may be prohibitively expensive to solve the problem by conceding a uniform pay rise for all groups. This was, for example, a common issue in highly unionized petrochemical refineries where traditional notions of internal equity dictated that all time-served craftsmen should be paid on the same rate even though the earnings of their various trades in the outside labour market might be very different. In recent years, however, the decline of traditional apprenticeship, the weakening of trade unions and recourse to outsourcing has provided employers with greater discretion. It is now commonplace to find once privileged groups, such as delivery drivers in the newspaper industry, being paid what are typically termed 'market rates', much inferior to their traditional rates, and comparable with those of the world outside.

Second, the degree of discretion offered to an employer by product market conditions is permissive and not imperative. The influence of the product market over wages tends to be coercive downwards, but permissive upwards. An employer's monopoly strength is thus not necessarily reflected in relatively high wages. American studies have shown how companies in strong market positions have often been able to resist conceding high wages over long periods because, for example, the relatively few employers in the product market have found it relatively easy to combine to resist union demands (Levinson 1966; Ozanne 1968). Similarly, if an employer's monopoly strength *is* reflected in relatively high wages, one should not conclude that this is necessarily the result of a deliberate employer strategy. A study of British engineering firms demonstrated that some of them paid relatively high wages over periods of many years simply because their piece-work payment systems were hopelessly out of management's control. Their product markets were undemanding, with the consequence that their managements had never been forced to undertake the difficult and potentially very costly task of regaining control (Brown 1973).

The third point is that a firm's choice of pay and employment strategy is constrained by its broader production strategy. The management of a firm is a complex, skilled activity. Variations in productivity and labour performance are not simply reducible to differences in factor inputs (Clark 1980; Hodgson 1982). Even firms in direct competition with each other may adopt very different approaches to production and to labour control. Firms whose production is based on high value added, where competition tends to be quality-based, are likely to emphasize high standards of work performance, an ability to work with discretion, and low labour turnover. This, in turn, is likely to be reflected in levels of pay that are high relative to those prevailing locally because of the potential costs of employee disaffection (Ramaswamy and Rowthorn 1991). This will contrast with firms whose competitive strategy is based on the production of low value added, standardized goods where competition tends to be cost- rather than quality-based. It will contrast again with firms whose production is relatively capital-intensive, which will tend to provide relatively good terms of employment, including pay, in order to ensure uninterrupted production.

Fourth and finally, pay is usually used not as an isolated device, but as part of a package of complementary devices to elicit worker productivity. A central source of such differences in productivity lies in the variable nature of the output of labour. Labour cannot simply be hired and blithely set to work. In practice, managements have to devise an integrated bundle of coercive and motivational devices to elicit productive effort from the workers they have hired. Pay is usually an important component of this, but to varying extents. Its importance is likely to be greater where, for example, the work is intrinsically unrewarding, and less so where there is, for example, a strong vocational element.

In sum, a combination of factors prevents employers from being simply the passive recipients of pay rates from the labour market. Employers differ in the compromises they make in protecting internal wage structures from the external labour market. They operate in product markets that offer them different degrees of discretion, and they respond to that discretion in different ways. They adopt different competitive strategies in their productive markets. They use pay to different extents and in different ways in trying to win productivity from their workforces. The key to understanding the dispersion of pay between firms thus lies in investigating management's active use of pay as a means of securing productive effort. We address this by first looking at the management of payment systems and structures, before moving on to discuss the much wider issues involved in pay bargaining with trade unions.

Managing Pay as a Motivator

Payment systems are sets of rules with which employers link pay rates not only to job descriptions, but also to any of a great variety of indicators related to issues such as employees' competence, performance, and career expectations. For as long as there has been employment, payments systems have been the object of endless experimentation. Why is the choice and management of payment systems intrinsically difficult, and why is pay so fickle a motivator?

A recurrent theme in the literature on pay is the stability of relative pay levels over prolonged period of time (Phelps Brown and Hopkins 1981). Authors who have been actively involved in the bargaining process have long commented on the dominance of custom in shaping conceptions of 'fair' relative pay levels, and thereby contributing to this stability (Clay 1929). Relative pay is closely linked to social status and thereby to employee perceptions of self-esteem. Consequently, for both employer and employee, one enters a motivational minefield when one strays from the pattern of relative pay that, whatever its origins may have been, has become consolidated by custom. This is a major reason why relative pay levels generally respond sluggishly, if at all, to changes in the relative demand for different occupations in a labour market.

If we look inside the firm, the stability of the pay structure becomes even more important. Employees' sensitivity to relative pay is all the more acute because they are in daily contact with the people in their comparative reference groups. The closer the point of comparison, the closer it is watched. Unless they accept that some rationale of 'fairness' underlies the disturbance of established internal pay differentials, employees are liable to become distressed, demotivated and thereby less productive. This applies whether or not trade unions are present, although their presence tends to precipitate a more robust reaction.

It is, consequently, important for employers to avoid discordant disruptions of internal pay structures. If there are managerial reasons to introduce alterations, it is important that it is done on some sort of basis of rational justification. This is commonly done by means of a 'job evaluation' procedure. Although these come in many types, they generally combine systematic job analysis with some degree of employee involvement in establishing acceptable relative pay levels. Job evaluation generally incorporates a procedure to review alterations to job content so as to maintain the acceptability of the structure of relative pay under changing circumstances (Quaid 1993). The maintenance of an acceptable internal pay structure is, in large part, a political exercise. When correctly used, job evaluation provides a means of maintaining and legitimizing a negotiated order. It provides a means for establishing criteria with which to assess the 'fairness' of relative pay, with implicit conceptions of fairness that are specific to the individual firm or bargaining unit.

What makes the management of an internal pay structure so demanding is that external changes, in technological, organizational and in market circumstances, alter relative power relationships within the workforce. This, in turn, affects employees' relative pay aspirations and their conceptions of fairness (Brown and Sisson 1975). In brief, it is not simply that a stable internal pay structure is a precondition for a well-motivated workforce from management's point of view, although that is a useful starting point. The particularly demanding management skill is achieving an acceptable level of stability when changing circumstances alter what is acceptable.

The danger that mismanaged pay will demotivate a workforce is all the greater when the payment system has some sort of performance-related component. Payment by results and performance-related pay systems are notoriously fickle and often short-lived. They are difficult to monitor, often have dysfunctional side-effects, and can generate demotivating pay anomalies (Kessler 2000). There has been an increase in the use of performance-related pay schemes in recent years, partly following declining trade union influence. Their success depends on the extent to which the main desired aspects of performance can be both measured and linked to pay in a way that the worker perceives to be fair. This is often very difficult in practice. But whether at the level of the individual worker or of the enterprise, incentive pay schemes usually remain a relatively minor, if highly sensitive, part of a wider motivational package.

Important in understanding this paradoxically minor role that incentive payment schemes play in eliciting productivity is the fact that the main vehicle of long-term, sustained productivity growth is technological change. The introduction of an incentive scheme may achieve a step improvement in labour productivity. If it is successful it may even sustain productivity at that higher level for some time, but it cannot on its own continue to raise it. It is technological change that has brought the sustained and continuing improvements in labour productivity that we have witnessed in industrial societies over the past hundred or more years. Much (perhaps most) technological innovation affects labour productivity in an almost stealthy way through small improvements in materials, controls, organization, and so on. This changes jobs piecemeal, incrementally and irregularly. Managers tend to cope with this by manipulating grading structures pragmatically, with fresh job grades being created and old ones being suppressed with the passage of time.

Furthermore, this varied and elusive character of technological innovation means that there may be little association between the actual productivity improvement achieved and the worker's perception of the increased difficulty and stress, if any, associated with it. The pay rises that accompany technologically driven innovation in practice owe much more to the scale of social and psychological disruption that the innovation has caused the workers involved, and to the consequent need to buy their consent. Consequently the size of ostensibly productivity-related pay increases typically bears little relationship to any actual improvement in the productivity of the workers involved (Brown and Nolan 1988).

In summary, pay plays a complex part in the productive use of labour and if not managed astutely can be a powerful demotivator. This is true whether or not workforces are organized in trade unions. The presence of unions does, however, have a very distinctive impact on the management of pay. Whether or not workers are unionized may not influence their sense of grievance when a sensitive pay differential is adversely and perversely altered, but it does affect their ability to take action over it. Managements deal with trade union action through collective bargaining, to which we now turn.

The Restructuring of Collective Bargaining

'Collective bargaining' is the term used when employers deal directly with the trade unions representing their employees in order to regulate the conduct and terms of their work. As discussed in chapter 1, the Webbs originally conceived of collective bargaining as an essentially economic activity in which workers substitute a group negotiation over wages for individual bargains. Flanders (1970) argued that it was best seen as a political rather than an economic process, observing that the conclusion of a collective agreement does not bind anyone to buy or sell any labour. It sets out the terms and conditions that will prevail if and when labour is engaged. He considered a more appropriate term for collective bargaining to be the joint regulation of work. Pay rates are only a part of the resulting web of rules, which usually also covers issues such as job descriptions, hours of work, and often, explicitly or by implication, working practices, disciplinary standards and effort levels. Collective bargaining is thus concerned with the joint governance not only of pay but also, to a greater or lesser degree, of many other important determinants of labour productivity.

In Britain collective bargaining had, until the 1980s, enjoyed official support, with successive governments throughout the century upholding at least the principle of extending its coverage. Just what proportion of the workforce was covered by a collective agreement at any time has been less clear, with survey data only becoming available in the 1960s. Until the 1980s the percentage coverage of collective agreements was substantially greater than the percentage coverage of trade union membership, but this gap has narrowed substantially since the 1980s and, in aggregate terms, had vanished by 1998. The first row of table 8.1 provides data, some based on estimates, of collective bargaining coverage of employees in Great Britain since 1960. These overstate bargaining coverage for the whole workforce because they relate to establishments of 25 or more employees, and smaller establishments have become increasingly less likely to be covered by any collective agreement. It will be evident that coverage declined dramatically after about 1980.

Table 8.1   Employees covered by collective bargaining for pay-fixing and principal level of pay-bargaining: GB establishments of 25 or more employees, 1960–1998 (%)

	1960	1970	1980	1984	1990	1998
Collective bargaining	80	80	75	70	54	40
of which:						
industry level (multi-employer)	60	50	43	37	31	14
enterprise level (single-employer)	20	30	32	33	23	26
No collective bargaining	20	20	25	30	46	60

Estimates in italics.
Sources: Beatson (1993); Millward et al. (1992); Milner (1995); Millward et al. (2000); Brown et al. (2000).

What structure underlies this collective bargaining coverage? A fundamental strategic issue for any employer intending to establish agreements with trade unions concerns the choice of bargaining unit, by which is meant the categories of employees that are to be covered by a particular collective agreement. This has far-reaching managerial and economic implications because of the substantial standardization of wage rates and conditions of employment that is implied across all those employees included in a single bargaining unit.

The most critical question facing employers is whether they should bargain as a united group, with an industry-wide agreement, or whether they should bargain independently, concluding agreements that are exclusive to some or all of their own employees. The attraction of industry-wide bargaining arrangements comes from their potential to encompass whole product markets at regional or national level. From the early days of collective bargaining both unions and employers have appreciated the chance this offers to pass on some of the cost of wage rises in price rises, traditionally referred to as 'taking wages out of competition'. For unions, industry-wide bargaining has the attraction of establishing the notion of the 'rate for the job' and of encouraging the identification of their members with their wider occupational and labour market collective interests beyond the individual firm. It avoids some of the vulnerability of a workforce that bargains with its firm in isolation. For employers, besides the protection against being picked off by unions separately, there are additional benefits that have strong productivity implications. These are, first, that industry-wide agreements tend to reduce the influence of the union within the workplace and thus limit union impact upon detailed job control. Second, industry-wide agreements, with their accompanying standardization of job descriptions, make easier the industry-wide management of training which helps deal with the problem of 'free-riding' employers who do not train.

Until the 1960s there were few open challenges to this argument in the British private sector. Although there were some exceptions of companies that had their own 'single-employer' agreements, the overwhelming majority of employees were covered by industry-wide ('multi-employer') agreements. Elsewhere in Europe such agreements were to prove their resilience for many years to come, but in post-war Britain full employment was already placing them under excessive strain. At workplace level across much of the private sector there was a growing if covert challenge reflected in the 'wage drift' of earnings away from the rates decreed by increasingly unrealistic industry-wide agreements. Informal workplace bargaining was tending to sap management control over work. In 1968 the Royal Commission under Lord Donovan, having pointed out the weakness of some of the larger industry-wide agreements, argued that for many employers the best solution would be to break away into single-employer, or what is now commonly called 'enterprise', bargaining.

This provided official blessing to an emerging trend that came to dominate British collective bargaining. It is summarized with public and private sectors combined in the second and third rows of table 8.1. In the 1960s there was still a strong majority of employees who relied upon multi-employer (industry-wide) agreements. By the end of the 1990s this had been reversed. Not only had coverage fallen substantially, but only about a third of that coverage came from multi-employer agreements. In the public sector, because of centralized funding, multi-employer arrangements have continued to be important (see chapter 11). But in the private sector the shift from multi-employer agreements was particularly marked; by 1998, the coverage of such agreements was one-fifth that of enterprise bargaining.

Why should there have been so widespread a move to enterprise bargaining when the arguments for industry-wide agreements once seemed so strong? As noted in chapters 2 and 7, employer solidarity has always had shallower roots in Britain than in most other European countries. Britain has generally had weaker wage agreements and training arrangements and has had none of the employer association sanctions and strike insurance schemes that are often to be found elsewhere. In any case, both the advantages and the feasibility of an agreement constrained by national frontiers diminish when, as chapter 3 shows, international trade brings international product markets. For an ever-increasing range of private sector goods and services, wages can no longer be 'taken out of competition' by an employer organization based within a single country. Furthermore, as detailed in chapter 11, the shift of much of the public sector into private ownership, outsourcing, or decentralized trusts, agencies and the like has broken or weakened the national agreements that once regulated public employment.

The positive reasons for adopting enterprise ('single-employer') bargaining come less from any benefits on the wages front than from the potential it offers employers to improve labour productivity in the light of their particular business circumstances. It allows employers to cultivate internal labour markets. When much skill acquisition is on-the-job, and when technological change is constant and incremental, there are advantages in having fluid job titles, predictable career trajectories, and stable internal salary structures. Enterprise bargaining fits in with the more individualistic treatment of employees that is associated with the decline of manual employment and it provides a ready base for enterprise-related incentive schemes.

The changing structure within which bargaining is conducted in Britain is, however, the less dramatic feature of table 8.1. More remarkably, the last row shows the rapid growth in the proportion of the workforce covered by no collective bargaining at all. If we take account of small workplaces not covered by the table, it can be estimated that within a thirty-year period the proportion of British employees unprotected by collective agreements of any sort rose from about a fifth to over two-thirds. The two developments are, however, linked. Employees working for many smaller employers previously covered by multi-employer agreements have de facto moved outside the collective bargaining system with the ending of those agreements, because of the absence of trade union organization at their place of work. Furthermore, some larger employers have taken the opportunity provided by the move to single-employer bargaining to experiment with non-union, and therefore non-collective bargaining, arrangements when opening new sites (Marginson et al. 1993). What, more precisely, is the nature of this withdrawal from collective bargaining, and what is taking its place?

Withdrawal from Collective Bargaining

Until the 1980s it was almost unheard of for employers to withdraw from collective bargaining or, as it is usually termed, to 'de-recognize' trade unions. It was common enough for unions to fail to win recruits in a workplace, or to succeed in that but to fail to gain recognition from management for bargaining purposes. And even then the employer not infrequently chose to follow the terms of the relevant multi-employer agreement. But once collective bargaining had become established it was generally felt not to be worth the effort and acrimony involved in unravelling arrangements and scrapping agreements. In the early 1980s, despite the government's hostility to collective bargaining, acts of de-recognition were rare and were generally confined to a narrow range of industries; but by the end of the decade it was becoming more widespread, although in many cases negotiating rights were withdrawn not as a deliberate management strategy but through lack of support from employees, and this gathered pace until the prospect of a Labour government in the late 1990s (see further chapter 14).

More important than de-recognition in accounting for the retreat from collective bargaining was the fact that both new and existing employers opening 'greenfield' sites became less willing to grant recognition (Millward et al. 2000: 103–8). The proportion of young workplaces (defined as those less than 10 years old) with 25 or more employees granting recognition to trade unions more than halved between 1980 and 1998, from six out of every 10 to under three. By contrast, recognition rates amongst older workplaces (more than 10 years old) declined less markedly comparing 1998 with 1980 (Machin 2000: 634–5). Among large companies, a 1992 survey found that only a minority of those that currently recognized trade unions at some or all of their existing sites had granted unions recognition at new sites. Since decisions on union recognition

Table 8.2 Percentages of employees covered by different pay-fixing arrangements

Row % (excl. final column)	Collective bargaining more than one employer	Collective bargaining higher in organization	Collective bargaining at workplace	Set by management higher in organization	Set by management at workplace	Negotiated with individual employees	Other (e.g. pay review bodies)	% of total employees by industry
All employees	15	13	7	24	26	3	10	100
Public sector	40	17	4	12	3	0	22	31
Private sector	4	12	8	30	36	4	5	69
Manufacturing	5	13	18	16	43	2	2	23
Electricity, gas and water	9	69	7	7	2	0	2	1
Construction	26	5	2	28	20	3	15	3
Wholesale and retail	6	11	1	48	24	3	3	15
Hotels and restaurants	6	2	1	46	31	8	5	4
Transport and communication	15	32	8	20	19	2	3	6
Financial services	2	32	4	28	27	1	15	4
Other business services	2	5	1	30	45	7	8	10
Public Administration	36	28	2	12	1	1	17	8
Education	36	7	3	14	11	1	28	10
Health	28	11	6	17	15	1	20	14
Other services	19	6	6	30	27	2	8	3

Data weighted, based to population of Great Britain, workplaces with 10 or more employees.
The first seven rows do not add up to 100 per cent due to rounding errors.
Source: Brown et al. (2000), from WERS (1998).

were also reported to be highly centralized, this implies a distinct shift in employer policy (Marginson et al. 1993).

Even those employers still recognizing trade unions for collective bargaining have seen a change in recognition in the form of a diminution of trade union influence and a consequent narrowing of the collective bargaining agenda. For a start, the association between recognition and trade union membership diminished. The density of trade union membership in workplaces with recognized unions fell from 78 per cent in 1980 to 56 per cent in 1998. Furthermore, within workplaces where unions were recognized for at least a part of the workforce, the proportion of workers covered by collective bargaining declined: from 86 per cent in 1984 to 67 per cent in 1998 (Millward et al. 2000). But more important was the fact that the nature of recognition changed. The scope of bargaining – the range of issues affected by bargaining – diminished. By the late 1990s many workplaces with trade union recognition had ceased to have formal negotiations over pay, relying instead upon consultation with unions over the minor details of pay settlements within strict budgetary limits (Brown et al. 1998).

The diminishing scope of recognition is even greater if we look at non-pay issues. WIRS analysts concluded that 'when we were able to compare the scope of bargaining between one survey and another the indications were that its scope had declined within the unionized sector. Broadly speaking, fewer issues were subject to joint regulation in 1990 than in 1980' (Millward et al. 1992: 353). The 1998 WERS survey corroborates this picture. For example, where trade unions were recognized, the proportion of managers reporting that they negotiated over employee recruitment fell from 43 per cent in 1980 to 3 per cent in 1998 (Brown et al. 2000).

The arrival of a government in 1997 that was more sympathetic to trade unions, and the subsequent passing of the 1999 Employment Relations Act, has tended to reverse the trend towards complete withdrawal from collective bargaining, and even to encourage 're-recognition' of unions in many firms. But this reversal appears to be very much on terms laid down by employers, and at time of writing it is unlikely to lead to substantial changes in pay-fixing arrangements (Oxenbridge et al. 2001).

How, then, was pay being fixed in Britain by the late 1990s? Table 8.2 draws on the 1998 WERS to categorize pay-fixing arrangements by industrial sector, showing the proportion of employees (in workplaces with 10 or more) covered. It is evident that collective bargaining covered 61 per cent of the public sector workforce, but only 24 per cent of the private sector. Multi-employer bargaining arrangements remained of significance only in the public sector (particularly local government, education and health). In the public sector too, statutory pay review bodies are important in determining pay, accounting for over one in five employees. Where collective bargaining is on a single-employer basis, in both the public and the private sectors, it is arrangements at higher levels of organizations covering a number of sites that are more important, in terms of numbers of employees covered, than arrangements based on individual workplaces. In other words, centralized bargaining within organizations is more prevalent than decentralized site-by-site negotiations.

For 50 per cent of all employees, and 66 per cent of the private sector, management fixed pay unilaterally. In the absence of collective bargaining it appears that relatively more employees are covered by decentralized than centralized pay-setting arrangements within organizations. Even so, 30 per cent of all private sector employees have their pay unilaterally set centrally within the organization (management at a higher level) as compared with 36 per cent whose pay is unilaterally set by management at the workplace. Strikingly, despite the considerable rhetoric and attention devoted to the individualization of the employment relationship (see chapters 12 and 14), negotiation of pay with individual employees was a rarity, accounting for less than 5 per cent of employees in the private sector.

The reality for the vast majority of employees who work in the private sector in Britain is that management, not trade unions, now determines their pay. In 1998 only one in five workplaces in the private sector engaged in collective bargaining, whereas four in five had pay set unilaterally by management (Cully et al. 1999). No new institutional arrangement has emerged in the place of collective bargaining through which individual employees can jointly determine their pay with their employer. Personal contracts, in which individual employees negotiate their pay with management, are found in only a small minority of that large proportion of private sector workplaces where there is no collective bargaining. In practice, 'individualization' means that trade unions are procedurally excluded from fixing pay and conditions, not that employees each receive substantively non-standard, pay and conditions packages (see chapter 12). The absence of any structure of employee representation in the great majority of non-union workplaces is reflected in the finding from a survey of the electrical engineering and insurance sectors, that non-union employee representatives were consulted by management when setting pay in just 5 per cent of cases (Cully and Marginson 1995). We now turn to how, in an era of diminished trade union influence, pay-setting is managed and controlled.

Management Control and Co-ordination of Pay-Setting Arrangements

How are pay-setting arrangements managed? There are two main dimensions to this: first, the control of pay within the firm and, second, how pay is positioned in relation to other employers. The question of internal control is especially important in large multi-site, multi-divisional firms. The growing fragmentation of pay-setting arrangements in the private sector since 1980 has increasingly been offset in multi-site organizations by substantial co-ordination control of local pay determination by management at corporate and divisional offices. A study of large companies operating in the UK in 1992 found that half conducted pay negotiations at site level in at least part of the enterprise. Yet two-thirds of these reported that higher, corporate management was involved in local-level negotiations, either directly participating or, more commonly, establishing parameters within which local managers had to negotiate (Marginson et al. 1993).

Even where local management within large organizations appears to enjoy autonomy over pay-setting, it usually has to operate within a corporate framework of budgetary control. The same survey of large UK companies found that the corporate finance function was extensively involved in setting and negotiating the payroll budgets that shape pay settlements. Moreover, when asked about the assumptions on pay, productivity and employment on which payroll budgets are based, corporate finance managers in over half of these large companies were able to give precise estimates of the assumptions employed. Local managers engaged in decentralized pay-setting probably have discretion over the trade-off between pay, productivity and headcount within their part of the business, but the budgetary constraints of the trade-off are either set by or negotiated with corporate headquarters.

Controlling pay within the firm is one matter; positioning pay levels and pay increases competitively with regard to other firms is quite another, especially in the absence of the sectoral agreements which once provided at least a common reference point for pay. An initial expectation would be one of greatly increased diversity in pay and in pay settlement levels, since the rationale of decentralized pay setting at enterprise level is to tie pay more closely to the particular business requirements. To some extent this appears to have been fulfilled. A study of pay settlements that the CBI monitored over the period 1980 to 1994 suggested that dispersion did increase after 1990. But annual settlements remained the norm, and the use, and apparent impact, of comparisons with other firms remained significant and strong in the 1990s, although now driven less by union pressures than by employer 'bench-marking' (Ingram et al. 1999).

Another study compared two sectors where multi-employer bargaining arrangements have ceased to operate (engineering and retail distribution) with two sectors where national agreements over pay remain in force (printing and the health service), finding there to be still a recognizable annual pay round and no significant difference in variation in average pay between, for example engineering and printing (Arrowsmith and Sisson 1999). In other words, a sector effect on pay-setting lived on in the sectors that had abolished national bargaining arrangements. In part this 'convoy' effect arises from the similar nature of product markets, labour requirements and technology within sectors. But it also reflected the durability of established ways of doing things; the shadow of the respective national agreements was clearly evident in the payments systems and job structures found amongst firms in the engineering and retail sectors.

Information on other employers' pay levels and movements becomes particularly important in a context of decentralized pay-setting in providing an alternative set of benchmarks for management (Arrowsmith and Sisson 1999). In a survey of pay determination arrangements in electrical engineering and insurance, Cully and Marginson (1995) found that four out of every five workplaces used information on other employers' levels of pay. The most common means were national salary surveys, employers' association reports and other industry-specific salary surveys. A majority of workplaces also participated in local salary surveys. Beyond such surveys firms also participated in industry and local networks, and in informal discussion with other companies. Decentralized pay-setting appears to have encouraged these information and networking arrangements.

Pay Determination in the Face of European Economic Integration

Given increasingly international product markets, and given the transnational character of the operations of many large companies in Britain, are employers beginning to set their pay levels by reference to what employers in other countries are doing? Within the European Economic Area, are there signs that economic integration is stimulating particular European practices such as cross-border pay comparisons and pay structures (see Marginson and Sisson 1998)? Are trade unions as well as management driving forward developments?

Pay determination arrangements are almost universally single-employer based, either at company or site level, in the sectors where competition is most clearly international in scope and production is increasingly integrated across borders, such as chemicals, engineering, food manufacturing and banking and financial services. Amongst the multinational companies (MNCs) which dominate these sectors, the collection of data on labour-related aspects of performance, including pay, productivity and labour costs, by MNCs' international corporate or business headquarters is widespread. This is particularly the case for MNCs with integrated production systems or which network services across borders, and where personnel managers from operations in different countries are in frequent contact and regularly meet together (Marginson et al. 1995). Such data are deployed by international management in the form of inter-plant comparisons to exert pressure on the local management and workforce to deliver performance- and flexibility-enhancing measures in local negotiations. This arises in a European, and sometimes global, context where sites are competing for production mandates and future investment from the MNC. However, such inter-plant comparisons appear to be primarily brought to bear in bargaining over working practices and working time arrangements and much less so on pay as such (Coller 1996; Mueller and Purcell 1992).

Such international benchmarking of employee performance appears to be reasonably common in the engineering sector, but unusual in printing and rare in retail (Arrowsmith and Sisson 2001). The latter two sectors are much less exposed to international competition than the first. In engineering, although international comparisons of pay were more widespread, they had relatively little influence on pay settlements among companies in the sector. Of considerably greater significance was the use by companies of international comparisons of overall labour costs. Arrowsmith and Sisson (2001) conclude that British employers appear to be engaged in two processes in managing pay in an international context. First, pay settlements (and employee expectations) themselves continue to be shaped by local and national considerations. Second, labour costs are then aligned with international benchmarks through parallel adjustments both to the numbers employed and to changes in working practices and working time arrangements, sometimes negotiated and other times not.

An earlier study of British-based multinationals found that many were using common job-evaluation systems for white-collar and managerial employees across Europe, indicating that there may be advantages in harmonizing career and control structures within a company. But this is a quite separate matter from that of harmonizing pay levels. The multinationals surveyed were acutely aware that differences in pension arrangements, taxation and social security represented a substantial impediment to any such harmonization, differences that remain even after economic and monetary union (Walsh et al. 1995). Firms were generally hostile to the idea of European co-ordination of pay bargaining across their companies, partly because of the risk of comparability claims from trade unions. Five years later, managers interviewed in nine multinational companies operating in the UK largely echoed these views and concerns (Sisson et al. 1999). Intensified use of cross-border comparisons in negotiations over working practices and working time was anticipated by managers, especially in the automotive sector, but movement towards common rates of pay in different European countries was seen to remain a 'distant prospect' for most types of employee. The exceptions were said to be managers themselves, and some groups of technical staff.

Trade unions for their part are deploying cross-border comparisons of working time and working practices in company and site negotiations among some of the more internationally integrated multinational companies. For example, this was evident in UK claims in the late 1990s for reduced working time at the major automotive manufacturers, where explicit comparisons were drawn with practice at company plants in other European countries (Sisson et al. 1999). As on the management side, however, the use of international comparisons does not appear to have extended to negotiations over pay. British trade unions are involved in developing bargaining co-operation and the exchange of bargaining data and relevant information with their counterparts in other European countries. But the UK is unlikely to be at the forefront of sustained moves by Europe's trade unions to develop a cross-border dimension to pay bargaining across the European Economic Area. This is for two reasons. First, the UK remains outside the single currency, and national and local settlements are therefore unlikely to be particularly influenced by the greater wage transparency that the introduction of the euro is bringing about. The second reason is the difference between the sector-based, multi-employer bargaining structures which still prevail in most other EEA countries and the single-employer pay determination arrangements that now predominate in the UK. For trade unions, the meshing of these two types of structure that the development of a European dimension to pay bargaining must entail represents a substantial future challenge.

Collective Bargaining and Wage Inequalities

We now return to the issue of income distribution with which we started. What have been the consequences of diminishing trade union influence over pay? The contraction of collective bargaining in Britain has been accompanied by a marked growth in wage inequalities, reversing moves towards greater equality in the distribution of earnings that characterized the post-war period up to the late 1970s. Wage inequality rose dramatically in the 1980s, with the result that by the end of the decade the gap in earnings between the highest- and lowest-paid male workers was greater than it had been over a century earlier (Machin, 1996; Johnson, 1996). A growth in the spread of earnings has occurred at both the bottom and top of the wages distribution. Consequently, while those employees at the bottom decile of the earnings distribution have received relatively modest rises in real wages, those in the top decile have experienced dramatic increases in the level of their real earnings. The Low Pay Commission, for instance, estimated that real hourly wages for those employees in the bottom decile of the wages distribution had risen by 20 per cent since 1978 compared with 66 per cent for those in the top decile (LPC 1998: 189).

If unearned income is taken into account, including, for example, income from share options received in payment, the picture becomes even starker. The top 1 per cent of income recipients saw their share of total income in the UK, which had been falling steadily since the 1910s, double from about 5 per cent to about 10 per cent between 1980 and 1998 (Atkinson 2001). This is consistent with the view that an important dynamic in the contemporary pay-fixing system may be 'top down' pay pull whereby the interlocking membership of company directors' pay review bodies may be pulling up top salaries through self-serving and self-reinforcing awards (McCarthy 1993).

Many countries experienced growing earnings inequalities in the 1980s and 1990s. Apart from Britain and the United States, however, the increase in inequality was quite modest. Indeed, Machin's (1999) analysis of trends in male wage inequality from the late 1970s to the mid-1990s suggests that the dispersion of earnings widened dramatically in Britain and the US, but that the structure of wages in other countries, notably in Continental Europe, remained relatively stable. While a variety of factors may underlie rising wage inequalities, the weakening of the collective institutions of pay determination appear to have been crucial in the British context. Wage bargaining serves to compress the structure of earnings for employees both within and across firms, occupations and industries. This is commonly referred to as the 'sword of justice' effect of trade unions (Flanders 1970: 15). The tendency of trade unions to encompass lower-waged employees within the scope of collective agreements, as well as their efforts to tie pay rates to jobs rather than individual productivity or performance criteria, have typically led to a compression of the wages distribution. Accordingly, a range of studies has indicated that trade unions in Britain have, through collective bargaining, served to 'equalize' earnings (Stewart 1987, 1991; Gosling and Machin 1995). As a result, the earnings of unionized workers have been less dispersed than those of their non-unionized counterparts. Such effects were buttressed by legislative mechanisms – such as the Fair Wages Resolution repealed in 1983 (see chapter 6) – that extended the terms of collective bargaining agreements to firms not directly involved in such agreements.

This equalizing impact of unions has been undermined by falling membership and by the withdrawal by employers from collective bargaining. Drawing on WIRS data, Gosling and Machin (1995) found a considerable widening of the gap in the spread of earnings across union and non-union plants between 1980 and 1990, estimating that around 15 per cent of the rise in the dispersion of semi-skilled earnings between 1980 and 1990 was attributable to the decline in unionization. Machin's (1997) analysis of the British Household Panel Survey from 1983 and 1991 attributed between 20 and 37 per cent of the rise in wage inequality to falling unionization. It also suggested that, while wage inequality among individuals rose within both the union and the non-union sector, the spread of earnings increased at a faster rate in the non-union sector. The increase in the relative size of the non-union sector over this period appears therefore to have been an important determinant of the overall rise in wage inequality.

Such findings are consistent with the international evidence. In the United States, Card (1991) and Freeman (1993) found that declining unionization accounted for approximately one-fifth of the rise in male wage inequality between the 1970s and 1980s. For Australia, Borland (1996) found that the decrease in union density over the period 1986 to 1994 explained approximately 30 per cent of the increase in the dispersion of male weekly earnings and 15 per cent of the rise in female earnings dispersion. As in Britain, the main cause of the increase in wage inequality was a rise in the spread of earnings for non-union employees. As discussed in chapter 17, there is also evidence that unionization helps to reduce gender pay inequality.

All this suggests that the weakening of trade unions has had a substantial effect on the distribution of earnings. If we now turn to the bargaining structures within which trade unions operate, it appears that the decentralization of wage determination has served to widen wage differentials. Rowthorn (1992) compared labour market performance in 17 OECD countries between 1973 and 1985 and concluded that countries with highly decentralized wage-setting arrangements have generally been associated with high earnings dispersion. Such findings are reinforced by Blau and Kahn's (1996) analysis of international trends in male wage inequality. In accounting for the higher level of earnings dispersion in the US compared to other OECD countries, they emphasize the role of institutional forces, including the coverage of collective bargaining, union pay policies and government labour market policies, in determining international differences in wage inequality. The decline of collective bargaining and of trade unions has had profound consequences for the structure of pay and the depth of wage inequality.

Conclusions

In this chapter we have described the demise of the system of multi-employer bargaining over pay in Britain, a structure of pay-setting which continues to prevail in many other west European countries, and its replacement by company-based systems for determining pay. We have also shown how, in a growing proportion of these company-based arrangements, pay is not determined through collective bargaining with trade unions but unilaterally by management. The influence of collective bargaining on pay has diminished considerably.

Explanations of pay rooted in the efficient workings of the labour market, which tend to dominate accounts in economics texts, have been shown to be partial and incomplete. It was argued that the factors determining the level at which employers set their pay awards, and whether in large organizations pay is determined at the level of the wider group or individual site, are closely connected to management's competitive strategy in the product market. Accordingly, any future 'Europeanization' of pay-setting is likely to arise from the further integration of product markets that economic and monetary union brings, and not through the imminent creation of a European labour market.

Changes in the structure and coverage of collective bargaining, and declining trade union influence in wage-setting, have permitted a marked increase in wage inequality in Britain since 1980. Statutory measures to support union recognition for collective bargaining and the introduction of the National Minimum Wage constitute important changes to the institutional landscape of pay determination in Britain. Whether their longer-term effects will serve to reverse the rise in wage inequality remains an open question.

References

Abowd, J., Kramarz, F. and Margolis, D. 1999: High wage workers and high wage firms' *Econometrica*, 67 (2), 251–333.

Akerlof, G. 1984: Gift exchange and efficiency wage theory: four views, *American Economic Review* (Papers and Proceedings), 74 (2), 79–83.

Akerlof, G., and Yellen, J. 1986: *Efficiency Wage Models of the Labor Market.* Cambridge: Cambridge University Press.

Arrowsmith, J., and Sisson K. 1999: Pay and working time: towards organisation-based employment systems? *British Journal of Industrial Relations*, 37 (1), 57–75.

Arrowsmith, J., and Sisson K. 2001: International competition and pay, working time and employment: exploring the process of adjustment, *Industrial Relations Journal*, 32 (2), 136–53.

Atkinson, A. B. 2001: Top incomes in the United Kingdom over the twentieth century. Mimeo, Nuffield College, Oxford.

Beatson, M. 1993: Trends in pay flexibility. *Labour Market Trends*, September, 405–28.

Blanchflower, D., Oswald, A. and Garrett, M. 1990: Insider power in wage determination, *Economica*, 57 (2), 143–70.

Blau, F. D., and Kahn, L. M. 1996: International differences in male wage inequality: institutions versus market forces, *Journal of Political Economy*, 104 (4), 791–837.

Borland, J. 1996: Union effects on earnings dispersion in Australia, 1986–1994, *British Journal of Industrial Relations*, 34 (2), 237–48.

Brown, W. 1973: *Piecework Bargaining.* London: Heinemann.

Brown, W., Deakin, S., Hudson, M., Pratten, C. and Ryan, P. 1998: *The Individualisation of the Employment Contract in Britain.* Department of Trade and Industry, Employment Relations Research Series 5. London: DTI. Available at <www.dti.gov.uk/er/emar>.

Brown, W., Deakin, S., Nash, D. and Oxenbridge, S. 2000: The employment contract: from collective procedures to individual rights, *British Journal of Industrial Relations*, 38 (4), 611–29.

Brown, W., Hayles, J., Hughes, B. and Rowe, L. 1980: Occupational pay structures under different wage fixing arrangements: a comparison of intra-occupational pay dispersion in Australia, Great Britain and the United States. *British Journal of Industrial Relations*, 18 (2), 217–30.

Brown, W., Hayles, J., Hughes, B. and Rowe, L. 1984: Product and labour markets in wage determination: some Australian evidence, *British Journal of Industrial Relations*, 22 (2), 169–76.

Brown, W., and Nolan, P. 1988: Wages and labour productivity: the contribution of industrial relations research to the understanding of pay determination, *British Journal of Industrial Relations*, 26 (3), 339–61.

Brown, W., and Sisson, K. 1975: The use of comparisons in workplace wage determination, *British Journal of Industrial Relations*, 13 (1), 23–53.

Card, D. 1991: The effect of unions on the distribution of wages: redistribution or relabelling? Princeton University Industrial Relations Section Discussion Paper 287.

Card, D., and Krueger, A. 1995: *Myth and Measurement: The New Economics of the Minimum Wage*. Princeton: Princeton University Press.

Carruth, A., and Oswald, A. 1989: *Pay Determination and Industrial Prosperity*. Oxford: Oxford University Press.

Clark, K. B. 1980: The impact of unionization on productivity, *Industrial and Labor Relations Review*, 33 (4), 451–69.

Clay, H. 1929: *The Problem of Industrial Relations and Other Lectures*. London: Macmillan.

Coller, X. 1996: Managing flexibility in the food industry: a cross-national comparative case study in European multinational companies, *European Journal of Industrial Relations*, 2 (2), 153–72.

Cully, M., and Marginson, P. 1995: Pay determination in unionised, contractual and unilateral workplaces. Report prepared for the Employment Department.

Cully, M., Woodland, S., O'Reilly, A. and Dix, G. 1999: *Britain at Work*. London: Routledge.

Doeringer, P. B., and Piore, M. J. 1971: *Internal Labor Markets and Manpower Analysis*. Boston: Lexington.

Flanders, A. 1970: *Management and Unions: The Theory and Reform of Industrial Relations*. London: Faber & Faber.

Freeman, R. 1989: *Labour Markets in Action*. New York: Harvester Wheatsheaf.

Freeman, R. 1993: How much has deunionization contributed to the rise in male earnings inequality? In S. Danziger and P. Gottschalk (eds), *Uneven Tides: Rising Inequality in America*. New York: Russell Sage Foundation.

Gosling, A., and Machin, S. 1995: Trade unions and the dispersion of earnings in British establishments 1980–90, *Oxford Bulletin of Economics and Statistics*, 57 (2), 167–84.

Groshen, E. 1991: Five reasons why wages vary among employers, *Industrial Relations*, 30 (3), 350–81.

Hicks, J. 1932: *The Theory of Wages*. London: Macmillan.

Hodgson, G. 1982: Theoretical and policy implications of variable productivity, *Cambridge Journal of Economics*, 6 (3), 213–26.

Ingram, P., Wadsworth, J. and Brown, D. 1999: Free to choose? Dimensions of private sector wage determination 1979–1994, *British Journal of Industrial Relations*, 37 (1), 33–49.

Johnson, P. 1996: The assessment: inequality, *Oxford Review of Economic Policy*, 12 (1), 1–14.

Kessler, I. 2000: Remuneration systems. In S. Bach and K. Sisson (eds), *Personnel Management*. Oxford: Blackwell.

Lester, R. A. 1952: A range theory of wage differentials. *Industrial and Labor Relations Review*, 5 (4), 483–500.

Levinson, H. M. 1966: *Determining Forces in Collective Wage Bargaining*. New York: Wiley.

Lindbeck, A., and Snower, D. 1986: Wage setting, unemployment and insider–outsider relations, *American Economic Review*, 76 (2), 235–9.

LPC (Low Pay Commission) 1998: *The National Minimum Wage: First Report of the Low Pay Commission*, Cmnd. 3276. London: HMSO.

Mackay, D., Boddy, D., Brack, J., Diack, J. and Jones, N. 1971: *Labour Markets under Different Employment Conditions*. London: Allen & Unwin.

Machin, S. 1996: Wage inequality in the UK, *Oxford Review of Economic Policy*, 12 (1), 49–62.

Machin, S. 1997: The decline of labour market institutions and the rise in wage inequality in Britain, *European Economic Review*, 41 (4), 647–57.

Machin, S. 1999: Wage inequality in the 1970s, 1980s and 1990s. In P. Gregg and J. Wadsworth (eds), *The State of Working Britain*, Manchester: Manchester University Press.

Machin, S. 2000: Union decline in Britain, *British Journal of Industrial Relations*, 38 (4), 631–45.

Marginson, P. 1984: The distinctive effects of plant and company size on workplace industrial relations, *British Journal of Industrial Relations*, 22 (1), 1–14.

Marginson, P., Armstrong, P., Edwards, P. and Purcell, J., with Hubbard, N. 1993: *The Control of Industrial Relations in Large Companies: An Initial Analysis of the Second Company Level Industrial Relations Survey*. Warwick Papers in Industrial Relations, 45. Coventry: IRRU, University of Warwick.

Marginson, P., Armstrong, P., Edwards P. and Purcell J. 1995: Extending beyond borders: multinational companies and the international management of labour, *International Journal of Human Resource Management*, 6 (3), 702–19.

Marginson, P., and Sisson, K. 1998: European collective bargaining: a virtual prospect? *Journal of Common Market Studies*, 36 (4), 505–28.

McCarthy, W. E. J. 1993: From Donovan till now: or twenty-five years of incomes policy, *Employee Relations*, 15 (6), 3–20.

Millward, N., Bryson, A. and Forth, J. 2000: *All Change at Work?* London: Routledge.

Millward, N., Stevens, M., Smart, D. and Hawes, W. R. 1992: *Workplace Industrial Relations in Transition*. Aldershot: Dartmouth.

Milner, S. 1995: The coverage of collective pay setting institutions in Britain 1895–1990, *British Journal of Industrial Relations*, 33 (1), 69–92.

Mueller, F., and Purcell, J. 1992: The Europeanisation of manufacturing and the decentralisation of bargaining, *International Journal of Human Resource Management*, 3 (1), 15–24.

Nolan, P., and Brown, W. 1983: Competition and workplace wage determination, *Oxford Bulletin of Economics and Statistics*, 45 (3), 269–87.

Oxenbridge, S., Brown, W., Deakin, S. and Pratten, C. 2001: Collective representation and the impact of law. Paper to the British Universities Industrial Relations Association annual conference.

Ozanne, R. 1968: *Wages in Practice and Theory*. Madison: University of Wisconsin Press.

Phelps Brown, E. H., and Hopkins, S. V. 1981: *A Perspective of Wages and Prices*. London: Methuen.

Quaid, M. 1993: *Job Evaluation: The Myth of Equitable Assessment*. Toronto: University of Toronto Press.

Ramaswamy, R., and Rowthorn, R. 1991: Efficiency wages and wage dispersion, *Economica*, 58 (4), 501–14.

Rowthorn, B. 1992: Corporatism and labour market performance. In J. Pekkarinen, M. Pohjola and B. Rowthorn (eds), *Social Corporatism: A Superior Economic System?* Oxford: Oxford University Press.

Rubery, J. 1997: Wages and the labour market, *British Journal of Industrial Relations*, 35 (3), 337–62.

Sisson, K., Marginson, P., Arrowsmith, J., Edwards T. and Newell, H. 1999: The industrial relations impact of economic and monetary union in the UK. Report prepared for the European Foundation for the Improvement of Living and Working Conditions, December.

Slichter, S. 1950: Notes on the structure of wages, *Review of Economics and Statistics*, 32 (1), 80–91.

Stewart, M. 1987: Collective bargaining arrangements, closed shops and relative pay, *Economic Journal*, 97 (1), 140–56.

Stewart, M. 1990: Union wage differentials, product market influences and the division of rents, *Economic Journal*, 100 (4), 1122–37.

Stewart, M. 1991: Union wage differentials in the face of changes in the economic and legal environment, *Economica*, 58 (1), 155–72.

Stewart, M. 2001: Estimation of the individual-level employment effects of the introduction of the National Minimum Wage. Final report to the Low Pay Commission, April.

Thomson, A., and Sanjines, C. 1990: Earnings by size of company and establishment. In M. Gregory and A. Thomson (eds), *A Portrait of Pay, 1970–82*. Oxford: Clarendon Press.

Walsh, J., Zappala, G. and Brown, W. 1995: European integration and the pay policies of British multinationals, *Industrial Relations Journal*, 26 (2), 84–96.

Weiss, A., and Landau, S. J. 1984: Wages, hiring standards and firm size, *Journal of Labor Economics*, 2 (4), 477–500.

9
TRADE UNION ORGANIZATION

JEREMY WADDINGTON

Nowhere in western Europe were trade unions confronted by such a concerted neo-liberal assault as in the United Kingdom between 1979 and 1997. As discussed in chapters 2 and 5, institutions of the post-war consensus were dismantled by successive Conservative governments, which implemented economic and political policies that forced unions on to the defensive. No fewer than nine separate pieces of legislation were enacted in the UK to curtail union organization and activity. Employers exploited the opportunities presented by the Conservatives' policies to restrict union activity and to resist the extension of union organization. The impact of these measures was, as explained in chapter 10, particularly damaging to workplace representation, the bedrock of British union strength, which was not legally underpinned as in many countries of western Europe. It has been claimed that the combined effect of these measures is no less than the 'dissolution of the labour movement' and the secular ascendancy of individualism (Phelps Brown 1990).

Employment shifts away from manufacturing towards private sector services, coupled to high levels of unemployment, resulted in continuous annual membership decline between 1979 and 1998. In sectors where unions were recognized, employers decentralized bargaining to the detriment of union cohesion and articulation. In private sector services and other areas of employment growth, many employers resisted unionization. Although high levels of job insecurity pervade the economy, unions have been unable to attract workers in expanding areas of the labour market into membership. Furthermore, through the introduction of new management practices, employers have isolated or bypassed shop stewards and union workplace organization in all but the most densely unionized sites.

The election of the Labour government in 1997, and its subsequent re-election in 2001, offered unions some hope of respite from the neo-liberal challenge. In its pursuit of the 'Third Way', the government reversed the UK's opt-out from the Social Protocol of the Maastricht Treaty and enacted legislation to facilitate trade union recognition (see chapter 6). The Labour government, however, is committed to retaining much of the legislation introduced by the Conservative governments to regulate trade unions, and opposed the draft directive of the European Commission (EC) on national-level information and consultation. There is also no likelihood that the social contract between the previous Labour government (1974–9) and the trade unions will be renewed or that the government will enact measures to encourage the re-establishment of national multi-employer collective bargaining. Instead, the government has 'distanced' itself from the unions, which are treated as a special interest group rather than as being an integral part of a labour movement. The 'contentious alliance' (Minkin 1991) between the unions and the Labour Party is, once again, in a state of flux.

Trade unions were initially slow to meet the neo-liberal challenge, with the consequence that its impact was amplified. A wide-ranging process of reform is, however, now under way at all levels of trade unionism. The Trades Union Congress (TUC)[1] has abandoned much of its committee structure in an attempt to adopt a more campaigning role. It was also instrumental in reversing the opposition of many British unions to the European Union (EU). Trade union mergers have continued apace, together with the reform of internal systems of representation. In addition, extensive organizing campaigns have been implemented with the object of developing recruitment and retention activities. New forms of 'partnership' have also been sought with employers. These measures have neither restored the political influence of trade unions nor reversed the decline in membership. Trade unions in the UK thus remain on the defensive.

The decoupling of trade unions from their traditional sources of influence promoted crises in the ways in which unions *aggregate* the interests of their members and then *represent* these interests to employers and government. In particular, increasing membership heterogeneity has necessitated the establishment of internal union structures to promote participation among more diverse groups of members and the development of mechanisms whereby a wider range of interests are reconciled within bargaining agendas. In addressing the crises of interest aggregation and representation, unions have embarked on a series of reforms to policy, structure and activity. A key and, as yet, unresolved tension within the reform agenda is between policies and activities characteristic of Anglo-Saxon trade union practice and those resonant of unions operating within the European social market model. Trade unions advocate social partnership with employers *and* the 'organizing model' of union behaviour. The tenets of social partnership are borrowed, albeit in a modified form, from west European trade union practice and view employers as partners in a search for mutual benefits. In contrast, it is the threat the employer poses to the employee that underpins the appeal of the organizing model, which assumes that the employee will join a union in order to seek protection from the activities of the employer. The same tension is evident in the simultaneous promotion of the 'single channel' (union only) and the 'dual system' (embracing systems not based solely on unions) of representation. Furthermore, the expanding range of individual legal protections emanating from the EU and the government is resulting in increasing demands on union organization to 'police' the legislation on behalf of members.

These demands also impinge on union reform and the processes of interest aggregation and representation. This chapter assesses the contradictions in trade union policy and activity that arise from these tensions in the reform agenda and argues that the character of interest aggregation and representation is in the process of a marked transformation.

This chapter addresses these issues in three sections. The first section examines the effects of the neo-liberal policy agenda. Although it argues that many of the intended effects were not realized, it acknowledges that a range of union activities, structures and policies in existence before 1980 are now rejected by many trade unionists. It also reviews the effects of these measures on unionization, merger activity and industrial conflict, and thus identifies the nature of the challenge faced by unions in the UK if they are to regain influence. The second section traces the development of Labour Party policy and examines how this is likely to affect trade union organization. It argues that elements of both US market capitalism and the European social model are present in Labour government policy. The former represent continuity with the policies of the previous Conservative governments, whereas the latter present opportunities to develop union organization. However, limitations in the capacity of British unions to mobilize and the 'distancing' of the Labour Party from the unions have curtailed the influence of unions on government policy formulation. The third section identifies four areas of reform introduced by trade unionists: the reorientation of the TUC, the shift in policy in favour of Europe, the adoption of social partnerships with employers and the establishment of an organizing culture within which recruitment can be extended to hitherto unorganized sectors of the economy. The argument of this section is that significant shifts in policy have been introduced, but they have not yet led to any widespread reverse of membership decline, nor have they addressed the key issues of union cohesion and articulation.

The Challenge of the Neo-Liberal Assault

This section traces the impact of measures of union exclusion in four stages. The first stage examines the impact of the Conservative political programme on the exclusion of unions at national and workplace levels. The subsequent stages review the impact of these measures on unionization, trade union restructuring by mergers and strikes.

The scope of the political challenge

The three principal political objectives of Conservative governments were the exclusion of unions from any role in national policymaking; to change the character of internal union democracy by compelling unions to adopt representative forms of democracy at the expense of participative forms; and to encourage management to assume greater control within the workplace. The last is not considered here (see chapters 7 and 8). The exclusion of unions from macro-economic and social policy formulation was achieved soon after 1979. As discussed in chapter 5, many of the institutions central to even the dilute forms of corporatism that characterized the UK during the 1970s were dismantled, principal among which were the Industrial Training Boards, the National Enterprise Council and, in 1992, the National Economic Development Council. The TUC attempted to re-establish links with the government and employers around the time of the 1983 Congress. This approach, termed 'New Realism', had the intention of formulating tripartite policies to address the high rate of unemployment. Its rejection was symbolized by the banning of unions from the Government Communications Headquarters (GCHQ) in 1984.[2] The Conservative government's concerted action against the year-long coal strike in 1984–5, for which it been planning since 1978 (Adeney and Lloyd 1986: 72–4), further heightened enmity between it and the trade unions. The TUC derived much of its authority over affiliated unions through its role as a conduit to government during the 1960s and 1970s. The political exclusion of unions after 1979 was thus felt particularly hard within the TUC.

A second objective pursued by Conservative governments after 1979 was the regulation of union decision-making and electoral procedures. Under the rubric of 'returning unions to their members' (DE 1983), a series of measures was enacted which collectively comprises the most comprehensive regulation of union government ever attempted in the UK. The central pillar of this approach is the independently scrutinized, fully postal, individual membership ballot that is now required every five years in the election of union executive committees, union presidents and union general secretaries (see chapter 6; Hendy 1989). By such means, it was anticipated that militant and unrepresentative union leaders would no longer be elected to positions of influence (DE 1983: 1–2). Individual union members were also afforded a range of statutory rights enforceable against unions. A Commissioner for the Rights of Trade Union Members (CROTUM) was appointed to assist union members in enforcing these rights.

Legislation intended to realize the individualist conception of union democracy advocated within the neo-liberal programme has had mixed effects. Legislative changes have led to the increased centralization of union government. The introduction of postal ballots has resulted in lower levels of membership participation in elections for senior positions in many unions, and there was a decline in the role and influence within the democratic process of intermediary levels, such as regions and districts (Undy et al. 1996: 240–4). The introduction of fines when the balloting requirements were contravened also accentuated central controls, particularly as the finances of many unions were parlous (Willman et al. 1993). Furthermore, very few applications for assistance were made to the CROTUM,[3] suggesting that member dissatisfaction with union practice and procedures was relatively limited. There is also no consistent evidence to suggest that the legislation reduced the impact of the political left during union elections (Undy et al. 1996: 188–90).

The political implications of the legislation for the union movement were wide-ranging. Until 1987 the majority of unions openly opposed the legislation and hoped for the election of a Labour government that would repeal it. Reform in unions was accordingly limited. Only the Amalgamated Engineering Union (AEU) and the Electrical, Electronic, Telecommunication and Plumbing Union (EETPU) were prepared to accept the Conservative legislation and financial support from the state to conduct ballots. This acceptance almost led to the expulsion of the AEU from the TUC in 1986, and was a key factor in the expulsion of the EETPU in 1988. In addition to the divisions among unions provoked by the balloting measures, the failure of the Labour Party in the 1987 and 1992 general elections led to a series of policy reviews, an outcome of which was the acceptance of the legislation on balloting by the Labour Party.

The reforms of the public sector discussed in chapter 11 complemented these measures and served as a political example to the private sector. The overarching objective was to bring market pressures to bear on a wide range of public services (Carter and Fairbrother 1999). Privatization, compulsory competitive tendering and the establishment of internal markets removed some workers from the ambit of public sector unions while among those remaining the proportion employed on short-term or temporary contracts rose sharply (Foster and Scott 1998).

The impact of these measures can be gauged in terms of their effects on the coverage of bargaining, union recognition and workplace practices. As discussed in chapter 8, employers withdrew from multi-employer bargaining, and collective bargaining coverage fell. The rise in the number of bargaining units arising from the decentralization of bargaining has placed an additional burden on union organization, as union support services have become more thinly spread. In particular, the relatively few full-time officers employed by trade unions in Britain have been unable to provide sufficient support to members. Furthermore, several unions have encountered difficulties in recruiting adequate numbers of shop stewards and providing those that do come forward with sufficient training. In the absence of both full-time officers and shop stewards in adequate numbers, the internal co-ordination of many union activities has been jeopardized by the decentralization of bargaining.

The proportion of workplaces at which employers recognized trade unions fell sharply. In 1984 unions were recognized at 66 per cent of workplaces. By 1990 this proportion had fallen to 53 per cent and to 45 per cent in 1998 (Cully et al. 1999). This was partly due to the direct de-recognition of unions, which was, however, limited to specific sectors and occupations, where unions were weak or where employers introduced individual bargaining for specific grades of employee (Claydon 1996). Employer resistance to unionization in new workplaces appears to be a more significant factor in the decline. For example, in 1998 unions were recognized at 32 per cent of workplaces that had existed for 25 or more years. This proportion fell to 22 per cent in workplaces of between 10 and 24 years' duration and to only 18 per cent in workplaces established during the last 10 years (Cully et al. 1999: 240).[4] The extent of employer rejection of a union presence was thus broader than at any time since 1945. Furthermore, where unions maintained a presence, management isolated or bypassed many union representatives, thus excluding them from any consultation or negotiation processes associated with workplace change (Smith and Morton 1993; Cully et al. 1999; Millward et al. 2000: 138–83).

Accompanying the decline in union recognition have been extensive changes at the workplace. As argued in chapter 12, trends towards individualization have tended to weaken the place of the union in the relationship between employer and worker. Several other developments, notably the wage inequality and insecurity discussed in chapter 1, present opportunities for unions. Attitudes towards management are also hardening as fewer workers feel their workplace is well managed and that relations between managers and workers are good, while an increasing number of workers feel that managers will 'try to get the better of them' if given the chance (Kelly 1998). Even where individualized pay arrangements are in place, workers want unions to establish a framework within which individual pay is settled fairly and equitably (Waddington and Whitston 1996), although there is no evidence to suggest that trade unions have been able to meet this requirement.

Plummeting unionization rates

Table 9.1 shows the movements in unionization in Great Britain since 1948. Between 1948 and 1965 increases in membership were slightly smaller than rises in employment, with the result that density fell slowly from 46 per cent to 43 per cent. Rapid membership growth between 1965 and 1979 led to a density level of 56 per cent. The period 1980–98 is the longest period of continuous annual membership decline since 1892, when records were first compiled. The membership gains secured between 1965 and 1979 were lost in half the time it had taken to achieve them. Trade unions currently organize less than three in 10 of the British labour force. The periods of steepest decline after 1979 were during the first few years of both the 1980s and 1990s, when the level of unemployment rose sharply during recessions. It is noteworthy, however, that declines in membership and density were also recorded during periods of employment expansion. The relationship between unionization and unemployment was thus not direct after 1979. During the mid-1990s the rate of decline slowed and several unions reported small membership increases.

In 1999 the first increase in trade union membership was reported since 1978/9. This increase of 105,000, however, was insufficient to raise density, which fell a further 0.1 per cent. British unions now represent a smaller proportion of the labour force than at any time since 1937.

A range of explanations has been advanced for the extent of the aggregate decline. There is a complex web of interrelationships between these explanations, which precludes the identification of their individual effects. It is apparent, however, that the impact, either directly or indirectly, of the measures associated with the Conservative political project had a wide-ranging influence on the decline in unionization. A direct effect of government policy in promoting membership decline is claimed by Freeman and Pelletier (1990: 155). This effect is seen as independent of other factors. They argue that the abolition of the statutory recognition procedure in 1980, the gradual removal of immunities protecting the closed shop, and restrictions on secondary action accounted for 'effectively the entire decline in UK density in [the period 1980–6]'.

Table 9.1   Union membership: Great Britain,[a] 1948–2001

Year	Membership[b] (000s)	Annual % change	Density[c] %	Annual % change
1948	9,102		45.5	
1950	9,003		44.3	
1955	9,460		44.5	
1960	9,437		44.0	
1965	9,715		43.0	
1970	10,672		48.5	
1975	11,561		52.0	
1979	12,639		55.8	
1980	12,239	−3.2	54.5	−1.3
1981	11,628	−5.0	54.4	−0.1
1982	11,138	−4.2	53.3	−1.1
1983	10,766	−3.3	52.3	−1.0
1984	10,336	−4.0	49.8	−2.5
1985	10,282	−0.5	49.0	−0.8
1986	9,995	−2.8	47.4	−1.6
1987	9,874	−1.2	46.3	−1.1
1988[d]				
1989	8,939		39.0	
1990	8,835	−1.2	38.1	−0.9
1991	8,602	−2.6	37.5	−0.6
1992	7,956	−7.5	35.8	−1.7
1993	7,767	−2.4	35.1	−0.7
1994	7,530	−3.0	33.6	−1.5
1995	7,309	−2.9	32.1	−1.5
1996	7,244	−0.9	31.2	−0.9
1997	7,154	−1.2	30.2	−1.0
1998	7,155	−0.0	29.6	−0.6
1999	7,277	+1.7	29.5	−0.1
2000	7,351	+1.0	29.4	−0.1
2001	7,295	−0.8	28.8	−0.6

[a] The data refer to Great Britain, rather than the United Kingdom.
[b] Union membership excludes unemployed and retired workers that retain membership. Until 1987 this exclusion is undertaken on the basis of union membership records and is unlikely to exclude all such members. After 1988 the Labour Force Survey data is based on those in employment and thus excludes all unemployed and retired workers.
[c] Union membership expressed as a proportion of all employees, except those serving in the armed forces.
[d] The difference in membership and density data between 1987 and 1989 can be explained in terms of membership decline *and* the transfer from one data source to another (see sources below for details).
Sources: Waddington (1992) for 1948–87 data; Labour Force Survey for 1989–2001 data.

Three factors undermine this explanation. Firstly, the decline in union density preceded the initial legislation (Disney 1990). The decline in density *may* thus have facilitated the enactment of the legislation, not vice versa. Secondly, if legislation was the sole influence on the decline in unionization, the rate of decline would be expected to rise as the cumulative effects of successive legislative measures restricted union organizing opportunities. Table 9.1 shows that this is not the case; the rate of decline is uneven rather than accelerating. Thirdly, the effects of the legislation enacted during the 1980s are contradictory and closely related to other developments (Brown and Wadhwani 1990). The case of the closed shop illustrates the point. Legislation on the closed shop was claimed to have had a marked effect on membership decline by Freeman and Pelletier. Yet between 1980 and 1984 almost all of the steep decline in the coverage of closed shops was due to compositional and structural effects, rather than legislative reform (Millward and Stevens 1986).

The legal explanation, however, should not be dismissed outright. As was mentioned above, employers at new sites appear to have used the legislation to resist union recruitment initiatives. It is difficult, however, to separate this effect from other concurrent developments (Disney et al. 1998). One of these effects is the shift in the composition of employment. Similarly to developments in much of western Europe, there has been a significant shift in employment away from manufacturing towards private sector services. Associated with this shift are trends towards more employment at small sites and more employment of women, part-time workers, workers on temporary contracts, and young workers. Each of these structural factors tends to be associated with lower levels of unionization. Changes in the composition of employment are shown to account for between about 25 and 30 per cent of the decline in unionization during the 1980s (Waddington 1992).

Workers in private sector services join unions for similar reasons to those in manufacturing and the public sector (Waddington and Whitston 1997), suggesting that it is not only the shift in the composition of employment that is at issue. Other factors, such as employer resistance or the absence of unions and union recruitment campaigns, are also influential. Employers in private sector services have been resistant to unionization for many years. This resistance may have been facilitated by the presence of structural factors, such as the prevalence of small sites, and the absence of unions and organizing campaigns. In recent years legislation may have also assisted employers in resisting unions. What existing research has been unable to do is to separate the effects of employer resistance from those of other influences. For example, the average density among part-time women workers is less than 30 per cent, but where a union was available for them to join the rate doubled (Green 1990). Similarly, where management is pro-union over 60 per cent of workers are unionized, but where management opposes unionization the level falls to 7 per cent (Cully et al. 1998). Thus, although the evidence is not conclusive, it seems likely that employer resistance has prevented unions from securing a presence at many workplaces and, hence, extending unionization throughout private sector services. This factor would also explain the incapacity of unions to record membership increases during periods of employment growth since 1979 (Disney et al. 1995; Disney et al. 1998).

The abandonment of any political commitment to full employment by the Conservative government was a further contributory factor to the decline of unionization. Unemployment rose sharply from 5.2 per cent in 1979 to 11.5 per cent in 1983 and did not fall beneath 10 per cent until 1988. Many of the jobs were lost from areas of union strength such as manufacturing and losses affected male, full-time workers. As unions in the UK offer very few services to unemployed members and there is no unemployment insurance administration conducted by unions, the majority of unionists made redundant abandoned their union membership. Associated with high levels of unemployment was the closure of many large workplaces within which trade union membership was concentrated (Machin 1995). Analysis reveals a close association between membership decline and rising unemployment during the 1980s (Carruth and Disney 1988). Furthermore, during the recession of the early 1990s extensive workforce restructuring was most likely to be undertaken by those companies that were adversely affected by the recession, thus accelerating membership decline (Geroski et al. 1995).

Union restructuring by merger

Membership decline was accompanied by a fall in the number of unions from 454 in 1979 to 218 in 1999–2000 (Certification Office 1980 and 2001).[5] Although more than 70 unions dissolved during this period, the principal reason for the decline in the number of unions is merger activity. The intensity of merger activity has been high in the UK since the mid-1960s (Waddington 1995). In the UK a merger may be completed by means of an amalgamation, in which two or more unions acting as equal partners combine to form a new union, or through a transfer of engagements, in which a large union acquires a smaller union.[6] Mergers completed using the transfer of engagements procedure account for about three-quarters of the decline in the number of unions due to mergers, but less than 15 per cent of the membership involved in the merger process (Undy et al. 1996: 45).

Factors associated with membership decline and its effects on financial viability have promoted many recent mergers. Membership contributions continue to constitute a substantial proportion of union income, but competition for members between unions often precludes increases in the level of membership contributions, thereby exacerbating financial weakness. Mergers are seen as a means of achieving some economies of scale. Proponents of mergers also claim that they may form a base from which the post-merger union may expand into areas of employment growth. There is no consistent evidence to suggest that this objective has been achieved. More likely is that mergers have merely mitigated the effects of membership loss among the larger unions.

A diverse range of merger policies have been implemented, with the consequence that the notoriously complex structure of British trade unionism has not been markedly 'simplified' by this extensive merger activity (Waddington 1995).

There is a tendency for union memberships to become more heterogeneous, even as membership declines. This tendency is clearly illustrated by the large number of unions that have now adopted some form of internal sectional system of representation, whereby groups of members are allocated to different sections according to their industry or occupation. A consequence of this development is that a wider range of support services is required at a time of membership decline and financial stringency, thus placing greater pressure on union resources.

The two traditional 'general' unions, the Transport and General Workers' Union (TGWU) and the General, Municipal and Boilermakers' Union (GMB), have acquired other unions since 1979. Although the TGWU was most active during the 1960s and 1970s, the GMB was more active after 1979, acquiring unions organizing groups as diverse as boilermakers, clerical workers, textile workers, tailors and garment workers and managers in local government. In order to absorb these unions, an internal structure based on sections was established. This complemented the traditional regional structure of the GMB and represented the adoption of a structure similar to the Trade Group system of the TGWU. A proposal to merge the TGWU and the GMB met with strong resistance from within specific regions of both unions.

The Amalgamated Engineering and Electrical Union (AEEU) was formed by an amalgamation in 1992. This merger combined two unions that originally recruited craft workers, although both had extended their recruitment activities throughout much of manufacturing prior to the merger, and several small white-collar unions that organized in a range of industries had been acquired. The AEEU is thus almost as wide in coverage as the two general unions, although its leadership still tends to be drawn from among former craft workers. A sectional structure has been adopted in order to incorporate an increasingly heterogeneous membership. This heterogeneity was widened with the merger of the AEEU with Manufacturing, Science and Finance (MSF), which was overwhelmingly ratified in an amalgamation ballot during March 2001. In practice this means that there are now three unions with a significant coverage in manufacturing; the TGWU, GMB and the union resulting from the AEEU–MSF merger. The next merger involving any two of these three unions is thus likely to determine which union will be the dominant union in manufacturing industry for the foreseeable future.

The amalgamations to form UNISON, the Graphical Paper and Media Union (GPMU), the Communication Workers' Union (CWU) and Public Commercial Services Union (PCS) unified groups of workers from within the same industry or sector. UNISON organizes across most of the public sector. The civil service is outside UNISON's ambit. It has particular concentrations of members in the National Health Service and local government. The merger brought together manual and white-collar workers in these industries, although the majority of nurses are outside and organized by the Royal College of Nursing (RCN). Similarly, the amalgamation to form the GPMU was the final merger, of a long series, that combined craft and unskilled workers within the printing industry. The formations of the CWU and PCS represent further stages in the unification of

workers in communications (post and telephones) and the civil service respectively. Each of these mergers was accompanied by the adoption of internal sections,
established to represent the interests of specific groups of workers. It remains to
be seen whether these new structures are the basis for cohesion between the
different membership groups or whether they inhibit the co-ordination of activities involving members from different groups.

UNISON has introduced a particularly wide-ranging series of constitutional
devices, designed to retain cohesion among a diverse membership. The constitution of the union incorporates representation on the basis of occupation, pay-
bargaining group, gender and status group. Also integral to the constitution is
the principle of proportionality in the composition of committees, conferences,
delegations and meetings. Many other unions have also introduced committee
structures through which under-represented groups, such as women and young
workers, can be encouraged to participate in union activities. The outcome of
these measures is far from uniform. Increases in the proportion of women shop
stewards have been recorded by several unions. The number of these women to
have secured more senior positions, however, remains marginal.

The merger process is associated with attempts to develop new forms of cohesion and articulation among heterogeneous memberships. The impact of the
legislative change in promoting the centralization of union government has been
amplified by the post-merger structures adopted in several unions. Tiers of management have been removed from union structures and an increasing number of
union officials have attended management schools for customized training. While
such managerial approaches may result in much-needed cost savings, it remains
to be seen how they impinge on union articulation. What is more certain is that
mergers will continue to be a preferred method of union structural adaptation.

Strike trends: a return to industrial peace?[7]

Strikes are a widely discussed indicator of organized collective action, and since
virtually all recorded strikes in the UK involve unions they are conveniently discussed here. They are not the only indicator of industrial conflict, and chapter 13,
for example, indicates continuing tensions over the introduction of new working
practices. But they remain an indicator of the conduct of industrial relations.

Table 9.2 shows that strike activity in the UK is at its lowest level since the
initial compilation of strike statistics in 1891. Although strike activity declined
throughout much of western Europe during the 1980s and 1990s, the decline in
the UK is steeper than elsewhere. During the run-up to the election in 1997,
Conservatives suggested that the election of a Labour government would lead to
a rise in strike activity. Although the number of days lost through strikes rose in
1998, because of strikes on the railways, London Underground and in construction, the overall trend continued downward, which proponents of social partnership took as evidence of a maturity in relations between managers and workers,
and as confirming the 'partnership mood', an issue to which this chapter will
return. In 1999 and 2000, however, the number of strikes and workers involved
increased.

Table 9.2 Strike trends in the United Kingdom, 1946–2000 (annual averages)[a]

Year	Strikes (no.)	All industries Workers involved (000s)	Days lost (000s)	Working days lost per 1,000 workers Mining, energy and water	Manufacturing	Services
1946–52	1,698	444	1,888			
1953–9	2,340	790	3,950			
1960–8	2,372	1,323	3,189			
1969–73	2,974	1,581	12,497			
1974–9	2,412	1,653	12,178			
1980	1,348	834	11,964	259	1,691	42
1981	1,344	1,513	4,266	374	396	117
1982	1,538	2,103	5,313	649	352	211
1983	1,364	574	3,754	2,212	345	39
1984	1,221	1,464	27,135	38,425	529	114
1985	903	791	6,402	7,518	183	86
1986	1,074	720	1,920	293	220	46
1987	1,016	887	3,546	482	124	181
1988	781	790	3,702	536	339	116
1989	710	727	4,128	165	156	199
1990	630	298	1,903	245	228	44
1991	369	177	761	87	52	30
1992	253	148	528	97	23	24
1993[b]	211	385	649	91	28	31
1994	205	107	278	2	15	13
1995	235	174	415	6	17	20
1996	244	364	1,303	8	24	70
1997	216	130	235	9	21	7
1998	166	93	282	1	8	13
1999	205	141	242	0	14	7
2000	212	183	499	17	13	20

[a] Strikes lasting less than one day or involving fewer than 10 workers are excluded from the UK statistics, unless the total numbers of days lost exceeds 100.
[b] Industrial data were classified according to the SIC 1980 for 1980–93, whereas figures for 1994 onwards are classified to SIC 1992.
Sources: Edwards (1995: 439) for 1946–79 data; Davies (2001) for 1980–2000 data.

Although strike activity has declined over the last decade, the distribution of reasons that underpin strikes has remained fairly constant. Strikes resulting from disputes over pay accounted for 51 per cent of working days lost in 1988 and 69 per cent in 1999 (Davies 2001). The most significant change over the period was the decline in the proportion of working days lost due to 'staffing and work allocation', which fell from 33 per cent to 2 per cent between 1988 and 1999. This decline suggests that management controls may be limiting workers' ability to mobilize around these issues within the workplace. 'Redundancy questions' were the cause of a further 14 per cent of working days lost in 1999. No other single reason was the cause of more than 10 per cent of working days lost in 1999.

Why has strike activity in the UK declined so sharply? As with the explanation of membership decline, no single explanation accounts for the entire downward trend in strikes. A variety of contributory factors have influenced the pattern of decline. The first of these is the changing composition of employment. Several strike-prone industries have lost jobs, with the result that there are fewer workers to influence aggregate statistics. Nowhere is this more apparent than in the coal industry. Between 1969 and the end of the miners' strike in 1985, for example, strikes in coalmining accounted for over 80 per cent of the total number of strikes (Edwards 1995: 439). The sharp decline in mining employment thereafter meant that there were fewer strikes in mining, thus contributing to the overall decline. This explanation is only partial, however, as even when changes in the level of employment are taken into account, the number of working days lost per 1,000 workers in mining, energy and water also shows a marked decline after 1985 (see table 9.2).

A second explanation builds on the shift in the balance of power. The rise in unemployment, the decline in unionization and changes in the law are component parts of this explanation. The evidence of a relationship between unemployment and strikes is mixed, although there is greater consistency in the relationship between unemployment and the number of strikes, than with other strikes indices (Shalev 1992; Edwards 1995). A review of the evidence suggests that there may be some decline in strikes due to the law, although separating the impact of legal changes from other influences remains fraught (Dunn and Metcalf 1996). What is clear is that the requirement for pre-strike ballots has changed the phase of the negotiation process that precedes the calling of a strike. The period within which employers can improve their offer to forestall a strike is now more clearly defined (between the result of the strike ballot and the date of the strike), which may assist in defusing what would otherwise be a strike.

A third explanation is that the industrial relations climate has improved. Within the terms of this broad explanation is suggested an increase in trust, commitment and co-operation; a reassertion of managerial prerogative; and a reordering of the workplace to eliminate some of the causes of strikes. This is a very complex bundle of factors. As other chapters in this volume show, there is some evidence that HRM is associated with employee commitment, but at the same time there is little evidence of a wholesale rise in trust, while growing insecurity might be expected to work in the other direction. In any event, the links between employee attitudes and whether or not a strike breaks out at a particular time and place are highly indirect and contingent. Strikes call for mobilization around a particular issue as well as some generalized discontent (Edwards 1995). The safest conclusion is that the entrenched adversarialism that characterized some sectors of the economy to 1979 has been weakened and that the resort to the strike is less 'natural' than it was, but that strike trends in themselves say little about the 'quality of industrial relations': strikes almost by definition reflect a breakdown of 'normality', but the absence of strikes says nothing about the underlying character of workplace relations.

Conclusion

To summarize, the Conservative assault on trade unions, aided and abetted by employers' policies, had wide-ranging effects. At national level, trade unions were excluded by government and by employers. Where unions retained a workplace presence, shop stewards came under increasing pressure. The resistance of employers in private sector services and at new companies prevented unions from recouping the membership losses sustained from the decline of manufacturing. Furthermore, membership levels and strike activity fell to post-war lows. The extent of the decline in these measures suggests that the capacity of unions to mobilize is, at best, restricted to specific sectors of the economy. The search for an agenda appropriate to these circumstances is the subject of the final section. The next section examines whether the election of a Labour government in May 1997 and its re-election in June 2001 represents a sea-change in the political position of trade unions.

New Labour: New Opportunities for Unions?

To understand the Labour government's industrial relations programme and its relations with trade unions, it is necessary to place them in the context of the 1970s. Several senior members of the present Labour government consider the weak form of corporatism that developed in the UK throughout the 1970s to be inappropriate. Furthermore, trade unions are held responsible by some for the 'winter of discontent' (1978–9), during which there were extensive strikes in the public sector and which is seen as being instrumental in the defeat of the Labour Party at the 1979 general election. In particular, the relationship between the then Labour government and trade unions was publicly seen to break down. Before 1979 Labour ministers regarded this relationship as a key element in the formulation of public policy that could not be replicated by a Conservative government (Minkin 1991). Many Labour ministers now view this relationship suspiciously, if not as a liability. In consequence, the Labour Party has 'distanced' itself from the unions.

It is thus certain that there will be no return to the politics of the 1970s by the current Labour government. What is more debatable is the categorization of Labour's 'Third Way' and its impact on union organization. In one of the leading expositions of the 'Third Way', there is no mention of trade unions (Giddens 1998). Where unions are mentioned, it tends to be, in the prime minister's words, in relation to their role in 'protecting individuals against arbitrary behaviour' (Blair and Schroeder n.d.); by contrast the French prime minister envisaged a wider role for unions in the regeneration of the economy (Jospin 1999). Present policies of the Labour government also suggest a rejection of any Keynesian approach in favour of a commitment to orthodox economic management, thus retaining continuity with much of the policy of the previous Conservative governments. Within this approach neo-liberal elements of an economic agenda are emphasized, epitomized by the pre-election commitment to the same public expenditure plans as envisaged by the Conservatives in 1997 and tough monetary and fiscal policies; the partnership with business, intended to foster the support of 'middle England'; and the advocacy of individual, rather than collective, relationships in policy formulation (McIlroy 1998; Leys 1996).

These features of market capitalism are qualified by policies more akin to a European social model. Among these policies are the emphasis on training, partnership between unions and employers, and the revitalization of the education and health sectors; the use of the windfall tax on public utilities to promote employment; and a desire to be at the centre of European policy developments (Coates 1996; Undy 1999). Tension between these competing policy elements is reviewed below in two stages. The first stage examines the development of the relationship between trade unions and the Labour Party. It shows that the distance between the two restricts the capacity of unions to exert an influence on policy. The second stage assesses the implications for trade unions of policy measures on the National Minimum Wage, the Social Chapter and union recognition. This discussion serves as an introduction to the next section, which examines the new policy agenda emerging among British unions.

The relationship between unions and the Labour Party

At a formal level, the share of trade union votes at the Labour Party conference was reduced from 70 per cent to 50 per cent. Support for this measure from the unions enabled the party to introduce it. Furthermore, at a succession of union conferences Mr Blair went to some lengths to explain that Labour Party conference decisions are not binding on a Labour government (McIlroy 1998). Sponsorship by trade unions of Members of Parliament was also stopped by the party, thus further distancing the unions. Instead of these formal and collective linkages, emphasis is placed by Labour Party representatives on the involvement of individual trade unionists who are Labour Party members in the affairs of the party. It is envisaged that this involvement will be based more on local 'influence and networks' than conference resolutions (Taylor and Cruddas n.d.).

This distancing was not shared by the unions. The case of the Trade Union Act 1984 illustrates the point. This Act required a ballot of union members every 10 years in order that a union could maintain a political fund. Unions drew on such funds to provide financial support to the Labour Party. During two rounds of such ballots, in 1985–6 and 1994–6, not a single union voted to abandon its political fund and several unions established such a fund for the first time. The intention underpinning the legislation was thus not achieved. To the contrary, more unions established funds to facilitate a linkage with the Labour Party. During the TUC Congress of 1999 only a single trade union general secretary,

Ken Cameron of the small Fire Brigades Union, suggested that trade unions should examine their relations with the Labour Party with a view to restricting the extent of funding that the unions provide. As the Labour Party remains largely dependent on the trade unions for income, this was a threat intended to 'bring the party into line'. This rallying call, however, did not attract other unions.

On policy questions the difference in emphasis between the Labour Party and the unions is apparent. Whereas union representatives emphasize the collective, Labour Party spokespersons tend towards the individual. Although the Labour Party initially welcomed the notion of stakeholding, for example, it was quick to distance itself from suggestions that unions were the representative organizations of workers through which they could stake a claim in economic management, and that stakeholders could expect more job security than is currently prevalent in the UK (Thompson 1996). The Labour government is also taking steps to introduce private funding of public sector organizations, such as hospitals. Many trade unionists see this as privatization 'through the back door' and are strongly opposed. Indeed, the GMB has cut funding to the Labour Party by £250,000 per year for four years from 2001 because of this initiative. Furthermore, UNISON and the Fire Brigades Union are reviewing their financial support of the Labour Party as a result of concern over the same issue.

The modernization of trade unions, as envisaged by several senior Labour Party representatives, also involves turning away from the collective. Instead emphasis is placed on trade union modernization through the provision of individual or friendly society benefits, such as advice on pensions, or through individual services, for example training. In addition, the influence of shop stewards is called into question within sections of the Labour government. My current research suggests that shop stewards are viewed as driving the union agenda, but as being unrepresentative of trade union members. This criticism echoes arguments cited by the Conservative governments when introducing their legal restrictions of union activities, and implicitly argues that a 'modernized' union movement is one that moves further away from participative forms of representation towards more parliamentary forms of representation. As discussed below, such a move would also mean adopting a 'servicing' model to the exclusion of the alternative 'organizing' model.[8] How the tension between these two competing emphases is resolved remains an open question. What is clear, however, is that the capacity of trade unions to exert influence is weaker than during the 1974–9 Labour government: membership and strike activity have declined; formal voting strength is reduced; and the Labour Party has distanced itself from trade unions. Unions are more reliant than hitherto on an active caucus of Members of Parliament, which lobbies on their behalf.

Towards a new regulatory regime?

The legislative programme of the Labour government incorporates several measures of trade union regulation that were introduced by the Conservatives. In particular, the regulations on balloting, secondary action and the closed shop remain in place. Some measures were repealed; for example, the rights to trade union membership at GCHQ are now restored; the triennial renewal of check-off arrangements are no longer required;[9] and workers dismissed during industrial action are allowed to take their case to an Employment Tribunal. While the repeal of these measures was welcomed by trade unionists, three further measures are more central to the new regulatory regime: the National Minimum Wage (NMW), ending the opt-out from the Social Chapter, and legislation on union recognition.

As discussed in chapter 17, unions came to favour the principle of the NMW during the 1980s. The rate set was, however, well below the £4.61 per hour requested by major unions. Furthermore, the manner of settlement of the rate and the intended method of uprating constitute a procedural point of departure. The Low Pay Commission, which recommended the terms of the NMW to government and is currently charged with the uprating, comprised unionists, employers and independents. Whereas the tripartite institutions of the 1970s included unionists (and employers) acting as representatives, the unionists who served on the Low Pay Commission did so as individuals, rather than as representatives. While unions welcomed the upratings of the NMW in 2000 and 2001, their prime concern is that an automatic formula for the uprating be introduced, thereby ensuring that the role of the Low Pay Commission is limited on the uprating issue.

At the Amsterdam Summit in June 1997 the Labour government committed itself to ending the UK's opt-out from the Social Chapter. Given the UK tradition of voluntarism and the Conservatives' policies of deregulation, the impact of the Social Chapter is likely to be as great, if not greater, in the UK than elsewhere. The unions welcomed this shift in policy as a means of providing some basic protections to workers (TUC 1997). Prior to this commitment, unions in the UK had successfully pursued a number of cases to the European Court of Justice (ECJ) in an attempt to stem the deregulatory tide of Conservative policy. The ending of the opt-out broadens the range of issues on which the unions can campaign with support from European measures. For example, a TUC-co-ordinated initiative led to two ECJ rulings on the rights of part-time workers to join pension schemes. The TUC is now expanding this initiative by developing programmes to assist in the recruitment and representation of part-time workers, which incorporate elements from the Part Time Work Directive and other aspects of the Social Chapter (Heery 1998a).

In addition to its new obligations under the Social Chapter, the government implemented the Working Time Directive. Thus, for the first time, the UK has a statutory framework for the regulation of working hours and annual holidays. As workers in the UK work the longest hours in Europe, the measure is likely to have wide-ranging effects (Arrowsmith and Sisson 2000). At the behest of employers' organizations, the government sought to maximize flexibility and exclusions in applying the directive in the UK. The TUC welcomed the directive, but argued that many of those on long working hours in professional and white-collar occupations would be excluded from its coverage by the terms of the transposition and, thus, the effect of the directive would be limited (TUC 1999a).

The introduction of a union recognition procedure was a key pledge of the Labour Party before the 1997 election. Such a measure was viewed within unions as a basis on which membership could be extended into private sector services. As detailed in chapter 6, the Employment Relations Act establishes procedures for statutory union recognition. The Act did not go as far as the unions wished, notably in the extent of employee support required before recognition could be imposed and in the restricted range of issues on which bargaining was required once recognition was achieved. While these points were contested by the unions, their absence of political leverage limited the extent of the concessions they were able to secure. Furthermore, the government also proposed that employers be granted a right to de-recognize unions in a manner similar to the de-certification arrangements that operate in the United States. The measure raises the prospect of 'union-busting' firms operating in the UK and unions having to compete against their activities (Adams 1999). Given the extent of employer resistance to unionization, this measure constitutes a significant new challenge to union organization, particularly where less than 50 per cent of a workforce is unionized.

A Union Transformation in the Making?

Three key points arise from the current analysis. First, unions were weakened by the neo-liberal assault. They now have a much-reduced capacity for action and represent a declining section of the labour force. Second, employers have contributed to the weakening of unions in that they have resisted unionization in expanding areas of the economy and, where unions are present, have limited the influence exerted by union representatives. Third, the option of retreating to traditional union practices has been cut off, as unions have been largely decoupled from their traditional sources of influence: the Labour Party, access to government and collective bargaining. In consequence, unions in the UK have sought a new agenda and have introduced internal reforms through which this agenda might be delivered, with the object of establishing new forms of interest aggregation and interest representation.

Four items are central to this agenda: the transformation of the TUC; widespread, but not universal, support for the European social dimension and deeper European integration; the development of social partnerships with employers; and the adoption of organizing campaigns intended to reverse the decline in unionization and in the participation of members in union activity. By no means are these reforms complete, nor are they without their contradictions. Several tensions inform their development. In particular, tensions persist between policies associated with the pursuit of adversarial trade unionism, that characterize US market capitalism, and the adoption of more features characteristic of a European social market model. The argument advanced here is that central to these developments is the well-being of union organization at the workplace and its articulation with activity at other levels of union organization.

Transforming the TUC

Throughout the 1960s and 1970s the TUC acted as a conduit to government. The TUC, for example, convened union representation to government on legislation and the formulation of the terms for incomes policies. Affiliation to the TUC thus allowed access to government. Second, the TUC administered the Bridlington Principles[10] whereby inter-union relations and disputes were regulated. In undertaking these functions the TUC gained some influence over affiliated unions. This influence went some way to making up for the absence of formal constitutional authority granted by affiliates to the TUC (Martin 1980). Apart from powers of expulsion, the TUC relies on argument and persuasion to maintain its position vis-à-vis affiliated unions. The political changes of the 1980s weakened the TUC's role in undertaking these functions. In particular, the dismantling of tripartite institutions and the rejection of any trade union role in macroeconomic policy by the Conservative government eliminated the TUC's role as a conduit to government. Moreover, the Trade Union Reform and Employment Rights Act 1993 gave workers a right to join any union that organized the same class of worker, thereby overriding the Bridlington Principles. Although the principles were reformulated to incorporate the impact of the legislation, the 1993 Act marked a significant step away from self-regulated competition between unions and, hence, from TUC administrative influence.

In the absence of these influences the TUC has sought new forms of influence in order to maintain cohesion. The central feature of the new approach is the transformation of the TUC into a campaigning organization (Heery 1998b) and the identification of what the TUC has termed as its 'millennial challenge'. To this end the TUC initiated campaigns for part-time workers, the establishment of minimum standards at work, social partnership with employers, building the organizing model, youth and anti-racism policies, and deeper involvement in Europe. Affiliated unions have been encouraged to participate in these campaigns, although co-ordination and direction remain in the hands of the TUC. Task groups, drawn from TUC staff and representatives of affiliated unions, are responsible for developing campaigns. As part of this development much of the TUC's standing committee structure was jettisoned. The General Council was also 'slimmed down' and now meets less frequently than in the past.

During the 1970s the TUC claim that it represented British labour was substantiated by density rates of around 50 per cent. It is more difficult to sustain this position today, particularly as it is in the areas of employment growth that unions are at their weakest. In addition to the organizing initiatives, which are examined below, two approaches have been adopted to address this weakness. First, the TUC has fostered a range of alliances with organizations whose interests overlap. For example, joint initiatives have been taken by the TUC with such bodies as the Consumers' Association, the National Association of Pension Funds, Help the Aged and Stonewall.[11] The purpose of these alliances is to raise the profile of the TUC and to engage more effectively on a wider range of public policy issues.

Second, the TUC has encouraged new affiliations. At the end of 1979 there were 109 unions affiliated to the TUC out of a total of 454. By 1998 TUC affiliations had dropped to 76 and the total number of unions to 233. While mergers influenced these figures, no fewer than 15 unions joined the TUC between 1995 and 1999.[12] Largely as a result of the affiliation of the Association of Teachers and Lecturers (ATL), membership affiliated to the TUC increased between 1997 and 1998. Among the unions with more than 100,000 members, only the RCN is now outside the TUC. The TUC has been particularly successful in persuading unions from service industries to affiliate. A broader basis is thus in place from which to launch recruitment campaigns into these areas. Associated with the encouragement of new affiliations is the provision of a wider range of union support services by the TUC. In addition to training provisions made available to shop stewards and the supply of briefing information, the TUC has established an effective Campaigns and Communication Department to assist unions. Training provisions have also been extended to full-time officials and staff in order to improve the management practices of unions. Such approaches are particularly welcomed by the smaller unions, which are unable to provide an extensive range of support services in-house (TUC 1997b).

The TUC also views the introduction of the new recognition procedure as a potential source of influence in relation to affiliated unions. The opportunity for unions to approach employers with a view to reaching a recognition agreement is available within the terms of the Employment Relations Act. A major challenge for unions is to avoid a free-for-all, in which recognition agreements are sought by unions competing with each other. Such a development would be seized on by both employers and those that question the union role within the Labour government as evidence of indiscipline within trade unionism. In the light of its historical role as adjudicator of the Bridlington Principles, the TUC proposed that it assume a role in the co-ordination of activities directed towards recognition. It remains to be seen how affiliated unions respond to this proposal. Many employers, however, have sought voluntary recognition agreements. As unions have already ratified many of these agreements, the opportunity for developing a co-ordinated approach is rapidly disappearing.

A longer-term option on the TUC's agenda is the introduction of a flat-rate membership of the TUC for individual members, which could be topped up with membership of an affiliated union. For this flat-rate contribution the member would have access to services such as information on rights at work, a stakeholder pension scheme and careers advice.[13] Underpinning this initiative is the idea that the member would retain TUC membership as s/he moved from job to job, but would change the top-up membership taken with affiliated unions. An employee would thus only need to be recruited once. Loyalty and commitment would primarily be generated between member and TUC, rather than, as now, between member and affiliated union. Elements of this approach resemble, and are based on, the policy of the Federatie Nederlandse Vakbeweging in the Netherlands and the Österreichischer Gewerkschaftsbund in Austria, in so far as the confederation is expected to undertake more wide-ranging functions. As affiliated unions are likely to lose influence were such a development to be enacted, it seems unlikely that they would support it. However, affiliated unions will have to improve the quality of their support services if they are to thwart this initiative altogether.

The TUC has thus attempted to restore some lost influence by adopting a campaigning role, entering into alliances with other campaigning groups, and by accepting more unions into affiliation. Proposals regarding the operation of the new recognition procedure may also restore some influence over inter-union relations. While these measures illustrate the extent of change within the TUC, three policy initiatives indicate the effect of the campaigning style on union policy in the UK. It is to these initiatives that we now turn.

The quest for European regulation

The invitation to Jacques Delors to speak at the TUC Congress in 1988 marked a significant step in the transition from an anti- to a pro-EU union movement in the UK. Following the defeat of the Labour Party at the election in 1987, a pro-EU policy was seen as a means of mitigating the deregulatory thrust of Conservative policy. The growing social agenda emanating from the EU allowed British unions to secure a number of legal advances, particularly in the fields of health and safety, equality and atypical workers, by reference to the ECJ. Subsequently, the TUC was the first major public institution in the UK to voice support for British entry into the single currency, although several unions with membership in the public sector are more reticent. If Britain were to join the euro, TUC representatives argue, the social protections available to workers in Europe would be transferred to their British counterparts. Similarly to most other national union confederations, the TUC advocates the development of national channels of representation within the European Trade Union Confederation (ETUC). Such an approach would consolidate the position of the TUC, rather than the alternative expansion of structures based on European Industry Federations, which rely on sectoral rather than national linkages between individual unions and the European-level policymaking institutions, and would curtail TUC influence. In accord with its pro-EU stance, the TUC, along with a small number of affiliated unions, has established an office in Brussels through which many of its activities concerning Europe are co-ordinated.

The issue of workplace representation is central to the relationship between British unionism and developments in the EU. European measures on working time, health and safety, and redundancy compensation assume a system of works councils, and cut across the traditional single-channel, union-only approach of the UK. This is likely to be exacerbated by the Council directive to establish a framework for national information and consultation rights, which is intended to extend the dual system. Although the European Parliament supported the draft directive, the Labour government opposed it, in alliance with the governments from Germany, Ireland and Spain. When the German government withdrew from this blocking alliance the position crumbled and the Labour government was compelled to accept the measure.

In its campaign to support the introduction of the measure, the TUC presented a joint statement with union confederations from Germany, Ireland and Spain, which was used to lobby within European institutions. The TUC thus welcomed the directive, a position supported by many affiliated unions. An earlier report of a TUC task group had prepared much of the ground on the issues of information and consultation, without explicitly examining the cases for and against the single channel and the dual system of representation (TUC 1995). However, within the two largest affiliated unions, UNISON and the TGWU, opposition to the directive is widespread, as it rests uneasily with the single channel of representation, which opponents of the directive wish to see maintained. Several smaller left-led unions take the same position for the same reason. Furthermore, a significant proportion of active members within unions that formally support the measure at national level remain unconvinced of the merits of the dual system. Whether support for the directive outweighs opposition thus remain a very open question.

Further compounding sensitivities on this issue is the stance of employers. The Confederation of British Industry (CBI) and the Institute of Directors (IOD) oppose the directive. The CBI campaigned in opposition to the measure within Union of Industrial and Employers' Confederations of Europe (UNICE) and successfully lobbied the Labour government to the same effect. This national-level position, however, is not uniformly replicated among companies. A survey of 481 businesses showed that 36 per cent of employers thought compulsory works councils to be a good thing, compared to 28 per cent who opposed them and a further 36 per cent who were undecided (Industrial Society 1998). Furthermore a growing number of employers have established company councils, company forums or similar arrangements, which represent a move away from the single channel of representation, as elements of social partnership arrangements (IDS 1999). Whether these arrangements have been introduced as a means of excluding unions or in preparation for the later introduction of a directive remains a moot point. For unions the issue is that, in practice, they are already confronted by a growing number of employers who have introduced workplace structures which are not usually associated with the single channel.

Commitment to the European regulatory framework may raise a significant challenge in the form of substantially reforming, if not abandoning, the single channel of representation in favour of a system more akin to the dual model. The role of the unions in 'policing' minimum labour standards at the workplace also represents a further shift away from traditional approaches based on voluntarism and requires unions to provide support capable of handling such matters through legal processes. Many full-time officers and shop stewards are now required to undertake duties with which they have little familiarity and, in many cases, they are insufficiently trained. Should the European Company Statute be enacted, this trend is likely to be exacerbated.

Social partnership: a new compromise with employers?

Early proposals for social partnership with employers assumed that areas of 'common interest' between unions and employers could form the basis of partnerships of mutual benefit (GMB/UCW 1990). Included among these issues were job security, training, productivity, and health and safety. Agreements settled on the basis of partnership tended to involve an exchange of union concessions on workplace flexibility for undertakings on job security (Williamson 1997). Several unions opposed the principle of partnership on the grounds that it offered few benefits for members and unions at the expense of traditional sources of workplace bargaining strength. Furthermore, proposals for partnership beyond the workplace, embracing tripartite working groups to discuss major policy issues of the day or a return to national bargaining, were rejected by employers.

The election of a Labour government prepared to advocate social partnership marked a change from the approach of the Conservatives, but also sustained some continuities. In particular, the government remained apart from any national-level developments in partnership and tended to emphasize the more individual aspects at the workplace (McIlroy 1998). In the TUC, however, the idea of social partnership was developed through the six principles discussed in chapter 7 and summarized for convenience below (TUC 1999b):

- shared commitment to the success of enterprise;
- a recognition that interests of the partners may legitimately differ;
- employment security;
- focus on the quality of working life;
- commitment to transparency, including information-sharing and consultation;
- adding value.

Prime Minister Blair endorsed this package in principle, although he questioned whether trade union participation was essential for workplace participation (Hall 1999). Thus for the Labour government the parameters of social partnership are far narrower than in union circles.

Employers are also prepared to endorse the principle of social partnership. The director-general of the CBI called for partnership between the TUC and the CBI to deal with EU social policy in a speech to Congress in 1997 (see Taylor 1998). He later viewed the cases cited by the TUC as demonstrating 'what can be achieved by companies and trade unions working in partnership' (TUC 1999b: 4). Furthermore, the number of companies at which partnership arrangements with unions are in place is claimed to be increasing (IPA 1997; Knell 1999). Evidence collected by the author, however, suggests that many new agreements concluded with employers have the title 'partnership agreement' attached to them simply because of the political climate rather than the content of the agreement. In other words, it is far from certain that the growth in the number of partnership agreements is a useful measure of any significant change in industrial relations practices. The rate of increase in such agreements appears to have accelerated more recently as employers enter into voluntary social partnership agreements to forestall the imposition of the terms of the Employment Relations Act. This is not to suggest, however, that there is a uniform position among employers. The director-general of the CBI also suggested that the TUC emphasis on union involvement was misplaced and too rigid, in arguing that partnership may be based on direct communication with employees or through share-ownership schemes (Hall 1999). The then president of the CBI added to this position in directly questioning whether a union was necessary for partnership.

Many of the issues associated with social partnership replicate those from a traditional collective bargaining agenda. As such, a similar initiative launched in any other EU member state would not attract much attention. Why then has the social partnership initiative assumed a high profile in the UK? The answer is that it is a proactive union policy directed towards addressing the issue of union exclusion by employers; that is, a key source of union weakness. Furthermore, it does so with qualified support from the Labour government, thus necessitating that employers at least engage in the debate. As even critics of the policy acknowledge, an alternative based on union militancy and supported by industrial action is not viable in the current climate (Kelly 1996).

Social partnership is, however, a policy with significant risks for unions and is thus contested within the TUC. First, differences in approach between unions and employers persist. Whereas the union view on social partnership exhibits consistent pluralist tendencies, employers waver between pluralist and unitarist interpretations (see chapter 12; Ackers and Payne 1998). Compounding this issue is the level at which social partnership operates. Employers see partnership as a workplace issue, as discussed in chapter 10, while unions have a view that embraces national-level activities. The only area where employers have proposed a partnership at national level is to address the issue of European social policy. Indeed, for employers to enter into partnership at national level would necessitate reversing the policies of national de-recognition implemented throughout the 1980s. As the government also tends to define social partnership in terms of the workplace, a risk for unions is that it remains purely a workplace issue. In such circumstances social partnership would not provide a source of cohesion between activities at different workplaces, which may remain, or become, isolated.

A second contested area is that searching for the partnership agenda may undermine union activities at well-organized sites, which are founded on adversarial union–management relations. Although the TUC and several affiliated unions have embarked on extensive training programmes to address this issue (see e.g. Fisher 1997), there is little evidence of growing trust and mutual commitment between unionists and managements (Kelly 1998). In the context of the short-termism that is characteristic of the UK economy, the generation of this trust may be undermined by the external demands of shareholders or changes in management following a company merger or take-over. Social partnership is thus likely to be more precarious in the UK than in economies where a longer-term perspective informs management decision-making. This short-term outlook among many employers has led some unions to question whether any long-term benefits can be generated from partnership. Scepticism among this group of unions was heightened during the sale of Rover, where the partnership agreement was overridden by commercial decisions, and by evidence which suggests that the benefits of partnership arrangements are heavily weighted in favour of management (Guest and Peccei 2001).

A third contested area associated with the partnership agenda concerns its relations with union organization. The union position assumes a well-organized union presence at the workplace in order to develop the partnership agenda. Indeed, Sir Ken Jackson, president of the AEEU and one of more bullish advocates of social partnership, claimed that social partnership, coupled with the new recognition procedure, would lead to a 50 per cent increase in membership of the AEEU in the 18 months after February 2000 (*Guardian*, 3 February 2000). The risk arises if such a presence cannot be established. In such circumstances, John Edmonds, general secretary of the GMB, suggested that unions would be marginalized (quoted in Taylor 1994: 215). Thus, associated with social partnership are campaigns to reverse the decline in unionization, to which this chapter now turns.

Moving towards an organizing approach

Table 9.3 illustrates the range in union density across the British labour force in 1991 and 1999. Two points are apparent from the data. First, the areas of union weakness in the expanding sectors of the economy mirror the pattern seen in much of western Europe. In private sector services, among young workers, part-time workers, temporary workers and sales employees union organization is relatively weak. In practice, there are two target groups to recruit in private sector services: the relatively secure, high-paid, technical staff, typically working in finance or computing-related employment; and low-paid, unskilled and insecure workers, employed in catering, hotels or cleaning. Second, in contrast to the situation elsewhere in Europe, where unions remain embedded in their traditional heartland, unions are now weak in many areas traditionally associated with strength. For example, in 1999 not a single occupation was unionized to 50 per cent, manufacturing was only 28 per cent unionized and one-third of full-time workers were unionized. In other words, the recruitment task facing unions is twofold: to extend union organization into sites with no union presence, and to deepen unionization at sites where unions have established a presence. Recent estimates suggest that more than 3 million workers are non-members but are employed at workplaces where unions have secured recognition (Bland 1999). Similarly, over 1 million workers are not union members although their pay is set by collective agreement.[14]

In broad terms, two approaches have been employed to address these tasks, the servicing model and the organizing model, both of which are intended to deepen and extend union organization (for details, see Bronfenbrenner et al. 1998; Midwest Center for Labor Research 1991). The servicing model relies on the provision of union support and services to members at their workplaces from sources external to the workplace, such as full-time officers or through facilities available in trade union structures beyond the workplace. In contrast, union support and services in the organizing model are made available from within the workplace by local representatives and members, who receive training, guidance and advice from their union to undertake these roles. In the UK these two approaches are not mutually exclusive and have been pursued as different

Table 9.3 Union density in Great Britain by individual, job-related and workplace characteristics[a]

Characteristic	1991	1999
Men	42	31
Women	32	28
Aged 16–24 (1991); under 20 years (1999)	22	6
Aged 25–34 (1991); 20–29 (1999)	37	19
Aged 30–39		31
Aged 35–49 (1991); 40–49 (1999)	42	39
50 years and over	42	34
Full-time employees	42	33
Part-time employees	33	20
Permanent employees	38	31
Temporary employees	17	18
Workplaces of:		
fewer than 25 employees	18	15
25 or more employees	47	37
Managers and administrators	32	20
Professionals	53	49
Associate professionals/technical	55	43
Clerical and secretarial	38	23
Craft and related	57	32
Personal and protective service occupations	46	28
Sales	25	11
Plant and machine operatives	59	37
Other occupations	49	27
Agriculture, forestry and fishing	15	9
Mining and quarrying	42	37
Manufacturing	36	28
Electricity, gas and water supply	78	52
Construction	19	21
Wholesale and retail trade	14	12
Hotels and restaurants	10	6
Transport and communications	55	42
Financial intermediation	34	30
Real estate and business services	11	11
Public administration	63	61
Education	55	54
Health	63	45
Other services	N/A	24

[a] The data in the Labour Force Surveys of 1991 and 1999 were collected on different bases. In particular, the Standard Industrial Classification changed between the two dates and the form of the questions on occupation and to define the sector in which people work were changed. The 1991 data are thus estimates based on the classification that was then in use.
Source: Labour Force Surveys (1991 and 1999).

elements of a unionization strategy. The distinction between the two models is thus analytical rather than practical (see Boxall and Haynes 1997). As is shown below, however, there has been a shift of emphasis in recent years away from the servicing model towards the organizing model.

In the years after 1987 the Special Review Body (SRB) of the TUC published a series of reports which advocated that affiliated unions offer a range of financial services as a means to entice workers in private sector services into membership. These reports anticipated that financial services would attract potential members from across the occupational spectrum by appealing to the more 'individualized' consumer interests of the new workforce. In accord with the recommendation of the SRB, most affiliated unions started to offer packages of financial services, which included discounted insurance on holidays, cars and housing; credit card facilities; personal loans and mortgage arrangements; and independent tax, financial and pensions advice. The individual financial services were offered in addition to benefits covering injury, funeral costs and sickness that many unions had offered throughout much of the twentieth century. Initial emphasis was, thus, placed on the extension of the servicing model.

As is apparent from table 9.3, this broader range of individual services has had no significant effect on the rate of unionization in either the expanding areas of the economy or the areas of traditional membership strength. A range of research results confirmed that packages of financial services were not attractive to either potential or existing members (Kerr 1992; Sapper 1991). For example, financial services were cited by 3 per cent of new members as being one of the two principal reasons for joining a trade union. By comparison, over 72 per cent of new members cited 'support if I have a problem at work' and 36 per cent mentioned 'improvements in pay and conditions' (Waddington and Whitston 1997). Packages of financial services are thus marginal to the recruitment of new members. They are also of little attraction to existing members. Only 3 per cent of members cite financial services as being one of the two principal reasons for remaining in membership, whereas 64 per cent cite 'support if I have a problem at work' and 40 per cent refer to the fact that 'most other people at work are members' (Waddington and Kerr 1999a). Neither recruitment nor retention is thus significantly influenced by the provision of financial services. Indeed, the old-style industrial benefits were more effective in both recruitment and retention than were financial services.

In the light of these research findings and in the absence of any widespread membership growth, there has been a shift in emphasis away from the servicing model towards the organizing model. This shift comprised activities at the TUC and within affiliated unions.

In this context, a key TUC initiative is the establishment of an Organizing Academy. This builds upon similar ventures launched by the American Federation of Labor–Congress of Industrial Organizations (AFL–CIO) and the Australian Council of Trade Unions (ACTU) (see Bronfenbrenner et al. 1998; Mort 1998). The weaknesses addressed by the Organizing Academy are the shortage of time and the inadequate resources available within many affiliated unions. Membership decline has led to financial constraints, and the decentralization of bargaining has increased the demands on full-time officers and shop stewards. It is now difficult for many of these representatives to engage extensively in recruitment activities, as they are fully occupied dealing with existing members (IRS 1996; Kelly and Heery 1994). In addition, many employers have curtailed the amount of facility time available to shop stewards, thus further restricting their opportunities to recruit. Furthermore, many unions have been unable to sustain workplace organization and representation at many sites. Recent estimates, for example, indicate that union representatives were present at 28 per cent of all workplaces and at only 64 per cent of workplaces where a union was recognized (Cully et al. 1999: 96). Supplementing scarce resources and addressing inefficiencies in union organization are thus key objectives of the Organizing Academy and the organizing model.

Within the framework of the Organizing Academy trainees are provided with the skills necessary to undertake recruitment. Each trainee is sponsored by an affiliated union, thus enabling him or her to gain fieldwork experience to supplement the formal training provided at the Organizing Academy. After graduating from the Organizing Academy, the trainees may become recruitment officers for their sponsoring union. Trainees are selected so that they are similar to the target groups of potential members, on the basis that 'like best recruits like'. The intention underpinning the initiative is that trainees will be able to concentrate on recruitment in the unorganized sectors of the economy. Initial results, however, suggest that sponsoring unions tend to employ the trainees for deepening recruitment in partially organized sectors. No major non-union company has yet succumbed and granted recognition under pressure from activities associated with the organizing model (Heery et al. 2000). Several unions have also elected not to recruit the trainees that they sponsored through the Organizing Academy, thereby bringing into question the viability of the specific approach adopted by the TUC.

Active members, shop stewards and local full-time officers are key to the success of the organizing approach. Unions have thus attempted to create conditions for a more active membership and have directed more resources to support local unionists in implementing the approach. Although it is difficult to assess how much additional funding has been provided, at present it is likely to be less than that provided by unions in the US to their recruitment activities. However, additional training has been made available to existing shop stewards, and campaigns have been launched to convince more members to become shop stewards. In order to relieve some of the pressure on shop stewards, several unions have offered financial incentives to members to encourage them to become involved in recruitment activities. Furthermore, in recognition that many workplaces have no shop stewards, telephone help-lines have been installed, whereby members can contact a union for advice. Of course, this last point illustrates the interconnections between the organizing and servicing models, as it is a servicing approach, in the form of the central provision of telephone advice, that is used to address a shortfall in shop stewards.

There are other challenges to be faced before the organizing model can be implemented on a wide-ranging basis. A significant proportion of members are dissatisfied with the extent of contact with shop stewards and full-time officers, and regard the provision of information by unions as inadequate (Waddington and Kerr 1999a). Furthermore, a large number of members are shown to leave the union because of shortcomings in union organization at the workplace: inadequate support provided by trade unions to members at their workplace is a reason cited by about 25 per cent of the members who leave Britain's largest union every year (Waddington and Kerr 1999b). The recent legislation on recognition allows a worker to be accompanied by a union representative throughout grievance or disciplinary hearings. In several unions this was seen as an opportunity to extend recruitment, the argument being that if the union representative performed well, the worker would join and encourage others to do the same. However, if existing members are dissatisfied with the quality of support that they receive, it seems unlikely that union representatives will be able satisfactorily to meet additional demands from non-members.

The legislative promotion of parliamentary forms of representation also runs counter to the thrust of the organizing model, because postal ballots have lowered participation rates in union elections compared to those achieved through workplace ballots (Undy et al. 1996: 241–4), and allow members to vote without directly participating in any union forum. A further outcome of Conservative legislation was the weakening of regional and district levels of union organization, as unions sought to centralize decision-making and, hence, avoid exposure to sequestration (Undy et al. 1996). As a precondition of the organizing model is an articulated union structure, its operation is threatened where these levels function inadequately. It thus seems likely that more resources and new forms of internal operation are required, if the organizing model is to secure membership growth in private sector services.

What is clear, however, is that recent organizing initiatives launched by both the TUC and affiliated unions have engaged more members than earlier initiatives which raised the profile of membership recruitment as a priority among full-time staff of the unions, rather than embracing the active membership who actually do much of the recruiting (Snape 1995). It remains to be seen whether the centralized setting of recruitment targets (Waddington and Kerr 2000) or other 'models of implementation' adopted for the organizing model in the UK (Carter 2000) will involve sufficient members to reverse the long-term decline in membership.

Associated with the promulgation of the organizing model is the development of institutions within trade unions to promote participation in union affairs among under-represented groups. Many unions have now introduced representative structures specifically for women, young workers and members from ethnic minorities. Such measures have assisted in the articulation of members' interests within branch and wider union organization (Munro 1999). The engagement of women in workplace learning initiatives also offers the potential for new forms of workplace organization with higher rates of participation among women (Munro and Rainbird 2000). Significant issues need to be addressed before such arrangements generate member participation at the levels required to further the organizing model. For example, separate structures have been associated with the marginalization of issues of importance to the groups represented therein (Briskin and McDermott 1993; Cunnison and Stageman 1995), they have proved inadequate to prevent the items they generate for bargaining agendas being among the first to be dropped during negotiations (Colling and Dickens 1998) and are not associated with a marked increase in the number of people from these groups assuming senior positions within trade unions (Garcia et al. n.d.). Furthermore, women are more likely to cite shortcomings in union organization as a reason for leaving a union than are men (Waddington and Kerr 1999b). In short, considerable progress is still required before issues of concern to these groups are mainstreamed within union organization and activity, thus facilitating the widespread adoption of the organizing model.

Conclusions

The social and political influence of trade unionism in the UK is dependent upon its strength at the workplace and on articulating this strength throughout the different levels of trade union organization. The neo-liberal assault weakened trade union organization in terms of its coverage and influence within the workplace. Where workplace union organization remained, it was too often isolated as mechanisms to articulate union activity decayed. Isolation of organization at the workplace accentuated membership decline, as potential members were unable to see the benefits of union membership.

Unions were also excluded from national-level engagement by both government and employers. The practices and activities that guided British trade unions in the 1970s were thus undermined at both workplace and national levels. The election of a Labour government has certainly mitigated some of the most adverse elements of neo-liberal policy. However, the political distance from the unions sought by the Labour government as it strives to maintain support from employers has necessitated that the unions develop a role that no longer relies on traditional ties with Labour. Furthermore, both the Labour government and employers oppose any widespread restoration of national-level exchange through which unions may exert influence.

Central to the union programme of reform is reversing the decline at the workplace. While the new recognition procedure will assist in securing additional members, it is the generation of an organizing approach that is likely to sustain membership growth and address the issues arising from the exclusionary policies of employers. A range of measures is in place directed to establishing the organizing approach, but its effects are qualified by limited resources and inadequate facilities. Furthermore, the means of union articulation are far from secure, thus raising the prospect of isolated activity undertaken in different workplaces with inadequate internal inter-linkages.

Other elements of the union agenda will be influenced markedly by the nature and extent of the recovery in the workplace. As some proponents of social partnership acknowledge, a robust workplace presence is required to ensure that the terms of partnership are mutually beneficial. Similarly, when national-level information and consultation arrangements are introduced, unions will be able to attain positions of influence only if workplace organization secures the majority of representative positions for unionists.

New approaches to interest aggregation and interest representation underpin the policy options pursued by trade unionists. Rising membership heterogeneity and the requirement to 'police' a widening range of individual legal rights within an environment of decentralized bargaining raise fresh challenges for under-resourced union organization. Key to success in these areas is the engagement of larger numbers of better-trained shop stewards and the provision of appropriate support to shop stewards at their workplaces.

The new agenda emerging among unions in the UK exhibits several key differences from the policies of the 1960s and 1970s. Although reforms have been implemented, many of the institutions and vested interests that operated during the earlier period remain in place. Pursuit of the new agenda is thus far from being unproblematic. Among the tensions that persist are those involved in the transition from a US-style market capitalism to one more akin to the social market models of western Europe. The debate between the single channel and a dual system of workplace representation, the pursuit of social partnership, when more employers than ever before reject even a union presence, and the adoption of an organizing approach in conjunction with both social partnership and support for wider juridification, all pose questions for the coming years. Furthermore, unions have yet to shed the pattern of male dominance that continues to inform activity at all levels, and have failed to address the interests of young workers. Only when marked progress in these areas has been achieved will unions be able to extend organization into private sector services on the basis of high rates of membership participation.

Appendix: The Changing Pattern of Industrial Action

This appendix develops the analysis presented in the main body of the chapter in three specific areas. Firstly, it assesses the post-war pattern of strike frequency and shows that in the 1990s strike rates were at lower levels than at any time during the post-war years, even other periods characterized as ones of industrial peace (Edwards 1995; Knowles 1954). Secondly, it examines the duration of strikes since 1946 and, in particular, traces the decline of the long, large-scale strike. Thirdly, the incidence of strikes at establishments with recognized trade unions is reviewed. Reference to these data allows a more detailed understanding of strike causation and the different forms of engagement of trade unions and trade unionists. Marked changes in the pattern of strike activity over the period indicate a range of forms of union engagement and mobilization. In particular, industrial conflict has tended to decline, even where a union presence has been maintained, suggesting that industrial conflict is, at best, only a partial function of a union presence.

Strike trends since 1946

Figure 9A.1 illustrates the overall trend in strike frequency since 1946. It is apparent that the number of strikes peaked during the early 1970s, having gradually increased from the

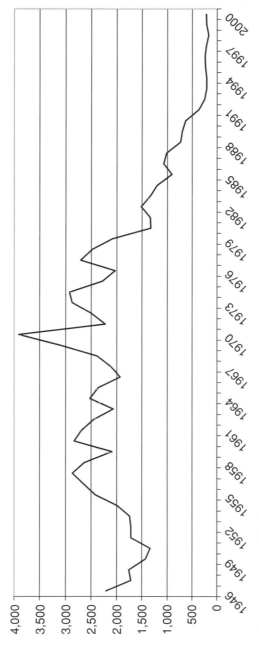

Figure 9A.1 Strike frequency, 1946–2000

1950s. From the late 1970s the number of strikes steadily declined to the lowest level on record during the 1990s.[15] In terms of the entire post-war period, the fifteen years between 1965 and 1979 were exceptional in so far as the number of strikes, workers involved and days lost were markedly higher than in either the preceding or subsequent periods (see also table 9.2).

Four distinct periods of strike activity were identified by Durcan et al. (1983), each of which is characterized by peculiarities in the extent, form and reasons for strike activity. The breaks between these periods, however, are blurred and uneven. The characteristics of one period are gradually transformed into those of another, rather than occurring as an abrupt schism.

- *1946–1952.* A period of industrial peace with five specific industries accounting for half of the total number of non-coal strikes (non-electrical engineering, shipbuilding, motor vehicles, docks and road passenger transport). Approaching 40 per cent of strikes were over wages and a further 21 per cent involved trade union principle.
- *1953–1959.* The number of strikes rose sharply after 1953. Other strikes indices fluctuated markedly under the influence of the first national industry-wide stoppages since 1926 in engineering (where there were two), shipbuilding and printing. Similarly to the 1940s, wages and issues of trade union principle were the primary reasons that underpinned strikes.
- *1960–1968.* A relatively small increase in the total number of strikes compared to the previous period. Although there were no national industry-wide stoppages, marked increases were recorded in the number of working days lost and workers involved indices, reflecting the growth in unofficial disputes led from the shop floor. Eight industries accounted for over half of the non-coal stoppages and about three-quarters of the days lost and workers involved (docks, motor vehicles, shipbuilding, aircraft, non-electrical engineering, electrical engineering, locomotives, carriages, etc. and iron, steel and other metals). Wage issues remained the principal reason for strikes, accounting for 48 per cent of the number of strikes during the period.
- *1969–1973.* Both the magnitude and form of strike activity between 1969 and 1973 differed from previous periods. In addition to the unofficial disputes of the previous period, a number of large-scale and official industry-wide stoppages were called, leading to a sharp increase in the number of days lost. The industrial concentration of strike activity lessened as industrial conflict spread to previously unaffected industries. Wage issues were the cause of 57 per cent of strikes during the period.

In addition to these periods identified by Durcan et al. (1983), several further periods may be isolated to take the data through to the present.

- *1974–1979.* The number of strikes fell, but the presence of a large number of industry-wide stoppages ensured relatively high levels of days lost and workers involved. This period culminated in the so-called 'winter of discontent' of 1978–9, when national strikes were called in the engineering industry and several parts of the public sector. Pay remained the primary issue that underpinned strikes, as public sector workers attempted to restore differentials with their private sector counterparts, which had widened between 1960 and 1973. The periods 1969–73 and 1974–9 are often grouped as constituting the 'formal challenge' to industrial relations practices in operation at the time.
- *1980–1987.* All the main strike indices tended to fall, with the number of strikes falling below the levels of the 1940s. The proportion of strikes on the issue of wages fell and

workplace issues assumed greater importance. This period of 'coercive pacification' (Hyman 1989) was marked by three significant defeats for organized labour: in 1980 at British Steel, as management dismantled industry-wide bargaining; in 1984–5 within coalmining, as the National Union of Mineworkers resisted pit closures; and 1986–7 in newspaper printing, when the Fleet Street print unions were unable to prevent the relocation of the industry. During this period, however, settlements in manufacturing following strikes resulted in higher pay increases than settlements achieved without a strike (Ingram et al. 1993). Furthermore, the extent of these gains tended to outweigh the costs incurred by strikers (Metcalf et al. 1993).

- *1988–2000*. Further declines in all strike indices. Strike frequency fell to about 15 per cent of that recorded during the 1940s, leading proponents of partnership to suggest that the conditions are in place for a wide-ranging partnership approach to be introduced. Strikes over workplace issues outnumbered strikes over pay for most years in this period. Strikes during this period thus primarily arose from discontent over the (re)organization of work.

An important element of the cyclical pattern of overall strike frequency is variation in the duration of strikes. As table 9A.1 illustrates, there were about 740 strikes per year lasting no more than a day until 1952. This number rose to more than 1,000 per year during the 1950s, before falling back to 700 per year between 1969 and 1973. From 1974 until 1990 strikes lasting no more than a day continued at a fairly stable level (average 411 per year) before falling again to a consistently lower level during the 1990s (average 138 per year).

The pattern of strikes lasting more than one day but less than three days is similar to that of strikes of shorter duration in so far as there was a rise to an annual peak of 882 per year between 1953 and 1959. The number of strikes lasting more than one day but less than three days, however, tended to remain fairly stable until the mid-1970s, whereas their shorter counterparts fell away during this period. The number of the longer strikes also dropped markedly during the 1980s and 1990s. Strikes of three days or less comprise roughly 70 to 75 per cent of the total number of strikes throughout the periods 1946–68 and 1985–2000. Strikes of more than three days' duration accounted for about half of the strikes during the 1970s as disputes within industrial or national levels of bargaining led to protracted disputes, often concerned with incomes policies or the terms of legislation.

The steepest decline in strike frequency is among those strikes of more than three days' duration. During the 1980s and 1990s, these strikes almost disappeared, amounting to about 25 per cent of all strikes compared to over 55 per cent during the second half of the 1970s when engineering and public sector workers participated in long, industry-wide stoppages.

The change in the frequency and the duration of strikes indicates variation in the form of union engagement. The steep growth in the number of short strikes during the 1960s, for example, resulted from initiatives taken by shop-floor trade unionists, whereas the extent of longer strikes, coupled with increases in the number of days lost, between 1969 and 1973 suggests more formal or official union engagement in the calling and co-ordination of industry-wide stoppages (Hyman 1984; Durcan et al. 1983). Table 9A.2 allows examination of a further aspect of the variation in the form of union engagement by showing changes in the pattern of industrial action between 1980 and 1998 at workplaces where at least one trade union was recognized.[16] The separation of strikes from other non-strike forms of industrial action allows assessment of whether trade unionists have replaced strikes with other forms of industrial action.

Table 9A.1   Strikes by duration, 1946–2000

Year	Not more than one day	% of total	One day, but not longer than three days	% of total	More than three days	% of total	Total (all strikes)
1946–52	5,174	43.5	3,997	33.6	2,712	22.8	11,883
1953–9	7,112	43.4	6,177	37.7	3,094	18.9	16,383
1960–8	7,532	35.3	7,630	35.7	6,182	29.0	21,344
1969–73	3,502	24.0	4,333	29.6	6,785	46.4	14,620
1974	436	14.2	815	27.9	1,671	57.2	2,922
1975	399	17.5	529	23.2	1,354	59.3	2,282
1976	397	19.5	544	26.7	1,094	53.8	2,035
1977	461	17.1	647	23.9	1,595	59.0	2,703
1978	447	18.1	600	24.3	1,424	57.6	2,471
1979	412	19.8	462	22.2	1,211	58.1	2,085
1980	356	26.8	327	24.6	647	48.6	1,330
1981	415	31.0	327	24.4	596	44.5	1,338
1982	566	37.2	353	23.2	602	39.6	1,521
1983	467	34.9	285	21.3	585	43.8	1,337
1984	357	29.6	266	22.1	583	48.3	1,206
1985	328	36.3	186	20.1	389	43.1	903
1986	522	48.6	204	19.0	348	32.4	1,074
1987	440	43.3	238	23.4	338	33.3	1,016
1988	331	45.4	175	24.0	223	30.6	729
1989	345	49.2	144	20.5	212	30.2	701
1990	302	47.9	134	21.3	194	30.8	630
1991	184	50.0	58	15.7	127	34.4	369
1992	118	46.6	50	19.8	85	33.6	253
1993	119	56.4	41	19.4	51	24.2	211
1994	118	57.6	47	22.9	40	19.5	205
1995	139	59.1	43	18.3	53	22.6	235
1996	118	48.4	61	25.0	65	26.6	244
1997	106	49.1	56	25.9	54	25.0	216
1998	68	41.0	50	30.1	48	28.9	166
1999	108	52.7	61	29.8	36	17.6	205
2000	103	48.6	65	30.7	44	20.8	212

Sources: Data 1946–73: Durcan et al. (1983); data from 1974, various issues of *Labour Market Trends*.

Reference to the 'all workplaces' data shows that the proportion of workplaces with recognized unions that experienced industrial action of any form declined from 25 per cent to 4 per cent between 1980 and 1998. Between 1980 and 1990 the principal source of this decline was in non-strike industrial action rather than strike activity, which remained fairly stable. Between 1990 and 1998, however, all indices of industrial conflict declined. In other words, this evidence does not suggest that other forms of industrial action have replaced strike activity. Instead the evidence points to widespread labour

Table 9A.2   Industrial action in workplaces with recognized unions, 1980–1998

	1980	1984	1990	1998
All workplaces				
None	75	69	80	96
Non-strike action only	10	8	4	2
Strike action only	9	11	11	2
Both strike and non-strike action	7	11	5	*
Private sector manufacturing				
None	62	70	88	95
Non-strike action only	11	14	10	5
Strike action only	15	9	*	0
Both strike and non-strike action	12	7	3	0
Private sector services				
None	89	85	93	97
Non-strike action only	5	4	1	1
Strike action only	5	8	1	2
Both strike and non-strike action	1	3	5	1
Public sector				
None	73	61	67	95
Non-strike action only	12	7	4	2
Strike action only	8	14	23	2
Both strike and non-strike action	8	17	6	*

Data refer to workplaces with 25 or more employees where there are recognized trade unions and are reported by managers to the WERS research team. No distinction is made between official and unofficial industrial action. The data thus record the incidence of all industrial action.
Source: Millward et al. (2000: 178). By permission of Routledge.

quiescence. However, record levels of cases taken to Employment Tribunals suggest that other means of expressing dissatisfaction may be gaining in significance. No fewer than 130,000 people made Employment Tribunal claims in 2000, with a disproportionately large number of claims coming from non-union workplaces (TUC 2001a).

By 1998 there were few differences between private manufacturing, private services and the public sector in terms of the occurrence of some form of industrial conflict. No industrial action was experienced by at least 95 per cent of workplaces in all sectors. Between 1980 and 1998, however, rather different trajectories had been followed. In private sector manufacturing there was a steady trend of declining industrial action, which, with the exception of 1984, was consistent in terms of both strike and non-strike action. A broadly similar pattern is found in private sector services, albeit at consistently lower levels of industrial action. The private sector contrasts with the public sector, as strike activity remained relatively high and increased until 1990, before falling dramatically between 1990 and 1998. Until 1990, therefore, industrial action was most prevalent where trade unions were most densely organized in the public sector. Whether this relationship is a function of union organization per se or a feature of the public sector remains a moot point. The link between union organization and industrial action is sustained for the whole economy, however, in that industrial action affected only 1 per cent of workplaces unionized to less than 25 per cent in 1998, compared to 8 per cent of workplaces with a level of union density of 90 per cent or more (Millward et al. 2000: 179).

Explanations and future trends

There are several competing interpretations of these data, each of which has rather different policy implications and expectations for the future pattern of strike activity. Four of these are briefly considered below: long wave theory, partnership, and two interpretations based on the effects of legislation. The future pattern of strike activity anticipated from each interpretation is also presented to highlight the range of outcomes analysts of industrial conflict are prepared to suggest.

Those who argue that long waves of economic development underpin many developments in industrial relations cite the cyclical pattern of strike activity as supporting their explanation (Screpanti 1987; Franzosi 1995; Kelly 1998). It is argued that 'aggressive' industrial action will peak at the top of each long wave of economic activity, with fewer and more defensive actions occurring during the subsequent downswing. The 'aggressive' pursuit of strikes over pay and trade union principle during the upswing of the long wave and the subsequent peak in the period 1965–79, followed by more 'defensive' strikes thereafter, is consistent with long wave theory. Proponents of this position anticipate steady growth in industrial conflict in the near future as the long downswing from about 1973 shifts into the upswing of the subsequent long wave during the late 1990s or immediately thereafter.

Taking an entirely different tack, advocates of partnership interpret the low and declining levels of strikes after 1990 as evidence of 'success' of the partnership arrangements that are already in place. As the decline in strike activity certainly preceded any widespread introduction of partnership agreements, this is not an argument about the reasons for the decline in strikes, but is about a means to ensure low levels of strike activity in the future. In practice, advocates of this position assume that there has been a change in the climate of industrial relations, which can be sustained by the extension of partnership arrangements.

Two explanations are based on the legislative changes introduced by the Conservative governments of 1979–92 and maintained, in large part, by subsequent Labour governments. The first of these explanations assumes that the trade unions have been 'tamed' and the strikes have been 'struck out' by the legislation (Hanson 1991). This approach assumes that the legislation introduced during the 1980s has restricted the trade union room for manoeuvre to the extent that strikes will no longer be a 'problem'. While it is far from clear that the legislation has been as effective as these authors suggest (see chapter 9), they would expect a continuation of the low levels of strike activity if the extant legislation remains on the statute book.

Another argument draws on the legislation, but incorporates an analysis of internal union practices. During the 1960s and early 1970s the growth of unofficial strikes was linked to union weakness, in particular the failure of formal union practices and procedures to fulfil their functions satisfactorily (Allen 1966: 115). As the legislation of the 1980s has made unions legally accountable for actions taken in their name, the distinction between a lawful strike and an official strike has become increasingly difficult to draw. In other words, the legislation has enabled formal unions to restore control (Undy et al. 1996). The central issue within the terms of this explanation is, can formal trade union practices remain dominant? If so, low levels of strike activity can be anticipated, but if not a return to more unofficial forms of industrial action is more likely.

What is clear is that the extent of any industrial action will be influenced by changes in union membership and the extent of adherence to the balloting provisions. Recent evidence suggests that currently this is the case. During the year to May 2001 there were 1,926 strike ballots compared with 983 during the previous year (TUC 2001b). In 86 per cent of these cases trade union members voted for industrial action, although most of the ballots were for action short of a strike, such as overtime bans. Furthermore, where a ballot took place, trade unions won some of their demands in 76 per cent of cases.

Notes

1 Formally, the TUC covers Great Britain and thus excludes Northern Ireland from its coverage. In practice, however, many TUC-affiliated unions organize members in Northern Ireland and several also organize in the Irish Republic; they would count these members in their affiliation to the TUC.

2 GCHQ is a government centre involved in monitoring and eavesdropping operations. Because of the national security implications arising from many of the activities undertaken there, the Conservative government deemed that it was inappropriate for the workforce at GCHQ to be represented by trade unions.

3 Between 1988 and 1996, 382 applications for assistance were made to the CROTUM, an average of 42 per year. The three most common applications for assistance related to breaches of union rules concerning election to, or removal from, union office; breaches of rules concerning disciplinary action; and a union's failure to comply with statutory duties for election of certain union offices (for details, see IRS 1996).

4 These data refer to workplaces at which 25 or more people are employed. As union recognition at smaller workplaces is lower than that at larger sites, these data exaggerate overall levels of union recognition.

5 The annual reports of the Certification Officer report data applicable to December of the year until the 1999 report, which includes data until 1998. Thereafter, these reports also include returns from trade unions with year-ending dates ranging from October to September. In consequence, there is no complete data set available for the year end.

6 Trade union mergers are regulated by law. In order to complete an amalgamation, a simple majority must be achieved among the members who vote in all the participating unions. For a transfer of engagements a simple majority is required only among the members of the smaller union.

7 See the appendix to this chapter for a fuller discussion of strike activity, trends and causation.

8 Also included in Labour's modernizing agenda for trade unions is the further restructuring of trade unions through mergers. Given the existing complexity of union structure and the absence of any constitutional authority within trade unionism to develop and impose a single framework of structural reform, it seems unlikely that an all-embracing co-ordinated strategy can be implemented.

9 Check-off arrangements allow an employer to deduct union contributions directly from the wages of employees and forward the sum to the union. The union is thus released from the obligation of collecting membership contributions. The majority of trade union members pay their contributions through the check-off. The Trade Union Reform and Employment Rights Act 1993 required that each worker paying his/her contributions through check-off arrangements must provide written consent every three years. While there is no evidence to suggest that large numbers of members

were lost as a result of this procedure, there is no doubt that it required a huge administrative effort by unions to complete.

10 The Bridlington Principles were originally agreed at the annual congress of the TUC in 1939, which was held in Bridlington. These principles stipulated that the Disputes Committee of the TUC was the arbiter of disputes between affiliated unions over members. Although the principles were periodically amended, the complexity of British union structure and the growth in the number of unions that organised across several industries and occupations led to much criticism from within unions about their operation.

11 Stonewall is an organization that campaigns on behalf on gay men.

12 Affiliations to the TUC since 1995 include: Professional Footballers' Association; Community and Youth Workers' Association; Community and District Nursing Association; UNIFI; Independent Union of Halifax Staff; Society of Chiropodists and Podiatrists; British Dietetic Association; Association of Flight Attendants – Heathrow Local; Association of Teachers and Lecturers; Alliance and Leicester Group Union of Staff; and the Association of Educational Psychologists.

13 These proposals were discussed by Francis O'Grady, Head of Organization and Services at the TUC (*Times*, Thursday 2 March 2000) and Matthew Taylor, director of the Institute for Public Policy Research (*Unions Today*, March 2000).

14 These figures are from the Labour Force Survey 1998. The number of employees in workplaces with union recognition is 10.1 million and the number of employees whose pay is determined by collective agreement is 8.0 million. The number of trade union members, estimated from the same source, is 6.8 million.

15 Consistent records on strike activity in the UK are available since 1891.

16 These data are drawn from successive workplace industrial relations surveys, the first of which was undertaken for 1980, hence the starting date for the data.

References

Ackers, P., and Payne, J. 1998: British trade unions and social partnership: rhetoric, reality and strategy, *International Journal of Human Resource Management*, 9 (3), 529–50.

Adams, R. 1999: Why statutory union recognition is bad labour policy: the North American experience, *Industrial Relations Journal*, 30 (1), 96–100.

Adeney, M., and Lloyd, J. 1986: *The Miners' Strike 1984–5: Loss without Limit.* London: Routledge.

Allen, V. 1966: *Militant Trade Unionism.* London: Merlin Press.

Arrowsmith, J., and Sisson, K. 2000: Managing working time. In S. Bach and K. Sisson (eds), *Personnel Management.* Oxford: Blackwell.

Blair, T., and Schroeder, G. n.d.: *Europe: The Third Way / Die Neue Mitte.* London: Labour Party.

Bland, P. 1999: Trade union membership and recognition 1997–98: an analysis of data from the Certification Officer and the Labour Force Survey, *Labour Market Trends*, July, 343–53.

Boxall, P., and Haynes, P. 1997: Strategy and trade union effectiveness in a neo-liberal environment, *British Journal of Industrial Relations*, 35 (4), 567–92.

Briskin, L., and McDermott, P. (eds) 1993: *Women Challenging Unions: Feminism, Democracy and Militancy.* Toronto: University of Toronto Press.

Bronfenbrenner, K., Friedman, S., Hurd, R., Oswald, R. and Seeber, R. 1998: *Organizing to Win.* Ithaca: ILR Press.

Brown, W., and Wadhwani, S. 1990: The economic effects of industrial relations legislation since 1979, *National Institute Economic Review*, February, 57–70.

Carruth, A., and Disney, R. 1988: Where have two million trade union members gone? *Economica*, 55 (1), 41–62.

Carter, B. 2000: Adoption of the organising model in British trade unions: some evidence from Manufacturing, Science and Finance, *Work, Employment and Society*, 14 (1), 117–36.

Carter, B., and Fairbrother, P. 1999: The transformation of British public sector industrial relations: from 'model employer' to marketized relations, *Historical Studies in Industrial Relations*, 7 (1), 119–46.

Certification Office. Various: *Annual Report of the Certification Officer*. London: Certification Office.

Claydon, T. 1996: Union derecognition: a re-examination. In I. Beardwell (ed.), *Contemporary Industrial Relations*. Oxford: Oxford University Press.

Coates, D. 1996: New Labour, or old? *New Left Review*, 219, 62–77.

Colling, T., and Dickens, L. 1998: Selling the case for gender equality: deregulation and equality bargaining, *British Journal of Industrial Relations*, 36 (3), 389–412.

Cully, M., O'Reilly, A., Millward, N., Forth, J., Woodland, S., Dix, G. and Bryson, A. 1998: *The 1998 Workplace Employee Relations Survey*. London: HMSO.

Cully, M., Woodland, S., O'Reilly, A. and Dix, G. 1999: *Britain at Work: As Depicted by the 1998 Workplace Employee Relations Survey*. London: Routledge.

Cunnison, S., and Stageman, J. 1995: *Feminizing the Unions*. Aldershot: Avebury.

Davies, J. 2001: Labour disputes in 2000, *Labour Market Trends*, June, 301–14.

DE (Department of Employment) 1983: *Democracy in Trade Unions*. Cmnd. 8778. London: HMSO.

Disney, R. 1990: Explanations of the decline in trade union density in Britain: an appraisal, *British Journal of Industrial Relations*, 28 (2), 165–78.

Disney, R., Gosling, A. and Machin, S. 1995: British unions in decline: determinants of the 1980s fall in union recognition, *Industrial and Labor Relations Review*, 48 (3), 403–19.

Disney, R., Gosling, A., Machin, S. and McCrae, J. 1998: *The Dynamics of Union Membership in Britain*. Employment Relations Research Series, Research Report 3, Department of Trade and Industry. Available at <www.dti.gov.uk/er/emar>.

Dunn, S., and Metcalf, D. 1996: Trade union law since 1979. In I. Beardwell (ed.), *Contemporary Industrial Relations*. Oxford: Oxford University Press.

Durcan, J., McCarthy, W. and Redman, G. 1983: *Strikes in Post-War Britain*. London: George Allen & Unwin.

Edwards, P. 1995: Strikes and industrial conflict. In P. Edwards (ed.), *Industrial Relations: Theory and Practice in Britain*. Oxford: Blackwell.

EWCB 1999: Draft directive on employee consultation, *European Works Council Bulletin*, 19 (January/February), 8–12.

Fisher, J. 1997: The challenge of change: the positive agenda of the TGWU, *International Journal of Human Resource Management*, 8 (6), 797–806.

Foster, D., and Scott, P. 1998: Competitive tendering of public services and industrial relations policy: the Conservative agenda under Thatcher and Major, 1979–1997, *Historical Studies in Industrial Relations*, 6 (1), 101–32.

Franzosi, R. 1995: *The Puzzle of Strikes*. Cambridge: Cambridge University Press.

Freeman, R., and Pelletier, J. 1990: The impact of industrial relations legislation on British union density, *British Journal of Industrial Relations*, 28 (2), 141–64.

Garcia, A., Hacourt, B. and Lega, H. n.d.: *The 'Second Sex' of European Trade Unionism*. Brussels: European Trade Union Confederation.

Geroski, P., Gregg, P. and Desjonqueres, T. 1995: Did the retreat of UK trade unionism accelerate during the 1990–1993 recession? *British Journal of Industrial Relations*, 33 (1), 35–54.

Giddens, A. 1998: *The Third Way: The Renewal of Social Democracy*. Cambridge: Polity.

GMB/UCW 1990: *New Agenda: Bargaining for Prosperity in the 1990s*. London: GMB and the Union of Communication Workers.

Green, F. 1990: Trade union availability and trade union membership in Britain, *Manchester School*, 58 (3), 378–94.

Guest, D., and Peccei, R. 2001: Partnership at work: mutuality and the balance of advantage, *British Journal of Industrial Relations*, 39 (2), 207–36.

Hall, M. 1999: TUC's partnership agenda wins qualified support from government and employers, *EIROnline*, June. <www.eiro.eurofound.eu.int>.

Hanson, C. 1991: *Taming the Trade Unions*. Basingstoke: Macmillan.

Heery, E. 1998a: Campaigning for part-time workers, *Work, Employment and Society*, 12 (2), 351–66.

Heery, E. 1998b: The relaunch of the Trades Union Congress, *British Journal of Industrial Relations*, 36 (3), 339–60.

Heery, E., Simms, M., Delbridge, R., Salmon, J. and Simpson, D. 2000: The TUC's Organising Academy: an assessment, *Industrial Relations Journal*, 31 (5), 400–15.

Hendy, J. 1989: *The Conservative Employment Laws: A National and International Assessment*. London: Institute of Employment Rights.

Hyman, R. 1984: *Strikes*. 3rd edn. London: Fontana.

Hyman, R. 1989: *Strikes*. 4th edn. London: Fontana.

Hyman, R. 1999: Strikes in the UK: withering away? *EIROnline*, July. <www.eiro.eurofound.eu.int>.

IDS (Incomes Data Services) 1999: Company councils, *IDS Studies*, 672 (July).

Industrial Society 1998: *Managing Best Practice 49: Works Councils*. London: Industrial Society.

Ingram, P., Metcalf, D. and Wadsworth, J. 1993: Strike incidence in British manufacturing in the 1980s, *Industrial and Labor Relations Review*, 46 (4), 704–17.

IPA (Involvement and Participation Association) 1997: *Towards Industrial Partnership: New Ways of Working in British Companies*. London: IPA.

IRS (Industrial Relations Services) 1996: Trade unions on trial, *IRS Employment Trends*, 608 (May), 11–16.

Jospin, L. 1999: *Modern Socialism*. Fabian Pamphlet 592. London: Fabian Society.

Kelly, J. 1996: Union militancy and social partnership. In P. Ackers, C. Smith and P. Smith (eds), *The New Workplace and Trade Unionism*. London: Routledge.

Kelly, J. 1998: *Rethinking Industrial Relations: Mobilization, Collectivism and Long Waves*. London: Routledge.

Kelly, J., and Heery, E. 1994: *Working for the Union*. Cambridge: Cambridge University Press.

Kerr, A. 1992: Why public sector workers join trade unions: an attitude survey of workers in the Health Service and local government, *Employee Relations*, 14 (2), 39–54.

Knell, J. 1999: *Partnership at Work*. Employment Relations Research Series 7. London: Department of Trade and Industry. Available at <www.dti.gov.uk/er/emar>.

Knowles, K. 1954: *Strikes: A Study in Industrial Conflict*. Oxford: Blackwell.

Leopold, J. 1997: Trade unions, political fund ballots and the Labour Party, *British Journal of Industrial Relations*, 35 (1), 23–38.

Leys, C. 1996: The British Labour Party's transition from socialism to capitalism, *Socialist Register*, 7–32.

Machin, S. 1995: Plant closures and unionization in British establishments, *British Journal of Industrial Relations*, 33 (1), 55–68.

Martin, R. 1980: *TUC: The Growth of a Pressure Group 1868–1976*. Oxford: Clarendon Press.

McIlroy, J. 1998: The enduring alliance? Trade unions and the making of New Labour, *British Journal of Industrial Relations*, 36 (4), 537–64.

Metcalf, D., Wadsworth, J. and Ingram, P. 1993: Do strikes pay? In D. Metcalf and S. Milner (eds), *New Perspectives on Industrial Disputes*. London: Routledge.

Midwest Center for Labor Research 1991: An organizing model of unionism, *Labor Research Review*, 17 (Spring), 97 pp.

Millward, N., Bryson, A. and Forth, J. 2000: *All Change at Work*. London: Routledge.

Millward, N., and Stevens, M. 1986: *British Workplace Industrial Relations 1980–1984*. Aldershot: Gower.

Minkin, L. 1991: *The Contentious Alliance*. Edinburgh: Edinburgh University Press.

Mort, J. (ed.) 1998: *Not Your Father's Union Movement*. London: Verso.

Munro, A. 1999: *Women, Work and Trade Unions*. London: Mansell.

Munro, A., and Rainbird, H. 2000: The new unionism and the new bargaining agenda: UNISON–employer partnerships on workplace learning in Britain, *British Journal of Industrial Relations*, 38 (2), 223–40.

Phelps Brown, H. 1990: The counter-revolution of our time, *Industrial Relations*, 29 (1), 1–14.

Sapper, S. 1991: Do members' services packages influence trade union recruitment? *Industrial Relations Journal*, 22 (1), 63–78.

Screpanti, E. 1987: Long cycles in strike activity: an empirical investigation, *British Journal of Industrial Relations*, 25 (1), 99–124.

Shalev, M. 1992: The resurgence of labour quiescence. In M. Regini (ed.), *The Future of Labour Movements*. London: Sage.

Smith, P., and Morton, G. 1993: Union exclusion and the decollectivization of industrial relations in contemporary Britain, *British Journal of Industrial Relations*, 31 (1), 97–114.

Snape, E. 1995: The development of 'managerial unionism' in the UK, *Work, Employment and Society*, 9 (3), 559–68.

Taylor, M., and Cruddas, J. n.d.: *New Labour New Links*. Discussion Paper. London: Unions 21.

Taylor, R. 1994: *The Future of the Trade Unions*. London: André Deutsch.

Taylor, R. 1998: Annual review article 1997, *British Journal of Industrial Relations*, 36 (2), 293–312.

Thompson, N. 1996: What New Labour really means, *New Left Review*, 216, 37–54.

TUC 1995: *Representation at Work*. London: Trades Union Congress.

TUC 1997a: *Britain and Europe: Next Steps*. London: Trades Union Congress.

TUC 1997b: *Congress Report*. London: Trades Union Congress.

TUC 1999a: Government should 'think again' on working time changes and get to grips with long hours culture. Press release, 20 August. London: Trades Union Congress.

TUC 1999b: *Partners in Progress: New Unionism in the Workplace*. London: Trades Union Congress.

TUC 2001a: TUC Response on Employment Tribunals, <www.tuc.org.uk>.

TUC 2001b: *Trade Union Trends 2001*. London: Trades Union Congress.

TUC. Various. *Annual Report*. London: Trades Union Congress.

Undy, R. 1999: New Labour's 'industrial relations settlement': the third way? *British Journal of Industrial Relations*, 37 (2), 315–36.

Undy, R., Fosh, P., Morris, H., Smith, P. and Martin, R. 1996: *Managing the Unions*. Oxford: Clarendon Press.

Waddington, J. 1992: Trade union membership in Britain, 1980–1987: unemployment and restructuring, *British Journal of Industrial Relations*, 30 (2), 287–322.

Waddington, J. 1995: *The Politics of Bargaining*. London: Mansell.

Waddington, J., and Kerr, A. 1999a: Membership retention in the public sector, *Industrial Relations Journal*, 30 (2), 151–65.

Waddington, J., and Kerr, A. 1999b: Trying to stem the flow: union membership turnover in the public sector, *Industrial Relations Journal*, 30 (3), 184–96.

Waddington, J., and Kerr, A. 2000: Towards an organising model in UNISON? A trade union membership strategy in transition. In M. Terry (ed.), *Redefining Public Sector Unionism*. London: Routledge.

Waddington, J., and Whitston, C. 1996: Collectivism in a changing context: union joining and bargaining preferences among white-collar staff. In P. Leisink, J. Van Leemput and J. Vilrokx (eds), *The Challenges to Trade Unions in Europe: Innovation or Adaptation*. Cheltenham: Edward Elgar.

Waddington, J., and Whitston, C. 1997: Why do people join unions in a period of membership decline? *British Journal of Industrial Relations*, 35 (4), 515–46.

Williamson, J. 1997: Your stake at work: the TUC's agenda. In G. Kelly, D. Kelly and A. Gamble (eds), *Stakeholder Capitalism*. Basingstoke: Macmillan.

Willman, P., Morris, T. and Aston, B. 1993: *Union Business*. Cambridge: Cambridge University Press.

10

EMPLOYEE REPRESENTATION: SHOP STEWARDS AND THE NEW LEGAL FRAMEWORK

MICHAEL TERRY

For generations the dominant institution for the representation of employee interests in the United Kingdom has been the trade union, and for many workers the most important and familiar agent in that process was and is the local union representative, still often called the shop steward. Elected by fellow workers and accountable to them, responsible for union recruitment and local organization, representatives in matters individual and collective, strike leaders and advice counsellors, shop stewards have always been trade union activists of many parts. Heroes or villains, they have been and remain the dynamic heart of the British union movement. The characteristic decentralization and workplace-centredness of British industrial relations discussed in chapter 2 have under-pinned the central role of the steward; in principle, as decentralization increased during the 1980s and 1990s (see chapters 7 and 11), their significance might have been expected to increase.

In fact the reverse has happened; shop stewards' role and activity have diminished over the last two decades. The central purpose of this chapter is to chart the changes and assess their significance. The stark reduction in the coverage and impact of systems of employee representation (the 'representation gap' – see Towers 1997) will be examined in the light of three key factors: the shifting characteristics of employment in the United Kingdom; the altered managerial environment; and unions' own structural strengths and weaknesses. This chapter focuses on *trade union* structures, which remain much the most common workplace representative bodies, but it also looks briefly at the significance of non-union forms of employee representation. At present in the UK these have two dimensions: first there are those companies that do not recognize a trade union but which have instituted a system of indirect employee representation, often called a 'company' or 'factory' council; second, as discussed in chapter 6, there are those representative structures that have developed as a consequence of European legislation conferring rights on *employees* to be informed and consulted in various ways. The best-known of these structures is the European Works Council, but other legislation has implicitly presumed the existence of structures for employee representation by insisting on consultation with employees in specific circumstance. Potentially even more significant is the directive on national information and consultation procedures, sometimes referred to as the 'works council' draft directive, that was finally adopted in June 2001 despite the evident unhappiness of the British government.

The chapter will not examine in detail other changes in the legal environment. One long-standing aspect of the legal framework in the UK is, however, central to our understanding of the trajectory of steward history. The *recognition* of trade unions by employers has, with only very brief exceptions, been a 'voluntary' act; there were no legal powers through which unions and their members could insist that it happen. Employers over the years may have been forced into dealing with stewards as representative agents through trade union deployment of collective strength, or they may have agreed to or even initiated it out of commitment to 'pluralist' industrial relations strategies, but, with the recent exception of representation in the area of health and safety, discussed later, the law has rarely intervened. This is in sharp distinction to virtually all other EU member states, where systems of employee representation, involving unions directly or indirectly, generally enjoy universal legal guarantee. In the UK, the relationship between employer and union within the enterprise or workplace, of its nature more fluid, is one of the two defining parameters of shop steward organization and influence (the other being that between union members and their representatives). The significance of this point will be elaborated later.

This chapter will argue that we are witnessing two trajectories of indirect employee representation in the UK. On the one hand we have the traditional voluntarist system, based overwhelmingly in the recognition of trade unions as employees' accredited representative agents, alongside a small number of employer-created non-union systems. On most measures this system has been in decline for two decades, as measured both by its coverage of the UK workforce and by the influence it can exert on its behalf. Much recent writing has been directed at exploring whether and under what circumstances the system can be revived or renewed. On the other hand we can see at least the potential for the development of a system of representation based in legal rights conferred not on a trade union but on the collectivity of individual employees in a workplace or an enterprise. The relationship between these two systems, and in particular whether the new developments represent a further threat to the viability of the traditional system, has been the subject of much debate, and will be discussed later. But first it is useful to sketch out the current state of employee representation.

Table 10.1 Types of worker representatives, by trade union presence (%)

	No union present	Union present no recognition	Recognized union	All
Union and non-union representatives	–	–	10	4
Union representatives only	–	–	64	28
Non-union representatives only	11	19	1	7
No worker representatives	89	81	25	60

Base: All workplaces with 25 or more employees.
Source: Cully et al. (1999: 96). By permission of Routledge.

Employee Workplace Representation in the UK

Where?

The 1998 WERS found that employee representatives were found in 40 per cent of workplaces employing more than 25 people (see table 10.1). Slightly up on the 38 per cent reported in 1994, it is a substantial decline since the 54 per cent in 1984 (Millward et al. 1992: 110). The actual number of stewards appears to have fallen less fast. In 1978 Clegg estimated that there were over 250,000 stewards in the UK (Terry 1983: 68) while the estimate for 1998 is 218,000 (Cully et al. 1998: 16). Nearly a quarter of a million workers can still be found to take on this often thankless work, even after 20 years of decline in union power and, it is sometimes claimed, in public esteem.

The presence of an employee representative at the workplace is plainly heavily dependent on trade union recognition, though it is notable that in a quarter of workplaces with a recognized union no representative is present. In 10 per cent of workplaces where unions are recognized there are both union and non-union representatives. In non-union workplaces access to a representative is very much the exception. The traditional 'size effect' continues: in the smallest size category (25–49 employees) employee representatives were present in 19 per cent of workplaces with trade union recognition while in those with 500 or more the figure was 65 per cent. Combining these figures with data on the presence of recognized unions, the WERS shows that access to a system of employee representation (a 'shop steward') is generally available to employees in the public services, the privatized utilities and services, in large manufacturing workplaces and, to a lesser extent, in finance and banking. Otherwise it is rare.

Of equal importance is the proportion of employees who may have access to a system of employee representation, and this is shown in table 10.2. The close association between union membership and access to a representative is confirmed, although nearly a fifth of union members do not have such direct access. At the same time, over half of all employees are employed in workplaces with at least some form of employee representation, although not all will enjoy direct

Table 10.2   Distribution of employees across workplaces with different forms of employee representation (%)

	All employees	Union members	Not union members
Union and non-union representatives	7	10	5
Union representatives only	46	74	29
Non-union representatives only	9	4	12
No worker representatives	39	13	54

Base: all workplaces with 25 or more employees.
Source: WERS 1998 data, special calculations by John Forth of the National Institute for Economic and Social Research.

access to it; non-union members, for example, will rarely be represented by union representatives even when they are present.

Other data from the survey, such as the incidence of joint consultation committees (Cully et al. 1999: 99–100) confirm the close relationship between this form of representation and workplace trade union presence while also making clear that in certain sectors, such as financial services, consultation is also widespread, but largely at corporate, rather than workplace, level. This is a useful reminder that in sectors with a significant proportion of small workplaces within large organizations representation by union full-time officials rather than shop stewards is the norm, with concomitant differences in the role of local representatives and indeed in the overall pattern of union member access to representation. We are thus not dealing with only one 'model' of union representation. Indeed, for significant parts of the private service sector the 'shop steward model' of trade union organization, often assumed to be virtually coterminous with trade unionism itself, may not be viable.

Finally, the survey shows that in respect of the specific issue of health and safety, representation is significantly more widespread in non-union workplaces than it is for other issues; in workplaces with no union members 31 per cent had joint health and safety committees and 27 per cent had elected safety representatives (Cully at al. 1999: 96). While lower than for workplaces with union recognition, these figures provide striking evidence of the potential impact of legislation, since it is only since the enactment of the Health and Safety (Consultation with Employees) Regulations in 1996 that employers who do not recognize trade unions have been under a general legal obligation to consult their employees on this issue. Significantly, the effect has been particularly marked in small workplaces and those without union recognition (Millward et al. 2000: 117).

Who?

In this chapter an employee representative is taken to mean an employee elected or nominated by a designated constituency of fellow employees. In the particular but numerically dominant case of the trade union representative (shop steward) the constituency consists only of fellow trade union members. Election and accountability combine with the close identification between representative and represented to underpin their particular legitimacy and authority, buttressed in the case of trade unions by identification with an independent organization charged with representing member interests. This is a point of difference with the 'works council' model of employee representation found in many other European countries, where both the detail of election procedures and the nature of the employee representative role are prescribed by law, which thus confers on representatives an additional, or different, source of representative legitimacy.

In the WERS data the typical (senior) union representative was male (65 per cent), and had been employed at his workplace for 11 years (i.e. since 1987), for six of those as a representative (i.e. since 1992). The vast majority of even senior stewards thus have little memory of their alleged heyday in the 1970s; their work and union experience are firmly set in the different environment since the late 1980s. The typical senior representative was formally elected into the position and had at some time received shop steward training. He typically did not hold an official position with his union either at national, regional or district level (Cully et al. 1999: 195).

The average size of representative constituencies fell slightly between 1990 and 1998 from 32 to 29 union members per representative (Millward et al. 2000: 154), although this 'density of representation' figure may be affected by union representatives' preparedness in certain circumstances to represent non-members, of whom there were growing numbers. More significantly perhaps the most recent data show a significant *occupational* differentiation, indicating that professional and white-collar workers have more representatives than their union membership numbers might suggest and that the reverse is true for many manual workers. Professional employees constitute 13 per cent of union members but they make up 33 per cent of all representatives; the comparable figures for 'plant and machine operatives' are 21 per cent and 11 per cent (Cully et al. 1999: 196). This does not necessarily indicate that 'manual' employees lack representation. In many trade unions that organize both professional and manual workers a disproportionate number of professional representatives may be found, but they are in theory and often in practice required to represent all that union's members. The public service union UNISON would be a typical case. One obvious reason for such 'professional over-representation' is that professional workers often have, by virtue of the work they do, access to facilities such as phones, word processors and photocopiers, and the time and opportunity to integrate union activities into work routines. At a time when managers appear to be limiting the resources and time available for union duties this could be crucial.

At the same time the 'gender gap', often noted in the past in respect of lay as well as full-time union officials, appears to be closing fast. By 1998, 36 per cent of union representatives were women, only slightly lower than the proportion of union members who were women (39 per cent), and in workplaces with a majority of female employees, 59 per cent of union representatives were women (Cully et al. 1999: 196–7). These figures must reflect, among other things, the serious efforts many unions have been making, in the face of strong allegations of their earlier ineffectiveness in properly representing women, to improve the situation. This is in turn directly relevant to arguments as to whether the representativeness of systems such as these is affected by an identity (of occupational status, gender, ethnicity) between representatives and represented. There are strong arguments that it is, most clearly articulated in the case of women (Munro 1999). The work of Heery and Kelly (1988), looking at union full-time officers rather than shop stewards, provides empirical support for the contention that women are better than men at representing women's interests. In that respect the quality of local trade union representation has improved significantly in recent years. At the same time, concern is being voiced in some union quarters at the increasingly inadequate representation of manual workers (Jones 2000: 126). Greater sensitivity to the need to develop effective structures for groups excluded from participation increases unions' representative capacity while at the same time reconfiguring the central political issue for any system of employee representation, namely the construction of organizational unity out of the effective representation of diversity.

What do shop stewards do?

As the old maxim has it, in a decentralized union system such as that of the UK, 'the shop steward *is* the union': the point of contact for individual advice and support and the conduit through which the collective benefits of union membership are channelled. What local union representatives do, and how effective they are perceived by their members to be in pursuing their interests, is vital to the health of local trade union organization; ineffective union representatives may have problems in retaining members.

At first glance the 1998 survey data suggest that shop stewards' 'job description' is little changed from earlier years; they spend the bulk of their time dealing with problems raised by the treatment of employees by management, employment security, health and safety issues, and maintaining employee wages and benefits (Cully et al. 1999: 201–2). It is for support and assistance with such issues that working people have always joined, and continue to join, trade unions (Waddington and Whitston 1997). However, the 1998 survey probed deeper than its predecessors, trying to uncover the *effectiveness* of such activity. For the first time employees were asked to indicate whether or not 'unions make a difference to what it is like at work'. Only 46 per cent of union members, 30 per cent of employees who had never been union members and 26 per cent of employees who had previously been union members agreed that they do (Cully et al. 1999: 212). This impression of relative ineffectiveness derives at least indirect support from managerial estimates of their own ability to organize work in workplaces with recognized trade unions. Between 70 per cent and 80 per cent of managers identified no union-derived constraints, a figure little changed from 1990 (Millward et al. 2000: 174–5). Recent time-series analysis shows that unions' long-established ability to reduce wage differentials (the 'gap' between high and low earners) through collective bargaining has disappeared

(Millward et al. 2000: 220) and that the so-called 'union mark-up' (pay generally higher in unionized than equivalent non-unionized workplaces) has also gone in all but the most highly organized workplaces (Millward 2001). On the other hand a local union continues to be effective in tempering managerial treatment of employees; both dismissals and disciplinary sanctions are significantly less common in unionized than non-union workplaces (Millward et al. 2000: 128) and there is some support for an association between employment security and trade union presence (Millward et al. 2000: 79).

This general picture of declining union effectiveness, including that of local representative structures, is hugely important in a country where employees join unions largely for pragmatic reasons. The traditional picture of shop stewards portrays them as bargaining agents first and foremost, locked into processes of virtually continuous negotiation with managers over a range of terms and conditions of employment to the evident benefit of their members. This picture, given its most concrete expression on the analysis of the 1967 Donovan Commission Report, appears to be no longer sustainable. This is made dramatically clear in just one set of data from the 1998 WERS survey. Managers were asked whether they negotiated with or consulted or provided information to workplace representatives on each of nine issues. In half of the workplaces with union representatives, there was no negotiation on any issue, and in a further 17 per cent there was negotiation on pay alone. This indicates that consultation rather than negotiation is now the dominant collective workplace relationship (see Brown et al. 2000: 615–18) and that, on many issues many stewards do not even have that. The differences between union and non-union representation, hitherto generally presumed to exist, seem to have disappeared, although this figure is based on managerial responses and they may exaggerate the effectiveness of systems they have themselves created.

Thus, as measured by *outcomes* shop stewards in the late 1990s appear relatively ineffective in comparison with our earlier picture of their activity, often ignored or sidelined by management. This conclusion is in line with data and arguments produced during the last two decades alleging managerial marginalizing of the role of trade unions, bypassing of shop stewards as communication channels to the workforce, and flouting of procedural presumptions of consultation or negotiation with trade union representatives before the implementation of change. The decline of shop steward influence seems incontrovertible, as does the claim that this decline has been most marked in the areas of historical strength; the nature and extent of change in less well researched areas with a degree of union presence (banks, supermarkets and so on) may be less dramatic. And certainly, as discussed below, they have been more marked in the private than the public sector.

In order to understand why these changes have occurred the next section will analyse the decline in traditional systems of representation in the unionized sectors, private and public, and will briefly comment on non-union workplaces. It will then examine the potential for the emergence of a new form of employee representation drawing its structures and rationale from European Union legislative development. The final section will assess, in the light of the analysis of the decline of the traditional system and the introduction of new legal rights, the prospects of survival for shop-floor-based union organization. It will pay particular attention to the recent vogue for the model of 'partnership'.

The 'Voluntary' System: Irreversible Decline?

Employee representation based around access to representatives of recognized trade unions in their workplace has declined, on all measures of coverage and effectiveness, since the late 1970s, and most markedly since the mid-1980s, in line with the fall in unionism more generally. What has caused the decline of a system that, after two decades of expansion had, by the end of the 1970s, come to be seen, whatever its strengths and weaknesses, as a permanent, expanding, presence in UK industrial relations? This analysis will focus on three factors: structural change in the UK economy; changing managerial practices; and features of the shop steward system itself.

Structural change

The argument that unions have been weakened as a consequence of a shift of employment from sectors where unions were traditionally strong into those where they were weak sounds like a truism but contains an important analytical insight, drawing our attention to the need to identify the structural impediments to strong workplace trade unionism in the latter sectors.

Briefly stated, the conventional argument is that effective steward organization flourished in environments that afforded both the necessary resources for independent existence and the ability to take or to threaten effective collective action (Terry 1983). Central to the former was the size of the workforce, since the basic resources for steward organization come from the members themselves. As noted above, surveys have revealed a strong association between workplace size and shop steward presence, an unsurprising finding in a voluntaristic system where union existence and structure derive from internal strength, rather than from legally guaranteed provision. While the evidence concerning the decline in workplace size is mixed (Millward et al. 2000: 28) there has been a significant decline in the proportion of employees in manufacturing and extractive industries in workplaces employing 500 or more (from 17 per cent to 10 per cent between 1980 and 1998). More importantly, employment has been shifting towards sectors associated with characteristically smaller than average workplaces, such as hotels, restaurants, and the wholesale and retail sector. However, the picture is sufficiently varied to make clear that a workplace size/resource argument alone is not an adequate explanation of the presence or absence of union representative systems.

More important is the argument that the period since the late 1970s has witnessed a decline in stewards' (and unions' generally) bargaining strength, not only in the UK but with particular consequences for UK shop-floor-based trade unionism in a voluntarist institutional setting. The ability to take or threaten effective workplace-based collective action (not necessarily strikes), seen for much of the 1970s as the shop steward's stock-in-trade 'resource', is vital, not least because a compelling case can be made that historical patterns of workplace unionism reflect patterns of workplace employee bargaining power and its expression. While not a complete explanation, this simple argument must go some way towards explaining why we find shop steward organization in manufacturing but less in private services.

An account of the exogenous factors underpinning workplace union bargaining power points up three of particular significance: the labour market power of the employees (how skilled, trained, replaceable they are); the product market location of the enterprise (product 'perishability', the likelihood of loss of market share to competitors, etc.); and the organizational structure and vulnerability of the company. This last factor covers production-related issues such as the supply chain, the degree of production integration, and the ability to transfer production and/or investment, and other organizational issues such as the economic contribution of individual workplaces to corporate viability or profitability. In both the manufacturing and service sectors it may be true that more streamlined, 'leaner' production systems have made them more vulnerable to localized disruption. At the same time, however, there is wide agreement that the increasingly fluid and flexible structures of modern capitalism, the ability rapidly to transfer and relocate production (and hence employment) are providing a real challenge to traditional sources of worker and union organizational strength (see chapter 13 and also Marginson et al. 1996: 188–9; Hyman 1996a: 61–2). Decentralized workplace-based trade unionism such as is found in the UK has been particularly weakened by such developments.

Analogous considerations of corporate structure and (in-)vulnerability constitute a starting point in understanding the long-standing lack of effective workplace organization in much of the private service sector. National or global restaurant chains or shops, for example, appear economically relatively invulnerable to local action, since any one workplace contributes only a small proportion of total revenue or profit. British trade unions, even in relatively well-organized sectors, have always experienced severe problems in co-ordinating activity across multiple workplaces. Employees in small firms, as distinct from small workplaces in large enterprises, face even greater problems, lacking the resources required to organize and recruit members, and in many cases facing more hostile managers and employers (Cully et al. 1999: 265).

It is therefore in the changing structure of the UK economy that one of the central drivers behind the growing 'representation gap' can be found. In the absence of the legal underpinnings of workplace representation workers have only their collective leverage on which to rely. There is a strong case that the factors that facilitated this in the past are increasingly rare today.

Managerial attitudes and priorities

By 1979 it appeared that employers generally, but most especially in the manufacturing and public sectors, had accepted the case made forcefully a decade or so earlier by the Donovan Report and subsequently accepted as public policy, of the need to recognize the reality and legitimacy of shop steward existence. This was to be achieved through the formalization of industrial relations at enterprise and workplace levels and through acceptance of the benefits that such systems could bring to stable workplace governance and the reduction of conflict. The growth in managerial support for steward organization – through improved facilities and time off for union and training activities – appeared to reflect this (Terry 1983).

There can be little doubt that the decline in shop steward organization since the mid-1980s, as reflected in surveys and case studies, owes much to the rapid and radical reversal of employer and management encouragement. A plausible case can be argued that this is simply a reversion to an earlier and more durable ideology of hostility to trade union organization on the part of UK employers, a hostility temporarily set aside during a period of union strength and political endorsement, but rapidly returned to as these two diminished. The dynamic underlying this reversion can in turn be traced to the dramatically changed priorities of employers, especially in the manufacturing sector, in the 1980s and 1990s. To grasp this it is necessary to understand also one characteristic of UK trade unions and collective bargaining. In no other European country is the decentralization of collective bargaining so advanced and in no other European country are the trade union priorities in bargaining so clearly set by the day-to-day priorities of the parties in the workplace, unconstrained by legal restrictions (see chapter 7). One corollary has been that, in the UK, collective bargaining has covered not only the terms and conditions of employment (pay, holidays, and so on), but has in many cases also extended into trade union influence over issues such as the organization and pace of work, technological innovation and a wide range of issues relating to control over the processes of production, as well as encroaching into areas of managerial responsibility such as recruitment, work allocation, and the exercise of disciplinary sanctions. It is worth remembering that one of the favourite metaphors for workplace industrial relations in the 1960s and 1970s was that of the 'frontier of control'. In many other European countries, by contrast, not only is collective bargaining over major distributive issues (pay and conditions) handled primarily at sectoral level, but many of the other areas identified, in particular those relating to the nature of work, are excluded by law from collective bargaining and are instead treated through the formally consensual consultative procedures of works councils, although, as has been noted, this pattern is beginning to change. Sometimes, as in Germany, such workplace processes operate within the context of peace and good faith obligations towards the employer. The essentially adversarial character of union–management relationships with regard to work-related issues is particularly marked in the UK.

During the 1980s and 1990s the industrial and political context encouraged and facilitated the reassertion of managerial control over work-related issues in ways that prompted a particular employer offensive against British systems of workplace representation not matched in other European countries. Prompted by the manufacturing crisis of the late 1970s and early 1980s, the dramatic possibilities offered by computer-based production systems, and strongly influenced by Japanese production and organizational methods, UK managers increasingly rejected collective bargaining and consultation in favour of the unilateral implementation of change. A strong case can be made for arguing that the much-discussed 'roll-back' of shop stewards that took place in much of manufacturing industry in the 1980s was motivated above all by a managerial desire to re-establish unilateral control over issues of work and work organization and the introduction of new systems and new technologies (see e.g. Edwardes 1983). Workplace trade unionism was portrayed as obstructive, leading to productive inefficiency and consequent corporate failure in increasingly competitive product markets. It is no coincidence that the so-called 'managerial offensive' with regard to these matters was most marked in shipbuilding, the iron and steel industry, engineering and, above all, the print industry, sectors where unions had exercised significant influence over such work-related issues. From the 1980s onwards British managers' acceptance of a degree of joint regulation as the 'least bad' approach to industrial governance and the management of change was significantly eroded, with the consequence that, by the late 1990s, as noted above, unions had been effectively excluded, even when recognized, from the handling of such issues.

The significance of the withdrawal of managerial support for shop stewards can be seen in, among other things, the evidence suggesting a decline in the resources provided by employers to support local union activity, including office facilities generally (Cully et al. 1999: 207), and, more importantly, the time available for union activity. Although some time off is guaranteed by law, the amounts are not generous; additional time is at management discretion. Senior representative responses indicated that 18 per cent spent more than 10 hours a week on union business but that 52 per cent spent two hours or less, which seems very little.

The dependence of shop steward organization on managerial support has often been noted. It is another characteristic difference between the UK and many other countries, where unions or works councils can draw on resource support guaranteed by law. In the UK, during times of union weakness, if indifferent or hostile managements withdraw support it can be very difficult to maintain viable union organization. The external unions themselves rarely have the resources to compensate for the lack of employer assistance.

Shop steward organization

Shop steward autonomy and local union policy Shop-steward-based trade unionism has been noted, often celebrated, for its autonomy. Historically workplace union organization, especially in manufacturing industry, frequently operated independently of national union structures and policies. Its hallmark, the unofficial strike (i.e. a strike not sanctioned by the national union leadership), was a totem of this, as was the oft-quoted reluctance of shop stewards to involve full-time union officials, local or national, in their affairs. The historic hostility between 'rank and file' and 'bureaucracy', though often exaggerated, was real enough in many large workplaces to sustain the notion of the self-sufficient, autonomous local union. In the context of the 1980s and 1990s the viability of this autonomous model was called into question as union strength and resources waned.

The strike legislation of the 1980s effectively restored control of the strike weapon to national union leaderships, and successive surveys revealed the increasing dependence of shop stewards on full-time officials (IRS 1992, 1993). This latter development took place as unions, losing members in catastrophic numbers, were forced to cut back on their provision of just such services, leaving many steward organizations exposed.

Such 'vertical' autonomy was not the only dimension of shop stewards' organizational independence. Historically stewards have, despite heroic efforts, experienced great difficulty in creating stable, long-lasting horizontal linkages with other steward bodies. The faltering efforts to create so-called 'combine committees', linking workplace bodies within multi-workplace enterprises, have been documented elsewhere (Terry 1985). The individual workplace and its problems and priorities continued to reassert themselves against efforts to extend the organizational boundaries of workplace unionism. Recent research suggests that this tendency is now being experienced within the operation of European Works Councils (Hancké 2000).

Such 'factory chauvinism', as Flanders called it 50 years ago, appears as an immanent characteristic of 'classical' shop steward organization. In a system based on the democracy of members in the workplace and the accountability of stewards to those who elected them, priorities are set by the immediate concerns of groups of union members, and those concerns were often parochial, limited, and directed above all towards short-term, 'economistic' objectives, and in particular pay (see Terry 1994 for a fuller discussion). In the context of the 1960s and 1970s these limited objectives provided both a basis for successful union organization and action and considerable purchase on managerial and government priorities. Steward organization was well suited to pay bargaining; it was straightforward, requiring only the formulation of simple demands and the mobilization, when necessary, of membership support. It did not require any particular organizational unity; indeed, decentralized, occupation-based unions were able to do much with bargaining over the maintenance of differentials between different groups.

However, as suggested above, issues related to the organization and control of work bulked larger in managerial priorities of the 1980s. Local union policies with regard to this were also set by the day-to-day priorities of their immediate members, and could be expressed simply in the trade union concept of the 'maintenance of the status quo', most clearly expressed in the famous 'mutuality' clause of the agreements at BL (later Rover) that prevented any change to working methods until union agreement had been reached. Workplace unions, again reflecting their members' priorities, tended to respond with hostility or caution to proposals for work restructuring – understandably, since in the UK, in contradistinction to some other European countries, they almost inevitably presaged job losses. In the context of the manufacturing crisis of the early 1980s and accompanying managerial offensive, not only was steward bargaining power significantly reduced by high unemployment, but in many cases the traditional union response of seeking to delay or block organizational change failed to convince or mobilize membership support at a time when it appeared obvious that without radical change many manufacturing companies would simply cease to exist. The repertoire was no longer adequate (Terry 1989).

Union representativeness   A voluntaristic system of the kind found in the UK leads not only to the development of steward organizations in sectors and workplaces where employees enjoy a significant degree of bargaining power and other resources, but also often to representative *differentiation* between employee groups within those sectors and workplaces. In particular, groups with lower degrees of bargaining power (unskilled, part-time, 'peripheral', and generally 'disposable' employees), even when union members, found themselves and their particular interests less well represented than their better-placed workmates. Such disadvantaged groups – in particular women and ethnic minority workers who were and are disproportionately consigned to unskilled, part-time and temporary employment – were in many ways excluded from the systems and priorities of workplace unionism. British trade unions at all levels, but perhaps particularly within manufacturing workplaces, tended to press the interests of their male, white, full-time and relatively permanent members. Over the last 20 years, prompted both by pragmatic needs and by a realization of the injustice perpetuated by such institutional exclusion, unions have been making strenuous efforts to reform their governance structures at all organizational levels (McBride 2001). As noted above, there is clear evidence of an impact on shop steward structures.

The exigencies of workplace unionism and decentralized bargaining in a voluntarist environment have contributed to the marginalization and under-representation of important sectors of the workforce. The legacy of these weaknesses persists, despite real efforts to change. Recent research has shown that new national policy initiatives with regard to issues such as equal opportunity may be slow to diffuse downwards and influence local union agenda (Kelly and Heery 1994).

Shop stewards and the 'new managerial agenda'   The 1980s and 1990s witnessed the rapid introduction (and often equally rapid disappearance) of a bewildering array of new forms of work organization (see chapter 13). They shared an interest in reconfiguring the micro-organization of work in a variety of ways, all designed to enhance labour usage, labour productivity, or quality. For much of the 1980s employers preferred to introduce these without union involvement, and indeed unions feared them as devices to bypass or weaken shop stewards, although from the late 1980s onwards some companies did start to consult unions over such initiatives (for a discussion of this process in Rover see Scarbrough and Terry 1997).

But in general there is considerable evidence to suggest that UK shop-steward-based trade unionism, in part for reasons argued above, confronts particular problems in responding to such initiatives. In this respect UK workplace representation again shows marked contrasts with its European, and in particular northern European, counterparts (Terry 1994). So, for example, it can be argued that British shop stewards lack the resources, the expertise, and the independence (from management and from their members) to develop and articulate a union position on such holistic, strategic issues. By contrast, a union such as the German engineering union IG Metall possesses the necessary resources to develop and promulgate a carefully argued trade union alternative to an initiative such as teamworking, *and* the necessary institutional base and legal rights (the works council and 'codetermination') through which to respond proactively to managerial initiatives on such issues. Confronted by the new managerial change agenda, unions' early response, of hostility and rejection, came to be replaced by a grudging acceptance (Martinez Lucio and Weston 1992). But even now that has not developed into a union approach comparable to that found in Sweden or Germany. Much of the responsibility for that lies with management, who generally remain hostile to union engagement with such issues (as confirmed by their WERS data above), seeing union intervention in production-related matters as both undesirable and unnecessary (see e.g. Grant 1994). But part of the explanation is also to be found in the nature of UK workplace unionism itself. The implications of these arguments for the future are discussed below in the context of 'Social Partnership' initiatives.

Leadership, participation and mobilization   The foregoing analysis highlights the role of external structures (management and markets) and history. Yet workplace unionism has its own dynamic and scope for action. Recent analyses (e.g. Greene et al. 2000; Darlington 1994) provide compelling evidence of the continuing importance of leadership and participation. These authors stress the need for shop stewards to assert their commitment to membership interests and their responsibility to oppose managerial proposals if necessary, not excluding the possibility of strike action. Being perceived as too close to management, too associated with its proposals for change and unprepared to oppose them, risks membership disenchantment and consequent union ineffectiveness. Greene et al., in analysing the constant and difficult balancing act that stewards have in managing the 'contradictory relationship with management that comprises different roles involving both resistance and accommodation' (2000: 77), are clearly sensitive to the great pressures that steward leaderships come under to become closer to management, especially when significant corporate restructuring is taking place.

On the reverse of the leadership coin is membership participation in shaping steward activity. Fosh (1993) argues for a 'participative style' of steward behaviour (the sharing of information and facilitation of membership participation in meetings), and she stresses that inability to participate may lead to membership indifference or hostility. Other analyses, particularly of the role of women, have similarly urged unions to rethink and restructure their traditional ways of working to facilitate the participation and representation of previously excluded groups.

It follows from the arguments of the preceding pages that the maintenance of an oppositional stance to management and the facilitation of a participative style are harder and more time-consuming for stewards now than in earlier decades. The pragmatic pressures for accommodation to managerial policies at a time of general union weakness are immense; for many stewards oppositional tactics would appear to invite the withdrawal of management support and, potentially, union derecognition. In many cases also, managerial proposals for change, especially those for restructuring to meet global competitive threat, appear irresistible, and a convincing pragmatic case can be made that acceptance is more likely to further members' interests than opposition. At the same time managerial pressures for continuous production reduce the scope and time for workplace meetings, and the legislative emphasis on individual secret ballots for key union decisions has reduced mass meetings and other participative opportunities. British unions enjoy none of the legal rights enjoyed by many Continental European unions for membership meetings, such as the right to hold mass meetings in company time provided in Italy.

Effective leadership and opportunity for democratic membership participation are essential for the health of workplace union organization. But in practice the nature and the exercise of leadership are tightly constrained by material conditions. And the opportunities for participative activities may be sharply reduced by managerial policy at a time when unions have lost much of the bargaining power previously deployed to insist on such rights. In a voluntarist context managerial action (or inaction) is as important as union behaviour in shaping the extent and expression of workplace activity. This too continues to pose problems for workplace unionism.

The public sector: the exception to the rule?

Though the decline in trade unionism and union organization in the UK has been general, it has been more marked in the private than the public sector. A recent estimate claimed that the public sector, accounting for 18 per cent of the UK workforce, also accounted for over half the union members in the country (Mathieson and Corby 1999: 208). There is also strong evidence that union *organization* has also survived better. The WERS 1998 data showed a recognized union present in 99 per cent of workplaces in public administration and 86 per cent in education, compared with 30 per cent in manufacturing and 7 per cent in hotels and restaurants (Cully et al. 1999: 92). Only 11 per cent of workplaces in public administration appeared to have no system of joint consultation, compared with 64 per cent for manufacturing (Cully et al. 1999: 99).

When the first edition of *Industrial Relations in Britain* (the first volume in the present series) appeared in 1983 the big story was the explosive growth in shop steward organization in the public sector after decades of underdevelopment, alongside the huge growth in public sector militancy of the 1970s and early 1980s. It was argued then that this indicated a convergence between public and private on a shop-steward-based model of unionism. Twenty years later what tends to stand out more is the distinctiveness of the public sector unions and their structures. Three factors can be identified to explain this: the relative protection of the public sector from global and national competitive market forces; the persistence, albeit in a heavily modified form, of the public sector managerial tradition of the 'good employer' (see chapter 11); and the continued relative centralization of collective bargaining pay arrangements.

Much has of course changed, and workplace public sector unionism has faced many of the challenges of its private sector counterparts. But it has done so in a more stable employment context, by and large, and in a managerial environment generally less exposed to global pressures and the need for rapid and radical organizational change. Public sector workplace unionism also had a very different starting point. The partial decentralization of public sector collective bargaining encouraged during the 1980s and 1990s increased the formal responsibilities of stewards, although by the time of the 1998 survey only 4 per cent of local representatives in education and 8 per cent in health were involved in pay determination, compared with 75 per cent in manufacturing. Certainly local representatives had to deal with a wide range of new and problematic issues, including the introduction of compulsory competitive tendering. Stewards were frequently forced into accepting agreements that, in order to keep work 'in house', resulted in significant deterioration in their members' pay and conditions, with the consequent risk of membership disenchantment.

Despite these pressures, public sector workplace unionism has been able to develop in a structural and managerial environment generally more supportive of unionism than that found in the private sector. Paradoxically it may be suggested that this relative health is also a consequence of the persistence of the importance of national union and bargaining structures. This means that, in general, workplace unionism is more integrated into, and dependent upon, external union support than in much of the private sector. Indeed Park has recently argued, on the basis of a detailed study of UNISON branches, that 'autonomous' (i.e. classical private sector) shop steward organization is not a viable model for public sector unionism since the problems and grievances of public sector workers are often created by, and in turn require for their resolution, a national political decision (Park 1999; for a contrary view see Fairbrother 1996).

One possible consequence of this different environment is that public sector unions have been able to demonstrate a degree of innovation and radicalism in their structures and behaviour, not least at workplace level, in response to new challenges. This has been particularly noticeable in the development of participative and representative structures for the participation of women, black workers and other groups often, as in the case of UNISON, the largest public sector union, through changes designed and agreed at national level (see McBride 2001; Terry 1996). Equally striking have been the beginnings of local innovative approaches to work and work organization, by unions themselves, often built around equal opportunities initiatives and rethinking the relationship between work and the domestic sphere (Terry 2000). This is not unique to the UK; indeed there is evidence to suggest that public sector unions in Sweden, Germany and elsewhere have been yet more adventurous in developing such local initiatives. The trajectory of workplace unionism in the public sector has thus been different from that in the private. At the start of the twenty-first century the latter appears to be facing a genuine crisis; the former a series of problems.

The non-union sector

A small but persistent minority of non-union employers have for a number of years created their own systems of indirect employee representation (for a recent summary and overview see Terry 1999). A recent example was Sainsbury's introduction in 1996 of employee councils in all its supermarkets and other workplaces as well as at higher levels in the company. Generally non-union systems tend to be found in companies whose size and market environment are of the kind still associated with a trade union presence. They may be associated with Japanese companies interested in collective representation but not wanting to recognize trade unions (Broad 1994), with companies whose owners, for reasons of personal conviction, favour employee representation but not unions, and with companies that have recently derecognized trade unions (Lloyd 2001). The contemporary significance of these systems does not lie in their numbers; until recently they would have been dismissed as an oddity not worthy of serious discussion, and might still but for two reasons: the perceived decline of the union-based system and the potential emergence of a system of representation based not on unions but on universal employee rights.

Until recently any suggestion that a non-union system could be as effective in representing members' interests as a union one would have been easily dismissed. The dominant analysis was that these bodies were primarily motivated by a managerial interest in union avoidance and that they offered merely a form of 'pseudo participation' (Ramsay 1980). The few case studies we have of such bodies in the 1980s (summarized in Terry 1999) support this view: non-union representatives saw themselves as weaker and worse resourced and trained than their union counterparts. Managers appear to have often treated them with relative disdain, frequently reluctant to share important information with them and, devastating to the councils' credibility, bypassing them completely when the going got tough, and resorting to unilateral managerial imposition. The independence, and hence the democratic legitimacy, of many such bodies are also open to serious question. In a number of cases non-union representatives are appointed by management rather than being elected or even nominated by members.

Case study work appears to confirm this picture. One of the few pieces of research that compares the effectiveness of union and non-union representatives confirms the relative weakness of the latter, and argues that they could match union representation only if supported and protected by a much more comprehensive set of legal rights (Kidger 1992). Lloyd's recent study of a non-union council introduced by a company in the wake of union de-recognition shows that manual workers and their union representatives dismissed the new structure as weak and irrelevant compared to union representation, although the white-collar employees and their representatives were more ambivalent in their views, suggesting that the new system removed some of the old barriers (Lloyd 2001). Formally, this council, as many others, enjoyed similar rights to union structures (negotiation rights, even reference to ACAS in the event of stubborn disagreement), but in practice all involved (managers, representatives, employees) agreed that it was different as a consequence of union exclusion. Managers saw it as less conflictual, a view shared by staff employees, while representatives and manual employees argued that they had lost effective power and influence.

Despite the widespread persistence of the view that union and non-union systems are different, and, in particular, from the point of view of employees and their representatives that the former are more powerful, the preceding discussion about the decline in the effectiveness of union-based systems does raise the question of how justified this view is. Although there are evident structural and organizational differences between union and non-union representation, the possibility, once unthinkable, that union representation may be little better than non-union forms at speaking for and advancing the interests of its constituents is a reminder of how much things may have changed.

The Growth of a Statutory System of Employee Representation?

As the coverage and activity of the voluntary system have declined, a development novel to the United Kingdom has emerged, namely the burgeoning of *legal* rules designed to provide employees with statutory rights to consultation and information. These have emerged as a direct consequence of the UK's membership of the European Union. In many other countries much of this legislation has passed relatively unnoticed, since it adds little to existing domestic legislation providing similar (or stronger) rights. The main exception to this has been the European Works Council, a genuinely novel development in all countries, which is discussed later. But first this chapter will look at the emerging legislative framework for national systems of domestic (workplace and enterprise) representation.

Legislative change

The fundamental organizational discrepancy between the traditional system and the new one is that the former was founded on the 'single channel' of employee representation by trade unions. If employees chose not to join trade unions, or found themselves in workplaces where management refused to recognize unions, they had no access to a representative system. This system, historically strongly defended by trade unions and the Labour Party and accepted, though for reasons unrelated to a desire to promulgate unionism, by the Conservative government of the 1980s and by employers, came into sharp conflict with European Union provisions. These start from the presumption that employees should enjoy basic rights to information and consultation irrespective of union membership or recognition.

In 1994 the European Court of Justice held that the existing British legislation on consultation in the event of redundancy failed to comply with European directives on the subject, since it required consultation only when unions were recognized (Hall 1996). The consequence was the Collective Redundancies and Transfer of Undertakings (Protection of Employment) (Amendment) Regulations 1995 which made provision for 'the designation of employee representatives for the purposes of information and consultation . . . in situations where there are no recognized unions' (Hall 1996: 17). The Conservative government that introduced these regulations did so in a manner seen by some commentators to be negating their potential for underpinning stable and effective representation structures (O'Hara 1996: 26–7) as well as taking the opportunity to reduce consultation by increasing the threshold number of redundancies that would require mandatory consultation. The Labour government has since strengthened the regulations, in particular by insisting that where a union is recognized it must be consulted over redundancies (the earlier regulations had allowed employers to bypass such recognized unions, although this rarely happened (Hall and Edwards 1999)), and by strengthening the election requirements for non-union representatives.

Since 1995 further legislative developments have added to the complexity of the picture. The 1996 Health and Safety (Consultation with Employees) Regulations extended consultation rights in this area to all employees and provided a rather more stable structural basis than the other regulations, provoking the Association of British Chambers of Commerce into claiming that they would 'introduce works councils through the back door' (cited in James 1996: 13). More recently still the Working Time Regulations 1998, introducing into the UK the provisions of the EU Working Time Directive, and regulations implementing the EU Parental Leave Directive in 1999 both contained the novel (for the UK) concept of so-called 'workforce agreements' on these matters to cover all or part of a workforce not represented by a union in collective bargaining. The precise mechanisms for such workforce agreements are not clearly specified, and there is no evidence yet of their widespread adoption, but in conforming to the EU norm that rights to engagement with such issues extend to all employees, not just those represented by a union, they prefigure potential systems of non-union representation, operating on a statutory basis.

Important though these are, they deal only with specific issues and do not necessarily imply stable mechanisms of employee representation other than at moments of handling the particular issues. Employee representation for health and safety issues, requiring continuous activity, may be an important exception to this. As noted above, events since 1996 in this field provide important evidence of the success of legislative intervention in stimulating representative development in workplaces where it would almost certainly not have happened on a voluntary basis. This in turn suggests a much greater potential significance to the enactment, finally agreed in June 2001, of an EU directive on national information and consultation that would require 'all undertakings with at least 50 employees . . . to consult employee representatives about a range of business, employment and work organization issues' (Hall 2000). In effect that would mean introducing into the UK at least a weak form of the works councils so frequently found in other EU member states, potentially affecting the great majority of UK employees. Long-standing UK government opposition to the directive was eventually withdrawn early in 2001, in part facilitated by European agreement to allow countries such as the UK, with no 'general, permanent and statutory' system of information and consultation, nor of workplace representation, to phase in its introduction. The proposed arrangements were that undertakings with at least 150 employees (or establishments with at least 100) would be covered as from the directive's three-year implementation deadline (the normal period in such cases), but that smaller organizations would be covered after a longer period (two more years for undertakings with 100 or more employees or establishments with 50 or more). Full implementation (i.e. to undertakings with 50 or more employees or establishments with 20 or more) would wait another two years – i.e. for these organizations implementation would take place four years after the usual implementation date.

One point that may be of the greatest significance for the effectiveness of these employee-based statutory mechanisms will be the practical, and eventually the judicial, interpretation of the concept of consultation. In traditional UK usage it has, at least in trade union circles, connotations of ineffectiveness and weakness, since it allows unilateral managerial action notwithstanding the views expressed by employees or their representatives. From the Donovan Report onwards it has been seen by trade unions as a poor second best to 'full-blown' negotiation, the outcome of which was held to be joint regulation, the normative cornerstone of the voluntaristic system. But, as Wedderburn and others have noted, in the European context 'consultation' has a much 'stronger' meaning, as is clear in the wording of the Collective Redundancies Directive that requires 'consultation with a view to reaching agreement', the meaning of which requires (judicial) clarification (Wedderburn 1997: 19), but which is clearly more robust than conventional UK usage might suggest.

The challenge and opportunities that these developments offer to the traditional union-based system of shop steward representation can partly be seen in the implementation of the European Works Councils Directive, passed in 1994 but only implemented in the UK in 2000, following the Labour government's reversal of its Conservative predecessor's 'opt-out'. Briefly

> the objective of the Directive is to promote the establishment of EWCs (European Works Councils) or other information and consultation procedures in 'Community-scale' undertakings or groups with at least 1000 employees within the territorial scope of the Directive, including at least 150 in each of two or more Member States. 'Consultation' is defined as 'the exchange of views and establishment of dialogue' between employee representatives and management. (Carley and Hall 2000)

According to the Department of Trade and Industry (DTI 1999) some 230 UK-based multinationals are subject to the EWCs Directive. Of these, 95 are reported to have established EWCs (ETUI 2001). As with all the other EU-based rights summarized above, European Works Councils rights are universalistic in application, requiring the representative participation of union members and non-members alike. This poses little problem in most EU member states where existing workplace representation systems already embody this principle. In the UK, by contrast, it was necessary to create a new mechanism, the so-called Special Negotiating Bodies (SNBs), required under the directive to take responsibility in negotiations with management for the creation of an EWC. That mechanism is to be a ballot of all UK employees affected, unless there already exists a consultative committee whose members are elected by all relevant employees (Carley and Hall 2000: 115). As this chapter has suggested, in confirmation of Carley and Hall, such committees are likely to be very rare, so the employee-wide ballot is likely to become the norm, even where recognized trade unions and shop stewards are to be found, although there is a requirement that existing representatives be consulted over the balloting arrangements.

Despite the enormous potential impact of these developments we so far know very little about their impact on UK workplace industrial relations and the future role of shop stewards and other representatives. The most far-reaching of the initiatives so far introduced – the European Works Councils – are restricted to information and consultation on matters of relevance to the transnational organization; strictly national matters are not on the agenda. A recent evaluation of EWCs by the European Commission indicated that, despite a generally positive evaluation, problems persisted, among them the 'very low level of transnational information and consultation provided by some agreements' and the need for 'efficient information and consultation systems to exist at national level and for an effective flow of information between Community and national levels of worker representation' (EWCB 2000: 5). This latter point is particularly likely to pose problems within the UK, given the uneven and fragmented nature of many existing systems of national representation, as described above. In addition, recent cases have suggested that, the careful wording notwithstanding, the new rights are weaker than seemed. In the wake of the announcement during 2000 of large-scale redundancy fears at both Rover and Vauxhall, major motor vehicle companies, concern was expressed about 'the adequacy of the UK's legal framework for employee information and consultation' (Hall 2001), leading to calls for government strengthening of the rights.

More generally, there is considerable debate within the UK concerning the implications for trade unions of these new universalistic legal rights (see for example the debate between Hyman (1996b) and Kelly (1996a)). On the one hand there is concern that the new structures may be 'captured' by management and used, in effect, as tools of managerial influence and control, especially where trade unions are weak, a not uncommon situation in many private sector organizations, as argued above. On the other it is argued that a framework of legal rights is a necessary buttress against further decline and, more optimistically, that unions may be able to use 'works council' structures as a vehicle for advancing their own organizations. To a certain extent the argument is coloured by the vagaries of the European experience; those fearful of the negative consequences for unions point to the French comités d'entreprise, introduced in the 1980s, and allegedly largely controlled by management, while the optimists point to the German unions' success (at least among manual workers) in dominating elections to works councils (for a fuller version of other European experience see Terry 1994). Martinez Lucio and Weston (2000) have argued that both these models are inadequate, at least with regard to EWCs, since they fail to recognize the changing regulatory terrain, political and industrial, within which EWCs are being developed. That the potential exists for British employers, if they choose, to seek to use the new framework as a means of 'union avoidance' is undeniable, but whether unions could be successfully excluded at a time when their legal position is being strengthened and in a country where, as Lloyd's work on a non-union firm shows, there is still a profound belief in many workplaces that unions are more influential and powerful than union-free representation, remains to be seen.

One further legal development, unrelated to European initiatives, apparently less dramatic in its formulation but potentially more pervasive in its effects, is the 'right to representation' introduced by the 1999 Employment Relations Act, which 'creates a statutory right for a worker to be accompanied by a fellow worker *or trade union official of his or her choice* during in-company grievance and disciplinary hearings' (Hall 2000, emphasis added). The significance of this is that it gives non-union employees the right to introduce a trade union presence into local workplace affairs whether the employer approves or not. Given the immense importance attached by many union members' to shop stewards' support in grievance and discipline handling, this new right might provide significant support for the development of workplace representation.

It is clear that the terrain of workplace unionism and the job of the shop steward will for the foreseeable future be increasingly informed by legal rights and statutorily based structures. For shop stewards the issues are twofold: first are the problems of reconciling traditional representative structures based on the 'single channel' of unionism with the new universalistic rights, as illustrated in the case of the SNBs above. Shop floor unions and stewards may have to take on the role of electoral machines for the new structures and, once elected, assume the responsibility of speaking for all constituents; they may also have to accept the idea, once anathema, of working together with non-union representatives. Second, unions and stewards will have a greater range of legal rights at their disposal, to set alongside, or perhaps to compensate for the loss of, traditional tactics. This may require the development of new expertise, and of new language and tactics in dealing with employers. Significant change may be near.

'Social partnership': the workplace industrial relations of the future?

In addition to the arrival in the UK of legislation deriving not only from the political systems but from the industrial relations and labour law traditions of mainland Europe, a new phrase has in recent years jumped into the industrial relations lexicon. As noted in chapter 7, 'social partnership' derives from northern European experience (Germany, Austria, the Netherlands and, with some difference of emphasis, Scandinavia). It refers to the interlocking systems of collective relationship between unions, their confederations, and employers' associations at national, sectoral and workplace level that make up those countries' industrial relations systems. It includes structures for the negotiation of distributive issues (wages and other terms and conditions of employment), often largely at the sectoral/industrial level of the economy, and within that sphere recognizes and allows for conflict and its expression. But it also makes explicit provision for the development of collaborative, consensual processes between the social partners, both at macro-level (economic and social policy, training, environmental protection) and in the workplace. At the latter level its most sophisticated expression is probably the 'consensual' German works council, which is explicitly forbidden to bargain and which has the responsibility of handling structural change (technological innovation, organizational change) within a framework that recognizes the commitment of all parties to the commercial success of the enterprise. Almost always buttressed by legal rights and restrictions far more extensive than anything presently envisaged in the United Kingdom, the works council model (and the social partnership approach more generally) is claimed by its supporters to have enabled successful adjustment to structural change without conflict and without damaging the employment and working lives of employees (see Jacobi et al. 1992). Central to an understanding of the consensual workplace relationships are the strong legal protections for the works council and its members, the legally backed guarantees of security and stability for workers at times of economic restructuring, and the handling of wage-bargaining at sectoral level.

The application of the concept to the United Kingdom is problematic, since virtually none of the infrastructural elements obtains there. But the term has been advanced as embodying the Labour government's approach to industrial relations, and has been strongly endorsed by them, by many national trade unions, and by some employers (Brown 2000: 305; for the most thorough discussion of the concept see Tailby and Winchester 2000). As Brown indicates, in the UK it can be used in two distinct senses (there is so far none of the articulation between levels that characterizes other approaches): at national level, as in the work of the Low Pay Commission, in reaching agreement between employers and unions, and at local level. The TUC's six underlying principles for local partnership are listed in chapter 7. The debt to the Continental model is clear, in the shared commitment to commercial success, the balance between change (flexibility) and security, and the emphasis on dialogue and expertise. Less clear is how and where the conflictual, distributive issues of pay and conditions are handled. The emphasis is on consultation rather than negotiation and on persuading employers of the value of employee representation. As Brown notes, such an agenda, which most unions and stewards would have rejected two decades ago as hopelessly collaborationist, 'selling out' members' interests, is 'in part, a symptom of a weakened union movement' (2000: 307).

An explicit shared commitment to business success is at the heart of partnership agreements. The influential Blue Circle Cement agreement starts:

> The purpose of this agreement is to establish the framework within which constructive employment relations can be maintained and developed. It is designed to support the objectives of the business in its journey towards excellence.

On one reading this represents nothing new. As Hyman (1996a: 71) remarks, 'unions have rarely welcomed the bankruptcy of their members' employers'. For Kelly (1999: 9), by contrast, it represents a new and dangerous expression of the familiar tactic of employer co-optation:

> Once union officials and senior stewards have come to define the employers' interests as their own, the union organisation can be used as a mechanism for disseminating partnership ideology through the workforce, at the same time demobilising any resistance that may occur.

In practical terms the managerial interpretation of such a commitment tends to be first that unions will take formal account of commercial considerations in formulating pay claims and will actively co-operate in the introduction of organizational change seen as necessary to commercial success. This leads directly to a second central feature, the unions' active participation in the achievement of measures to promote flexibility. Here the traditional union response, summarized above, of caution and resistance, should be replaced by the co-management of change. For some union activists this goes too far in giving management carte blanche in day-to-day workforce management.

In exchange employers offer security, in two senses. For employees the advantage is employment security often, as with Welsh Water, explicitly linked to organizational flexibility. 'Essential to the agreement was union acceptance of the linkage between continued cooperation in the organisational and technological changes designed to promote efficiency and the No Compulsory Redundancy Policy' (IPA 1995: 2). This implies that shop floor unions do not merely not object to change, but are actively involved in it. The implications for the earlier argument concerning the 'closeness' of unions to management objectives and the potential damage to membership confidence are clear. The second strand of security is that of unions as organizations. Partnerships may be seen as involving an implicit exchange between greater managerial recognition of union rights in exchange for union concession on substantive issues. This can have substantial benefits. At the Tesco supermarket chain, following the overhaul of management–union relationships and the construction of a new top-to-bottom consultation structure built around union involvement, USDAW, the recognized union, claimed to have recruited 9,000 new members. This, for some commentators, is the key consideration. After decades of being marginalized, watching from the sidelines, the problem for unions was 'not . . . whether to fight or collaborate, but [how to] get a foot in the door and begin to advance their *institutional centrality* . . . social partnership presents itself as such a strategy' (Ackers and Payne 1998: 546, emphasis added).

Yet social partnership presents acute challenges for the traditional shop floor union model. First, both the language and the practice of partnership seem to shift local union representatives to a position closer to that of management than to the independent representation of members' interests. The balance between the two, noted by Greene et al. as central to the health of workplace unionism, may be fundamentally compromised. Second, the emphasis on consultation, corporate success and the other elements identified above indicates a union input based more on expertise and professionalism than on claims backed up by collective interest. This is problematic for fragmented, autonomous shop steward organization – from where is the expertise to come? No UK partnership agreements provide any rights to independent expertise such as are commonly found in northern Europe and, as noted, the provision of shop steward training appears to be declining. In these circumstances the potential for an enhancement of union influence in consultation over more strategic matters may be illusory. At the very least it may require a significant reconfiguring of the roles of shop stewards and union full-time officials.

Opinion in the United Kingdom on the implications for unions is divided. Ackers and Payne (1998: 544–5) argue that partnership 'marks out a favourable industrial relations terrain, in which unions can regain the initiative and work to rebuild their institutional presence in British society'. Kelly, by contrast, argues that it will further demobilize and debilitate shop steward organization, through embracing a managerial agenda that will distance stewards from their members and the effective representation of their interests (Kelly 1996b). Indeed, Kelly has gone further in an initial attempt to compare wages and employment security between partnership and non-partnership companies, and claims that on both counts the former fare worse (Kelly 1999, 2000), a claim rebutted by a senior shop steward at Blue Circle Cement (Warren 1999), who argues that Kelly fails to identify the unions' longer-term influence and membership benefits.

On the evidence of this chapter it is clear why partnership appears attractive to unions and also why it could increase rather than reduce their problems. Perhaps the critical new element here is the emergence of the statutory framework outlined above. The emerging 'works council' model may provide workplace unions in the UK the necessary minimum guarantees to avoid excessive dependence on management and to continue to speak and act with an independent, membership-based voice. Equally, British employers will not, for the foreseeable future, be able to operate in a context entirely devoid of collective rights to information and consultation for their employees; in that sense 'pure' managerial unilateralism may be off the agenda. Hyman (1996b: 81–2) has argued that, on the balance of evidence, just such a legal framework offers the only hope for private sector unionism since free collective bargaining offers none. But that, combined perhaps with the partnership approach, implies a profound reconfiguration of systems of workplace representation.

Conclusion

At the heart of what is sometimes called the European Social Model lie a number of fundamental values concerning the rights of employees to protection in their work against arbitrary treatment by employers, to advance by legitimate means their collective and individual interests, and to help shape the behaviour of the organizations to which they devote their working lives. Although laws and other regulatory mechanisms can play a part, which in some countries is a much larger one than in the United Kingdom, in the UK these rights have been embodied principally in the presence and activity of trade unions, and in particular of workplace-based trade union, shop steward activity. This chapter has charted the decline in quantitative and qualitative terms of this activity and with it of those rights. Its conclusions concerning future trends have not been overly optimistic. It has argued that, although the causes of decline are complex, and some are of the unions' own making, the principal reasons lie outside the unions' ability to influence. Although enlightened managerial self-interest may continue to support a form of workplace unionism, this is likely to be limited and contingent. It is possible that trends and developments not identified here will contribute to a resurgence of self-confidence and workplace militancy and with them the bargaining power to re-establish a form of voluntarist local unionism. But at present the portents are not good. The inescapable conclusion is thus that the effective future of workplace employee representation, and with it the employee rights summarized above, lies principally with governments, national and supra-national, and their legislative interventions.

References

Ackers, P., and Payne, J. 1998: British trade unions and social partnership: rhetoric, reality and strategy, *International Journal of Human Resource Management*, 9 (3), 529–50.

Broad, G. 1994: Japan in Britain: the dynamics of joint consultation, *Industrial Relations Journal*, 25 (2), 26–38.

Brown, W. 2000: Annual review article: putting partnership into practice, *British Journal of Industrial Relations*, 38 (2), 299–316.

Brown, W., Deakin, S., Hudson, M., Pratton, C. and Ryan, P. 1998: *The Individualisation of Employment Contracts in Britain*. DTI Employment Relations Research Series 4. Available at <www.dti.gov.uk/er/emar>.

Brown, W., Deakin, S., Nash, D. and Oxenbridge, S. 2000: The employment contract: from collective procedures to individual rights, *British Journal of Industrial Relations*, 38 (4), 611–29.

Carley, M., and Hall, M. 2000: The implementation of the European Works Council Directive, *Industrial Law Journal*, 29 (2), 103–24.

Cully, M., Woodland, S., O'Reilly, A. and Dix, G. 1999: *Britain at Work*. London: Routledge.

Cully, M., Woodland, S., O'Reilly, A., Dix, G., Millward, N., Bryson, A. and Forth, J. 1998: *The 1998 Workplace Employee Relations Survey: First Findings*. London: Department of Trade and Industry.

Darlington, R. 1994: *The Dynamics of Work Place Unionism: Shop Stewards' Organisation in Three Merseyside Plants*. London: Mansell.

DTI (Department of Trade and Industry) 1999: Implementation in the UK of the European Works Council Directive: a consultative document. URN99/926. London: DTI.

Edwardes, M. 1983: *Back from the Brink: an Apocalyptic Experience*. London: Collins.

ETUI (European Trade Union Institute) 2001: Multinationals database: inventory of companies affected by the EWC Directive. <www.etuc.org/ETUI/ewcfeb01.pdf>.

EWCB 2000: Commission assesses implementation of EWCs Directive, *European Works Council Bulletin*, 28 (July/August), 4–6.

Fairbrother, P. 1996: Workplace trade unionism in the state sector. In P. Ackers et al. (eds), *The New Workplace and Trade Unionism*. London: Routledge.

Fosh, P. 1993: Membership participation and work place trade unionism: the possibility of renewal, *British Journal of Industrial Relations*, 31 (4), 577–92.

Grant, D. 1994: New style agreements at Japanese transplants in the UK, *Employee Relations*, 16, 65–83.

Greene, A.-M., Black, J. and Ackers, P. 2000: The union makes us strong? A study of the dynamics of workplace union leadership at two UK manufacturing plants, *British Journal of Industrial Relations*, 38 (1), 75–93.

Hall, M. 1996: Beyond recognition? Employee representation and EU law, *Industrial Law Journal*, 25 (1), 15–27.

Hall, M. 2000: New right for workers to be accompanied at disciplinary and grievance hearings, *EIROnline*, October. <www.eiro.eurofound.eu.int>.

Hall, M. 2001: Government launches review of redundancy consultation laws, *EIROnline*, January. <www.eiro.eurofound.eu.int>.

Hall, M., and Edwards, P. 1999: Reforming the statutory redundancy consultation procedure, *Industrial Law Journal*, 28 (4), 299–318.

Hancké, B. 2000: European Works Councils and industrial restructuring in the European motor industry, *European Journal of Industrial Relations*, 6 (1), 35–59.

Heery, E., and Kelly, J. 1988: Do female representatives make a difference? Women full-time officials and trade union work, *Work, Employment and Society*, 2 (4), 487–505.

Hyman, R. 1996a: Changing union identities in Europe. In P. Leisink et al. (eds), *The Challenges to Trade Unions in Europe*. Cheltenham: Edward Elgar.

Hyman, R. 1996b: Is there a case for statutory works councils in Britain? In A. McColgan (ed.), *The Future of Labour Law*. London: Cassell.

IPA (Involvement and Participation Association) 1995: *Welsh Water, Towards Industrial Partnership*, 3. London: IPA.

IRS (Industrial Relations Services) 1992: The changing role of trade union officers 1: the devolution of pay bargaining, *Industrial Relations Review and Report: IRS Employment Trends*, 526 (December), 5–12.

IRS 1993: The changing role of trade union officers 2: collective bargaining and working practices, *Industrial Relations Review and Report: IRS Employment Trends*, 527 (January), 3–11.

Jacobi, O., Keller, B. and Müller-Jentsch, W. 1992: Germany: codetermining the future? In A. Ferner and R. Hyman (eds), *Industrial Relations in the New Europe*. Oxford: Blackwell.

James, P. 1996: Mixed responses to new safety consultation rights, *IRS Employment Review 607 / Health and Safety Bulletin 245* (May), 13–14.

Jones, M. 2000: Working with Labour: the impact of UNISON's political settlement. In M. Terry (ed.), *Redefining Public Service Unionism: UNISON and the Future of Trade Unions*. London: Routledge.

Kelly, J. 1996a: Works councils: union advance or marginalisation? In A. McColgan (ed.), *The Future of Labour Law*. London: Cassell.

Kelly, J. 1996b: Union militancy and social partnership. In P. Ackers et al. (eds), *The New Workplace and Trade Unionism*. London: Routledge.

Kelly, J. 1999: Social partnership in Britain: good for profits, bad for jobs and unions, *Communist Review*, Autumn, 3–10.

Kelly, J. 2000: The limits and contradictions of social partnership, *Communist Review*, Autumn, 3–7.

Kelly, J., and Heery, E. 1994: *Working for the Union: British Trade Union Officers*. Cambridge: Cambridge University Press.

Kidger, P. 1992: Employee participation in occupational health and safety: should union-appointed or elected representatives be the model for the UK? *Human Resource Management Journal*, 2 (4), 21–35.

Lloyd, C. 2001: What do employee councils do? The impact of non-union forms of representation on trade union organisation, *Industrial Relations Journal*, 32.

McBride, A. 2001: *Gender Democracy in Trade Unions*. Aldershot: Ashgate.

Marginson, P., Armstrong, P., Edwards, P. and Purcell, J. 1996: Facing the multinational challenge. In P. Leisink et al. (eds), *The Challenges to Trade Unions in Europe*. Cheltenham: Edward Elgar.

Martinez Lucio, M., and Weston, S. 1992: The politics and complexity of trade union responses to new management practices, *Human Resource Management Journal*, 2 (4), 77–91.

Martinez Lucio, M., and Weston, S. 2000: European Works Councils and 'flexible regulation': the politics of intervention, *European Journal of Industrial Relations*, 6 (3), 203–16.

Mathieson, H., and Corby, S. 1999: Trade unions: the challenge of individualism? In S. Corby and G. White (eds), *Employee Relations in the Public Services*. London: Routledge.

Millward, N. 2001: Paper to research seminar. IRRU, University of Warwick.

Millward, N., Bryson, A. and Forth, J. 2000: *All Change at Work?* London: Routledge.

Millward, N., Stevens, M., Smart, D. and Hawes, W. 1992: *Workplace Industrial Relations in Transition*. Aldershot: Dartmouth.

Munro, A. 1999: *Women, Work and Trade Unions*. London: Mansell.

O'Hara, J. 1996: *Worker Participation and Collective Bargaining in Britain: The Influence of European Law*. London: Institute of Employment Rights.

Park, T.-J. 1999: In and beyond the workplace: the search for articulated trade unionism in UNISON. Ph.D. thesis, University of Warwick.

Ramsay, H. 1980: Phantom participation: patterns of power and conflict, *Industrial Relations Journal*, 11 (3), 46–59.

Scarbrough, H., and Terry, M. 1997: United Kingdom: the reorganisation of production. In T. Kochan et al. (eds), *After Lean Production*. Ithaca: Cornell University Press.

Tailby, S., and Winchester, D. 2000: Management and trade unions: towards social partnership? In S. Bach and K. Sisson (eds), *Personnel Management*. Oxford: Blackwell.

Terry, M. 1983: Shop steward development and management strategies. In G. S. Bain (ed.), *Industrial Relations in Britain*. Oxford: Blackwell.

Terry, M. 1985: Combine committees: developments of the 1970s, *British Journal of Industrial Relations*, 23 (3), 359–78.

Terry, M. 1989: Recontextualising shopfloor industrial relations: some case study evidence. In S. Tailby and C. Whitston (eds), *Manufacturing Change*. Oxford: Blackwell.

Terry, M. 1994: Workplace unionism: redefining structures and objectives. In R. Hyman and A. Ferner (eds), *New Frontiers in European Industrial Relations*. Oxford: Blackwell.

Terry, M. 1996: Negotiating the government of UNISON: union democracy in theory and practice, *British Journal of Industrial Relations*, 34 (1), 87–110.

Terry, M. 1999: Systems of collective employee representation in non-union firms in the UK, *Industrial Relations Journal*, 30 (1), 16–30.

Terry, M. (ed.) 2000: *Redefining Public Service Unionism: UNISON and the Future of Trade Unions*. London: Routledge.

Towers, B. 1997: *The Representation Gap: Change and Reform in the British and American Workplace*. Oxford: Oxford University Press.

Waddington, J., and Whitston, C. 1997: Why do people join unions in a period of membership decline? *British Journal of Industrial Relations*, 35 (4), 515–46.

Warren, D. 1999: Blue Circle shows that dialogue really works, *IPA Magazine*, November <http://www.partnership-at-work.com>.

Wedderburn, Lord 1997: Consultation or collective bargaining in Europe: success or ideology? *Industrial Law Journal*, 26 (1), 1–34.

11
INDUSTRIAL RELATIONS IN THE PUBLIC SECTOR

STEPHEN BACH AND DAVID WINCHESTER

The election of the 1997 Labour government marked an important juncture for public sector industrial relations. Since Labour's previous period in office, large parts of the public sector had been privatized and the remaining public services had been restructured into semi-autonomous 'enterprises' with less predictable income streams. These reforms were accompanied by significant changes in employment relations. Conservative governments had encouraged the development of a more assertive tier of senior managers with greater discretion to reform work organization and pay systems. Public sector management had to operate within a more fragmented overall structure; for example, widespread organizational reform replaced a unified civil service with approximately 100 semi-autonomous agencies, and more than 400 health care trusts were established within the internal market of the National Health Service (NHS). Trade unions, although faring much better than most of their private sector counterparts, were excluded from national policymaking and often faced severe difficulties in safeguarding their members' terms and conditions of employment.

Even though the landscape of the public sector in 1997 was very different from 18 years earlier, four Conservative governments had been unable to convert their ideological hostility towards the public sector into a coherent programme of reform. They thus left a contradictory legacy. Despite the introduction of market-type incentives to foster change, traditional hierarchies and long-standing working practices remained intact in some parts of the sector. The centralized process of pay determination embodied in new pay review bodies for nurses and school teachers sat uneasily alongside frequent exhortation on the merits of decentralized pay-bargaining. And the emphasis on enhanced managerial autonomy in shaping human resource practices was undermined by frequent political intervention and the resistance of highly organized professional groups.

This chapter assesses the impact of the Conservatives' reform programme and the ways in which the modernization project of the 1997–2001 Labour government consolidated many of its predecessor's policies and redirected others. It outlines the main features of organizational and management reform, and the changing pattern of public service employment, and assesses whether previously distinctive features of employment regulation have been eroded. In particular, it explores recent attempts to develop a more decentralized and flexible system linking pay more closely to labour market conditions, individual employee performance, working practices and organizational efficiency, and the eradication of unequal pay between men and women.

Public services are by their nature in the public eye, and stories of staff demotivation in particular parts of the public sector are common. This chapter demonstrates the impossibility of saying whether reforms have 'improved' or 'worsened' employment conditions as a whole. First, there is enormous variation within the public sector. Second, some aspects of reforms have brought benefits to employees while others have entailed costs. Some surveys report relatively low commitment and satisfaction, which they explain in terms of the extent and depth of change (Emmott 2001). Such change has certainly been substantial, but it has not destroyed all aspects of public sector work. Compared to the private sector, many public sector workers enjoy relatively high job security, shorter working hours, and a smaller likelihood of discipline or dismissal, while low pay is also relatively rare. Developments in relation to such issues as equal opportunities are also relatively strongly marked in the public sector.

The State as Employer

In contrast to most European countries, there has never been a sharp legal distinction between industrial relations in the public and private sectors in Britain. Public service employees have enjoyed few special privileges and faced only selective legal restrictions on the right to join a trade union and strike (e.g. as in the armed forces and police). As discussed in chapter 2, for most of the twentieth century the 'voluntary' system covered the private sector and most of the public services. Similarly the rapid extension of employment regulation over the last 30 years has applied more or less equally to the public and private sectors. Thus, although some parts of public service employment had been viewed, in practice, as a lifetime career with predictable patterns of promotion and high levels of job security, such expectations were not established by statute, nor explicitly recognized in common law.

The absence of a strong and legally supported tradition of public administration has provided greater scope for governments in Britain, especially those with a clear electoral mandate, to implement far-reaching reforms of the public sector. Until the mid-1970s, however, the scope for radical reforms remained largely untested. This arose from a widespread acceptance of the distinctive features of public sector industrial relations that had been shaped by relatively favourable political and economic conditions in the 1960s and 1970s (Winchester 1983).

First, the provision of most education, health and social services developed as part of the rapid growth of the post-war welfare state. Alongside the emergency services provided by police, fire-fighters and ambulance staff, the funding and organization of public services were regulated by statute and had no private sector counterpart. The political sensitivity of the quality of public services encouraged stable industrial relations, uniform service standards, and a distinctive orientation to work linked to a commitment to the service provided. Public service employers had only a limited industrial relations role because the centralized systems of pay determination seemed to require little local personnel management expertise. Trade union membership was often encouraged by employers, and most of the civil service, teaching and health service professional associations and non-manual trade unions were outside the mainstream of the trade union movement until they began to affiliate to the TUC in the 1970s.

Second, the role of the state as an employer was distinctive in terms of the public accountability for its actions; decisions about the recruitment of staff and the way in which they were managed and rewarded were open to public scrutiny (Morris 2000). An important aspect of this accountability concerns the pay and conditions of public sector employees; the state has to reconcile the expectation that it should be a fair or 'model' employer with its duty to taxpayers as the guardian of the public purse. Until the 1980s, strong institutional support for trade unions and collective bargaining, relatively good conditions of service (e.g. pensions and sick pay), and the rapid expansion of public service employment partly concealed the less generous policies of governments concerning internal and external pay relativities and other conditions of employment (Bach 1999a; Carter and Fairbrother 1999).

From the late 1960s, economic conditions deteriorated and industrial relations in the public sector became much more uncertain and conflictual. In the context of rapidly fluctuating levels of inflation, the imposition of pay restraint policies on the public sector led to unprecedented and widespread wage militancy. A series of protracted disputes threatened co-operative patterns of trade union and management behaviour, and challenged traditional notions of the 'public service ethos' of staff. Government policies focused on restraining the growth of public expenditure, privatization and commercialization, and legal and administrative intervention to reduce trade union power and strengthen the position of management. For most commentators, the 1980s witnessed the collapse of the traditional pattern of public sector industrial relations, and the end of the 'model' employer aspirations of the state.

The Conservative Legacy

The first of four Conservative governments was elected in 1979 on a wave of anti-union sentiment following the disruption of public services during the previous 'winter of discontent'. It began a programme of public sector reform and privatization that continued until it lost office in 1997, the most notable feature of which was a sustained attack on trade union power. This policy was complemented by a strong critique of public sector management values and policies. It was argued that managers had been too submissive in their dealings with trade unions and professional groups; the interests of 'producers' had prevailed over those of the 'consumers' of public services (Self 2000).

The most visible part of the Conservative reform programme was a far-reaching programme of privatization. Following the sale of British Telecom in 1984, most nationalized industries and public utilities covering gas, water, electricity, steel, coal and many parts of the transport sector (including the railways) had been privatized by 1997. The scale of the privatization programme was much greater than that adopted by governments in other European countries, as were the complementary policies of liberalization designed to stimulate a competitive marketplace.

The industrial relations and employment consequences of privatization were uneven. It is difficult to disentangle the impact of deregulation, corporate restructuring and technological change from the consequences of changes in ownership. Nonetheless, in most cases the combined impact of these processes led to very substantial job losses, often facilitated by substantial redundancy payments. Collective bargaining remained the dominant form of pay determination in privatized companies, but it became more decentralized, and widespread enterprise restructuring was reflected in more disparate bargaining structures. The ability of trade unions to mobilize their members diminished, and senior and middle-management grades were often excluded from collective bargaining. Senior managers experimented with new forms of human resource management: some developed more abrasive styles of macho-management designed to marginalize trade unions (e.g. British Airways), while others (e.g. in water supply) sought to sustain co-operative relations with unions and the workforce through partnership agreements (Pendleton 1997).

In its first period of office, the Labour government did not reverse any of its predecessor's privatization policies; indeed, it proceeded with its own partial privatization of air traffic control, despite vociferous trade union opposition centred on concerns about safety. The government largely accepted the argument that privatization had improved efficiency and service quality, albeit at a cost of more intensive working practices and job losses. An important exception was the railway industry, over which public anger was ignited by declining service standards and lapses in health and safety standards, including several high-profile train crashes. The refusal of the government to consider any form of renationalization (until the financial collapse of Railtrack forced it do so in the early months of its second period of office) dismayed the trade union movement, already wary of government plans for increasing private sector involvement in the provision of public services.

The most contentious issue was the government's acceptance of its predecessor's policy that most new capital projects should not be funded directly by the Treasury. The Conservative government developed its Private Finance Initiative (PFI) in the early 1990s when the public sector borrowing requirement was more than £40 billion. Under the PFI system, private sector firms bid for contracts to finance, design, build and operate public service facilities – such as new hospitals, roads, prisons, and schools-related infrastructure – and the Treasury makes an agreed annual payment for the duration of the contract (e.g. 25–30 years). Such arrangements have been justified by the belief that specialist contractors can make efficiency savings, and share the initial risks of construction delays and escalating costs. Since 1997 the rationale of PFI contracts has been broadened to encompass a wider range of public–private partnerships (PPPs) under which public sector organizations commission and pay for services, but do not directly provide them (Treasury 2000).

Apart from technical questions concerning the relative cost of different ways of funding capital expenditure, trade union leaders and activists view public–private partnerships as another form of privatization. Given their experience of competitive tendering (see Foster and Scott 1998), they believe that public–private partnerships threaten the pay and conditions of their members and the organization and influence of the union. While employees' rights and conditions are legally protected on transfer from the public to the private sector, trade unions have argued strongly that new staff should have the same pay and conditions as the protected employees to avoid the creation of a 'two-tier' workforce (UNISON 2000).

Health service trade unions led the campaign to defend public services, not least because most new hospitals have been funded through PFI contracts, and in the autumn of 2001 they achieved a notable victory. The government agreed that pilot schemes would be implemented in three new hospitals in which all staff would remain employed on NHS terms and conditions of employment. In the education sector, the scope of private sector involvement is much less. Nonetheless, 600 schools were refurbished via PFI schemes, 20 local education authorities outsourced many of their management services, and three state schools – judged to be 'failing' by inspectors – were managed by private sector organizations. These developments were strongly opposed by teachers' trade unions. Perhaps the most dramatic changes took place in the prison service. Most of the new prisons built since 1997 have been funded by PFI arrangements, and the private sector companies involved were given the responsibility for custodial services, as well as ancillary and maintenance functions. In none of the nine privately managed prisons has the main trade union, the Prison Officers' Association (POA), achieved recognition for collective bargaining. In one case, the union claimed that 145 of the 250 employees were POA members, but the Central Arbitration Committee rejected the application as inadmissible because the employer had signed a collective agreement with the non-independent Securicor Custodial Services Staff Association.

A second important component of Conservative reform focused on increasing the authority, status and pay of senior managers, and the devolution of managerial responsibilities to more autonomous organizational units. The expectation that managers would assert their right to manage, and embrace policies of cultural change, was encouraged by the recruitment of senior managers from the private sector. The devolution of responsibility for personnel practice to local managers allowed greater scope to alter job roles and develop other forms of flexibility (Hegewisch 1999). These initiatives also reflected the more active role of line managers in developing workplace reforms (Bach 1999b). At the same time, however, central government accrued unprecedented levels of control over the funding and management of nominally independent service providers through strictly enforced cash limits and demands for annual 'efficiency gains'.

This partially explains the apparent paradox of increased central control set against the Conservative government's rhetorical support for management devolution.

Proposals for devolved management covered pay and terms and conditions of service, as well as the operational aspects of recruitment and selection. Managerial scope for innovation was increased by government exhortation, and facilitated by the relatively weak tradition of public administration in the UK in comparison with most other European countries (Bach and Della Rocca 2000). Professional associations and trade unions were also more willing to accept working practice reforms than concede the devolution or individualization of pay. Managers experimented with changes in work organization and working time arrangements (e.g. in hospitals), and made greater use of temporary employment – altering the composition of the workforce and the roles undertaken (Arrowsmith and Mossé 2000; Grimshaw 1999). There was also a harder edge to many of the reforms, with more control of sickness absence and increases in workload. These and other changes were reflected in the high levels of work intensification reported throughout the public sector and analysed by Green (2001).

The final component of the Conservative reforms was the diffusion of market-type mechanisms across the public services. Compulsory competitive tendering (CCT) for ancillary and support services was introduced in the health and local government sectors in the early 1980s, and was later extended in the latter to incorporate a variety of professional white-collar services, such as personnel and information management. In the civil service, the policy of 'market testing' increasingly excluded in-house bids, ensuring that a higher proportion of work was contracted out than in other public services. Regardless of whether a service was retained in house or outsourced, this policy led to substantial reductions in the workforce, and accompanying payroll savings (Colling 1999). The imposition of mandatory competitive tendering provided managers with an incentive to alter working practices, erode national terms and conditions of employment and, in their judgement, improve service quality by establishing more clearly defined and monitored performance standards (IRS 1998).

New Labour: Modernizing Government

Since 1997, the government's mantra has been the modernization of public services, signalling an important change from past Labour government policies. It accepted most parts of the radical organizational restructuring of the public services introduced under the Conservatives. The government's programme for 'modernising government' (Cabinet Office 1999), however, is designed to encourage a shift away from a narrow preoccupation with cost minimization towards an emphasis on improved service quality and tighter monitoring of service standards. In place of the competitive ethos fostered by earlier market-type reforms, it is envisaged that public service providers – especially the NHS and local authorities – should co-operate more effectively, straddling the boundaries between the public and private sectors, and between different parts of the public services. This is accompanied, however, by more rigorous scrutiny of organizational performance.

The Labour government's policy of 'best value' for local government services eases the prescriptive nature of CCT, seeking to build on previous reforms by extending the scrutiny of performance to all local authority services. In place of periodic market testing of services designed to specify costs and standards for the duration of a contract, local authorities are expected to engage in a more continuous process of performance reviews to increase service standards and achieve efficiency gains. Whereas CCT sometimes discouraged competition in practice, the Best Value regime encourages local authorities to develop broader tests of competitiveness, such as benchmark comparisons with similar public and private services, and to promote partnership and joint ventures between local authorities and private sector organizations. As Martin (2000) notes in his review of Best Value pilot programmes, the focus on citizen-centred services and performance measures based on outcomes for users, rather than cost inputs, frequently requires internal reorganization as well as more effective external collaboration. This complex process, therefore, has not always led to immediate improvements in service quality. The Audit Commission (2001a: 2) reports that while 'best value has helped to ensure that councils are more in touch with the needs and wishes of service users and council tax payers . . . over 60 per cent of the inspected services are found to be poor or fair, and there are still substantial variations in performance across different councils'.

In its first term in office, the government espoused a more positive policy on public expenditure. In the 1980s the Thatcher governments had argued that excessive public spending was at the root of Britain's economic ills, though their attempts to reduce the share of public expenditure as a proportion of GDP achieved rather mixed results. In its 1997 election manifesto, the Labour Party argued that it would retain the spending plans of the previous government for its first two years in office. This was justified partly by the need to reduce the substantial budget deficit it inherited, and partly to sustain its 'business-friendly' credentials by reducing expectations of an immediate hike in public sector pay. Between 1997 and 2001, public expenditure averaged 39.4 per cent of GDP compared with 44 per cent of GDP for the period 1979–97 (Mullard 2001). This indicates that the government kept a very tight rein on public expenditure, and partly explains the disappointment of public service employees and the simmering discontent of their trade unions during the Labour government's first period in office.

Following the early period of restraint, and at a time of strong economic growth, the government increased public expenditure very substantially, especially in the politically sensitive areas of hospitals and schools. This formed part of the Comprehensive Spending Review process that replaced annual departmental expenditure plans with three-year plans designed to facilitate longer-term planning. The process also included a new system of public service agreements (PSAs) between each department and the Treasury, linking increased investment to greater accountability in meeting specific targets, such as reduced hospital waiting lists or better examination results (Treasury 1998). This targeting of resources had important implications for pay policy; the Pay Review Bodies were encouraged to recommend pay increases differentiated by occupation and grade, resulting in less uniform pay settlements than has historically been the case (White 2000). In a period of relatively low inflation, a three-year spending cycle may encourage longer-term pay deals, and facilitate the phased implementation of radical and expensive proposals for the reform of pay structures.

In contrast to the Conservative government's emphasis on organizational reform and market competition, the Labour government regards effective human resource management policies as essential in delivering its modernization agenda (Cabinet Office 1999). It is anxious to distance itself from the legacy of the Thatcher period, when public service workers were denigrated and viewed as part of the problem, rather than a crucial resource for the improvement of services. In its first four-year period of office, however, the Labour government failed to secure the wholehearted support of many public service employees and their trade unions. The latter strongly criticized the government's initial caution in its public expenditure plans, the proliferation of performance targets and, in the face of growing recruitment and retention problems in many public services, the widespread demoralization of staff arising from increases in work intensity. These problems were exacerbated by declining pay relativities. Most public service employees received annual pay increases above the rate of price inflation, but until 2001 they did not match the increases received by comparable groups of qualified staff in the private sector (IDS 2001b).

Alongside this often acrimonious public criticism of government policies, trade union negotiators partially accepted the argument that pay systems had to be reformed, not least to meet some of their own objectives, as well as those of the government. Significant progress was made before the 2001 general election in negotiating the outlines of major reforms in salary structures and pay systems throughout the public services. These included new and simplified national pay spines based on job evaluation that facilitated local grading decisions and the removal of sex discrimination in pay practices, and procedures to link pay increases to individual or team performance. As Hatchett (2001: 37) argues, these and other proposals in the government's modernization programme were not entirely new, but were an attempt to give 'coherence and a hearty push forward to a set of ideas that have been fermenting over the past decade'.

A greater sense of urgency in pursuing such reforms was injected by a growing recognition of the severity of recruitment and retention problems amongst key groups (such as nurses, teachers and police), and by the availability of significant increases in public expenditure to finance the changes. The government also stressed the value of non-pay rewards, especially 'family-friendly' policies and attempts to improve the working lives of staff. Although most policies were targeted at individuals, the emphasis on partnership working aimed to alter the culture of employment relations and required senior management to review on a regular basis staff involvement and to undertake annual staff attitude surveys (DoH 2000). This higher profile for human resource management than had occurred under the Conservative administrations seemed to represent a distinctive phase in the process of increasing managerialism that unfolded during the 1979–97 period.

Public Service Employment

In exploring the distinctive characteristics of employment in the public sector it is useful to differentiate between three main sub-sectors. First, nearly 2.7 million staff are employed by local authorities. These are organizations with elected leaders who have the power to raise funds through rates, levies and taxes, and are responsible for the provision of education (schools), social services, police, fire and other services. Second, more than 1.5 million staff are employed in publicly owned and controlled corporations (identified below) which nevertheless have substantial freedom to conduct their activities along business lines. Third, almost 0.5 million civil servants provide services to the public (e.g. social security benefits and employment services), with a small group of senior staff providing information and advice to government ministers in support of policy development. In total, 5.1 million staff were employed in the public sector in 2000 (18 per cent of the UK workforce), 2 million fewer than in 1981 when the public sector accounted for nearly 30 per cent of the workforce (MacGregor 2001).

The allocation of functions between these three groups is partly an accident of history and has been affected by the public sector reforms discussed above. As can be seen in table 11.1, the decline in aggregate public sector employment since 1981 has arisen largely from the privatization of most of the nationalized industries within the public corporations category. Most health service staff were eventually reclassified into this group following the creation of NHS trusts in 1991, leaving the Post Office as the most significant employer of the surviving public corporations. Privatization and subcontracting also contributed to a decline of around 25 per cent in civil service employment and to a significant loss of manual workers' jobs throughout the public services. Employment in the NHS and in local authorities has declined less dramatically over the last two decades, and increased in 1999 and 2000, although these aggregate figures conceal changes in the occupational distribution of staff within both sub-sectors. For example, the number of senior hospital doctors in the NHS grew by 4 per cent per annum between 1990 and 2000, while the number of qualified nursing staff increased only by 0.3 per cent per annum over the same period (DoH 2001).

The data in table 11.1, derived from the classification of the UK national accounts, exaggerate slightly the decline in public service employment and growth in the private sector. For instance, the reclassification of polytechnics, further education and sixth-form colleges as 'private non-profit-making bodies' (alongside the old universities) arose because they are no longer 'wholly dependent' on government funding, or subject to local authority control. Nonetheless, these organizations are part of the public education system, highly dependent on expenditure decisions taken by central government, and covered by systems of pay determination and employment relations deeply rooted in public service traditions.

In the last decade, the proportion of women in the public sector workforce has increased from around 50 to 60 per cent. This reflects the privatization of

Table 11.1   UK Workforce jobs by sector, 1981–2000 (000s)

	1981	1990	1998	2000
Total workforce jobs	26,001	28,920	28,498	29,011
Private sector	18,816	22,868	23,554	23,918
Public sector	7,185	6,052	4,944	5,093
Public corporations	1,867	785	1,497	1,530
of which:				
National Health Service Trusts	–	–	1,123	1,145
Other	1,867	785	374	385
Central government	2,419	2,300	868	873
of which:				
HM Forces	334	303	210	207
National Health Service	1,207	1,221	77	79
Other (mainly civil service)	878	776	581	587
Local government	2,899	2,967	2,579	2,690
of which:				
Education	1,454	1,431	1,204	1,300
Social services	350	417	395	388
Police	186	199	207	204
Construction	143	114	61	59
Other	766	806	712	739

Source: MacGregor (2001).

nationalized industries – which employed mainly men – and the relative stability of employment levels in public services. Education, health and social services employ far more women than men, not only in professional posts (e.g. teaching and nursing), but also in less qualified and lower-status occupations (e.g. secretarial, cleaning and catering jobs). To a greater extent than in many parts of the private sector, employment in the public services expresses a complex pattern of gender segregation rooted in traditional – if changing – assumptions about appropriate employment for women and men. For example, women comprised 88 per cent of full-time classroom teachers and 59 per cent of head teachers in nursery and primary schools in England and Wales in 1999, while in secondary schools 55 per cent of full-time classroom teachers and 28 per cent of head teachers were women (DfES 2001). In the NHS, women comprised 22 per cent of the hospital medical consultants in England in 2000, but 79 per cent of the non-medical workforce – that is, nurses, therapeutic, administrative and ancillary staff (DoH 2001).

This pattern of horizontal and vertical segregation is replicated in other caring, nursing, teaching and domestic services provided by the public sector. In most parts of the public services, however, the gender pay gap and other expressions of women's disadvantaged position vis-à-vis men have declined over the last 20 years. Generally, public service employers have responded more positively than their private service counterparts to trade union pressures and adverse employment tribunal decisions in seeking to develop effective equal opportunities policies. Also, severe recruitment and retention difficulties in the late 1990s encouraged managers to offer more flexible employment conditions for their female staff, and gave a strong impetus to negotiations on the reform of national pay and grading systems to further reduce the gender pay gap (see further chapter 16).

The gender composition of the public service workforce is associated with the increase in part-time working, from around 25 to 35 per cent, over the last 15 years. There is no single explanation for this change – and there are wide variations in the use of part-time employees within different parts of the public services. Part-time working is not restricted to relatively low-paid ancillary and support staff; for example, 41 per cent of female doctors (GPs) were on half-time or three-quarter time contracts, or were job-sharing in 1999 (EOC 2001). The evidence suggests that both supply-side and demand factors are at work. Public service employers report that increases in part-time working arise from staff requests for job-sharing or reduced working hours, especially from women returning from maternity leave. Also, many employers have increased the use of part-time working to deal with labour shortages and budget constraints; the reorganization of working time can offer increased flexibility in meeting uneven service demands (Arrowsmith and Sisson 2000). The Labour government has also prompted employers to make part-time work available as part of its attempt to improve the quality of working life in the public services, and its attractiveness to employees may be further enhanced by the implementation of the European Union directive on part-time workers that removes most of the barriers to equal treatment of part-time workers.

Since 1990 there has been an increase in the number of temporary employees in the British labour market. By 1996 there were 1.6 million temporary employees in total; around 10 per cent of all staff in the public sector, compared with 5 per cent in the private sector. The majority of public service temporary employees were on fixed-term contracts, and many worked in professional occupations such as teaching (Sly and Stillwell 1997). Others obtained work through temporary employment agencies; for example, nurses and teachers have been recruited more often from private sector agencies, as well as from public service-organized supply sources, such as 'nurse banks'. Budget uncertainties, as well as the need to provide cover for absent staff (e.g. on maternity leave), provided the main motives for the increase in temporary employment in the mid-1990s (IDS 1996).

In recent years, many public service managers have tried to reduce the incidence of temporary employment because of its potentially detrimental impact on recruitment and retention and on service quality. The Labour government supported such attempts to reduce the use of temporary and short-term contracts, especially in the health service (IDS 1999), but in the context of chronic staff shortages in many health care occupations this was not achieved.

In the case of nursing, an Audit Commission (2001b) study found that NHS expenditure on agency staff increased by a third, and expenditure on bank staff by 14 per cent, in 1999/2000. On a typical day about 20,000 bank and agency nurses provided temporary cover for staffing shortfalls on 10 per cent of all shifts. The majority of temporary staff covered the gaps arising from unfilled vacancies and sickness absence; others were employed to meet peaks in work-load or to cover for staff on leave (i.e. holidays, maternity and study leave). The Audit Commission also found that the majority of bank and agency nursing staff already had full-time or part-time substantive contracts in the NHS. Many worked their additional shifts in familiar wards, facilitating consistency and continuity in patient care, although almost half of the staff who combined full-time posts with agency or bank employment worked more than 48 hours a week. Moreover, the methods by which temporary staff working less regularly were recruited, trained and appraised sometimes reduced the consistency and quality of patient care.

The growth of temporary employment and contingent contracts raises the broader question of the extent to which public service employment has become less secure over the last decade or so. The analysis of a wide range of survey data by Morgan et al. (2000: 106) shows that many public service workers have faced an increasing risk of job loss and deteriorating conditions of employment. Despite the growth of precarious employment in the public services in the 1990s, however, 'employees remain substantially more secure than their private sector counterparts'. As will be discussed later, relatively secure employment in the public services has been accompanied by substantial evidence of staff demoral-ization. This has been associated with increasing workloads, relatively low pay in relation to qualifications and experience, and the widespread belief of staff that the government, management, and the public do not sufficiently acknowledge the value of their work.

Pay Determination and Collective Bargaining

The unending process of public sector reform over the last two decades arose from the desire of governments to achieve a number of potentially conflicting objectives. For example, most governments simultaneously wanted to restrain the growth of public expenditure and encourage improvements in the quality of public services. Their policies, however, were shaped partly by short-term eco-nomic fluctuations, especially in the state of public finances and labour mar-ket conditions, and by changing ideological and political priorities. This section explores the ways in which government policies impacted on patterns of public service industrial relations. First, it examines changes in the institutional struc-tures and principles of public service pay determination, especially the extension of the pay review system to a million more public service employees. Second, it explores the extent to which pay determination has become more decentralized in the civil service, NHS and local authorities and compares the differing per-spectives of trade unions, employers, and governments towards the reform of collective bargaining.

Forms of pay determination

The institutional forms and principles of public sector pay determination have changed significantly over the last twenty years. The previous post-war system had several distinctive features. First, a centralized structure of collective bargaining covered almost all employees and managers in the public sector. The scope of bargaining was wide and included national grading and salary structures and other terms and conditions of employment that were outlined in great detail, and implemented relatively uniformly. Second, the bargaining principle of 'fair comparison' with pay levels and increases in the private sector was widely accepted. Its most elaborate institutional expression had been established in the civil service in the mid-1950s, but negotiations in other public services also focused mainly on comparability arguments. Third, arbitration procedures designed to avoid or resolve disputes were almost universal throughout the public services and contributed to the low level of conflict. While none of these features survives intact, the scope and direction of change have varied between different occupational groups and services.

As noted above, the 1979 Conservative government was elected after a decade of widespread and highly politicized public sector conflict. A few years earlier, fire service staff (following a lengthy dispute) and police (after threatening industrial action) were each granted large pay increases, and an indexation formula to protect their improved relative pay. The formulas linked pay increases to favourable measures of the annual growth in national earnings, and, despite several threats to end these pay indexation arrangements, they have survived. The Conservative government also inherited another institutional innovation – the Standing Commission on Pay Comparability. This had been established partly to resolve the public services disputes of the winter of 1978/9, but also to recommend procedures for establishing acceptable 'bases of comparison' for pay determination throughout the public services.

The Conservative government immediately signalled its intention to erode the principle of 'fair comparison' and emphasize 'affordability', defined by strictly enforced cash limits on public expenditure. The Comparability Commission was abolished, public service employers were encouraged to resist trade union wage demands, and the government seemed to relish protracted disputes with trade unions in the civil service in 1981, in the health service in 1982, and in schools in the mid-1980s. The government made few concessions to resolve these pay disputes (and none in the year-long dispute in the (then) publicly owned coal-mining industry concerning colliery closures and job losses in 1984–5). Partly for reasons of political expediency, however, it established an independent pay review body for nurses, midwives and professions allied to medicine in 1983, and one for school teachers (in England and Wales) in 1991.

Pay review bodies had previously covered only a relatively small number of public sector staff (i.e. the armed services, doctors and dentists, senior civil servants and judges) whose pay had never been determined by collective bargaining. All of the review bodies have a small group of members appointed by the government and are serviced by an independent civil service secretariat. Each year they invite written and oral evidence from interested parties, visit workplaces to meet managers and employees, and commission their own research. On the basis of such evidence they make recommendations on pay increases – and other matters identified in their terms of reference – which are not binding on the government.

The extension of the pay review system to nearly 1 million nurses and teachers had a significant effect on the development of public service pay determination. The pay review bodies have been successful in containing overt pay conflict, but they have discouraged the decentralization of pay bargaining and limited the erosion of the principle of 'fair comparison' – two key objectives of Conservative governments in the 1980s and 1990s (Bach and Winchester 1994). Members of the review bodies have often demonstrated their independence by rejecting the arguments of ministers and senior civil servants. For example, they have recommended pay increases above the level that could be funded by expenditure plans, and criticized government decisions to stage the implementation pay awards to keep the annual salary costs within cash-limited budgets. Moreover, when the Labour government issued more extensive and prescriptive terms of reference for most of the review bodies in 1998, the next report of the nurses' review body insisted bluntly that its primary role was to ensure fair pay. It argued that it must be free to give equal attention to the evidence of all the parties, and to make recommendations on pay increases that should not be constrained by a sum of money predetermined by government (White 2000: 96).

In comparison with traditional forms of national pay bargaining, the review body process has encouraged a more systematic analysis of a wider range of arguments and data. Alongside the parties' conflicting views on the importance of comparability and affordability arguments, the review bodies have analysed data on recruitment and retention, and on motivation, morale and workload. Partly for these reasons the pay review process for nurses and teachers seems to offer a more acceptable mechanism for determining public service pay than those that preceded it, although it has costs as well as benefits for each of the parties involved.

The government has been able to distance itself from direct pay negotiations with trade unions, but it has not avoided considerable political costs when it has staged the pay recommendations of the review bodies. Trade unions representing qualified nursing and teaching staff have influenced the review bodies sufficiently to achieve higher pay increases for their members than other public service groups excluded from the system – that is, covered by collective bargaining. For example, Elliott and Duffus (1996) show that doctors and qualified nurses achieved real earnings growth of more than 30 per cent between 1981 and 1992. In comparison, the real earnings of male scientists in the civil service and university academics increased by less than 10 per cent. Elliott and Duffus argue that the more favourable pay outcomes may be explained by the increasing demand for the services of doctors, nurses and (since the early 1990s) teachers, and their representation by powerful professional associations. They note also that overall changes in the relative pay of public and private sector employees follow a cyclical pattern. Significant improvements in the relative pay of public employees usually follow protracted periods of decline, and often occur during periods of slow economic growth or recession, when earnings growth in the private sector decelerates sharply (e.g. in the early 1990s).

Trade union leaders have often opposed some review body recommendations and arguments, but employers and managers in local government and the NHS have been much more critical of the pay review system. They have to meet the costs of recommended pay increases without having much influence on the process, and they have to manage the tension between groups of staff covered or excluded by pay review. Moreover, the pay review system has discouraged more decentralized and flexible systems of pay determination, and thus reduced the incentive for managers to embark on the reform of local pay structures (White 1999).

The reform of pay determination arrangements

The rationale for a centralized system of pay determination rooted in a strong commitment to national comparability arguments has been weakened over the last 15 years. As managers were given greater responsibility for budgets in which labour costs were the most significant component, the relevance of national pay and conditions arrangements was increasingly questioned. The restructuring and organizational fragmentation of public services, and the growing interest in private sector management 'best practice', added further weight to the arguments in favour of a more decentralized system of pay determination.

Across the public services, more decentralized and flexible arrangements for pay determination – and collective bargaining over non-pay issues – have developed, but in a piecemeal, uneven, and often inconsistent way. This can be explained partly by disagreements within each of the three main parties involved in the process, as well as by differences between them. First, the inconsistency in government policy arose from the tension between the Treasury's determination to sustain centralized financial control, and the frequent exhortation of departmental ministers in favour of greater local pay flexibility. Second, public service managers held different views on the proposed pace and direction of reform. All managers wanted to escape from highly prescriptive national pay and conditions agreements, but many preferred to negotiate incremental reforms to the existing system rather than embark on a radical and potentially hazardous shift to local pay determination. Third, while all trade union leaders and activists resisted proposals to dismantle national pay agreements, there were disagreements within and between unions on the scope for flexibility and managerial discretion within partially reformed national agreements.

The uneven progress towards more decentralized systems of pay determination can also be explained by distinctive features of different parts of the public service sector. There have always been variations in the procedural and substantive content of national agreements between the civil service, the NHS and local authorities – as well as between different groups of employees within these services (e.g. for doctors, nurses, and ancillary workers within the NHS, and for teachers, fire service, manual and clerical staff in local authorities). All of the separate agreements have been shaped by past conflicts between central government, public employers and trade unions, and reflect the different occupational and labour market characteristics of each group of employees.

The analysis of bargaining reforms and attempts to modernize pay systems considers separately developments in the civil service, the NHS and local authorities (including the distinctive case of school teachers). Four themes or issues have driven the move towards more decentralized pay systems in each of these sub-sectors at different times over the last decade or so. The first concerns variations in labour market pressures and recruitment and retention problems. The second arises from the desire of governments and employers to replace automatic pay increments based on service with some form of performance-related pay. The third focuses on the reform of grading and salary structures to reflect or encourage changes in work organization and skills, and the removal of sex discrimination in pay systems. The fourth concerns the link between pay systems and working practices, patterns of working time, workload, and employee motivation. The impact of these four issues on developments in different parts of the public services has varied, and the influence of each cannot easily be separated from that of the others.

The civil service

The reform of pay determination arrangements has been more comprehensive in the civil service than in other parts of the public sector, mainly because government ministers have been able to exercise more direct control than elsewhere. In the years following the lengthy 1981 dispute, the government experimented with various 'flexibility' initiatives to deal with recruitment and retention problems, and introduced a performance-related pay scheme for senior managers. By the end of the 1980s, individual civil service unions and the Treasury had reached agreements that, in the words of Kessler (1993: 306), 'incorporated the two competing traditions of pay determination – one rooted in a concern for comparability, the other in the pursuit of flexibility as a management tool'.

These tentative steps towards a more decentralized pay system were followed by two major reforms. First, after the civil service was reorganized into semi-autonomous executive agencies, legislation in 1992 enabled the Treasury to delegate its direct responsibility for negotiating pay and conditions to individual departments and agencies. Civil service-wide pay determination ended in 1996, except for the newly created Senior Civil Service comprising 3,000 of the most senior managers and professional staff, who were covered by a pay review body. Second, individual performance-related pay (PRP) was extended under 'delegated bargaining'. The traditional system of automatic progression through the pay scales on the basis of annual increments was abolished and replaced by the assessment of individual performance against agreed objectives.

Trade union representatives in the civil service strongly criticized the introduction of PRP schemes, arguing that their individualist assumptions would undermine the teamwork values and public service ethos of staff. Numerous studies have since identified the practical problems of sustaining effective schemes: for example, the time-consuming process in setting objectives and measuring performance; the limited financial resources available to reward good or excellent performance; and the demoralization of staff who believe that they have been treated unfairly (Marsden and French 1998). For these and other reasons, the link between pay and performance has become increasingly blurred.

In allocating the budget for annual pay increases approved by the Treasury, agencies and departments have recently accorded a high priority to dealing with low pay and recruitment problems, and facilitating the faster progression of staff to the top of the pay band. Time and money have also been committed to resolving equal pay problems. In some departments grading structures have been reformed to provide a more robust defence against equal value claims, and managers have had to respond to research evidence of biased performance assessments, relating to ethnicity and disability, as well as gender, throughout the civil service (IDS 2001a). The resources available to fund individual PRP schemes thus diminished at time when there was a widespread recognition that they had failed to achieve many of their anticipated benefits in the civil service and elsewhere.

Government ministers and senior civil servants, however, remain strongly committed to systems of performance management. As part of the 'modernising government' agenda, a team led by the finance director of Pearson plc examined the operation of performance-related pay in four major government departments. The report recommended that team-based performance bonuses should replace individual PRP schemes, and that the bonuses should not be consolidated into base salaries because they relate only to recent performance (Makinson 2000; IRS 2000a, 2000b). Some civil service departments and agencies have begun to explore the ways in which team-based bonuses could be related to operational targets set out in public service agreements, while others have revised their existing PRP schemes by introducing non-consolidated individual bonuses.

The National Health Service

The pressures to decentralize collective bargaining and reform pay systems in the NHS were similar to those in the civil service. Pay and conditions were negotiated nationally in 10 functional Whitley Councils (i.e. bargaining units covering the main occupational groups) and, after approval from the Secretary of State, were applied in a prescriptive and uniform manner. The government's policy of strict cash limits and its willingness to resist union wage claims, precipitated a nine-month campaign of demonstrations and 'days of action' in 1982. The dispute temporarily united TUC-affiliated unions and non-affiliated professional associations, especially the Royal College of Nursing (RCN), but its settlement created the conditions for a return to deeply rooted expressions of organizational rivalry. The government sanctioned a higher pay increase for nurses than for other staff and, more important, created two new pay review bodies in 1983 – one for nurses and midwives, and another for 'professions allied to medicine'.

As noted earlier, this initiative provided a distinctive framework within which future proposals for the reform of pay determination in the NHS had to be considered. The review body for nurses and midwives did not exclude all forms of collective bargaining; indeed, the most significant improvement in their relative pay arose from the 1988 clinical grading review, discussed at length within the national Whitley Council. As pay review bodies covered more than half the NHS workforce, however, their recommendations inevitably constrained attempts to decentralize collective bargaining. By the early 1990s, national negotiations had modified wage and salary structures, producing more flexible job definitions and allowing local pay supplements to deal with recruitment and retention problems in particular occupations and locations. The creation of a new grade of 'health care assistant', the pay and conditions of which were excluded from national agreements, also provided a modest push towards local pay determination. The development of the 'internal market', and the reorganization of NHS service provision into 400 nominally independent trusts, however, raised expectations of a much more extensive devolution of pay bargaining, but these expectations were not realized.

By the end of the decade it was clear that progress towards devolved bargaining had been very limited, despite strong pressures from Conservative governments up to 1997 (Duncan 2001). In the years immediately following the NHS reorganization, the scarcity of management resources and skills undoubtedly inhibited bargaining reforms: managers had to deal with the complexity of the new internal market; and they knew that any proposals for local pay determination would meet with opposition from employees and their trade unions. The strength of opposition was revealed in 1995 when the nurses' pay review body recommended a national pay increase of only 1 per cent in the expectation that local bargaining over efficiency and flexibility might produce an overall increase of between 1.5 per cent and 3 per cent. After threatening industrial action, the trade unions demanded, and in most cases achieved, unconditional local pay increases of 2 per cent.

The review body pursued a similar two-tier approach in 1996, but hardly any serious negotiations took place; pay increases were delayed and severely restricted by financial constraints. The abject failure of this 'hybrid two-tier system' for dealing with annual pay increases for nurses led to its abandonment by the Conservative government before the 1997 general election (Thornley et al. 2000), and a promise from the Labour Party to restore national pay determination. The review body continued to support the principle of local pay determination, but since 1997 it has recommended only national pay increases. As it reported in 1998, the government had persuaded NHS employers and trade unions to begin discussions on 'a new pay system which would command the confidence of all interested parties and would combine national pay and local flexibility' (NPRB 1998: p. iv).

The Labour government published *Agenda for Change* in early 1999, outlining the case for a comprehensive modernization of NHS pay systems. Since then lengthy discussions between government, employers and trade unions have generated broad support for the main elements of a new system. First, the separate pay structures for different occupational groups would be replaced by just three pay spines: one for doctors and dentists; one for nurses and professions allied to medicine; and one for all other staff. It is assumed that pay increases for the first two groups would continue to be based on recommendations of the review bodies, and the pay of all other staff would be negotiated in a single negotiating council. Second, grades within the three pay spines would be determined locally on the basis of a single, NHS-wide job evaluation scheme. Third, service-based incremental progression might be modified by progression based on new responsibilities and competencies, thus improving the links between education and development and pay progression. Finally, a set of 'core' conditions of service would be determined at national level with others subject to variation and negotiated locally. Apart from other potential benefits, such as reducing the barriers to cross-functional working, each of these proposals would make it easier for managers to comply with equal pay legislation.

The scope and ambition of the *Agenda for Change* negotiations – and the assumption that 'nothing is agreed until everything is agreed' – have led to delays in the planned timetable for provisional agreement, consultation, pilot sites of 'early implementers', and full implementation. Even if provisional agreement is reached in 2002, the reforms are unlikely to be implemented fully before 2005. This timetable has already complicated the process of pay review and the response of the parties to urgent problems. For example, the RCN argues that recruitment and retention problems arise not only from inadequate pay in relation to comparable groups elsewhere, but also from unfair grading decisions and inadequate staffing levels leading to excessive workloads and unpaid excess hours (RCN 2001). The government would prefer to leave changes in grading to the *Agenda for Change* negotiations, and argues that workload problems are best addressed by improving work organization and skill-mix at local level. Nonetheless, it introduced 'cost of living supplements' for qualified staff working in London and other high-cost areas and, in its evidence to the review body in 2001, argued that additional incremental points should be awarded to nursing auxiliaries who have acquired new skills.

Local authorities

Proposals for the modernization of pay in the NHS were influenced directly by the example of the local government 'single status' agreement of 1997. This signalled the reform and integration of the two principal collective agreements covering 1.3 million manual workers and administrative, professional, technical and clerical (APT&C) staff. In the decade before 1997, the national agreements had become more flexible and less prescriptive for several reasons. First, local authorities employed an occupationally heterogeneous workforce in more than 400 councils, varying in size from nearly 50,000 to a few hundred staff. Second, strongly organized trade union branches in urban areas were able to raise their members' pay through 'grading drift' for APT&C staff and bonus schemes for manual workers, especially when local labour market conditions were favourable. Third, in comparison with the civil service and the NHS, the strategies of local authority employers often reflected the party political values of their elected members. In the tight labour market conditions of the late 1980s, for example, Conservative-controlled councils in the south-east of England exerted strong pressure for a more flexible national agreement. After the lengthy national dispute with APT&C staff in 1989, more than 30 councils withdrew from the national agreement and implemented local agreements.

The 'single status' agreement was greeted by employers and trade unions as a major turning-point for employment relations in local government in 1997. A national pay spine, based on a jointly agreed job evaluation scheme, was designed to provide a framework within which each local authority could seek local agreement on a grading structure covering all staff. Alongside the harmonization of basic conditions such as working time and holidays, the agreement greatly increased the prospect of equality of employment between men and women, as well as between manual and white-collar staff. Over the last four years, however, progress on the local implementation of the agreement has been slow.

This can be explained partly by the time-consuming and practical difficulties encountered in integrating two groups of disparate occupations in a single pay structure, especially in local authorities that employ a large number of former manual workers. Equally important, insufficient funding was provided by central government to meet the cost of moving to single-status pay and conditions. The measures proposed by some local authorities to offset these costs – for example, to increase productivity or reduce allowances – were invariably resisted by employees and union representatives (Hatchett 2001). This opposition was exacerbated by the anxieties of some groups of white-collar employees, who expected to gain nothing from assimilation onto a single pay spine, and the fears of manual workers that they would lose their bonus payments and allowances. While these problems were not insoluble, they had to be confronted alongside other pressures on employers and trade unions – for example, reviewing the quality of services to meet Best Value guidelines, and dealing with severe recruitment and retention difficulties. A small number of local authorities had fully implemented the agreement by 2001, and a minority of the others had made considerable progress towards local agreement. Nonetheless, the obstacles that have delayed the implementation of the local government agreement – and the inconclusive *Agenda for Change* negotiations in the NHS – reveal the vast scope and complexity of the government's pay modernization proposals.

School teachers

Reforms in the system of pay determination for 400,000 teachers were shaped by problems found elsewhere in local government, but also by distinctive features of the teaching profession and the character of teachers' trade unionism. Frequent disputes in the mid-1980s were fuelled by intense inter-union rivalry, and political conflict between Labour-controlled local authorities and the Conservative government. Following the failure of the negotiating parties to reach an agreement in 1986, the government abolished the statutory national forum for pay negotiations (the Burnham Committee) and, after a transitional period, established the School Teachers' Review Body (STRB) in 1991. Its terms of reference were to make recommendations on pay and on conditions of service relating to the professional duties and working time of teachers (White 2000).

In the last few years the pay and career structure of classroom teachers and leadership group teachers (i.e. heads, deputies and assistant heads) has been substantially reformed. The changes have been driven by severe recruitment and retention problems, and have evoked sharply conflicting views on the ways in which they can be ameliorated. The five trade unions representing classroom teachers argue that teacher supply problems have been caused by inadequate salaries, slow and limited career progression, and poor conditions of service. On the latter, they point to workload pressures arising from large class sizes, excessive working hours, and an insufficiently constrained obligation to cover for absent colleagues. The trade unions believe that a higher starting salary – comparable to the average for all graduates – and a simplified salary structure facilitating faster progression through fewer points of the main scale, would provide the best solution to recruitment and retention problems.

In contrast, while the government accepts that recruitment and retention problems can be addressed partly by annual pay settlements, it argues that 'solutions need to be effectively targeted on problem areas, with the result that higher pay increases should be tightly focused on specific shortages rather than paid across the board' (DfES 2001: 6). The shortages refer mainly to subjects (maths, science, technology etc.) and location (high cost areas, especially London), but also to career phases (the number of applicants for teacher training, resignations after teaching for only a few years, qualified teachers returning from other jobs etc.). Government initiatives targeted on these areas include training salaries or bursaries for undergraduate and postgraduate trainees, 'golden hellos' for teachers in shortage subjects, bonuses for qualified teachers returning to schools, and funds to help teachers in London buy homes. These measures, and the discretion within the pay system to award additional allowances on the basis of recruitment and retention problems (rarely used outside London), were rejected by the trade unions as a grossly inadequate response to the problem.

The trade unions directed their greatest hostility, however, towards government plans to link teachers' pay to performance. The policy developed performance management arrangements that allow faster progression through the main pay scale on the basis of 'excellent performance', as well as the established criteria of qualifications and experience. More important, the government proposed that, once teachers had reached the top of the main pay scale, they could apply to cross a 'performance threshold' and, if successful, receive an immediate £2,000 pay increase by moving to a new upper scale with a maximum salary 25 per cent above the top of the main scale.

The opposition of teachers' unions to these proposals focused especially on the inclusion of 'pupil progress' as one of the eight standards to be assessed – alongside subject knowledge, teaching and assessment, professional effectiveness, etc. Teachers also criticized aspects of the assessment process, such as the complexity of the application forms, and demanded the right to appeal to external assessors to minimize the risk of bias on the part of head teachers. Despite the widespread reservations of teachers, almost 200,000 (80 per cent of those who were eligible) had applied to cross the threshold by the middle of 2000. The process was delayed when the High Court ruled in favour of the claim by the National Union of Teachers (NUT) that there had not been 'due consultation'. In October, the STRB produced a special report clarifying aspects of the procedure, and endorsing the government's policy. A few months later, 97 per cent of the teachers who had applied were told that they had met the performance standards and, in the spring of 2001, received the threshold payment of £2,000 and progressed to the upper pay scale.

The outcome of the first round of threshold assessment raises several questions about the hostility it had generated. First, it seems that the rhetoric with which trade union leaders and activists mobilized such strong opposition was based on little substance. The performance threshold assessment is not a return to the practice of 'payments by results' last used for teachers in the nineteenth century, and it has little in common with discredited individual performance-related pay schemes in the civil service and elsewhere. The intensity of the opposition was probably sustained by other grievances concerning conditions of work and education policy reforms. Second, although the government achieved some success in establishing procedures for better performance management in schools, the system will generate further conflict if it is not developed to encompass acceptable rules for progression through the upper pay scale, and if the government commitment to 'appropriate and sustained funding to support the new arrangements' is not sustained (STRB 2001: p. viii). Finally, the teachers' threshold assessment should not be viewed simply as another form of performance-related pay; its success will be judged on its contribution to the reform of the salary structure and career progression, and thus on its impact on recruitment and retention.

A few general points arise from the above summaries of attempts to reform pay determination in different parts of the public services. First, comprehensive pay reforms in sectors with a heterogeneous workforce (e.g. local authorities and the NHS) require a large investment of management time and resources, a high degree of inter-union agreement, and additional funding from central government. In the absence of one or more of these conditions, incremental and piecemeal reform can be agreed, although often it leads to anomalous outcomes. Second, most innovations in pay systems – for example, individual PRP schemes or major changes in salary structures – have a relatively brief shelf-life and require frequent amendment or fine-tuning. Finally, cyclical changes in labour market conditions and public expenditure growth interact with service-specific pay problems in ways that may undermine the initial rationale of reforms or their later impact.

Trade Union Organization and Policies

Throughout this chapter, frequent reference has been made to the response of trade union leaders and members to changes in government policies and

Table 11.2   Membership of the 12 largest unions in 1979, 1992 and 1999 (000s)

	1979	1992	1999	% women in 1999
UNISON – the Public Services Union*	1,658	1,487	1,272	72
Transport and General Workers Union (TGWU)	2,086	1,037	872	21
Amalgamated Engineering and Electrical Union (AEEU)	1,310	884	727	10
GMB – General Union	967	799	694	38
Manufacturing, Science and Finance (MSF)	691	552	416	32
Royal College of Nursing (RCN)	162	299	310	92
Union of Shop Distributive and Allied Workers (USDAW)	470	316	310	60
Communication Workers Union (CWU)	203	179	281	21
Public and Commercial Services Union (PCS)*	397	295	258	59
Graphical, Paper and Media Union (GMPU)	112	270	201	17
National Union of Teachers (NUT)	291	214	201	76
Schoolmasters and Women Teachers (NAS/UWT)	152	191	181	60

* The 1979 and 1992 figures for UNISON and PCS are the aggregate membership of the unions involved in the mergers in 1993 and 1998 respectively.
Source: Certification Officer Reports; Equal Opportunities Review (2000).

management strategies in different parts of the public service. This section briefly explores some more general aspects of trade union organization, membership density and policies, and examines the relationship between national and local union organization. It also comments on 'union renewal', that is, whether the restructuring of public services has eroded the power of trade unions, or created the conditions for more participative forms of workplace trade unionism and membership representation.

The importance of public service union membership within the British trade union movement can be expressed in several ways. First, table 11.2 shows that six of the largest 12 trade unions organize mainly in the public service sector, and that in comparison with the large general unions that recruit mainly in the private sector, they have suffered much smaller membership losses over the last two decades. Nonetheless, organizational and financial problems led to important trade union mergers in the mid- and late 1990s, creating UNISON and the PCS, which represent the majority of trade union members in local authorities and the civil service respectively. Table 11.2 also indicates that these two unions – and the single-occupation trade unions for classroom teachers and nurses (i.e. the NUT and the NAS/UWT, and the RCN, which is not affiliated to the

Table 11.3   Union density by sector, autumn 2000 (%)

	All	Private sector	Public sector
All employees	29	19	60
Manufacturing	27	27	58
Electricity, gas and water	53	52	–
Transport/Communication	42	36	75
Public administration	59	24	61
Education	54	26	58
Health	46	17	64

Source: Sneade (2001).

TUC) – have a much higher proportion of women members than other large trade unions. Thus, although some the most powerful public sector unions of the 1970s (e.g. coalminers and steelworkers) experienced very large membership losses through industrial restructuring and privatization, public service trade unions today have a high public profile and an influential role in the TUC and in its relationship with government. Moreover, the largest general unions – the TGWU, and the AEEU and MSF (due to merge to form Amicus in 2002) – also organize significant groups of public service employees.

Second, using data from the Labour Force Survey, table 11.3 shows that, while aggregate trade union density in 2000 was under 30 per cent, the figure for the public sector was 60 per cent, much higher than union density of less than 20 per cent in the private sector. It also shows that the small, but growing, 'privatized' parts of public administration, education and health services have a much lower union density than the core services delivered by direct public provision. This partly explains why most public service unions oppose public–private partnerships and the outsourcing of functions and services to the private sector. In recent years trade unions have had some success, however, in 'following their members' into the private sector, as is reflected in the name chosen by the civil service unions that merged to form the Public and Commercial Services Union.

The organizational capacity of trade unions to protect the interests of their members has undoubtedly been threatened by public service reforms. Trade union organization in the 1950s and 1960s was highly centralized and bureaucratic, reflecting the structure and character of collective bargaining. The emergence of union branch activism and workplace bargaining were both a cause and an effect of the public service disputes of the 1970s, but attempts to develop local union organization were limited and uneven, not least because they depended partly on management support and facilities. Over the last decade, in response to the devolution of management authority, the move to more decentralized negotiations, and the increasingly fragmented structure of public service provision, trade unions have invested far more resources in servicing local branches and workplace representatives.

It is extremely difficult to assess the effectiveness of these initiatives and to generalize about the current strength of public service trade unionism. In each trade union, the relationship between leadership and policymaking at national, regional and branch levels, and the day-to-day consultation and negotiations involving workplace union representatives and managers, is complex (Fairbrother 2000). The co-ordination of union activities and the provision of external support for local initiatives are therefore difficult, and are complicated further by multi-unionism (e.g. in the NHS). Moreover, the differences in trade union practice between the civil service, the NHS and local authorities are exceeded by variations in the character of workplace employment relations within each of these sectors. It is thus not surprising that some studies have found evidence of strong workplace organization effectively supported by union officials, while other research findings have identified examples of chronic trade union weakness and uncertainty. Furthermore, in some circumstances 'union renewal' may be structured around a more active 'partnership' approach with employers, encouraged by the modernization agenda of the Labour government, while elsewhere it may be based on the mobilization of more active members against specific policies of the government or employers.

Conclusions

This chapter has explored the impact of the continuous process of reform on public service employment relations over the last 20 years. It has focused on the political rationale of far-reaching changes in the organization and management of public services, and examined in some detail recent attempts to modernize systems of pay determination. The scope and pace of the reforms initiated by four Conservative governments from 1979 were intensified – albeit in modified forms – by the Labour government of 1997–2001. This disappointed public service employees, managers and trade union officials, most of whom would have welcomed a period of organizational stability and more generous funding so that they might recover from 'reform fatigue'.

The policies of the Labour government were driven partly by short-term recruitment and retention problems for key groups of public sector employees, but also by the need to respond to a widespread perception of a 'public service in crisis'. A constant stream of critical reports on the limited availability and uneven quality of public services was produced by public agencies and pressure groups, and the problems were magnified by opposition parties and the mass media. Trade unions and professional associations contributed actively to this critique of policy, and argued that substantial additional resources were required to increase pay and staffing levels and thus reduce excessive workloads and improve conditions of employment and morale.

The most optimistic interpretation of this critical view of the quality of public services is that it is based on higher expectations than in the past, and that a broad consensus is emerging in support of higher future levels of public expenditure to meet these increasing aspirations. In support of this view, it can be argued that public service provision today is more focused on the needs of 'users' (e.g. patients, pupils and benefit recipients), and that much of the evidence of inadequate service standards emerged mainly as a result of reforms that created more effective forms of accountability and measures of performance. In industrial relations, the piecemeal reform of collective agreements and pay systems often produced benefits for staff, as well as increasing flexibility for managers seeking to improve the quality of labour-intensive services. For the next few years at least, significant increases in public expenditure may also facilitate the implementation of more ambitious pay reforms in local authorities and the NHS, and ameliorate the recruitment and retention problems throughout the public services.

A more pessimistic view of the scale of the problems, and the prospect of successful further reform, can be inferred from the uneasy relationship between government ministers and public service managers. Labour government ministers share the predilection of their predecessors for constant intervention from the centre, often justified as a means of encouraging greater local flexibility and management discretion. The unrelenting stream of initiatives and short-term service targets irritates and disorientates managers, distracting them from medium- and long-term policy development. This problem inhibited the emergence of a more strategic conception of human resource management in many parts of the public service. The Labour government announced ambitious plans to raise the profile of human resource issues (e.g. on equal opportunities and family-friendly policies, especially in the NHS), but the need to use limited managerial and financial resources to deal with day-to-day staffing problems and meet politically sensitive targets inhibited policy development.

Over the last 15 years, the boundaries between public and private sector organization and service provision have changed significantly, and many of the reforms in public service pay systems have been designed to emulate aspects of private sector practice. It can be argued that a partial convergence between private and public sector employment relations has occurred, but the diversity of institutional arrangements and employment practices and outcomes within both sectors seems more notable than the similarities. It is also apparent that the degree of public scrutiny, and the amount of political intervention in key public services, has no equivalent in the private sector. This public scrutiny is likely to continue to influence change in employment relations.

References

Arrowsmith, J., and Mossé, P. 2000: Hospital reform and the working time of hospital nurses in England and France, *European Journal of Industrial Relations*, 6 (3), 283–307.

Arrowsmith, J., and Sisson, K. 2000: Working time. In S. Bach and K. Sisson (eds), *Personnel Management: A Comprehensive Guide to Theory and Practice*, 3rd edn. Oxford: Blackwell.

Audit Commission 2001a: *Changing Gear: Best Value Annual Statement 2001*. London: Audit Commission. Available at <www.audit-commission.gov.uk>.

Audit Commission 2001b: *Brief Encounters: Getting the Best from Temporary Nursing Staff.* London: Audit Commission.

Bach, S. 1999a: From national pay determination to qualified market relations: NHS pay bargaining reform, *Historical Studies in Industrial Relations*, 8, 99–115.

Bach, S. 1999b: Personnel managers: managing to change? In S. Corby and G. White (eds), *Employee Relations in the Public Services.* London: Routledge.

Bach, S., and Della Rocca, G. 2000: The management strategies of public service employers in Europe, *Industrial Relations Journal*, 31 (2), 82–96.

Bach, S., and Winchester, D. 1994: Opting out of pay devolution? Prospects for local pay bargaining in UK public services, *British Journal of Industrial Relations*, 32 (2), 263–82.

Cabinet Office 1999: *Modernising Government.* Cm 4310. London: Stationery Office.

Carter, B., and Fairbrother, P. 1999: The transformation of British public sector industrial relations: from model employer to marketized relations, *Historical Studies in Industrial Relations*, 7, 119–46.

Colling, T. 1999: Tendering and outsourcing: working in the contract state? In S. Corby and G. White (eds), *Employee Relations in the Public Services.* London: Routledge.

DfES (Department for Education and Skills) 2001: *Database of Teacher Records.* Available at <http://www.dfes.gov.uk>.

DoH (Department of Health) 2000: *The NHS Plan.* Cm 4818-I. London: Department of Health.

DoH 2001: *NHS Hospital and Community Health Services Non-Medical Staff in England: 1990–2000.* London: Department of Health.

Duncan, C. 2001: The impact of two decades of reform of British public sector industrial relations, *Public Money & Management* (January–March), 27–34.

Elliott, R., and Duffus, K. 1996: What has been happening to pay in the public-service sector of the British economy? Developments over the period 1970–92, *British Journal of Industrial Relations*, 34 (1), 51–85.

Emmott, M. 2001: Woeful in Whitehall, *People Management*, 8 February, 39–40.

EOC (Equal Opportunities Commission) 2001: *Women and Men in Britain: Professional Occupations.* Manchester: EOC. Available at <www.eoc.org.uk>.

Equal Opportunities Review 2000: *Women in the Unions*, 94 (November/ December), 34.

Fairbrother, P. 2000: *Trade Unions at the Crossroads.* London: Mansell.

Foster, D., and Scott, P. 1998: Competitive tendering of public services and industrial relations policy: the Conservative agenda under Thatcher and Major, 1979–97, *Historical Studies in Industrial Relations*, 6, 101–32.

Green, F. 2001: It's been a hard day's night: the concentration and intensification of work in late-twentieth century Britain, *British Journal of Industrial Relations*, 39 (1), 53–80.

Grimshaw, D. 1999: Changes in skills-mix and pay determination among the nursing workforce in the UK, *Work, Employment and Society*, 13 (2), 295–328.

Hatchett, A. 2001: A test of determination, *People Management*, 8 February, 36–9.

Hegewisch, A. 1999: Employment flexibility: push or pull? In S. Corby and G. White (eds), *Employee Relations in the Public Services.* London: Routledge.

IDS (Incomes Data Services) 1996: Public sector labour market survey. *IDS Report*, 725, 25–30.

IDS 1999: Public sector labour market survey. *IDS Report*, 799, 10–19.

IDS 2001a: Pay in central government. *IDS Report*, 826, 15–21.

IDS 2001b: Public sector pay in 2001. *IDS Report*, 839, 8–15.

IRS (Industrial Relations Services) 1998: Goodbye CCT. *Employment Trends*, 647 (January), 5–11.

IRS 2000a: Merit malaise: performance pay in the public sector. *Pay and Benefits Bulletin*, 493, 5–10.

IRS 2000b: Civil service pay: from individual to team reward. *Pay and Benefits Bulletin*, 499, 5–9.

Kessler, I. 1993: Pay determination in the British civil service since 1979. *Public Administration*, 71 (3), 301–18.

MacGregor, D. 2001: Jobs in the public and private sectors, *Economic Trends*, 571, 35–50.

Makinson, J. 2000: *Incentives for Change: Rewarding Performance in National Government*. London: Treasury.

Marsden, D., and French, S. 1998: *What a Performance: Performance-Related Pay in the Public Services*. London: Centre for Economic Performance, LSE.

Martin, S. 2000: Implementing 'Best Value': local public services in transition, *Public Administration*, 78 (1), 209–27.

Morgan, P., Allington, N. and Heery, E. 2000: Employment insecurity in the public services. In E. Heery and J. Salmon (eds), *The Insecure Workforce*. London: Routledge.

Morris, G. 2000: Employment in public services: the case for special treatment. *Oxford Journal of Legal Studies*, 20 (2), 167–83.

Mullard, M. 2001: New Labour, new public expenditure: the case of cake tomorrow, *The Political Quarterly*, 72 (3), 310–21.

NPRB (Nurses' Pay Review Body) 1998: *Fifteenth Report*. Cm 3832. London: HMSO.

Pendleton, A. 1997: What impact has privatisation had on pay and employment? A review of the UK experience. *Relations Industrielles*, 52 (3), 554–79.

RCN (Royal College of Nursing) 2001: *Evidence to the Review Body for 2002*. London: RCN. Available at <www.rcn.org.uk>.

Self, P. 2000: *Rolling Back the Market. Economic Dogma and Political Choice*. London: Macmillan.

Sly, F., and Stillwell, D. 1997: Temporary workers in Great Britain, *Labour Market Trends*, September, 347–54.

Sneade, A. 2001: Trade union membership 1999–2000: an analysis of data from the Certification Officer and the Labour Force Survey, *Labour Market Trends*, September, 433–44.

STRB (School Teachers' Review Body) 2001: *Tenth Report*. Cm 4990. London: Stationery Office. Available at <http://www.dfee.gov.uk>.

Thornley, C., Ironside, M. and Seifert, R. 2000: UNISON and changes in collective bargaining in health and local government. In M. Terry (ed.), *Redefining Public Sector Unionism: UNISON and the Future of Trade Unions*. London: Routledge.

Treasury 1998: *Modernising Public Services for Britain: Investing in Reform*. Cm 4011. London: Stationery Office.

Treasury 2000: *Public Private Partnerships: The Government's Approach*. London: Stationery Office. Available at <www.hm-treasury.gov.uk>.

UNISON 2000: *Contracting Out and the Two-Tier Workforce*. London: UNISON.

White, G. 1999: The remuneration of public servants: fair pay or new pay? In S. Corby and G. White (eds), *Employee Relations in the Public Services*. London: Routledge.

White, G. 2000. The pay review body system: its development and impact, *Historical Studies in Industrial Relations*, 9, 71–100.

Winchester, D. 1983: Industrial relations in the public sector. In G. Bain (ed.), *Industrial Relations in Britain*. Oxford: Blackwell.

12

INDIVIDUALISM AND COLLECTIVISM IN INDUSTRIAL RELATIONS

IAN KESSLER AND JOHN PURCELL

Over recent years the distinction between individualism and collectivism has come to form one of the key axes along which debates among industrial relations academics, as well as policymakers and practitioners, have been conducted. The starting point for these debates has often been, as discussed in chapters 5 and 8, the apparent unravelling of an industrial relations system based on state-sponsored collective principles and voluntary collective employer and employee institutions. This unravelling has exposed and indeed to a considerable extent been driven by a preference amongst certain key actors for alternative means of regulating the employment relationship, in particular those founded on a direct and unmediated relationship between the employer and the individual employee.

However, beyond this point of departure, discussion on the balance between individualism and collectivism has been wide-ranging and contested. These key terms and related developments have been subject to varying interpretations and have been used in often contrasting ways by different types of literature falling more or less directly within mainstream industrial relations. More specifically, debates have tended to address three main themes. First, attention has been given to the nature of collectivism and individualism. This is largely a definitional and conceptual exercise constituting an essential foundation for the meaningful consideration of any reconfiguration of employment relations. What aspects or dimensions of the employment relationship are captured by the terms? Second, interest has concentrated on the extent and character of any change in the relationship between individualism and collectivism and why it might have taken place. Has there, for example, been a shift away from particular forms of collectivism and if so, what has this shift been towards? How have social, political and economic factors of a structural, attitudinal and behavioural kind interacted to stimulate change? Finally, concern has focused on the respective roles played by the main industrial relations actors in the process of change. To what extent have employees, trade unions, the state and more especially employers driven change and how has change impacted upon these actors?

This chapter seeks to address these questions. It utilizes the notions of individualism and collectivism as a means of characterizing management style and evaluating how such style has developed in recent years. The term 'management style' is designed to highlight the possibility that managers, as agents of the employing organization, are able to exercise some degree of choice in the fundamental approaches to the way employees are managed, although, as we shall show, all choices are constrained and influenced by environmental factors and the actions and reactions of the other parties to the employment relationship (see the discussion of rules and negotiation in chapter 1). More specifically, the chapter first provides a conceptual framework to define management style in terms of individualism and collectivism. It then uses this framework to evaluate the extent and nature of shifts in the expressed preferences and choices of certain key industrial relations actors – employees, unions and employers – as they relate to management style. Finally it considers evidence on actual and current management practice as a reflection of this style.

It will be argued that the relationship between individualism and collectivism or the prevailing management style represents a configuration of preferences and choices among industrial relations actors embedded in a particular set of social, economic and political circumstances which both shape the nature of these preferences and choices and the power available to the respective parties to impose them. As circumstances have changed in Britain so have expressed preferences and the ability of different stakeholders to assert them through the choices they have made.

A shift from a management style largely based on adversarial collectivism has been accompanied by the emergence of alternative prescriptive models based on union exclusion combined with high-commitment management practices, or on a more co-operative relationship with the unions again complemented by a high-commitment approach to the individual employee. However, there is very limited evidence to indicate that either model has been widely adopted, with opportunistic and cost-driven management approaches to employment relations largely predominating. While changing conditions may have provided new choices, these very same conditions have allowed management to fall back on an almost atavistic preference for the assertion of its prerogative at the workplace. This pursuit of managerial prerogative, sometimes combined with the practical and normative difficulties faced by organizations in disentangling themselves from well-established and embedded ways of regulating the employment relationship, has often undermined the meaningful development of partnership arrangements with the unions and weakened the purposeful implementation of 'softer', commitment approaches.

Definitions and Meanings

An 'ism' is 'a body or system of principles and practices' (*New Oxford Dictionary of English*, 1998). This is a useful starting point for an understanding of the terms individualism and collectivism, for it raises questions about the subject of such principles and practices, who holds and adopts them, and what substantive form they take. Recent conceptualizations of these questions can be traced directly to the work of Fox (1974), who was one of the first researchers to focus on management ideology and strategy in an industrial relations context. Fox highlights the importance of frames of reference as a mean of understanding the attitudes and behaviours of managers and indeed employees at the workplace. These frames comprise certain perceptions mediating action and rooted in specific assumptions, beliefs and values related to the nature of organizations, how they operate and the place of employees and managers within them. Two predominant frames are distinguished, one based on unitarism and the other on pluralism.

The unitarist frame of reference is founded upon a presumed harmony of interest between employees and management and therefore an assumption of shared goals, so denying the legitimacy of conflict and any group or groups which might express it. In contrast, the pluralist frame of reference recognizes the inevitability of diverse employee and management interests related to competition over the allocation of scarce resources such as time, reward and effort. As a consequence, it accepts different goals and the legitimacy of conflict, and of groups and processes which might articulate and regulate it.

The possibility that managers and workers might hold different perspectives encourages Fox (1974: 296) to elaborate on the unitarist–pluralist distinction by identifying a range of potential patterns of management–employee relations. These are:

- *traditional* (unitary perspective on the part of both management and employees);
- *classical conflict* (unitarist management and pluralist employees, the former displaying a deep-rooted distrust in their workers and their representative and tending therefore to oppose trade unions);
- *continuous challenge* (unitarist management and pluralist employees, the latter displaying a deep-rooted distrust in their managers as agents of the owners which encourages an ongoing challenge to management prerogative);
- *sophisticated modern* (pluralist perspective on the part of both management and employees);
- *standard modern* (managerial ambivalence and fluctuation between unitarism and pluralism);
- *sophisticated paternalist* (pluralist management and unitarist employees).

The link between the unitarist–pluralist dichotomy and notions of individualism and collectivism has tended to rest on the nature of the relationship between interests and representation. Individualism has been viewed as closely associated with unitarism in that this frame of reference suggests shared interests and therefore a preference for a relationship between the individual employee and the manager which is direct and unmediated by collective employee representation. Pluralism has been seen as being related to collectivism in that this perspective implies conflicting employee–management interests and consequently a preference for collective institutions and procedures in the form of trade unions and collective bargaining or state-sponsored works councils which represent and regulate these conflicting interests. Seen in these terms unitarism/individualism and pluralism/collectivism emerge as mutually exclusive: interests are either shared or they are not; collective mechanisms are either present or they are not.

More recently, however, it has been argued that the tendency to equate unitarism with individualism and pluralism with collectivism in this way fails to do justice to the complexity of management approaches as they relate to the individual and the collective at the workplace (Purcell 1987). Interpreted in a somewhat broader and more refined sense, notions of individualism and collectivism have increasingly been used to characterize distinct but related dimensions of the employment relationship. More specifically, Purcell and various colleagues (Purcell and Sisson 1983; Purcell and Ahlstrand 1994) have presented individualism and collectivism as complementary rather than mutually exclusive approaches. Thus, individualism directs attention to how employers manage the individual employee while collectivism encourages a focus on how employers address and deal with collective or representative institutions. In short, managers in most organizations need to decide on how they deal with *both* the individual employee and the collective, representative organization. The way in which approaches to the individual and the collective are combined has come to be conceptualized as management style.

Purcell and Ahlstrand's (1994) style matrix represents an attempt at further refinement, by characterizing the different approaches that might be adopted to the treatment of the individual and the collective. Thus, along each dimension three options or choices are distinguished. Collectivism might take the form of union absence or a non-union situation; an adversarial relationship based on an ongoing but institutionalized conflict between unions and management; or a co-operative relationship where clearly unions and management develop more consensual relations and seek shared means to pursue their objectives. Individualism might take the form of cost minimization with the worker being utilized in a 'hard' and efficient way; paternalism with staff welfare to the fore; or a high-commitment approach with employees being treated as a resource to be developed in an effective and supportive manner. These different options are presented in the management style matrix (figure 12.1).

It can be seen that combining different approaches to the individual and the collective in this way gives rise to a number of substantive management styles. A non-union approach along the collective dimension combines with different orientations toward the individual employee to provide three management styles: *traditional*, where cost minimization leads to low pay and low job security and a fear of and hostility towards the union which might challenge this situation; *paternalist*, with an 'enlightened' management approach to the employee, albeit viewed in a dependent and subordinate way, rendering the union an irrelevance; and *sophisticated human relations*, where a developmental approach to the employee is designed to meet all employment needs and aspirations, fostering loyalty and making union representation simply unnecessary.

An adversarial relationship with the union in association with a cost-driven or paternalistic approach to the individual leads to *bargained constitutionalism*. This is

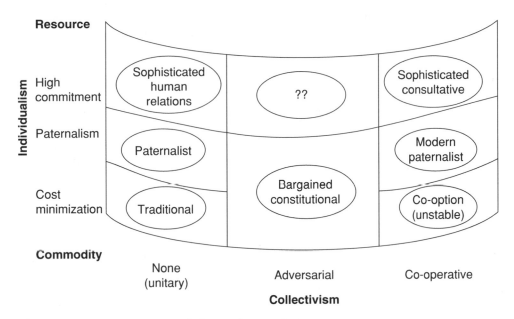

Figure 12.1   Management style in employee relations

Source: © John Purcell and Bruce Ahlstrand 1994. Reprinted from *Human Resource Management in the Multidivisional Company* by John Purcell and Bruce Ahlstrand (1994) by permission of Oxford University Press.

characterized by highly developed formal negotiating procedures and mechanisms designed to regulate and facilitate the purposeful and effective pursuit of distinctive employee and management interests. However, where adversarialism is combined with a high-commitment approach to the individual, an unstable situation is likely to arise. The treatment of the employee in a 'caring' way does not sit easily with conflictual union relations. In such circumstances, management is either seeking to exclude the union or develop a more co-operative relationship with it.

Finally, a co-operative approach to the union gives rise to three further possible styles. In combination with a cost-driven approach to the individual it generates *co-option*. While unions may well be reluctant to co-operate with management where employees are being treated as a cost, there are circumstances where management might seek such involvement, say in cases of redundancy or restructuring, as a means of legitimizing and facilitating their activity. Where co-operation is underpinned by paternalism (*modern paternalism*) unions are more likely to play a role in influencing rather than determining decisions, with involvement taking the form of consultation as opposed to negotiation. Finally, in association with a high-commitment approach, co-operation with the union is conceptualized as a *sophisticated consultative* style. In this case unions and management are assumed to have a shared interest in supporting and developing the individual employee, consequently seeking joint means and solutions to this end.

These refinements and the related matrix have been subject to some critical comment. For example, Marchington and Parker (1990) find that in practice management treatment of both the individual and the collective, the union, can contain aspects of all three approaches on the respective dimensions. This leads them to a reconstituted analytical scheme based on continua related to the degree to which managers invest in staff (high–low) and adopt a partnership approach to unions (high–low). Nonetheless, this critique does not undermine the fundamental principle underpinning the Purcell and Ahlstrand matrix, which is management's need to address both the individual employee and the collective in the form of the union. The matrix, therefore, retains its value in generating a number of important issues at micro- and macro-levels which have been pursued with varying degrees of explicitness and intensity by industrial relations researchers.

First, and at the micro- or firm level, the identification of different style options raises the issue of whether any given organization adopts more than one such style. More specifically, will an organization pursue different styles for, say, different occupational groups? In Atkinson's (1984) work on the flexible firm, for example, there is a prescriptive assumption that 'core' workers should be treated in a developmental way or, in the language of the style matrix, a high-commitment manner, in contrast to 'peripheral' employees who should be dealt with more as a cost to be minimized. More recently, Lepak and Snell (1999: 45) have made a similar point, noting that, although 'some firms may manage all employees in the same way, regardless of their value and uniqueness, we anticipate that most firms make significant distinctions in the methods they use for different skill sets'. Certainly, there is strong empirical evidence to suggest that the incidence of particular employment policies and practices does vary by occupational group. Thus, WERS highlights the fact that managerial and professional staff are much more likely to have off-the-job training and performance appraisal than clerical staff and operatives (Cully et al. 1999: 60–72).

Second, and partly related, the changing shape of companies with the emergence of the 'extended' organization (Colling 2000) raises questions about which management one is talking about when referring to management style. Thus the increasing use of contractors and outsourcers at a given workplace suggests that at any given point in time styles from a number of different 'managements' might be 'in play' (Rubery et al. 2000). Outsourcing and contracting out appear to be increasing in many sectors (Cully et al. 1999; Colling 2000), while case-study evidence from the local government sector, for example, has highlighted the managerial issues and tensions that can arise where staff work in the same organization but for different employers with contrasting styles (Kessler et al. 1999).

Third, the style matrix directs attention towards variation in management style across space or, more specifically, across organizations in the British economy at any point in time. Thus the matrix explicitly envisages the predominance of different management styles according to sector, product market, technology and ownership patterns (Purcell and Ahlstrand, 1994; Kessler and Purcell, 1995). For example, the traditional style might be viewed as fairly common in some labour-intensive contract or franchise firms as well as in the hotel and catering industry; sophisticated human relations has often been seen to characterize American electronic or information firms and high-technology and professional service organizations; while bargained constitutionalism has typically been found in the public service sector as well as in mass production or large batch manufacturing firms.

Finally, the matrix encourages an interest in not only variation of style across space but also shifts in style over time. It is crucial to recognize that management style represents a contingent set of preferences. In other words, a range of social, political, economic and technical factors combine to influence power relations between the main industrial actors, encouraging a stable but potentially fragile configuration of preferences. A shift in circumstances can readily alter power relations, leading to a new configuration of preferences or management style. Figure 12.2 provides some indication of the various kinds of movement in management style which might occur at organizational or micro-level. However, this chapter focuses more broadly on shifts in preferences at the systemic level. The style matrix appears well suited to this task.

Debate on recent developments in industrial relations has been framed in terms which equate quite closely with those presented in the style matrix. For example, in relation to collectivism, discussion has often focused on shifts from adversarial to co-operative relations between management and unions, while competing views on the treatment of the individual have concentrated on whether labour should be treated as a cost, exposed to the full force of market pressures, or as a key resource internalized, protected and developed. The application of this conceptual framework to shifts in the pattern of management style in British industrial relations comprises a number of parts. Initially consideration needs to be given to the expressed preferences or the espoused rhetoric of the main industrial relations actors. The matrix helps us map any move in these style preferences. Once shifts in expressed preferences have been outlined consideration can be given to whether practice supports this rhetoric.

Shifting Preferences?

As discussed in chapter 2, the predominant British management style was premised on collectivism but a distinctive form of collectivism based on adversarial rather than co-operative union–management relations. The treatment of the individual employee was typically cost-driven or to a lesser extent paternalistic. In other words, the predominant style in terms of the matrix was a form of bargained constitutionalism. The dramatic unravelling of this system, particularly along the collective dimension, is now difficult to contest (see chapters 8 and 9). There has been considerable debate on the causes of the shift away from adversarial collectivism and whether indeed this shift is irreversible or simply part of cycle of events (Heery 1996; Kelly 1998). It has been suggested that change has been driven more by fundamental changes in the structure of industry, product markets and workforces than by the expression of new actor preferences. Yet shifts in the balance of power caused by such changes have allowed the main industrial relations actors to alter their preferences as they relate to the principles and practices associated with individualism and collectivism.

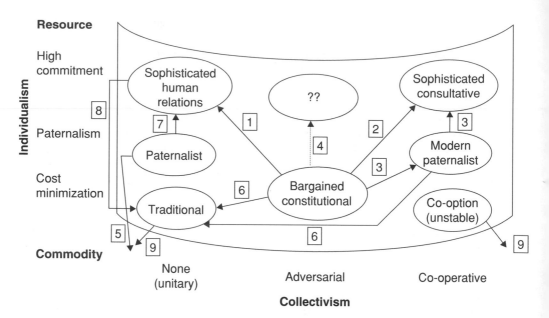

Figure 12.2 Changes in management style in employee relations

Source: © John Purcell and Bruce Ahlstrand 1994. Reprinted from *Human Resource Management in the Multidivisional Company* by John Purcell and Bruce Ahlstrand (1994) by permission of Oxford University Press.

Notes

1 Employees encouraged to sign new contracts and union recognition for bargaining purposes withdrawn. New work practices, recruitment, selection, appraisal and training initiatives implemented in accordance with high-commitment management.

2 Co-operative, consultative relations with trade unions/works councils/company councils developed alongside the introduction of high-commitment-type policies.

3 Co-operative, consultative relations initiated with unions as a prelude to subsequent initiatives to introduce high-commitment management. The new relationship is often triggered by a crisis in the competitive position of the firm such that choice is forced. Competitive analysis reveals that the strength of the major firms in the market is based in part on high-commitment management.

4 Unstable conditions exist as unions are bypassed in the change programme to introduce high-commitment management policies. Subsequently either union membership declines and recognition is withdrawn, or both unions and management 'learn' to modify their behaviour to each other to emphasize partnership, or initiatives fail and the bargained constitutional pattern is reinforced.

5 Growing competition, falling profit margins and declining market share force a reappraisal of employment policies leading to the introduction of cost minimization, reduction in job security and reduced employee benefits.

6 A new tough regime is introduced often triggered by a change in ownership, competitive tendering, subcontracting or acquisition. Union recognition is withdrawn and cost minimization policies reinforced, with employees working under worse conditions.

7 Emphasis placed on employee productivity achieved through high-commitment policies and technical change based on a realization that it is desirable to encourage employees to use diagnostic skills and their knowledge for the benefit of the business and to satisfy customers.

8 Rapidly falling market share in a depressed or mature market leading to substantial loss of profitability forces major reappraisal of employment policies. A change in top management is often a precursor to the abandonment of the high-commitment policies, and substantial cuts in employee investment.

9 Cost pressures and benchmarking lead to outsourcing of functions (catering/IT/transport/documentation/payroll etc.) and/or insourcing of certain types of labour, usually low- or generic-skilled. Specific organizational knowledge is not needed.

The intensification of product market competition, and particularly the mobility of capital across borders, has fundamentally shifted the balance of power in favour of management. However, the past and present preferences of other key actors have played a crucial part in influencing management style. Indeed, Howell (1995) suggests that the rapid demise of a century-long tradition of British collectivism over barely a generation can only be explained by the distinctive character of state intervention in the UK and a trade union movement which had chosen to organize and act in ways which made it particularly vulnerable when the character of that intervention changed. State preferences are covered in earlier chapters of this volume. Attention will therefore focus here on union and employee preferences before moving on to those of management.

Union and employee preferences

Any understanding of union preferences and choices raises issues related to the nature of employee affiliation to the union (Newton and Shore 1992) and more specifically directs attention to what employees seek and expect from their union and, perhaps in a broader sense, from collective action. In important respects the notions of individualism and collectivism as embodied in the style matrix do not do justice to the complex interaction between employee, member and union preferences, suggesting the need to briefly revisit the meanings attached to these terms.

In this context, individualism is perhaps the more pivotal of the two terms. Thus, in wider debates on social developments the notion of individualism has been seen as one of the defining characteristics of (late) modernity (Giddens 1991; Beck 1992), with the suggestion that established identities, loyalties and structures are breaking down, leaving the employee or citizen isolated and atomized. Although part of a wider sociological debate on the nature of the modern condition, changes in the labour market have been seen as a key feature of and contributor to this growing individualization. As Beck (1992: 142) notes, the 'individual situations that come into existence are thoroughly dependent on the labour market'. He continues, 'the system of standardized full employment is beginning to soften and fray at the margins into flexibilization of its three supporting pillars: labour law, work site and working hours'. These views echo those voiced in a mainstream employment relations context by Phelps Brown (1990), who suggested that the growing strength of individual values in the light of social, economic and political change had undermined the traditional collectivism of British industrial relations.

The assumptions informing some of these pronouncements, particularly those related to the individualization of the labour market, remain questionable. For instance, the implication that employees have become more dispersed and isolated in the labour market with the emergence of new forms of employment such as teleworking, casualization and other types of contingent working finds limited empirical support. While these forms of employment have been increasing, they still cover only a very small proportion of the workforce (Casey et al. 1997). Nonetheless, it remains important to distinguish between the different ways in which the notion of individualism within this broader social context has informed debates in the industrial relations sphere, and especially those linked to an assessment of employee, member and union preferences and choices.

First, an emphasis on individualism raises questions about the propensity of employees to join and remain members of a trade union; in other words, do employees prefer to pursue their goals through individual rather than through collective effort? A number of years ago Edwards (1986) distinguished between individual and collective worker orientations, acknowledging that combining and acting in concert with colleagues is by no means the only employee option. In this sense individualism might be seen to constitute the non-union option on the collective dimension of the style matrix. Clearly, such unitarism is not a meaningful union preference, although any reluctance on the part of employees to join or remain within the union is an issue the union would need to face.

Consideration of employee preferences to join and stay with the union in the context of declining union membership and as a reflection of a broader societal trend towards individualism relates to wider debates on the causes of this decline and the relative influence of structural, attitudinal and behavioural factors. Such debates are largely beyond the scope of this chapter, although the specific question of whether employees are generally inclined to join union remains very much open. While public support for unions appears to have increased (Bryson 1999), evidence on employee orientations towards trade unions needs to be treated with some care. Thus various surveys (Gallie 1996; Cully et al. 1999; Bryson 1999) have suggested that existing members have a fairly positive view about their union in terms of its workplace influence and activity, while non-union members in unionized workplaces and employees in non-union organizations are less supportive.

In analytical and conceptual terms, consideration of employee preferences to join and remain within a union has reawakened interest in the contingent nature of collective action. This is implied in Edwards's (1986: 227) work, but has more recently been used to challenge the assumptions underpinning the drift towards individualization. As Hyman notes:

> The plausibility of the disaggregation thesis depends heavily on a mythologized vision of the past: a golden age when workers were spontaneously collective and labour organizations joined ranks in a unifying class project. History of course was never like this. (1992: 159)

Indeed, the problematic and contingent nature of collective action has encouraged the search for frameworks helping to explain the process by which it emerges. Thus, Marchington (1982: 97) and more recently Kelly (1998), drawing upon Tilly's mobilization theory, have used similar frameworks to suggest that collective action requires the identification of shared interests and the willingness and ability to organize in meaningful pursuit of such interests, which in turn is associated with relative power resources.

The notion of individualism has also informed debates on employee and union preferences and choices in terms of the underlying purpose or meaning of union

membership. In this respect, a crude distinction can be made between individualism beyond and within the 'factory gates'. The style matrix does not directly
cover the individualistic rationale for union membership beyond the 'factory
gates'. However, it can be seen as represented in a view of the union as a
provider of individual member services covered in greater detail in chapter 9 of
this volume.

Within the 'factory gates' we are back on the 'home territory' of the style
matrix with its familiar distinction between different forms of individualism.
Thus, within this context, consideration might be given to whether employees
and, where appropriate, their unions seek the 'relational' relationship (MacNeil
1985) with the organization implied by the high-commitment approach to the
individual, or the 'transactional' relationship suggested by the cost-minimization
approach.

The research on employee, member and union preferences can be characterized in a number of ways. First, it has concentrated primarily on the preferences
of union members and has not therefore touched on the preferences of employees more generally. It has usually asked union members why they joined
and why they have retained union membership, tending not to pose questions
to non-members on, for example, why they remain outside the union and what
might encourage them to join. Second, it has tended to equate individualism
in this context with a member preference for the union as a provider of individual member services rather than with how they are treated at the workplace.
Information on member perceptions of management strategies towards the
individual employee remains limited. This focus on individual member services
has typically been juxtaposed with a collective union orientation focused on the
pursuit of workplace issues and more particularly those concerned with terms and
conditions of employment. Finally, the research has essentially been concerned
with ends rather than means, in that it has sought member views on substantive union goals or aims rather than on how they might be achieved. Member
views on adversarial and more co-operative union approaches have not therefore
generally been sought.

Structured and conceptualized in this way, such research (Williams 1997;
Waddington and Kerr 1999) has highlighted the ongoing importance of traditional collective goals tied to improved terms and conditions as more important
in recruiting and retaining members than the provision of individual services.
Indeed, Waddington and Whitston (1997: 539) conclude from the most extensive survey of member preferences that there is

> little support (for) those arguing that individualization has dissolved the labour
> movement since 1979. On the contrary, collective reasons remain central to union
> joining and individual services are secondary to the joining process.

Combined with the finding, also common to much of this work, that solidaristic
and ideological goals do not figure prominently alongside an interest in the
union pursuit of improved terms and conditions, these results might be interpreted as reflecting the continuity of an 'instrumental collectivism' seen by Fox

(1985) as traditionally characterizing British unionism, and confirmed over the years by findings on the orientation of specific groups of employee such as Roberts et al.'s (1972) 'reluctant militants'. It is a view which finds further expression in Hyman's observation that:

> While trade union activists and ideologues may have traditionally viewed collectivism as a moral value in its own right, it is perhaps realistic to assume that – apart from moments of enthusiasm of mass mobilization – most union members have adhered to collective organization for instrumental reasons: the most effective means of realizing individual needs and aspirations. (1992: 160)

This analysis presents the recently articulated union preference for a new approach to joint workplace relations in an interesting light. While views have varied within and between unions, these preferences have tended to coalesce around a partnership model sponsored by key policymakers such as the TUC and actively pursued by the leadership of certain unions, including the GMB, UNIFI, AEU, and USDAW. This model can be seen be seen as corresponding fairly unambiguously with a 'sophisticated consultation' style of management with its preference for co-operative rather than adversarial collective relations and for high-commitment rather than cost-driven individual employment practices. Thus it is an approach apparently based on a degree of reciprocity involving, for example, union endorsement of greater employee flexibility in return for great job security and more supportive employee policies. As the TUC general secretary John Monks (1994) has noted, unions have nothing to fear, and indeed would welcome a management approach recognizing the value of employees and consequently treating them in a supportive way:

> Human resource management as described in business school theory apparently has much to commend it the union movement. Treating workers as assets rather than factors of production, developing a wider range of communication systems, involving employees in the organization and planning of their work are laudable objectives.

This partnership approach makes some quite significant assumptions about the nature of employee and member workplace interests. As noted, our knowledge of the relative preference amongst workers for a cost-driven or 'transactional' relationship with the organization as opposed to high-commitment or 'relational' one remains fairly limited. Certainly classic studies, for instance by Goldthorpe et al. (1968), have warned against the assumption that employees are necessarily seeking the latter type of relationship. At the same time, internal union research by the GMB, for example, has highlighted the importance attached by its members to developmental or work-related issues, perhaps accounting for the observations of its general secretary John Edmonds, who noted that:

> What we are trying to do is construct a system based on the concept of social partnership, where non-wage issues such as training, promotion, job satisfaction and development are very important. (quoted in Mitchell 1998: 30)

Union sponsorship of a partnership or sophisticated consultant model, with its emphasis on a more conciliatory, joint problem-solving approach, also makes assumptions about the preferred means by which members see their goals as being pursued. Again as stressed above, there is limited evidence available on how members view their interests as being best advanced. It might be argued that the 'instrumental collectivism' of British trade unionists precludes a major concern with means as long as desired ends are achieved. Indeed, social partnership might simply be interpreted as a pragmatic union response to new and more difficult circumstances. The approach becomes more contentious, however, where some blurring or diminishing of worker and management interests is assumed and where the ability of employees to advance their goals is seen as compromised.

Management preferences

The scope for employers to pursue their preferred style of management will be constrained by a range of structural, historical and demographic factors. Indeed, it is noteworthy that moves away from collectivism, as reflected in non-unionism, are most marked in greenfield sites relatively unconstrained by the past or inertia (Millward et al. 1992), although even in these circumstances instances of constraint are available. Thus the Japanese companies setting up in Wales and the north-east still felt the need to grant union recognition, albeit often on a single-union basis, given regional traditions and employee expectations (see chapter 4). Accepting these constraints, it is nonetheless apparent that with the shift in public policy towards an emphasis on managerial discretion in the selection of a 'suitable' style and the relative power resources at the disposal of employers, increasing attention needs to be paid to management choices. As Millward et al. (2000: 236) have stated, 'our most likely expectation is that the economy will continue to generate more workplaces in which the nature of the employment relationship is almost exclusively a matter for managerial choice'.

In exploring the way in which this choice has been exercised it is naturally important to distinguish between an expressed preference and the exercise of that preference as a choice. Certainly in terms of expressed managerial preference, this has not always been clearly or consistently expressed. There have been some calls for a move towards non-union forms of individualism, particularly among key employer organizations. Howell (1995: 163) notes how in the late 1980s the Institute of Directors called for:

> the almost complete individualization of industrial relations, meaning individual pay contracts and merit pay in place of national agreements and collective bargaining, employee shareholding, individualized training, and either the elimination of any role for the trade unions or a minimalist role in which trade unions provide services for their members but do not engage in collective bargaining and have a limited right to strike.

As Howell (1995: 163) continues, 'the Confederation of British Industry is scarcely less radical with its call for an "individualization of workplace relations"'.

However, some care is needed in equating these general peak-level prescriptions with the preferences of actual managers. Indeed, managerial views on trade unions rarely appear to be characterized by hostility, tending to range more between neutrality and acceptance. Cully et al. (1999) found that only 5 per cent of managers were not in favour of union membership, with the rest being fairly evenly split between acceptance (54 per cent) and neutrality (41 per cent). Moreover, once recognized, unions are more likely to be seen by managers as contributing to organizational well-being than undermining it. Over 40 per cent of managers agreed that unions helped find ways to improve performance with under a third (30 per cent) disagreeing.

There also appears to be a difference in the forms of individualism being advocated by management. Specifically, two forms can be distinguished. The first might be seen as an integrative form based on employee development and revolving around what have been labelled high-commitment practices. The list used in the Workplace Employment Relations Survey (Cully et al. 1999) provides an indication of the kind of practices covered and includes the use of personality and performance tests, formal off-the-job training, profit-related pay, employee share-ownership schemes, regular appraisal, autonomous work groups, single status, guaranteed job security and group-based team-briefing and problem-solving groups. Such practices do not necessarily undermine collectivism, and WERS famously found that they were more common in union than non-union workplaces.

However, as practices which seek to change employee attitudes, their intended effect on unionism may be more pernicious. It was Guest (1989) who pointed out that, of all the 'human resource management' goals, commitment was the one that posed the greatest threat to unions in seeking to create the company as the single and unambiguous source of worker loyalty. While dual commitment has been found amongst employees in certain circumstances (Deery and Walsh, 1999), the power of these practices to create this kind of allegiance is perhaps heightened when harnessed to calls for a culture-driven approach to the management of staff. Such an approach seeks to create shared company values and has led Provis (1996) to distinguish between 'interest unitarism' and 'value unitarism', the latter arguably being a more potent management strategy, locking employees into the organization less through economically rational and instrumental means and more through emotional and normative mechanisms. In the long run, then, high-commitment practices may undermine the perceived need for unions.

This integrative and inclusive individualism is very different from the second form of individualism within management rhetoric, which sees the individual employee as much more disembodied or detached from the organization. In other words, it is an individualism which has its foundation beyond the boundaries of the firm and is based much more on self-direction on the part of the employee and, some have argued, on notions of identity-formation (Madsen 1997). As the human resources manager for Mobil UK has noted:

> A neo liberal view of the world has forced people to see what is right for the individual employee. Where previously it was a corporate identity for the person,

now it is an individual identity. The centre of gravity has shifted towards the employee and his or her needs. (*Personnel Today* 1998)

Thus management may be forced to respond to an individual's lifestyle approach, reflecting a desired home–work balance. More typically perhaps, it represents an attempt by management to shuffle off its traditional responsibilities onto the employee, placing the onus on workers to shape their own career opportunities in the external labour market. Du Gay (1996: 65) has drawn attention to the CBI call for 'greater individual responsibility on the part of all employees and, in consequence, the development of self-management at all levels' as a necessary accompaniment of the pursuit of lower manning levels and more flexible job specifications needed to improve productivity. As he notes, 'the message is clear: the free ride is over, you're on your own. From now on it's up to individuals to secure their own futures through their own efforts.'

This type of individualism does not readily fall within the style matrix but is partly reflected in figure 12.2 by arrows where employment is externalized. It does not necessarily imply a low-investment or commodity-driven approach to the employee. Indeed, one of the most obvious examples of this form of individualism can be seen in the recent prominence given to the notion of employability (Rajan 1997), which in some firms involves a heightened investment in staff training and development as a means of increasing workers' marketability once they have been discarded by the company. In other cases, however, 'employability' is associated with the closure of training departments as individuals are made responsible for their own development, often in their own time. This is reflected in the views of one management commentator, who notes that:

> Individuals wishing to ensure their employability no longer have the option of sitting on their laurels . . . The key to success is continuing professional development and those who fail to act and react will only have themselves to blame. (Young 1995: 5)

This form of individualism does suggest that the treatment of the individual is based on a fragile and finite employee attachment to the organization rather than on attempts to bind the employee into the company for the foreseeable future.

Style in Practice

There is certainly strong evidence to suggest that Britain has moved away from a management style based upon adversarial collectivism. As Millward et al. (2000: 234) state:

> [the] system of collective relations, based on the shared values of the legitimacy of representation by independent trade unions and of joint regulation, [has] crumbled [in the last] eighteen years to such an extent that it no longer represents the dominant model.

There is, however, less evidence to suggest the emergence of a new or pervasive style of management. Millward et al. (2000) remain uncertain as to what British industrial relations has been transformed into. Our review of trends in expressed preferences suggests two potential contemporary outcomes which might readily be located on the style matrix. The first is a co-operative form of collectivism combined with high-commitment management captured, although not exclusively so, by current notions of partnership or, in the terms of the style matrix, a form of sophisticated consultation. The second is a 'soft', 'enlightened' and often inclusive or culture-driven human resource management based on high-commitment management in a non-union environment and seen as sophisticated human relations. However, despite the highlighted rhetoric which has propelled these models to the fore, any examination of practice may well reveal alternative styles. Both models rely upon a high-commitment approach to employees. The failure of such an approach to emerge raises the possibility of management continuing to adopt a cost-minimization approach to its employees. In the context of union withdrawal or exclusion such a style readily becomes characterized in terms of the matrix as a traditional approach.

Evidence as it relates to the sophisticated consultative and then the sophisticated human relations models is presented below. It will be seen that, despite data to suggest that these styles enhance organizational performance (see chapter 19), take-up remains low. Change is clearly slow, incremental and at best patchy. This suggests that barriers to the development of new management styles remain. These barriers can be traced to deeply embedded managerial attitudes and behaviours characterized by a concern with the reassertion of managerial prerogative. As union power weakens and becomes less effective in modifying managerial actions, we are left not with new partnerships where unions remain, or 'enlightened', caring approaches where they do not, but with managerial attempts to reimpose a cost-driven control.

Sophisticated consultative

The search for a sophisticated consultative style would suggest the need for evidence on the presence of employee development or high-commitment practices and on union co-operation in their implementation. Certainly WERS (Cully et al. 1999: 111) found evidence to suggest the presence of high-commitment practices in unionized workplaces. Thus where at least half of the itemized practices were in place, union density averaged 47 per cent, compared with 35 per cent where it was below this number. Moreover, joint negotiation with unions was more likely to take place where over half these practices were present, suggesting perhaps that the introduction of such practices may be related to a degree of union support. Specific examples of union involvement in the development of high-commitment or developmental practices can be cited. Thus, the Korean high-tech company LG electronics has used the AEEU to provide training to managers and staff on new working practices (*Personnel Today* 1999b), while UNIFI, the banking union, has signed a 'learning partnership' for its members at the HSBC. Indeed there is more robust and more general evidence to suggest that union presence is associated with higher levels of training (Green et al. 1999).

The compatibility of high-commitment practices and union presence might be explained in a number of ways. First, the implementation of such practices may well require a considerable degree of trust between employees and management, facilitated and generated by union presence and involvement. In their own right such practices involve a significant departure from established employment relations approaches, but they are also often linked with fundamental changes in the organization of work, necessitating some underlying legitimation which unions can perhaps provide. Indeed, it is noteworthy that in the US major changes in employment and work relations were, with some degree of success, introduced at a number of locations, including at the Ford Cleveland engine plant and Northeast Ohio Council with considerable union support and participation (IRS 1998).

Second, such compatibility may be linked to the fact that the use of a particular practice is not in its own right an indication of management intent. Any given practice may well be used to pursue a wide variety of managerial objectives. In the past there has been a temptation to view certain techniques as indicative of a non-union individualism. This is perhaps most apparent in relation to individual performance-related pay and, to a lesser extent, profit-related pay and share-ownership schemes. Yet, it is clear that these systems are used in very different ways by management (Kessler and Purcell 1995). There are certainly high-profile examples of organizations such as the then British Rail, where the introduction of individual performance-related pay was accompanied by union de-recognition. Moreover, Brown et al. (1998) did find that individual performance-related pay was more likely to be found in non-union than in union organizations. However, union exclusion has rarely been the primary objective of individual performance-related pay (Thompson 1992).

Such schemes have been used to pursue a wide array of goals (Kessler and Purcell 1992). These include recruiting and retaining staff by boosting earnings potential and selectively rewarding; encouraging the development of certain process skills amongst managers such as communication and judgement; and reinforcing and encouraging certain desired attitudes and behaviours often associated with, for example, new product market needs and circumstances. The compatibility of such schemes with union presence is further reflected in continued union involvement in pay determination. This might take the form of negotiation over the size of the general paybill increase or over the revalorization of grade point minima and maxima, leaving management free to distribute pay or movements within grade according to individual performance.

Profit-sharing and employee share-ownership schemes have often been presented as even more directly concerned with creating an alternative source of employee allegiance through linking employee pay to the performance of the company rather than the efforts of the union (Poole 1989). However, in reality these schemes have proved to be much less threatening to unions than individual performance-related pay. Again such schemes have been informed by various managerial objectives. As popularized in the 1980s through the work of

Weitzman (1984), profit-sharing was seen as more about cost minimization than union exclusion, ensuring that companies gave increases when they could afford to do so. It has also been seen as a tax-efficient means of reward, with approved schemes attracting certain tax benefits (Smith 1986).

Moreover, in practical terms such schemes appear much less likely to encroach on the bargaining agenda. In contrast to certain individual performance-related pay schemes, they are rarely traded off against bargained increases, being seen more as an addition or 'top-up' to the negotiated rise. As such they may even be welcomed by the unions in providing members with an additional bonus. Indeed, they have also been seen by some unions as providing a degree of bargaining leverage. Thus where members' pay depends on company profit the unions might argue they should have a say over strategic factors determining profit but traditionally excluded from the bargaining agenda (IPCS 1988).

Yet while union presence and the implementation of high-commitment practices remains a perfectly credible combination, it is nonetheless equally clear that such a combination is extremely rare. Cully et al. (1999), for example, found that only 4 per cent of workplaces had a majority-unionized workforce, where local representatives negotiated with managers and where at least half of the high-commitment practices had been implemented. A survey by Guest and Peccei (1998) reveals further evidence of a lack of diffusion of this type of approach. Drawing more explicitly on a partnership model, a survey of members of the Involvement and Participation Association (IPA) (who might as a consequence be expected to adhere to such a style) found that only around a quarter of their companies had followed this path in full.

It is perhaps an irony that this same survey revealed that, where organizations had adopted a partnership model, business performance was positively affected. This raises questions about why, despite its apparent effectiveness in these terms, there has been such a low take-up of the sophisticated consultative or partnership approach. The reasons have been well rehearsed (Kelly 1998; Claydon 1998; Tailby and Winchester 2000; chapter 10 above), and do not require a detailed restatement here. In brief, however, partnership agreements appear to operate in the shadow of the predominant trend in British industrial relations for management to seek to reassert its prerogative. Where management has the power to assert its prerogative it is likely to do so. Partnership might be seen as a 'best case' managerial strategy in increasingly rare instances of ongoing union strength. As Claydon (1998) has pointed out, management has traditionally shown little inclination to involve unions in the handling of such issues as training and development. Where management is in a powerful position, it has little need to become engaged in partnership arrangements. Indeed, Bacon and Storey's (2000) case-study work confirms the way in which certain high-profile partnership agreements bear the imprint of managerial prerogative. Thus, in a number of organizations such as Cadbury-Schweppes, the Co-operative Bank and National Power, partnership agreements were seen as a response to failed management attempts to impose a more individualistic approach to the regulation of the employment relationship. In other organizations such as the (then) Royal Mail and InterCity, where a union-based collectivism remained significant, such agreements were viewed by management as unlikely to check their longer-term interest in re-establishing their prerogative.

Finally, the fragility of the partnership model, particularly in delivering key elements such as job security in face of perceived corporate imperatives linked to competitive pressure, is likely to test its credibility in the eyes of unions and their members and call into question management commitment to this type of model (Tailby and Winchester 2000). Thus, in one of many examples that could be quoted, Centrica announced 1,500 job losses following the closure of all 243 of its shops just four months after a signing a partnership agreement 'maximizing employment security' (*Personnel Today* 1999a).

In short, management commitment to pursue a policy of partnership with unions combining co-operation with high-commitment employment practices is rarely the product of a frame of reference based on an acceptance of the values of pluralism as Fox first described them. Rather, it is likely to be a pragmatic and conditional response to the prevailing form of unionization in the firm, sector and location, underpinned by labour law.

Sophisticated human relations

The widespread emergence of the non-union workplace signalled by the third Workplace Industrial Relations Survey (WIRS) (Millward et al. 1992) and confirmed by the most recent Workplace Employment Relations Survey (Cully et al. 1999) has inevitably encouraged interest in the form taken by employment relations in such workplaces. In the 1980s, high-profile cases of non-union organizations, especially in the high-tech sector, pursuing what might in retrospect be viewed as a high-commitment approach, provided the basis for a potent prescriptive model (Peters and Waterman 1982). There is, however, limited evidence to suggest that organizations in general have been able or willing to adopt such a model.

Certainly, there appear to be circumstances in which a high-commitment approach remains an option. Guest and Hoque (1994), for example, found that, on relatively new sites, employers were significantly more likely to adopt a 'good' approach involving the 'strategic' use of 'innovative' employment practices than a 'bad' approach combining ad hoc-ism and a low take-up of such practices. Yet the broader picture suggests that non-union firms are unlikely to pursue such a high-commitment or developmental approach for the bulk of their workforce. The third WIRS (Millward et al. 1992) highlighted that non-union workplaces were more accurately characterized as a 'Bleak House' (Sisson 1993) than havens of enlightened 'good practice'. Here employees are more likely to have an accident or be dismissed and less likely to be communicated with. Indeed this approach, closer to traditional than to sophisticated human relations, is reconfirmed in the recent WERS, which notes 'the diffusion of high commitment management practices was not especially widespread ... For most employers, it might be best to characterize their approach as one of retaining control and doing what they could do to contain costs' (Cully et al. 1999: 295).

It is again noteworthy that evidence from the US and more recently from the UK (Thompson 2000) suggests a relationship between the use of high-commitment practices and positive employee attitudes and improved organizational performance, raising the question as to why such practices are not used more extensively. A number of possible reasons have been proposed (Appelbaum and Batt 1994). At the macro-level, there are institutional barriers, which inhibit the investment of time and resources needed for these practices to be effectively implemented. Organizations are driven to bottom-line costs and short time horizons by systems of financial and corporate governance, which demand the short-term servicing of shareholder needs (Storey and Sisson 1990). At the micro-level, such practices are sometimes seen to constitute a threat to established patterns of authority. Thus, middle management resistance has been seen as one of the reasons for the failure of quality or problem-solving circles. As Scott (1994: 129) noted in relation to his cases, 'even where managers were keen to introduce the new industrial relations, their commitment to innovative approaches co-existed with a desire to preserve conventional aspects of management authority'.

The universal applicability of such practices might also be called into question. A more contingent approach suggests that such practices might be viewed as more appropriate in certain industries and for specific occupational groups where employee commitment is explicitly linked to organizational performance and well-being. More profoundly perhaps, low diffusion may reflect the difficulties faced in changing the character of workplace employment relations, which are usually rooted in long-standing, entrenched and complex patterns or networks of relations, traditions, habits, norms and managerial beliefs (Scott 1994).

The apparent absence of a non-union high-commitment model in practice raises questions about the character of management style and particularly the nature of individualism in the non-union environment. As already suggested, survey evidence suggests that this environment essentially remains cost-driven and far from 'enlightened'. Qualitative research providing a feel for the texture of working life in this context, with a few notable exceptions (McLoughlin and Gourlay 1994), remains limited. What evidence is available, however, suggests that the extent to which the treatment of the employee has been individualized needs to be treated with some care.

This is highlighted by Brown et al. (1998) in their discussion of individual performance-related pay in non-union organizations. The distinction they make between procedural and substantive individualization is useful in this respect. Thus, while the general introduction of performance-related pay in their sample of non-union firms constituted a form of procedural individualization, in substantive terms employees continued to be treated in a fairly standard way with little variation in the pay increases received.

Indeed the presence of high-commitment practices in a non-union environment should not be seen as necessarily leading to the adoption of a 'softer' developmental approach. This is very much associated with the earlier suggestion that given practices may be used as vehicles for different approaches to the management of employees. A number of case-study projects have revealed a gap between espoused and operational policies in this respect. Thus, Bacon's (1999:

17) case study of a 'mini-steel' company found evidence of the use of standard high-commitment practices following union de-recognition. However, these provided the veneer for a fairly harsh management regime:

> The detailed operation of policies and practices at the mini-steel [company] revealed a sense of the nature of work at odds from that formally presented by the company ... Measured by current survey questions mini-steel is a 'good' non-union human resource management employer. However this description did not match the reality revealed here.

These findings receive confirmation in Scott's (1994: 146) work on a food-processing factory, where the realities and complexities of everyday workplace life simply did not lend themselves to the meaningful implementation of policies based on a direct relationship between management and employees:

> By the admission of both managers and workers, in most instances, the direct relationship existed more in theory than it did in practice. There were too many people on each shift for the manager to know most individuals at all well. For many, annual appraisals tended to concentrate on discussion of hard measures of workers' performance such as timekeeping and sickness rather than matters which required managers to have some detailed knowledge of workers' strengths and weaknesses.

Where individualized practices have, however, been implemented the effects, particularly as perceived by employees, have been at best uneven. In general terms, this is reflected in Guest and Conway's (1999) work drawing on self-report data from around 1,000 employees. This suggests that, while trade union membership appears to be associated with 'poorer' employment relations, it also is correlated with longer tenure and lower experience of redundancy. More specifically, the variable impact of such practices on the quality of workplace relations is well illustrated by reference to one such practice: communication.

Along with individual performance-related pay, the use of non-union and especially direct forms of communication and consultation has perhaps been seen as the mechanism most clearly reflecting and embodying a more individualized approach to employment relations. Certainly the use of direct voice arrangements such as briefing groups and employee attitude surveys, in particular, is not necessarily inimical to a trade union presence. Analysis of the third Workplace Industrial Relations Survey by Sisson (1993) found that such arrangements were more likely to be found in unionized workplaces, while WERS (Cully et al. 1999) found that a combination of representative and direct voice mechanism remained the most common institutional set-up in workplaces. There does appear, however, to have been a marked increase in the use of non-union arrangements only and direct voice mechanisms only in recent years. For example, WERS revealed that the proportion of workplaces with non-union-only arrangements had risen from 16 per cent to 40 per cent between 1984 and 1998, with use of direct voice mechanisms increasing from 10 per cent to 30 per cent over the same period.

The variable impact of these mechanisms is apparent in contrasting perceptions about their implications for the quality of the communication process and the more general handling of employees. More specifically, non-union and direct voice arrangements appeared to be associated with a more proactive management approach to consulting employees (Millward et al. 2000: 131) and with a greater management responsiveness to employee proposals. However, it was equally apparent that a union presence was closely related to employee perceptions of fair treatment. The fact that the only combination of voice mechanisms independently associated with ratings of fair treatment was union recognition and union representation on a consultative committee leads Millward et al. (2000: 134) to conclude that union influence 'may well be the critical factor'. It is a finding that has some plausibility in the context of earlier discussion on union presence as a crucial mediating force in forging a degree of trust between management and the workforce. Union involvement might well be seen as contributing towards perceptions of procedural justice, thus contributing to an acceptance of new and changing employment and work practices.

Summary and Conclusions

During the past 20 years the predominance of a state-supported management style characterized as bargained constitutionalism, and combining an emphasis on adversarial collectivism with a cost-driven individualism, has clearly been undermined, thus providing the opportunity for a realignment of such preferences and choices. This new 'space' appears to have been colonized by two new normative models, one based upon a sophisticated consultative style revolving around high-commitment practices in a co-operative union environment and the other related to a sophisticated human relations style also reflecting high-commitment practices but in a non-union context.

It might be argued that these are economically rational models with much, therefore, to commend them, particularly from a managerial perspective. Thus the high-commitment management and union partnership approaches were both found to improve organizational performance. Indeed, a union presence seemed to be particularly important in encouraging efficient and effective management. It was not only associated with the more extensive use of high-commitment practices but was also seen as necessary in encouraging perceptions of organizational fairness or justice often crucial in gaining employee acceptance of the kind of changes required to meet new competitive pressures and firm needs.

Despite these findings, however, the pursuit of such styles appears to be rare. As Fox indicated when he first developed the idea of pluralistic and unitary frames of reference, behind the veneer of economic rationality are much deeper managerial beliefs about control and prerogative. Since 1979 changes in the state's conception of 'good industrial relations', linked to the precipitous decline in union strength, have reinforced these beliefs and allowed management greater choice over which style of employee management to adopt. There are many examples of enlightened managements developing more sophisticated approaches, some with unions, and some without. In some cases domestic or global competitive pressures have forced a reappraisal of management style towards 'higher' values and employee inclusion. But these are still the exception. Indeed, evidence suggests that managements are driven more by a cost-minimization and opportunistic approach to employees, reflecting more than anything a traditional style. It is far from clear what would trigger a major change in underlying managerial values and beliefs.

References

Appelbaum, R., and Batt, E. 1994: *The New American Workplace*. Ithaca: ILR Press.

Atkinson, J. 1984: Manpower strategies for flexible organizations, *Personnel Management*, August, 28–31.

Bacon, N. 1999: Union de-recognition and new human relations: a steel industry case study, *Work, Employment and Society*, 13 (1), 1–18.

Bacon, N., and Storey, J. 2000: New employee relations strategies in Britain: towards individualism or partnership? *British Journal of Industrial Relations*, 38 (3) 407–28.

Beck, U. 1992: *Risk Society*. London: Sage.

Brown, W., Deakin, S., Hudson, M., Pratten, C. and Ryan, P. 1998: *The Individualisation of the Employment Contract in Britain*. Department of Trade and Industry, Employment Relations Research Series 4. London: DTI. Available at <www.dti.gov.uk/er/emar>.

Bryson, A. 1999: Are unions good for industrial relations? In R. Jowell, J. Curtice, A. Park and K. Thomson (eds), *Who Shares New Labour's Values?* British Social Attitudes Survey, 16th report. Aldershot: Ashgate.

Casey, B., Metcalf, H. and Millward, N. 1997: *Employers' Use of Flexible Labour*. London: PSI.

Claydon, T. 1998: Problematising partnership: the prospects for a co-operative bargaining agenda. In P. Sparrow and M. Marchington (eds), *Human Resource Management: The New Agenda*. London: Financial Times/Pitman.

Colling, T. 2000: Personnel management in the extended organization. In S. Bach and K. Sisson (eds), *Personnel Management in Britain*. Oxford: Blackwell.

Cully, M., Woodland, S., O'Reilly, A. and Dix, G. 1999: *Britain at Work*. London: Routledge.

Deery, S., and Walsh, J. 1999: The decline of collectivism? A comparative study of white collar employees in Britain and Australia, *British Journal of Industrial Relations*, 37 (2), 245–70.

Du Gay, P. 1996: *Consumption and Identity at Work*. London: Sage.

Edwards, P. K. 1986: *Conflict at Work*. Oxford: Blackwell.

Fox, A. 1974: *Beyond Contract: Work, Power and Trust Relations*. London: Faber & Faber.

Fox, A. 1985: *History and Heritage*. London: George Allen & Unwin.

Gallie, D. 1996: Trade union allegiance and decline in British urban labour markets. In D. Gallie, R. Penn and M. Rose (eds), *Trade Unionism in Recession*. Oxford: Oxford University Press.

Giddens, A. 1991: *Modernity and Self Identity*. Cambridge: Polity.

Goldthorpe, J., Lockwood, D., Bechhofer, F. and Platt, J. 1968: *The Affluent Worker: Industrial Attitudes and Behaviour*. Cambridge: Cambridge University Press.

Green, F., Machin, S. and Wilkinson, D. 1999: Trade unions and training practices in British workplaces, *Industrial and Labor Relations Review*, 52 (2), 179–93.

Guest, D. 1989: HRM: its implications for industrial relations and trade unions. In J. Storey (ed.), *New Perspectives on Human Resource Management*. London: Routledge.

Guest, D., and Conway, N. 1999: Peering into the black hole: the downside of the new employment relations in the UK. *British Journal of Industrial Relations*, 37 (3), 367–90.

Guest, D., and Hoque, K. 1994: The good, the bad and the ugly: employment relations in new non-union workplaces, *Human Resource Management Journal*, 5 (1), 1–13.

Guest, D., and Peccei, R. 1998: *The Partnership Company*. London: Involvement and Participation Association.

Heery, E. 1996: The new new unionism. In I. Beardwell (ed.), *Contemporary Industrial Relations*. Oxford: Oxford University Press.

Howell, C. 1995: Trade unions and the state: a critique of British industrial relations, *Politics and Society*, 23 (2), 149–83.

Hyman, R. 1992: Trade unions and the disintegration of the working class. In M. Regini (ed.), *The Future of Labour Movements*. London: Sage.

IPCS (Institution of Professional Civil Servants) 1988: *Fair Shares? Negotiator Guide to Profit Sharing*. London: IPCS.

IRS (Industrial Relations Services). 1998: Labour–management co-operation in the USA, *IRS Employment Trends*, 656.

Kelly, J. 1998: *Rethinking Industrial Relations*. London: Routledge.

Kessler, I., Coyle Shapiro, J. and Purcell, J. 1999: Outsourcing and the employee perspective, *Human Resource Management Journal*, 9 (2), 5–19.

Kessler, I., and Purcell, J. 1992: Performance-related pay: objectives and application, *Human Resource Management Journal*, 2 (3), 34–59.

Kessler, I., and Purcell, J. 1995: Individualism in theory and practice. In P. Edwards (ed.), *Industrial Relations: Theory and Practice in Britain*. Oxford: Blackwell.

Lepak, D., and Snell, S. 1999: The human resource architecture: toward a theory of human capital allocation and development, *Academy of Management Review*, 24 (1), 31–48.

MacNeil, I. 1985: Relational contracts: what we do and do not know, *Wisconsin Law Review*, 14 (4), 483–525.

Madsen, M. 1997: The relationship between working life and individualization: a study among Danish union members, *Work, Employment and Society*, 11 (2), 197–218.

Marchington, M. 1982: *Managing Industrial Relations*. London: McGraw Hill.

Marchington, M., and Parker, P. 1990: *Changing Patterns of Employee Relations*. London: Harvester Wheatsheaf.

McLoughlin, I., and Gourlay, S. 1994: *Enterprise without Unions*. Buckingham: Open University Press.

Millward, N., Bryson, A. and Forth, J., 2000: *All Change at Work?* London: Routledge.

Millward, N., Stevens, M., Smart, D. and Hawes, W. 1992: *Workplace Industrial Relations in Transition*. Aldershot: Dartmouth.

Mitchell, A. 1998: New model unions, *Management Today*, July, 28–32.

Monks, J. 1994: The union response to HRM: fraud or opportunity, *Personnel Management*, September, 42–7.

Newton, L., and Shore, L. 1992: A model of union membership: instrumentality, commitment and opposition, *Academy of Management Review*, 17 (2), 275–98.

Personnel Today 1998: 24 September.

Personnel Today 1999a: 26 August.

Personnel Today 1999b: 7 October.

Peters, T., and Waterman, R. 1982: *In Search of Excellence*. New York: Harper & Row.

Phelps Brown, E. H. 1990: The counter revolution of our time, *Industrial Relations*, 29 (1), 1–14.

Poole, M. 1989: *The Origins of Economic Democracy*. London: Routledge.

Provis, C. 1996: Unitarism, pluralism, interests and values, *British Journal of Industrial Relations*, 34 (4), 473–96.

Purcell, J. 1987: Mapping management styles in employee relations, *Journal of Management Studies*, 24 (5), 533–48.

Purcell, J. and Ahlstrand, B. 1994: *Human Resource Management in the Multi Divisional Company*. Oxford: OUP.

Purcell, J., and Sisson, K. 1983: Strategies and practice in the management of industrial relations. In G. S. Bain (ed.), *Industrial Relations in Britain*. Oxford: Blackwell.

Rajan, A. 1997: Employability in the finance sector: rhetoric vs reality, *Human Resource Management Journal*, 7 (1), 67–78.

Roberts, B., Loveridge, R. and Gennard, J. 1972: *Reluctant Militants*. London: Heinemann.

Rubery, J., Earnshaw, J., Marchington, M., Cooke, F. and Vincent, S. 2000: *Changing Organizational Forms and the Employment Relationship*. SCASE Conference Paper. London: LSE.

Scott, A. 1994: *Willing Slaves?* Cambridge: Cambridge University Press.

Sisson, K. 1993: In search of HRM, *British Journal of Industrial Relations*, 31 (2), 201–10.

Smith, G. 1986: Profit sharing and employee share ownership, *Employment Gazette*, September, 308–85.

Storey, J., and Sisson, K. 1990: Limits to transformation: human resource management in the British context, *Industrial Relations Journal*, 21 (1), 60–5.

Tailby, S., and Winchester, D. 2000: Management and trade unions. In S. Bach and K. Sisson (eds), *Personnel Management in Britain*. Oxford: Blackwell.

Thompson, M. 1992: *Performance Related Pay: The Employers' Experience*. Brighton: IMS.

Thompson, M. 2000: *The UK Aerospace People Management Audit 2000*. London: SBAC/DTI.

Waddington, J., and Kerr, A. 1999: Membership retention in the public sector, *Industrial Relations Journal*, 30 (2), 151–65.

Waddington, J., and Whitston, C. 1997: Why do people join unions in a period of membership decline? *British Journal of Industrial Relations*, 35 (4), 515–46.

Weitzman, M. 1984: *The Share Economy*, Cambridge, Mass.: Harvard University Press.

Williams, S. 1997: The nature of some recent trade union modernization policies in the UK, *British Journal of Industrial Relations*, 35 (4), 494–514.

Wood, S. 1999: HRM and performance, *International Journal of Management Reviews*, 1 (4), 387–413.

Young, R. 1995: It's time to learn to help yourself, *Management Today*, November, 5–6.

13

NEW FORMS OF WORK ORGANIZATION: STILL LIMITED, STILL CONTROLLED, BUT STILL WELCOME?

JOHN F. GEARY

When the first edition of this book was produced in 1995, the literature on work organization was to a large degree polarized in its analysis of the extent to which work had been reorganized and its consequences for employees. On the one hand, there were a variety of upbeat accounts in Britain and elsewhere identifying the transformative capacities of new work systems, creating a 'new industrial relations', transforming management–employee relations and granting employees the means to be self-managing in their day-to-day work (Kochan and Osterman 1994; Wood and Albanese 1995; Pil and MacDuffie 1996; Whitfield 1998). Here the impetus for change was seen to lie with management efforts to restructure the employment relationship in accordance with 'new' managerial thinking in the face of intensified competition. As to the consequences for employees, this optimistic perspective argued that the intention was to empower employees, to make work more rewarding and to create a better and more challenging work environment. Employers were seen therefore as being determined to move away from old ways of organizing work around Taylorist principles to create a distinctly new form of work organization. The sharpest expression of this transformation thesis is Walton's (1985) claim that there has been a shift from the 'management of control' to the 'management of commitment'.

Critical engagement with this 'empowerment' literature was not always easy; its claims were often grandiose, vague and difficult to pin down and there often coexisted an uneasy combination of observation, theoretical analysis and prescription. The simplistic and unitarist biases of these accounts have been commented on elsewhere and will not be added to here (Webb 1996). Apart from this critique, however, this literature has led to two responses. First, there is what might be termed the 'intensification' literature; second, there is a more nuanced and middle position, which was proposed in the first edition of this book, arguing for a so-called 're-regulation' view, where work reorganization gives rise to a mixture of costs and benefits (Geary 1995).

The 'intensification' view makes short shrift of the optimism of the empowerment literature and argues that management's intentions are not so noble, that an extension in management control is the primary motive, and that there is no managerial need or desire for tapping employees' discretionary efforts or tacit skills. The consequences of the introduction of new work structures are seen to be detrimental to employees' welfare, resulting in job losses and effort intensification. In this sense, it is claimed, management's motives are the same as they have always been; all that has changed is the means used to pursue them. Few benefits are seen to accrue to workers. Rinehart et al.'s (1997) study of 'lean production systems' (defined below) in CAMI Automotive in Canada, for example, dismisses many of the great claims made for lean production. J. Hyman and Mason (1995: 191, 193) in their review of employee involvement have argued that 'basically and critically, empowerment becomes a euphemism for work intensification' and that similar practices are being 'used to disguise workers' growing occupational impoverishment'.

This polarization of views has, more recently, given way to a more nuanced and context-sensitive understanding of new work structures and employee involvement (Geary 1995; Marchington et al. 1994). Edwards et al. (2002) have, for instance, argued that management initiatives are 'more limited and controlled than the enthusiasts claim, but more constructive than the critics admit'; essentially, the intentions and consequences of management's actions are more complex and variable than allowed for by either camp. New forms of work organization, it is argued, do not have uniform effects but are likely to be contingent on a series of factors, such as the manner in which change is introduced; whether employees and their representatives are involved; employees' prior experiences and expectations; whether any provision is made for employment security, and the extent to which human resource policies are adapted to support their introduction. Generally, it would now seem to have been accepted that this re-regulation view is closer to capturing the dominant patterns of work reorganization.

In the course of this chapter a number of studies will be reviewed in an attempt to illustrate how this re-regulation approach works where new forms of work reorganization have been introduced. The chapter begins, however, by examining the incidence and shape of new work practices in Britain; where possible, comparisons with other countries, particularly elsewhere in Europe, are made.

The present concern with new work practices focuses on those initiatives in which employees have some active participation in defining the nature of work tasks and the way in which they are to be carried out. Thus this chapter concentrates on the more 'advanced' forms of work organization such as teamwork, quality circles (QCs), problem-solving groups, and total quality management (TQM). These are accepted indices of innovation in work organization and are frequently cited as key dimensions of the new production model (see e.g. Osterman 1994, 2000; Geary 1999; Ichniowski et al. 1996). The significance of these practices is that they – potentially, at least – alter the structure of work and supervision in a very fundamental way, primarily through granting employees more discretion to organize, plan and execute work tasks. In addition, their introduction has the potential to overcome rigidities often associated with Taylorist traditions of job specialization and work boundaries. The significance of such innovations will naturally vary depending on the starting points of a country's tradition of work organization and industrial relations.

The importance of this focus may be highlighted by reference to the debate on lean production. Such a system is based on the elimination of waste and the pursuit of continuous improvement. As discussed in chapter 4, it is widely associated with Japanese methods, and, as is now well established, some of the early claims were that these methods also entailed 'high-commitment' HR practices. Yet a stream of research, such as the CAMI study mentioned above, shows clearly that jobs remain narrowly defined and that workers' ability to participate actively in the organization of work is tightly constrained. Ackroyd and Proctor's (1998) review of lean organization in Britain highlights the intensification of managerial control based on cost minimization and the narrow range of skills required of employees, We touch below on some issues around lean production, but focus on more advanced forms of teamwork; chapter 4 has summarized the evidence on the use of Japanese methods on the shop floor.

Survey Evidence of New Work Practices

Before considering the survey evidence, it is important to address a number of points in relation to method. The findings from a number of national and international surveys will then be examined and compared. Particular attention will be given to the recently completed WERS survey and the EPOC cross-national survey of 10 EU member countries.

Methodological issues

A major problem in the analysis of new work practices has been the weakness of the survey evidence. First, new forms of work organization are notoriously difficult to define and measure. It is not unusual in some surveys to see respondents being asked simply, 'Do you have teamworking?', without seeking to reduce the 'elasticity' of such labels by adding a more precise definition or description as to what might be meant by such concepts. Understanding of what constitutes such popular labels, however, varies enormously.

Second, if new forms of work organization are difficult to define, it becomes virtually impossible to measure their diffusion. For it is not just a question of the simple incidence of new practices that is at issue. Knowing that a workplace has teamwork, for example, tells us nothing about the nature of the practice: whether, for example, the team is a loose grouping who work together from time to time or a formally designated and relatively permanent unit; whether the team is semi-autonomous in its working or under close management supervision, and so on. Consider, for example, the work of Scarbrough and Terry (1997) on the UK car industry. Their survey of seven plants of the major car-producing companies revealed a strikingly uniform picture in respect of the introduction and operation of team-based work organization where supervisory roles were significantly altered or done away with. Their more detailed case-study investigation of Rover, however, revealed a more mundane and complex picture: elements of a new model of work organization had been introduced and the workplace regime had changed in a manner which challenged many traditional job controls and demarcations, but many of the model's key features had remained underspecified, its introduction had been piecemeal, and views as to its form and operation were contested and the focus of much dispute.

Third, there is the 'quality of response'. This depends on the identity of the respondent and the unit of analysis. It would seem reasonable to argue that what is critical in a survey is that the chosen respondent is familiar with the policy, and close to the practice, of new work practices. In most of the surveys cited here, as with the WIRS surveys in Britain and Australia, the respondent was the senior workplace manager with responsibility for IR/HRM matters. The unit of analysis was the workplace. In contrast, and in spite of having the same unit of analysis, the much-cited Lawler et al. (1992) and Huselid (1995) studies in the US relied on a respondent at the level of corporate HQ. In this instance, the quality of responses must be suspect as the respondent is likely to be more familiar with company policy than with workplace practice and, in answering in respect of the former and not the latter, may be more likely to overstate the diffusion or depth of new work practices.

This points to a fourth issue. Where the subject of study is the extent of workplace innovations, it is certainly likely that, where such changes have been introduced, their champions may be anxious and eager to have their efforts recorded. Organizations not associated with such innovations, however, may be less likely to agree to participate in a survey. There is therefore the possibility of overestimating the diffusion of workplace change. Of course, there is also the additional problem that the reality of new work practices may bear little resemblance to their protagonists' proclamations. To act as a check for such exaggeration, the British and Australian workplace surveys have not relied solely on the views of a member of management; an employee representative is also interviewed and, more critically, the most recent surveys have included an employee survey.

Fifth, there is the importance of a study's sampling frame. A number of studies often rely on drawing their sample from a list of top-performing companies or the largest 1,000 firms: Oliver and Wilkinson's (1989) study of the extent of Japanese practices in the UK used the *Times 1000* index for its sample, and Lawler et al. (1992) study drew its sample from the *Fortune* 1,000 companies in the US. One would obviously need to exercise extreme caution in making statements as to the diffusion of new practices when using such sampling frames. After all, such firms are most likely to support, and have present, the conditions necessary for the introduction of new work practices. In such circumstances, the diffusion of new practices is again likely to be overstated.

Sixth, there is the durability of new forms of work organization. Unfortunately, there are few surveys with a longitudinal or panel design that can help us provide information on this area. The exceptions are, in the US, Osterman's (2000) replication of a previous survey first conducted in 1992 (Osterman 1994) and the WIRS series in Britain and Australia, both of which contain a panel sample (see Millward et al. 2000). This not only allows us to examine the survival rates of new work structures, but carries the additional advantage of allowing us to discriminate between two major sources of change, whether that is 'within-unit' change or compositional change. Most of the other surveys looked at here are one-off and, therefore, only permit a measure of the diffusion or incidence of new practices at one point in time.

Finally, and perhaps most importantly, there is the problem of comparison and, in particular, cross-national comparison. The great majority of the studies have been country-specific. Inevitably, as well as suffering from a number of the general weaknesses identified above, they tend to reflect the national concerns not only of researchers but also of policymakers. Thus issues such as the 'quality of working life' have been very much to the fore in European studies, while 'transformation' has tended to be uppermost in their US equivalents. This makes it extremely difficult to compare the extent of new forms of work organization in different countries.

In brief, then, it is not only difficult to define and measure new work practices accurately, but the quality of the survey data available varies tremendously. Data of the quality and authority of the UK WIRS and AWIRS are hard to come by.

New work practices in Britain

Up until the late 1980s and early 1990s, findings from the UK WIRS series suggested that new work practices were not widely diffused and had not penetrated the UK workplace to any great extent. The 1990 survey, for instance, found that 'semi-autonomous work groups' existed in only 2 per cent of establishments (Millward et al. 1992). The most recent workplace survey, however, suggests that use of new work practices, such as teamworking and problem-solving groups, has increased to a significant degree (Cully et al. 1999: 42–4). The proportion of workplaces using problem-solving groups grew significantly, from a very low base in the early 1980s to 35 per cent in 1990 and to 38 per cent of workplaces in 1998. Interestingly, the panel element of the survey revealed an even greater increase, from 36 per cent in 1990 to 49 per cent in 1998, suggesting that the so-called continuing workplaces have been particularly innovative in this area (Millward et al. 2000: 119). The proportion of workplaces reporting that 'formally designated teams' had been introduced – 83 per cent where at least some employees in the largest occupational group worked in teams and 65 per cent where most employees in the group worked in teams – also points towards a significant move by employers to reorganize work and to promote employee involvement. However, once progressively stringent definitions are adopted, the proportion of British workplaces using teams is steadily whittled down. A reasonable approximation to the model of semi-autonomous teams embraces teams:

- where members work together, *and*
- have responsibility for a specific product or service, *and*
- jointly decide on how work is done.

One-third (35 per cent) of workplaces qualified, a very significant increase on the WIRS 1990 figure cited above. However, adding the criterion that teams elect their own leaders dramatically cut the figure to 3 per cent. When occupational categories are taken into account, teamworking is much more prevalent among professionals, technicians, sales, clerical and secretarial staff than among plant and machine operatives, crafts, and personal and protective services (Cully et al. 1999: 44).

The WERS study was also able to examine by using three measures – task variety, autonomy and control over the pace of work – the level of influence enjoyed by individual employees in their work (Cully et al. 1999: 40–2, 140–3). Both management respondents and employees in the employee opinion survey were asked broadly comparable questions. The latter, drawing from a sample of 28,237 respondents, found that 30 per cent of employees had a lot of influence over their work, 43 per cent had some influence, while the remaining 27 per cent had little or no influence. Not surprisingly, while the level of influence workers had over work was in large measure a feature of employees' occupational group, it was also found to be related to the manner in which job responsibilities were conveyed to employees. Thus where individual objectives and targets were applied, job influence was higher than where supervision and standard operating procedures were used.

The Employment in Britain Survey provides a valuable addition to the WIRS series (Gallie et al. 1998). The data, derived from a national representative survey of 3,458 employees of between 20 and 60 years of age, provide a rare insight into the effects of workplace innovations on the nature of the labour process. In respect of the incidence of new practices, it was found that 20 per cent of employees participated in QCs or similar groups, with some significant variations across occupational categories. But notwithstanding the limited reach of QCs, the study revealed that their effects were quite profound: employees felt they had a significant say over the way in which their work was organized, members were more willing to use their discretion and initiative, and they enjoyed their work more than non-members. To this extent, the study's findings indicate that QCs can be highly effective in promoting employees' sense of involvement.

When the authors looked at the wider issue of changes in skill levels, they found evidence for a striking upskilling of UK employees together with a significant devolution of responsibilities in relation to decisions about work tasks in a manner which would suggest that the 'most prevalent employer policy with regard to work organization has been a move towards "responsible autonomy"'

(Gallie 1996: 156). Notwithstanding this, a less positive and more mixed picture emerges once the wider consequences of these changes in work organization were analysed: on the plus side, employees enjoyed more autonomy, made greater use of their skills and had more opportunities for self-development, but on the negative side, there was an extensive and expanding use of control systems as well as considerable intensification of effort levels. But perhaps the most striking finding from this study was the rarity with which employees were permitted to take part in decisions that involved changes in work organization: only a third felt they could exercise some significant influence and nearly half were dissatisfied with their level of influence. And when it came to those employees (46 per cent) who reported that they were a member of a work group, no more than 15 per cent worked in a group that had a 'lot of responsibility'. There was also evidence to suggest that the level of employee participation had not increased from the mid-1980s, and may in fact have declined.

The finding that performance management practices were also being used, particularly, although not surprisingly, among those employees who enjoyed high task discretion is also interesting. It would suggest that, although management were willing to decentralize work task decision-making within organizations, there was also an attempt to reassert control over erstwhile autonomous employees. It was thus a highly ambivalent process with employers relaxing or replacing immediate controls with more remote controls. Managerial control, therefore, was not being revoked but was being recast – sometimes in a more sophisticated way – and, in some important respects, intensified.

It was also found that there was no simple polarization as between employers who might have adopted high control and low discretion strategies and others who might have preferred low control and high discretion. There was not therefore, a

> simple trade-off between discretion and control. . . . Employers' practices about task discretion do not appear to map in any straightforward way onto their policies of control. Depending on the type of control used, higher control might be associated with lower discretion, higher discretion or something in the middle. (Gallie et al. 1998: 71)

It should also be emphasized that all categories of employees had experienced high or growing control.

Britain in comparative perspective

Prior to 1996, it was very difficult to compare the extent of new work practices in Britain with other countries, as the great majority of studies had been country-specific. With the completion of the so-called EPOC survey, however, it became possible for the first time to make cross-national comparisons. Critically, the same instrument was used to survey managers in workplaces in 10 European countries. It was also designed to overcome many of the limitations of previous surveys, especially to go beyond the simple incidence of practices and

Box 13.1   Four forms of direct participation

Group consultation

'Temporary' groups	groups of employees who come together for a specific purpose and for a limited period of time, e.g. 'project groups' or 'task forces'
'Permanent' groups	groups of employees who discuss various work-related topics on an ongoing basis, such as QCs

Delegation

Individual	individual employees are granted extended rights and responsibilities to carry out their work without constant reference back to managers – sometimes known as 'job enrichment'
Group	rights and responsibilities are granted to teams of employees to carry out their common tasks without constant reference back to managers.

to take into account dimensions of coverage, scope and autonomy. We are thus in a position to reliably compare the extent of workplace innovation in Britain with the other countries surveyed.

The main objective of the EPOC study was to examine the nature and extent of 'direct participation'. 'Direct participation' was seen to constitute two forms: (1) *consultative participation* – management encourages employees to make their views known on work-related matters, but reserves the right to take action or not; (2) *delegative participation* – management grants employees increased discretion and responsibility to organize their work without the requirement to refer back. Both consultative and delegative participation can involve employees as individuals or in groups of a temporary or permanent status. Box 13.1 details four relatively advanced forms of direct participation (for further details, see Geary and Sisson 1994).

The size threshold for the larger countries was 50 employees, but this was lowered to 20 employees in small and medium-sized countries. Over 32,000 workplaces were surveyed. The study covered all areas of the private sector and public services. An overall response rate of 17.8 per cent was achieved. In Britain, the survey achieved a response rate of 16.6 per cent, 812 workplaces in all. All questions were asked in respect of the firm's largest occupational group.

It was found that, in the area of consultative participation, 'temporary groups' such as project groups or task forces, were present in 33 per cent of firms and 'permanent groups' such as QCs were used in 41 per cent of enterprises in Britain. This compared with a 10-country average of 31 per cent and 30 per cent respectively. 'Delegative participation' involving individual employees and organized around team structures was found in 53 and 37 per cent of British organizations respectively, which was very similar to the average scores of 55 and 36 per cent in the study as a whole (see table 13.1). When coverage is taken into account – that is, whether the participation initiative involved more than

Table 13.1   Incidence of group consultation and delegation in Europe (% of workplaces)

	Group consultation: temporary groups %	Group consultation: permanent groups %	Individual delegation %	Group delegation %
10-country average	31	30	55	36
France	40	34	54	40
Germany	26	31	64	31
Italy	42	21	44	28
United Kingdom	33	41	53	37

Source: European Foundation for the Improvement of Living and Working Conditions (1997: tables 4.9–4.11).

50 per cent of the largest occupational group – the figures for Britain are again close to the average. For example, 47 per cent of UK workplaces reported that at least half their largest occupational group was covered by teamworking, a figure identical to the 10-country average.

One of the most novel features of the EPOC survey was its attempt to measure the intensity of teamworking. Two indicators were used. The first was the 'scope' of teamworking, which measured the number of rights of employees to make decisions on how they performed their work without reference to immediate management in areas such as scheduling and allocation of work. The second was the degree of autonomy permitted to employees to choose their own team members and to decide which issues the group might address. Where high levels of discretion were allowed to employees this form of teamworking would approximate closely to semi-autonomous work groups. Of those British enterprises using teamworking only 16 per cent were found to have a high level of intensity; most (52 per cent) had a medium level and a third had a low level of intensity (see table 13.2). Of all workplaces, the proportion with semi-autonomous teamworking was closer to 5 per cent, a figure that confirms the results of Cully et al. (1999).

Finally, it is important to relate another revealing finding from the EPOC study. While the survey found no association between the presence of direct participation and whether a company was foreign-owned or not, distinct country differences were identified: in Germany, Italy, the Netherlands and Sweden, the proportion of foreign-owned workplaces with direct participation was above average; it was lower in countries characterized by weaker industrial relations systems, including Britain (Edwards et al. 2002). In the case of Britain, it would appear, in line with the arguments in chapter 4, that a desire or urgency for innovation in work structures among foreign companies is tempered by an opportunity to gain competitive advantage by other means. In the absence of a restraining industrial relations regime and without the requirement to offset costs

Table 13.2 The intensity of group delegation

	Score (% of workplaces)		
	Low %	Medium %	High %
10-country average	27	51	22
France	32	54	14
Germany	32	46	22
Italy	47	40	13
United Kingdom	32	52	16

Source: European Foundation for the Improvement of Living and Working Conditions (1997: figure 4.9).

associated therewith, it might not come as a surprise that a variety of competitive postures and forms of work organization with varying degrees of novelty would be identified. This issue will be addressed in some more detail below.

Summary

In summary, the data reported here demonstrate that British employers' use of new work practices has increased in recent years and that current levels of innovation are considerable. The overall picture is one of significant experimentation. That said, however, emphasis needs to be given to two points. First, in a comparative context Britain occupies a lower-middle ranking behind, on most measurements of delegative participation, Sweden, Holland, Ireland, and Denmark. Thus, in comparison to other European countries, Britain does not stand out as being to the fore in introducing new forms of work organization; it is very much an 'average performer'. Second, while the overall incidence of new work practices is impressive, when one probes behind measures of the distribution of practices, a significantly different picture emerges. While change is evident, it is of a form which would suggest that new work practices have not reached 'critical mass' in respect of the extent to which employers have adopted these new initiatives, whether they are of an advanced form and permit employees a significant degree of autonomy, and also as regards just how deeply embedded they have become in the labour process. Overall, it seems clear that the advanced forms of teamwork that have dominated so much of the debate to date are very much the exception rather than the rule. And, even in those instances where employees have been entrusted with increased discretion, it has not been accompanied with a relaxation in management control. Control remains as pervasive as ever, albeit organized in a different and sometimes more distant and less immediate manner. It is not a story of either/or, but both/and. That is, the dynamics of change are not such that we have moved from a model of control and rigidity to one of empowerment and flexibility. Alternatives are not so neatly packaged.

Consequences of Work Reorganization

In examining the consequences of new forms of work organization, particularly as they affect employees' working lives, the next section concentrates primarily on case-study evidence. There are a number of advantages which case-study analysis has over survey research in such an examination. Edwards et al. (2002) have pointed to the following. First, case studies are often capable of identifying causal links by adopting sharper definitions of both dependent and independent variables than is normally possible under survey research. Consider, for example, the view of Osterman (1994, 2000) that job security was not important in determining the incidence and the shape of new work practices in his survey. Other studies, particularly those using case-study methodologies, have suggested the reverse (Marchington et al. 1994; Collinson et al. 1998). To understand why this might be so, case-study research can focus very closely on the precise meaning of teamworking for employees and, in turn, can examine the qualitative effect on employees of the presence of job security provisions or perhaps the effects of job losses. The key point is that case-study research can reveal the links between dependent and independent variables and explore whether those relations are causal or not.

Second, to understand the dynamics of teamworking and its implications for employee empowerment and management control, close and detailed enquiry into experience on the ground is needed:

> understanding the nature of any teamworking initiative is insufficient on its own, as we also need to appreciate the context within which teamworking is implemented and the objectives that underpin its operation . . . there is a need to remove the blinkers and put teamworking initiatives into the context of each organization, studying not only what is meant by the term to those involved but also how its operation might be influenced by internal and external factors. (Marchington 2000: 77)

Four issues are addressed in this section. First, on the consequences of work reorganization for employees' autonomy and management control, it is argued that the introduction of new work practices has led to a re-regulation of the labour process; new forms of work organization entail both autonomy and control, and embraced within this is a series of inherent tensions and ambiguities. Second, there is the important issue of whether new work practices are 'gendered' in their consequences. There are a number of ways in which this might occur. In the simplest sense, as women tend to be concentrated in jobs that are low-skilled and offer few opportunities for advancement they are less likely to benefit from new work structures. But there may also be a more subtle process at work, whereby definitions of job content – in terms of skill and autonomy – are shaped by (male) gender assumptions. Third, the discussion turns to considering the economic effects of work reorganization. Finally, some consideration is given to the factors necessary for the successful introduction of new forms of work organization.

Granting autonomy and increasing control: understanding why

There are a number of studies which reveal the complexities associated with work reorganization. One study which leans towards an 'empowerment' perspective but which also is keenly aware of the tensions and limits of work reorganization is Clark's (1995) study of Pirelli's greenfield facility in South Wales. Pirelli management introduced a Total Quality programme which allowed for job flexibility, multi-skilling and self-supervision. The outcomes were largely positive for employees. In interviews, they expressed 'overwhelming support for self-supervision and [were] strongly committed to involvement in the day-to-day management of product quality' (1995: 234). Job satisfaction had also increased, even though employees experienced an intensification of effort levels. There were also benefits for management, primarily as the new work practices helped to smooth the flow of production. But there were also tensions: flexibility between the main occupational categories was not achieved, only flexibility within them, and even then early ambitions of attaining full flexibility were abandoned; the system of self-supervision was abused by some employees and a failure on the part of management to address the issue led to a lowering of morale amongst other employees committed to the new working practices; the skill-based pay system was in 'direct conflict with the need for thorough training, skilled working in particular areas, and team spirit and cooperation' (1995: 233); the vast majority of employees, union and non-union alike, felt powerless in relation to matters of pay and staffing levels to the extent that a substantial minority came to question the relevance of the union's role. The case of Pirelli, then, nicely illustrates the costs and benefits associated with work reorganization: plainly one did not come without the other. It also points to the limitations of a management strategy of empowerment. What is also clear is that workers valued the new system for its order and coherence, and that when that was jeopardized by management's failure to confront employees' abuse of the system, their regard for management was diminished.

This idea of workers welcoming a more orderly and better-managed work process – even where it results in increased effort – is one that figures prominently in the case-study literature (Collinson et al. 1998; Rosenthal et al. 1997; Geary and Dobbins 2001). Collinson et al. have coined the term 'the disciplined worker model' to capture this tendency. In their study of six organizations in the manufacturing and service sectors which had introduced TQM they found that, in contrast to an exploitation view, those workers working the hardest and most subject to explicit performance standards were more likely to express satisfaction with TQM. Their results are explained in these terms: workers welcomed a sense of order and managerially defined disciplines, and were prepared to accept limits to the exercise of discretion and increased effort levels where they could see a value and benefit in so doing. Employees may, therefore, see less reason to resist than they may have done in the past. While this may be due to a variety of factors, the possibility that management have better organized the work and addressed many of the old irritants which gave rise to conflict is often not considered by those who support an exploitation thesis. Employees may thus welcome a reassertion of managerial authority where this results in a better organization of work.

To this extent, new forms of work organization bring new benefits as well as costs, but they also entail contradictions. This emerges from Korczynski et al.'s (2000) examination of two different types of frontline service worker: 'knowledge workers' in the financial services industry and computer engineering, and less skilled 'mass-customized service workers', working in call centres. The former's work organization was thought to approximate to that of semi-autonomous teams and the latter to that of high-skill autonomous groups. The analysis highlights tensions associated with management's attempts to enroll the customer as a mechanism for controlling employees' efforts. The challenges management confronted included, first, the problem of variability – as individual customer preferences vary it is not always possible to prescribe mechanistic or bureaucratic solutions. This problem is more acute with knowledge work and less so, though by no means absent, with mass-customized services. Second, there is the problem of observability: direct observation of the labour process is likely to be costly; monitoring employees' efforts requires detailed information on the nature and quality of the employee–customer interaction, and there is also the risk that the physical presence of a supervisor might compound the problem by impairing the quality of the service provision. The difficulties associated with observation and variability give rise to a third problem, that of output measurement: as the quality of output is intimately connected to customers' perceptions of their interaction with an employee, it is likely to be difficult for management to unequivocally assess employees' behaviour.

The mechanisms for enlisting the customer as a solution in controlling the labour process varied between Korczynski et al.'s cases. In mass-customized service work, management tried to inculcate and encourage appropriate behaviour by using the norm of customer empathy, while in knowledge work the customer played a less central role, but information from customers as to the behaviour and performance of employees was supplied to management. The adoption of a pervasive system of monitoring and data measurement was accepted by employees on the basis that it was designed ultimately to meet customers' concerns. There was then considerable identification by employees with managerial objectives. Tensions arose, however, over competing definitions of what constituted good customer service. While management was concerned to reduce queuing or waiting times, workers were more anxious to see through to completion customer problems and queries. Employees preferred this approach as it gave them greater job variety, but also because they had come to develop a strong empathy with individual customers. In the end, management pressed ahead with imposing its conception of customer care over that of the workers, control was intensified and considerable ill-feeling was generated, to the extent that it risked leading, as one manager conceded, to an increase in stress levels and staff turnover.

The management of the labour process proved equally, if not more, problematic in the knowledge work sites, where the imposition of a strict regulatory regime proved less feasible. The principal difficulty for management was that any attempt to elicit information from the client company about the services provided by its employees might have been to concede that the assigned workers were not fully competent for the task in hand. Thus, the opportunity in such circumstances to use the customer as a mechanism of control was severely limited; other mechanisms had to be devised.

Similar results emerge from S. Taylor's (1997) study of workers in two customer service organizations that had introduced TQM, and from McKinlay and P. Taylor's (1996) study of teamworking in an American-owned microelectronics plant in Scotland. In the latter, a strict regulatory regime was introduced alongside teams, principally through the operation of a peer review system. And, as in Korczynski et al.'s cases, employees were quick to use managerially sanctioned rhetoric, in this case of teamworking and empowerment, as well as the concrete performance benefits to have arisen from their participation in teams, against management's efforts to use peer review as a surveillance mechanism. In essence, teams were used by workers to protect – as they saw it – the integrity of the team concept from an intensification of management control. Following the subversion of the peer review system, management moved to redesign the system and with it imposed a more codified and detailed surveillance system. As the authors emphasize, the introduction of teamworking involved both autonomy and control:

> There is never simply a stark alternative between 'empowerment' and 'emasculation', nor is this categorisation conclusive and irreversible. Empowerment is both an ideological construct and part of the daily experience of the [firm's] workforce. [The] employees endorsed key elements of teamworking as an ideology and as practice while decisively rejecting its disciplinary objectives. (McKinlay and Taylor 1996: 298)

In S. Taylor's study, workers were given responsibility for the detailed planning of work tasks, but at the same time there was a centralization of strategic control through the use of surveillance and the setting of hard performance targets. Crucially, these two forces were not separate but were part of what Taylor terms a dialectic of control: they were necessarily intertwined, and in combination reflected a new way of managing the age-old tension between the granting of autonomy and the exercise of managerial control.

The implication in many of these studies is that, where work is reorganized, it is often in a modest and pragmatic way. Workers assume greater responsibility for their work and are permitted greater involvement in work organization. This does not, however, lead to wider empowerment. Managerial authority has been redefined and reasserted, but rarely in some crude fashion. Management continues to confront the perennial problem of identifying the apposite balance between consent and control. But nor is it a case of management simply reassembling or juggling existing practices. There is a new dynamic, but one cast within the familiar terrain of management seeking to maintain control by granting employees discretion so that their commitment and creativity might be harnessed, but also restricting this so that this same discretion might not be used in ways which run against management's interests. New work practices

> have their own contradictions: specific ones, such as balancing individual responsibility against loyalty to teams, or reconciling work team autonomy and the need to meet externally imposed targets; and more generic ones around the balance between control and autonomy and the extent to which management can insulate autonomy in the labour process from the pressures emanating from capitalist competition. New forms of work organization are a re-regulation of work, not the end of regulation. (Edwards et al. 2002: 116)

Gender and new work practices

There is now substantial evidence, from both survey and case-study research, which demonstrates that the consequences of work reorganization differ substantially between men and women. There are a number of reasons for this. First, women are more likely to be concentrated in occupations and industries which require less skill and fewer qualifications (Gallie et al. 1998: ch. 2) and where employers remain rooted to cost-based business strategies. As it is skilled work that is likely to be the focus of management's efforts to compete on the basis of quality and innovation, it is men's work which is more likely to be associated with new forms of work organization. Second, as argued by Wajcman (2000), not only is the construction of jobs inherently related to gender, but the organizations in which they are located are also 'gendered' and the control of the labour process is intimately related to the gender of workers involved. Thus, the gender stereotyping of jobs is deeply embedded in the structure of work. As she emphasizes, 'pre-existing relationships of men and women to skilled labour and technology mediate the effects of new forms of work organization' (Wajcman 2000: 191). Third, there are the more subtle processes involved in work reorganization, particularly with teamworking, where notions of 'fitting in' assume a particular importance. Citing the leading study of Cockburn (1986), Jensen (1989: 154) makes the point that it is often very difficult for women to be accepted by teams of men who are used to working with one another in single-sex work groups:

> To the extent that work groups constitute themselves around ideas of who 'fits in', mixed groups are unlikely to form, both because notions of masculinity and femininity exclude the possibility of female competence ('she couldn't pull her weight') and because managers and workers recognize implicitly that the very process of group bonding includes reinforcement of gender identities ('she wouldn't like the language and the jokes of the lads'). Thus sexual difference, often carried by a discourse of sexual innuendo, becomes a powerful limit to the development of mixed work groups.

Indeed in instances where teams enjoy the freedom to select their own team members the gendered character of new forms of work organization may become even more pronounced.

Gallie et al.'s (1998) survey research also shows that most changes in work organization have been 'gendered' in that male employees in Britain were more likely to have recorded an increase in skills, task discretion and responsibility. Generally this gendered disadvantage was apparent across virtually all occupational categories, with the partial exception of professional and managerial positions. Thus, women's disadvantage is not only a consequence of their occupational distribution; gender inequality was evident *within* the majority of occupational categories. Further, while the evidence would suggest that over time gender differences in skill levels have tended to diminish, there was no evidence of any improvement with respect to responsibility over work decisions. It would seem, then, that as reticent as employers are generally to relinquish control to employees, where they are prepared to increase employees' discretion, they are more likely to privilege male over female employees.

Economic performance and new work practices

There is considerable evidence both in the US and Europe to suggest that where organizations introduce new work practices, the improvement in organizational performance is considerable (Appelbaum and Batt 1994; Huselid 1995; Delery and Doty 1996; Ichniowski et al. 1996; European Foundation 1997; Cully et al. 1999; Appelbaum et al. 2000; Guest 2000). That said, however, the benefits which accrue to firms from such changes can rarely, if ever, be attributed to one causal factor; rather, it is in combination or in 'bundles' that these changes have their greatest impact. Pil and MacDuffie (1996), for example, argue that changes in work practices are more effective in contributing to organizational performance where they 'fit' with, or are supported by, other changes in management practice. According to Ichniowski et al. (1996: 322), 'There are no one or two "magic bullets" that are *the* work practices that will stimulate worker and business performance. Work teams or QCs alone are not enough. Rather, whole systems need to be changed' (emphasis in original).

But as to answering the question *how* it is that new work practices 'fitted' with particular HR and business practices, or how 'bundles' of HR practices work, we are at some distance from knowing. 'Fit' implies the notion of strategic contingencies, that particular policies suit particular circumstances. The notion of 'bundles', on the other hand, suggests that there is a set of HR practices which bring consistently superior results, regardless of circumstances. Arguably, we are not helped a great deal by the available research as there is evidence to support both approaches. There is also some ambiguity as to whether practices should bundle in one specific way rather than another, or whether certain elements of the bundle are more important than others, and, as for 'fit', how tight a fit is necessary. As Edwards and Wright (2001) argue, until we examine the relevant processes and the complex ways in which new work practices and HR practices come together and in turn are linked to outcomes we can only answer whether they 'work', but, arguably, not why, and how it is that they might enhance organizational performance.

The recent work of David Guest and colleagues (Guest 2000; Guest et al. 2000a, 2000b) does, however, represent a significant attempt, albeit within the realm of quantitative evidence, to get beyond these constraints. Essentially Guest argues that greater consideration needs to be given to employee commitment, employee quality and employee response to work organization and that measures thereof should be developed and included in statistical models testing for links between high-performance systems and organizational performance. While his research, using data from WERS 1998 and from a survey of corporate managers of 237 companies, shows indeed that the presence of HR practices has a positive impact on employees' attitudes and behaviour which is in turn associated with particular performance outcomes, it does suffer, as he acknowledges, from its reliance on cross-sectional data. As such it is not possible to identify the direction of causality: improved performance may thus be antecedent to and not a consequence of new forms of work organization. It should also be noted that there was a strong, direct link from HR practices to performance, which was unmediated by employee attitudes (cf. Inchiowski et al. 1996; Godard and Delaney 2000).

But the search to identify determinate effects, whether they arise from individual practices, their fit, or their bundling with other practices, may be to miss the point. Consider, for example, Storey et al.'s (1997: 217) discussion of the influence of management development and career planning in Japanese and British companies on performance. They prefer to eschew the pursuit of 'causality' *sensu stricto*, that is, that management development is an independent or direct 'cause' of competitive advantage. Where such effects are identified, it is because they are seen as a *concomitant* of performance: a factor which interacts with other processes and which is itself sustained by continued competitive success. One of the authors of that research notes elsewhere:

> Career structures in Japan had outcomes because they were part of a wider set of company policies. They cannot be understood outside this context, and they do not have independent effects. Indeed, any effect reflected their long-established role . . . they were part of a process in which there was a systematic long-term view of business policy; this meant that they were allowed to become embedded in the fabric of the organization; and this in turn allowed benefits to emerge, which finally reinforced their existing approach. (Edwards 1998: 18)

Identifying the conditions for new forms of work organization to take root and prosper

We now turn to identifying the conditions under which employees welcome and benefit from the introduction of new forms of work organization.

Job security   Among the most critical would appear to be job security. The clearest demonstration of this in Britain is perhaps Marchington et al.'s (1994) study of employee involvement in six organizations which included a survey of 249 workers. In three organizations where the initiatives were successfully introduced employees felt secure in their positions. Conversely, in those other organizations where employees' attitudes were negative, there had been job losses or the future competitive circumstances of the companies appeared bleak. In the case of the latter companies, one, 'Southern Shoe', had had enjoyed good relations with employees, consulted widely and had considerable experience of employee involvement initiatives. However, more recent attempts by management to intensify employees' effort levels, to implement factory closures and generally undermine employees' sense of security was sufficient to undo the feeling of the company being a 'caring employer'. Other studies, too, highlight the importance of job security, Collinson et al. (1998) in respect of TQM, and Geary and Dobbins (2001), Cutcher-Gershenfeld et al. (1998), and Shaiken et al. (1997) in studies of teamworking. Other changes to HR practice would also seem to be important (Kinnie and Purcell 1998). For example, a focus on training to support teamworking was considered essential by management in Mueller and Purcell's (1992) study of European automotive engine plants. Other studies show how a managerial failure to adapt HR practices to support work reorganization is likely to result in the initiative failing. Bélanger and Dumas (1998) show, for example, how the development of teamworking in Alcan in Canada was constrained by the persistence of old regulations governing job evaluations and wage structures, as well as an adherence to particular seniority principles. Lloyd and Newell's (2000) study of teamworking, albeit of a limited form, among staff in a sales force at a pharmaceutical firm also demonstrates how a failure to align HR policies alongside teams was one important reason for its failure; in particular, teamworking was imposed on the sales force and – as in the Southern Shoe case – it breached the expectations that employees had of their work.

Technology and the nature of the production process   It would now appear clear that it is often difficult for teamworking to take root in low-skilled, routine fabrication operations (McArdle et al. 1995; Pollert 1996; Proctor and Mueller 2000; Scott 1994). What the relevant studies found was important, but they tended to assume that the work intensification that they observed was universal. It is ironic, as Proctor and Mueller (2000: 10) emphasize, that, as the debate on teamworking has centred to a considerable degree on the automotive industry and thus on assembly-line technology, it is precisely in such environments where it is most difficult to operate teamworking successfully. One might be more precise, however, and suggest that particular types of teams are more likely to work in different production environments. Thus, for example, in assembly operations where employees' autonomy is constrained and where team leaders exercise considerable influence, off-line teams and lean production teams are perhaps more likely, but in continuous production operations, autonomous teamworking may be more likely to develop (see Cutcher-Gershenfeld et al. 1998: ch. 4).

Wright and Edwards's (1998) study of Alcan's aluminium smelter in Lynemouth, and Geary and Dobbins's (2001) study of an American pharmaceutical firm in Ireland, demonstrate how capital-intensive, continuous-process techno-logy seems to be particularly apposite for the development of teamworking. There are two main reasons. First, the nature of employees' work is to monitor the production process such that there is often the time and space to interact and engage in team activities. Further, employees often work in small groups and in a common work area which encourages information-sharing and problem-solving activities. The second relates to the important issue of workers' prior orientations and experiences. In both these studies, even before management had introduced teams there was already an appreciation of team principles amongst the production workforce, and natural work groups had developed informally on the shop floor. Teamwork, therefore, was introduced into a 'receptive' labour process and where it had a natural affinity with employees' preferred ways of working. That said, however, prior experience of teams did raise employees' expectations – which were not always met – of what a 'formal' teamworking initiative might look like. In contrast, the absence of prior experience may work to promote employee support for teamworking. In the Geary and Dobbins study, junior administrative office staff, who had little prior experience of working in teams, derived considerable satisfaction from the new initiative, but for the reason that it introduced some novelty, as well as increased discretion, into their daily routines.

There are also examples of where workers' prior experience of 'teamworking' clashes with managerial definitions of the 'introduction' of teams. Consider Martinez Lucio et al.'s (2000) study of management's attempts to introduce teamworking at Royal Mail in the face of employee resistance. Workers' objec-tions were twofold: first, teams already existed, albeit 'introduced' and organized by workers themselves; second, these were seen to be more worker-friendly than the form of teamworking proposed by management. This study, along with others (e.g. Rinehart et al. 1997), shows not only how work groups often have clearly defined norms governing effort levels and that these groups perform important social functions, but also how competing conceptions of teamwork are rooted firmly in the issue of control. Two more general lessons might then be drawn from this: first, workers are unlikely to respond passively to 'new' management ideas; second, new initiatives continue to remain part of a relation-ship of control.

Management choices and strategies   Third, there is the issue of management choices and the strategies management pursues. As Geary and Dobbins (2001) explain, management at their case-study site made a conscious and deliberate attempt to reposition the competitive strategy of the company around the manufacture of small-batch, high-margin, high-quality goods. To support this strategy manage-ment invested in new technology, introduced teamworking, made an enhanced commitment to employment security and employee training, and made con-siderable efforts to restructure industrial relations. This integration of teamworking with other elements of HR practice and the company's wider business strategy had the advantage of conveying a reasonably coherent set of messages to the workforce. In contrast, Knights and McCabe's (1998) study of organizational innovation in the financial services sector found that employees remained poorly committed to quality as management's approach was characterized by a series of inconsistencies: teamwork was undermined by an insistence on measuring individual employee performance and a concentration on quantity of output as opposed to quality.

The climate of industrial relations   Finally, there is the climate of industrial relations and the manner in which change is introduced in unionized organizations. The predominant reading of the available case-study evidence would suggest that a poor industrial relations climate and an attack on trade unions is usually inimical to the successful implementation of new work practices. The success of team-working at Alcan's Lynemouth plant, for example, followed a marked improve-ment in the quality of management–union relations and was, in part at least, attributable to management's willingness to work with shop stewards in the introduction of change (Wright and Edwards 1998). Similarly at Geary and Dobbins's (2001) pharmaceutical site, management had enjoyed good relations with the trade unions and the strategy of introducing teamworking with trade union involvement and co-operation through a steering committee achieved considerable success. In contrast, where management has tried to bypass and marginalize trade unions in the introduction of new work structures, or where their implementation was designed to reduce union influence, then it is often difficult for new innovations to take root (Collinson et al. 1998).

In sum, it would seem that where management introduces new forms of work organization without giving due attention to employees' views and welfare, either by denying employees an input into the design of the new practices or by making no provision for employment security, the innovations may be seen simply as a crude device to intensify work and engage in downsizing (cf. Marchington et al. 1994; Wilkinson et al. 1997). The implication of this would appear therefore to be clear: arguments for the introduction of new work practices which rely solely or primarily on efficiency criteria, but which do not consider the issue of equity or mutual obligations, are unlikely to succeed in the long term.

Why Are New Work Practices Not Adopted More Widely?

Given the overwhelming evidence that the introduction of new work practices brings substantial economic benefits, why is it that they are not used more widely? There have been a number of attempts to answer this question, most notably Ichniowski et al. (1996), Pil and MacDuffie (1996), Edwards (1998) and Geary (1999). The following factors would seem to be the most important.

Destroying existing competencies

First, there are the difficulties associated with learning new practices and unlearn-ing old ones. Pil and MacDuffie refer to this process, where an organization puts to one side the competencies and understandings obtained under an older system of work organization, as 'competence-destroying'. As a consequence, organizational performance, at least at the early stages, is likely to suffer as management and employees grapple with the demands of introducing new work practices. In anticipation of the difficulties and costs – and perhaps with no clear or shared view of the potential benefits – of introducing such a new system, it is not surprising that many organizations should seek to adopt single practices incrementally. In doing so, employers are, unwittingly perhaps, judging the contribution of individual practices in isolation from the potential of a total system. The danger is that, as the individual parts of the new system are taken up and are subsequently judged not to have generated economically important effects, they are dropped before the value of a new system can be properly established.

Limited space to invest

Second, the financial costs of introducing new work practices, particularly as part of a comprehensive package that includes extensive training and which makes provision for employment security, are considerable. For many organizations, however, the short-term pressures of maintaining and maximizing the current stock price are of a level to make such long-term investments very difficult. The problem for employers is that, while they might recognize the benefits of introducing new work practices and of establishing collaborative relations with employees and their representatives, these are difficult-to-measure initiatives, have a long lead time before their benefits can be identified and are not easy to justify to portfolio investors.

That said, some firms have obviously been able to experiment and innovate in significant ways. One group is typically high-tech companies competing on the basis of value-added, customized products – many of whom are subsidiaries of large US MNCs – who have, for reasons indicated in chapter 4, been able to escape some of the pressures of short-termism, 'suspend market rules' and be innovative in terms of product design, work organization and competitive strategies. Such firms have often been able to construct social communities within themselves such that provision is made for employment security, the development of internal labour markets and investment in skills. Crouch and Streeck (1997) refer to these companies as 'institutional firms', to distinguish them from mainstream hierarchical companies. In a way, then, these companies would seem to be able to secure an adequate level of organizational loyalty. That these practices have been successfully reproduced outside their country of origin would also suggest that they are to a degree independent of a national 'exoskeleton of rule-setting institutions'.[1] Yet, as chapter 4 shows, the practices are not context-independent: they may not flourish in a hostile environment, and they will require some adaptation to survive. A second group of firms consists of those who have faced a severe crisis and who have been pushed into workplace innovation. The difficulty with this, however, is that such a response can quite easily slip into, or be backed into, innovation as a cost-containment measure where jobs are lost, employees are expected to work in teams so that they can perform more tasks, and effort levels are intensified. Changes are introduced only at the margin: the fundamental nature of work organization and management–employee relations remain unchanged; nor does it seem to lead to a great deal of success in the long run (Appelbaum and Batt 1994: 22–3) and may serve only to undermine employee co-operation and motivation.

Management difficulties

It is well recognized that changes to work systems pose particular difficulties for middle and line management (Strauss 1998; Marchington 2000). There are a number of elements here. First, the practice of sharing information, authority and decision-making responsibility does not come easy to many managers. Such tendencies are accentuated where the introduction of new work practices leads to 'delayering' and the flattening of hierarchical structures. Second, managers' desire to hold on to information and a tendency not to trust their staff is not, as Edwards (1998) argues, just some kind of psychological quirk, but reflects rather an absence of structured career paths and a need to prove oneself in competition with others. Third, the incentive structure rewards what Smith (1991) terms 'managerial opportunism', where managers are rewarded for taking action that will improve the bottom line in the short term: as a result, change of a more fundamental and radical kind is rarely countenanced (Appelbaum and Batt 1994). Finally, management (in)action and inertia may be a consequence of an inability to understand what is required to transform work systems so that greater flexibilities and efficiencies may be achieved. An important element here is that in many organizations people-management issues are at best secondary to, and at worst remain disconnected from, decisions in respect of other organizational objectives. The most recent workplace survey, for instance, found that the proportion of organizations employing employee relations specialists at board level had fallen steadily in recent years. The fall was most marked amongst smaller, indigenous firms and those without union representation; perhaps surprisingly, newly established workplaces were less likely to have board-level personnel representatives (Millward et al. 2000: 76–7).

Market contexts and competitive strategies

New work practices are more likely to be adopted where organizations' products or services are highly specialized and change over short periods, but are perhaps less appropriate or less of a necessity in the production of standardized goods, or in the provision of uniform services, or in stable market environments (Osterman, 1994; European Foundation 1997; Geary 1999; Appelbaum et al. 2000). As the predominant route to gaining competitive advantage in the UK – although this is not often conceded publicly – is through price competition and the production and delivery of standard goods and services (Prais 1995; Williams et al. 1990; FMI/DTI/IBM 1996), there may be little incentive or perceived need to adopt innovative work systems. Indeed Ackroyd and Proctor (1998) make the point that British firms often eschew the production of complex products and that many are systematically withdrawing from manufacturing high-value-added capital goods (see p. 74 above).

There are two important reasons why British employers continue to persist with low-value-added, low-quality production strategies. First, there is the structure of domestic demand (Keep and Mayhew 1998; Keep 1999). Inequality in income distribution in the UK – a fifth of Europe's poor (using EU definitions) reside within the UK – means that there are many people who simply cannot afford to buy high-quality goods and services. Thus, in contrast to other European countries, notably Scandinavia and Germany, where incomes are generally higher and more equally distributed, British companies have less opportunity and incentive to pursue high-value-added production strategies. Consider the example of retail banking, offered by Keep and Mayhew (1998: 5), where the 'current holy grail is to achieve the lowest possible cost base in order to compete effectively in what is a cost-based marketplace'. To this list could be added other sectors, including leisure and tourism, distribution, hotel and catering, and finally, increasingly significant parts of the airline industry. Keep (1999: 8) makes the point forcefully:

> Far from being dead, Fordism and neo-Fordism is a growing and powerful model of competitive advantage within the UK economy, especially within large swaths of the service sector. While mass production may have declined as the dominant model for the manufacture of consumer goods, it offers, in combination with economy of scale advantages, the promise of salvation to many major UK retail chains, retail banks, and insurance companies.

To this extent, therefore, there are important demand-side impediments to the adoption of new work practices in Britain.

The second important factor relates to the opportunity, afforded by a deregulated labour market and flexible industrial relations regime, to use labour costs and effort-intensive forms of work organization as competitive levers. There are a number of elements here. For example, as discussed in chapter 15, the training system is poorly equipped to extricate the UK from a low-skill equilibrium (Green 1998; Keep 1999). In many cases, firms are only looking for a narrow range of low-level skills and do not require their employees generally to take responsibility or exhibit discretion (Dench et al. 1998). There is therefore much to suggest a meeting point has been reached between what the training system can deliver and what individual employers want.

The tendency, therefore, for large sections of British industry, is to look at what has worked in the past and to simply seek more of it. The option of introducing significant changes in work practices, in contrast, is seen to be too costly and too risky in a financial environment where few have the luxury of time to await the potential economic benefits. To this extent, large portions of British industry are likely for the foreseeable future to remain locked within what have been termed 'competency traps' (Pil and MacDuffie 1996). Keep (1999: 15) offers the following conclusion:

Instead of flat, team-working organizations utilizing the knowledge and skills of the entire workforce as a source of competitive advantage, the general trend continues to be to rely upon the brainpower of a relatively small elite to devise systems, procedures and ways of working that routinize work and minimize opportunities for thought and discretion, and thereby to consign the rest of the non-managerial workforce to the role of willing hands or drones in a non-participator hierarchy.

Conclusions

The key implications of this analysis are as follows. First, while interest in new forms of work organization has increased significantly in recent years, British employers remain reluctant to adopt advanced forms that permit employees considerable discretion and autonomy. In comparison to other European countries, Britain lags some way behind, being very much a middle-ranking performer. While the reasons for this are complex and varied, this chapter has stressed that the conditions conducive to innovation are in large part absent in Britain. In their place are competitive strategies which give emphasis to cost minimization and the delivery of mass products and services, a financial system which is inimical to patient investment in training and skills acquisition and an industrial relations regime which permits employers the option of eschewing high-commitment strategies in favour of more traditional labour-use strategies. These factors combined represent significant structural impediments in the face of workplace innovation in Britain. These will not be easy to overcome and the likelihood must be that the adoption of advanced forms of work reorganization will remain confined to a minority of organizations.

Second, the success or otherwise of new work practices within the workplace is crucially dependent on: the provision made for employment security; employee and employer expectations of, and previous experience with, new forms of work organization; a genuine commitment on the part of management to increase employees' autonomy; the place of and influence exercised by employees and their representatives; and finally, the ability to integrate work structures and HR practices in a coherent manner. The economic context of the firm is also important, principally whether companies compete through product innovation and quality as opposed to cost-based strategies and also whether organizations can insulate themselves from short-term financial pressures. Clearly, given these conditions initiatives such as teamworking are unlikely to flourish outside a modest number of organizations, and as firms' circumstances vary, so, too, does the shape of new forms of work organization. Plainly, then, new work practices are likely to take a variety of forms.

But while organizations' economic circumstances are indeed an important mediating factor in explaining the incidence of teamworking, to deduce from this that, where similar conditions are present, teamworking will take root is perhaps too unidirectional and simple (Edwards et al. 2002). There is nothing inevitable here. Consider, for example, Springer's (1999) argument that, as the German auto industry moved to adopt a German version of lean production, there was in tandem a 'roll-back to Taylorism' with a return to the classical assembly line operating with standardized, short work cycles. The reason, he suggests, is that as labour markets slackened and competition intensified the focus of management's attention shifted from considerations of the quality of work life to production efficiency. One German manager complained recently: 'quality used to give us a 20 per cent premium on the price: now it's about 5 per cent' (quoted in Dore 2000: 231), indicating that the once stark differentiation between different competitive postures, one based on cost minimization and the other on quality and innovation, is less sustainable today. But employers are stuck with wage levels predicated on that 20 per cent premium. In such a context it is perhaps not surprising that companies should focus increasingly on production efficiencies and perhaps less on quality of work life considerations. That said, while the economic context is undoubtedly important, it is not a determining influence; it may be that, depending on the economic or labour market context, either or both might be the key factor. Moreover, the same point can be used to emphasize that management's motivation for introducing new work practices is informed by many considerations and that it is only likely to introduce change where it sees good reason and foresees some benefit.

Third, re-regulation has altered the blend of control and consent. Over two decades ago Burawoy (1979) in the US and Cressey and MacInnes (1980) in Britain made the point that management is not simply about controlling employees, it is also about tapping into and releasing employees' discretionary effort and creativity. An employer strategy that is exclusively based on direct control – or responsible autonomy – is not open to management. To use Burawoy's words, 'coercion must be supplemented by the organization of consent' (1979: 27), and while employers have usually combined trust and constraint 'in an uneasy combination' (Hyman 1991: 269), the search for a solution is, at the very least, the search for a better, if more pragmatic, combination. Thus while management has an incentive to grant employees increased autonomy in their work, it is unlikely to cede anything like full autonomy. It is for this reason, then, that we must continue to talk about control *and* autonomy, but not in the stark terms conceived by some of the more extreme critics. The problems of labour regulation are not escaped; tensions and ambiguities remain.

Finally, there are the consequences of new forms work organization for employees. The central argument is that they have middling and complex effects. The common tendency to see new work practices as being either exploitative or transformative is to exaggerate their intentions and consequences; the claim is that it rests within more mundane and modest effort to re-regulate labour. Nor is it simply a matter of seeing it as a zero-sum game. There are elements of new forms of work organization which are of benefit to employees and may be welcomed, but there are also aspects which impose new demands and which may not be seen to be so advantageous. But the balance of costs and benefits is not simply six of one and half a dozen of the other; employees' response and the ultimate shape of new work practices is influenced by, and is connected to, the way work is being reorganized and the expectations employees hold. This chapter has underlined the importance of the latter; seemingly 'strong' forms of work reorganization may be treated with scepticism and hostility by employees where they have exercised traditional skills, perhaps within work groups sharing strong norms governing effort and self-discipline, to which they are committed, while 'weaker' forms, introduced into a work environment where employees have enjoyed little or no discretion, may be welcomed. There is thus no one new, distinct, self-contained model: new forms of work organization assume different forms in different settings, and have variable effects. Where employees buy into new practices and accept the need for a more disciplined work environment co-operation between employees and employer may occur, but not necessarily of a form which leads to a transformation in employees' trust in management. But this might be enough for both parties, management and workers!

Note

Some of the material used in this chapter draws on work jointly authored with Paul Edwards and Keith Sisson.

1 That is, independent of the institutional structures and political context of a particular country's industrial relations system. The phrase is Streeck's (1997: 52).

References

Ackroyd, S., and Procter, S. 1998: British manufacturing organisation and workplace industrial relations: some attributes of the new flexible firm, *British Journal of Industrial Relations*, 36 (2), 163–83.

Appelbaum, E., Bailey, T., Berg, P. and Kalleberg, A. 2000: *Manufacturing Advantage: Why High-Performance Work Systems Pay Off.* Ithaca: Cornell University Press.

Appelbaum, E., and Batt, R. 1994: *The New American Workplace: Transforming Work Systems in the United States.* Ithaca: ILR Press.

Becker, B., Huselid, M., Pickus, P. and Spratt, M. 1997: HR as a source of shareholder value: research and recommendations, *Human Resource Management*, 36 (1), 39–47.

Bélanger, J., and Dumas, M. 1998: Teamworking and internal labour markets: a study of a Canadian aluminium smelter, *Economic and Industrial Democracy*, 19 (3), 417–42.

Burawoy, M. 1979: *Manufacturing Consent: Changes in the Labor Process Under Monopoly Capitalism.* Chicago: University of Chicago Press.

Clark, J. 1995: *Managing Innovation and Change.* London: Sage.

Cockburn, C. 1986: Women and technology: opportunity is not enough. In K. Purcell, S. Wood, A. Waton and S. Allen (eds), *The Changing Experience of Employment.* London: Macmillan.

Collinson, M., Edwards, P. and Rees, C. 1998: *Involving Employees in Total Quality Management.* DTI Employment Relations Research Series, 1. London: DTI. Available at <www.dti.gov.uk/er/emar>.

Cressey, P., and MacInnes, J. 1980: Voting for Ford. *Capital and Class*, 11, 5–33.

Crouch, C., Finegold, D. and Sako, M. 1999: *Are Skills the Answer? The Political Economy of Skill Creation in Advanced Industrial Countries.* Oxford: Oxford University Press.

Crouch, C., and Streeck, W. (eds) 1997: *Political Economy of Modern Capitalism.* London: Sage.

Cully, M., Woodland, S., O'Reilly, A. and Dix, G. 1999: *Britain at Work*. London: Routledge.

Cutcher-Gershenfeld, J., et al. 1998: *Knowledge-Driven Work: Unexpected Lessons from Japanese and United States Work Practices*. New York: Oxford University Press.

Danford, A. 1998: Teamworking and labour regulation in the autocomponents industry, *Work, Employment and Society*, 12 (3), 409–32.

Delery, J. E., and Doty, D. H. 1996: Modes of theorizing in strategic human resource management, *Academy of Management Journal*, 39 (4), 802–35.

Dench, S., Perryman, S., and Giles, L. 1998: *Employers' Perceptions of Key Skills*. IES Report 349. Brighton: Institute of Employment Studies.

Dore, R. 2000: *Stock Market Capitalism – Welfare Capitalism: Japan and Germany Versus the Anglo Saxons*. Oxford: Oxford University Press.

Doty, D., and Delery, J. 1997: The importance of holism, interdependence, and equifinality assumptions in high performance work systems: toward theories of the high performance workforce. Manuscript. Fayetteville, Ark.: University of Arkansas.

Edwards, P. K. 1988: Patterns of conflict and accommodation. In D. Gallie (ed.), *Employment in Britain*. Oxford: Blackwell.

Edwards, P. K. 1998: The future of the employment relationship, seminar paper, University College, Dublin.

Edwards, P., Geary, J. and Sisson, K. 2002: Employee involvement in the workplace: transformative, exploitative, or limited and controlled? In J. Bélanger, A. Giles, P. Lapointe and G. Murray (eds), *Work and Employment Relations in the High Performance Workplace*. London: Continuum International.

Edwards, P. K., and Wright, M. 2001: High-involvement work systems and performance outcomes, *International Journal of Human Resource Management*, 12 (4), 568–85.

European Foundation for the Improvement of Living and Working Conditions 1997: *New Forms of Work Organisation. Can Europe Realise its Potential? Results of a Survey of Direct Employee Participation in Europe*. Luxembourg: Office for the Official Publications of the European Communities.

FMI (Foundation for Manufacturing Industry)/DTI/IBM 1996: *Tomorrow's Best Practice: A Vision for the Future for Top Manufacturing Companies in the UK*. London: FMI.

Gallie, D. 1996: Skill, gender and the quality of employment. In R. Crompton, D. Gallie and K. Purcell (eds), *Changing Forms of Employment: Organisations, Skills and Gender*. London: Routledge.

Gallie, D., and White, M. 1993: *Employee Commitment and the Skills Revolution: First Findings from the Employment in Britain Survey*. London: Policy Studies Institute.

Gallie, D., White, M., Cheng, Y. and Tomlinson, M. 1998: *Restructuring the Employment Relationship*. Oxford: Clarendon Press.

Geary, J. F. 1995: Work practices: the structure of work. In P. Edwards (ed.), *Industrial Relations*. Oxford: Blackwell.

Geary, J. F. 1999: The new workplace: change at work in Ireland, *International Journal of Human Resource Management*, 10 (5), 870–90.

Geary, J. F., and Dobbins, A. 2001: Teamworking: a new dynamic in a familiar (contested) terrain, *Human Resource Management Journal*, 11 (1), 3–21.

Geary, J. F., and Sisson, K. 1994: *Conceptualising Direct Participation in Organisational Change*. Luxembourg: Office for Official Publications of the European Communities.

Godard, J., and Delaney, J. T. 2000: Reflections on the 'high performance' paradigm's implications for industrial relations, *Industrial and Labor Relations Review*, 53 (3), 482–502.

Green, A. 1988: Core skills, key skills and general culture: in search of the common foundation in vocational education, *Evaluation and Research in Education*, 12 (1), 23–43.

Guest, D. 2000: Human Resource Management, employee well-being and organisational performance. Paper presented at IPD Professional Standards Conference, University of Warwick, July 2000.

Guest, D., Michie, J., Sheehan, M. and Conway, N. 2000a: *Employment Relations, HRM and Business Performance: An Analysis of the 1998 Workplace Employee Relations Survey*. London: IPD.

Guest, D., Michie, J., Sheehan, M. and Conway, N. 2000b: *Human Resource Management and Performance: First Findings from the Future of Work Study*. London: IPD.

Huselid, M. 1995: The impact of human resource management practices on turnover, productivity, and corporate financial performance, *Academy of Management Journal*, 38 (3), 635–70.

Hyman, J., and Mason, B. 1995: *Managing Employee Involvement and Participation*. London: Sage.

Hyman, R. 1991: Plus ça change? The theory of production and the production of theory. In A. Pollert (ed.), *Farewell to Flexibility*. Oxford: Blackwell.

Ichniowski, C., Kochan, T., Levine, D., Olson, C. and Strauss, G. 1996: What works at work: overview and assessment. *Industrial Relations*, 35 (3), 299–333.

Jenson, J. 1989: The talents of women, the skills of men: flexible specialisation and women. In S. Wood (ed.), *The Transformation of Work?* London: Unwin Hyman.

Keep, E. 1999: Britain's VET policy and the 'Third Way': following a high street trajectory or running up a dead end street? Paper presented at CEROP Research Seminar, Michael Smurfit Graduate School of Business, University College Dublin, March 1999.

Keep, E., and Mayhew, K. 1998: *Was Ratner Right? Product Market and Competitive Strategies and their Links with Skills and Knowledge*. London: Employment Policy Institute.

Kinnie, N., and Purcell, J. 1998: Side effects, *People Management*, 30 April, 34–6.

Knights, D., and McCabe, D. 1998: Dreams and designs on strategy: a critical analysis of TQM and management control, *Work, Employment and Society*, 12 (3), 433–57.

Kochan, T., and Osterman, P. 1994: *The Mutual Gains Enterprise*. Cambridge, Mass.: Harvard Business School Press.

Korczynski, M., Shire, K., Frenkel, S. and Tam, M. 2000: Service work in consumer capitalism: customers, control and contradictions, *Work, Employment and Society*, 14 (4), 669–88.

Lawler, E., Mohrman, S. and Ledford, G. 1992: *Employee Involvement and Total Quality Management: Practices and Results in Fortune 1000 Companies*. San Francisco: Jossey-Bass.

Lincoln, J. R., and Kalleberg, A. L. 1996: Commitment, quits and work organization in Japanese and US plants, *Industrial and Labor Relations Review*, 50 (1), 39–59.

Lloyd, C., and Newell, H. 2000: Selling teams to the salesforce: teamworking in the UK pharmaceutical industry. In S. Procter and F. Mueller (eds), *Teamworking*. Basingstoke: Macmillan.

Marchington, M. 2000: Teamworking and employee involvement: terminology, evaluation and context. In S. Procter and F. Mueller (eds), *Teamworking*. Basingstoke: Macmillan.

Marchington, M., Wilkinson, A., Ackers, P. and Goodman, J. 1994: Understanding the meaning of participation. *Human Relations*, 47 (8), 867–93.

Martinez Lucio, M., Jenkins, S. and Noon, M. 2000: Management strategy, union identity and oppositionalism: teamwork in the Royal Mail. In S. Procter and F. Mueller (eds), *Teamworking*. Basingstoke: Macmillan.

McArdle, L., Rowlinson, M., Procter, S., Hassard, J. and Forrester, P. 1995: Total Quality Management and participation: employee empowerment or the enhancement of exploitation? In A. Wilkinson and H. Wilmott (eds), *Making Quality Critical: New Perspectives on Organisational Change*. London: Routledge.

McKinlay, A., and Taylor, P. 1996: Power, surveillance and resistance: inside the 'factory of the future'. In P. Ackers, C. Smith and P. Smith (eds), *The New Workplace and Trade Unionism*. London: Routledge.

Millward, N., Bryson, A. and Forth, J. 2000: *All Change at Work?* London: Routledge.

Millward, N., Stevens, M., Smart, D. and Hawes, W. R. 1992: *Workplace Industrial Relations in Transition*. Aldershot: Dartmouth.

Mueller, F., and Purcell, J. 1992: The drive for higher productivity, *Personnel Management*, May, 28–33.

Oliver, N., and Wilkinson, B. 1989: Japanese manufacturing techniques and personnel and industrial relations practice in Britain: evidence and implications, *British Journal of Industrial Relations*, 27 (1) 73–91.

Osterman, P. 1994: How common is workplace transformation and how can we explain who adopts it? *Industrial and Labor Relations Review*, 47 (1) 173–87.

Osterman, P. 1999: *Securing Prosperity. The American Labor Market: How it has Changed and What To Do About It*. Princeton: Princeton University Press.

Osterman, P. 2000: Work reorganization in an era of restructuring, *Industrial and Labor Relations Review*, 53 (2), 179–96.

Pil, F. K., and MacDuffie, J. P. 1996: The adoption of high-involvement work practices, *Industrial Relations*, 35, 423–55.

Pollert, A. 1996: 'Team work' on the assembly line: contradiction and the dynamics of union resilience. In P. Ackers, C. Smith and P. Smith, (eds), *The New Workplace and Trade Unionism*. London: Routledge.

Prais, S. J. 1995: *Productivity, Education and Training*. Cambridge: Cambridge University Press.

Procter, S., and Mueller, F. 2000: Teamworking: strategy, structure, systems and culture. In S. Procter and F. Mueller (eds), *Teamworking*. Basingstoke: Macmillan.

Rinehart, J., Huxley, C. and Robertson, D. 1997: *Just Another Car Factory? Lean Production and its Discontents*. Ithaca: ILR Press.

Rosenthal, P., Hill, S. and Peccei, R. 1997: Checking out service: evaluating excellence, HRM and TQM in retailing, *Work, Employment and Society*, 11 (3), 481–503.

Scarbrough, H., and Terry, M. 1997: United Kingdom: the reorganisation of production. In T. A. Kochan, R. D. Lansbury and J. P. MacDuffie (eds), *After Lean Production*. Ithaca: ILR Press.

Scott, A. 1994: *Willing Slaves? British Workers under Human Resource Management*. Cambridge: Cambridge University Press.

Shaiken, H., Lopez, S. and Mankita, I. 1997: Two routes to team production: Saturn and Chrysler compared, *Industrial Relations*, 36 (1), 17–45.

Smith, S. 1991: On the economic rationale for codetermination laws, *Journal of Economic Behaviour and Organisation*, 16 (2), 261–81.

Springer, R. 1999: The end of new production concepts? *Economic and Industrial Democracy*, 20 (1), 117–46.

Strauss, G. 1998: Participation works – if conditions are appropriate. In F. Heller, E. Pusic, G. Strauss and B. Wilpert (eds), *Organisational Participation: Myth and Reality*. Oxford: Oxford University Press.

Streeck, W. 1997: German capitalism: Does it exist? Can it survive? *New Political Economy*, 2 (2), 237–56.

Storey, J., Edwards, P. and Sisson, K. 1997: *Managers in the Making*. London: Sage.

Taylor, S. 1997: 'Empowerment' or 'degradation': Total Quality Management and the service sector. In R. K. Brown (ed.), *The Changing Shape of Work*. Basingstoke: Macmillan.

Wajcman, J. 2000: Feminism facing industrial relations in Britain. *British Journal of Industrial Relations*, 38 (2), 183–201.

Walton, R. E. 1985: From control to commitment in the workplace, *Harvard Business Review*, 53 (2), 77–84.

Webb, J. 1996: Vocabularies of motive and the 'NEW' management, *Work, Employment and Society*, 10 (2), 251–71.

Whitfield, K. 1998: High performance work systems: disentangling the bundles. Paper to British Universities Industrial Relations Association annual conference, University of Keele.

Wilkinson, A., Godfrey, G. and Marchington, M. 1997: Bouquets, brickbats and blinkers: Total Quality Management and employee involvement in practice, *Organization Studies*, 18 (5), 799–819.

Williams, K., Williams, J. and Haslam, C. 1990: The hollowing out of British manufacturing and its implications for policy. *Economy and Society*, 19 (4), 456–90.

Wood, S., and Albanese, M. 1995: Can we speak of high commitment management on the shop floor? *Journal of Management Studies*, 32 (2), 215–47.

Wright, M., and Edwards, P. 1998: Does teamworking work and, if so, why? A case study in the aluminium industry. *Economic and Industrial Democracy*, 19 (1), 59–90.

14

MANAGING WITHOUT UNIONS: THE SOURCES AND LIMITATIONS OF INDIVIDUALISM

TREVOR COLLING

This chapter develops the analyses already presented in chapters 8, 9 and 12 in two main ways. The first moves in what may be called a 'macro' direction, relating analyses of the specifics of industrial relations systems to wider developments in society. Specifically, it addresses a stream of writing which claims that the decline in collectivism reflects, not just the institutions of industrial relations, but also more fundamental shifts in social identities, particularly a collapse in collective and class-based loyalties. If such a view were correct, explanations deriving from industrial relations phenomena would be at best partial. In fact, however, the evidence does not sustain claims of a collapse of collective identities. The empirical focus in this chapter is British, but it should also be noted that the more sweeping claims are often made about modern capitalism as a whole. But if one examines attitudes towards collectivism across the industrialized world it is clear that the decline of collective institutions has been still less marked than in Britain. To claim a shift in attitudes across modern capitalism is to claim too much.

The second aspect of the chapter moves in the opposite direction: a 'micro' examination of the nature of employment relations in two non-union and potentially 'individualized' firms. Chapter 12 has shown that individualization often contains collective strands and that it cannot be equated with a high-trust employment relationship. The chapter also underlined cost pressure as a key driver that could undermine employer rhetoric about skills and training. The present analysis develops such themes, showing in particular what individualization meant to employees and that its nature varied according to context, sometimes in surprising ways.

The two strands of the chapter together reveal the complexities behind an apparently simple idea such as individualism. The second strand also acts as a concrete example of the case-study method in industrial relations that can be used as an introduction to more specialist research literature.

Explaining the Decline of Collectivism

That the decline in collective employee relations has been steep is beyond dispute. Explaining this trend involves tackling some complex issues, many of which go beyond simple measures of institutional health. Which explanation, or combination of explanations, is preferred depends too upon the frame of reference one starts from and implicit definitions of interests (see chapter 1). Those who see the interests of managers and employees as mainly complementary and mutually reinforcing will tend to see the emergence of collectivity as the result of specific factors such as the failure of communication. There is also a long-established strand of writing that sees discontent as peaking either during early industrialization or with the arrival of large-scale Fordist work organization. Whichever particular view is taken of the exact mechanism at work, the emphasis is on secular and broad patterns of social change that are now eroding former bases of solidarity. On the other hand, those who see fundamental conflicts of interest in the workplace will tend to emphasize shifts in the balance of power between workers and their employers, supported by public policy. The middle ground will see conflicts arising from time to time and focus on whether and how managers in the workplace have addressed them. Each of these perspectives is now examined in turn, focusing first on the evidence of a secular rise in individualism.

A secular trend?

The collapsing incidence of collective organization and conflict in the workplace is often attributed to the declining influence of class interests and identities. This has a number of facets: the rise of acquisitive, consumption-based individualism; changes in the composition of labour markets; and the changes in the structure and social context of workplaces. That these trends have affected deeply collective identities and organization is not denied here, but their novelty is. Placed in historical perspective, they are arguably part of an ongoing process. While class identities have changed in form and extent, there is little evidence that their foundations have been eradicated.

Throughout the 1980s, reflection on the issue of social change tended towards the epochal. Social and economic change was altering not just the expression of class identity but its very basis (for a typical example of this kind of discussion, see Hebdige 1989). Dissatisfaction with unions was high. Media and policymakers allocated to them almost exclusive responsibility for the protracted industrial and political conflict of the late 1970s (Claydon 2000). Workplace studies suggested that aspects of union decline were attributable to negative public perceptions of them (McLoughlin and Gourlay 1993). On its own, this could have been a transitory phenomenon; union popularity had waxed and waned in the past, usually in relation to patterns of industrial conflict (Edwards and Bain 1988). But the nature of economic recovery from the mid-1980s apparently did nothing to reinstate enthusiasm for collective organization. Recovery was consumer-led, fuelled by house price inflation, wage growth for those on above-average incomes and the increasingly easy availability of credit. The array of consumer products, and the retail environments in which they were offered, changed and expanded. Commentators became preoccupied with consumption (or 'lifestyle shopping') as an expression of individual and collective identities (Williamson 1985). According to some, the omens for trade unions were not good:

> It was a consequence of the political and cultural changes in the 1960s and 1970s that personal identity and individual self-assertion became highly valued goals of human experience in the west. But this emphasis not only challenges authority structures such as the family, the school, the monarchy, the police, and courts and so on; it also questions the basis of joining and participating in collective organizations such as trade unions. (Urry 1989: 100)

Underlying trends in consumer expenditure were social changes of a more substantial kind. Long-term shifts in the sectoral composition of the economy intensified during late 1970s and this was sustained through most of the 1980s. Measured as a proportion of gross domestic product, manufacturing declined by 10 percentage points over that period so that it now accounts for less than a quarter (Mayes with Soteri 1994: 378). Some have suggested that this process alone accounted for up to 50 per cent of union membership decline in Britain during the 1980s (Visser 1992: 26).

Three sets of factors supporting claims of this kind can be identified. First, consequent upon changes in sectoral composition, white-collar work and workers became preponderant at the expense of manual workers who had provided the core of the union movement. An established line of argument suggests that the labour market position of white-collar workers, and thus the norms and terms under which they are engaged, foster workplace dynamics of a different character. The rapid diffusion of information technology, coming on top of the shift to service working, has given perspectives of this kind added weight and momentum. Paid work that used to be characterized primarily by physical effort is now more likely to involve social (or, 'people') skills, 'emotional' labour, and the manipulation and interpretation of different kinds of 'knowledge'. Since these skills are difficult to define and prescribe in advance, they are said to be less amenable to direct control. For these reasons, supervision and overt expressions of managerial authority over employees are less of a feature in modern white-collar employment relationships: 'The knowledge carried by the employee becomes a real and controlling resource, perhaps a decisive factor in production, but it *remains with the employee* and in no real sense is it ever of the firm' (Despres and Hiltrop 1995: 11, emphasis added). Frenkel et al. (1995: 773) observe a trend towards 'knowledge work *and* people centredness' (emphasis added). Rising levels of skill and education combined with different employer strategies thus give rise to meritocratic workplace cultures. Traditional bases of collectivism, stemming from alienating work processes and the experience of managerial direction, are eroded.

The second key change was the decline of the 'male breadwinner'. This refers not to relative pay but to patterns of employment. Male participation in the labour market declined overall as older and younger men increasingly fell out of employment (Crompton 1997: 25). Women's employment, though, increased steadily alongside the growing availability of part-time work (see chapter 16). These two factors together undermined the assumptions governing employment relationships, particularly in traditional manufacturing settings, that revolved around predominantly male workforces in full-time employment assumed to be providing the sole 'family wage' (Barrett and McIntosh 1982).

These two factors impinge upon the operation of labour markets. A third set of issues is more about the size and spatial distribution of workplaces. Services-based employment is associated with the decline in establishment size. Low start-up costs, or the easy availability of venture capital, permit waves of small entrepreneurs in some parts of the service sector. But a significant part of the trend to smaller workplaces is accounted for by restructuring within large companies (Shutt and Whittington 1987). Call centres, which have become almost emblematic of service sector working, are most likely to be a part of larger organizations (Gall and MacKay 1999). Whatever the underlying cause, smaller workplaces have quite specific implications for unions since they are more difficult (that is, expensive) to organize than a smaller number of larger ones. Geroski et al. (1995: 40) find that company characteristics account for 40 per cent of the decline of union recognition and that firm size explains almost all of this.

Shifts to services-based employment also involved changes to the spatial balance of employment as jobs moved from urban areas in the north to the south and to less populated areas everywhere. For manufacturing unions, 'in itself, this [was] some kind of loss of identity, of history' (Massey and Miles 1984: 20). Throughout the 1950s and 1960s, sociologists highlighted how working-class communities linked the public and private aspects of class identity, the workplace with the home, in ways that highlighted class-based differences in social power and status: 'down below, on the main road running straight into town, the bosses' cars whirr away at five o'clock to converted farm houses ten miles out in the hills; the men stream up into their district' (Hoggart 1957: 59–60). Whether, as discussed below, social symmetry was generally this neat is open to question (Clarke 1979; Critcher 1979; Stedman-Jones 1983), but de-industrialization certainly affected deeply communities built around specific industries such as coal, steel and shipbuilding, and unions could not rely on collective traditions emerging organically in the south and south-east.

Taken together, these pressures are often taken to denote a fatal fracturing of collective identity. Leadbeater (1989: 140), for example, argued that 'the economic restructuring of the 1980s has produced deep divisions within the working class. Established occupational, sexual and cultural identities, sources of solidarity and common identification are dissolving.' These 'new' divisions are contrasted with the relatively homogeneous working-class and trade union cultures that preceded them. Thus, Phelps Brown talks of 'the sense of common interest and common purpose' that united union members in the past (1990: 11) and depicts post-war British trade unionism as

> a movement, and not simply a federation of bodies with common purposes. Its members were accustomed to address each other as brothers and sisters, and they did indeed feel a fraternal obligation to support one another. Within the ground rules of democracy, they saw themselves as committed to an adversarial approach in industrial relations and to a radical change in social and economic institutions. (1990: 4)

The problem with such perspectives is that they overstate the previous strength of collective identities and, in doing so, depict the current crisis of collectivism as being without precedent and unfathomably deep. Sherman expresses this vividly from a trade unionist's viewpoint, 'if the giants lived yesterday then, by implication, we are pygmies today' (1987: 7). But class structures and expressions of identity have always been complex and have always varied over time in terms of their form and relative strength (Hyman 1978: 66). Fraser (1974: 213) quotes the contemporaneous observations of W. R. Greg, who in the late nineteenth century insisted on referring to the 'working *classes*' because there was, 'less of sympathy, of sense of common interest, or even mutual respect, between the upper and lower strata of the working classes – between, say a skilled and intelligent artisan and an ignorant and half-pauper labourer, than there is between several of the higher strata of those who are spoken of as one class and some of the strata of those spoken of as another and dissimilar class'.

The fragility of collective identities has carried at least three consequences for patterns of trade union membership. First, it has been prone to periodic crises before this most recent one. For example, union membership was halved to just 4 million following the economic depression in the 1920s (Winchester 1989: 498) and over one-third of this loss was sustained in just three years following 1920 (Kelly 1988). Second, collective identities organized through unionism often confirmed sectional and exclusionary attitudes rather than confronting them. Skilled engineers resisted opening their union to non-skilled 'helpers' and viewed their attempts at independent union organization with 'undisguised hostility' (Hinton 1983: 29). Semi-skilled machinists were only admitted to the Amalgamated Engineering Union (as it was called then) in 1922 following a major dispute and a lockout that was lost by the union. 'Unskilled men had to wait until 1926 and women until 1942' (Gardiner 1981: 324). Finally, collective institutions seeking stability tended to value bureaucratic anchors over those provided by active membership allegiance and commitment (Fairbrother 2001). Contrary to the assertions of writers such as Phelps Brown, this is especially so of the relatively brief 'golden age' of trade unionism during the immediate post-war period – the model that, implicitly at least, provides their point of departure when asserting a secular decline in collectivist values. Industrial relations scholars such as Flanders (1970) suggested that the growth of unionism in the

1960s and 1970s was largely one of *organization*. That is, it was characterized primarily by the co-ordination and regulation of members and the development of sanctions to ensure their compliance. By contrast, unionism as a *movement* (which 'implies a common end or at least a *community of purpose*') largely ossified (Flanders 1970: 43).

There are dangers then in deducing a shift towards individualism from a crisis in particular forms of collective identity. But, in the absence of obvious widespread demand for union organization, what contemporary evidence exists to support such an analysis? It is necessary to recall the different aspects of class formation, structure, and identity. The first can be evaluated by analysis of the distribution of wealth and power. Clearly, if this is becoming more even, then collective identities will be weakened, but there is no evidence for such a claim. Indeed, as noted in chapter 1, inequalities intensified throughout the 1980s and into the 1990s. Average incomes for the poorest 10 per cent of the population increased by 9 per cent between 1979 and 1995 while the richest 10 per cent became 59 per cent better off (TUC 1998). Wages of the lowest paid rose as a consequence of the National Minimum Wage, but early indications are that it has done little to diminish differentials between them and the highest paid (McKay 2001: 288). As in the United States, there is evidence that increased earnings inequality is causally connected to the decline in trade union organization and joint regulation (Leslie and Pu 1996; Wadsworth 1997).

The existence of social inequalities does not of itself ensure stable class identity. This depends upon their *recognition* by those affected and the ability or *opportunity* to react to them (see Kelly 1998). Interest recognition is not a straightforward process and can be mediated by the kinds of overlying divisions just discussed, based on status, race or gender. Moreover, employers can act to exaggerate these, intentionally or otherwise. Based on current data, however, there is little evidence to suggest that the kernels of class identity have been eradicated. British Social Attitudes data reveal general awareness of increased inequality and disapproval of it. Evans (2000: 55) distinguishes between the views of the salariat, the self-employed, and the working class. Perhaps the most striking finding is the widespread belief that the gap between high and low incomes has become too large – a view shared by 83 per cent of working-class respondents and, interestingly, 79 per cent of the salariat. Fewer than one in five accepted the view that earnings inequality was necessary for economic prosperity, and respondents felt that they were personally affected by inequality; 57 per cent of working-class respondents felt they were paid less than a 'fair' wage.

This general awareness may not manifest itself automatically in positive attitudes towards trade unions. But research amongst union members specifically shows growing rather than diminishing attachment to their unions. Gallie (1996: 144–6) found that very few trade union members (15 per cent) felt their unions had become less important to them over the previous five years. More than twice as many members (39 per cent) felt their unions had become still more important. Perhaps this is not the most important source of evidence – remaining members of declining institutions often become still more devout. British Social Attitudes Survey data captures the views of both members and non-members (Bryson 2001: 92–3). Over almost a 10-year period, between 1989 and 1998, the proportion of employees feeling that unions had too much power in their workplace began as negligible (4 per cent) and declined further (to 2 per cent). The proportion sanguine about the position of unions also declined, with fewer than half (45 per cent) believing unions had the right amount of power. Correspondingly, the proportion feeling unions had too little power increased significantly, from 32 per cent to 41 per cent. Within these limits, employee evaluations of union effectiveness appear relatively generous. Majorities of members (67 per cent) and non-members (55 per cent) consider unions recognized in their workplaces to be 'doing their job well'. The gap between those groups, at 12 percentage points, is smaller now than it was in 1989 (21 percentage points) with most of the change coming in the form of more positive evaluations amongst non-members.

On the basis of this evidence, it is difficult to conclude that declining union organization is the consequence of fracturing class identities alone. At the very least, such explanations require buttressing with those of a different character.

A trend towards successful HRM?

If the identification of distinct and contending interests is key, then the behaviour of employers is of central interest. Individualism in relation to management style is the central theme of chapter 12. Discussion here is of a more general kind and focuses on the circumstances in which employees might develop collective orientations. Where employers act to reduce the basis for conflict in the workplace, to identify and meet employee concerns, and to develop their commitment to the enterprise, employees may be less inclined or less able to assert alternative or contending claims. Some have identified just such a trend:

> A number of developments have served to bring about a heightened identification of workers in the private sector with their firms. This has in turn encouraged a commitment to the career chances given by the firm's internal labour market, to becoming employee shareholders and to collective bargaining at the level of the individual enterprise. (Urry 1989: 99)

Analysis of this kind is particularly influential in the US, where non-unionized employment relationships are practically the norm. Jacoby (1997) explores the phenomenon of welfare capitalism, a particularly sophisticated variant of non-unionism that he argues is especially characteristic of the American business system. It is argued that non-unionism in US welfare capitalist firms is a largely consensual affair. The exceptional history of immigration and its consequences, in terms of the fragmentation of the American working class, means that individualism is innate within American culture. Since demand for collective representation is said to be weak, employers are sowing on fertile ground when they encourage and reward individualized approaches to work through paternalistic approaches to the workforce, high pay, opportunities for employee involvement and the wide provision of employee benefits. In this way, welfare capitalist companies are identified as the pioneers of modern, high-commitment approaches to human resource management. Indeed, one of the most innovative aspects of the book is to trace the development of such practices in key case studies and their subsequent diffusion. Thus, Jacoby's thesis suggests that individualized approaches to workforces can develop into a virtuous circle: sophisticated and enlightened approaches by employers garner organizational commitment from employees and a willingness voluntarily to forgo collective representation. Care has to be taken not to overstate this case, particularly in the American context where managers generally have not been reputed for their reciprocal approach to employee relations, and recent union decline is attributed conventionally to sustained anti-union offensives (see Bronfenbrenner 2000; Colling 2001; Davis 1986; Goldfield 1987). Nevertheless, analysis of this kind highlights the complexity of workers' orientations to their employers, even in contexts where managerial prerogative predominates.

Of course, employees in the UK also place trust in their employers and managers, sometimes in preference to collective organization. In research that generally emphasizes the continuing appeal of unions, Whitston et al. (1999) find significant proportions of workforces who feel that managers, rather than unions, represent their views on a range of work-related issues. This is significant because it is a survey of union members in highly unionized industries, the postal service and telecommunications. There was some differentiation by issue. Majorities of respondents felt that their union represented them best on *market relations* issues, such as pay, job security and pensions. Other significant issues relating to the organization of work and management of the business, however, including training and new technology, were seen as the natural domain of management.

Evidence that employers have sought to build on this innate inclination to trust (as in Jacoby's thesis) and to establish sophisticated individualism is hard to find (Gall and MacKay 1999). The Workplace Industrial Relations Survey series (WIRS and WERS) picked up some time ago that the spread of high-commitment HR practice was far from virulent and was concentrated in unionized, rather than non-union workplaces – a finding that led Sisson famously to describe non-union employee relations in the UK as 'Bleak House' (1993: 207). Such a characterization seems to have held true for the findings from the most recent survey too. Measured by the presence of a range of 'high-commitment' strategies (such as team-briefing, performance management, and family-friendly working), sophisticated HR practice is still most common in large organizations, with a large personnel function and recognized trade unions. Nearly half of all workplaces without a union (41 per cent) deployed only between one and three high-commitment strategies. Very few unionized workplaces (15 per cent) deployed as few as this; 25 per cent of workplaces with a recognized union had eight or more high-commitment strategies (Cully et al. 1999: 48–82, 110).

The absence of formal procedures does not in itself indicate that non-union employment relationships are experienced as exploitative or that contending interests are inevitably apparent. Storey (2000) analyses firms where take-up of HRM is limited and joint regulation is entirely absent, yet aspects of employment practice associated with staff cost minimization are not prominent. Echoing other research, notably from WERS, she found only a minority of her sample of 54 engineering firms adopting high-commitment HR practices. The majority, however, paid at or above market rates and offered some form of job security. Over two-thirds of the sample exhibited management systems that offered advantages to employees, despite their informality. More generally, the research on small firms reviewed in chapter 18 shows that workplace relations are often informal and non-union but also have distinctive sources of tension; such workplaces are neither havens of harmony nor sites of straight managerial domination.

Without joint regulation or formal procedures, however, managerial prerogative is fettered only by voluntary restraint, and this is easily disturbed where circumstances change quickly. It is important to recognize, therefore, that while high-trust relationships are possible in such circumstances, they are also highly contingent (see Rose 1996: 65). Indeed, one of the most striking accompaniments to the de-collectivization of employee relationships in the UK has been the increased reliance by individuals upon the law to seek redress. The year before the Employment Relations Act 1999 was enacted, claims to employment tribunals increased by 31 per cent and the government was forced to appoint 17 per cent more lay members (ACAS Annual Report 1998: 132). During 1999–2000, claims increased again by 32 per cent over the previous year and ACAS (the Advisory, Conciliation and Arbitration Service) dealt with 170,000 cases, the largest workload ever recorded by the organization (ACAS Annual Report 2000; McKay 2001).

An orchestrated trend?

A final set of explanations coheres around the idea that the rise of individualism is more properly understood as a forced process driven by state policy and employer prerogative. If, as suggested by the social attitudes data discussed above, perceptions of inequality in the work environment have not been eradicated, then the continued decline of union organization might be explicable by the withdrawal of *opportunities* to act on those perceptions (Kelly 1998). Thus an important point of emphasis arises; according to such an analysis we are witnessing not so much the rise of individualism as the 'de-collectivization' (Smith and Morton 1993, 2001) of employment relationships coupled with the 'de-mobilization' of collective organizations (Kelly 1998).

Labour law is the primary medium through which state policy on the employment relationship is communicated, and other chapters in this volume cover that topic extensively. Two things are important for us to note. First, that state support for collective bargaining, and thereby for trade unions, was extensive for most of the post-war period. True, rights to trade union membership and activity were not expressed positively, as in some European states; they were merely tolerated through the use of exemptions from legal liability. But collective bargaining was promoted in a variety of other ways. Duties established for statutory bodies such as ACAS obliged them to foster collective employment relationships via trade unions. Similar obligations were written into the statutes of the nationalized industries, such as rail and electricity (see chapter 11), and collective agreements in the public services were effectively extended to the private services with which they dealt via mechanisms such as the Fair Wages Resolution. Second, reorientation of employment law through the 1980s and early 1990s stripped away these supports and went further to promote individualized relationships through restrictions on trade union activity, regulation of their governance and the limited promotion, instead, of individual employment rights. The changing orientation following the election of the Labour governments in 1997 and 2001 has loosened some of the constraints on unions but falls far short of positively promoting collective employment relations (McIlroy 2000; Smith and Morton 2001).

Such a policy context, of course, has both conditioned and been conditioned by employer preferences. Their operating environments have become much more pressured as a result of intensifying product market competition, rapid changes in technologies and consumer demand, and, for publicly quoted companies, increased pressure to provide short-term returns to shareholders (see Brown et al. 1999). To the extent that de-collectivization offers discretion to managements responding to such pressures, its appeal to them has grown. Though a majority of managers surveyed by WERS described themselves as neutral on the issue, Cully et al (1999: 87–8), note that sizeable minorities (38 per cent) disagreed that unions improved workplace performance, and that nearly three-quarters (72 per cent) said they preferred to consult directly with employees rather than through trade unions. De-recognition of unions is the ultimate expression of this. In a review of the available survey evidence up to the early 1990s, Claydon (1996) distinguishes between two forms of de-recognition. Reactive de-recognition involves partial and usually opportunistic responses by management to shifting orientations of their workforces and the consequences of employment or organizational restructuring. Purposive de-recognition involves a more concerted attempt to drive out unions across the organization, irrespective of occupational and geographical boundaries. The former strategy explains a substantial proportion of union decline through the 1980s, as employers pursued grade-specific de-recognition or resisted the extension of bargaining to newly developed business streams. In the 1990s, however, Claydon finds evidence of purposive de-recognition in some selected sectors, notably petro-chemicals and provincial newspapers (see also Smith and Morton 1990). He concludes that 'there seem to be grounds for thinking that purposive de-recognition might become more widespread, since the circumstances which encourage it and make it practicable appear to be spreading' (1996: 170). Geroski et al. (1995) corroborate this. They found accelerated trends towards de-recognition that were not explicable by the usual business cycle factors.

These explanations of declining collectivism raise important questions. Whether recent social and economic change has destroyed the basis for collective identity in any general or novel sense must be open to doubt. Sectoral change generates important ramifications in terms of labour market restructuring and has influenced prevailing patterns of union organization. Recognition of differing interests remains, however, and there is no evidence of any generally weakening approval of trade unions. Neither is there much evidence of concerted or strategic action by employers positively to reinforce individualistic inclinations within workforces. Employers have increased the breadth of their prerogative in the workplace by marginalizing and de-recognizing trade unions, but this has not generally been overlaid with high-commitment strategies. We are left with the consequences of a series of interlocking changes that cannot support epochal or simplistic conceptualizations of individualism. We are not witnessing the emergence of some Brave New World in employment relationships. De-collectivization appears to be driven by opportunism and ad hoc responses ventured under intensifying competitive pressure (McLoughlin and Gourlay 1994). It is important, then, to examine these developments in specific and concrete circumstances, to highlight their different dimensions and the meanings attributed to them in the workplace. The case-study approach is especially suited to such a task and the chapter turns now to an examination of individualism in two distinct organizations.

Individualism in Practice: Two Case Studies

This section explores two case studies of individualism in practice.[1] 'Posh Nosh' is a prestige contract caterer operating executive and staff dining rooms in the City of London and the West End. 'Knowco' is an information technology (IT) company offering consultancy and skills training to a variety of companies nationwide.[2] These are not representative of non-collective employee relations in any all-encompassing sense but they do encapsulate many of the features of the 'new' workplace just discussed. First, they are both essentially service-based companies and have benefited substantially from the general growth of the sector. (Whether the production of food is a service or a manufacturing process is an intriguing point, but Posh Nosh was marketed explicitly as a provider of catering and hospitality services.) Second, both are small businesses. Knowco employed 300 people at the time of the research and Posh Nosh approximately 700. As picked up in the preceding analysis, though, this small scale is belied by the fact that both are parts of much larger organizations. Knowco developed as part of a large IT manufacturer employing 24,000 people and had traditionally delivered training programmes to purchasers of its mainframe and networked computer systems before its designation as an 'autonomous' business in 1992. Posh Nosh is a subsidiary of the UK's largest contract catering company which employs 40,000 people. Third, they allow us to explore some of the specific characteristics of service-sector working. Posh Nosh employs a predominantly craft-based workforce, though the hospitality (or 'front of house') side of the business relies also on 'people' skills. Knowco's workforce is made up of 'knowledge workers': technicians, software designers and lecturers involved in developing skills and imparting information. Finally, and most important, both organizations are characterized by avowedly non-collectivized employee relations, and trade unions are not recognized for collective bargaining. The evidence is more conveniently presented in the reverse order to the preceding section.

An orchestrated trend?

There was little evidence of an ideological opposition to unions in either organization. For differing reasons, managers had dealt with unions before and
expressed a pragmatic approach towards them. Collective bargaining had been
established across Knowco's parent company. Posh Nosh's parent continued to
bargain collectively in those contracts where unions had been established
previously, particularly in the public sector, for example. But the operational
environments of the two businesses provided quite specific pressures towards
non-collectivized employee relations. Both operated through portfolios of projects
and contracts with a range of different customers. These could be for varying
levels of service over different contract periods. Satisfying a range of differently
configured customer preferences was central to both businesses and generated
an imperative to retain flexibility and managerial discretion.

This was new to Knowco. As well as adapting to new market opportunities,
they had been forced to change the nature of their product. Previously, Knowco's
sales had been entirely dependent on the purchase of hardware products manufactured by the parent company. Knowco, then, simply had to advertise a schedule
of courses to customers who sent their staff to the national training centre. As
the parent company withdrew from manufacturing, Knowco was obliged to
provide generic IT training across a much broader range of hardware and software products. Delivery modes also changed, since customers preferred shorter,
often bespoke, courses held on their own premises at times of their choosing.
Employment relationships in Knowco were re-created relatively recently by
deliberate management strategy. Staff had been represented by MSF previously,
who also negotiated their terms and conditions of employment. Once designated an 'autonomous' business, however, Knowco managers de-recognized the
union and issued new contracts of employment to staff. Grading structures were
reviewed, as were procedures governing promotion and pay progression. In each
case, the objective was to increase flexibility between job roles and to create
direct relationships between staff and their managers.

Markets and products had changed less quickly in Posh Nosh, but the expectations of customers were deeply influential and could be expressed still more
directly. Unions were almost entirely absent from Posh Nosh's immediate environment. Staff were recruited specifically from restaurants and hotels in London's
West End, and the company's operations were primarily in the City of London.
Posh Nosh managers did not expect to deal with unions but neither, significantly, did their clients, and contractual arrangements made this particularly
significant. Two broad forms of contract are conventional in catering, fixed-price
and cost-plus, with a variety of hybrids in between. The majority of Posh Nosh's
contracts were offered on a cost-plus basis, that is, clients were free to alter their
requirements to accommodate particular arrangements, such as ad hoc corporate
hospitality, for which Posh Nosh was paid at cost plus a management fee. Under
these arrangements, client managers retained rights to oversee food and labour
costs. They were free to question decisions made by contract managers and, on
some issues, were involved in taking them jointly. Client managers could request

disciplinary action against staff, and they were frequently involved in pay reviews for those Posh Nosh staff within their contract: 'any movement on pay reflects on the client's bottom line and that is why they are involved in it' (managing director, Posh Nosh). Staff, however, were never involved directly in these discussions. In this way, non-collective employee relations were embedded through the preferences of the direct employer under detailed pressure from clients.

Successful HRM?

The form taken by non-collectivized employee relations was influenced in part by the ethos established by their parent companies corporately and was supported by their resources. Both parent companies were market leaders and encouraged sophisticated approaches to human resource management across their businesses. Corporate personnel policies cohered around quality assurance and skills development. Both organizations have established reputations for their investment in skill development and the usual marks of public recognition for quality (such as Investors in People) were much in evidence. Corporate personnel policies emphasized commitment to individual employees and to their development within the company. 'Throughout [Posh Nosh]', the company's promotional literature proclaimed, 'we encourage creative talent and an exchange of ideas.'

Contextual pressures influenced deeply the way in which these systems operated in practice. First, exemplifying the points of chapter 12, both businesses were subject to intensifying controls over financial performance. A significant proportion of Posh Nosh's customer base had reviewed their support services contracts, including catering, with a view to extracting savings. Increasingly, such reviews were prompted and managed by consultants promising only to take fees as a proportion of the savings made. Knowco's parent company set quarterly targets for the business but, in the context of poor corporate performance overall, these were reviewed monthly to maximize contributions to earnings. So emphatic was this focus that it conditioned managerial interpretations of broader company objectives. During the fieldwork period, the corporate board cascaded four key 'breakthrough' targets. Expressed somewhat cryptically, they included: boosting margin, delighting customers, achieving promises, and valuing people. Asked what each of them meant in practice, one manager responded promptly and unambiguously to argue that they were all about money.

> 'Achieving promises' means, 'You give us the money. We give you a budget; you agree that budget; that is a promise that you will make that budget. You will achieve it.' It sounds sort of woolly and nice to say, 'Well, I will keep my promise to you', [laughs] but what it actually means is 'You will cough up the money at the end of every quarter!'

Second, general employment credos were administered in both businesses through rather threadbare infrastructures in terms of support from human resources or personnel specialists. This too can be explained by the focus on financial performance and the specific inflection this is given in project environments (for a discussion of personnel functions in 'lean' organizations, see Legge 2000). Competition for contracts was frequently decided on price, and the proportion of the overall price accounted for by overheads received particular scrutiny. Financial and quality functions could be justified in terms of benefits to the customer, but the costs of a personnel function were perceived to be potentially problematic. Personnel functions in both organizations were small, under-resourced, and focused on administrative matters. Posh Nosh sourced its personnel advice on a service basis from the neighbouring division. Knowco retained a personnel function, but this was staffed by one personnel officer at the time of the research.

Responsibility for HR matters resided firmly with line managers in both organizations and, specifically, with the project managers overseeing particular contracts. Knowco relied upon self-employed 'associate' staff to deliver large proportions of their training projects (see below) and this was managed exclusively at project level. The HR function had no knowledge of the numbers of associate staff working at any one time and held no contact details for them. In Posh Nosh, decisions over recruitment, discipline, and access to training were all taken locally: 'our philosophy within the division is one of flexibility, it is a flexible approach' (account executive, Posh Nosh).

This context carried two consequences for the nature of non-collective employee relations. First, it generated a preoccupation with containing employment costs. There were significant differences between the businesses in terms of how these underlying imperatives were communicated and perceived. Managers in Posh Nosh consistently displayed a paternalistic approach to their employees. The fact that operations were geographically concentrated facilitated such approaches, since even senior managers were able to visit staff in the units frequently, but they were driven primarily by the very tight local labour markets. In order to attract and retain staff, Posh Nosh differentiated itself from its key competitors by offering regular working hours (with little evening or weekend work), permanent contracts of employment, and generally full-time employment too. Great importance was attached to internal labour markets and developing managers through the ranks. Over two-thirds of Posh Nosh managers (70 per cent) had been with the company for five years or more; one-fifth (22 per cent) had over 10 years service. Cost controls in Posh Nosh tended to focus on physical productivity. The survey of workers revealed that staff almost uniformly reported working harder than they did three years ago. Craft/operative staff were especially likely to report increased work effort; nearly half (44 per cent) said they were working 'a lot harder'. This pattern of hard work but regular employment illustrates the particular form of the effort bargain here, which is more complex than notions of individualization can grasp. As shown in chapter 13, new forms of work organization can have benefits as well as costs for employees.

In Knowco, however, intensifying cost controls were pursued in an atmosphere of increasing insecurity. Lecturers had once been subject experts and used to transferring between technical and teaching roles. The switch to generic applications training, coupled with new modes of delivery such as on-line training, meant that 'the older, far more expensive, tutor/lecturer is not in demand' (managing director, Knowco). Nearly two-thirds of the lecturing workforce was made redundant and re-engaged as self-employed 'associates' on an 'as and when' basis. In contrast to Posh Nosh, internal labour markets for those staff remaining were disrupted as managers sought to satisfy demand for specific skills externally. This had important implications for training, for example: an overwhelming majority of staff (79 per cent) disagreed with the proposition that their training needs were met as a result of appraisal; one-third of these disagreed strongly. One lecturer recalled,

> Well, they said to me, because I was an experienced lecturer, they couldn't afford to have me not earning revenue and then paying me my normal salary for the amount of time it would take them to train me. . . . So, if I went to train in a new area, that is an investment they didn't seem prepared to make.

In this instance, the tactical devices adopted by line managers to secure business and deliver on their 'bottom line' was directly at odds with the HR ethos of personal and professional development promoted by the corporate centre.

Limited HR support contributed to the second consequence: clear limits to the extent to which non-collective employee relations could be truly individualized. As discussion in the introductory sections highlighted, employee relations can be exclusively individualized or collectivized only in very rare circumstances. Employees themselves think in complex ways, pursuing personal objectives on some issues and broader, shared ones on other issues or at other times (for a social psychological study of these matters, see Kelly 1998). Employers will have similar inclinations, but the issue of costs and benefits will also be key. To put it simply, supporting a wholly individualized set of employment practices across the whole of their workforces was simply not a viable proposition in either Posh Nosh or Knowco. Training and development were undoubtedly important in Posh Nosh, but individual appraisals were confined to key staff, those working at the business's head office, account managers and senior catering or 'front of house' staff from the units. Training needs for staff below this level were seen as more general, driven primarily by food hygiene and safety regulations, and were met by standardized training packages for groups of staff, often held on site.

Devotion to individualism was particularly marked in Knowco, but this too had definite limits. References to associate staff were saturated with the vocabulary of entrepreneurship but, in fact, most worked only for Knowco and were retained on standard contracts that left little room for individual negotiation. Great importance was attached to the individual performance-related pay for direct employees, but the extent to which individuals could demonstrate particular creativity or ingenuity was constrained in practice. While clients' information technology and training needs could be quite specific, the drive to reduce risk generated pressures towards standardization in terms of training delivery. Courses for one major public sector customer were said to involve standard course handouts, a set of standard demonstrations, a set of standard exercises, and course kit guide to [lecturers] as to how the course should be run. We do that because we have to get the course approved by [the customer] and we have to have a definitive set of documentation that says this is what the customer's course is like, this is what it would look like *no matter who runs it*. So the lecturers have to conform to that. (project manager, Knowco; emphasis added)

Pay data was not made available to the research, but there was a strong perception that earnings did not vary significantly to reflect individual perform-ance. Rather, an apparently individualized pay system was perceived as a guise for containing or reducing the pay bill overall. As one lecturer reflected,

my view, and that of other people, is that, despite what is said . . . it is not neces-sarily associated with 'this person has worked extremely hard . . . let's give them some recognition'. There is not much scope for people to be able to do that, it seems to me.

Such perceptions were partially confirmed by senior managers, who talked about the need to reorient pay structures and the points of comparison drawn previously by employees. Moving away from corporate pay systems offered the opportunity to do this, since 'we benchmark against other consultancy and training companies; we don't benchmark against IT companies or anything we are not' (managing director, Knowco).

Secular?

Some workforce characteristics were consistent with a thesis that there was little demand for collective employee relations. But this did not extend to a general-ized faith in management or commitment to the organization.

Two aspects of the workforce characteristics potentially weakened demand for collective channels. First, both workforces were relatively youthful. One-third of the Knowco workforce was under 30 years of age; nearly two-thirds were under 40. The characteristic was particularly apparent in Posh Nosh, where less than one-fifth of the workforce was more than 40 years of age and well over a third (38 per cent) were under 30. Almost all Posh Nosh managers (93 per cent) were under 40. Second, these were also relatively mobile workforces, in that small proportions had been in the company for long periods. Again, this was particu-larly the case for Posh Nosh, where half of the workforce overall had been with the company for less than five years, most of these having under three years' service.

As figure 14.1 illustrates, very small proportions of these workforces were union members but, despite these workforce characteristics, there was little evidence of hostility towards unions. The slightly higher incidence of union membership in Knowco (6 per cent) was due to some staff retaining their membership independently following de-recognition of the union by management. More broadly, employees were asked to offer reasons for their non-membership ranked in order of importance (for this reason, values total more than 100).

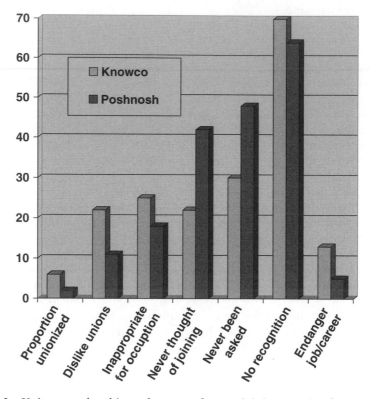

Figure 14.1   Union membership and reasons for not joining a union by company

Only minorities expressed dislike of unions in principle or thought that unions were not appropriate to their specific occupation. In both cases, the absence of union membership is explained overwhelmingly (60–70 per cent of respondents) by employer preferences, that no union was recognized by their employer or in their establishment. This finding echoes broader findings: the reason for non-membership of trade unions offered most frequently by employees is that they have never been asked to join (for a general discussion, see p. 221 above and Waddington and Whitston 1997). The importance of employer preferences is further indicated in Knowco by the small proportion that felt that union membership would endanger their chances of career progression.

Were non-collective employee relations to be the result of employee preferences, we would expect to find high levels of trust between staff and their managers. In fact, both workforces displayed scepticism on this point. As shown in figure 14.2, the largest proportions of staff in each case were noncommittal, describing relationships merely as 'fair'. Relatively few thought there was a lot of trust, and complete trust was expressed only by a small minority of Posh Nosh staff. Substantial numbers, however, pointed to low levels of trust, and this was particularly marked in Knowco, where nearly half of staff overall (47 per cent) felt there was little or no trust. In both cases, managers tended to profess a more

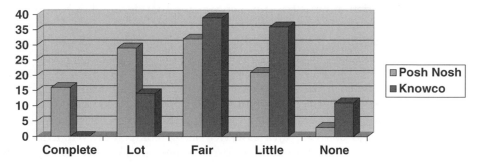

Figure 14.2   Employee perceptions of trust between staff and managers

favourable view than non-managerial staff; craft and operative staff in Posh Nosh were three times more likely than management staff to express little or no trust. Lecturing staff in Knowco, the largest non-management group, had a particularly jaundiced view of their managers. Nearly one-third of them claimed there was no trust between them and managers; a further half said there was little trust.

Despite this, the propensity to challenge management decisions certainly was not widespread. Employees appeared most likely to leave the company altogether or seek another position internally. Around two-thirds of each workforce had considered leaving their present position, the proportion in Knowco being slightly higher (69 per cent) than in Posh Nosh (62 per cent). Moreover, the desire to quit appeared relatively 'hard': around three-quarters of those expressing such a view in each business said they were serious or very serious about the prospect. But a key difference underlies these figures. Prospective quits in Knowco planned to leave the company altogether. Asked where they would like to move to, only one-third said they would stay within Knowco or the parent company. The remainder were looking to move externally to another computing services company (29 per cent), to set up a business (19 per cent) or to change careers entirely (19 per cent). Movements in Posh Nosh, by contrast, appeared to be linked to career progression within the company and the opportunity to move between contracts. Over half of those wishing to move said they would stay with the company. This option was preferred overwhelmingly by management staff, 80 per cent of whom said they would stay, but it was also the second most favoured option amongst craft/operative staff wishing to move on. In any event, the company's most immediate competitors appeared unlikely to benefit from Posh Nosh quits. Less than 15 per cent of the workforce as a whole had considered moving to restaurants/hotels or to other contract caterers.

Discussion and Conclusions

This chapter has set out to explore the decline in collectivized employee relations and the reasons for it. Three variants of explanation were identified, though these tend to overlap in practice. Those suggesting that decline has been secular emphasize the absence of demand for collective channels of representation and explain this by shifts in the composition of the economy and labour markets. Others point to high-commitment strategies and the extent to which employers have been successful in garnering the trust and allegiance of their employees. Some see the trend as a strategic one, created by deliberate employer actions, facilitated by state policy, to secure managerial prerogative and close down joint regulation. These themes from the general literature were explored further through case studies of two growing service-sector companies. What does this material tell us about the nature of non-collective employee relations in the United Kingdom? Three conclusions may be made.

First, broad general explanations are not wholly satisfactory and potentially mask important complexities and variations in practice. Looking at general outcomes, we know that de-collectivization is associated strongly overall with increased inequalities in terms of treatment and pay, but what explains employees' acquiescence or consent? Some theses can be dealt with relatively easily. The social attitudes data discussed earlier undermine the notion that employees are opposed, or even indifferent, to collective channels; this result finds an echo in this case-study material. In each case, non-collective employee relations were attributable to employer preferences and to the policy and business environments in which they developed. Because these conjunctural factors are critical, as chapters 12 and 13 have argued, there is no single, overarching model of individualized employment relationships. Interestingly, the sectoral and labour market pressures influencing our two cases operated counter-intuitively. The catering industry is generally famed for its short-term approach to employees and unfettered use of managerial prerogative (Lucas 1996) while the 'knowledge work' thesis, discussed earlier, suggests meritocratic workplaces. Differences were found in these cases, but they were precisely the reverse of these stereotypes in terms of their character. Relative stability in product markets and extremely tight labour markets encouraged a paternalistic approach to employees in Posh Nosh in which considerable importance was attached to employment security and strong internal labour markets. Managerial prerogative was guarded and HR strategies were focused tightly on minorities of key professional and managerial staff. Nevertheless, the managerial approach generally depended upon demonstrated reciprocity in the employment relationship. Knowco was subject to rapid and intense change in terms of demand for its product and relationships within its parent organization. Management here had created non-collective employee relations, via de-recognition, in the context of employment restructuring and reorientation of the business. The consequence was intensified employment insecurity and markedly low levels of trust between staff and managers. In short, individualism simply does not comply with one single recipe. There are several different forms and employee relations will tend to comprise different mixes of authority and trust, prerogative and reciprocity in each case.

Second, despite their differences, these case studies emphasize that non-collectivized employee relations is not synonymous with individualized employee relations. Individualized and collectivized aspects of the employment relationship continue to coexist, even in the absence of formal joint regulation. Brown et al. (1999) distinguish between *procedural individualization*, the removal of collective channels, and *substantive individualization*, which implies actual differentiation in the terms and conditions of individual employment contracts. The second of these is potentially extremely expensive to pursue since, for it to be meaningful, it requires the management capacity to negotiate, monitor and review a portfolio of individual contracts. Brown et al. find that such capacity is not generally available, and this was markedly true of these two case studies. Non-collective employee relations tend to focus therefore on the removal of collective channels. This may provide considerable managerial discretion to deal with changeable trading environments, but this is not without its costs. Indeed, it creates potentially extremely volatile circumstances internally by diminishing trust and commitment. Staff in both organizations demonstrated a propensity to quit. In Posh Nosh, this appeared to be associated as with internal career progression and could involve moves between contracts rather than beyond the organization. Large proportions of Knowco staff, however, wished to leave the organization altogether.

Finally, though it is not claimed that these cases are representative, it is possible to draw some inferences about the prospects for trade union renewal. Certainly, as writers such as Machin (2000) have argued, it is far too easy to be dazzled by the shift to service working. Partly, this is a question of definition. When one moves beyond generalities, distinctions between services and manufacturing settings become much less clear-cut. Many services depend upon manufacturing, they may be delivered in manufacturing establishments, and their labour processes may even contain elements of manufacture themselves, as in the creation of meals in Posh Nosh kitchens. It is also a question of employment relationships, and these case studies demonstrate the difficulty of generalizing on this point. The development of collective identities in the workplace is dependent upon three key factors: dissatisfaction with terms and conditions of work; fear of exposure to managerial prerogative; and the availability of unions to join (Kelly 1998). Evidence of the first two were found readily in these two services companies. The key issue is the last one. Staff had never been asked to join unions and employers were unwilling to recognize them. New rights may change the former circumstance, but to what extent? Unions, of course, are now responding with greater energy and ingenuity to the imperative to recruit, but limited resources may incline many of them to concentrate on deepening organization in their heartlands, rather than extending membership into new areas (Colling and Claydon 2000; Heery et al. 2000). Even where they do so, experience from the US suggests that such activity will be subject to close cost-benefit analysis. Either way, the prospect of high-profile recognition and recruitment campaigns in the City of London, for example, appears remote. Everything turns therefore on the orientation of employers. Where managers are expressly opposed to unions, density levels remain extremely low at around 5 per cent and this increases only modestly to 15 per cent where managers remain neutral (Cully et al. 1999: 89–90). Majorities of the workforce become union members only in the minority of workplaces where managers positively endorse membership. While the ideological opposition to unions found in the USA has yet to materialize in any sustained way in the UK, there is little chance of this kind of endorsement emerging as a consequence of enlightened self-interest alone. As these case studies demonstrate, the attractions of *procedural individualization* are strong indeed for managers under pressure to sustain or improve organizational performance, and the costs of such strategies are often obscured at this level. De-collectivization may have been stanched for the time being. The prospects, though, that joint regulation will develop from beyond its small circle of wagons depends on the case made by unions and, to a greater extent, on the positive support of government.

Notes

I am indebted to Tim Claydon and to the students we have worked with on the MA in Human Resource Management at Leicester Business School, De Montfort University. Ideas underpinning this chapter have developed as a consequence of discussion with them. Thanks also to Paul Edwards, whose suggestions improved earlier drafts. Responsibility for errors or omissions remain with me.

1 Fieldwork was conducted between 1996 and 1997 as part of the Industrial Relations Research Unit's project, Competitiveness and Workplace Change, supported by the Economic and Social Research Council. This chapter draws particularly on interviews with managers at corporate, business and project level and with selected panels of employees in each business. Full surveys of each workforce were also conducted and data from these are also referred to.

2 'Posh Nosh' and 'Knowco' are pseudonyms used to preserve the anonymity requested by the organizations studied. Any similarity with companies bearing those names is purely coincidental.

References

Barrett, M., and McIntosh, M. 1982: The 'family wage'. In E. Whitelegg, M. Arnot, E. Bartels, V. Beechey, L. Birke, S. Himmelweit, D. Leonard, S. Ruehl and M. Speakman (eds), *The Changing Experience of Women*. Oxford: Martin Robertson.

Bronfenbrenner, K. *2000: Uneasy Terrain. The Impact of Capital Mobility on Workers, Wages, and Union Organizing*. Report to the US Trade Deficit Review Commission. New York School of Industrial and Labor Relations, Cornell University.

Brown, W., Deakin, S., Hudson, M., Pratten, C. and Ryan, P. 1999: *The Individualization of Employment Contracts in Britain*. Employment Relations Research Series, 4. London, Department of Trade and Industry. <http://www.dti.gov.uk/er/emar>.

Bryson, A. 2001: The foundation of partnership? Union effects on employee trust in management. *National Institute Economic Review*, 176, 91–104.

Clarke, J. 1979: Capital and culture: the post-war working class revisited. In J. Clarke, C. Critcher and R. Johnson (eds), *Working Class Culture: Studies in History and Theory*. London: Hutchinson.

Claydon, T. 1996: Union derecognition: a re-examination. In I. Beardwell (ed.), *Contemporary Industrial Relations: A Critical Analysis*. Oxford: Oxford University Press.

Claydon, T. 2000: Tales of disorder: the press and the narrative construction of industrial relations in the British motor industry, 1950–79. *Historical Studies in Industrial Relations*, 9, 1–36.

Colling, T. 2001: *'In a state of bliss, there is no need for a ministry of bliss': Non-Unionism, Power and Consent in the American Business System*. Occasional Paper 67. Leicester Business School, De Montfort University.

Colling, T., and Claydon, T. 2000: Strategic review and organisational change in Unison. In M. Terry (ed.), *Redefining Public Sector Unionism: Unison and the Future of Trade Unions*. London: Routledge.

Critcher, C. 1979: Sociology, cultural studies, and the post-war working class. In J. Clarke, C. Critcher and R. Johnson (eds), *Working Class Culture: Studies in History and Theory*. London: Hutchinson.

Crompton, R. 1997: *Women and Work in Modern Britain*. Oxford: Oxford University Press.

Cully, M., Woodland, S., O'Reilly, A. and Dix, G. 1999: *Britain at Work: As Depicted by the 1998 Workplace Employee Relations Survey*. London: Routledge.

Davis, M. 1986: *Prisoners of the American Dream*. London: Verso.

Despres, C., and Hiltrop, J. M. 1995: Human resource management in the knowledge age: current practice and perspectives on the future, *Employee Relations*, 17 (1), 9–23.

Edwards, P. K., and Bain, G. S. 1988: Why are trade unions becoming more popular? Unions and public opinion in Britain, *British Journal of Industrial Relations*, 26 (3), 311–26.

Evans, G. 2000: The working class and New Labour: a parting of the ways? In R. Jowell, J. Curtice, A. Park, K. Thomson, L. Jarvis, C. Bromley and N. Stratford (eds), *British Social Attitudes, the 17th Report: Focusing on Diversity*. London: Sage.

Fairbrother, P. 2001: *Trade Unions at the Crossroads*. London: Mansell.

Flanders, A. 1970: *Management and Unions: The Theory and Reform of Industrial Relations*. London: Faber & Faber.

Fraser, W. H. 1974: *Trade Unions and Society: The Struggle for Acceptance, 1850–1880*. London: Allen & Unwin.

Frenkel, S., Korczynski, M., Donaghue, L. and Shire, K. 1995: Re-constituting work: trends towards knowledge work and info-normative control, *Work Employment and Society*, 9 (4), 773–96.

Gall, G., and MacKay, S. 1999: Developments in union recognition and derecognition in Britain 1994–1998, *British Journal of Industrial Relations*, 37 (4), 601–14.

Gallie, D. 1996: Trade union allegiance and decline in British urban labour markets. In D. Gallie, R. Penn and M. Rose (eds), *Trade Unionism in Recession*. Oxford: Oxford University Press.

Gardiner, J. 1981: The development of the British working class. In S. Aaronovitch and R. Smith (eds), *The Political Economy of British Capitalism*. London: McGraw-Hill.

Geroski, P., Gregg, P. and Desjonqueres, T. 1995: Did the retreat of UK trade unionism accelerate during the 1990–1993 recession? *British Journal of Industrial Relations*, 33 (1), 35–54.

Goldfield, M. 1987: *The Decline of Organised Labor in the United States*. Chicago: University of Chicago Press.

Hebdige, D. 1989: After the masses. *Marxism Today*. January, 48–53.

Heery, E., Simms, M., Delbridge, R., Salmon, J. and Simpson, D. 2000: Organizing unionism comes to the UK, *Employee Relations*, 22 (1), 38–57.

Hinton, J. 1983: *Labour and Socialism: A History of the British Labour Movement 1867–1974*. Brighton: Wheatsheaf.

Hoggart, R. 1957: *The Uses of Literacy*. Harmondsworth: Penguin.

Jacoby, S. M. 1997: *Modern Manors*. Princeton: Princeton University Press.

Kelly, J. 1988: *Trade Unions and Socialist Politics* London: Verso.

Kelly, J. 1998: *Rethinking Industrial Relations: Mobilization, Collectivism, and Long Waves*. London: Routledge.

Leadbeater, C. 1989: Power to the person. In S. Hall and M. Jacques (eds), *New Times: The Changing Face of Politics in the 1990s*. London: Lawrence & Wishart.

Legge, K. 2000: Personnel management in the lean organisation. In S. Bach and K. Sisson (eds), *Personnel Management: A Comprehensive Guide to Theory and Practice*. Oxford: Blackwell.

Leslie, D., and Pu, Y. 1996: What caused rising earnings inequality in Britain? Evidence from time series, 1970–1993, *British Journal of Industrial Relations*, 34 (1), 111–30.

Lucas, R. (1996) Industrial relations in hotels and catering: neglect and paradox? *British Journal of Industrial Relations*. 34 (2), 267–86.

Machin, S. 2000: Union decline in Britain, *British Journal of Industrial Relations*, 38 (4), 631–45.

Massey, D., and Miles, N. 1984: Mapping out the unions, *Marxism Today*, May, 19–24.

Mayes, D., with Soteri, S. 1994: Does manufacturing matter? In T. Buxton, P. Chapman and P. Temple (eds), *Britain's Economic Performance*. London: Routledge.

McIlroy, J. 2000: New Labour, new unions, new left, *Capital and Class*, 71, 11–43.

McKay, S. 2001: Between flexibility and regulation: rights, equality and protection at work, *British Journal of Industrial Relations*, 39 (2), 285–303.

McLoughlin, I., and Gourlay, S. 1993: Why do employees in non-union firms not join unions? Paper presented to conference on 'Unions on the Brink: The Future of the Union Movement', Cardiff Business School, September.

McLoughlin, I., and Gourlay, S. 1994: *Enterprise Without Unions: Industrial Relations in the Non-Union Firm*. Buckingham: Open University Press.

Phelps Brown, H. 1990: The counter-revolution of our time. *Industrial Relations*, 29 (1), 1–14.

Rose, M. 1996: Still life in Swindon: case studies in union survival and employer policy in a 'sunrise' labour market. In D. Gallie, R. Penn and M. Rose (eds), *Trade Unionism in Recession*. Oxford: Oxford University Press.

Sherman, B. 1987: *The State of the Unions*. Chichester: Wiley.

Shutt, J., and Whittington, R. 1987: Fragmentation strategies and the rise of small units: cases from the North West, *Regional Studies*, 21 (1), 13–23.

Sisson, K. 1993: In search of HRM. *British Journal of Industrial Relations*, 31 (2), 201–10.

Smith, P., and Morton, G. 1990: A change of heart: union exclusion in the provincial newspaper sector, *Work, Employment and Society*, 4 (1), 105–24.

Smith, P., and Morton, G. 1993: Union exclusion and the de-collectivisation of industrial relations in contemporary Britain, *British Journal of Industrial Relations*, 31 (1), 97–114.

Smith, P., and Morton, G. 2001: New Labour's reform of Britain's employment law: the devil is not only in the detail but in the values and policy too, *British Journal of Industrial Relations*, 39 (1), 119–38.

Stedman-Jones, G. 1983: *Languages of Class: Studies in English Working Class History 1832–1982*. Cambridge: Cambridge University Press.

Storey, J. 2000: Is paternalism alive and well? People management in non-union workplaces. Paper presented to British Universities Industrial Relations Association Annual Conference, University of Warwick, July.

TUC (Trades Union Congress): 1998: A briefing on inequality. Welfare Reform Series, 12. London: TUC.

Urry, J. 1989: The end of organised capitalism. In S. Hall and M. Jacques (eds), *New Times: The Changing Face of Politics in the 1990s*. London: Lawrence & Wishart.

Visser, J. 1992: The strength of labour movements in advanced capitalist democracies: social and organizational variations. In M. Regini (ed.), *The Future of Labour Movements*. London: Sage.

Waddington, J., and Whitston, C. 1997: Why do people join unions in a period of union decline? *British Journal of Industrial Relations*, 35 (4), 515–46.

Wadsworth, J. 1997: Over the top? Wage inequality in the UK, *Economic Review*, 15 (1) September, 24–8.

Whitston, C., Roe, A. and Jefferys, S. 1999: Job regulation and the managerial challenge to trade unions: evidence from two union membership surveys, *Industrial Relations Journal*, 30 (5), 482–98.

Williamson, J. 1985: *Consuming Passions: The Dynamics of Popular Culture*. London: Marion Boyars.

Winchester, D. 1989: Sectoral change and trade union organization. In D. Gallie (ed.), *Employment in Britain*. Oxford: Blackwell.

15
TRAINING

EWART KEEP AND HELEN RAINBIRD

Training and the Role of Regulation

Nowhere has the pace of change within the British industrial relations system since 1979 been more rapid or sweeping than in the field of training. In 1981 Britain possessed a training system based on a national tripartite focus for policymaking, and statutory industrial training boards (ITBs). Today every single major element of that system has either vanished or been radically altered. In some cases, the institutions introduced to replace the earlier tripartite system have themselves subsequently been replaced or radically modified. The pace of change has continued unabated since the election of the Labour government in 1997. It has set itself ambitious targets for increasing the proportion of young people in higher education and for widening participation and is introducing institutional changes in the financing of post-16 education and training. Perhaps more significantly, with political devolution to Scotland, Wales and Northern Ireland, it is no longer meaningful to talk of a UK training system, but rather of four separate systems with different dynamics. Whereas the version of this chapter which appeared in the first edition of *Industrial Relations in Britain* did deal with Great Britain, the emergence of a federal system means that the main focus of this chapter is England.

Change has not only encompassed the institutional landscape, but has also included new methods of delivering training (such as computer-based learning and open learning), a massive decline in the craft apprenticeship system, and moves towards multi-skilling and the erosion of traditional job, skill and training demarcations in the workplace. Since 1997, shifting attitudes towards the role of unions in training have emphasized their role in stimulating demand, but this does not extend to rights to consultation and information on workplace training plans, nor to paid educational leave.

Given the scale and pace of change, and the often transitory nature of many institutional mechanisms within the new British training system, this chapter cannot cover all aspects of these developments in detail. The aim is to focus on the major underlying trends in the structure of training policymaking and supply, some of the most important features of the evolving systems of training delivery in the workplace, and the implication of these developments for relations between employers and unions. The chapter opens by addressing the regulation and deregulation of training and the role of the 'social partners'. We then offer a brief account of the creation of the new training system. The chapter then turns to the decline of traditional apprenticeships and new developments, such as multi-skilling, open learning and personal development programmes, which have consequences for the structure of occupations and the distribution of skills in the workforce. Finally, we review trade unions' changing attitudes towards and policies on training.

Elsewhere in Europe (and in the past in the UK), training policy has been viewed as a classic area for the development of corporatist arrangements, whereby the state devolves the responsibility for policy development and implementation to the representative organizations of labour and capital (see chapter 5). The reason for this is that individual employers, acting on a rational basis, may not invest enough in training since they can find it cheaper to recruit skilled labour from other employers. State intervention is therefore believed to be necessary in order to secure sufficient training of adequate quality to meet the needs of the economy. However, since state intervention alone is often bureaucratic and lacks adequate information, the devolution of responsibility to employers, on the one hand, and trade unions, on the other, ensures that the parties which are most directly involved in the production process have a stake in the decision-making process and thus an interest in the successful implementation of policy. Although the form of regulation varies considerably from one European country to another, most exhibit some form of state intervention and incorporation of the 'social partners' into training policy and institutions.

The ideological context framing the British debate has been bound up with the role of the state. As the first country to industrialize, Britain initially entrusted the provision of education to religious charities and training to employers. While an involvement of the state in education gradually evolved, training remained on a voluntarist basis and outside the ambit of government funding and control. By contrast, in Germany, France and Japan, the state rejected a laissez-faire approach and took the lead in stimulating industrial development; as part of these efforts, it invested in vocational education and training (VET) (Coates 2000: 107–21). More recently, many European states have chosen to provide some form of statutory backing to training. This often involves trade unions, for two reasons. First, it helps to secure co-operation in changes to training programmes. Second, since union members' interests are best served through the development of skills which have wide recognition in the labour market, as opposed to the task- and firm-specific requirements of employers, the incorporation of unions is conducive to driving the training system towards meeting long-term skill requirements rather than employers' immediate needs (Streeck 1989).

In Britain voluntarism has been the dominant approach to training. The exception was the interlude between 1964 and 1988 during which the tripartite

Industrial Training Boards operated a system of training levies, and public training programmes were administered through the Manpower Services Commission (see below). Although union interests were incorporated into the policymaking process during this period, after the Conservative government came to power in 1979 there was a systematic process of exclusion of unions from authoritative decision-making with respect to training policy (Rainbird 1990). Individual employers were seen as having primary responsibility for training decisions in their own organizations. They were also awarded a dominant role in the residual areas of public training policy aimed at the unemployed and young people through their involvement in the Training and Enterprise Councils.

Since the Labour government came to power, there have been continuities with the approach of the Conservatives as well as new departures. In its policy documents the government has given high priority to education, lifelong learning and the skills needs of the economy. The main focus of its interventions has been to emphasize the role of state in increasing participation in formal education and reform of the funding mechanism for post-16 education and training through the establishment of the Learning and Skills Council (LSC). As far as workplace learning is concerned, it supports a voluntary approach and incentives to individual learners to engage in the learning market, rather than encouraging a statutory framework of entitlements. The overall climate is more conducive to the development of social partnership. Nevertheless, it has adopted a piecemeal approach: providing funding for trade union innovation on workplace learning (the DfES's Union Learning Fund), supporting the development of partnership approaches more generally (the Department of Trade and Industry's (DTI's) Partnership Fund), using example in the public sector (for example, employee involvement and workforce development in the NHS) and exhortation elsewhere.

These changes have been motivated by a range of concerns about education and training performance (NSTF 2000a and b). Such concerns have been with us for at least the last 150 years (Perry 1976), but have intensified in the last two decades. They include international comparisons that appear to show that, relative to many other developed countries, standards of basic literacy and numeracy are low, and that levels of qualification across the workforce are low, except at degree level and above (Campbell et al. 2001). It also appears that about one-third of the adult UK workforce rarely receives much in the way of training (Keep 1999a). These weaknesses have been linked to policy agendas concerned with both social inclusion (largely employability), and economic performance (largely centring on productivity).

Since the late 1970s a broad consensus has emerged that improvement of the UK's skills base is a prerequisite for economic success, and, more latterly, that without more and better education and training for some sections of the population unemployment will continue to be a problem. The means by which such improvements might best be secured have not been subject to the same level of consensus, and the role of the state and degree to which training can be left to market forces has been the focus of controversy.

Changes in Policymaking and Delivery Structures

The development of the national training system prior to 1979

As outlined above, until the 1960s the role of the state in training in peacetime was minimal, with responsibility for training provision resting with individual employers. However, a growing awareness of the need for improvement in Britain's training performance, and the slow pace of change being generated by voluntary training arrangements, led in 1962 to the Conservative government's White Paper on training, which in turn led to indirect state intervention in the form of the Labour government's 1964 Industrial Training Act (see Perry 1976 for details). The Act gave ministers the power to create Industrial Training Boards (ITBs) – sectoral bodies made up of employers and trade union representatives, which were empowered to establish a levy on firms within their industry. This levy funded the boards' operating costs and sectoral training activity via training grants to companies whose training plans and provision met standards laid down by the ITB. By 1969 there were 27 ITBs covering 15 million employees (mainly in manufacturing) out of a national workforce of 25 million (Lindley 1983).

In 1972, following criticisms about excessive bureaucracy and the inability of the ITB system to accommodate the problems and requirements of small firms, the operation of the ITBs was reviewed. As a result, the Employment and Training Act 1973 replaced the levy/grant system with a new system based on exemptions from the levy for all small firms and for those companies whose training met criteria specified by the ITB. The state would in future meet the ITBs' operating costs (see Perry 1976; Senker 1992).

The Act also created a new national, tripartite body – the Manpower Services Commission (MSC) – to oversee manpower planning, the operation of government training schemes and employment services, and the activities of the ITBs. The MSC rapidly became involved in measures aimed at reducing persistent cyclical skill shortages in the economy, and in devising various special temporary employment measures and training schemes aimed at the unemployed (for details, see Ainley and Corney 1991; Evans 1992).

The creation of the MSC reflected a belief that there was a role for more direct state intervention in training, and that planning at national level was a necessity. Both the ITBs and the MSC also embodied the concept that training policy and delivery were best tackled via institutions that embraced both sides of industry, as well as, in some cases, the interests of educationalists and local government.

Changing policies and institutions after 1979

The election in 1979 of a Conservative government committed to ending the post-war consensus signalled a dramatic shift in training policies. The government's approach to training was shaped by a number of beliefs. These include the assumption that market forces, rather than statutory rights and duties, were the best means of determining the type and amount of training undertaken; that it was the responsibility of employers, and to a lesser extent individuals, to decide their levels of investment in training; that the role of the state in training should be limited to supporting provision for disadvantaged groups (such as the long-term unemployed), helping with pump-priming funding to aid innovation, and exhortation; and finally, that VET should be employer-led and employer-controlled, with the influence of educationalists and trade unions being sharply reduced (for a concise statement of government beliefs on training, see ED 1988).

This approach to training can be seen as part of a wider continuum of policies aimed at increasing the efficiency of the British labour market through increasing deregulation and greater labour market competition. Thus the diminution of trade union influence upon training policy cannot be viewed in isolation from wider attempts by the Conservative government to weaken the power of trade unions within the British labour market.

The move from ITBs to NSTOs to ITOs to NTOs   The initial indicator of a new approach to training came in 1981, with the decision to abolish the majority of the ITBs. Seventeen were abolished, with more being wound up in 1988, leaving only the Construction Industry Training Board. (The Engineering Construction section of the Engineering Industry Training Board set up its own training board.)

The voluntary sectoral bodies that replaced the statutory ITBs were originally styled Non-Statutory Training Organizations (NSTOs), then Industry Training Organizations (ITOs). They were designed, run and financed by employers, and, in contrast to the ITBs, involvement in them by trade unions and educationalists was not guaranteed but was available only at the invitation of the employers. Employer membership of these bodies was entirely voluntary, as was the decision to support or participate in their activities. The ITOs had no powers to raise a levy, or to compel companies to train or to co-operate with their plans. Their main roles proved to be the dissemination of information on training, helping to define future sectoral skill needs, organizing group training schemes, and encouraging and exhorting firms to do more training. By the early 1990s there were about 120 ITOs. They were estimated to cover five-sixths of the national workforce (Berry-Lound et al. 1991: 535).

Did these arrangements work? Evidence to support the Conservative government's view, that 'the Training Boards . . . have not succeeded in raising the standard and quantity of training in the sectors they covered to the level of our major competitors overseas' (ED 1988: 34), is limited. The official reviews of ITB operation conducted in 1972, 1980 and 1981 all reached the general conclusion that the ITBs had, on the whole, made a major contribution to improving the quantity and quality of training, but that in some important areas, such as cross-sectoral skills, adult training and apprenticeship reform, progress had been limited. The blame for this situation may not have rested with the boards. As Senker (1992) points out, their inability to take effective initiatives in these areas often stemmed from employers' conservatism and unwillingness to countenance and pay for change (see also MSC 1981; Lindley 1983). Senker also argues that government policies, in particular the replacement of the levy/grant system with levy exemptions, and the tensions between the MSC's national policies and the needs of individual sectors, made the ITBs' task more difficult (see also Perry 1976; MSC 1981).

What is known about the performance of the ITOs does not suggest that they represented an improvement in the effectiveness of sectoral training arrangements in Britain. Research in the mid-1980s suggested that the majority of the voluntary sectoral bodies were ineffective when judged against the MSC's targets for their activities (Rainbird and Grant 1985; Varlaam 1987).

There is some evidence that their effectiveness subsequently improved, but significant problems remained and resulted in the Labour government taking steps to rationalize them. They are now referred to as National Training Organizations (NTOs) and their numbers have been reduced by forced merger by the government. They are supposed to be employer-led, but they have been created and, in some cases funded, by the DfEE/DfES.[1] Although they have responsibilities for producing workforce development plans for their sectors, a reading of the reports of the National Skills Task Force (NSTF 1998, 1999, 2000c) suggests a declining role for employers in the training system and an increasing move towards a state-led system with resources concentrated on education. There is to be no compulsion on employers and the responsibility of the new Learning and Skills Council is to fill the gaps in employer provision, in this way creating a new variation on the old theme of voluntarism in the workplace and state intervention on the supply side.

The development of vocational qualifications   The second decisive development in the creation of a new training system came with moves towards a unified system of national vocational qualifications (NVQs). An MSC-sponsored review of existing vocational qualifications concluded that provision was complex, confusing to employer and trainee, offered patchy coverage, gave limited access to training for adults, made little provision for the accreditation of prior learning, and laid too much stress on the testing of knowledge rather than skills and competences (MSC/DES 1986).

In 1986 the government set up the employer-led National Council for Vocational Qualifications (NCVQ) to tackle these problems through the creation of a system of NVQs in England, Wales, and Northern Ireland. In Scotland an existing body – the Scottish Vocational Education Council (SCOTVEC) – was charged with creating parallel Scottish vocational qualifications (SVQs). The NCVQ adopted a radical approach, based on the formulation of an NVQ framework of employer-designed, competence-based qualifications at five (initially four) levels. The NCVQ has since merged with the Schools Curriculum and Assessment Authority (SCAA) to become the Qualifications and Curriculum Authority (QCA).

NVQs and SVQs are based on standards of competence, as defined by employers, that are needed to undertake specific jobs. NVQs must be modular, and be broken down into component 'units of competence'. The trainee acquires an NVQ by achieving the standards for each of these units, for which a credit is received. Credits can be accumulated through undertaking training, through the accreditation of prior learning (APL), or both. The competences required for an NVQ are normally assessed in the workplace, rather than the classroom or through written examinations, and assessment of the ability to perform tasks is generally expected to be undertaken by the candidate's supervisor or other managerial staff. As a result of this competence-based approach NVQs and SVQs are grounded and specified in terms of the outcomes of learning, rather than the processes through which the learning takes place. They are hence specified independently of any particular location, mode and duration of training delivery (Jessup 1991).

The NCVQ did not itself design the qualifications: it simply recognized and approved existing and new qualifications that fitted within its framework. The QCA works in the same manner. The design of the qualifications for each industry originally rested with employer-led Industry Lead Bodies (ILBs), a role now taken over by the NTOs. To deal with areas of employment such as clerical and administrative work which cover many industries, cross-sectoral bodies have been created.

The system of competence-based NVQs was a radical innovation, and a great deal of effort and political capital has been invested in it. The official view was that NVQs would raise the status of vocational qualifications in comparison to traditional academic qualifications, and encourage investment in training by promoting flexible provision (Debling 1991; Jessup 1991). Moreover, NVQs were to provide the glue that bound together the new devolved training system. As the focus of policy shifted to local delivery mechanisms, the role of national standards as a means of ensuring coherence increased. NVQs formed the key element in monitoring the success of national training policies, and of companies' training efforts.

NVQs have not been without their critics. Some academics accused employers of defining competences in a very narrow, task-specific way, in contrast to their European counterparts, who appear to desire a broader mix of training and general education (Prais 1989; A. Green 1998). Some employers echoed these criticisms (CBI 1989). It is alleged that NVQs often require the minimum level of skill needed to perform a particular job, rather than encouraging broader-based learning in transferable skills (McCool 1991), and Callender (1992) suggests that there may be an inherent conflict between the short-term needs of individual employers and the longer-term needs of trainees and the national economy. There has also been concern that the levels of skill being specified are sometimes low, particularly when contrasted with those required by overseas employers. Doubts have also been expressed about the status and credibility of workplace assessment (Prais 1989, 1991), and about the ability of the personnel and training systems within many workplaces to deliver the support that NVQ training and assessment requires (Callender 1992).

One of the main indicators of the success of NVQs is the extent to which they have been adopted by employers. Since their introduction in 1987 about 3.1 million NVQs have been awarded. In the UK in 1999–2000 more than 1 million vocational qualifications (VQs) were awarded, of which 117,000 were GNVQs, 450,000 were NVQs and just over half a million were other VQs. Of these, 32 per cent were awarded at level 1, the lowest level, and 40 per cent at level 2.

The higher levels, levels 3 and 4, represented 23 and 5 per cent respectively (*Statistical Bulletin* 2000). Their use for initial training has been relatively strong, but this reflects the fact that the major part of vocational education and training for young people is state-funded and, as a result, the achievement of a qualification has been made a requirement. The proportion of young people undertaking work-based, employer-sponsored training has declined since the beginning of the 1990s and this now represents a minority route (see Evans et al. 1997). As far as adult workers are concerned, a major part of training continues to be informal and on the job, and is often uncertified. Even where it is more formalized it is often linked to company-specific or task-specific requirements, and is not appropriate to NVQ certification. There is also relatively little evidence of employers using APL as a means of certifying the existing skills of the workforce and encouraging progression. In some instances NVQs have been linked to the introduction of systems of Total Quality Management (Keep 2000). The care sector is one in which the government has set targets for the achievement of a qualified workforce via the NVQ route: it has stipulated that all workers should be qualified to NVQ level 2 in Social Care and to NVQ level 3 in Child Care as a means of meeting quality standards (TOPSS 1999).

Alongside NVQs, traditional vocational qualifications, such as City and Guilds, have continued to flourish. There are around 840 NVQs, approximately 1,800 VQs sufficiently in line with NVQ criteria to be approved for government funding through the further education system, and more than 17,000 other VQs. There has also been a rise of new qualifications offered by commercial companies rather than traditional awarding bodies. Certification for successful completion of Microsoft training courses would be one example. The QCA is now working to implement a national qualification framework, into which all qualifications, academic and vocational, can be slotted, and it is hoped that this may result in some reduction in the overall number of qualifications on offer.

To summarize, the key features of NVQ usage are as follows. Surveys suggest that about half of employers use NVQs, though for widely varying proportions of their employees. There are considerable sectoral variations in usage (Steedman 1998; Winterton and Winterton 1998) with low levels of take-up in small and medium-sized firms. The split between the number of NVQs and VQs awarded annually seems to have settled at a ratio of roughly 50 : 50.

Despite the emphasis placed on the redesign of the vocational qualification system, the real engine for growth in the qualification levels of the UK workforce has been elsewhere. Overall, in 1999 the proportion of academic qualifications held by the workforce had risen relative to vocational qualifications, with 49 per cent of those in employment holding academic qualifications as against 31 per cent who had vocational qualifications. In 1979 the figures were 29 per cent and 26 per cent respectively (Keep 2000). The continued expansion of higher education and, in particular, two-year degree programmes delivered through further education colleges, is likely to reinforce the continuing marginalization of work-based qualifications and their inferior status relative to educational qualifications.

The end of the MSC and moves to a locally based system   In spite of the Conservative government's desire to disengage itself from responsibility for training, events during the early and mid-1980s conspired to render this goal problematic. In particular, the rise in youth and adult unemployment created a political require-ment for the government to be seen to be tackling the problem via large-scale, government-funded training and work experience programmes, such as the Youth Training Scheme (YTS) (Keep 1994). The MSC as a consequence found itself acting as the main agency for managing the problems of unemployment.

However, following the 1987 general election. and with youth unemployment no longer rising, the government fulfilled a manifesto commitment by restruc-turing the MSC and removing its responsibility for employment service func-tions, renaming the organization the Training Commission to denote its new focus of activity. In September 1988, following a refusal by TUC representatives on the Commission to endorse the proposed Employment Training (ET) scheme for the long-term unemployed, the government announced the outright aboli-tion of the Commission and its intention to shift decision-making away from national and sectoral levels towards a new focus on local labour markets. The chief component of the new system was to be a network of Training and Enter-prise Councils (TECs) in England and Wales, and in Scotland a broadly similar set of bodies to be styled Local Enterprise Companies (LECs).

TECs and LECs were set up as employer-led bodies, with the legal status of limited companies. Two-thirds of the members of each TEC's board had to be the chairs or chief executives of private sector companies. Trade union participation was by invitation. Members of a TEC board served in a personal capacity and were not deemed to represent their company or organization. The functions of TECs and LECs were to administer government training and work experience schemes for the unemployed, to monitor and address skill requirements in the local labour market, to encourage companies to invest in training, and to act as a catalyst for local economic growth and regeneration. TECs and LECs had a contractual relationship with the Employment Department, from whom they received funding for training schemes for the unemployed, plus a small basic grant to cover operating costs and promotional activities. There were initially 82 TECs covering England and Wales, and 20 Scottish LECs.

Over time the TECs evolved into an extremely varied and diverse group of institutions, about which generalizations are hence difficult to make. That this should be the case is hardly surprising: as local bodies they tended to mould their activities and methods of operation to meet local circumstances and prior-ities (Keep 1999a: 12; for a detailed overview see Jones 1999).

A distinctive feature of the TECs was that they were not constituted as repre-sentative bodies. Many TEC boards were not representative of local employers. Initial analysis of the composition of TEC boards (Emmerick and Peck 1991) indicated that private sector manufacturing industry was often over-represented in relation to the proportion of employment it provided in the locality. At a broader level, TECs were designed by the Conservative government to be explic-itly unrepresentative of other stakeholders in VET – educationalists, trade unions, community groups, local authorities and the unemployed. Some TECs made efforts to overcome these problems and evolved advisory structures in order to allow representation for non-employer stakeholders. Nevertheless, their legal status as limited companies, the merger of many of them with their local chambers of commerce and industry, and the lack of any compulsory requirement for formal linkages with representative bodies in the localities within which they operated, meant that their accountability to their local communities was at best uncertain.

Perhaps the greatest success of the TEC movement was to harness the interest and energy of large numbers of senior private sector executives (NTTF 1992; Wood 1992). On the debit side, problems included cuts in government funding, conflicts with the Employment Department and later the Department for Education and Employment (DfEE) over departmental supervision of their activities, and difficult relations with other parts of the training system, such as the sectoral bodies. However, the greatest single difficulty which TECs faced was that nine-tenths of the government funding they received was committed to schemes that were, in the main, aimed at the unemployed, and which only covered entrants or re-entrants to the labour market rather than existing members of the workforce. The TECs were relatively unsuccessful at attracting funding from non-governmental sources. Summarizing these problems, an OECD report pointed out that, although TECs and LECs did create some inventive opportunities for young people, there was 'sometimes excessive competition between training providers and intermediary bodies which can be costly and which raises equity problems with regard to access to further and higher education and training'. It concluded that they had contributed little to ameliorating Britain's poor record in equipping young people for the world of work. In 1998, 20 per cent of young people were dropping out of education within a year of the end of compulsory schooling and 40 per cent of young people aged between 19 and 24 had not reached what the OECD considered to be a minimum level of qualification (*Guardian*, 11 February 2000).

Faced with these problems, and keen to increase the government's capacity for direct intervention in and leverage on the VET system, the Labour government's White Paper *Learning to Succeed* (DfEE 1999) announced the abolition of the TECs in England and Wales. In their place came a Learning and Skills Council (LSC), with 47 Local Learning and Skills Councils (LLSCs) at local level, bringing together responsibility for funding all post-16 education and training (see below).

New schemes and targets   The two remaining major elements of the training system – Investors in People (IIP), and the Learning Targets – although employer-led in their development, have included a role for participation and endorsement by the TUC.

The Investors in People initiative (IIP) is a national standard for effective investment in employees. It was developed by the National Training Task Force, the strategic body set up to oversee the establishment and operations of the TECs, in collaboration with CBI members, the Association of British Chambers of

Commerce (ABCC), the TUC, ITOs, and other training organizations. IIP was launched in November 1990. The aim was to encourage organizations to invest in training, to help them to do so more effectively, and to reward this commitment with a nationally recognized 'kitemark' of training quality.

To achieve IIP status an organization's owner or chief executive must make a public commitment to develop all employees in order to achieve business objectives, and the organization must regularly review the training and development needs of all its employees, demonstrate action to train and develop individuals, and provide evidence that the organization regularly evaluates and reviews its investment in training. Until 2001, assessment of most organizations in England and Wales applying for IIP status is made by their local TEC, though large companies dealt with a national Employment Department unit. In Scotland, IIP assessment is undertaken by a national body, Investors in People (Scotland). The award of IIP status is made for three years, after which it is necessary for the organization to provide evidence of continued achievement and development.

IIP has been taken up by a significant proportion of large and medium-sized enterprises. Data from IIP UK indicate that, as at the end of January 2001, 89 per cent of all organizations (public and private sector) with 200 or more employees had achieved (56 per cent) or were committed to achieving (33 per cent) the standard. Among organizations with 50 or more employees, the relevant figures were that 55 per cent had achieved the standard (33 per cent) or were committed to doing so (22 per cent). Penetration among smaller employers is much weaker.

IIP was important to the TECs because it provided them with their chief lever for attempting to improve the training of the employed workforce. It is likely to be expected to perform much the same role by the LSC, which has assumed overall responsibility for promoting IIP to large and medium-sized employers and supporting them to achieve the standard. The Small Business Service will undertake this role for smaller companies, upon whom much effort is expected to be focused.

IIP's weakness lies in the fact that, as a voluntary measure, it is a mechanism for badging the training practices of organizations that are committed to providing the training necessary to deliver their business strategies. It has little scope for influencing the business strategies themselves, particularly in organizations that are dependent on price competition rather than the quality of their products and services. More importantly, the attainment of IIP does not require any new commitment of resources to training and development. It merely requires that training needs are considered and are appropriate to business need. As a result, many employees, particularly on the lower salary grades, continue to have little access to training and development because their jobs do not require it (Rainbird et al. 1999).

The National Learning Targets. One of the features of the VET system in the last two decades has been a growing dependence upon the use of targets as a management tool. This is most noticeable in the introduction of sets of overarching national targets. The earliest manifestations of these were the National Education and Training Targets (NETTs).

Table 15.1 LSC's National Learning Targets

	Target 2004	Actual 2000
16–18 year olds in structured learning	80%	75%
At level 2 by age 19	85%	75%
At level 3 by age 19	55%	51%
Raise literacy and numeracy skills	750,000 adults	n.a.
Adults at level 3	52%	47%

Level 2 denotes NVQ level 2 or its academic equivalent – 5 good GCSEs.
Level 3 denotes NVQ level 3 or its academic equivalent – 2 A levels.

The original NETTs for the year 2000 were formulated in 1989 by the CBI follow-ing bilateral talks with other employers' groups, trade unions and educational bodies. They were launched in the summer of 1991 with endorsement from the TUC. The government subsequently decided to offer its support to the targets. The targets have been updated and revised on a number of occasions, basically as it became apparent that a significant number were not going to be met.

They are now called the National Learning Targets, and, following the aboli-tion of the committee that used to set them (NACETT – the National Advisory Committee for Education and Training Targets), responsibility has passed to the LSC. The new National Learning Targets for 2004 are given in table 15.1, along with current levels of performance. Their aim is to extend participation in learn-ing, increase the engagement of employers in workforce development, raise achievement levels among young people and adults, and raise the quality of VET and increase user satisfaction. The targets form the centrepiece and main-spring of the LSC's Corporate Plan (LSC 2001a). Further targets for measuring employer engagement, adult participation in VET, and baselines and targets for raising quality and user satisfaction, will be set by the LSC in 2002.

There has never been any independent evaluation of what impact the National Learning Targets or their predecessors might or might not have had upon the volume of VET, and the value of such targets is open to doubt. In a sense, they are simply an institutionalized form of exhortation. The underlying assumption is that the existing patterns of decisions taken by employers and young people are relatively easy to change and that the main requirement is more and better information on what VET opportunities are available and the benefits they can bring (LSC 2001a). As mentioned above, many of the earlier targets were not met, though this fact was disguised because the targets had been revised by the time the deadline for achievement arrived. These earlier failures point to the possibility that existing patterns of training may be deeply rooted in existing structures of employment, product market strategies, work organization and job design (Keep and Mayhew 1998), and as such extremely difficult to change.

The LSC The latest rejigging of the institutional landscape focuses on the LSC. As mentioned above, the LSC and its local arms – the LLSCs – have replaced the

TECs and some other bodies. The LSC is responsible for funding all post-16 provision except higher education, with a budget in excess of £5.5 billion. Its scope includes sixth-form colleges, school sixth forms, adult and community learning, education–business links, adult advice and guidance, further education, and publicly funded training by employers. Its remit embraces setting and achieving the National Learning Targets, better matching the supply of VET with demand at national, sectoral and local levels, and the inspection of publicly funded training. It has been given a statutory duty to encourage participation in learning and to encourage employer participation in the provision of education and training.

The largest single grouping of members on both the LSC (and its central committees) and the LLSCs is employers, who make up 40 per cent of the total membership. Other interests represented include trade unions, local authorities, education institutions, and community and voluntary groups. The relationship between the LSC and its local arms is as yet unclear. Although the LSC's first Corporate Plan talks about the importance of both top-down and bottom-up planning, and stresses the desire 'to establish a culture in which there is maximum local freedom and flexibility, within a nationally-determined set of standards for quality and outcome' (LSC 2001a: 2), a recent LSC press release described the LSC as 'a national organization operating through 47 local offices' (LSC 2001b). What may prove crucial is the degree of local budgetary discretion that LLSCs are allowed to exercise. Recent figures have suggested that discretionary funds over which the LLSCs will have total control may amount to no more than about 1 per cent of the LSC's total budget.

Despite the restructuring of the funding arrangements for the supply side of the education and training system, some of the problems which have dogged it remain unresolved. The involvement of two government departments in this policy arena seems likely to raise problems of co-ordination and demarcation of responsibilities between them. The DfES is responsible for the LSC and LLSCs that are charged with developing workforce development plans for their local areas. The DTI is responsible for the Regional Development Agencies (RDAs) which control a relatively small Skills Development Fund and various streams of European funding, and also the Small Business Service (SBS) which will be responsible for developing wider business strategies for the SME sector. It is also relatively easy to set the LSC the task of creating the perfect funding mechanism to cover all routes within the VET system, but quite another matter to actually design, create and administer such a mechanism.

What are the prospects for the LSC? As detailed above, previous attempts to introduce systemic change through institutional reform suggest a need for caution. In all the cases discussed, high hopes at the time of their introduction were not subsequently fully met, and none of the new structures functioned quite as their designers had intended. Just as a new agency to distribute child benefit might not, of itself, be able to bring about an end to child poverty, so a new planning and funding mechanism for VET may not be able to solve the many deep-seated problems with skills in the UK economy.

Having examined the structural changes through which the mechanisms of training policy and delivery have been going, we now turn to see whether there are any indications that the reforms are producing concrete results in terms of changes taking place in the volume and quality of training being delivered.

The Scale and Scope of Training Activity

Data on the quality and quantity of training are both extensive and patchy, and the quality of some are open to question (Felstead et al. 1997). Some aspects are monitored in detail, while for others only the sketchiest indicators are available. For example, we know something about the volume of formalized training (both on and off the job), but next to nothing about the volume of informal learning that takes place, save that it is very substantial (Eraut et al. 1999). The picture that emerges is extremely complex. What follows tries to give a very brief overview (see further Campbell et al. 2001).

Recent developments

The level of qualifications held by the workforce has increased considerably over the last two decades. In 1979 more than 40 per cent of the economically active population did not possess any qualifications. By 2000, this had fallen to 15 per cent. Although this in part reflects rising levels of VET among older workers, the main drivers have been better examination results at the end of compulsory schooling (age 16), increased staying on rates in post-compulsory education, and the massive expansion of the higher education system.

That said, the overall volume of employer-provided training activity has undoubtedly risen over recent times. Participation rates have grown, with the proportion of the UK workforce receiving training in the four weeks preceding the Labour Force Survey rising from 8.3 per cent in 1984 to 15.9 per cent in 1999 (CBI 2000). The rate at which this improvement has taken place has varied. Between 1985 and 1994 the increase was 5 per cent, but only 1.8 per cent between 1995 and 1999 (NSTF 2000b: 72).

However, much of the training being provided appears to be either induction training or related to health and safety matters (DfEE 2000: 53; Felstead and Ashton 1996). Other indicators suggest that there may be problems with the quality of the training and/or the level at which it is being pitched, since 38 per cent was for a period of a week or less (*Labour Market Quarterly*, Winter 2000: 7), and work by Francis Green (1999) suggests that the duration of training episodes may have been falling in recent years. About 39 per cent of employer-funded training leads to either a whole qualification or a credit towards a qualification; the International Adult Literacy Survey (IALS) indicated that 'most training received was at a very low level and often is of relatively low duration' (NSTF 2000b: 76).

A further key feature is that training opportunities are distributed extremely unevenly across the workforce. Put simply, the rule is that unto those who already have, more shall be given. The recipients of the most intensive training are those who hold the highest educational qualifications and who have jobs near the top of the occupational ladder. Those least likely to be trained are those in low-status jobs, and those working for small firms (see Keep 1999a; NSTF 2000b; Campbell et al. 2001). It seems that at least a third of the adult workforce receives little or no training whatsoever – the Spring 1998 Labour Force Survey recorded that 72 per cent of UK employees had received no job-related training in the 13 weeks preceding the survey, and of these just under half (48 per cent) reported that they had never been offered any type of training by their current employer (DfEE 1998a: 33).

The issue of how much employers are investing in skills remains a vexed one. There are massive problems with the data, not least because many employers keep either no or only the sketchiest of records on how much they have spent on training, and the basis upon which such costs are calculated varies from organization to organization. Thus, although surveys come up with figures, these are often based on employers' guesstimates rather than anything that resembles hard accounting. The *Training in Britain* survey (Training Agency 1989) suggested that employers (public and private sector combined) spent about £14.4 billion on training in 1986/7. In 1993 a further survey was conducted, unfortunately using a different sample of employers and defining training costs in a manner that rendered comparisons with the earlier survey next to impossible. This exercise, the results of which were not published until 1997, revealed that employer spending in 1993 was £10.6 billion (IFF 1997). The latest estimate comes from the Learning and Training at Work 2000 survey (IFF 2000), again conducted using a sample and methodology that render direct comparisons with the earlier surveys extremely problematic. It suggested that, for employers with more than 10 employees, combined annual training expenditure has now reached £23.5 billion. The unreliability of these estimates means that it is not meaningful to develop measures of expenditure on training as a percentage of sales or payroll.

Relative performance

As outlined above, the last century and a half has witnessed concern that levels of skill in the workforce are lower across the whole of the UK than in competitor nations. This concern has sharpened in the last two decades, with a series of less than flattering comparisons emerging from OECD statistics, as well as from government-commissioned research (see e.g. IMS/MSC/NEDO 1984; DfEE/Cabinet Office 1996). Despite often substantial progress in some areas of VET provision, the overall prognosis remains gloomy. Campbell et al. (2001) conclude in a study for the DfES that, 'it appears that the UK's overall position is not particularly strong and that it is "falling behind" over time'. The data that follow come from this report.

Positive aspects include:

- the proportion of 50–54-year-olds in our workforce who have achieved tertiary-level qualifications;
- the participation rate in lifelong learning (for those aged between 16 and 65) is the sixth highest in the OECD (behind Finland, Denmark, Sweden, Norway and New Zealand);

- the participation rate for adults aged over 35 is the second highest in the 22 OECD countries for which figures are available;
- the UK has the highest participation rate in job-related continuing education and training.

The minus points are as follows.

- although the UK has the highest participation in training among the over-35 group, the average number of hours of training undertaken per person is the second lowest;
- the record on adult literacy is poor: the IALS survey suggests that, overall, the UK ranked seventeenth out of 22 countries across the entire range of skills being measured;
- the worst problems, however, relate to the proportion of young people attaining the equivalent of what is termed 'upper secondary education' (or training). Here, the UK's 25- to 29-year-old population achieved 64 per cent, compared to an OECD average of 72 per cent. This means that out of 26 countries ranked by the OECD, the UK finished nineteenth, ahead of only Turkey, Mexico, Portugal, Iceland, Spain, Italy, and Poland. Moreover, relative performance is worsening over time.

How do some of these figures relate to training rather than education, and to the actions of employers? It could be argued that poor adult literacy and weak levels of achievement among young people simply reflect failings in the education system. Undoubtedly education plays a part in both these problems, but so too do the action and demands of employers.

On adult literacy, as McIntosh and Steedman show, many adults with literacy difficulties 'work in jobs that fail to provide them with the motive or the opportunity to develop reading skills through reading tasks' (2001: 97). McIntosh and Steedman conclude that job improvement measures are required if progress is to be made in tackling the worst aspects of poor literacy among those in low-skilled jobs.

On the UK's poor showing on the proportion of young people achieving the equivalent of upper-secondary education, the role of employers is important in two ways. First, one of the weaknesses of provision in the UK, compared to countries such as Germany, concerns the lack of a strong work-based route for initial VET for young people. In countries where there is a well-founded apprenticeship system, such as Germany or Denmark, there is a high-quality alternative to school or college which can motivate sections of the young population to higher levels of achievement.

In the UK over the last two decades, faced with a sharp and continuing decline in traditional apprenticeships, there has been a succession of government initiatives aimed at revolutionizing the quality of what is on offer via work-based initial VET. These have included the Youth Training Scheme (YTS), Youth Training (YT), National Traineeships (NTs), Modern Apprenticeships (MAs), and now Foundation and Advanced Modern Apprenticeships (FMAs and AMAs). On the whole, these have often proved less successful than was hoped, and it remains to be seen whether a viable, high-quality work-based route can be constructed and maintained in more than a few sectors (Unwin and Fuller 2000; Keep and Payne forthcoming). Current evidence from official evaluations of MAs suggest that employers in many sectors have limited comprehension of what a high-quality work-based route would look like (Sims et al. 2000; Kodz et al. 2000). For example, as Winterbotham et al. (2000: 3) report, in the retailing sector only 6 per cent of modern apprentices attend college as part of their apprenticeship and 'a third appear to have no formal training of any sort (formal here meaning training beyond merely being supervised while doing day-to-day work)'.

The second reason why employers are implicated in the UK's poor performance on achieving the equivalent of upper-secondary schooling is that they set the structure of demand in the labour market. Put simply, the chief reason why most other developed countries have higher levels of achievement is because employers in those countries demand higher standards from young entrants to the labour market. In many countries the entry level to non-graduate occupations is the broad equivalent of UK level 3 (two A levels). In the UK it is often level 2 or below. By sending the signal that there are many jobs that can be gained with relatively limited qualifications, and by continuing to offer a relatively substantial number of entry-level jobs that carry with them either limited or no training, employers create incentives for young people, especially the less able, to under-achieve.

Training, Skill and Industrial Relations

Within these overall trends, one development that has had significant implications for industrial relations has been the decline of the craft apprenticeship system which traditionally constituted the main form of training for skilled manual workers. Outside this, training for manual workers had primarily been provided on the job, with little access to structured learning. In Britain, the concept of 'skill' traditionally derived from the production system rather than from vocational qualifications, and was associated, in particular, with the regulation of apprenticeship by craft unions. Skilled work was therefore associated with membership of a craft union and, since apprenticeship has normally been restricted to white male workers, access to training and to skilled work was not open to other groups of workers.

The Conservative government's policy on the reform of the apprenticeship system in 1983 aimed to remove craft union restrictions on training. In particular, it aimed to replace traditional time-serving, the system whereby the trainee was recognized as a skilled worker on completing a number of years as an apprentice, by tested standards, and to remove restrictions limiting the age of entry to 16-year-olds. These changes, alongside the development of the Youth Training Scheme, did not have the effect of boosting the number of apprentices, but consolidated their long-term decline. Between 1970 and 1983, when the reforms were introduced, the numbers of apprentices halved from 218,000 to 102,100 and by 1990 numbers had reduced to 53,600, less than a quarter of the 1970 level (figures compiled from various issues of the *Employment Gazette*).

In the early 1980s these reductions partly reflected the fall in manufacturing employment and redundancies among trainees in particular. Nevertheless, it is clear that the decline in apprenticeships has been disproportionate to the reduction in manufacturing employment. Whereas in 1980 apprentices accounted for 2.3 per cent of the workforce, this had dropped to 1 per cent by 1990. Between 1979 and 1991 membership of the three main craft unions declined sharply (see also chapter 9).

Developments in new technology and multi-skilling have consequences for industrial relations and trade union organization (Rainbird 1988). The organization of unions along occupational lines has imposed constraints on occupational mobility and, in particular, limited the possibilities for unskilled and semi-skilled workers to upgrade their jobs. Where companies are restructuring or introducing multi-skilling, access to training will determine which unions benefit most from these changes and, as a corollary, the groups of employees who are most at risk from redundancy. Moves towards increased flexibility and multi-skilling may be perceived as a threat to the spheres of influence of different trade unions and bring them into conflict with each other.

Training and collective bargaining

Training is rarely the primary purpose of collective agreements, and this is reflected in managers' claim that they rarely negotiate on training and development with union representatives. The 1998 WERS survey found that, in 43 per cent of cases where union representatives were present, managers provided no information on training, let alone consulted or negotiated on it (Cully et al., 1999: 105). Nevertheless, case-study evidence suggests that many workplaces are covered by collective agreements which may have consequences for training and development or which have clauses referring to it (Rainbird et al. forthcoming).

In the 1990s there have been a number of ways in which training and development have become incorporated into the collective bargaining agenda. Employers have introduced various forms of competence-based pay into collective agreements on wages and, in this way, training and development have been incorporated into the traditional bargaining agenda and mechanisms for dealing with it (e.g. grievance procedures, consultative committees). It is also present, but less centrally, in agreements on multi-skilling, flexibility, new technology and equal opportunities. Training and development has also been an arena in which partnership approaches have been encouraged by government, at least at the rhetorical level and with some financial support (see the section on partnership and the lifelong learning agenda below). Partnership arrangements on a specific learning agenda are often separate from the traditional mechanisms of collective bargaining. They may have more in common with the joint problem-solving approach to dealing with issues such as health and safety and may require union representatives to work with managers as well as using their traditional bargaining skills (Sutherland and Rainbird 2000). Training concerning the company's business needs is usually initiated by managers and is often seen as an area of management prerogative. In contrast, measures promoting workforce employability in a wider sense are more likely to be initiated by the unions, or through a joint approach and joint management structures (Rainbird et al. forthcoming).

Although, as indicated earlier, access to continuing training has been limited, there have nevertheless been a number of well-publicized examples of training and education schemes which have been designed to increase workers' adaptability to change, and willingness to learn. The Ford Motor Company's Employee Development Assistance Programme (EDAP), agreed in 1987, is an example which has attracted widespread interest within the trade union movement, partly for its joint approach (it is managed through a series of joint union–management committees) and partly for its enthusiastic take-up among Ford's manual workers. Although it concerns education and personal development rather than vocational training, it has had the effect of encouraging manual workers to return to learn through the allocation of funds for courses. Other major companies such as Rover and Peugeot introduced similar personal development programmes for their employees, though they are not all jointly managed. The development of open learning methods also has the potential to open up opportunities for learning in the workplace, though this is often in the workers' own time and takes an individual rather than collective form. Some trade unions such as the Amalgamated Engineering and Electrical Union (AEEU) and UNISON provide training and development as a service to members.

Union policies on training

The low levels of occupational training in Britain mean that not all unions have had coherent and clearly articulated policies on training, because their members have not been accustomed to dealing with it as a workplace issue (Rainbird 1990). Historically, the major form of training has been apprenticeship and, as a consequence, unions organizing skilled workers such as the AEEU and the Union of Construction and Allied Trades and Technicians (UCATT) had more highly developed policies on training than unions representing semi-skilled and unskilled manual workers, and they were able to represent their members' interests in the structures that were available to them. The general unions had less highly developed policies on training as well as a more heterogeneous membership. Therefore they did not use their rights to representation on ITBs and the MSC structures as effectively as they could have done.

During the 1980s, union policies often focused on the relationship between initial training programmes such as apprenticeship and the government-funded Youth Training Scheme. Concerns were raised by the threat to youth pay rates posed by trainee allowances and the possibility of job substitution. Craft unions were concerned to guarantee that apprentices completed their full period of training so that training and skill standards were maintained. In these circumstances, bargaining focused on the wages and conditions of trainees, rather than on the content of training itself (Rainbird 1990). During the 1990s concern shifted to training as an item on the 'new bargaining agenda' (Storey and Bacon 1993) and the extent to which it could help unions to appeal to new groups of workers – women and the highly qualified, in particular – who were perceived as having different interests to those of traditional male manual workers.

A number of factors came together to contribute to an increased interest in training. The first of these was the Labour Party's and TUC's analysis which identified low levels of investment in training and education as contributing to the structural weakness of the British economy. Second, the demand for rights to initial and continuing training in the European Union's social charter made Europe a point of reference for trade unions which were able to make little progress on statutory entitlements under the Conservative government at home. Even though the Conservatives 'opted out' of the social chapter of the Maastricht Treaty, the 'social dialogue' between employers' associations and unions at European level concerned training. This was echoed by the TUC's endorsement of the CBI's national training targets even before 1997 and the Labour government's signature of the social chapter. Third, unions had to respond to developments such as YTS, NVQs, modern apprenticeships and IIP. Although much of this has been defensive, there is some evidence of the development of more offensive strategies, particularly with respect to the development of NVQs and IIP, for example through the TUC/TEC Bargaining for Skills projects (see below). Fourth, the generally weakened bargaining position of unions meant that strategies on training complemented wage bargaining. Finally, the development of policies on training is part of a new relationship with both members and employers discussed in chapters 9 and 10. On the one hand, training increases the range of services offered to members. On the other hand, it is part of an approach to employers which allows unions to demonstrate their ability to co-operate in a productivist strategy. Training and the 'new bargaining agenda' were very much a part of the 'new unionism' aimed at refocusing union activities on services to individual members and promoting more co-operative relationships with employers. Nevertheless, not all initiatives relating to partnerships with employers on training and development can be interpreted within the framework of individual services to members, and traditional collectivist approaches retain their salience (Munro and Rainbird 2000).

Whereas trade unions, and the craft unions in particular, have had an interest in initial training through their involvement in apprenticeship, the ITBs, YTS and its successors, there has never really been any national or sectoral forum for discussing continuing training. In addition, employee representatives had no formal role in decision-making on training and development in the workplace. It was in relation to continuing training and development that unions began to develop an interest in the workplace as a locus of decision-making for training and, from the beginning of the 1990s, began to make demands for workplace training committees and rights to training (see e.g. TUC 1992). In the run-up to the general election in 1992 the TGWU and the GMB issued a joint demand for workers to have the right to five days' training per year. Unions sought to influence training in three main ways: through representation of members' interests where institutional structures have permitted it; through collective bargaining; and, more recently, through the development of partnerships with employers on lifelong learning. Paradoxically, the formal exclusion of trade union interests from training bodies under the Conservatives coincided with unions' increased interest in, and awareness of, training as a bargaining issue.

Representation of members' interests   Although the arenas in which unions can represent their members' interests on training have been reduced, unions have always retained some representational rights. They did not have equal representation rights with employers but, as outlined earlier, they had seats by invitation on the TEC and LEC boards and their committee structures. Many unions have been involved in the development of NVQs for their sectors through their participation in the ILBs. They are represented on the NTOs.

With the change of government in 1997, trade unions have been drawn into the policymaking process at national level, though not as equal partners with employers. Through their participation in a number of bodies, trade unionists have contributed to formulating policy on lifelong learning (the National Advisory Group on Continuing Education and Lifelong Learning – NAGCELL – which contributed to the publication of the DfEE's *The Learning Age*: DfEE 1998b), on widening participation (which contributed to the Kennedy Report 1997) and on basic skills (which contributed to the Moser Report 1998). Indeed, the Moser Report recognized that unions have a key role to play in reaching parts of the workforce that other bodies are unable to involve in workplace learning. They have also participated in the National Skills Task Force, though their support for statutory intervention on training has not been shared by the employer representatives nor accepted by the government (NSTF 2000a). They are represented, along with other stakeholders such as the voluntary sector and educationalists, in the new LSC and LLSCs, where they have had to apply on a competitive basis for seats. Although employers also have to apply on the same basis, employers' representatives have been allocated 40 per cent of seats. In October 2000, the membership of the national Learning and Skills Council was announced: John Monks, General Secretary of the TUC, had a seat and chaired the Adult Learning Committee.

Partnership and the lifelong learning agenda   Given the formal exclusion of union interests from training institutions, unions have increasingly turned to alternative methods of influence. The Manufacturing, Science and Finance union (MSF) has argued that 'as long as access to training is not a statutory entitlement, employees depend to a large degree on trade unions to secure this right for them as part of their contract of employment' (MSF 1988: 20). The TUC's preferred form of involvement is that of workplace training committees and a number of unions such as MSF and the TGWU have incorporated this demand into collective bargaining strategies. Despite the growth in interest in training as a bargaining issue, much of the impetus came from national leaderships rather than from grassroots trade union members. Winterton and Winterton's examination of training and collective bargaining in the UK found that the 'new policy initiatives have clearly established training as part of the "new agenda"', but concluded that 'trade union aspirations for involvement are more extensive than any collaboration agreed in practice to date' (1994: 6, 45).

One way in which trade unions have become involved in training in companies has been through the TUC/TEC Bargaining for Skills projects. Initially set up as a means of mobilizing trade union support for the national training targets, Bargaining for Skills has become a mechanism for extending the use of the Investors in People award and NVQs through trade unions campaigning for their take-up in their workplaces. A model has emerged whereby trade unions approach the employer to introduce IIP and NVQs as a means of contributing to training for business need. Trade union representatives have also gained new sources of expertise to support these developments, for example in conducting training needs analysis and NVQ assessment. This has often been accompanied by the setting up of a learning centre on company premises, which is seen as contributing to training for employees' needs. In some cases joint committees have been set up to oversee these developments, in which trade union representatives, managers and sometimes training providers (such as further education colleges) have been represented. The Bargaining for Skills projects have also used the resources available for trade union innovation on training through the DfEE's Union Learning Fund to develop the role of learning representatives in the workplace. Learning representatives have new roles, such as negotiating with the employer on training and development, providing advice and guidance to members, and developing collective mechanisms for delivering learning opportunities through collective forms of Individual Learning Accounts. The TUC is also involved in some University for Industry 'learning hubs'.

Individual unions have been developing strategies to enable lifelong learning in the workplace and community. UNISON has built on its tradition of professional training for members (developed by the National and Local Government Officers Association (NALGO)) and membership development for manual workers (the Return to Learn programme, initially developed by the National Union of Public Employees (NUPE)) to develop partnerships with public sector employers on employee development. Initially these programmes were developed as a service to members and were extended to partnership with employers on a pragmatic basis (Munro et al. 1997). The first partnerships were established with employers in 1996, and by 2000 there were over 250, including an agreement with the National Health Service in Scotland to provide Return to Learn in every NHS trust and Health Board in Scotland. The range of provision has been extended to access courses into higher education, as well as the development of work-based routes into professional qualifications in social work and nursing.

The DfEE/DfES's Union Learning Fund, set up in 1998, has provided impetus to developments which were already under way in many unions. In the first two funding rounds £4.2 million was allocated to projects supporting trade union innovation on learning. This supported a range of initiatives aimed at building union capacity on lifelong learning (see Shaw 1999 and Cutter 2000 for evaluations of the two phases). As a result of these developments, in 2001 the government issued proposals to give union learning representatives a legal right to paid release from work. The then Secretary of State for Education and Employment, David Blunkett, saw their role as 'footsoldiers' for raising skills and 'workplace experts' on skills issues (*Guardian*, 28 August 2000).

Since the Labour government came to power in 1997 there have been significant moves to involve trade unions in the policymaking process, and a shift towards a rhetoric of social partnership, based on a facilitative rather than a statutory approach. By this we mean that the principal mechanism remains a voluntary one, although financial support has been made available to support innovative developments (for example, the Union Learning Fund and the Partnership Fund). A consequence of this has been that a wide range of practices has been emerging, often at the initiative of national union officers. Since resources are available for innovation, the question of how these new practices are consolidated and embedded in workplace practices and union branch structures is problematic. At the workplace level there are no formal institutional mechanisms for union representatives to be informed or consulted on their employers' training plan. Unlike their European counterparts, British workers still have no entitlement to paid educational leave, and in 2000 the trade union movement launched a campaign to secure this.

There is some evidence to suggest that trade unions have been using learning initiatives to build union organization and to recruit workers in sectors which are hard to organize (see some of the examples of the Union Learning Fund projects in Cutter 2000). Nevertheless the 1998 WERS survey shows evidence of their de facto exclusion from training in the bulk of workplaces (Rainbird et al. forthcoming), to say nothing of their absence from many areas of the economy. Although there has been progress, and this may be supported by placing union learning representatives on a statutory footing, so far it has been limited not only to unionized workplaces, but to those where unions have a conscious strategy on training and development.

Conclusions

What conclusions can be drawn about the changes that have taken place in British training? The first is that training policies between 1979 and 1997 under the Conservative government represented a decisive rejection of legislative backing for training, and of any notions of social partnership and tripartite control of training design and delivery. By so doing, they were in marked contrast to those common in the rest of the European Union, where legislative underpinning for training and the active involvement of the social partners are more often the norm. Since 1997, the Labour government has given greater priority to education, training and lifelong learning. It is more favourably disposed to approaches based on social partnership, but (in line with its broader policies analysed in chapters 5 and 6) has so far relied on encouragement and facilitation rather than a legislative approach. It can be argued that if the active participation of all stakeholders in the VET system is an essential precondition for making sustained progress in improving the supply and usage of skills in the UK, then the British training system continues to be an inadequate vehicle for securing that participation and support.

A second conclusion is that while there undoubtedly has been progress in increasing the amount of training that takes place within the British economy, doubts remain concerning the quality of what is being provided. In particular, the level of education and training required of young entrants into many non-managerial and non-professional jobs is low compared to that found in most other developed countries. At the same time progress on creating a work-based route for the development of intermediate skills, where many have argued Britain's skills gap compared to its overseas competitors is most acute (Ryan 1991, 2000; NSTF 2000a, 2000b), has not been very marked.

Finally, the main thrust of Conservative policy was to pursue sweeping institutional reform in the belief that the creation of a market-based, employer-led training system could, of itself, deliver a fundamental change in the quantity and quality of training in Britain. The pace and scale of this wave of institutional reforms and the activity which it generated have perhaps served to focus the attention of both policymakers and commentators on the supply of training, to the detriment of the consideration of more fundamental questions concerning the often relatively weak demand for skills in the British economy. Indeed, in some senses, it can be argued that endless rounds of institutional change have acted as a form of displacement activity, diverting attention from the underlying causes of the UK's relative weaknesses in VET.

The Labour government has continued to pursue the dual goals of institutional reform and improvements to the supply of labour, but with greater emphasis on the role of the state and the education system. It can still be argued (Keep and Mayhew 1998; Keep 1999b) that numerous structural factors within the British economy limit the demand for skills, and that unless these factors are addressed there is a danger that any increased investment in the supply of skills will produce an inadequate rate of return, whether for individuals, firms or society as a whole. Many of these structural inhibitors are identified in this book. They include developments within the labour market, such as the growth of small firms and part-time work, and the erosion of skilled manual employment. Equally, the structure of consumer demand within the British economy, where the large numbers subsist on relatively low incomes, results in many firms concentrating on cost-centred competitive strategies. Other factors affecting firms include the difficulties in calculating returns on investment in training, the limited adoption of the high-performance workplace model, the frequent lack of internal labour markets and opportunities for progression and the dominance of internal cost-control structures. For multinational companies, the increasing marginality of their UK operations and the ease of making British workers redundant may reinforce these predispositions. At the same time, the capacity of the public sector to train is being undermined by the extension of its role as a commissioner rather than a direct provider of services.

In the light of these structural brakes on demand for higher levels of skill within the economy, the need is for policies that go beyond attempts to boost the supply of skills, and which aim to address the current limits to demand. As

Coffield suggests, this means that 'high skill formation calls for more than technical adjustments to the supply of skills; it calls for nothing less than a new national settlement between government, employers, trade unions and the British people' (2001: 11). This would mean policies that encompassed issues such as product market strategies, job design, work organization, and wider systems of personnel management and labour utilization. Thus, rather than defining the problem as being simply about the supply of education and training, a more productive approach would be a broader focus on ways in which the design and organization of production and employment can be improved, thereby enhancing demand for, and usage of, skills. Such a focus would require a significant degree of leadership and intervention by government and its agencies, which brings us back to the issue with which this chapter began – the vexed question of the role of the state.

Note

1 Following the re-election of the Labour government in 2001, the Department for Education and Employment became the Department for Education and Skills. For details of how this affected its remit, see the DfES website at <http://www.des.gov.uk> and the Learning and Skills Council website at <http://www.lsc.gov.uk>.

References

Ainley, P., and Corney, M. 1991: *Training for the Future: The Rise and Fall of the Manpower Services Commission.* London: Cassell.

Berry-Lound, D., Chaplin, M. and O'Connell, B. 1991: Review of industrial training organisations, *Employment Gazette,* October, 535–42.

Callender, C. 1992: *Will NVQs Work? Evidence from the Construction Industry.* IMS Report 228. Brighton: Institute of Manpower Studies.

Campbell, M., Baldwin, S., Johnson, S., Chapman, R., Upton, A. and Walton, F. 2001: *The State of Skills in England 2001.* Sudbury: DfES.

CBI (Confederation of British Industry) 1989: *Towards a Skills Revolution.* London: CBI.

CBI 2000: *Fact not Fiction: UK Training Performance.* London: CBI.

Coates, D. 2000: *Models of Capitalism: Growth and Stagnation in the Modern Era.* Cambridge: Polity.

Cockburn, C. 1987: *Two-Track Training: Sex Inequalities and the YTS.* Basingstoke: Macmillan.

Coffield, F. 2001: Raising the potential of lifelong learning. In F. Coffield (ed.), *What Progress are we Making with Lifelong Learning? The Evidence from Research.* Newcastle: Newcastle University, Department of Education.

Cully, M., Woodland, S., O'Reilly, A. and Dix, G. 1999: *Britain at Work.* London: Routledge.

Cutter, J. 2000: *A Second Evaluation of the Union Learning Fund.* DfEE Research Report RR208. Nottingham: DfEE.

Debling, G. 1991: Developing standards. In P. Raggatt and L. Unwin (eds), *Change and Intervention: Vocational Education and Training.* London: Falmer Press.

DfEE (Department for Education and Employment) 1998a: *Labour Market and Skill Trends, 1998/99.* Nottingham: DfEE.

DfEE 1998b: *The Learning Age: A Renaissance for a New Britain.* Sudbury: DfEE.

DfEE 1999: *Learning to Succeed: A New Framework for Post-16 Learning.* Sudbury: DfEE.

DfEE 2000: *Labour Market and Skill Trends 2000.* Nottingham: DfEE.

DfEE/Cabinet Office 1996: *The Skills Audit: A Report from an Inter-Departmental Group.* Competitiveness Occasional Paper. London: DfEE/Cabinet Office.

ED (Employment Department) 1988: *Employment for the 1990s.* Cm 540. London: HMSO.

Emmerick, M., and Peck, J. 1991: *First Report of the TEC Monitoring Project.* Manchester: Centre for Local Economic Strategies.

Eraut, M., Alderton, J., Cole, G. and Senker, P. 1999: Learning from other people at work. In F. Coffield (ed.), *Learning at Work,* Bristol: Policy Press.

Equal Opportunities Commission 1988: Submission to the House of Lords Select Committee on the European Communities, *Vocational Training and Retraining.* London: HMSO.

Evans, B. 1992: *The Politics of the Training Market: From Manpower Services Commission to Training and Enterprise Councils.* London: Routledge.

Evans, K., Hodkinson, K., Keep, E., Maguire, M., Raffe, D., Rainbird, H., Senker, P. and Unwin, L. 1997: *Working to Learn: A Work-Based Route for Young People.* Issues in People Management, 18. London: Institute of Personnel and Development.

Felstead, A., and Ashton, D. 1996: Training implications of regulation compliance and business cycles. In A. L. Booth and D. J. Snower (eds), *Acquiring Skills: Market Failures, their Symptoms and Policy Responses.* Cambridge: Cambridge University Press.

Felstead, A., Green, F. and Mayhew, K. 1997: *Getting the Measure of Training.* Leeds: University of Leeds, Centre for Industrial Policy and Performance.

Green, A. 1998: Core skills, key skills and general culture: in search of a common foundation for vocational education, *Evaluation and Research in Education,* 12 (1), 23–33.

Green, F. 1999: Training the workers. In P. Gregg and J. Wadsworth (eds), *The State of Working Britain.* Manchester: Manchester University Press.

IFF Ltd. 1997: *Employer Provided Training in the UK: 1993.* London: IFF (mimeo).

IFF Research Ltd. 2000: *Learning and Training at Work 1999.* London: IFF.

IMS/MSC/NEDC (Institute of Manpower Studies/Manpower Services Commission/National Economic Development Office) 1984: *Competence and Competition.* London: MSC.

Jarvis, V., and Prais, S. 1989: Two nations of shopkeepers: training for retailing in Britain and France, *National Institute Economic Review,* 128, 58–74.

Jessup, G. 1991: *Outcomes: NVQs and the Emerging Model of Education and Training.* Brighton: Falmer Press.

Jones, M. 1999: *New Institutional Spaces: TECs and the Remaking of Economic Governance.* Regional Policy and Development Series 20. London: Jessica Kingsley/Regional Studies Association.

Keep, E. 1994: The transition from school to work. In K. Sisson (ed.), *Personnel Management in Britain,* 2nd edn. Oxford: Blackwell.

Keep, E. 1999a: *Employers' Attitudes to Training.* Skills Task Force Research Paper 15, Nottingham: DfEE.

Keep, E. 1999b: UK VET policy and the 'third way': following a high skills trajectory or running up a dead end street? *Journal of Education and Work,* 12 (3), 323–46.

Keep, E. 2000: The uses of vocational qualifications by employers and government in Britain. Paper presented to the Conference on the Certification of Vocational Qualifications in France and the United Kingdom. CEREQ, Marseilles, March.

Keep, E., and Mayhew, K. 1998: Was Ratner right? Product market and competitive strategies and their links with skills and knowledge, *Economic Policy Institute Economic Review,* 12 (3), 1–14.

Keep, E., and Payne, J. (forthcoming): Policy interventions for a vibrant work-based route, or, when policy hits reality's fan (again). In K. Evans (ed.), *Learning for Work*. London: Kogan Page.

Kennedy, H. 1997: *Learning Works: Widening Participation in Further Education*. Coventry: FEFC.

Kodz, J., Tackley, N. D., Pollard, E., Dench, S., Tyers, C. and Dewson, S. 2000: *Modern Apprenticeships and National Traineeships: Skills Utilization and Progression*. DfEE Research Report RR204. Nottingham: DfEE.

Lindley, R. 1983: Active manpower policy. In G. S. Bain (ed.), *Industrial Relations in Britain*. Oxford: Blackwell.

LSC (Learning and Skills Council) 2001a: *Learning and Skills Council Strategic Framework to 2004, Corporate Plan*. Coventry: LSC.

LSC 2001b: LSC sets new ambitious learning and skills for the nation. News Issue 22. Coventry: LSC (mimeo).

McCool, T. 1991: Making standards work together. Presentation to CBI Conference on Leading Standards Forward. London, December.

McIntosh, S., and Steedman, H. 2001: Learning in the workplace: some international comparisons. In F. Coffield (ed.), *What Progress are we Making with Lifelong Learning?* Newcastle: Newcastle University Department of Education.

Moser, C. 1998: *Improving Literacy and Numeracy: A Fresh Start*. Report of the working group chaired by Sir Claus Moser. Sudbury: DfEE.

MSC (Manpower Services Commission) 1981: *A Framework for the Future*. London: MSC.

MSC/Department of Education and Science 1986: *Review of Vocational Qualifications in England and Wales*. London: HMSO.

MSF (Manufacturing, Science and Finance) 1988: *Campaigning for Training*. London: MSF.

Munro, A., and Rainbird, H. 2000: The new unionism and the new bargaining agenda: UNISON–employer partnerships on workplace learning in Britain, *British Journal of Industrial Relations*, 38 (2), 223–40.

Munro, A., Rainbird, H. and Holly, L. 1997: *Partners in Workplace Learning: A Report on the UNISON/Employer Learning and Development Programme*. London: UNISON.

NACETT (National Advisory Committee for Education and Training Targets) 1999: *Business Plan, 1999–2000*. Sheffield: NACETT.

NSTF (National Skills Task Force) 1998: *Towards a National Skills Agenda: First Report of the National Skills Task Force*. Sudbury: DfEE.

NSTF 1999: *Second Report of the National Skills Task Force: Developing Skills for All*. Sudbury: DfEE.

NSTF 2000a: *Skills for All: Proposals for a National Skills Agenda*. Sudbury: DfES.

NSTF 2000b: *Skills for All: Research Report from the National Skills Task Force*. Sudbury: DfEE.

NSTF 2000c: *Third Report of the National Skills Task Force: Tackling the Adult Skills Gap. Upskilling Adults and the Role of Workplace Learning*. Sudbury: DfEE.

NTTF 1992: Draft copy of the Cleaver Report (mimeo). London: NTTF.

Perry, P. J. C. 1976: *The Evolution of British Manpower Policy*. London: Eyre & Spottiswoode.

Prais, S. J. 1989: How Europe would see the new British initiative for standardising vocational qualifications, *National Institute Economic Review*, 129, 52–3.

Prais, S. J., 1991: Vocational qualifications in Britain and Europe: theory and practice. *National Institute Economic Review*, 135, 86–92.

Rainbird, H. 1988: New technology, training and union strategies. In R. Hyman and W. Streeck (eds), *New Technology and Industrial Relations*. Oxford: Blackwell.

Rainbird, H. 1990: *Training Matters: Union Perspectives on Industrial Restructuring and Training*. Oxford: Blackwell.

Rainbird, H., and Grant, W. 1985: *Employers' Associations and Training Policy*. Coventry: Institute for Employment Research.

Rainbird H., Munro A., Holly, L. and Leisten, R. 1999: *The Future of Work in the Public Sector. Learning and Workplace Inequality*. ESRC Future of Work Programme Discussion Paper 2. Leeds: University of Leeds.

Rainbird, H., Sutherland, J., Edwards, P. K., Munro, A. and Holly, L. (forthcoming): *Employee Voice and its Influence over Training Provision*. Department of Trade and Industry, Employment Relations Research Series.

Ryan, P. (ed.) 1991: *International Comparisons of Vocational Education and Training for Intermediate Skills*. London: Falmer Press.

Ryan, P. 2000: The institutional requirements of apprenticeship: evidence from smaller EU countries, *International Journal of Training and Development*, 4 (1), 42–65.

Senker, P. J. 1992: *Industrial Training in a Cold Climate*. Aldershot: Avebury.

Shaw, N. 1999: *An Early Evaluation of the Union Learning Fund*. DfEE Research Report RR113. Nottingham: DfEE.

Sims, D., Golden, S., Blenkinsop, S. and Lewis, G. 2000. *Barriers to Take-Up of Modern Apprenticeship and National Traineeships by SMEs and Specific Sectors*. DfEE Research Report RR205. Nottingham: DfEE.

Statistical Bulletin 2000: Vocational qualifications in the UK, *Statistical Bulletin*, 5 (May).

Steedman, H. 1998: A decade of skill formation in Britain and Germany, *Journal of Education and Work*, 11 (3), 275–92.

Storey, J., and Bacon, N. 1993: The 'new agenda' and human resource management: a round table discussion with John Edmonds, *Human Resource Management Journal*, 4 (1), 63–70.

Streeck, W. 1989: Skills and the limits of neoliberalism: the enterprise of the future as a place of learning, *Work, Employment and Society*, 3 (1), 89–104.

Sutherland, J., and Rainbird, H. 2000: Unions and workplace learning: conflict or cooperation with the employer? In H. Rainbird (ed.), *Training in the Workplace: Critical Perspectives on Learning at Work*. Basingstoke: Macmillan.

TOPSS 1999: *Modernising the Social Care Workforce*. TOPSS, the National Training Organization for Social Care, October. <www.topss.org.uk>.

Training Agency 1989: *Training in Britain: Employers' Activities*. Sheffield: TA.

TUC (Trades Union Congress) 1992: *Bargaining for Skills: A Call for Action*. London: TUC.

Unwin, L., and Fuller, A. 2000: *National Report on Apprenticeships: Great Britain*. Leicester: Centre for Labour Market Studies (mimeo).

Varlaam, C. 1987: *The Full Fact-Finding Study of the NSTO System*. Brighton: Institute of Manpower Studies.

Winterbotham, M., Adams, L. and Lorentzen-White, D. 2000: *Modern Apprenticeship: Exploring the Reasons for Non-Completion in Five Sectors*. DfEE Research Report RR217. Nottingham: DfEE.

Winterton, J., and Winterton, R. 1994: *Collective Bargaining and Consultation Over Continuing Vocational Training*. London: Employment Department.

Winterton, J., and Winterton, R. 1998: *Validation and Recognition of Competences and Qualifications in the UK*. Edinburgh: Napier University, Employment Research Institute.

Wood, L. 1992: Urgent need found for government to examine TECs' funding, *Financial Times*, 25 March.

16

THE INDUSTRIAL RELATIONS OF A DIVERSE WORKFORCE

SONIA LIFF

The numbers of women in the UK workforce, now approaching parity with men, should change the way we think about the subject of industrial relations. Feminist writing on industrial relations in the UK (Dickens 1989, 1998; Rubery and Fagan 1995; Woodall 1996; Wajcman 2000), in moves also evident in related academic disciplines, has argued that this should mean more than some additional studies of women workers to supplement those of men. Two further, inter-related, features have been highlighted: first the extent to which the typical worker and his (*sic*) interests have been conceptualized unreflexively as those of a white, able-bodied, heterosexual man with a wife and family; second, the need to develop an understanding of the way in which organizations and the main parties to the processes of industrial relations embody assumptions about gender, race and other social characteristics within their structures and practices so as to favour some groups of workers and marginalize others. By comparison, and in contrast to North America, writing on race and ethnicity in the workplace is less developed. However, high-profile cases relating to the police service's treatment of the ethnic minority population raised related issues about institutional racism in the late 1990s. An increased interest in notions of identity (Jenkins 1996) and greater emphasis on individualism in employee relations (see chapter 12) have also reinforced the significance of understanding diversity within the workforce.

There is considerable evidence that different social group membership continues to affect people's opportunities, experiences and achievements at work. Some of this data is described below. However, as Wajcman (2000) argues, it is important to look beyond these differences to the social processes which sustain them and, I would add, those which might disrupt them. These issues have become more salient in the light of experience of over a quarter of a century of legislation intended to outlaw discrimination. While progress has certainly been made, continuing patterns of disadvantage suggest the need for some new thinking about measures designed to promote equality.

This chapter begins by reviewing the changing context for workplace equality in terms both of the formal measures in place and the approaches and commitment of the various parties involved. It moves on to review the data on different experiences in the workplace and to discuss the research which contributes to an understanding of the workplace and the wider social processes which sustain them. In the light of this it concludes with an assessment of the achievements and limitations of dominant approaches to promoting greater workplace equality and considers the potential of approaches that give greater weight to the acknowledgement of workplace diversity.

The Changing Equality Agenda, 1970–2000

Historically there is evidence that women were deliberately excluded from some areas of work and targeted for others (see e.g. Bradley 1989). Such exclusion was not simply the result of management preferences but was actively pursued by male trade unionists (Walby 1983). Wartime experience showed that women were able to do many jobs from which they had been previously excluded, particularly where adequate training was provided and minor adjustments made. Nevertheless, they were excluded again after the war, not simply as a result of trade union agreements but also through management choice (Summerfield 1989). Trade unions long defended differential wages for women on the grounds that men needed to be able to provide for their families whereas women were 'secondary' wage-earners (despite the TUC's long-standing formal commitment to equal pay). As for other aspects of disadvantage, in the immediate post-war period legislation was introduced that was supposed to ensure that people with disabilities were adequately represented in the workforce. However, employers claimed such targets were not achievable and were regularly granted exemptions from their obligations. In the 1950s and 1960s African Caribbean people were encouraged to come to Britain and specifically channelled into jobs which the indigenous population considered unattractive (Fryer 1984). Developments from the 1970s onwards began to challenge the acceptability of these patterns.

Legal and political changes

Legal changes have had an important influence on the development of employment practices. Most obvious in this field is the introduction of anti-discrimination and equal pay legislation in the 1970s. The Equal Pay Act was introduced in 1970 and came fully into force in 1975. This provided for equal pay for men and women doing 'like work' for the same employer, or doing jobs which had been rated equal by a job evaluation scheme. 1975 also saw the introduction of the Sex Discrimination Act, which included provision for the equal treatment of men and women in most spheres. Discrimination was defined in two ways. Direct discrimination involves treating a person differently from the way a person of the other sex has been, or would have been, treated in the same circumstances. Indirect discrimination involves applying a term or condition equally to all, but with the effect that a substantially larger proportion of those of one sex can fulfil it than the other, that this is to their detriment and cannot otherwise be justified. In 2001, as a result of an EU initiative, the burden of proof for establishing such discrimination shifted from employee to employer. In 1976 the Race Relations Act was passed, giving similar protection against discrimination on the grounds of ethnicity to that granted on the grounds of sex. The government announced proposals in 2000 to extend the ways in which this law applies to public authorities, which included a requirement to promote race equality. These Acts also led to the establishment of the Equal Opportunity Commission (EOC) and the Commission for Racial Equality (CRE). As well as pursuing cases themselves, these bodies have established Codes of Practice which, as will be discussed below, have provided the framework for most organizations' own equal opportunity policies. The 1970s also saw legislation giving at least some women protection against being dismissed while pregnant and the right to their job back after maternity leave.

The period during which anti-discrimination legislation was passed was politically favourable to the establishment of formal rights for workers. In contrast (as discussed in chapter 6), the focus during successive Conservative governments in the 1980s and 1990s was on the removal of 'unnecessary burdens' from industry. Despite this the 1980s saw an important amendment to the Equal Pay Act, providing for equal pay for work of equal value following an EC ruling on the inadequacy of British equal pay legislation. This allowed a person to ask for their job to be independently evaluated against a specified job undertaken, for the same employer, by a person of the opposite sex. The mid-1990s also saw the establishment of new legislation covering people with disabilities in the form of the Disability Discrimination Act 1995. This provides similar protection to that contained in sex and race legislation and in addition requires employers to make 'reasonable adjustment' to accommodate those people who, say, with a minor modification to the built environment or with some specialized equipment would be perfectly capable of doing a particular job.

The election of a Labour government in 1997 brought a somewhat more positive approach to European initiatives to increase protection for certain groups. Most significant in terms of gender equality have been the Maternity and Parental Leave Regulations 1999 and the Part-Time Workers Regulations 2000. The former increased the period of maternity leave and reduced the period of employment necessary for a woman to qualify to take such leave. It also provided, under certain circumstances, for either parent to take a defined amount of unpaid leave while their child is under the age of 5. There are also provisions in the Employment Relations Act 1999 for employees to take a reasonable amount of time off (although again with no necessity for it to be paid) to deal with emergencies such as illness, injury or disruption to the normal care arrangements for dependents. 'Dependents' here includes not only children but also a spouse, parent or anyone else in a household who would normally rely on the employee for care in such circumstances. The Part-Time Workers Regulations make it unlawful for employers to treat part-time workers less favourably than comparable full-time workers in respect of their terms and conditions of employment unless such treatment can be objectively justified. A new Race Directive was formally adopted in 2000, making racial discrimination unlawful throughout the EU for the first time. Future European-led changes include a directive (passed by the European Council of Ministers in 2000 with a requirement that it be implemented by the end of 2003) to combat discrimination on grounds including religious belief, age and sexual orientation. None of these criteria are covered by current anti-discrimination legislation in Britain, although some protection may be established under the Human Rights Act that came into force in October 2000.

In other ways the approach of the Labour government shows continuity with changes that occurred at the beginning of the 1990s. When anti-discrimination legislation was introduced in the 1970s it was seen primarily in terms of the promotion of social justice. While not entirely negating such moral arguments, the dominant discourse during the 1990s has been that equality should be promoted because it makes sound business sense. The statutory bodies have sought to promote this approach: the Equal Opportunities Commission sponsored research on the economics of equal opportunities (Humphries and Rubery 1995) which attempts to demonstrate the financial benefits to be achieved from equality initiatives; and the Commission for Racial Equality created a Standard for Racial Equality for Employers which sets out the business case for race equality. A parallel development has been the stress on 'mainstreaming' equality issues, particularly within the European Union (Rees 1998). This is commonly understood as meaning that equality issues should be considered within existing policy areas rather than seen as something separate. The Labour government has not introduced new anti-discrimination legislation on age, despite a clearly expressed intention to do when in opposition (Loretto et al. 2000). Instead it has introduced a voluntary Code of Practice which claims to show employers how the elimination of discrimination in this area will lead to the employment and retention of the best person for the job.

Labour market and socio-economic changes

Changing industrial structures, patterns of work and social norms have also dramatically changed the context for equal opportunities. The trend for married women to work in the formal economy both before their children are born and again once they are established at school has increased throughout the post-war period. What has been distinctive about the more recent period has been the larger number of women who are economically active while their children are under the age of 5; in 2000, 58 per cent of such women were economically active, a rise of 10 percentage points over 1990 (Twomey 2001b). This has been in part facilitated by maternity leave provisions, but is also strongly related to levels of qualification and broader social changes in the perception of women's role. It is now much more acceptable for women to go out to work while their children are young than it was for earlier generations.

Broader changes in the availability of jobs have also been an important factor in increased female participation in the workforce, in particular the long-term decline of employment opportunities in manufacturing relative to services. In 1998 there were 4.3 jobs in services for every 1 in manufacturing, and women made up 56 per cent of service sector workers (Partington and Mayell 2000). The reasons for this are complex, but one factor that sustains this association is the number of such jobs which are part-time: 44 per cent of women but only 12 per cent of men work part-time. The Labour government is currently reinforcing the centrality of work for groups whose participation rates have traditionally been low by encouraging single mothers and those with disabilities to find work and generally stressing that economic activity is the only sustainable route out of poverty and disadvantage.

Social attitudes towards the contribution women can make in the workplace have also changed. A survey by the Institute of Management (Charlesworth 1997) found that over 60 per cent of managers (of both sexes) felt that women managers were no different to men in the workplace, and over 80 per cent agreed that all managers should receive equal treatment irrespective of family responsibilities. This contrasts interestingly with Hunt's (1975) earlier survey of managers formulating or implementing personnel policy. She found that only 11 per cent responded positively to the statement 'Do you think it would be a good or bad thing if more women occupied senior positions?'

In a range of ways, then, Britain is a very different place in terms of workplace equality than it was in the 1960s. Legislation exists outlawing certain forms of discrimination and, whatever its limitations, has been significant both in allowing exclusion to be challenged and in changing attitudes. Women in particular are now taking up types of jobs and achieving success at levels that would not have not have seemed possible 30 years ago. Yet company boardrooms, and to a large extent the senior levels of trade unions and government bodies, remain predominantly white male preserves. The regularity of media reports and tribunal hearings relating to the exclusion of women and ethnic minorities from opportunities for promotion, and to workplace cultures characterized by harassment and victimization, suggests that discrimination cannot be dismissed as a historical phenomenon. To understand this picture of both change and continuity it is necessary to pursue two issues: first, the ways in which the legislative developments described above have been translated into workplace equality policies by the social partners; second, the patterns of inclusion and exclusion facing different social groups and the practices which sustain them. These issues are the focus of the next two sections.

Workplace Equality Policies

Codes of Practice

The equality policies which developed in the 1980s and 1990s take a form that can be derived largely from a traditional approach to industrial relations, based as they are on the application of formal rules and procedures in a uniform way for all employees. The dominant approach derives from Codes of Practice issued by the Commission for Racial Equality and the Equal Opportunities Commission

(CRE 1984; EOC 1985a). These outline procedural approaches to avoid discrimination and promote equality. They include measures considered necessary to comply with the anti-discrimination legislation and initiatives compatible with, but not required by, legislation which are thought likely to enhance the opportunities of previously disadvantaged groups.

To avoid discrimination organizations are encouraged to issue a policy statement which describes their intentions in relation to equal opportunities. In practice such statements range from the minimalist ('we are an equal opportunities employer') to a more elaborate statement saying which areas of employment policy are to be addressed and which social groups covered, and some of the measures that will be taken to put it into practice. The importance of such a statement is said to lie in its indication of senior management support and commitment. Organizations are also advised to instruct their staff not to discriminate, and to provide them with some guidance as to how this is to be achieved. This is usually an elaboration of personnel best practice in areas such as selection. Many organizations stop at this point. However, Codes of Practice recommend that the policy should be monitored, as should the make-up of the workforce, so that any remaining problems can be identified.

In order to promote equality in a more active way organizations are encouraged to undertake policies which address the particular disadvantages or specific employment patterns of women and ethnic minorities. The law requires equal treatment in most circumstances, so such approaches cannot be about providing specific benefits for only certain groups (except for the provision of training in some limited circumstances or to make reasonable adjustments for those with disabilities) or reserving jobs for them. Instead they are about adapting employment practices so that they are more open to these groups.

Suggestions include allowing a wider range of jobs to be carried out on a part-time basis; providing career breaks whereby jobs are held open during unpaid leave; advertising jobs more widely, for example in the ethnic minority press; ensuring that advertisements and publicity material show diverse images of employees; allowing flexible holidays so that workers can observe their own religious festivals; and providing specific training for those groups who have been traditionally under-represented in a particular occupation and who are missing the necessary pre-qualifications. It is also possible to establish targets for increasing the proportion of particular groups within certain occupational areas as long as this does not extend to setting quotas or establishing reserved places, which would be unlawful.

Codes of Practice have been influential in the development of workplace equality policies but have never been a requirement for legal compliance. Policies and practices which follow the Codes closely are taken as evidence of good practice in tribunal hearings judging discrimination cases. However, the number of cases taken and won is small, in part due to the way the law is framed and in part due to the limited resources of the statutory bodies involved. To understand the development of workplace policies it is important to look also at the interests and motivations of employers and trade unions.

Employers' adoption of equality policies and the role of business case arguments

Sixty-four per cent of workplaces surveyed for the 1998 WERS had equal opportunities polices (Cully et al. 1999), and for the most part these will follow closely the approach suggested by Codes of Practice. Organizations are increasingly extending this approach to ensure compliance with the more recent Disability Discrimination Act. Some have gone further, to develop policies to cover those still outside legislation such as older workers, gay men and lesbians. For example, a survey of policies (which because of its methodology probably over-represents those most active in the field) found that 76 per cent of equality policies covered age, 81 per cent sexuality and 86 per cent religion (*EOR* 1999a). However, even in such organizations, initiatives for groups not subject to statutory protection may be less comprehensive than those relating to gender, race and disability. For example only around half the organizations monitored recruitment on the basis of age or had ensured that benefits were available to same-sex partners on the same basis as different-sex ones (*EOR* 1999a).

A number of employer-led bodies with an equality focus were formed during the 1990s in parallel to the statutory bodies discussed earlier. Opportunity 2000, renamed Opportunity Now in 1999, is primarily concerned with gender equality, Race for Opportunity with equality issues affecting ethnic minorities, and the Employer's Forum on Age with discrimination on the basis of age. These bodies allow organizations to identify themselves as in the vanguard of 'best practice' in relation to equality. A central claim of such organizations and their members is that equality initiatives bring business benefits. There is no single business case for equality: arguments have included being an 'employer of choice' able to recruit and retain the best employees; reduced absenteeism; improved productivity and innovativeness; and greater customer satisfaction. The consequences of promoting a business case rationale for equality are contradictory. They are arguably a more persuasive way of encouraging organizations to take action in this area than is available through moral censure or a legal system which relies on individual claimants pursuing cases and for the most part low levels of fines. It is also striking that some of the initiatives supported by Opportunity Now and others, such as targets, are more radical than the basic approach required by Codes of Practice. On the other hand, as Dickens (1999) and others have pointed out, to argue that organizations should pursue equality initiatives which make business sense carries with it the corollary that if benefits cannot be identified there is no need to implement them. This risks equality initiatives being differentially available to those who are fortunate enough to have specialist skills, or who work in an area of labour market shortage or for an organization pursuing a quality or innovation competitive strategy.

The focus of employer-led equality bodies also challenges the approach advocated by Codes of Practice, albeit implicitly. For example, Opportunity Now only requires member organizations to set targets, demonstrate senior management commitment to them, and monitor their progress towards them. The determination of goals and the way they should be achieved is seen as best determined by the particular organization on the basis of its business strategy and priorities. It is not clear where this leaves the Codes, which advocate a fixed set of procedures that should be followed to achieve predetermined goals. The Codes of Practice could also be seen as out of step with employee relations approaches, which try to take a more individualistic approach or to achieve an internal fit between a series of human resource policies. In both cases there are likely to be conflicts with the 'one best way' prescriptive approach of the Codes. All these tensions are evident in those approaches to managing diversity which claim to be providing a new approach to equality. In contrast to traditional approaches, Kandola and Fullerton (1998) argue that every initiative should have a clear business rationale and be based on seeing employees as individuals rather than members of social groups with needs derived from that membership.

The role of trade unions

Historically trade unions' promotion of equality issues has been at best equivocal. In part this reflected the perceived divisiveness of an issue which appeared to benefit some members at the expense of others (of course this argument itself reflects a blindness to the way this was occurring in any case through the promotion of some bargaining issues rather than others). However, with the growth in the number of women in the workforce and a decline in traditional members, most trade unions are now keen to demonstrate their commitment to recruiting a more diverse membership, representing their interests, and promoting their own internal equality policies (Cunnison and Stageman 1995). Women now comprise 40 per cent of members of TUC-affiliated unions, and their numbers are growing while men's decline (see chapter 9). Most accounts of equality initiatives by trade unions have focused on their significance for women. However, some unions at least are also pursuing equality issues with respect to ethnicity and sexuality (Colgan 1999; McBride 2001).

Kirton and Greene (2000: 162) draw on existing writing on gender equity in collective bargaining (Colling and Dickens 1998; Bercusson and Dickens 1996) to define equality bargaining as 'the collective negotiation of provisions that are of particular interest or benefit to disadvantaged groups and/or are likely to facilitate equality at work'. They distinguish between equality benefits that come from traditional bargaining objectives and agendas and equality bargaining which seeks to introduce or strengthen agreements or policies with a specific equality focus. An example of the former would be bargaining aimed at tackling low pay. Though not explicitly encompassing an equality dimension, this approach is likely to benefit disadvantaged groups more than others because they are concentrated in low-paid jobs (see chapter 17). Kirton and Greene (2000) draw on a range of evidence to suggest that workplaces where unions are recognized have more equitable payment systems and/or above-average wage rates for all workers which benefit those on the lowest pay.

In terms of bargaining to institute or improve equality policies and provisions, earlier work by Colling and Dickens (1989) concluded that such activity was rare. Their research suggested that management-initiated equal opportunity measures were often excluded from the bargaining arena. Nevertheless Dickens (1999) makes a strong case for believing that social regulation could lead to equality gains, and sees some encouraging signs that unions are taking up this opportunity. In the context of the rise of 'business case' justifications for equality, she argues that unions can change employers' cost-benefit analysis through increasing the cost of not taking action. They may also play an important role in extending benefits which management grants to limited sections of the workforce on a business case rationale (for example career breaks for women managers) to other employees. Importantly, collective bargaining also provides the potential for disadvantaged groups to shape the equality agenda rather than merely being recipients of management agendas and priorities. Weiler (2000) provides examples, from across Europe, of collective agreements which promote gender equality not only in relation to pay but also across a wide range of issues, including segregation and work–home balance.

Recent research has started to identify the circumstances which make it more likely that trade unions will play this positive role in promoting gender equality through collective bargaining. Given the traditional lack of attention to equality issues, concern has been as much with the circumstances internal to trade unions that lead to the inclusion of equality issues in the collective bargaining agenda as with the achievement of successful bargaining outcomes. Dickens (2000), reviewing the findings of a Europe-wide study of gender equality and collective bargaining, finds that progressive agreements are more likely to be achieved in circumstances where the bargaining relationship is based on social partnership rather than adversarial principles. In common with earlier studies she identifies the importance of women in negotiating positions (rather than women members per se) as necessary to ensure that equality issues reach the bargaining agenda. This issue, conceptualized as the importance of internal equity (women's presence and power in trade unions) for external equity (the capacity of trade unions to promote equality through collective bargaining), highlights the need for trade unions to change themselves as well as the employment situation of their members. Greater presence of women in negotiating positions is unlikely to occur without some internal equality measures and, as with employing organizations, these can take a variety of forms. In some cases women may reach positions of power only by downplaying their concerns with equality issues (or by not having any in the first place), or may find it difficult to create a consensus for pursuing such issues even from a negotiating position. In this context the concern of some unions with providing structures for the self-organization of traditionally excluded groups is significant. In the UK this has probably been pursued most fully by UNISON. Colgan and Ledwith (2000) review the interrelationships between women's self-identity (in terms of ethnicity, sexuality and disability as well as gender) and the role of self-organization with officers and activists in UNISON. They conclude that this organizational form is significant for involving new groups in active union membership and helping such members to clarify and develop their sense of identity and associated interests. They are more cautious about the extent to which these changes will lead to equality outcomes, particularly where such 'identity politics' leads to fragmentation rather than coalition between different excluded groups.

Differing Experiences of the Employment Relationship

To understand the successes and failures of workplace equality policies it is necessary to look in greater detail at the types of inequalities they seek to address and the processes which appear to create and sustain them. The following section investigates two key aspects of the employment relationship: the allocation of work, as shown by data on unemployment, occupational segregation and the processes of recruitment and selection; and the assessment and reward of ability and performance, as shown by data on remuneration and the operation of appraisal systems and performance-related pay. It explores the ways in which the experience of these aspects of employment differs depending on characteristics such as gender, ethnicity, and disability rather than just by individual differences in qualifications and ability to do the job. Where such difference is present, the processes through which it occurs are explored.

There is certainly extensive evidence that not only the likelihood of having a job, but also the type of job obtained and the benefits received, vary with different social group membership. The nature of this evidence varies, and this is reflected in the discussion below. Differences between the employment position of men and women are regularly and extensively documented in statistical sources. Statistical data are also collected about ethnic minorities, although they are far less prevalent than data on women. Evidence on people with disabilities is becoming more widespread since they have been subject to anti-discrimination legislation. In all cases such data need to be supplemented with evidence from occasional surveys and case studies to clarify the processes involved. In the case of some social groups such evidence is the only kind available. Often even this is limited. For example, there is considerable anecdotal evidence that gay men and lesbians face discrimination in the workplace. However, there is very little systematic research which explores this issue.

Unemployment

Between 1990 and 2000, the economic activity rate of women of working age rose slightly (from 71 to 73 per cent) while the rate for men fell (from 88 to 84 per cent) (Twomey 2001b). Such figures have led to the suggestion that the world of work is becoming increasingly feminized and that, far from facing discrimination, women are now in an advantageous situation. Unemployment figures seem to bear this out, with 2000 figures showing a male unemployment rate of 6.1 per cent and a female one of 4.9 per cent (Twomey 2001b). However, such figures need to be treated with caution. The definition of unemployment used (from the International Labour Office) requires that a person is not only without a job but has looked for one during the previous four weeks and, crucially, is available to start work in the next two weeks. Many women who are neither in work nor unemployed on this definition (and hence classified as economically inactive) are looking after children or other dependents. The Labour Force Survey of spring 2000 found that 29 per cent of these women said that they would prefer to be working (Twomey 2001b). Another survey found that two-thirds of mothers of children under the age of 15 would prefer to work if they had access to good-quality, convenient, reliable and affordable childcare (La Valle et al. 2000).

Unemployment figures are higher for both men and women from ethnic minorities than for the equivalent white group. For example, in the year to spring 2000, white men had an unemployment rate of 6 per cent, compared to that for men from ethnic minorities of 13 per cent. There was also considerable variation between different ethnic minority groups, with rates for those identified as black being 17 per cent (Twomey 2001a). These differences cannot be explained by differences in qualification levels: men from ethnic minorities have a higher unemployment rate than white men at each qualification level. In the most extreme example a Caribbean man with qualifications of A levels or higher is twice as likely as a similarly qualified white man to be unemployed, and indeed more likely to be unemployed than a white man with no qualifications (Modood 1997).

Data on people with disabilities have improved with clearer definitions provided by the Disability Discrimination Act. People are considered disabled if they have a physical or mental impairment which has a substantial and long-term adverse effect on their ability to carry out normal day-to-day activities. The 2000 Labour Force Survey found that this applied to 19 per cent of the working-age population (Twomey 2001c). Forty-seven per cent were in employment compared with 82 per cent of those without long-term disabilities. The unemployment rate of people with disabilities was nearly twice that of the able-bodied population. As with women with dependents, unemployment rates may misrepresent the situation. Over a third of those with disabilities who were classified as economically inactive (neither in work, nor unemployed) said that they would like to work, rising to half of those who saw themselves as being able to work (Meager and Hibbett 1999).

Occupational segregation

In 2000, women made up 44 per cent of all those of working age in employment, but this near equality in terms of total numbers hides many differences in distribution between occupational groups. Women form the majority of workers in clerical and secretarial occupations (74 per cent), personal and protective services (66 per cent) and sales (64 per cent). In total over half of working women are in these occupational groups compared with 19 per cent of men. Conversely there are areas where women are significantly under-represented such as construction, engineering and machine operators (Bower 2001). Differences are not just between occupational areas (described as horizontal segregation) but are also related to levels in the organizational hierarchy (vertical segregation). So, for example, 20 per cent of all men in employment are managers compared with 12 per cent of women. These figures themselves disguise a further under-representation at the most senior levels. In the year 2000 there was only one female chief executive in a FTSE 100 company. Opportunity Now, reporting on the achievements of its member companies (who claim to be in the vanguard of gender equality), found 8 per cent of executive directors and 14 per cent of board members were women (*EOR* 2000a). The details of which jobs are done by men and which by women vary between countries, but the existence of segregation and its general characteristics are pervasive across Europe.

Men and women also display different patterns of working hours. Women are much more likely to work part-time than are men in all EC countries (Clifford et al. 1997). Britain has one of the highest proportions of women working part-time, accounting for 44 per cent of the female labour force; between 1990 and 2000, part-time employment for women rose by 12 per cent, compared to 4 per cent for full-time jobs (Twomey 2001b). There is no necessary association between these different working hours and occupational segregation, but in practice part-time working has been found to be much more prevalent in sectors which have an over-representation of women workers. In autumn 1998, 23 per cent of those working in manufacturing were part-time compared with 54 per cent of those working in banking, finance and insurance (Partington and Mayell 2000). Thus those seeking part-time work may find that this form of working is difficult to find outside a limited range of occupations traditionally seen as appropriate to women.

Women's participation rates vary with their domestic circumstances. While more women than ever are going out to work while their children are young, hours of work are still strongly correlated with presence of, and age of, dependent children. Women with children under the age of 5 are twice as likely to be working part-time than full-time, a ratio that does not equalize until children are over 16 (Twomey 2001b). With an ageing population many women are increasingly faced with responsibility for elderly or sick relatives which may also affect their ability to go out to work. These patterns again vary between countries, but in all cases are distinctive from men's engagement with waged work over their lives (O'Reilly and Fagan 1998). There may be no necessary link between these patterns and occupational segregation, but longitudinal research suggests that breaks in paid employment have been associated with downward occupational mobility for women (Dex 1992).

Ethnic minorities make up less than 7 per cent of the British population of working age (Twomey 2001a) and so it is easiest to judge whether occupational segregation exists by looking at the proportion of the ethnic minority workforce within a particular occupation compared with the proportion of the workforce overall. This shows some areas of similarity but also significant areas of difference, compounded by different profiles for different ethnic groups. With respect to ethnic minority men, Modood (1997: 109) says, 'none is quite like any other or akin to white males. Moreover, not only does each minority have some economic sectors in which it is particularly concentrated, but each has a more restricted distribution than do white men.' Overall, ethnic minority men are largely absent from the primary sector, construction, and much of manufacturing.

Modood shows from a 1994 survey that, by contrast, 60 per cent of all Bangladeshi men and 23 per cent of Chinese men were employed in hotels and catering (as against only 2 per cent of white and 3 per cent of Caribbean men). Again there is a vertical dimension to this segregation. A TUC analysis of the Labour Force Survey showed that more black employees have higher-level qualifications than white workers (30 per cent compared with 26 per cent), but only a quarter are managers or supervisors compared with a third of white workers (IRS 2000a).

Women and ethnic minorities are the groups which are most commonly considered in relation to distinctive employment patterns. However, there are other groups to which a similar analysis can be applied. For example, 16 per cent of men with work-limiting disabilities are managers compared with 23 per cent of those without (Labour Market Spotlight 1999). For any worker over the age of 50 a period of unemployment can mean the end of their career. A study of those leaving the unemployment register found that claimants of that age were less likely than their younger counterparts to leave the register for full-time work, education or training and more likely to leave to receive other benefits (Hatch 1999).

Processes of recruitment and selection

Evidence of different experience is not necessarily evidence of discrimination. Discrimination suggests that these patterns are the result of the exclusion of individuals from areas of employment on the basis of their social group membership. Alternative explanations of differential patterns could be that they reflect the qualifications and abilities of different groups, or that they reflect choices on the part of members of groups to engage in some areas of work in preference to others, or their degree of attachment to work and a career compared with other aspects of their lives, or to their willingness to acquire training. Studies of the recruitment and selection process provide a way of exploring the causes of the differential allocation of work.

The first part of the process relates to the methods and forms of recruitment. The Commission for Racial Equality has drawn attention to the possible consequences of recruitment methods based on internal, or extended internal, labour markets. If the current workforce is not ethnically mixed then recruiting internally will simply perpetuate this situation. Asking current workers to recommend friends or family members for vacancies is similarly likely to lead to a reproduction of the current social mix of the workforce. The suggestion is not that white people are deliberately discriminating by refusing to tell black people about vacancies, rather that people are most likely to be part of social networks dominated by people from the same ethnic group as themselves. As such these forms of recruitment could constitute indirect discrimination. Even where formal advertising does occur, the way an organization portrays itself in recruitment material may well give some potential applicants the message that they are not expected to apply.

Sex, race and disability discrimination legislation make it unlawful, in most circumstances, to advertise explicitly for someone of a particular gender or ethnic group, or to exclude from consideration people with disabilities who, with reasonable accommodation, are able to do the job. However, for some groups there is no such protection. A voluntary Code of Practice on Age Diversity in Employment is currently in force. As part of the consultation process involved in its establishment, participants highlighted the use of terms such as 'newly qualified' and 'recent graduates' as disguised ways of identifying the desirability of a certain age profile for applicants (IRS 1999).

Even where the law prevents explicit exclusion there is evidence that some employers distinguish between applications from different social groups. A number of studies have involved sending applications from fictitious candidates with equivalent qualifications and experience, but different ethnic backgrounds, to a range of employers. In the early 1980s Brown and Gay (1985) used this approach to target employers advertising non-manual or skilled manual vacancies for men and women. Any invitation to take the application further (for example sending an application form) was treated as a positive response. Even at this level the results suggested that 35–45 per cent of employers discriminated against either one or both of the notionally black or Asian candidates. More recent studies have looked at the treatment of those with higher-level qualifications. Noon (1993) sent speculative enquiries to the 100 largest UK companies from two men apparently completing their MBAs, one with a name that suggested an Asian ethnicity, the other which suggested the applicant was white. In this case there was no significant difference in the likelihood of either candidate being sent a response. However, when the 'quality' of the responses was analysed (fullness of the response, extent to which it addressed the questions asked etc.) there was a significant difference in favour of the white candidate. This study was repeated six years later (Hoque and Noon 1999), when no evidence of discrimination in favour of either applicant was found. The extent to which positive conclusions about improvements in the treatment of ethnic minority candidates can be drawn from this needs to be somewhat tempered by the additional finding that it resulted from changes in the composition of the top 100 companies rather than changes in the practice of those surveyed at the earlier date.

Interviewing has received much attention as a possible site for discrimination in the selection process. Interviews are generally criticized for being a poor method of selection. Research has shown that one reason for this is that people tend to appoint in their own image. Other research has drawn a distinction between decisions based on specific job-related qualifications or experience (known as suitability criteria), and assessments about whether the person will fit in with the organization, other workers, or customers, known as acceptability criteria (Jenkins 1986). This has shown that acceptability criteria are particularly likely to be disadvantageous to ethnic minorities, leading to the recommendation that selection should focus on suitability criteria. Research by Jewson et al. (1990) showed that acceptability criteria continued to be used to the disadvantage of ethnic minorities. Moreover, they found that the assessment of suitability criteria was based on stereotyped assumptions about the characteristics of particular ethnic groups. Overall nearly one in five ethnic minority workers believe they have been refused at least one job for racial or religious reasons (Modood 1997).

In the case of women some research has shown that even where applicants fulfil pre-defined suitability criteria some managers seem to find it difficult to believe that a woman could possibly be the best candidate. Collinson et al. (1990), during detailed observation of interviews, found that managers used different (gender-based) criteria to assess whether applicants were able to meet the job requirements. For example a form of behaviour described as 'showing initiative' and assessed as desirable when demonstrated by a male applicant, in a woman applicant was seen as 'pushy' and undesirable. Similarly Curran (1988: 344) showed that managers often found it hard to separate the assessment of a characteristic such as leadership from the concept of masculinity, or a 'requirement for a pleasant personality and one for a pretty girl with a smile'. What is important about these findings is that they show that for some managers at least gender becomes part of their assessment of suitability criteria. As with the related findings on ethnicity, this raises questions about claims (central to the approach of Codes of Practice) that recruiters can avoid discrimination by assessing only those criteria necessary to do the job. If these criteria themselves embody gendered or race-based assumptions then this may be a necessary but not sufficient condition. Such findings also reduce the force of the prescriptive advice to excluded groups that they can succeed simply by gaining the necessary skills and demonstrating their ability at job-related tasks.

In other cases women may be disadvantaged because the criteria chosen to assess suitability involve behaviour patterns that are gender-specific. In Britain, managers often work extremely long hours and the length of time at one's desk has become, for many organizations, a measure of commitment. Research shows that, despite the increase in the number of women in paid work, housework, childcare and care of the sick and elderly are very unevenly divided between men and women (see Pilcher 2000 for a review). In these circumstances women's ability to demonstrate their commitment to work as conventionally defined may be less than men's (or achieved at a higher cost). Liff and Ward (2001) discuss an organization where, despite a high-profile commitment to equality, women managers felt that even discussing the possibility of having children would be detrimental to one's career prospects. For some writers (most notably Hakim 1996) commitment to work becomes almost by definition a male characteristic by an approach which sees it as in contradiction to commitment to one's family.

One might assume that more 'scientific' approaches to selection, such as psychometric tests, would not be subject to these problems. However, research suggests that the use of many of these tests can also lead to indirect discrimination (Baker and Cooper 1995; Wood and Baron 1992; Wood 1996). There are a number of ways in which this can occur. The simplest may just be about how familiar different groups of applicants are with taking tests and with the best approach for getting a high score. Research suggests that people do better if they have been told in advance that tests will be administered and given samples of the types of test involved so that they can prepare themselves. This is true for all applicants, but seems to have a particular significance for reducing the adverse impact on ethnic minorities. Other problems can occur when a test embodies a higher language requirement than is needed for the job. For example, reasoning skill may be measured through a written test, and for those for whom English is their first language this may be a perfectly acceptable method. However, some people may score badly not because they lack reasoning skills but because they have limited written language skills. Women may be similarly disadvantaged by tests that draw primarily on experience and expertise more likely to be held by men.

Remuneration

The most obvious way to look at whether members of different social groups gain different benefits for their performance is to look at the pay they receive. The usual way to compare pay is via a comparison of rates for similar time periods. On this basis women's hourly pay in Britain is 74.5 per cent of men's in full-time manual occupations and 69.2 per cent in full-time non-manual occupations (*EOR* 2000b). This general difference is repeated in most countries, although the percentage difference varies. There is little systematic data collected on earnings for ethnic minorities, but Modood's (1997) study shows lower average earnings but suggests that, in contrast to earlier surveys, the disadvantage for ethnic minority male employees is now only evident in non-manual jobs. Blackaby et al. (2000) found significant differences between the earnings of able-bodied employees and those with disabilities even when levels of education and other factors were controlled.

Again there are a number of explanations of these differences in pay other than straightforward discrimination. One is that they are a reflection of the fact that the occupations within which disadvantaged social groups are concentrated require fewer skills or less experience than those in which white men are found and that the remuneration received is a reflection of these relative requirements. However, before accepting such an explanation one needs to ask whether an objective assessment of the skills and abilities needed to perform different jobs successfully has been carried out. Job evaluation was thought to offer a way of assessing whether pay levels were objective and is an option available under the Equal Pay Act in relation to gender differentials. However, research suggests that such schemes conventionally embody a system of values which rates activities most commonly found in jobs that tend to be done by men, such as those requiring physical strength, more highly than those commonly found in jobs done by women, such as caring for others (EOC 1985b; Morris 1983), and this has led to a greater awareness of the ways in which definitions of skill are gender-biased. However, research in North America and Australia (where 'comparative worth' has a longer history) continues to demonstrate the difficulty of producing a gender-neutral system and the limitations of this approach to equal pay (Burton 1991; Kahn and Meehan 1992).

Even in areas where skills are recognized and the same job is being done, the pay of people from different social groups is not always equal. A statistical study of men from certain Asian ethnic groups in the US with very high levels of qualification and high levels of pay showed they were still earning less than white men when matched for occupation and industry (Duleep and Sanders 1992). A longitudinal US study of negotiations over starting salaries showed that ethnic minority candidates were less successful than white candidates in achieving improvements to their original offer, but that much of the difference could be accounted for by whether the individual had social ties to existing organizational members (Seidel et al. 2000). They suggest that this is likely to be due to the benefits such social ties bring in terms of increased information and influence. In the UK a typical woman with GCSE qualifications earns £241,000 less than her male counterpart over a lifetime simply on the basis of gender; having two children leads to an additional £140,000 loss (*EOR* 2000c).

A different kind of explanation for why there should be pay differences even when individuals are doing the same job is that they reflect different degrees of merit in performing those jobs. In assessing evidence for this it is necessary to look at the objectivity of methods used to assess job-holders' performance and whether they embody hierarchies based on gender and ethnicity.

Appraisal and performance-related pay

Appraisal systems raise many similar issues to those discussed in relation to selection techniques above. The more informal the appraisal system used, the greater is the opportunity for bias to enter judgements about merit. Even when a person is being assessed against specific criteria it is possible for views of the characteristics and abilities of different social groups to affect a manager's perceptions of an individual's abilities (Townley 1990).

In contrast to most selection situations, an appraiser will generally have knowledge of the appraisee over a considerable period of time. This should be valuable in overcoming the 'instant' judgements made in selection decisions. However, greater familiarity does not necessarily seem to lead to any greater objectivity. A study of assessment linked to performance-related pay found that managers of both sexes valued different attributes in men than they did in women (Bevan and Thompson 1992). Those attributes tended to be ones that reinforced gender stereotypes. This led to different merit awards for men and women – not always to women's disadvantage. They also found some cases where jobs which were sex-typed as male were associated with higher than average merit increases and vice versa. Recent interest in forms of multi-rater appraisal raise some additional questions. While such an approach might help to remove random bias or favouritism, the case for their ability to eliminate systematic bias based on stereotyping is less convincing (since such bias is widely distributed). There is also considerable evidence that women tend to rate themselves less positively than do men (Fletcher 1999), raising issues about the comparability of such measures between men and women.

A different issue is raised by Skinner's (1999) study of the treatment of part-time staff. She found that no guidance was available to line managers about how to measure a part-timer's output in relation to that of full-timers. Managers found this particularly problematic in relation to those whose contracts included extended periods of absence, such as those working in term-time only. It was also clear that the managers' assessment of whether a part-time employee should be offered a development opportunity or was ready for promotion was coloured by assessment criteria which implicitly incorporated a sense of 'time served'. Another example of managers' uncertainty and discomfort about dealing with equality issues in relation to performance assessment comes from a study of local authorities (Tamkin 2000). Despite excellent records for employing ethnic minority staff these organizations found that disproportionately high numbers of such employees were being disciplined. An analysis of the approach taken by managers found that, when compared to their practice with white employees, some managers were much more reluctant to initiate the use of disciplinary procedures with ethnic minority staff, in case their decisions could be interpreted as unfair, while others moved much more quickly to formal procedures to ensure everything was 'on the record'. In either case this was likely to lead to the situation being handled inappropriately and in some cases to minority employees' perception that they were being treated more harshly.

Assessing Equality Approaches

It is very difficult to assess the impact of legislation with any certainty. The small number of cases reaching employment tribunals and the relatively low success rate of those that do (*Labour Market Trends* 1999) might encourage cynicism. However, the effect of legislation extends further, to include changes in attitudes and approaches in organizations which may never face a legal challenge. So for example the Disability Discrimination Act seems to have led to a substantial increase in the proportion of organizations that have equality policies relating to those with disabilities and to a widespread review of recruitment and selection procedures to ensure compliance (IRS 2000b). The impact of Codes of Practice raises similar questions. In the case of discrimination based on gender and ethnicity they have provided a guide to the types of policies and practices that are thought to lead to compliance with the letter and spirit of the legislation. As such their influence can be seen in the widespread adoption of organizational equality policies which closely follow their approach. In the case of the Code of Practice for Age Diversity in Employment there is currently no supporting legislation. Loretto et al. (2000) draw on research on an earlier industrial relations code to assess its likely impact. This suggests that a code is likely to be successful if its creation has involved widespread consultation, there is consensus about its objectives and there are supporting institutions in place to ensure its full application. Loretto et al. argue that, while consultation was pursued, there are disagreements over both which age groups need to be protected against discrimination and whether a code is the best approach, and an absence of supporting mechanisms. They conclude that tackling age discrimination in this way is likely to have limited impact. However, for all groups with little collective power in the workplace any formal endorsement of their equality claims is likely to have some value.

Attempts to measure the effectiveness of equal opportunity policies are also problematic. As argued above, there are often a number of possible explanations for different employment patterns. Similarly it is difficult to attribute any particular distribution to a specific policy initiative. On the positive side the 1998 Workplace Employee Relations Survey (Cully et al. 1999: 26) found a correlation between presence of an equal opportunities policy and a high proportion of women in the workforce. Annual reports from Opportunity 2000/Opportunity Now show that their members, who tend to be adopting a wider range of equality initiatives than the average organization, have improved equality outcomes. For example, in 1999 over a third of managers in member organizations were women compared to a national figure of 18 per cent (*EOR* 1999b). However, a survey of top UK companies found that those which said that they were actively involved in the management of diversity had not employed more ethnic minorities, women, people with disabilities or older people in the last five years than companies without such policies (*EOR* 1999c). Most of the recent attempts to assess the impact of equality policies have done so not from the perspective of equality objectives but rather from a concern to demonstrate the business benefits that flow from such an approach (Humphries and Rubery 1995; Metcalf and Forth 2000). The latter study reports that benefits can certainly be identified, but that they depend on the business context. So a company which operates in an area with a high ethnic minority population, selling to ethnic minority customers, or seeking to recruit younger workers, will gain more from ethnic equality initiatives than an organization without these characteristics. Such research is important for understanding how organizations might be persuaded to introduce equality policies, but cannot really be said to be providing an evaluation of the policies per se. In fact they demonstrate a major limitation of the business case rationales – that they are likely to be adopted selectively and hence will not provide a secure basis for ensuring opportunities across the board.

Explanations of the coexistence of anti-discrimination legislation, equal opportunities policies and continuing evidence of differential experiences of the employment relation, which cannot be attributed solely to individual choice, take two broad forms. The first suggests policies are fine in principle but that problems arise in their implementation. There is now a considerable body of research which has tried to unravel the ways in which equality policies can be compromised in practice (much of it reviewed in Kirton and Greene 2000). Recurrent themes are the problematic relationship between line managers and personnel whereby equality initiatives highlight different priorities and conflicts over who controls decision-making; tensions between those priorities and approaches demanded by equality policies and those indicated by business imperatives, for example open recruitment versus filling posts internally or payment systems based on job evaluation rather than market requirements; and resistance from employees not benefiting from the initiatives. It is usually suggested that such problems can be tackled by greater commitment from the top, better training of line managers and closer monitoring of their decision-making, and better integration of equality policies into mainstream business strategies. The second response takes a more critical stance to the dominant approach to equal opportunities. This suggests a need to reflect on the understanding of discrimination embodied in equality approaches and the goals of equal opportunities policies.

Analytical perspectives

What type of equality are mainstream equal opportunities policies aiming for? Jewson and Mason (1986a) characterize the approach outlined in the Codes of Practice as 'liberal'. By this they mean that equality is understood as treating everyone the same. Cockburn (1989) also discusses this approach under the title of the 'short agenda'. Jewson and Mason contrast the approach taken by the Codes with one they call 'radical'. Here equality is conceived as equal outcomes. They argue that this approach involves a commitment to achieving fair distributions (as established by quotas) of under-represented groups within the workforce. This is likely to constitute positive discrimination and as such is usually unlawful under British legislation. For this reason one does not find examples of organizations explicitly building an equal opportunity policy around such an approach, although Jewson and Mason argue it is expressed by workers.

This dichotomy is problematic for a number of reasons. It suggests that 'liberals' are indifferent to the outcomes that flow from their fair procedures whereas it would seem more likely that they support equal treatment because they believe it is the best way to secure 'fair' outcomes. Radicals are presented as just wanting equal outcomes regardless of merit. However, it seems more likely that they are unconvinced of the ability of 'fair procedures' to demonstrate the abilities of under-represented groups or of employers' commitment to accept evidence of that ability without added sanctions.

There is an alternative to the radical approach which captures better the limitations of the liberal approach. This sees equality as allowing people to compete on equal terms. Such an approach has been explored by Webb and Liff (1988) in their critique of Jewson and Mason (1986a) and is characterized by Cockburn (1989) as the 'long agenda'. It embodies the idea that, although people may be treated equally, this may not necessarily result in 'fair' outcomes. Treating people the same is insufficient if the way competition for jobs is structured disadvantages members of one group by being organized around the normal practices of the dominant group of workers. For example, if an able-bodied person is competing against a wheelchair-user for a job located in a building with steps up to it, then although they are being treated equally, few would find the situation fair. However, fairness is not ensured by giving the person in the wheelchair the job regardless of the applicants' relative merits (which is what the radical approach seems to imply should happen if people with disabilities were under-represented) but rather, this approach suggests, by providing a way for all applicants to gain access to the building. The employer can then judge the applicants equally on job-related terms.

Managing diversity approaches have the potential to address such concerns in a distinctive way by arguing for a recognition of, and a response to, differences between people that will allow each employee to make the most of their talents and potential (Ellis and Sonnenfeld 1994; Kandola and Fullerton 1998; Thomas

1990). Managing diversity remains a contested term (Liff 1997), but all approaches imply a need for organizations to adapt their approach to deal with just the type of barriers described above. Whether this occurs in relation to randomly distributed individual differences or in relation to differences located predominantly within social groups varies between models (Liff 1997). It is also unclear what analytical alternative is being presented to the principle of treating everyone equally. The most obvious approach would appear to be some notion of equitable treatment, but there is little discussion about how this could be determined in practice. In much of the discussion it is assumed that some reconciliation can be achieved between the concepts of equal treatment and diversity management, but this proves difficult to tease out either analytically or practically (Liff and Wajcman 1996; Liff 1999).

The potential of managing diversity approaches

These difficulties notwithstanding, the importance of a recognition that disadvantage can be perpetuated through an organization's structure, culture and practices, rather than just through the biased decision-making of its managers, is crucial. As the studies reported above in relation to selection and appraisal show, when stereotypes based on social groups become embedded in the criteria which underpin decision-making (for example, as indicators of suitability for a particular job) then it is very hard for this to be overcome simply through improved procedures. What managing diversity approaches could do is raise awareness of the way the world of work is constructed around a particular type of worker. Most obviously the treatment of full-time (and often longer) hours as the norm (reflected, as Rees (1998) points out, in the designation of all other work patterns as 'atypical') assumes an availability for work which is very difficult to sustain if one has practical family commitments. Men with children are only able to work in this way because women have taken a greater share of domestic and caring work. The disadvantage suffered by such women who, as a consequence, have breaks in their employment and/or work part-time is seen as the result of a personal choice rather than discrimination on the part of employing organizations. That the problem lies in the incompatibility between current working practices and an involvement in family responsibilities is demonstrated by data which show that far fewer female managers have children than do male managers (e.g. Wajcman 1998), and research on the negative effects on men's salaries of their partner's choice to also pursue a career (Stroh and Brett 1996). Holt and Thaulow (1996) show that not only working patterns but also the form taken by 'family-friendly' policies and the support provided by co-workers are structured by the different forms of involvement of men and women in parental responsibilities.

As has been seen, feminist critics of liberal equality policies have long drawn attention to this type of problem. However, the solutions they have proposed, at least at the level of practical intervention, have tended to focus on positive action initiatives to 'level the playing field' or ensure fair competition. It could be argued that this approach does not provide a sufficiently explicit challenge to the dominant way of organizing. As a result organizations continue to be seen as 'fair' by most of their members (certainly those from dominant groups), and equality initiatives can be categorized as providing 'special help' to groups who could not compete on their own merits. This can lead to resentment from members of dominant groups, who are not forced to confront the way the system currently advantages them, and constructs others as being inadequate or having problems 'fitting in' (Cockburn 1991; Young 1990). Those who are appointed as a result of equality initiatives in such a context may come to be viewed as not up to the job and unlikely to succeed (Heilman et al. 1992). However, such reactions are not inevitable and well-designed initiatives whose purpose and rationale are clearly explained are likely to be successful (Crosby and Clayton 1990). Liff and Cameron (1997) discuss these issues in terms of the cultural assumptions and practices underlying organizational understandings of equality issues. They suggest initiatives that might disrupt such cultures, including audits which highlight the extent to which women's skills are under-utilized in their present jobs, the organizational costs of men's long hours in terms of health problems and relationship breakdown, and opportunities for men as well as women to explore the limitations of their current roles and behaviour and to develop solutions in relation to both business requirements and their life outside work. The importance of developing initiatives which command greater support is not just a desirable extra. The alternative of trying to ensure compliance by tighter controls on behaviour has been shown to be ineffective. Managers have shown themselves to be very adept at finding ways round such controls (Collinson et al. 1990; Burton 1991; Jewson and Mason 1986b; Liff and Dale 1994), and the high turnover of minority employees who face a hostile culture once appointed has been recognized to be a serious limitation on affirmative action approaches in the USA (Thomas 1990). The effect of hostile work cultures on minority employees is also becoming recognized in the UK in relation to the police (Holdaway 1997) and fire services.

Managing diversity approaches have aroused considerable anxiety and hostility in some quarters. It is feared that the promotion of the individual over the social group and the stress on diversity measures benefiting everyone, including white males, is intended to reduce awareness of, and commitment to redress, those inequalities between social groups which are still clearly evident. Writers stress the dominance of business models which have led managers to play up certain characteristics of different groups when they fit in with, say, a desire for flexibility but to ignore broader equality needs (Miller 1996; Webb 1997). There are also concerns that, claims about the promotion of cultural diversity notwithstanding, managing diversity involves the dissemination of a particular set of US cultural values which will undermine other models of equality between different ethnic groups (Jones et al. 2000). There is no doubt that there are good grounds for such concerns, but it is also important to recognize the limitations of previous equality models.

There is the potential to define managing diversity approaches in different ways and, as with any equality approach, the role of the state and of collective action is likely to be crucial in modifying dominant managerial approaches

(Dickens 1997). Rather than abandon the term there is a case for showing that it can be used in a progressive way. Though some have worried that 'mainstreaming' equality issues will simply lead to their being ignored, Rees (1998: 46) argues that it is about feminizing the mainstream. In relation to training she argues that it is a long-term strategy designed to place women's 'needs and the realities of their daily lives centre stage in the policy development of all education and training providers and in the design of all programmes through changing organizational cultures and institutions'. In its rhetoric at least managing diversity acknowledges that the workforce consists of different types of people and that organizations should reflect this in the rules governing employment. As Kirton and Greene (2000: 4) argue, the term can be used to conceptualize workplaces as 'composed of diverse social groups which share many employment experiences, but which simultaneously are also treated differentially, and at times require different treatment by, the labour market' rather than as a particular approach to equality. Understood in this way, it has the potential to lead to a change in the approach to studying 'mainstream' industrial relations which could make chapters such as this one irrelevant.

References

Baker, B. and Cooper, J. 1995: Fair play or foul? A survey of occupational test practices in the UK, *Personnel Review*, 24 (3), 3–18.

Bercusson, B., and Dickens, L. 1996: *Equal Opportunities and Collective Bargaining in Europe: Defining the Issues*. Dublin: European Foundation.

Bevan, S., and Thompson, M. 1992: *Merit Pay, Performance Appraisal and Attitudes to Women's Work*. IMS Report 234. Brighton: Institute of Manpower Studies.

Blackaby, D., Clark, K., Drinkwater, S., Leslie, D., Murphy, P. and O'Leary, N. 2000: Earnings and employment opportunities of disabled people. *Labour Market Trends*, March, 131–2.

Bower, C. 2001: Trends in female employment, *Labour Market Trends*, February, 107–18.

Bradley, H. 1989: *Men's Work Women's Work*. Cambridge: Polity.

Brown, C., and Gay, P. 1985: *Racial Discrimination: 17 Years after the Act*. London: Policy Studies Institute.

Burton, C. 1991: *The Promise and the Price*. Sydney, Australia: Allen & Unwin.

Charlesworth, K. 1997: *A Question of Balance*. London: Institute of Management.

Clifford, N., Moreley, M. and Gunnigle, P. 1997: Part-time work in Europe, *Employee Relations*, 19 (6), 555–67.

Cockburn, C. 1989: Equal opportunities: the short and the long agenda, *Industrial Relations Journal*, 20 (3), 213–25.

Cockburn, C. 1991: *In the Way of Women*. Basingstoke: Macmillan.

Colgan, F. 1999: Recognising the lesbian and gay constituency in UK trade unions: moving forward in UNISON? *Industrial Relations Journal*, 30 (5), 444–63.

Colgan, F., and Ledwith, S. 2000: Diversity, identities and strategies of women trade union activists, *Gender, Work and Organisation*, 7 (4), 242–57.

Colling, T., and Dickens, L. 1989: *Equality Bargaining: Why Not?* London: HMSO.

Colling, T., and Dickens, L. 1998: Selling the case for gender equality: deregulation and equality bargaining, *British Journal of Industrial Relations*, 36 (3), 389–411.

Collinson, D. L., Knights, K. and Collinson, M. 1990: *Managing to Discriminate*. London: Routledge.

CRE (Commission for Racial Equality) 1984: *Code of Practice*. London: HMSO.

Crosby, F., and Clayton, S. 1990: Affirmative action and the issue of expectancies, *Journal of Social Issues*, 46 (2), 61–79.

Cully, M., Woodland, S., O'Reilly, A. and Dix, G. 1999: *Britain at Work*. London: Routledge.

Cunnison, S., and Stageman, J. 1995: *Feminising the Unions*. Aldershot: Avebury.

Curran, M. 1988: Gender and recruitment: people and places in the labour market, *Work Employment and Society*, 2 (3), 335–51.

Dex, S. 1992: Labour force participation of women during the 1990s: occupational mobility and part-time employment. In R. Lindley (ed.), *Women's Employment: Britain and the Single European Market*. Research Series. Equal Opportunities Commission. London: HMSO.

Dickens, L. 1989: Women: a rediscovered resource? *Industrial Relations Journal*, 20 (3), 167–75.

Dickens, L. 1997: Gender, race and employment equality in Britain: inadequate strategies and the role of industrial relations actors, *Industrial Relations Journal*, 28 (4), 282–91.

Dickens, L. 1998: What HRM means for gender equality, *Human Resource Management Journal*, 8 (1), 23–40.

Dickens, L. 1999: Beyond the business case: a three-pronged approach to equality action, *Human Resource Management Journal*, 9 (1), 9–19.

Dickens, L. 2000: Collective bargaining and the promotion of gender equality at work: opportunities and challenges for trade unions, *Transfer*, 6 (2), 193–208.

Duleep, H. O., and Sanders, S. 1992: Discrimination at the top: American-born Asian and white men, *Industrial Relations*, 31 (3), 416–32.

Ellis, C., and Sonnenfeld, J. 1994: Diverse approaches to managing diversity. *Human Resource Management*, 33 (1), 79–109.

EOC (Equal Opportunities Commission) 1985a: *Code of Practice*. London: HMSO.

EOC 1985b: *Job Evaluation Schemes Free of Sex Bias*. Manchester: EOC.

EOR 1999a: Equal opportunities policies: an *EOR* survey of employers, *Equal Opportunities Review*, 87 (September/October), 14–23.

EOR 1999b: Opportunity 2000 relaunch, *Equal Opportunities Review*, 87 (September/October), 6.

EOR 1999c: Managing diversity firms not more diverse, *Equal Opportunities Review*, 87 (September/October), 5–6.

EOR 2000a: Fewer women in the boardroom, *Equal Opportunities Review*, 91 (May/June), 5–6.

EOR 2000b: Gender pay gap narrows, *Equal Opportunities Review*, 89 (January/February), 32.

EOR 2000c: Women forfeit £250,000 lifetime earnings, *Equal Opportunities Review*, 90 (March/April), 3–5.

Fletcher, C. 1999: The implications of research on gender differences in self-assessment and 360-degree appraisal, *Human Resource Management Journal*, 9 (1), 39–46.

Fryer, P. 1984: *Staying Power: Black People in Britain Since 1504*. Atlantic Highlands, USA: Humanities Press.

Hakim, C. 1996: *Key Issues in Women's Work: Female Heterogeneity and the Polarisation of Women's Employment*. London: Athlone.

Hatch, D. 1999: Destinations of claimant count departures: how the over-50s compare. *Labour Market Trends*, April, 169–74.

Heilman, M., Block, C. and Lucas, J. 1992: Presumed incompetent? Stigmatization and affirmative action efforts, *Journal of Applied Psychology*, 77 (4), 536–44.

Holdaway, S. 1997: Responding to racialized divisions within the workforce: the experience of black and Asian police officers in England, *Ethnic and Racial Studies*, 20 (1), 69–90.

Holt, K., and Thaulow, I. 1996: Formal and informal flexibility in the workplace. In S. Lewis and J. Lewis (eds), *The Work-Family Challenge: Rethinking Employment*. London: Sage.

Hoque, K., and Noon, M. 1999: Racial discrimination in speculative applications: new optimism six years on? *Human Resource Management Journal*, 9 (3), 71–82.

Humphries, J., and Rubery, J. (eds) 1995: *The Economics of Equal Opportunities*. Manchester: Equal Opportunities Commission.

Hunt, A. 1975: *Management Attitudes and Practices Towards Women at Work*. London: HMSO.

IRS (Industrial Relations Services) 1999: Managing a mixed-age workforce. *IRS Employment Trends*, 694 (December), 12–16.

IRS 2000a: Racism still widespread at work. *IRS Employment Trends*, 699 (March), 2.

IRS 2000b: New ways to manage disability. *IRS Employment Trends*, 708 (July), 9–16.

Jenkins, R. 1986: *Racism and Recruitment: Managers, Organisations and Equal Opportunity in the Labour Market*. Cambridge: Cambridge University Press.

Jenkins, R. 1996: *Social Identity*. London: Routledge.

Jewson, N., and Mason, D. 1986a: The theory and practice of equal opportunities policies: liberal and radical approaches, *Sociological Review*, 34 (2), 307–34.

Jewson, N., and Mason, D. 1986b: Modes of discrimination in the recruitment process: formalisation, fairness and efficiency, *Sociology*, 20 (1), 43–63.

Jewson, N. et al. 1990: *Ethnic Minorities and Employment Practice*. Department of Employment Research Paper No. 76. London: Department of Employment.

Jones, D., Pringle, J. and Shepherd, D. 2000: Managing diversity meets Aotearoa, New Zealand, *Personnel Review*, 29 (3), 364–80.

Kahn, P., and Meehan, E. (eds) 1992: *Equal Value/Comparable Worth in the UK and the USA*. London: Macmillan.

Kandola, R., and Fullerton, J. 1998: *Diversity in Action: Managing the Mosaic*, 2nd edn. London: Institute of Personnel and Development.

Kirton, G., and Greene, A.-M. 2000: *The Dynamics of Managing Diversity: A Critical Approach*. Oxford: Butterworth Heinemann.

La Valle, I., Finch, S., Nove, A. and Lewin, C. 2000: Parents' demand for childcare. *Labour Market Trends*, June, 293–6.

Labour Market Spotlight 1999: *Labour Market Trends*, February, 60.

Labour Market Trends 1999: Employment tribunal and employment appeal tribunal statistics 1997–98 and 1998–99. *Labour Market Trends*, September, 493–7.

Liff, S. 1997: Two routes to managing diversity: individual differences or social group characteristics, *Employee Relations*, 19 (1), 11–26.

Liff, S. 1999: Diversity and equal opportunities: room for a constructive compromise? *Human Resource Management Journal*, 9 (1), 65–75.

Liff, S., and Cameron, I. 1997: Changing equality cultures to move beyond 'women's problems', *Gender, Work and Organization*, 4 (1), 35–46.

Liff, S., and Dale, K. 1994: Formal opportunity, informal barriers: black women managers within a local authority, *Work Employment and Society*, 8 (2), 177–98.

Liff, S., and Wajcman, J. 1996: Sameness and difference revisited: which way forward for equal opportunity initiatives? *Journal of Management Studies*, 33 (1), 79–94.

Liff, S., and Ward, K. 2001: Distorted views through the glass ceiling: the construction of women's understanding of promotion and senior management positions, *Gender, Work and Organization*, 8 (1), 19–36.

Loretto, W., Duncan, C. and White, P. 2000: Industrial relations codes of practice: the 1999 age discrimination code in context. *Employee Relations*, 22 (2), 146–59.

McBride, A. 2001: *Making a Difference? Gender Democracy in Trade Unions*. Aldershot: Ashgate.

Meager, N., and Hibbett, A. 1999: Disability and the labour market: findings from the DfEE Baseline Survey. *Labour Market Trends*, September, 467–76.

Metcalf, H., and Forth, J. 2000: The business benefits of race equality at work. *Labour Market Trends*, June, 297–9.

Miller, D. 1996: Equality management: towards a materialist approach, *Gender, Work and Organization*, 3 (4), 202–14.

Modood, T. 1997: Employment. In R. Berthoud et al. (eds), *Ethnic Minorities in Britain: Diversity and Disadvantage*. London: Policy Studies Institute.

Morris, J. 1983: *No More Peanuts*. London: NCCL.

Noon, M. 1993: Racial discrimination in speculative application: evidence from the UK's top 100 firms, *Human Resource Management Journal*, 3 (4), 35–47.

O'Reilly, J., and Fagan, C. 1998: *Part-time Prospects: An International Comparison of Part-time Work in Europe, North America and the Pacific Rim*. London: Routledge.

Partington, J., and Mayell, C. 2000: Annual Employment Survey 1998. *Labour Market Trends*, June, 273–95.

Pilcher, J. 2000: Domestic divisions of labour in the twentieth century: 'change slow a-coming', *Work, Employment and Society*, 14 (4), 771–80.

Rees, T. 1998: *Mainstreaming Equality in the European Union*. London: Routledge.

Rubery, J., and Fagan, C. 1995: Comparative industrial relations research: towards reversing the gender bias, *British Journal of Industrial Relations*, 33 (2), 209–36.

Seidel, M.-D., Polzer, J. and Stewart, J. 2000: Friends in high places: the effects of social networks on discrimination in salary negotiations, *Administrative Science Quarterly*, 45 (1), 1–24.

Skinner, D. 1999: The reality of equal opportunities: the expectations and experiences of part-time staff and their managers, *Personnel Review*, 28 (5/6), 425–38.

Stroh, L., and Brett, J. 1996: The dual-earner dad penalty in salary progression, *Human Resource Management*, 35 (2), 181–201.

Summerfield, P. 1989: *Women Workers in the Second World War*. London: Routledge.

Tamkin, P. 2000: Institutional racism: daring to open Pandora's box, *Equal Opportunities Review*, 92 (July/August), 19–23.

Thomas, R. R. 1990: From affirmative action to affirming diversity, *Harvard Business Review*, March/April, 107–17.

Townley, B. 1990: A discriminating approach to appraisal, *Personnel Management*, December, 34–7.

Twomey, B. 2001a: Labour market participation of ethnic groups, *Labour Market Trends*, January, 29–42.

Twomey, B. 2001b: Women in the labour market: results from the spring 2000 LFS, *Labour Market Trends*, February, 93–106.

Twomey, B. 2001c: Disability and the labour market: results from the summer 2000 LFS, *Labour Market Trends*, May, 241–52.

Wajcman, J. 1998: *Managing Like a Man: Women and Men in Corporate Management*. Cambridge: Polity.

Wajcman, J. 2000: Feminism facing industrial relations in Britain, *British Journal of Industrial Relations*, 38 (2), 183–201.

Walby, S. 1983: *Patriarchy at Work*. Cambridge: Polity.

Webb, J. 1997: The politics of equal opportunity, *Gender, Work and Organization*, 4 (3), 159–69.

Webb, J., and Liff, S. 1988: Play the white man: the social construction of fairness and competition in equal opportunity policies, *Sociological Review*, 36 (3), 543–51.

Weiler, A. 2000: Innovative agreements on equal opportunities: new horizons of collective bargaining? *Transfer*, 6 (2), 209–26.

Wood, R. 1996: Psychometrics should make assessment fairer, *Equal Opportunities Review*, 67, May/June, 27–33.

Wood, R., and Baron, H. 1992: Psychological testing free from prejudice, *Personnel Management*, December, 34–7.

Woodall, J. 1996: Human resource management and women: the vision of the gender-blind? In B. Towers (ed.), *The Handbook of Human Resource Management*, 2nd edn. Oxford: Blackwell.

Young, I. M. 1990: *Justice and the Politics of Difference*. Princeton: Princeton University Press.

17
LOW PAY AND THE NATIONAL MINIMUM WAGE

JILL RUBERY AND PAUL EDWARDS

Low Pay in Britain

Earnings inequality in the UK widened persistently and markedly over the final two decades of the twentieth century (OECD 1993, 1996; Bazen et al. 1998), more than offsetting the trends towards more equal earnings distribution in the 1970s (Machin 1999). This increase in earning inequality resulted both from a rising share of relatively well-paid workers and a rising share of low-paid workers. That is, the gap between the top of the earnings distribution and the median, and the gap between the median and the bottom, both grew. The growth of low pay was associated with various labour market developments, including: a much higher level of unemployment than that which prevailed up until the end of the 1970s; a growth of service sector employment; a continued growth in part-time jobs; and finally a major increase in the share of the labour force whose pay was determined by management without the protection of minimum wage standards established by voluntary agreement or by legal regulation. As noted in chapter 8, by the middle of the 1990s there were more employees who were outside the voluntary collective bargaining system than employees covered by collective bargaining, and all forms of legal minimum wage protection had been abolished, except for those covering agricultural workers. It was against this background that the Labour government was elected in 1997 with a mandate to introduce a National Minimum Wage, and it was only in 1999, the first year in which a National Minimum Wage was implemented in the UK, that there was any evidence of a reversal of this trend towards greater inequality.

Definitions of Low Pay

Low pay is necessarily a relative concept. There is no absolute standard of fair pay or indeed reasonable minimum living standards; all definitions depend on the conditions specific to a particular society and time period (Wedderburn

1974). This point is worth stressing. It is widely argued that one reason for growing inequality of pay is a shift in demand, with employers' needs for unskilled labour falling (Machin 1999). There is certainly convincing evidence here, but such demand shifts do not determine the size of the pay gap between the skilled and the unskilled. Wage structures differ between countries and over time, and there is no objective definition of the size of pay differentials; given that differentials were already wide in Britain, it is not clear why further widening was needed to attract labour to the more skilled and higher-paying jobs (Rubery 1997: 347).

However, to recognize that we are here talking about relative and not absolute levels does not solve the problem; there is also the issue that discussions of low pay tend to revolve around two quite separate definitions of low pay: one relative to the earnings of other workers, and one relative to the standards of living enjoyed by other workers. However, standards of living do not just depend on an individual's earnings; also important are the individual's family situation and the access of the individual and other family members to other sources of income and resources. Some argue that low pay is not a problem if it does not result in the individuals who are low-paid living in poverty; from this perspective low wages are only issues of social concern if the end result is the inability of families to achieve minimum acceptable consumption standards (Layard et al. 1978; Johnson and Stark 1991). The emphasis on family income draws attention away from the issue of how much effort or how much time should have to be expended to achieve reasonable living standards: should there be a maximum number of hours of labour as well as a minimum consumption standard? Many low-paid workers and families may get by simply by working very long hours, sometimes in a range of different jobs, and women workers may add to long hours of domestic labour by taking on paid work at low wage rates. Often these wage rates are justified by employers on the grounds that the women are working 'only for extras' or for 'pin money'.[1] Yet without these extras many more families may fall into poverty. Nor is it necessarily fair that people should receive much lower rates of pay for similar effort and time spent at work. The principle 'a fair day's work for a fair day's pay' may be said to apply irrespective of an individual's family circumstances. The notion that pay should be proportional to the work done and not influenced by the presumed income needs of the person employed is also the basis for the principle of equal pay for equal work between men and women (a principle included in the UK's 1970 Equal Pay Act as well as the European Community's Treaty of Rome and the International Labour Office's set of labour standards). Low pay is thus best defined in terms that are independent of family or household living standards.

Even though we have argued that low pay should be defined by reference to wage norms, several definitions and approaches to the measurement of low pay can still be used. The most common approach is to define low pay as covering all those working at a wage below a certain percentage of the average earnings level; the level most frequently chosen, and adopted as the Council of Europe's standard of decency, is around two-thirds of average (mean) wages. In practice many studies adopt the more modest definition of two-thirds of median earnings. Another approach is to look at what has been happening over time to the lowest

10 per cent of the labour force: has their pay been increasing or decreasing over time relative to median or average pay?

Low Pay in the UK in Comparative Perspective

To assess the extent of the problem of low pay in the UK it is important to place the distribution of earnings in a comparative context (Dex et al. 1999). However, a major problem with data on earnings is that even the most comprehensive data fail to provide a fully integrated distribution of earnings in the labour market. These problems apply both to UK sources of data and to international comparative data. Most data refer only or mainly to full-time employees, even though low pay is often common among part-timers. Moreover, both the share of part-time workers and their concentration among the low-paid varies between countries (Gornick and Jacobs 1996; Rubery 1998; Grimshaw and Rubery 1997). Comparisons that only include full-time employees are therefore inadequate to give a full picture of the relative extent and the form of the low-pay problem in the UK. It is therefore necessary to provide separate comparisons for full-time and part-time employees.

Table 17.1 shows the distribution of earnings for full-time employees in selected OECD countries for five-year intervals from 1980 to 1995. It is the UK,

Table 17.1   Earnings distribution in OECD countries, 1980–1995

Country D9/D1	1980	1985	1990	1995
Australia	2.84	2.72	2.81	2.92
Austria	2.83		2.89	2.95 (1994)
Belgium		2.00	1.97	
Canada	4.01 (1981)	4.45 (1986)	4.40	4.19 (1994)
Denmark	2.14	2.17	2.17	
Finland	2.45	2.50 (1986)	2.50	2.38 (1994)
France	3.26	3.12	3.26	3.28 (1994)
Germany		2.62	2.52	2.32 (1993)
Italy	2.64	2.50 (1986)	2.42 (1991)	2.80 (1993)
Japan	2.91	3.11	3.16	3.02 (1994)
Netherlands		2.51	2.61	2.59 (1994)
New Zealand		2.84 (1986)	3.05	3.05 (1994)
Norway	2.06		1.98 (1991)	
Portugal		3.61	3.49 (1991)	4.05 (1993)
Sweden	2.04	2.07	2.01	2.13 (1993)
United Kingdom	2.78	3.06	3.29	3.38
United States				4.39

D1 and D9 refer to the upper earnings limits of, respectively, the first and ninth deciles of employees ranked in order of their earnings from lowest to highest.
Source: OECD (1996: table 3.1).

together with the US, which have witnessed the sharpest widening of wage differentials. Thus while in 1980 in the UK the top decile of earnings was 2.78 times greater than the earnings of the lowest decile, by 1995 this ratio had risen to 3.38. Data for the whole distribution were not available for the earlier years for the US, but taking male and female earnings separately we find a rise between the top and bottom decile for men from 3.26 in 1980 to 4.34 in 1995, with the female earnings ratio rising from 2.92 to 3.96 over the same period. In 1995 the US, together with Canada and Portugal, had the widest degree of earnings inequality, followed by the UK. In contrast, the width of the earnings distribution had remained relatively constant in the majority of OECD countries for which we have data, even though they started the period with very different patterns of earnings inequality. For example, France, which started the period with one of the widest distributions, and Sweden which had one of the narrowest, each experienced a change in the D9/D1 ratio of less than 0.1 over the time period. There was, therefore, neither a consistent trend pattern within OECD countries towards wider or narrower earnings distributions nor evidence of a process of convergence in earnings distributions over these two decades.

Table 17.2 shows the shares of low-paid workers, defined as earning less than two-thirds of the median wage, all for full-time employees only. These shares follow the pattern of earnings inequality revealed in table 17.1, with the UK and the North American countries having much higher shares of low-paid workers than most Continental European countries, and in particular much higher shares

Table 17.2   Incidence of low pay by gender and age (% of relevant group)

Country	Total	Men	Women	Under 25	25–54	55 and over
Australia 1995	13.8	11.8	17.7	34.5	8.8	12.5
Austria 1993	13.2	7.0	22.8	19.5	12.1	9.6
Belgium 1993	7.2	3.9	14.2	22.2	5.3	4.9
Canada 1994	23.7	16.1	34.3	57.1	20.1	20.8
Finland 1994	5.9	3.3	8.7	27.1	5.5	4.4
France 1995	13.3	10.6	17.4	49.5	10.6	10.5
Germany 1994	13.3	7.6	25.4	50.4	6.7	5.4
Italy 1993	12.5	9.3	18.5	27.0	6.7	7.4
Japan 1994	15.7	5.9	37.2	36.4	9.6	19.8
Netherlands 1994	11.9					
New Zealand 1994/5	16.9	14.4	20.7	41.3	11.6	15.6
Sweden 1993	5.2	3.0	8.4	18.7	4.3	2.9
Switzerland 1995	13.0	6.8	30.4	44.0	9.0	9.2
United Kingdom 1995	19.6	12.8	31.2	45.8	15.0	22.9
United States 1994	25.0	19.6	32.5	63.0	21.2	23.7

The share of low-paid workers refers to full-time employment only. Low pay is defined as less than two-thirds of median earnings for all full-time employees.
Source: OECD (1996: table 3.2).

than the Nordic countries of Finland and Sweden. The factors associated with the low incidence of low pay in Scandinavian countries include the presence of comprehensive collective bargaining systems, the policy within the collective bargaining system of favouring narrow differentials for skills or between sectors, the small size and socially homogeneous structure of the societies concerned and the strong commitment to gender equality.

The high incidence of low pay in the UK becomes even more evident once we attempt to take into account part-time as well as full-time employees. Data on part-time earnings are particularly difficult to obtain on a comparative basis. The OECD has made a recent attempt to assess relative pay for part-timers using a combination of the 1995 European Structure of Earnings Survey and a range of other national sources for non-European countries. The Structure of Earnings Survey excludes public sector employees and therefore provides only a partial comparison. Moreover, for part-timers we do not have exact measures of the share of low-paid workers falling below low-pay thresholds; instead we have only a proxy for the likely impact of part-time work on low pay, that is a comparison of the median hourly rate of pay for part-timers compared to full-timers. Table 17.3 shows that median part-timers' pay is lower than median

Table 17.3 Part-time earnings and part-time employment, 1995

Country	Part-time median hourly wages as % of full-time workers			Part-time employment as % of all employment	
	Men	*Women*	*All*	*Men*	*Women*
Australia			89.4	14.7	41.2
Belgium	74.7	86.8	78.4	4.8	32.3
Canada	46.9	69.8	55.9	10.5	29.4
Denmark	74.2	76.4	74.2	11.1	24.2
Finland	76.5	90.2	82.6	6.0	10.6
France	73.2	81.7	73.0	5.9	25.2
Germany	78.4	87.5	82.5	3.7	29.9
Greece	79.6	108.8	86.6	4.8	14.1
Italy	83.1	103.0	87.4	5.1	22.2
Luxembourg	78.6	77.5	69.5	2.1	24.7
Netherlands	69.8	93.1	73.2	11.1	54.8
Portugal	80.8	113.0	90.0	5.1	16.5
Spain	66.4	84.0	67.8	3.1	16.8
Sweden	88.7	92.3	87.2	8.1	24.9
United Kingdom	54.2	69.6	58.0	8.2	40.9
United States	44.0	62.5	54.3	8.3	19.5
Unweighted average	71.3	86.4	75.6	7.0	26.7

Source: OECD (1999: tables 1.5 and 1.A.4).

full-timers' pay, for both men and women and for all employees combined, with the exception of female part-timers in three southern European countries where the part-time incidence is relatively low. These data also show that the position of part-timers in the UK and North America is much worse than is the case in Australia and all the other European OECD countries. If it were possible to include part-timers within the data on low-paid workers presented in table 17.2, there would be an even wider gulf between the UK and the North American countries and the rest. There is no clear relationship between the differential between part-timers' hourly pay and that of full-timers and the actual incidence of part-time work. The Netherlands, for example, has the highest incidence of part-time work for women but female part-timers receive over 93 per cent of female full-timers' median pay compared to only 69 per cent in the case of the UK. Countries such as Germany and Sweden have moderately high incidences of part-time working, but also have relatively high ratios of part-time to full-time median earnings. The US has the lowest part-time to full-time pay ratio but a relatively modest level of part-time working. The argument that the UK has traded off pay equality for part-time workers in return for greater job opportunities for part-timers does not appear to hold up once it is recognized that other countries have managed to combine part-time work opportunities with higher relative pay for part-timers.

Labour Market Regulation and Low Pay

The high incidence of low pay in the UK by the time of the implementation of the National Minimum Wage in April 1999 must be considered the consequence of the overall pattern of economic development in the UK (Rubery 1994) and the specific approach to employment regulation and protection. Here we will focus primarily on the regulatory explanations for the growth of low pay. However, the tendency for the UK economy to generate low-skilled jobs both in mass-production manufacturing and in service sectors can be considered a major contributory factor (see chapter 3). This tendency is, of course, not independent of the pattern of employment regulation which facilitates the development of low-wage employment; the interactions between the pattern of economic development and the industrial relations system are considered in more detail in chapter 5. Recent research on the incidence of low pay, using the 1998 WERS survey, reveals the significance of workplace characteristics in the share of low-paid workers. Workplaces most likely to be low-paying were 'single [i.e. not part of a larger firm] private-sector establishments, in competitive product markets, which have limited collective industrial relations institutions' (McNabb and Whitfield 2000: 605); of these institutions, collective bargaining coverage was most important.

Turning to the history of the employment and wage regulatory system, we find that much of the distinctive development of the UK in its pattern of wage dispersion relative to other European countries can be attributed to a particular industrial relations history and tradition, namely voluntarism combined with active, state-led deregulation. Investigation of that tradition reveals that the historical development of wage regulation has been by no means linear, but can be divided into different stages and patterns. In some periods or sectors there has been a complementary strengthening of both voluntary collective bargaining and legal regulation; in others the focus was on the potential for competition between voluntary and legal systems. Finally in the 1980s there is a descent into a complementary or reinforcing decline of both voluntary and legal forms of wage protection, associated with the de-institutionalization of wage-fixing and protection in the UK labour market.

Voluntarism and legal regulation: complementary or competitive approaches?

The trade union movement in Britain has traditionally had an ambivalent attitude towards the protection of the low-paid and the unorganized. The preference for voluntary systems of collective bargaining and regulation in Britain has involved a choice not to pursue the development of universal, legally enforceable employment rights for all workers irrespective of their affiliation to unions or employment in firms engaged in collective bargaining. In Britain all parties involved in industrial relations have traditionally been reluctant to develop compulsory systems of regulation requiring enforcement by the state (see chapter 2). Despite this reluctance, at certain times and in certain sectors trade unions have recognized that voluntary collective bargaining was more an aspiration than a reality. As such there was perceived to be a need for some interim arrangements, both to provide protection of those employed in low-paid and unorganized sectors and to protect the voluntary systems of regulation in place. The state has been persuaded to step in to set up regulatory mechanisms which were held to be temporary substitutes for a voluntary system. In this sense legal regulation and voluntary collective bargaining could be seen as developing in a complementary way, with legal regulation providing the basis for protecting and fostering the voluntary system.

The most obvious example of how the voluntarist system was extended through state and legal intervention to provide wage protection for the low-paid and unorganized is found in the Wages Council system. Originally known as Trade Boards, these bodies were set up to fix legal minimum wages in industries which were regarded as not able to establish voluntary systems of collective bargaining. The first four boards were established in 1909. Instead of establishing general legal minimum wages, legal minimum wage protection was established only in those sectors where low pay or 'sweating' was regarded as a general problem and where there was no evidence of effective voluntary regulation. Moreover, in keeping with the voluntarist principle, these bodies were established as quasi-collective-bargaining institutions, consisting of two 'sides', employers and workers, in practice consisting of employers' association representatives and trade union representatives, even though these were largely unorganized industries. The Trade Boards or Wages Councils only differed from collective bargaining institutions in two main respects: independent members were present to ensure that a wage rate was eventually set even if bargaining broke down, and once set the wage rates became legally enforceable, through the operation of a Wages Inspectorate who had the power to inspect the wages records of any company whose business fell mainly within the scope of a Wages Council.

The conversion from Trade Boards to Wages Councils came in 1945 and a major expansion of the system was introduced to cover service industries as well as manufacturing. The result was that Wages Councils were established in most of the industries where low pay is both concentrated and dominant: in particular in retail, catering, clothing, hairdressing and laundry as well as other miscellaneous manufacturing and service trades. Similar bodies called Wages Boards set minimum rates of pay in agriculture. By 1986, Wages Councils covered 2.5 million workers, or about 11 per cent of the labour force. Some smaller industries also noted for low pay were never brought within the Wages Council net (for example parts of retail, dry cleaning) but also excluded were low-paid workers and unorganized firms in industries where collective bargaining was well established for the majority of firms. Thus the Wages Council system was set up to supplement and not to supplant the voluntary system of regulation and was far from universal in impact.

The establishment of more comprehensive minimum wage protection covering services as well as manufacturing after 1945 was consistent with trade union policies of providing for fair pay and employment rights, and indeed with the wider political agenda of developing the welfare state and the social market in the post-war period. However, perhaps paradoxically, up until the election of the first Thatcher government in 1979 the main threat to the continuation of the Wages Councils came from the trade union movement. Pressure had begun to mount in the late 1960s to abolish certain Wages Councils. They were regarded as setting too low rates of pay, and many unions came to the view that instead of fostering collective bargaining, they discouraged firms from engaging directly in collective bargaining and workers from joining trade unions. Legal regulation and voluntary collective bargaining began to be seen as competitive rather than complementary systems of regulation. Full employment and the general spread of collective regulation were argued to have turned Wages Councils into an anachronism. This view was propagated in Bayliss's classic study of the Wages Councils in 1962: 'under full employment it is no longer the prime function of Wages Councils to provide a legally enforced level of wages and conditions markedly above that which would otherwise prevail' (1962: 74). By the mid-1990s many trade unionists had come to regret the time when they had such misplaced confidence in their ability to regulate the labour market without assistance from institutions such as Wages Councils.

Under pressure from the unions the government did agree to the abolition of a range of Wages Councils, mainly in manufacturing but also including one large service sector Wages Council, industrial and staff canteens. A study set up to investigate to what extent the claims of the trade union movement were justified found that, even before the major change in union fortunes in the 1980s, the claim that abolition would help the low-paid by bringing them properly within the voluntary collective bargaining net were not well founded (Craig et al. 1982). Not only did effective collective bargaining fail to develop in all but one of the six sectors studied following abolition, but there was also evidence that a significant share of workers would have been better off if the Wages Councils had been maintained.

By and large the Wages Councils provided the main means of legal protection in the UK against low pay from 1909 until their abolition in the early 1990s. The main alternative means to separate legal minimum wage systems to provide protection against low pay is to make collectively agreed minima legally binding even on organizations not party to the collective agreements, but this system, although widely used in many European Union member states, has generally not been used in Britain, in part because collective agreements are not even legally binding instruments on voluntary participants. However, there have been three exceptions to this general pattern. The first was the series of Fair Wages Resolutions by the House of Commons. The initial resolution was passed in 1891, but its modern version was passed in 1946. This required government contractors to pay fair wages and to respect the rights of their employees to be members of trade unions. Fair wages were usually interpreted as at least equal to the minimum rates set by the relevant industry-level agreement. This provision thereby both protected public sector employees from competition based on 'unfair wages' and at the same time encouraged the extension of industry-level collective agreements to firms that otherwise might have chosen to set pay independently.

The second way in which voluntary agreements have been extended to non-participating employers was through the provisions of the 1975 Employment Protection Act, in particular Schedule 11. This Act established a mechanism by which workers employed by firms which did not engage in collective bargaining could seek union recognition and the right to bargain collectively. If that failed, under Schedule 11 they could also seek the imposition on the employer of a requirement to at least match the 'general level' of pay for comparable workers in the district, a ruling in practice interpreted, when applied, as the relevant industry-level minimum rates. These provisions were not extensively used in the short period during which they were available in British law (1975–1980), in part because the mechanisms for implementing these rights were complex and unwieldy. A separate case had to be taken for each individual firm and there was no system for imposing the minimum rates on all firms in the industry.

The third method of extending agreements to non-participating firms was union action. This took various forms. For example, in the printing industry the unions were sufficiently well established to be able to organize boycotts of non-union firms. In the public sector, unions were sometimes able, at times through the political support of councillors, to ensure that public sector work was sub-contracted only to unionized firms or to those observing collective agreements. However, it was far from the case that all unions were active in ensuring that all firms in the labour market observed the collective agreements to reduce the threat of 'unfair competition'. Particularly in the 1970s the unions could be accused of having become complacent about collective bargaining at the industry level. Instead they put most of their energies into the organization of bargaining at the establishment or company level, supporting and encouraging the employers' decisions to move to decentralized bargaining, and in some cases to quit the industry employers' association.

Low pay is not only related to lack of regulation and absence of collective bargaining but also to such factors as sex and race discrimination. As discussed in chapter 6, rights not to be discriminated against on the basis of gender or race were introduced for the first time in the 1970s. Pay structures up until this date often included very specific references to the sex of the workers employed, while race discrimination was less explicit and thus less easily identified. The 1970 Equal Pay Act required firms to pay equal pay for the same work and to establish pay-grading structures, where they already existed, which were free from sex bias. The result of this legislation was a marked narrowing of the earnings gap between men and women between 1970 and 1975, the date of implementation. As women constitute the majority of low-paid workers this development clearly had a major impact on low pay, reducing the earnings spread by raising the minimum wages previously set for women's work closer to those established for men's work. Although the principle applied to all firms, in practice it was in the more regulated firms that there was the strongest effect, as a formal pay-grading structure was the most likely condition permitting action to eliminate a male and a female minimum wage rate (Craig et al. 1985). Where unions were present, strong pressure was put on employers to establish the new pay structure based on the previous male minimum rate; where employers were free to establish the rate without union regulation, the new minimum rate was more likely to have been established around the previous female minimum rate. Moreover, evidence suggests that much of the impact on women's wages arose through the generalization of the new wage structures through industry-level agreements and through Wages Councils (Zabalza and Tzannatsos 1985). Thus there was some reduction in low pay in the 1970s as a consequence of an effective interaction between new individual rights and the system of voluntary regulation. The widespread impact of these changes relied on mechanisms that allowed the unions to generalize the benefits to workers found in relatively unorganized as well as organized firms.

Another source of protection against low pay in the 1970s can be considered, at least by 1990s standards, a relatively generous unemployment benefit system. The unemployed were entitled not only to a basic benefit, but also to an earnings-related supplement for the first six months. This higher level of benefit was designed to help the newly unemployed search for suitable work without pushing them straight away into low-paid jobs.

Trade unions also sought to protect adult workers from competition from young people who may be willing to work at very low wages rather than remain unemployed. Young people are often anxious to obtain some form of labour market experience and may be willing to work for very little as they will receive support from their families. For these reasons trade unions in Britain have historically aimed to link youth wages to adult wages. By the 1970s they had succeeded in setting youth rates at relatively high percentages of adult rates (Ryan 1987; Marsden and Ryan 1991). In the 1980s both these methods of reducing 'competition' at the bottom of the labour market were to be challenged by the incoming Thatcher government.

From voluntarism to deregulation

The voluntarist system of regulation as it existed in the post-war period up until 1979 was by no means an ideal or effective system of protection against low pay. Much of the labour market remained outside any system of legal compulsion to pay fair wages, and even within the Wages Council sector pay was often low and underpayment widespread, in part at least because of the sheer complexity of the Wages Council orders (Pond 1983). Trade unions failed to understand the depth of the problem of regulating pay in small firms and competitive industries and seemed content to rely on the mystical powers of full employment to keep up a reasonable floor to wages. Nevertheless, there was a general commitment to the existence and extension of labour standards. Above all there was a commitment to collective bargaining and a belief that those workers outside its net should be as far as possible integrated into the system and paid comparable or fair wages.

The changes that occurred in the 1980s and much of the 1990s involved a rejection of all these principles and objectives. The new principle was that employers should be free to decide whether or not to recognize unions and to determine their own rates of pay according to their own individual circumstances. Any mechanisms that encouraged co-ordination of pay rates between firms or that enshrined the principles of comparability or fair pay were to be regarded as suspect. Mechanisms that encouraged workers to compete against each other on the basis of pay, or employers to reduce pay rates for existing or new staff, were to be looked upon favourably. The problems with Wages Councils were no longer that they set too low pay and discouraged collective bargaining; instead they were deemed to set too high wage rates and to discourage employment growth. Out of this turnaround in approach came a series of measures which reversed the tendencies described above.

As Wages Councils represented the most blatant deviation from the notion of a free market and a voluntarist system of regulation it is perhaps surprising that it was not until 1986 that there was a serious attempt by the Thatcher government to abolish the councils, and even then this resulted only in legislation to reduce their powers.[2] In 1988 a plan to abolish was again withdrawn and it was only in 1993 under John Major's government that the complete abolition of the system was effected. One reason for the survival of the Wages Councils was the support that the system received from the employers' associations in the industries concerned, certainly at the time that abolition was mooted in 1986. With no particular constituency supporting abolition, the government perhaps felt it was too much trouble to take the steps to abolish the councils in the 1980s, especially in the run-up to the 1987 election. But in 1993, with much of their other legislation on labour markets already on the statute books, the government could see no good reason for further maintaining a system to which it was ideologically opposed.

The arguments that the government put forward in favour of abolition were threefold: first that it would stimulate jobs, second that the Wages Councils were an anachronism which no longer affected pay except for a small minority, and third that most people who worked in Wages Council industries were not living in poverty, and thus there was not a social justice argument for maintaining the system. This argument about social justice sits uneasily with principles such as equal pay for equal work which require there to be a fair reward for work irrespective of the effect on living standards. Moreover, research evidence contradicted the view that falls in Wages Council rates would not hurt low-income households. Indeed the anticipated effect of abolition was unclear, even to the government. On the one hand, Wages Councils were argued to be an irrelevance such that their abolition would have little impact on pay; on the other hand, the beneficial effect of abolition was argued to come through job creation stimulated by wage cuts. One of the reasons why it was argued that the effect of abolition would be relatively small was that most workers in Wages Council industries received rates somewhat in excess of Wages Council orders. However, this may have reflected the fact that many firms set their wages with regard to Wages Council rates but aimed to pay slightly above this floor. Once the floor to wages was removed, wages for the majority of the workforce were in principle at least free to begin to fall, particularly as few firms, including even the large firms in Wages Council sectors, had systems of voluntary collective regulation of wages. The period from the abolition of Wages Councils to the introduction of a minimum wage was too short to actually test out these effects, but such research as was carried out did point to a relative decline in pay rates at the bottom of the labour market segments (Lucas and Radiven 1998).

While Wages Councils survived until the final years of the Conservative administration, the Fair Wages Resolution was rescinded in 1983 and the provisions for extensions of collective agreements under Schedule 11 of the Employment Protection Act abolished in 1980. The repeal of the fair wages clause was important in paving the way for another major policy of the 1980s – the introduction of compulsory competitive tendering into many areas of public sector services. The explicit aim of this policy was to reduce costs, particularly in ancillary services. Public sector employers were considered likely to be paying wages in excess of the rates at which private firms could recruit workers in sectors such as cleaning, catering and construction. The repeal of the resolution was intended to remove any scrutiny of the wage rates set by the tendering firms and to introduce competition based on lower wage costs. Even those public sector workers that fought off the competitive threat did so at the cost of reduced remuneration and/or increased work effort. One of the main ways in which the remuneration package was cut was through reduced holiday pay (Crompton and Sanderson 1990), and also bonuses. However the Transfer of Undertakings legislation placed new and unanticipated constraints on the competitive tendering process. This legislation protected the terms and conditions of workers transferred from one employer to another but was originally limited only to private sector undertakings. New case law established that it should have been extended to public sector employees. This reduced the extent to which competitive tendering could be based on straightforward cuts in remuneration packages.

In addition to limiting the influence of industry-level agreements to public sector contractors, the government also took steps to prevent unions taking action against firms that refused to recognize unions, operate closed shops or respect industry-level agreements. Regulations against secondary picketing and 'blacking' of non-union firms reduced the ability of unions to prevent the entry of non-union firms into the labour market, for example in printing.

However, the Conservative governments were not only opposed to the extension of collectively agreed minima to non-participating firms but to the whole concept of industry- or occupation-based minimum wage standards, believing that each firm should set its own rates of pay according to what it could afford. This stance against industry-level agreements had little direct effect in the first instance, but as the 1980s progressed many industry-level collective agreements disappeared as large employers took government advice and withdrew and as small employers felt under less pressure or obligation to agree to a settlement and were willing to contemplate what in earlier times would have been unthinkable, the permanent demise of the industry agreement. The outcome was that many firms, particularly small ones, were left without any guidance at the industry or national level as to what wage rates or wage increases to pay. The policy that each firm should decide for itself what to pay was turned from an option into a necessity with the disappearance of the standard benchmarks as to what was a reasonable minimum rate of pay, provided by Wages Councils and by national agreements.

These regulatory changes considerably narrowed the scope and influence of wage protection mechanisms that had set a floor to wages in the 1960s and 1970s. The impact of these regulatory changes has been reinforced by changes in the structure and composition of employment, away from manufacturing and towards services, and away from large and towards small firms. These have reduced the scope and scale of collective regulation, although the maintenance of public sector service sector employment, where unionization remains high, has to some extent offset these effects.

Part-time work has also increased, again increasing problems of organization. Growth of female employment is also often cited as a reason for reductions in union coverage, but, as discussed in chapters 9 and 10, the lower rates of unionization among women are more associated with the type of industry in which they are employed, and their involvement in part-time work, than with gender differences per se, and the gender gap in unionization is narrowing, not widening. However, women constitute the bulk of low-paid workers, many of them being low-paid even when covered by forms of collective bargaining (McNabb and Whitfield 2000). Thus the increase in female employment may itself be considered to expand the potential pool of low-paid workers. Women workers may be vulnerable to low pay in part because they are often ineligible for unemployment benefits, due to part-time or intermittent participation in employment. Thus they may be willing to take low-paid jobs if the choice appears to be no other source of income. Changes to benefit and pay structures in the 1980s and 1990s further increased competition in the low-paid segments of the labour market. Firstly the link between young people's pay and adult workers' pay was targeted in a series of policies, including the removal of young people from the scope of Wages Councils, the payment of a low allowance to young people on the Youth Training Scheme, well below the rates previously set for trainees in collective agreements, and the Young Workers Scheme (in operation from 1983 to 1985), which provided a subsidy to employers who took on young people provided they paid a wage below a fixed amount. These measures, coupled with the impact of high unemployment among young people in the early 1980s, resulted in a significant widening in the rates of pay between adult and youth labour, turning young people into a source of low-wage competition in the labour market.

More pressures have also been placed on the unemployed to take low-wage jobs, and the cushion of the earnings-related supplement to unemployment benefit was removed. The large increase in the numbers of unemployed in the early 1980s, and again in the 1990s, in itself added considerably to competitive pressure on wages at the bottom of the labour market.

The National Minimum Wage

Britain's first comprehensive National Minimum Wage (NMW), as contrasted to the patchy coverage of the Wages Councils, was introduced in April 1999. This section discusses the process through which the NMW was established, its key components, and views of its effects.

The principle of an NMW has been discussed among low-pay pressure groups and trade unions for many years. Proposals 'were at the centre of industrial relations debate in the late 1960s and early 1970s, although enthusiasm . . . subsequently evaporated among trade unions' as part of their opposition to the wages policies of the governments of the time (Pond 1983: 206). Union opposition to an NMW, reflecting a fear that it would undermine the role of collective bargaining, effectively blocked further discussion. But, as discussed above, by the early 1980s unions representing the low-paid came to the view that, even where it existed, collective bargaining was not resolving the problem of low pay, and that the problem of extending bargaining to sectors without it was proving intractable. In 1986 the TUC endorsed the principle of an NMW, which was also part of Labour Party election manifestos in 1992 and 1997.

The Labour government elected in 1997 appointed the Low Pay Commission (LPC) in July, and the Commission's recommendations were published a year later. The LPC was initially appointed simply to recommend on the level and coverage of the NMW, but it has since continued in being. It has nine members, from employer, employee and academic backgrounds. It claims that it 'embodies the principle of social partnership' (LPC 1998: p. ix) through its composition and its endeavours to reach agreed recommendations. At the time of its introduction, the NMW was highly controversial, with employer opposition centring on potential cost rises and job losses and implying a low level for the NMW, while proponents sought a significantly higher rate. Yet the Commission reached a unanimous conclusion. Independent commentators have also remarked on the value of this joint approach, the result being that the NMW has not been a major source of political dispute. The Conservative Party announced in early 2000 its conversion to the principle of the NMW.

The LPC's recommendations were largely accepted by the government. The rate for adult workers (those aged over 21) was set at £3.60 an hour, though there was no commitment to any formula for increasing this rate. The rate was increased to £3.70 in October 2000, with a much more significant rise of 40 pence to £4.10 from October 2001. Workers aged 18–21 initially received a rate of £3, rising to £3.20 in June 2000. Workers aged under 18 were excluded from coverage. The £3.60 was roughly equivalent to half of male median earnings, in contrast to the level of two-thirds of the median which is the widely accepted measure of low pay. Stewart (1999: 226) notes that two-thirds of full-time median pay would have been £5.13 or £4.57 per hour in 1997, depending on which of two data sources is used.

The coverage of the NMW is broad: all workers, including homeworkers for example, are covered, and it excludes only the genuinely self-employed. In its second report, the LPC (2000: 63–71) noted some particular issues of coverage, for example workers in the voluntary sector and seafarers, but no major problems. Pay counting towards the NMW comprises all standard earnings, that is basic pay and incentives such as piecework payment. Premium payments for overtime and shift working are excluded. Tips and gratuities are included only when they are paid through the payroll. Employers are required to define a pay reference period up to a maximum of a month. Standard pay received during the period is divided by the hours worked to produce an average hourly rate.

The NMW was set at a level which was believed to be acceptable to the majority of employers, many of whom had already raised wages in anticipation. The LPC (2000: 102) accordingly reports on the basis of several studies that it commissioned that 'most employers are complying'. Not surprisingly, compliance is lowest on the fringes of the economy and among groups such as homeworkers. One study (Gilman et al. 2002) found that compliance was weak in Asian-owned restaurants and parts of the clothing industry, reflecting the fact that many workers were employed 'off the books' and without any clear definition of hours of work. The most obvious means of evasion is to require workers to work longer hours than are in fact recorded. The study found that firms could move in one of two directions: employing all workers on formal contracts; or moving downmarket, to operate within the black economy and accede to the requests of some workers, who were also claiming social security benefits, to be paid cash in hand. As for homeworkers, the LPC-commissioned projects found that several had seen increases in their pay, though 'substantial numbers' continued to be underpaid (LPC 2000: 106). A key issue was that the legally required written agreements on working hours, aimed to prevent the working of unrecorded hours, were not being used.

Enforcement is in the hands of the Inland Revenue. In the first year of the NMW's operation, only a few cases came to public attention. This reflects the

Table 17.4   Minimum wages in selected countries, 1999

| | Rate per hour (£) | | As % median earnings |
	At current exchange rates	Purchasing Power Parity	
UK	3.60	3.60	43
Australia	3.79	4.83	54
France	3.97	4.10	57
Japan	3.74	2.57	31
Netherlands	4.19	4.56	49
USA	3.18	3.38	38

Source: LPC (1999: 210–12, 2000: 181), except for UK NMW as % median earnings, which is calculated from New Earnings Survey 1999.

generally high level of awareness of the NMW and the fact that, according to the LPC, most employers either comply after an initial approach from the Inland Revenue or do so after a threat of legal action.

This system has parallels with those in other countries. Some countries, notably France and the Unites States, have statutory minimum wages. In others, such as Germany, there is no NMW as such but the well-established principle of extending collective agreements across a whole sector means that there are effective floors to pay levels. The value of an NMW can be considered in terms of its absolute level and its relationship to the average pay level in a country. As shown in table 17.4, on both these measures the British NMW falls in the middle of the range of advanced industrial economies. In countries with statutory systems, variations of the minimum according to age are common, though in many some form of protection is provided to those aged under 18. In France, for example, 17-year-olds receive 90 per cent of the adult minimum (for the first six months of employment, followed by entitlement to the adult rate, which starts at the age of 18).

An NMW can have a wide range of effects. As shown in box 17.1, the most obvious are on the wages of people formerly paid below its level and on the wages of other workers as a result of the restoration of pay differentials. These two wage effects will then affect employers' pay bills and profits and, potentially, the number of jobs they can offer. Yet employers may be able to offset some costs. One possibility is that a rise in wages makes low-paying jobs more attractive, thus bringing forward more skilled workers and reducing the costs of recruitment (which can be considerable, given that low-paying jobs are often in sectors of very high labour turnover). A second offset could come from increased work effort, which embraces simply harder work during each working hour or reductions in former benefits such as paid rest breaks. A particularly controversial issue is productivity. Proponents of an NMW have long argued that it will tend to 'shock' firms into more efficient working practices, and there is some evidence (reviewed by Edwards and Gilman 1999) to sustain this view. Yet the alternative view, that if work practices were beneficial they would already have been introduced, is equally plausible. It is possible that making labour more expensive than other inputs will encourage firms to introduce labour-saving methods that would otherwise not be profitable, but the size of such an effect is hard to predict. Estimating each effect is difficult in itself. They will also interact with each other, and they will of course be influenced by the state of the economy as a whole. Finally, the effects discussed above are static, not dynamic. Yet some researchers argue, for example, that even if an NMW destroys some jobs it does so in the least efficient firms in a sector and is likely to affect whole sectors which have low productivity. The longer-run dynamic consequence may be to shift labour to more efficient operations.

Box 17.1   Potential labour relations effects of an NMW

Costs	Compensating changes
Increase in pay of those below NMW	Increased labour supply and/or lower labour turnover
Effect on pay differentials	Ease of recruitment
Employers' pay bill	Increased work effort
Effect on employment	Reductions in breaks and/or benefits in kind
Administration and enforcement	Productivity
	Reduced threat of 'unfair' competition

The bulk of research in countries with long-established minimum wage systems has focused on one particular effect, namely on employment, and has used econometric estimating techniques. Many studies find negative, albeit small, effects on employment, particularly that of young workers. Yet assumptions about such things as the effects on higher-paid workers and the specific form of estimating equations have significant effects on the size of estimates. There is also a body of literature, notably the work of Card and Krueger (1995) in the United States, which reports positive effects. The major explanation is that of monopsony power in the labour market (see Edwards and Gilman 1999 for details). Whereas monopoly power is the ability to set prices at above their competitive value, monopsony is the power to buy goods or labour at below competitive values. It exists, according to the theory, because of market imperfections and the fact that labour may not be able to move freely between employers as a result of geographical immobility or other factors. Where it exists in labour markets, wages will be below their market level, and an NMW will thus cut profits but not necessarily affect employment; employment could even rise if the supply of labour rose. UK research on the Wages Councils is consistent with the monopsony view (Dickens et al. 1999). A measure of Wages Council 'toughness' was defined as the ratio of council minima to average earnings. Conventional expectations would be that tough Wages Council rates would push up wages and thus cut employment. In fact, the research found that there was a positive association between toughness and employment levels, which the researchers interpreted in terms of monopsony effects.

The problem with such explanations is that they describe some aspects of labour markets but do not explain the origins of monopsony. As Card and Krueger admit, they depart only slightly from neo-classical economics. Yet, as shown in chapter 8, it is well established that labour markets rarely clear, and that a range of institutional mechanisms influence the level of wages (see also Rubery 1997). Employers have a range of indeterminacy in the setting of wages, reflecting the facts that employees take into account a wide range of factors as well as pay in judging where to work, that pay relativities are often vague and shifting, and that information on pay in other firms may be lacking. Research on small firms, which are disproportionately likely to be low-paying, discussed in chapter 18, shows that pay structures are often informal and that decisions on pay rates are shaped by personal relationships and rather broad standards of fairness as well as by market forces. The effects of an NMW are mediated by such factors and cannot be predicted mechanically.

More institutionally based explanations would stress the following. First, the effects of the NMW on differentials within a given firm will be shaped by the structure of pay-bargaining. Given that collective bargaining is rare across the economy and even rarer in the low-paying sectors (in 80 per cent of small businesses identified in WERS pay was set by management alone or through individual negotiation: Cully et al. 1999: 269), organized collective means to restore differentials will be weak. Differentials are also often stated in terms of ranks rather than percentage differences. Second, because of the fragmentation of pay-bargaining, pay rises in the low-paying sectors are unlikely to be translated into other parts of the economy. Third, the range of indeterminacy in firms affected by the NMW seems to be at least as large as it is in higher-paying organizations (Gilman et al. 2002). The scope for firms to adjust to the NMW without job losses is thus considerable.

Given that the British NMW has operated for only a short time, what can be said of its effects? First, the NMW clearly raised the pay of about 1.7 million workers; two-thirds of these were women, of whom two-thirds worked part-time. According to the LPC (2000: 16), even in the year to April 1999 'the gap in the average hourly pay of women relative to men narrowed by a full percentage point, the largest amount for almost a decade'. New Earnings Survey data up to 2000 show no change in the ratio of part-time to full-time female earnings, suggesting that any gains were shared by full- and part-timers. We also looked at NES data on the distribution of earnings. As discussed above (table 17.1), earnings became more unequal throughout the 1980s and 1990s. In 1995 gross hourly earnings at the lowest decile (D1) stood at 56.6 per cent of the median. This had risen to 57.6 by 2000. Plainly the reasons are complex, and we have highlighted above the complex interactions between an NMW and existing pay structures. Nonetheless, the reversal of a long period of decline is consistent with some role for the NMW in reducing inequality. Second, and clearly related, there has emerged a clear pay 'spike' at the NMW level, suggesting that wages are being concentrated at this point and hence that there has been an equaliza-tion of pay and that differentials effects have been small. Third, the research on Wages Council toughness and on the range of indeterminacy in pay-setting suggests that any effects on employment will be indirect and probably small.

As for effects within firms, some studies have found compensating effects such as the reduction of paid rest breaks or the consolidation of previous bonus payments (e.g. a firm formerly paying, say, £3 basic and £4 for overtime may now pay £3.60 for all hours). Just how extensive these effects are is impossible to say since many of them will be subtle. It appears that they are most likely where a firm faces financial difficulties, and they are unlikely to be very wide-spread. Efficiency effects are equally hard to pin down. Some current unpublished research suggests that small numbers of firms which face expanding markets or have the means to move upmarket may be able to make such improvements, such as introducing new equipment or increasing training (Arrowsmith et al. 2001). Yet some low-paying sectors such as hotels and catering lack any clear means to up-skill, while the fact that the NMW was introduced at an 'accept-able' level suggests that the incentive to make such changes will in many cases be small. As argued above and in chapter 3, moreover, the skills structure of British firms tends to discourage innovation, so that the contextual conditions promoting up-skilling are weak.

The LPC's research (2000: 28) indicated some efficiency improvements. But it is important to note what is meant here. The largest group among a survey of firms said that they had tightened control of labour costs (almost 40 per cent had done so to a significant degree). This does not mean efficiency in the strict sense, but rather increased work effort in the terms of box 17.1. About 30 per cent had changed work organization significantly, with much smaller proportions citing such things as increased investment in training and development. The implica-tion of these and other similar surveys is that a majority of firms have made few changes as a result of the NMW. Some have sought compensating increases in work effort and some have made genuine productivity improvements. There will also be firms on the margins of the economy which have ignored the NMW. The overall impact seems to have been a small but noticeable effect on effi-ciency, albeit highly variable between firms, together with only small effects on employment. This evidence of rather limited effects is of course consistent with the NMW having been set at a relatively low level.

Conclusions

International comparative research shows that the decline of trade unions has been a significant influence on the increase in pay inequality (Machin 1999). Research in Britain reveals in addition that low-paid jobs are rarely stepping-stones to higher-paying employment: some people are trapped in a cycle of low pay and no pay (Stewart 1999). Studies of low-paying firms (see chapter 18; also Gilman et al. 2002) suggest some of the reasons why. Labour markets are structured by occupation, gender and type of firm, and once people are placed in low-paying jobs they may lack the resources to escape. The processes generating low pay intensified during the 1980s and 1990s as a result of legislative change and the further weakening of collective bargaining.

The NMW is one of a series of measures aimed at altering the operation of the low-wage labour market. Others include the New Deal, which helps the unemployed into work, and the Working Families Tax Credit, aimed at reducing the disincentive to taking paid employment faced by unemployed people with children. The WFTC effectively protects low-income families from the impact of low wages on living standards. However, without an NMW the cost of the WFTC to the state could prove to be very high as employers might be happy to allow the state to make up the gap between low wages and acceptable living standards. Moreover some key low-paid groups, such as women in couples with employed partners and young people, are not eligible for WFTC and remain reliant on the NMW to protect their income levels. It is too early yet to judge the combined impact of these various measures on the low-wage labour market, but the level of the NMW will continue to be a critical factor for the majority of the recipients of low wages who remain ineligible for the new tax credit system.

The NMW was not designed to eliminate low pay, only to reduce its extent and intensity. It was deliberately set at a level which many firms believed to be manageable, with the aim of establishing a wage floor on which collective bargaining could operate. Low pay is also a reflection of other processes in the labour market, such as the extent of gender segregation and the organization of part-time work. To the extent that the NMW interacts with these processes, it may tend in the long run to reverse the rise in pay inequality observed after 1980. How far this happens will also depend on three factors. First and most crucially, it will depend on the level at which the NMW is set in the future. The experience of the first two years has already revealed the vulnerability of the determination process to political factors as well as to perceptions of the economic cycle. Electoral considerations and the relative buoyancy of the economy must be considered important factors in the decision in 2001 to allow a rise in the NMW above the rate of earnings inflation. It is equally possible to imagine other periods when the political and economic factors will lead to very different decisions. Protection against low pay requires the adoption of a genuinely independent decision-making process, based for example on some form of indexation, but the current government is not willing to contemplate the NMW being taken out of its political control. The second factor that will shape the pattern of wage inequality will be the kind of new jobs that are generated. Although there was no uniform trend in pay dispersion over the 1980s and 1990s, very few countries experienced a compression in pay and several saw a rise in dispersion. Some attribute this to changes in the structure and demand for skills, and no doubt the increase in wages in some advanced technology sectors can be related to an increased demand for those with key skills (Machin 1999). However, at the other end of the labour market the factors that drive the creation of particular forms of work, for example low-paid and often part-time work in the service sector, are related to a wide set of institutional arrangements in society, from the pattern of gender relations and the availability of childcare to the system of national insurance contributions and the promotion of private sector providers of public service employment. Thus the growth of low-paid part-time work in the UK is shaped by a whole range of factors which provide incentives to employers to organize work in this way (O'Reilly and Fagan 1998). Many people, particularly women returners, still remain underemployed in the labour market and have in any case little access to training opportunities to improve their labour market position. The third and related factor shaping the evaluation of wage inequality is the development of trade union organization and collective bargaining. The NMW may have been set at a level to allow collective bargaining to operate, but that space may not be taken up and utilized.

One further possibility is that there will be a polarization of labour market conditions. There are some suggestions that the NMW may sharpen the divide between 'legitimate' businesses which comply with it and illicit operations which ignore it or work on the margins, for example paying workers fixed sums per day and under-recording the actual hours of work. Evidence to date suggests that this latter group may be small, and concentrated in certain sectors such as restaurants and clothing. Yet it is unlikely to be removed, and it can draw on workers who lack the skills and experience to enter the mainstream labour market. The margins of the system are likely to be redefined, not eliminated.

One policy issue is thus to focus enforcement of the NMW in certain sectors of the economy. A different and more complex issue is the pursuit of positive effects of the NMW (Brosnan and Wilkinson 1987; Deakin and Wilkinson 1990; Sachdev and Wilkinson 1998). As this chapter has stressed, the dynamics of low pay reflect the interaction of legislation with a series of developments in firms and labour markets. Firms subject to the NMW are likely to be small and in competitive industries, conditions where it is most difficult to engage in training and other means of developing human capital. It should thus not be assumed that they will necessarily be 'shocked' into better labour relations policies, though the evidence suggests that this will be true of a minority. To increase the size of this minority may take efforts to encourage firms to consider changes in work organization and improved attention to training. The NMW is a major change in the contours of low-wage labour markets. Its possibilities will not be realized without further effort in a range of other policy areas.

Notes

1 The consultative document published by the government on the abolition of Wages Councils indicated that the fact that many of the workers covered by Wages Councils were part-timers, contributing a second income to the household, was a factor in the decision to abolish the councils.
2 The reform of the Wages Councils introduced in 1986 reduced their powers to set anything other than a minimum rate of pay and an overtime rate. Thus rates for skilled workers, regional differentials and holiday pay arrangements were no longer set by the councils. The other part of the reform was to take those under 21 out of the scope of the councils (previously minimum wages were generally applied at 18 and younger workers received a lower but regulated minimum wage).

References

Arrowsmith, J., Gilman, M., Edwards, P. and Ram, M. 2001: Regulatory change and employment relations in small firms. Unpublished paper, Industrial Relations Research Unit, University of Warwick, January.

Bayliss, F. 1962: *British Wages Councils*. Oxford: Blackwell.

Bazen, S., Gregory, M. and Salverda, W. (eds) 1998: *Low-Wage Employment in Europe*. Cheltenham: Edward Elgar.

Brosnan, P., and Wilkinson, F. 1987: A National Statutory Minimum Wage and economic efficiency, *Contributions to Political Economy*, 7, 1–48.

Card, D., and Krueger, A. B. 1995: *Myth and Measurement: The New Economics of the Minimum Wage*. Princeton: Princeton University Press.

Craig, C., Garnsey, E. and Rubery, J. 1985: *Payment Structures and Smaller Firms: Women's Employment in Segmented Labour Markets*. Department of Employment Research Paper 48. London.

Craig, C., Rubery, J., Tarling, R. and Wilkinson, F. 1982: *Labour Market Structure, Worker Organisation and Low Pay*. Cambridge: Cambridge University Press.

Crompton, R., and Sandersen, K. 1990: *Gendered Jobs and Social Change*. London: Unwin Hyman.

Cully, M., Woodland, S., O'Reilly, A. and Dix, G. 1999: *Britain at Work*. London: Routledge.

Deakin, S., and Wilkinson, F. 1990: *The Economics of Employment Rights*. London: Institute of Employment Rights.

Dex, S., Robson, P. and Wilkinson, F. 1999: The characteristics of the low paid: a cross-national comparison, *Work Employment and Society*, 13 (3), 503–24.

Dickens, R., Machin, S. and Manning, A. 1999: The effects of minimum wages on employment: theory and evidence from Britain, *Journal of Labor Economics*, 17 (1), 1–22.

Edwards, P. K., and Gilman, M. 1999: Pay equity and the National Minimum Wage, *Human Resource Management Journal*, 9 (1), 20–38.

Gilman, M., Edwards, P., Ram, M. and Arrowsmith, J. 2002: Pay determination in small firms in the UK, *Industrial Relations Journal*, 33 (1), 52–67.

Gornick, J. C., and Jacobs, J. 1996: A cross-national analysis of part-time workers' wages, *Work, Employment and Society*, 10 (1), 1–27.

Grimshaw, D. and Rubery, J. 1997: *The Concentration of Women's Employment and Relative Occupational Pay: A Statistical Framework for Comparative Analysis*. OECD Labour Market and Social Policy Occasional Paper 26.

Johnson, P., and Stark, G. 1991: The effects of a minimum wage on family incomes, *Fiscal Studies*, 12 (1), 88–93.

Layard, R., Piachaud, D. and Stewart, M. 1978: *The Causes of Poverty*. Royal Commission on the Distribution of Income and Wealth, Background Paper 5. London: HMSO.

LPC (Low Pay Commission) 1998: *The National Minimum Wage: First Report of the Low Pay Commission*. Cm 3976. London: HMSO.

LPC 2000: *The National Minimum Wage: The Story So Far*. Cm 4571. London: Stationery Office.

Lucas, R., and Radiven, N. 1998: After wages councils: minimum pay and practice, *Human Resource Management Journal*, 8 (4), 5–19.

Machin, S. 1999: Wage inequality in the 1970s, the 1980s and the 1990s. In P. Gregg and J. Wadsworth (eds), *The State of Working Britain*. Manchester: Manchester University Press.

Marsden, D., and Ryan, P. 1991: Youth pay and training in industrial countries. In P. Ryan, R. Edwards and P. Garonna (eds), *The Problem of Youth*. Basingstoke: Macmillan.

McNabb, R., and Whitfield, K. 2000: 'Worth so appallingly little': a workplace-level analysis of low pay, *British Journal of Industrial Relations*, 38 (4), 585–610.

OECD 1993: *Employment Outlook*. Paris: OECD.

OECD 1996: *Employment Outlook*. Paris: OECD.

OECD 1999: *Employment Outlook*. Paris: OECD.

O'Reilly, J., and Fagan, C. (eds) 1998: *Part-Time Prospects: Part-Time Employment in Europe, North America and the Pacific Rim*. London: Routledge.

Pond, C. 1983: Wages councils, the unorganised and the low paid. In G. S. Bain (ed.), *Industrial Relations in Britain*. Oxford: Blackwell.

Rubery, J. 1994: The British production regime: a societal-specific system, *Economy and Society*, 23 (3), 335–54.

Rubery, J. 1997: Wages and the labour market. *British Journal of Industrial Relations*, 35 (3), 337–62.

Rubery, J. 1998: Part-time work: a threat to labour standards. In O'Reilly and Fagan (eds), *Part-Time Prospects: Part-Time Employment in Europe, North America and the Pacific Rim*. London: Routledge.

Ryan, P. 1987: Trade unionism and the pay of young workers. In P. Junankar (ed.), *From School to Unemployment: The Labour Market for Young People*. London: Macmillan.

Sachdev, S., and Wilkinson, F. 1998: *Low Pay, the Working of the Labour Market and the Role of a Minimum Wage*. London: Institute of Employment Rights.

Stewart, M. B. 1999: Low pay in Britain. In P. Gregg and J. Wadsworth (eds), *The State of Working Britain*. Manchester: Manchester University Press.

Wedderburn, D. (ed.) 1974: *Poverty, Inequality and Class Structure*. Cambridge: Cambridge University Press.

Zabalza, A., and Tzannatsos, Z. 1985: *Women and Equal Pay*. Cambridge: Cambridge University Press.

18
EMPLOYMENT RELATIONS IN SMALL FIRMS

RICHARD SCASE

Our knowledge of industrial relations in small firms is highly limited for two major reasons. First, small businesses have received little attention in academic social research. Second, issues of employer–employee relations have been considered to be non-problematic on the grounds that 'harmony' prevails. This chapter queries this assumption and suggests that there is a diversity of attitudes and practices within the small firms sector which, in turn, affect the character of social relations that exist between employers and employees. It argues that there is a need for further detailed comparative research that will enable us to understand more adequately the diversity of employers' strategies and how these, within different contexts, are negotiated with employees to determine varying patterns of accommodation ranging from positive commitment to sullen acquiescence. The chapter concludes with some suggestions for further research, emphasizing the need for the study of employment relations in non-traditional small businesses where interpersonal relations are quite different from those of the small firms which have, to date, dominated research.

The Economic and Industrial Relations Context

Figures from the 15 EU states for 1994 show that 66 per cent of all employment was in businesses with fewer than 250 employees; half of these employees were in firms with fewer than 10 workers, with those with 10–49 workers accounting for a further 19 per cent (*EIRObserver* 1999: p. i). The UK's figures are slightly below the EU average but still substantial. The sector has been growing, for reasons including the growth of the sectors where small firms are particularly common (such as services and IT) and outsourcing by large companies.

A standard image of the employment relation in small firms is of informality based on close personal ties, which is contrasted with the formal procedures of large firms. This has always been a simplification. It has long been established that there is informality in large firms (Hill 1974), while the decline of collective

Table 18.1 Pay determination by size of organization (% of workplaces)

	Small businesses	Small multiples	Workplaces with >25 employees		
			All	Private	Public
Only collective bargaining	1	14	15	9	33
Only management decision	67	71	48	63	10
Only individual negotiation	13	1	3	3	0
Only other means	5	10	8	3	20
Mix of methods	14	5	26	22	37

Source: Cully et al. (1999: 109, 269). By permission of Routledge.

bargaining analysed in chapter 8 means that in such key areas as pay determination formal procedures are much less prevalent than they were in the past. It is certainly true that some standard features of industrial relations are less common in small firms than large ones. The Labour Force Survey (using size of workplace and not company as the criterion) shows that in 1997 union density was 16 per cent in workplaces of fewer than 25 employees, as against 38 per cent in larger workplaces. The 1998 WERS distinguished small businesses (independent sites with between 10 and 99 employees) and small multiples (workplaces of the same size owned by larger companies). Individual grievance procedures were present in 68 per cent of the former and 95 per cent of the latter. As for collective bargaining, table 18.1 sets out figures for these two groups and compares them with those for all workplaces with over 25 employees. Collective bargaining is rare across the whole of the private sector, and virtually unknown in small businesses.

Other features of small businesses complement this picture of overlap with large firms. Thus small firms are often seen as the home of managerial prerogative and harsh discipline. Yet the contrast between 'small businesses' and all workplaces with more than 25 employees in WERS is not great (e.g. 2.4 and 1.9 complaints to an employment tribunal per 1,000 workers employed). Multivariate analysis shows that a greater size of the workplace was associated with a high and not a low dismissal rate (Knight and Latreille 2000). Similarly, the link between size and low pay is more complex than often thought, with small establishments in small organizations having a lower than average proportion of low-paid employees (McNabb and Whitfield 2000). One reason is that small organizations are remarkably heterogeneous: it is true that small firms in some sectors pay low wages and have harsh discipline. But even then uniformity should not be assumed. One study of small firms in three low-paying sectors found a range of pay across the firms of a similar magnitude to that common between large firms: individual variation can be quite dramatic (Gilman et al. 2002). To understand small firms' employment relations we need to place them in context.

The Role and Nature of Small Firms

Until recently, small businesses were seen as a declining feature of the modern economy (Goss 1991a). Forces of modern capitalism, with their inherent tendencies to the concentration and centralization of production, would lead to the growth of monopoly and quasi-monopoly enterprises, contributing to the long-term decline of small-scale forms of production. This was a predominant assumption among many Marxist writers in the 1980s who, in their belief in inevitable historical tendencies, considered small firms to be of little intellectual interest. Indeed, they viewed them as a 'relic' of an earlier stage within the development of the capitalist mode of production (Wright 1978). Alongside increasing concentration of economic production, it was held that there is a growing polarization of labour markets as craft forms of work become superseded by tasks that require little in the form of skills. Accordingly, the deskilling of work went alongside the growth of large corporations, leading to the emergence of class structures wherein the petite bourgeoisie – the self-employed and the owners of small-scale enterprises – were becoming irrelevant (Scase 1982). Such theoretical assumptions among social scientists led them to focus almost exclusively upon the labour processes and the social relations of large-scale corporations, since it was these that were considered to be the 'motors' of economic development and the context within which major class struggles are acted out (Braverman 1974). The outcome has been an industrial sociology and an industrial relations which have as their underpinnings theories of labour process based on the social relations of large-scale corporations. Accordingly, with a few notable exceptions, the employment relations of small firms have been regarded as being of secondary or, indeed, peripheral interest.

It was not until the late 1980s that detailed and theoretically informed enquiries began to investigate the social dynamics of small firms. At that time, it was recognized that the economies of western Europe and the United States were undergoing a number of fundamental structural changes such that small-scale forms of economic organization were becoming more, rather than less, prevalent. Further, it was more readily admitted by social scientists that processes associated with the internal dynamics of large-scale organizations – which had been to the forefront of their preoccupations – could only be fully understood by reference to those same structural processes associated with the growth of small firms (Piore and Sabel 1984). Hence, it became accepted that small businesses constituted a legitimate area of academic enquiry because of a range of ideological and material functions that these fulfil in modern capitalist society.

The functions of small firms

Ideologically, small firms fulfil a key function in the modern economy because they sustain notions of competition and of the free market. As such, they conceal the dominance that quasi-monopoly corporations are able to exercise within many economic sectors. Equally, the possibilities for business start-up, absent as they were from the formerly state socialist countries of eastern Europe, underwrite claims that market economies are 'open' and offer opportunities for personal success for those who are prepared to extend the necessary 'effort and self-sacrifice'. Accordingly, the persistence of strata of self-employed and small-scale employers offers the 'promise' of personal achievement for those who for a variety of reasons are disadvantaged in the pursuit of more conventional careers within the more hierarchical structures of large-scale organizations (Burrows 1991). Women and members of ethnic minorities are often attracted to entrepreneurship and small-scale business proprietorship as a result of perceiving that, for reasons of prejudice, discrimination and social disadvantage, they are unlikely to obtain occupational success by means of more traditional career routes (Goffee and Scase 1985). As such, business start-up – as an ideological appeal – functions as a safety valve within the capitalist order.

But if entrepreneurship and small business ownership have a significant function in legitimizing the predominant capitalist order, their material contribution is even more pronounced. As noted above, small businesses employ approximately one-third of all workers in the European Union. Consequently, they fulfil a key function in determining the pay, working and living conditions of millions of workers and are thus highly significant in the structuring of labour markets. They are equally significant in the impact which they have upon the policies formulated by organizations representing the interests of large employers, unions and governments. Witness the role of the French farming community in the determination of EU agricultural policies, and similarly the lobbying of small business organizations in Britain in shaping the legislation affecting employment and social legislation.

But perhaps most importantly of all, small businesses often have close economic relationships with larger enterprises. Indeed, the profits and growth of the latter can be highly contingent upon their relationships with the former, as has become clear for example in Japan, where the position of large firms is dependent on a network of small ones which insulate the large firms from economic fluctuations. Often this will take the form of subcontracting, as in manufacturing, or of licensing and franchising, as in retailing. In the case of the former, various components are manufactured out of house before being assembled into completed products within large-scale work processes. Indeed, since the very beginnings of the industrial revolution, the growth of manufacturing has been characterized by the parallel processes of *centralization* and *decentralization* in productive activities.

In manufacturing, Fordist production methods, based upon the principles of scientific management and the standardization of products, have been heavily dependent upon subcontractors who, in competition with each other, provide the various components for later assembly. Emergence of the 'post-Fordist' flexible firm has merely reinforced this trend, as too has the growth of high-technology, knowledge-based companies. These trends have encouraged the fragmentation of labour markets, the differentiation of working conditions and employment relations, and the growth of enterprise-based payment systems. They create, in other words, the very material and ideological conditions that militate against the development of collective organization, action and consciousness among employees (Sabel 1982). Centre-periphery labour markets, with the periphery consisting of those engaged in lower-paid, insecure and usually unskilled jobs in small-scale enterprises, are a feature of almost all of the capitalist economies and tend to be a direct outcome of the relations of dependency and symbiosis that exist between large- and small-scale enterprises (Friedman 1977). Such features of national labour markets continue to persist, though they tend to be concealed beneath managerial rhetoric which extols the virtues of 'network' organizations, strategic alliances, joint ventures, 'externalizing' production and just-in-time methods of management.

Within these managerial strategies, small businesses become increasingly locked within webs of dependency, with their economic viability determined by the purchasing capacity of their major customers. It is a feature of the 'Information Economy' which largely goes unrecognized, particularly by the politicians of 'New Labour'.

Although not all small firms are located within such market conditions, in one way or another, the economic circumstances of the great majority are either directly or indirectly affected. Even those geared to trading within the areas of internet technologies and business services rather than in declining traditional manufacturing are constrained by the dictates of the market as shaped by the policies and strategies of large-scale companies. Indeed, the market context of small firms and the variable relationships between them and large corporations, constitute distinct categories which have been used for the purposes of analysing small businesses. According to Rainnie, it is possible to identify four types of such firms: *dependent, dominated, isolated* and *innovative* (Rainnie 1989). Although his typology was constructed for the purposes of analysing small firms in manufacturing sectors, it remains equally applicable to business transaction in the emergent 'service' and 'information' sectors of the economies of the twenty-first century.

Varieties of small firm

For Rainnie, *dependent* firms are of the kind discussed above. Their economic viability is determined by the larger customers with whom they trade. However, because they act as subcontractors (service providers), for example in the engineering and electronics industries, the nature of their internal work processes is also externally regulated through their purchasers' specifications about quality and quantity of output. Negotiated prices within usually highly competitive market circumstances clearly have knock-on effects for costs, including level of wages, fringe benefits and, hence, employer–employee relations. Even so, such constraints merely constitute parameters within which a variety of negotiated arrangements between staff and their employers can be determined. Often the owners, as service providers, can be little more than sub-agents for their larger customers. What has been enabled by the widespread adoption of internet technologies is the extent to which this progress can now operate on a global rather than a purely national or local basis. Many small firms in south China and the

Far East, for instance, are 'locked in to the global supply chains of large companies based in Europe and the United States' (Radice 2000).

Dominated enterprises, as in the expanding retail and service sectors, compete against larger organizations on the basis of their lower operating costs. Through their lower costs, they are able to maintain their position in the marketplace, but according to 'rules' dictated by larger employers. Accordingly, the proprietors of these smaller businesses are compelled by their market position to offer lower rates of pay and relatively poorer working conditions. For these reasons, they tend to attract employees whose bargaining position is weak and who have limited job opportunities. Such enterprises often require relatively unskilled labour and, as a result they tend to hire staff on a short-term, part-time and often temporary basis. Employees in such enterprises are potentially vulnerable to the exploitative demands of their employers but, again, the outcome can be a variety of employer–employee relationships, some of which are characterized by 'harmonious' modes of accommodation. This is usually important in order to provide 'good customer service'.

Rainnie describes *isolated* businesses as those trading in markets which larger enterprises have chosen to avoid for reasons to do with lack of profit margin or of potential for longer-term business growth. Small businesses trading in specialist and localized market niches will be constrained by costs which must be kept low since otherwise their competitive advantage will be destroyed. Many sectors of the leisure, hotel and catering industries can be described in these terms, consisting as they do of large numbers of isolated small businesses which are only able to survive because of their low prices and hence the lower wages which they offer. In these businesses there is an overwhelming tendency to employ staff on a short-term or part-time basis, offering jobs to those who are unable to obtain alternative employment. Yet differences from dependent and dominated firms are important, as Moule (1998), for example, shows in his analysis of a small firm making buttons which had secured a niche position in its market. This meant that workers enjoyed a degree of employment stability and the ability to negotiate details of the effort bargain.

Finally, Rainnie identifies *innovative* small businesses which operate in high-risk areas because of their commitment to developing new products and services. These are the enterprises that are given the greatest prominence in political debate and it is these which are seen to offer 'solutions' to macro-economic problems ranging from unemployment to lack of industrial innovation and modernization. They are viewed as capable of overcoming the so-called problems of large-scale enterprises because of their allegedly greater potential to respond to changing customer needs. Such small firms are often portrayed as the 'key' to Britain's economic success when large sectors of manufacturing have been destroyed by a variety of global and national economic and political processes. Undoubtedly, there are some small businesses that are established by those who, as engineers, scientists and experts in other fields, have identified niches in the market for new products and services. But such corporate ventures are far fewer than those which have close relations with larger corporate partners with whom they share various licensing and funding arrangements. More often than not, the innovative products and services developed by small firms are those which would be too costly or irrelevant for larger organizations to pursue. It is, for them, more cost-effective to cultivate 'arm's-length' relations with smaller enterprises so that when the development of an innovative product suggests profitable potential, they can take equity stakes, offer distribution facilities, and even take over the production of patented commodities. The electronics, computer software and biotechnology industries offer countless examples of large companies reducing both their risks and costs through their relationships with small firms.

In the analysis of small firms and the understanding of their role in a modern economy it is, then, necessary to understand the economic context within which they operate and the extent to which their viability is highly contingent upon the activities of larger enterprises that are dominant within different economic sectors. However, the study of small businesses tends to be undertaken in isolation from these broader processes, and political debate is inclined to regard them as highly autonomous enterprises which, in various ways, function to generate new and relatively autonomous economic and industrial sectors. It is through such reasoning that the Labour government's small business policies tend to be orientated towards regional neighbourhood and economic renewal. It hopes that business start-up in declining industrial regions can kick-start high-technology economic growth. But it is only by understanding wider economic processes that it is possible to identify the factors contributing to the growing popularity of small business start-ups at the beginning of the twenty-first century, and the reasons why an increasing proportion of the labour force is now self-employed or working in small firms.

Growth and survival

As already discussed, inherent processes of *concentration* and *disaggregation* characterize the capitalist mode of production. But the growth of small firms is also reinforced by forces of corporate restructuring which are leading to the break-up of forms of production that were previously assembled or manufactured 'in house'. The emergence of so-called 'flexible' firms, according to which 'core' work processes are retained while all other tasks are subcontracted or outsourced, is a feature of economic change in all of the market economies in the 1990s. Through processes of organizational fragmentation, large companies are reducing their operating costs through making their former fixed-cost in-house activities into variable costs. They are able to adopt practices of competitive tendering, to exercise tight constraints over quality control and to implement methods of just-in-time management, so that they retain all the advantages of in-house assembly and production but without the associated overheads. The adoption of internet technologies enables these 'business networks', created on the basis of operational collaboration between large and small firms in often global-based supply chains, to function more cheaply and efficiently than the in-house integration of disparate business processes (Goffee and Scase 1995).

Indeed, forces of organizational fragmentation are apparent not only in manufacturing but also in other key areas of economic activity (Tapscott 1996).

Within the financial services sector, for example, consisting of retail banking, insurance and personal savings, there has been a large increase in the numbers of those who are either self-employed as 'consultants' or engaged in partnerships and smaller business practices. Equally, in different sectors of the media industries, organizational fragmentation has led to the rapid growth of freelance workers, of the self-employed, of partnerships, and of other small-scale owner-managed enterprises. This trend has been particularly pronounced within the television and film industries, where the production and distribution of finished products consists of a series of interconnected cycles of work which have to be co-ordinated and integrated within project teams and which consist of various 'independent' small business units, many of which operate for only limited periods of time. At the end of particular programme projects or contracts, they disband, with their members regrouping for new short-term ventures. With the expansion of financial services, media and entertainment as well as of specialist business services (including information and communication technologies), the outlook for the formation and growth of small firms appears robust (Davis and Scase 2000).

The implications of these structural changes for the nature of work, employment and labour markets are far-reaching. For some commentators, they constitute the emergence of a postmodern economic order in which individuals are no longer constrained by the day-to-day drudgery associated with traditional employment relations (Handy 1984). Thus, freelances and the self-employed are able to vary their work patterns according to personal preferences and lifestyles. According to this view, they are released from the tight supervisory control and exploitative relations associated with traditional forms of large-scale manufacturing. As a result the emergence of such work patterns is claimed to render redundant the need for trade unions and institutional labour relations. Employment relations are becoming superseded by market relations according to which negotiations between parties determine the provision of technical, professional and expert services of one kind or another. There is, then, little need for collective bargaining as the forces of economic change are destroying the preconditions for organized collective labour. The break-up of traditional Fordist methods of production and the increasing abolition of standardized work tasks brings with it the decline of unionism. Indeed, according to this view, in the 'knowledge-based', postmodern, 'post-industrial' society the working class ceases to exist.

For other observers, however, the shift to self-employment, the fragmentation of large-scale enterprises through the development of forms of subcontracting and the subsequent emergence of small 'independent' (in fact, in the terms introduced above, often dependent) small firms is having quite the reverse ramifications (Goss 1991a). At best, it is reinforcing the nature of dependency and exploitation in labour markets and, at worst, creating an 'under-class' of the low-paid and unemployed. Although traditional Fordist methods of production were organized on the basis of rational capitalist criteria, the relative protection offered by trade unions and negotiated bargaining systems provided workers some security of employment. By contrast, the overwhelming majority of small firms, encapsulated as they are within dependent relations with larger corporations who are able to dictate the terms of trading, are compelled to offer insecure employment, albeit with the incentive of high short-term financial rewards. Computer specialists who contract their services to small firms which, in turn, are trading with larger companies are a case in point. The outcome is the emergence of a labour market consisting of growing numbers who are engaged on an increasingly short-term basis. Accordingly, it is argued that such trends, reinforced by the deregulation of labour markets and the decline of trade unionism, are leading to the fragmentation of labour markets and also the emergence of an 'under-class' of low-paid service workers. What, then, is the nature of employment relations within small-scale enterprises as these become of increasing significance in modern economies?

Patterns of Employment Relations

In reviewing these, it is useful to make a distinction between 'high-skill' and 'low-skill' small firms, since associated with each of these are rather distinctive employer–employee relations (Keeble and Kelly 1986). Research traditionally tended to focus upon low-skill manufacturing enterprises to the neglect of the other types of enterprise. More recently, however, the emphasis has been more upon small businesses established on the basis of high-technology, professional, expert and creative skills of one kind or another.

'Traditional small firms'

Small businesses trading in the more traditional, low-skill manufacturing sectors of the economy have attracted most attention, primarily because of their dependency either directly or indirectly on larger companies (Rainnie 1989). Their investigation, therefore, can be more readily incorporated within the traditional concerns of industrial relations and industrial sociology than other types of small firm. Hence, research has been directed to the study of small-scale manufacturing 'craft' or retailing enterprises. Even so, such a category of small firms incorporates a wide diversity of enterprises, which, again, makes it difficult to generalize about the nature of industrial relations. Scase and Goffee (1982, 1987) suggested a typology of small firms based upon the nature of proprietorial roles, since it is possible to identify particular types of labour relations associated with each of these. The categories they specify are the *self-employed*, *small employers*, *owner-controllers* and *owner-directors*. Each of these, they claim, represents differences in the relative mix of capital utilized and labour employed. As such, they consider their typology to be grounded in the Marxist theory of petty capital accumulation.

The *self-employed* constitute the largest proportion of small firm owners. By definition, they formally employ no labour. They are, however, usually dependent upon the unpaid services of partners and family members and the utilization of domestic resources for trading purposes. In a sense, there are no formal employment relations, but at the same time, the unpaid input of others demands the stipulation of a rudimentary division of labour according to which duties and tasks are undertaken. Often, gender-based authority relations as found within small business families incorporate both work and domestic roles. In other words, the 'deferential dialectic' (Newby 1977) defines not only what gets done within the home but also within the business.

Formal employment relations are obviously more explicit among *small employers*. These work alongside their employees and, in addition, undertake routine administrative and managerial tasks. They both labour and own their means of production and also employ wage labour. In such enterprises, the nature of employment relations is complex and, indeed, riddled with contradictions. On the one hand, proprietors act as employers while at the same time they work alongside their staff, performing productive work as though they themselves are employees. They perform the functions of both capital and labour, whereas in the large enterprise, by contrast, these are separately constituted. At the same time, such contradictions are reinforced by the fact that relations are personal and face-to-face. Embedded as they are within complex interpersonal networks often incorporating 'friends' and 'family members', they often generate severe constraints on rational decision-making and, potentially, there are tensions and interpersonal frictions associated with the exercise of proprietorial authority.

Owner-controllers, in many ways, typify the old-style 'classical' capitalists. They do not work alongside their employees but are responsible for the administration and management of their businesses. Unlike the self-employed and small employers, owner-controllers are more likely to depend upon personal managerial and financial expertise rather than trade- or craft-based skills. Because they do not work alongside their employees, they must devote more attention to the explicit development of employer–employee relations and, with this, mechanisms of supervisory control. Obtaining worker commitment and establishing appropriate rewards systems associated with an acceptable quality and quantity of employee performance is more problematic than it is for small employers. The latter, by working alongside their staff, are able not only to nurture close personal commitment but also to exercise tight supervisory control for determining work norms.

Finally, *owner-directors* manage and control their businesses through the implementation of formalized management structures. Administrative tasks are subdivided and delegated to managers, and these proprietors no longer personally undertake all of the functions of supervision and control. These, of course, tend to be larger enterprises which, since start-up, will have experienced considerable growth. Within such enterprises, the development of employment relations will be highly variable, ranging from an emphasis upon formal and more bureaucratic forms to more personal strategies dependent upon the 'charisma' and personal interventions of owner-directors. Often in such businesses, mechanisms of delegation can be underdeveloped even with the employment of managerial staff, to the extent that within such formalized structures management styles may be similar to those found among owner-controllers.

Even though it is possible to identify such types of proprietorial role, which, of course, tend to vary according to the size of the small business, it is evident that they share a number of common characteristics as far as the study of labour relations is concerned. Although every business will incorporate the fundamental feature of 'mixing' capital and labour, the articulation of these forces within the small firm is negotiated within patterns of interpersonal relations. Even within owner-director enterprises, with their greater dependency upon formal mechanisms and with a more evident split between capital (managers) and labour (workers), the limited size of such enterprises is still conducive to the generation of labour relations that are particularistic, informal and rarely institutionalized. Hence, in the study of employment relations in small firms there is the need to emphasize the importance of negotiated orders and how these function within the context of personal, face-to-face relations.

The study of small business growth, as it is usually linked with small employers becoming owner-controllers, requires an emphasis upon the changes which occur within the dynamics of these negotiated orders (Scase and Goffee 1982). Indeed, the success or failure of small business growth is often more associated with proprietors' ability to manage such transformations than it is to do with market opportunities or with various aspects of financial management. Such negotiated orders may be described in terms of *egalitarian* and *autocratic* strategies, both of which describe mechanisms, whereby, within the context of interpersonal relations, small business owners are able to obtain, or command, the allegiance of their staff. Each is characterized by particular employer–employee relations, according to which 'appropriate' work practices are established and rewards determined. However, as small businesses grow, such personal strategies become less relevant and, while small employers and owner-controllers may be able to continue to adhere to them, this is less likely for owner-directors. Indeed, many of the key conflicts within these 'larger' small firms hinge around ambiguous expectations associated with the parallel or partial use of both *interpersonal* and more *impersonal* forms of managerial control.

Egalitarianism and autocracy

In and *egalitarian* system owner-managers tend to work alongside their employees – as is the case with small employers. As a result of this working relationship, job duties and responsibilities become defined through processes of mutual adjustment, according to which 'psychological' and interpersonal hierarchical relations are largely absent. Employer strategies emphasize the overriding importance of 'commitment' and working for the survival of the company and nurture interpersonal relations accordingly (Goffee and Scase 1995).

They will emphasize the importance of 'teamwork' and, as members themselves of such 'teams' they will demonstrate their own productive contribution to the economic welfare of their businesses. They will deliberately relegate the undertaking of administrative tasks to the evenings and weekends in order to set examples of work norms and to demonstrate that, in working at the same level of output as their employees, they are not exploiting their staff for profit. Indeed, as small employers, they can often pay themselves a similar level of wages, reaping the rewards of proprietorship and compensating for the risk they endure as business owners through end-of-year profits. Even then, a strategy of egalitarianism is often maintained by giving employees a share in these year-end profits so that identification is reinforced and sources of employer–employee differentiation are minimized (Scase and Goffee 1982).

If strategies of egalitarianism are driven by the market situation of employees and hence their bargaining capacity, a similar set of factors accounts for the *autocratic* styles found in many other small businesses. When employees have dispensable skills, they are highly vulnerable to the stipulations and commands of their employers (Goss 1988). Their market capacity is weak and, in the absence of effective unionism, they are unable to bargain with their employers. As a result, employers are able to offer extremely low rates of pay and very poor work and employment conditions. This, of course, would seem to be the situation in many low-skill sectors of the economy such as clothing and textiles, many areas of hotel and catering, and retailing (Hoel 1982). Employees, being readily expendable by their small business owners, are compelled to accept the employment relation as this is determined by their employers.

How, then, is this relationship legitimized? According to Rainnie (1989), on the basis of his case studies of small firms in the clothing and printing industries, employers legitimize their actions by reference to the competitive forces of a market economy. In other words, they will openly acknowledge to their staff that the wages which they offer are unacceptably low but claim that these reflect circumstances beyond their own personal control. Such appeals have considerable legitimacy in periods when staff have little in the form of skills which make them either indispensable to their employers or capable of making job shifts between employers. For employees, it is a choice between low levels of remuneration and no job at all. This is particularly pertinent in circumstances when there are unfavourable preconditions for collective organization through unionism and when there is a very low statutory national minimum wage.

The relevance of skill and market conditions shaping the nature of employer–employee relations and, hence, the adoption of particular employer strategies, can be further illustrated by the research of Goss (1991b: 161). Like Rainnie, he has studied small firms in the printing industry. Unlike Rainnie, however, he identifies two quite contrasting sectors within this industry: 'On the one hand, there are those firms which are concerned with high-quality, technologically sophisticated work. These enterprises are likely to exhibit a strong craft-base, being heavily dependent upon skilled labour.' These firms tend to retain union agreements and to be at the capital-intensive end of the industry. Goss continues:

> On the other hand, there is a growing sector of the industry concerned with 'instant printing' which can more properly be seen as the industry's 'service wing'. . . . These enterprises have emerged primarily as a result of the simplification and automation of small-scale printing technology and the harnessing of this to electronic/computerized methods of typesetting, thereby eliminating the need for skilled labour.

Employees here generally lack formal training and are rarely unionized.

In view of the differences in markets, products and, hence, employers' relative dependency upon skilled workers, Goss demonstrates how these two sectors of the printing industry are characterized by very different employment relations. In the low-skill instant printing sector, there is the widespread use of younger workers who are unable to bargain, or to protect their interests either through collective action or by effective labour legislation. They are highly vulnerable to the commands of their employers and as a result, are compelled to comply with autocratic employer stipulations in terms of wages, work and employment conditions and quality of performance. Within the 'manufacturing' sector of printing, on the other hand, such autocratic strategies are inappropriate. Instead, employers are constrained to negotiate effective working relations and more favourable rewards with employees who are in a stronger bargaining position. Because of their bargaining capacity, employees are more indispensable and can better resist proprietorial prerogatives. Under such conditions, the more appropriate owner strategies are those associated with egalitarianism rather than the autocratic stances of those employed in the less skilled instant print sector.

But autocratic employer strategies are not inevitably associated with the employment of unskilled workers. They can also be the development of 'indulgency patterns' and high trust relations between small employers and their staff. In a recent study of the clothing industry, in an attempt to test some of Rainnie's claims about the general tendencies towards autocratic forms of control in low-skill businesses, Ram (1994: 213) collected data in a number of small clothing firms in the West Midlands. In this, he undertook case studies of ethnic enterprises where:

> Asians in the West Midlands [are] pushed into the clothing industry because of the absence of opportunity in mainstream employment rather than the possession of any cultural flair for enterprise. Observing employer after employer frantically attempting to balance the demands of a hostile market, an often chaotic system of production, a far from passive workforce and an indifferent banking system for very little reward leads me to the conclusion that few could have freely chosen such an existence.

According to Ram, the survival of these enterprises is highly dependent upon the use of low-paid female labour operating within the traditional patriarchal structures of Asian society. At the same time, manager–worker relations can only be understood by reference to this culture: for instance, the segregation of male and female workers, deference to older employees, the accommodation within work routines of various rituals and ceremonies, and the centrality of family relations.

Employer–employee relations in these Asian-owned businesses, therefore, are not characterized by autocratic forms of proprietorial control. But neither are they symptomatic of social harmony. Instead, ongoing bargaining between employers and employees determines, within the context of highly competitive and unpredictable market circumstances, work practices, levels of production and the exercise of authority on the shop floor. In each of the case studies Ram describes an 'indulgency pattern' whereby employers and employees become interdependent within complex relations of trust, obligation and mutual reciprocity. It is for this reason, he claims, that such small firms are often seen to be inefficiently organized and are criticized for failing to adhere to more 'rational' methods of production. However, as he suggests, attempts to rationalize work processes would break down the indulgency patterns according to which both employers and employees, through mutual reciprocity, achieve their separate goals. To destroy these patterns would be to destroy the business.

Creative and professional small firms

Managers, technologists, highly qualified specialists and professionals often quit the relative security of the large corporation to start up their own businesses. Many of them feel that their personal talents and skills are not being fully utilized. Middle-aged managers often accept redundancy and experiment with entrepreneurship, often with initial financial support from their previous employers. Younger managers, on the other hand, who have been encouraged to expect opportunities for creativity, challenge and self-fulfilment in their jobs, are often disappointed. They regard entrepreneurship as an alternative route for the achievement of these goals (Scase and Goffee 1989).

The growth of these businesses has been most pronounced in those economic sectors where there has been corporate fragmentation, downsizing and associated processes of outsourcing. The media offer many examples of these trends, with more than half of those working in this sector being freelance, self-employed or the proprietors and partners of small business enterprises. Television broadcasting companies, for example, now purchase programmes from producers and directors who in turn hire, on a project and temporary basis, freelance sound engineers, camera crews, and other staff. The television industry, once integrated on the basis of large corporations with both in-house production and broadcasting functions, has become an example of 'virtual' corporations, fragmented around networks of broadcasters who are little more than commissioning agents of programmes made by small-scale enterprises (Davis and Scase 2000).

A similar process is occurring within other media sectors such as newspaper, magazine and book publishing, advertising and the performing arts. Out-of-house freelance specialists are commissioned to contribute to specific projects which are co-ordinated by their clients. Areas of London, New York, Paris and other capital cities are taking on the features of closely knit occupational districts where networks of independent specialists are constantly grouping and regrouping to offer contractual services to commissioning clients. Equally, the financial services sector has become fragmented around a core of major insurance companies, finance houses and other banking institutions. Self-employed consultants and advisers, operating from home-based work stations, increasingly 'interface' between the purchasers and suppliers of corporate services. Often partnerships and small limited companies, offering specialist financial services within precisely designated market niches, are set up.

Demands for software and computer packages have generated a sector of small-scale providers who prefer to be self-employed rather than work in large corporations. Many university graduates with such skills obtain work experience in large companies before moving on to smaller software houses or setting up their own businesses, often in partnership with like-minded others (Slatter 1992). Similarly, more sophisticated consumer markets have led to the growth of public relations, promotion and marketing functions which, instead of being undertaken in-house, are outsourced to freelance specialists who often pool their personal talents. What, then, are the employment characteristics of these small firms?

The organization of work on the basis of specialist and changing customer needs tends to produce flexible work roles, duties and responsibilities. Instead of the performance of routine tasks, adaptiveness and job variety are the predominant characteristics of these enterprises. Equally, their small-scale nature means that little can be offered to employees in the form of conventional promotion prospects. If these are important sources of motivation for managers in large organizations, they are generally absent from small firms. In the latter, psychological rewards are obtained through *self-fulfilment* and individual *recognition.* This has ramifications for management styles, interpersonal relations between proprietors and employees, business cultures and structures, and growth strategies (Slatter 1992). Work roles tend to be broadly defined, with high levels of discretion and responsibility. Professional employees working in these small businesses are assumed to prefer personal autonomy, responsibility and recognition and, indeed, these are typically their motives for moving from employment in large organizations. Staff are encouraged to develop close working relationships with clients so that, in a relatively autonomous manner, they can exercise particular expert, creative and technical skills. As Grugulis et al. (2000) show, from a study of a management consultancy with 150 employees, there is an emphasis on skill, autonomy and even 'having fun at work', but also an effort to institutionalize the kinds of personal control discussed above. Employees are expected to accept the company's way of doing things, and there is a continuing tension between freedom and control.

Personal recognition is also an important reward because of the significance of broader 'professional' reference groups. In advertising, television, film, the performing arts, and public relations, there are numerous rewards and other tokens of recognition that constitute important motivators for those working in these industries (Davis and Scase 2000). Equally, professional bodies in some areas, such as law and accountancy, stipulate standards of conduct and criteria for terms of trade which shape relationships between the buyers and sellers of services. In other spheres, there are no such standards: Ram (1999: 893) argues that in the case of management consultancy knowledge is particularly hard to codify, with the result that uncertainties in the employment relationship may be greater than they are in the more established professions (Davis and Scase 2000).

Even though the creative energies of employees are the major asset of such businesses, and the need for self-fulfilment must be addressed, there must also be suitable financial rewards. However, the discretionary nature of work means that pay and performance can rarely be precisely measured. Further, the organization of work activities around client-determined projects can entail the cultivation of long-term relationships, since the assets largely comprise the owners' and their colleagues' expert skills. Hence, enterprises that trade with creative and expert skills are often set up as *business partnerships*. Partnerships also offer support systems and shared competences which reduce the risks inherent in business start-up, but more important is the fact that such partnerships enable individuals whose skills are indispensable for business success to have a stake in ownership. Although partners may pay themselves relatively low wages in the short term, they enjoy long-term benefits in the incremental increases in the value of their businesses. Ownership stakes are often extended to those employees who demonstrate high commitment and performance; equally, new staff are often attracted by the promise of them. In these ways participation in ownership is a means of incentivizing colleagues in enterprises where staff skills provide the bases for making profits. Without such arrangements, tensions can easily emerge, leading to staff resenting the fact that their talents and skills are being exploited by others for personal gain (Winch and Schneider 1993; Ram 1999).

In creative, professional and high-technology small businesses, the work process is broken down into 'projects', 'jobs', and 'accounts'. Work activities are organized according to client needs, for which particular individuals or groups within the enterprise will be responsible. Partners and employees organize their own and colleagues' work tasks according to these project requirements. There is little need for more direct forms of management control since workflows are constantly adapted according to the needs of clients. In this sense clients manage the work process and, as such, there is little need for explicit management control. Just as the division between owners and employees is dissolved through the operation of these businesses as partnerships, distinctions between managerial and non-managerial roles are blurred (Davis and Scase 2000).

If there are explicit forms of managerial control, these are applied to support staff such as secretaries, technicians, and other assistants. It is in handling these relationships that there are likely to be more workplace tensions, since hierarchical control is contrary to the predominant culture of these enterprises. Attempts to exercise formal management over support staff may cause resentment because this contrasts vividly with the apparently ill-defined personal relations between experts and professionals within the 'operating core'. Their jobs offer only limited opportunities for personal discretion and there are few other rewards in the form of personal recognition, challenge or self-fulfilment. They have few chances of promotion as they lack the professional qualifications and/ or the creative, technical or expert skills necessary to become members of the operating core.

Professionals tend to view their employing organization as a *resource* which can be used for delivering services to clients and for enhancing their own personal reputations. How, then, can their commitment to their businesses be obtained? Essentially, such businesses are integrated on the basis of informal social networks and work teams. In staff recruitment, it is often difficult to assess in any precise manner a person's skills because of the uncertain and ambiguous nature of creative, expert and professional tasks. Alongside personal testimonials and job histories, knowledge of job applicants through networks of personal contacts is often considered important in the recruitment process. Since work activities are project-driven, as in television production or advertising campaigns, it is important that specialists are able to work together, pooling their talents and skills in a creative and productive manner. Hence, trust relations are important, and ever-forming and temporary work teams are the chief means whereby they can be nurtured. In these teams, work roles are often stretched beyond specific personal technical and creative competencies, and hence colleagues become dependent upon each other for the achievement of their own goals (Davis and Scase 2000).

The creation of effective work groups built upon the complementary competencies and personalities of colleagues is the major management issue in many of these small businesses. This becomes even more significant when these enterprises expand. Because of the job expectations of creative, professional and highly skilled employees, growth has to be pursued without the development of a specialist management function, without formalized rules and procedures, and by avoiding the imposition of hierarchical control structures. However, processes of organizational growth often require the introduction of a management function which is positioned in order to support, rather than control, professional, technical and creative specialists. A challenging dynamic of business growth in these firms is to preserve professional autonomy while at the same time, introducing legitimate managerial processes (Goffee and Scase 1995).

Conclusions

In *traditional* small businesses, there are a variety of employer strategies, each of which shapes the nature of labour relations. But such strategies are themselves determined by a range of external factors which constrain the extent to which proprietors are able to impose their own particular patterns of control. It is rare for employers to manage their businesses in an entirely 'unfettered' autocratic manner, because of the bargaining capacity of their employees. Generally, within the context of personal relations that are face-to-face and highly particularistic, patterns of reciprocity and trust will emerge such that negotiated patterns of work, performance and productivity will become established. Generally, for reasons of employee skill, market capacity and the external threats that face small businesses in often highly competitive circumstances, forms of accommodation emerge between employers and employees which negate the imposition of autocratic forms of control. Instead, modes of egalitarianism more appropriately describe, albeit crudely, employer–employee relations in the majority of traditional small businesses.

In small businesses in the professional and creative sectors, employment relations are likely to be highly variable but also very different from those found in the more traditional sectors of the economy. Often, conventional employer–employee relations do not exist because many such enterprises are organized on the basis of co-ownership or partnership arrangements. In this way, those working in the business also have a stake in its ownership and this, of course, affects the nature of social relations. Further, such businesses often trade on the basis of various intellectual, creative, professional and expert skills which, through inter-personal team dynamics, constitute the trading assets of the business. Accordingly, on the basis of individuals' competencies, a rudimentary division of tasks emerges among partners, according to which various services are delivered to customers and clients. If there is a management process, this is *colleague-based*, with perhaps only a senior partner exercising more explicit forms of managerialism of the kind exercised by professional managers in large organizations, rather than the egalitarian or autocratic strategies of the owners of more traditional small firms. If managerial control is explicitly exercised by senior partners, it tends to be directed towards 'support staff' – secretaries, administrators, assistants – rather than towards the professional or expert colleagues who constitute the 'operating core' of the businesses. In smaller enterprises trading in high-technology products, employees are likely to be highly educated people who see themselves as mobile in both national and international labour markets. They are often anxious about the exploitation of their intellectual property rights and this provides the basis for highly individualistic negotiated orders in terms of reward systems and employment relations.

The theme of this chapter, then, has been the diversity of small firms and hence of their employment relations. Models which equate such firms with either autocracy or post-Fordist autonomy are far too simplistic. Although some small firm sectors have features that fit the post-Fordist model, many others do not. Not surprisingly, diversity and fragmentation constitute continuing tendencies in the small business sector, as this is shaped by broader economic and structured trends.

References

Braverman, H. 1974: *Labor and Monopoly Capital*. New York: Monthly Review Press.

Burrows, R. 1991: The discourse of the enterprise culture and the restructuring of Britain: a polemical contribution. In J. Curran and R. Blackburn (eds), *Paths of Enterprise: The Future of the Small Business*. London: Routledge.

Cully, M., Woodland, S., O'Reilly, A. and Dix, G. 1999: *Britain at Work*. London: Routledge.

Davis, H., and Scase, R. 2000: *Managing Creativity: The Dynamics of Work and Organizations*. Milton Keynes: Open University Press.

EIRObserver 1999: Industrial relations in SMEs. Update 3/99, supplement. Dublin: European Foundation for the Improvement of Living and Working Conditions. Further details at <www.eiro.eurofound.eu.int>.

Friedman, A. 1977: *Industry and Labour*. London: Macmillan.

Gilman, M., Edwards, P., Ram, M. and Arrowsmith, J. 2002: Pay determination in small firms in the UK, *Industrial Relations Journal*, 33 (1), 52–67.

Goffee, R., and Scase, R. 1985: *Women in Charge: The Experiences of Female Entrepreneurs*. London: George Allen & Unwin.

Goffee, R., and Scase, R. 1995: *Corporate Realities*. London. Routledge.

Goss, D. 1988: Social harmony and the small firm: a reappraisal. *Sociological Review*, 32 (1), 114–32.

Goss, D. 1991a: *Small Business and Society*. London: Routledge.

Goss, D. 1991b: In search of small firm industrial relations. In R. Burrows (ed.), *Deciphering the Enterprise Culture*. London: Routledge.

Grugulis, I., Dundon, T. and Wilkinson, A. 2000: Cultural control and the 'culture manager', *Work, Employment and Society*, 14 (1), 97–116.

Handy, C. 1984: *The Future of Work*. Oxford: Blackwell.

Hill, S. 1974: Norms, groups and power. *British Journal of Industrial Relations*, 12 (2), 213–35.

Hoel, B. 1982: Contemporary clothing sweatshops. In J. West (ed.), *Work, Women and the Labour Market*. London: Routledge & Kegan Paul.

Keeble, D., and Kelly, T. 1986: New firms and high technology industry in the United Kingdom: the case of computer electronics. In D. Keeble and E. Wever (eds), *New Firms and Regional Development in Europe*. London: Croom Helm.

Knight, K. G., and Latreille, P. L. 2000: Discipline, dismissals and complaints to employment tribunals, *British Journal of Industrial Relations*, 38 (4), 533–56.

McNabb, R., and Whitfield, K. 2000: 'Worth so appallingly little': a workplace-level analysis of low pay, *British Journal Industrial Relations*, 38 (4), 585–610.

Moule, C. 1998: The regulation of work in small firms, *Work, Employment and Society*, 12 (4), 635–54.

Newby, H. 1977: *The Deferential Worker*. London: Penguin.

Piore, M., and Sabel, C. 1984: *The Second Industrial Divide: Prospects for Prosperity*. New York: Basic Books.

Radice, H. 2000: Globalisation and national capitalisms: theorizing convergence and differentiation, *Review of International Political Economy*, 7 (4), 719–42.

Rainnie, A. 1989: *Industrial Relations in Small Firms*. London: Routledge.

Ram, M. 1994: *Managing to Survive*. Oxford: Blackwell.

Ram, M. 1999: Managing consultants in a small firm, *Journal of Management Studies*, 36 (6), 875–97.

Sabel, C. 1982: *Work and Politics*. Cambridge: Cambridge University Press.

Scase, R. 1982: The petty bourgeoisie and modern capitalism. In A. Giddens and G. Mackenzie (eds), *Social Class and the Division of Labour*. Cambridge: Cambridge University Press.

Scase, R., and Goffee, R. 1982: *The Entrepreneurial Middle Class*. London: Croom Helm.

Scase, R., and Goffee, R. 1987: *The Real World of the Small Business Owner*. 2nd edn. London: Croom Helm.

Scase, R., and Goffee, R. 1989: *Reluctant Managers*. London: Routledge.

Slatter, S. 1992: *Gambling on Growth*. Chichester: Wiley.

Tapscott, D. 1996: *The Digital Economy*. London: McGraw Hill.

Winch, G., and Schneider, E. 1993: Managing the knowledge-based organization, *Journal of Management Studies*, 30 (6), 923–37.

Wright, E. O. 1978: *Class, Crisis and the State*. London: Verso.

19
INDUSTRIAL RELATIONS, HRM AND PERFORMANCE

PETER NOLAN AND KATHY O'DONNELL

Britain's productivity profile, the subject of long-standing controversy, is once more at the centre of political and economic debate. Linked to a wider set of concerns about the performance and competitiveness of British-based industry, the productivity record has commonly served to direct attention to the possible sources of domestic under-performance. The historical evidence shows that the United States opened up a significant productivity gap with Britain early last century, and most major western European economies eclipsed Britain's performance 40 years ago. In staking its reputation on improving performance and closing the productivity gap with the other advanced economies, the present government is treading a well-worn path.

Successive post-war governments launched various initiatives to check the problem but with limited success, and by the late 1970s talk of a deep-seated crisis in production was commonplace. By the mid-1980s the climate of opinion had begun to change. The government of the day, led by Mrs Thatcher, claimed there had been a productivity breakthrough. With official statistics showing a domestic growth rate of 4 per cent, Britain was said to be top of the league table in Europe, ahead of the United States, and on a par with Japan, but the illusion was short-lived. The accumulating evidence revealed that the 'breakthrough' had been partial and was unsustainable. Long-standing weaknesses had resurfaced in a way that no amount of creative statistical manipulation could conceal.

In the past, industrial under-performance had been linked by many commentators to Britain's tradition of 'adversarial' industrial relations, and more commonly to the conduct of trade unions in the workplace. But latterly, in recognition of the important shifts in the character of employment relations in the 1990s, the focus of analysis and debate has been redirected to consider the effects of a wider set of social relations. What significance have new human resource management (HRM) practices had on the motivation, commitment and performance of employees? Is there a critical point at which such practices transform business practices and performance, and to what extent do companies in Britain systematically pursue HRM?

This chapter investigates the significance of the management of the employment relationship for economic performance. The first part examines the main theoretical perspectives and the second places Britain's post-war productivity record in context. Key conceptual and measurement problems are highlighted. The third part reviews the historical legacy and examines the role of unions and industrial relations in Britain's deteriorating economic performance. The fourth section examines the view that the reforms introduced by Mrs Thatcher's governments boosted economic performance. The final part engages with the latest findings that business performance has been improved by the application of human resource management practices in the 1990s.

Theoretical Perspectives

Industrial relations and performance

For at least a century, the performance consequences of industrial relations have been a central issue in Britain. The academic study of the complex relationships involved, however, remains seriously underdeveloped. Conceptual clarity and empirical rigour have been impeded by long-standing disciplinary and methodological differences and the limitations of the available data. Economics, the dominant perspective, has set the agenda and sharpened the analytical issues by spearheading the empirical study of the associations between measures of performance (profit, productivity, etc.) and the presence of institutional variables such as unions. But the theories underpinning such studies are relatively primitive and have been challenged in recent years by competing institutional and radical perspectives.

Conventional economic theory has little to say about industrial relations as a set of social relationships, but it claims to have a theory of the economic effects of trade unions. Cleansed of power relations, information costs and other so-called frictions, the labour market is depicted as an atomistic paradise in which wages are advanced for labour services in line with the forces of supply and demand. Against this backdrop, unions are demonized as monopoly sellers of labour. Their attempts to improve their members' terms and conditions are said to have the following deleterious consequences.

First, wage gains negotiated by trade unions will prompt employers to restore equilibrium between costs and revenue by cutting output (a *scale* effect). In the longer term employers will replace union workers with physical capital and cheaper non-unionized labour (a *substitution* effect). Confined at first to unionized establishments, these effects will have wider consequences. Displaced unionized workers will be absorbed into relatively low-paid, low-productivity jobs in non-unionized firms, and scarce capital will be reallocated to the unionized sector. The aggregate result will be an imbalance in the allocation of productive resources between the organized and unorganized sectors and non-trivial output losses.

Second, attempts by unions to influence directly the organization of work (staffing and effort levels, for example) are regarded as an unwelcome abrogation of management prerogative and a further potential source of economic losses. Seeing the work process as a technical relationship between inputs and outputs, neo-classical theory uncritically embraces a crude managerial perspective and defines any attempt at power-sharing and joint decision-making as an unwelcome deviation from best practice. The approach, analogous to the 'unitarist' frame of reference in industrial relations, condemns in the strongest terms any interruptions to production through strikes and work to rule. Following this line of reasoning, Hayek, a leading adviser to Mrs Thatcher in the 1980s, claimed that unions were 'the prime source of unemployment' and the 'main reason for the decline of the British economy in general' (Hayek 1980).

Third, efforts by unions to press their members' interests in the political arena are connected to major distortions in markets and macro-economic outcomes. Acquiescence by governments in their sectional demands, the argument runs, may well deliver short-term palliatives for their members, but the longer-term impact on the efficiency of markets and factor utilization will be negative. That the pressure-group activities of other organized interest groups (multinational companies, the Confederation of British Industry, and financial institutions) fail to attract so much as a footnote in such accounts is indicative of the limited scope and relevance of the theory to contemporary capitalist economies.

The central problem with the neo-classical perspective, as countless radical and institutionalist accounts record, is that it derives from a model of the economy that is abstract, ahistorical, and preoccupied with static, allocation issues. Responding to their critics, the leading exponents of the conventional approach concede that the model is merely a conceptual device or benchmark to better understand the workings of the real economy. But in practice the real economy is judged against the properties of the model rather than the other way round. Inserted into the analysis as 'imperfections', and deemed corrosive of economic performance, trade unions are presented as the prime impediment to efficiency that should be rooted out so that the economy may come to approximate the perfectly competitive ideal. Not only is this conclusion predetermined at the outset by the assumptions of the model, it is generated without any consideration of the dynamic properties of the system.

With scant attention to history, the conventional theory fails to provide any significant insights into the origins and effects of collective relationships in the workplace. The analogy drawn between unions and monopoly producers is especially misleading. Unions do not sell labour services nor do they pursue profit-maximizing objectives. Their primary role as intermediary institutions is, as stressed by the institutionalists Freeman and Medoff (1984), to negotiate with employers and redress the imbalance of power inherent in the employment relationship by giving employees a collective voice.

Institutional perspectives on the labour market were particularly influential in the United States in the 1940s and 1950s (see McNulty 1980). They received a welcome revival in the 1980s following the fresh investigations of researchers at Harvard University. Freeman and Medoff (1984), summarizing the results of numerous empirical studies, concluded that unions were good for productivity and economic efficiency. Inverting conventional theory, they argued that a union presence in the workplace provides workers with a collective voice and hence a channel of communications with management. Possible consequences include the establishment of proper grievance procedures, health and safety rules, and a more effectively managed internal labour market. Some of the Harvard research, for example by Kim Clark (1980a and 1980b), revealed that the introduction of unions into previously unorganized workplaces served to 'shock' sloppy managements into pursuing 'best practice' in respect of the alignment of technology and tasks, and the utilization of labour time.

Other studies of the role of unions in the economy tend to stress either their blocking role or their dynamic effects. Under the former, some radical accounts, deploying a zero-sum perspective on employment relations, assume that gains for labour in the workplace and wage arena will entail losses for business (Kilpatrick and Lawson 1980). Reproducing, in analytical method and substantive conclusions, the neo-classical approach, this perspective remains popular with many writers on trade unionism. The latter approach (e.g. Nolan 1996) is predicated on the idea that, by resisting the crudest forms of exploitation in production (such as intensification and the extension of unpaid working hours), and pushing for higher wages for their members, unions may have a transformative impact on the character of production and business strategies. Employers are constrained, so to speak, to pursue high-productivity, high-value-added routes to profitability. A further implication is that weak trade unionism tends to be correlated with poor management bred by complacency and the absence of adequate countervailing challenges.

HRM and performance

During the 1980s research on the performance implications of trade unions intensified, against the backdrop of their diminishing membership and influence in the United States, and in Britain and many other countries in Europe. By the 1990s, however, the contraction of collective bargaining, manufacturing decline, and the rapid growth of service industries provided the context for a new research agenda on the impact of management practices, focusing on individual rather than collective relationships in the workplace. As previous chapters testify, the new managerial agenda has had profound consequences for the study of the employment relationship, but the implications of this agenda for the understanding of performance outcomes remain tentative and contested.

The most basic (yet still remarkably common) approach presents a version of the unitarist frame of reference by postulating a positive correlation between effective leadership and co-operation in the workplace, enhanced commitment and performance gains. The essential elements of HRM are typically defined in opposition to Taylorism. The key ingredients of the latter system remain controversial in the historical and empirical literature, but stylized accounts point to its role in degrading work and workers in the expanding factories and offices of the twentieth century. Taylorism aimed to separate mental and manual labour, fragment, simplify and measure routine tasks, and control labour costs by the application of result-payment systems. HRM, by contrast, allegedly releases previously under-utilized sources of creativity and productivity by empowering individuals, fostering teamwork and rewarding personal initiative.

Taking this position forward, researchers have argued that the sources of the success of human resource practices are rooted in the application and consequences of 'high-commitment' and 'high-involvement' management systems. Sometimes presented as distinct strategies, these overlapping approaches are reckoned to have had a positive impact on performance through their effects on employee morale, behaviour and commitment. Implicitly assuming that workers are putty in their bosses' hands, the studies posit a line of causality running from new management initiatives through worker responses to business performance.

High-commitment management (HCM) is associated with measures aimed at diluting the range and intensity of direct managerial influence over the organization and control of work. It is also linked to the improvement of workers' welfare through, for example, the introduction of team-based work and family-friendly policies. Higher levels of employee commitment are expected *inter alia* to reduce levels of absenteeism and turnover, lift productivity and boost financial performance.

High-involvement management (HIM) is thought to deliver positive benefits through a different transmission mechanism. At its core is the application of new measures to empower employees, enhance training, share information and provide incentives that enable and encourage employees to take 'ownership' of key production and supply decisions. The gains in performance are attributed to changes in employee conduct, yet sceptics point out that direct measures of such behavioural shifts are rarely presented, and the theoretical underpinning of the assumed relationships tends to be left unspecified.

Recent research by Guest et al. (2000a, 2000b), focusing principally on measurement rather than underlying theoretical issues, has begun to fill the gaps. The studies highlight significant mediation effects between HRM practices and performance and point to the cumulative positive impact of the number of practices deployed. Organizations that successfully combine measures to support teamworking, a learning culture and performance-related pay are, on their findings, likely to outperform employers that do not. Consistent with the 'universalistic' model elaborated by Huselid (1995), their results have proved stable in a variety of national and organizational contexts, and thus contradict the 'contingency' approach favoured by, for example, Wood and de Menezes (1998). Whereas the latter perspective holds that the effects of HRM practices are context-specific and hence resistant to a generic theory of causal relations and effects, the universalistic model is held to apply irrespective of specific national and organizational structures.

Inviting comparisons with the 'black box' theory of production in neo-classical economic theory, the new studies of HRM and performance remain stubbornly silent on basic questions. If the performance benefits attributed to the effective implementation of HRM are so compelling, why are such practices far from ubiquitous? How should we interpret the interplay between the execution of HRM practices and the alleged changes in employee conduct? Do the apparent benefits derive from a change in 'hearts and minds', or are employees merely signifying their compliance to a lighter-touch regime and improved material incentives?

In a timely reminder that contemporary management practices are often little more than a repackaging of previously tried and tested means, Ramsay et al. (2000) suggest that the apparent performance benefits of HRM could be rooted in a different logic of control. Citing the work of Braverman (1974), Palloix (1976) and Friedman (1977), Ramsay and his colleagues sketch the outlines of a contemporary 'labour process' perspective and present this as a testable alternative to the more common narratives in HRM. The basic approach recalls Friedman's distinction between 'direct control' and 'responsible autonomy' (1977: 6). The former system embraces many aspects of Taylorism and attempts to limit the scope for worker autonomy. Responsible autonomy, by contrast, 'attempts to harness the adaptability of labour power by giving workers leeway and by encouraging them to adapt to changing situations in a manner beneficial to the firm'. Applying this argument to the contemporary world of work, Ramsay et al. note that:

> In common with the HPWS (High Performance Work Systems) account, the labour process interpretation posits a positive association between HPWS-style practices and employee discretion. This association is conceptualized as an enhancement of discretion arising from management's need to gain employee compliance and creative capability, in search of which it offers 'responsible autonomy' . . . To the extent that employees enjoy benefits, these will take the form of minor gains in discretion, granted as a means to gain compliance with managerial aims, which are far outweighed by work intensification, insecurity and stress. (Ramsay et al. 2000: 505)

In short, it is possible to account for the link between new management practices and gains in performance without assuming that the critical links flow from enlightened management initiatives to shifts in worker attitudes, increased commitment and more effective performance. A narrative pointing to new accommodations and worker compliance may be more compelling. Careful empirical analysis of the relevant relationships and their linkages is a necessary first step in testing the purchase of these competing theoretical perspectives. But, as the next section reveals, exposing the complex connections is fraught with difficulties.

The Empirical Record

Measurement issues

In common with the earlier studies of unions and productivity, the new research on HRM and performance has been constrained in important ways by the limitations of the available data. Drawing in the main upon large-scale surveys of workplaces and organizations, the analytical focus has centred on the comparison of performance within specific national systems, the UK and US for example. Do trade unions make a difference, and has HRM been good for the bottom line?

The data presented in the following section reveal that such questions, however important, are dominated by much greater and more persistent gaps in average performance levels between countries rather than between organizations within a national context.

The UK boasts one of the most reliable sources of representative data on the nature, dimensions and scope of changes in employment relations in the workplace, as a consequence of the four WIRS (now WERS) surveys conducted since 1980 (for details see Cully et al. 1999). The data generated by these surveys, frequently cited in previous chapters, are immensely rich, but remain limited in respect of performance outcomes. Based on management's views of the relative performance of their workplace as compared to that of their rivals in the same industry, the data are judged by some writers to be too subjective and impressionistic to draw firm conclusions about the precise performance consequences of competing systems of employee management. These criticisms are not without force, but the more 'objective' sources of information that have been used in studies of relative performance (whether at organization, industry or national level) are scarcely free from difficulties.

The analysis of productivity across time, establishments, industries and national frontiers is especially problematic. How should productivity be measured, what are the relevant procedures for aggregating heterogeneous inputs and outputs, and how in time series studies should trend and cyclical movements be disentangled? Given that productivity is the outcome of a collective social process, what significance should be assigned to the politics of production relations? This issue has scarcely been addressed, still less resolved in the empirical research literature.

The most commonly used statistics are labour productivity and total factor productivity. Labour productivity (or output per employee hour) is generally measured in price rather than physical units, and interpreted as a rough and ready index of labour efficiency. Do British employees work, on average, as efficiently as their counterparts overseas? Comparative data on labour productivity are often cited to support the view that they do not, but such a conclusion may not be warranted. Is the quality of management in Britain comparable to that elsewhere, are domestic factories equipped to the same standards, do British workers receive the same levels of training? Without a consideration of such issues, few meaningful conclusions can be drawn from the figures on labour productivity.

Labour is usually calculated on the basis of an extensive measure of labour input – the number of people or hours worked – and as such does not take account of the intensity of work. If the human effort expended per worker hour is raised, for whatever reason, then the total input of labour would have increased, and a failure to record this increase would produce biased estimates of the true relationship between output and labour input. Two implications follow. First, improvements in measured labour productivity may not imply a corresponding improvement in labour efficiency: what matters for efficiency is the ratio of output to input, including changes in labour intensity. Second, comparative productivity measures over time and place that fail to capture variations in labour intensities are likely to produce biased estimates.

Turning to the measurement of output, the usual procedure is to value heterogeneous products and services in nominal prices and then adjust the latter by appropriate price deflators to yield a measure of the real value of output. Two possible difficulties may arise with the procedure. First, value added may be distorted if the price of inputs rises at a different rate to the price of outputs (fuel would be an obvious example). To avoid such difficulties, Bruno (1984) and others have argued that separate (or 'double') deflators for inputs and outputs should be applied. Second, the existence of different price regimes in different countries introduces a further complexity when the value of output is converted into a common currency, the US dollar for example. Recent studies (e.g. Scarpetta et al. 2000) have addressed this problem by calculating purchasing power parity (PPP) exchange rates. The latter are formed on the basis of ratios of ex-factory prices for matched samples of products in each pair of countries under comparison. The effect is to reduce distortions in the valuation of output, country by country, that would otherwise surface as a result of exchange rate fluctuations. Table 19.1, which places Britain's labour productivity record in a wider international context, is based on this method.

Total factor productivity (TFP) is judged by many writers to yield more insights into the sources of performance changes (Oulton and O'Mahoney 1994). Defined as the rate of output growth minus the weighted sum of the growth of inputs – the weights being determined by each input's share of total income – TFP is said to capture the output gains accruing from changes in the methods of capital and labour utilization rather than changes in the quantities themselves. Critics note that TFP is estimated as a residual and hence tends to serve as a crude 'catch all' term. Usually the largest element in the estimated equation, it embraces 'advances in knowledge, personal characteristics such as effort and experience, union power, government regulation' (Alford 1988: 18), and as such provides a 'licence to speculate' about the causes of observed changes in measured productivity (Nolan 1989).

Britain's relative performance

Whatever the shortcomings of the available data, the latter suggest for the UK a picture of relative under-performance over many decades. In terms of output per head, the gap with the United States opened up early on last century. In 1960 the differential exceeded 40 per cent, but by the end of the last century had narrowed to 18 per cent. Table 19.1 reveals that the UK emerged as a relatively high-productivity economy within Europe in the second half of the twentieth century, but has since declined relatively. The latest figures thus highlight a deficit in GDP per person of between 20 and 25 per cent with France, Italy and Germany. Japan also emerges from the last century with a significant negative differential with respect to the US, which is perhaps surprising in view of Japan's dynamic manufacturing sector. Part of the explanation, as Fingleton argues, may be that the method of purchasing parity ratios is used 'to assign a lower-than-market valuation to wages earned by workers in Japan' (Fingleton

Table 19.1 Productivity levels in OECD countries, 1950–1998 (GDP per person hour relative to the United States)

	1950	1960	1973	1987	1992	1998
USA	100	100	100	100	100	100
Japan	15	20	45	60	67	68
West Germany	34	52	73	91	100	106
Germany					87	90
France	42	51	74	99	101	102
Italy	38	46	78	96	97	100
Sweden	50	55	78	84	82	84
UK	58	57	68	81	79	82

Source: Scarpetta et al. (2000).

Table 19.2 Manufacturing productivity levels in selected OECD countries, 1950–1998 (GDP per hour worked)

	1950	1960	1970	1980	1990	1998
USA	100	100	100	100	100	100
Japan	11.1	19.9	43.4	65.2	80.7	80.0
Germany[a]	28.5	57.9	77.6	94.8	87.5	86.5
France	35.5	49.8	71.0	87.8	92.1	92.8
Sweden	43.9	55.3	86.4	98.5	89.8	99.7
UK	40.3	45.9	50.9	52.6	63.2	57.0

[a] 1950–80 West Germany; 1990 and 1998 all Germany.
Source: Scarpetta et al. (2000).

1999: 10). A more common explanation is that advances in productivity outside manufacturing have been far less impressive.

The relative performance of manufacturing conventionally is considered the most reliable and crucial indicator of competitiveness. Comparing labour productivity levels in seven countries over the past 50 years, table 19.2 reveals the enduring strength of the US manufacturing sector, the remarkable productivity gains in Japanese manufacturing, and clear evidence of catch-up between France and, to a lesser extent, Germany and the United States. The pattern of convergence between the UK and the US is plainly more fitful, with some progress recorded until 1990 and then a further erosion of relative productivity since then. The gap, remaining stubbornly in excess of 40 per cent, provides the backdrop to the contemporary renewal of a long-standing debate.

Estimates of total factor productivity growth rates since 1980 are presented in table 19.3. The United States shows signs of improvement over the period,

Table 19.3   Total-factor productivity growth rates in selected OECD countries, 1980–1998 (average annual growth rates)

	1980–90		1990–8		1995–8	
	(a)	(b)	(a)	(b)	(a)	(b)
USA	0.8	0.8	1.1	1.0	1.1	1.0
Japan	1.6	2.0	0.7	1.6	0.8	1.6
Germany	1.1	1.6	1.0	1.4	1.1	1.5
France	1.6	2.1	0.9	1.1	0.8	1.1
Sweden	0.9	0.8	1.7	1.3	1.7	1.3
UK	–	–	1.2	1.3	1.3	1.4

(a) based on non-adjusted hours per employee
(b) based on adjusted hours per employee
Source: Scarpetta et al. (2000).

whereas France records a significant slowdown. The differences between countries are difficult to interpret, because, as indicated above, the figures are highly sensitive to cross-national variations in the measurement of outputs and inputs (hours worked, the quality of labour and capital deployed). The degree of sensitivity is revealed to some extent by the inclusion of separate estimates for 'adjusted' and 'non-adjusted' hours worked per employee. Accordingly, the figures in column (b) for each of the three years suggest that US performance is inferior to that of Japan, Germany, France and the UK when TFP is calculated to control for the (higher) number of hours worked by US employees.

The central conclusions to be drawn from this brief review of the latest statistical data on performance are twofold: the UK's historic position as a relatively low-productivity economy has not been reversed, and its manufacturing sector is, if anything, falling further behind the other leading capitalist economies. This is the empirical background against which past and present claims about the deleterious consequences of trade unions and the positive performance implications of HRM should be situated. The following sections examine the claims and counter-claims, the empirical evidence, and the wider historical context.

The Politics of Productivity

The United States, as indicated, established a commanding productivity lead over Britain early in the twentieth century. Many commentators (Chandler 1966; Lazonick 1991) linked the success of American business to four connected developments: the early and rapid diffusion of the techniques of 'scientific' management and the associated subjugation of craft unions; the decisive shift in key industries to capital-intensive methods of production; the growth of the vertically integrated firm; and the monopolization of markets which permitted the fuller exploitation of economies of scale. By contrast, in Britain's staple industries (cotton, coal, steel, shipbuilding), techniques of production were not radically transformed, craft practices partially survived, markets remained fragmented, and firms retained their traditional structures, rendering them on average small in scale and scope.

The accumulated weaknesses of domestic industry, especially the legacy of under-investment in new techniques and methods during the inter-war years, were rudely exposed during the Second World War. The incoming Labour government sought to deal with the most glaring deficiencies – in gas, electricity, coal and the railways – through nationalization. But for the bulk of industries, particularly manufacturing, which remained under private ownership, exhortation rather than direct intervention was the chosen lever for change.

In a context of severe labour shortages, Attlee's government, as Tomlinson (1991) argues, assigned a high priority to raising industrial productivity. But the initiatives that Labour took met with limited success. Labour's Production Campaign, which involved media advertising, conferences and factory newsletters, was launched in 1946. It was followed by plans to establish tripartite development councils to promote rationalization and renewal in key industries, but in the face of strong opposition from employers only four such councils were eventually created (Tomlinson 1991: 46–7). With American encouragement, notably from the Economic Co-operation Administration established to administer Marshall Aid, Labour set up in 1947 the Anglo-American Council on Productivity (AACP). The Council sought to promote awareness of American production methods, particularly 'scientific' management and mass production, by organizing visits (66 in total between 1949 and 1952) for British employers and trade unionists to American factories.

The reports from these missions identified major obstacles to the 'Americanization' of British industry: not the restrictive practices of labour as Crafts (1988) alleges, but rather the shortcomings of management (Coates 1994). Tomlinson points out that the AACP reports attracted hostility from the industrial community, particularly the Federation of British Industry, which had come to regard Labour's productivity drive cynically as the 'thin end of the wedge' and an attempt by the government to lay the blame for Britain's ills solely on management. With the return to power of the Conservatives in 1952, the findings of the AACP were shelved. Indeed during the 1950s there were no further major state-sponsored initiatives to boost productivity, although it was apparent to many commentators that productivity growth rates elsewhere were such that Britain's relative position was seriously at risk. What, if any, forces for modernization were at play?

Many commentators on this period stress the buoyant market conditions, at home and abroad (Kilpatrick and Lawson 1980; Tomlinson 1991; Grant 1991), which they claim served to weaken the pressures on firms to upgrade products and processes. Yet this argument does not help to explain why the techniques and business structures pioneered in the United States were so enthusiastically embraced elsewhere, in France for example (I. Clark 2000). Nor does it explain why the forces of competition, both domestic and international, were subverted. Even in buoyant market conditions, it must surely be to the advantage of at least some firms to exploit modern techniques to gain competitive advantage?

A trade union problem?

With the benefit of hindsight, it is possible to see that the sources of the domestic economy's developing weaknesses in the post-war period were complex, yet the character of the contemporary analysis and debate was such that many crucial considerations were crowded out by the search for immediate panaceas. In and of itself, the argument about market conditions is insufficient as an explanation of the increasingly sclerotic character of domestic industry. The other favoured explanation was (and remains) labour, or more particularly union obstructionism.

Typical of the genre was the 1958 pamphlet *A Giant's Strength*, produced by the partisan Inns of Court Conservative and Unionist Society, which recommended the erosion of the legal immunities that had protected trade unions since 1906 from criminal prosecution for most torts (civil wrongs). In the face of mounting pressure to do something to tackle the allegedly powerful and pernicious restrictive practices that unions were held to have put in place in the workplace, the then Labour government established the Donovan Commission to investigate the character of trade unions and employers' associations (see chapter 2). Understandably in the circumstances, it chose to focus primarily on the sources of workplace 'disorder'. Shortly before the commission began its work, Hugh Clegg, the principal architect of the final report, had this to say on the issue of 'restrictive' practices:

> Under-employment of labour is one of the major scandals of the British economy. There may be few workers – outside of the newspaper industry – who are paid to do nothing at all, but throughout British industry there must be hundreds of thousands of workers who are paid to do nothing for a considerable part of their working time . . . Then there are the new machines and changes in technology – many of them in use in other countries – which would be introduced here but for the limits placed by workers on their output. (Clegg 1964)

In the event the commission's report did not lay the blame for disorder solely at the feet of the unions. The analysis was more subtle. Senior management were held culpable for neglecting industrial relations issues and allowing foremen and supervisors to enter into covert and cosy deals with the rapidly expanding ranks of shop-floor trade union representatives. Stressing that management alone could put the situation to right, the Donovan Report argued for comprehensive factory agreements, the formalization of industrial relations procedures, and the integration of shop stewards into the machinery of collective bargaining.

Formalization, to be sure, was an important consequence of the changes sought by management in the 1960s and 1970s. Strategies of internalization were more pervasive and pronounced, and greater effort was made to cut costs by introducing work study techniques, job evaluation and pay policies more closely tailored to the needs of the enterprise (see chapter 3). Yet the weaknesses in industrial performance became more, not less striking. The substantive improvements in labour productivity that were expected to accompany the workplace reforms prescribed by the Donovan Report did not materialize, perhaps, as Metcalf (1989a) has suggested, because the benefits of formalization were subject to significant lags and only became apparent in the changed conditions of the 1980s. Others, for example Edwards (1983), have argued that the reform process itself may well have been self-defeating; attacks on the status quo may have provoked resentment and increased conflict in the workplace.

Whatever the true explanation – and part of it must be that the anticipated performance gains from formalization were massively overstated in the first place – the fact is that the apparent failure of the post-Donovan industrial relations reforms only served to build support for the case that more radical policies were required to attenuate the allegedly deleterious effects of union activities in the workplace. Many thought that the solution lay in the enactment of new laws designed to restrict unionism, and the 1971 Industrial Relations Act was the first major shift in that direction. Although its subsequent repeal in 1974 was erroneously thought to constitute clear evidence that the voluntarist tradition in British industrial relations was firmly embedded, support for tougher measures against unions continued to grow. The clearest manifestation was the election of Mrs Thatcher in 1979.

What theories and evidence were mobilized to support the case against workers and their unions? An examination of the literature for the period 1945–79 reveals a dearth of systematic and dispassionate findings. With respect to theory, the investigation of the connections between workplace struggles and accommodations, their wider impacts in the economy, and the role of mediating forces such as economic competition were remarkably primitive. What are the relevant bridging concepts in moving from isolated incidents in the workplace (strikes, job controls, etc.) to wider industrial and economic developments? One of the most immediate consequences of the lack of relevant theory is that the analysis of the impact of industrial relations on productivity has usually lacked specificity. What is the nature of the charge against British workers and unions? When exactly did unions develop the capacities to block change, and what is the nature of these capacities that supposedly enabled unions – however localized and partial in presence – to impede the forces of competition?

One obvious place to look is in the voluminous research reports provided for the Donovan Report, but these tended to take for granted that there was a vital connection between systems of workplace regulation and performance without any explicit analysis. Other contemporary studies (Mackay et al. 1971; Turner et al. 1967) failed to confirm the conventional wisdom. Turner and his colleagues focused on the car industry, which by the mid-1960s had come to symbolize the British malaise, yet they pointed to a complex set of connections between management strategy, the organization of work, and company performance. On the specific issue of the impact of strikes on output and productivity, Turner and his colleagues found a strong 'clear but inverse connection between striker days and production'.

Re-examining the evidence some twenty years later, Tolliday (n.d.) noted that 'the interruptions of production due to disputes do not seem to have had very serious effects on car-makers' performance'. By the 1960s, the manufacturers' 'main problem was not inadequate volumes of production but being able to sell the cars they made at a profit, and "beneficial strikes" could avoid the pile-up of unsaleable cars'. On the question of the impact of workers' job controls on productivity, he concluded that 'under piecework the pace and intensity of work were generally high', but the low levels of pay in the industry 'made it less attractive' for the manufacturers 'to invest in capital intensive methods'. In effect the low cost of labour functioned as a powerfully high exit barrier to inefficient firms.

New studies, focusing on developments in the 1960s and 1970s, provided seemingly conclusive evidence of the significant role of workers and trade unions in Britain's industrial decline. Pratten (1976) investigated the determinants of labour productivity differentials in 100 international firms with factories in Britain, France, Germany and the United States. He found that, as compared to Britain, labour productivity was higher by 50 per cent in the United States, 27 per cent in Germany, and 15 per cent in France. Strikes, restrictive practices and staffing levels accounted for 11 per cent of the differential with the United States, 12 per cent of the differential with Germany and 6 per cent of the differential with France.

Caves (1980) examined the causes of productivity differentials in 71 matched industries in Britain and the United States for the period 1967–72. He found that the factors which best explained the productivity shortfall in Britain were the number of strikes and days lost through strikes, the proportion of employment in Britain in 'older industrial regions', and the extent of the coverage of male manual employees by collective agreements. Prais (1981) studied 10 matched industries in Britain, Germany and the United States, and concluded that 'management seems not to be free to decide on how many (workers) to employ per machine, nor is it free to decide on what work to employ them' (1981: 269), yet he made no effort to check these perceptions with the relevant workers nor to specify clearly in what ways workers had blocked change.

The limitations of all three studies were exposed by Nichols (1986): Pratten relied almost exclusively on information provided by management; Caves's study was flawed by serious data limitations; and Prais's study is at odds with the more detailed accounts of the history of domestic industry. Hannah (1983) and Channon (1973), for example, point to various factors, including the enduring character of family-owned and managed firms, which stalled the rise of the modern integrated company, so-called M-form management systems, and the concentrated markets that permit the successful exploitation of economies of scale.

Even as these debates were taking place, there was a new mood taking root in government and the wider policy arenas. The arguments were led by new political forces that had embraced a more radical perspective on the deleterious role of unions and other obstacles to the free play of market forces. Elected in 1979 with a strong mandate to reform industrial relations, Mrs Thatcher's new Conservative government sought to remove, weaken, or radically reform any institutions that stood accused of inhibiting entrepreneurship and the performance of the British economy.

The Thatcher Revolution

The view that government policies in the early 1980s had induced a productivity breakthrough was first mooted by Muellbauer (1986). Although he was unable to specify the precise nature of the connections, his investigation pointed to a trend shift in total factor productivity (TFP) after the third quarter of 1980. According to Muellbauer, TFP averaged 2.76 per cent annually between 1980 and 1985, as compared to 0.62 per cent between 1973 and 1979. TFP, as noted, is estimated as a residual and hence is open to a number of possible interpretations. The one seized upon by Maynard (1988), among others, was that the Thatcher government's tougher approach to the unions had allowed previously unexploited gains in efficiency to be realized.

Echoing this perspective Metcalf claimed there was conclusive evidence 'that union presence is associated with lower labour productivity' (Metcalf 1989a). In his wide-ranging review of the changing character of post-war British industrial relations, he argued that Thatcher's policies – anti-union legislation, the freeing of market forces, and the permissive stance towards high unemployment – had wrought profound changes in workplace behaviour and practices. Disciplined by the 'fear' of unemployment and plant closures, workers were subjected to harsher work routines as management demanded increased effort and productivity. Comparing Thatcher's approach with the pluralist reform strategy of the 1960s and 1970s, Metcalf concluded that, whereas the latter had failed to yield any significant gains, Thatcher's policies 'seem to have done the trick' (1989b: 27).

In a similar vein Crafts claimed that Thatcher's 'get tough' approach to the unions would yield enduring benefits 'if the bargaining power of workers over manning levels remains weak' (Crafts 1991). Others, for example Nolan (1989) and Nolan and Marginson (1990), took issue with the emerging consensus. Noting that there was no evidence of any step increase in investment in plant, people and technology, they argued that Thatcher's reforms may have supplied a quick fix at the expense of the more fundamental structural reforms urgently required to reinvigorate the UK economy. The evidence reviewed above provides little support for the contention that the UK economy moved to a new sustainable growth trajectory in the 1980s.

Studies of the changing relationship between unions and performance at enterprise level also failed to confirm a positive 'Thatcher effect'. Nickell et al. (1989) and Wadhwani (1990), for example, examined the performance of 124 manufacturing companies between 1972 and 1986. Tracking changes in productivity during the second half of the 1970s (a period of relative union 'strength') and the first half of the 1980s (a period of relative 'weakness'), Wadhwani found that the 'pro-union' legislation of the 1970s did not discourage investment or inhibit productivity growth. Both studies noted that unionized firms in the first half of the 1980s experienced faster productivity growth than their non-unionized counterparts. Nickell et al. thus concluded that 'there is no simple association between unionism and productivity growth. . . . Contrary to what is alleged, unions do not consistently reduce productivity growth' (Nickell et al. 1989: 21, 29).

Machin and Wadhwani (1991) reported a 'positive association between union-ism and organizational change'. Such change is defined as 'substantial changes in work organization or work practices not involving new plant, machinery or equipment'. Three in 10 of the 721 private sector establishments they examined had experienced some changes between 1981 and 1984. Finding that the incidence of change was higher in unionized than non-unionized establishments, they considered two competing explanations. Change may have been more common in unionized workplaces because management had taken advantage of unions' enfeebled position to push through long overdue changes. Alternatively, as highlighted in the Harvard studies, union 'shock' effects may have been the primary impulse. Lacking direct evidence on the relevant social processes, Machin and Wadhwani concluded that 'both the above channels combine to give us a positive association between unionism and organizational change' (1991: 852).

Thereafter new contributions to the evidence base were few and far between. With data from WIRS 1990, Fernie and Metcalf (1995) examined the impact of unionism (and other workplace variables) on six performance measures (productivity levels and changes, employment, quit rates, absenteeism rates and the industrial relations climate). They found that, with the exception of quit rates, a strong union presence was associated with inferior performance. Machin and Stewart, also drawing on WIRS 1990, looked at the impact of unions on financial performance. Their results point to a negative union effect in enterprises with a closed shop or where management recommended the union. Anchored in the material conditions of the 1980s, both studies have been replicated for the more recent period with WERS 1998 data (Addison and Belfield 2001). Finding little support for the earlier conclusions, Addison and Belfield reported that union recognition was positively associated with productivity change and statistically insignificant with respect to financial performance. How are these radically conflicting results for the two periods to be interpreted?

Addison and Belfield suggest that the ebbing of union power in the 1980s and 1990s may have released previously entrenched constraints on performance. 'Equally', they continue, 'we should not be surprised to see some reversal of our results in the light of the more favourable environment for unions implied by the passage of the June 1999 Employment Relations Act' (2001: 357). Eschewing evidence from other European economies of positive outcomes from systems of collective regulation, the authors merely restate the stock neo-classical argument that strong or strengthened unions must be a source of economic inefficiency. More telling, however, is their observation that the findings on unions, productivity and performance are subject to the 'methodological constraints of cross-sectional analysis, the use of simple constructs to model complex phenomena, and – most important of all [the difficulties in modelling] – the dynamic nature of workplace management' (Addison and Belfield 2001: 361).

There are three separate issues. The first concerns the data-generation process. Is it not likely that the steep recession of the early 1990s, and the economic recovery that followed, shaped management perceptions – the sole source of the data on performance – in a way that rendered marginal rather than central workplace variables such as the presence or absence of a trade union? Remember WIRS 1990 was conducted in a period of severe economic recession, whereas the data for WERS 1998 were collected (October 1997–June 1998) after the election of a new Labour government and during a period of sustained prosperity. Contextual shifts of this order are not easily captured in a single equation model with or without the inclusion of a dummy variable.

The second issue concerns the structural stability of the hypothesized relationships between unions and performance. According to Addison and Belfield (2001: 358), the discrepancies between their findings and those of the studies based on WIRS 1990 may reveal that 'the relationships that once held may no longer do so'. Relevant in this context is the Harvard view that 'unionism per se is neither a plus nor a minus to productivity. What matters is how unions and management interact at the workplace' (Freeman and Medoff 1984: 179). Following a decade of profound political and economic upheaval – including a new accent on partnership in the workplace, wider shifts in the framework of labour law, and a partial revival of trade union fortunes – it would be surprising if the (estimated) relationships between unions and performance at the height of Thatcherism had the same purchase a decade later.

The third issue concerns the dominant research method. Limited to regression analysis, the studies cited above have no direct observations on the causal processes in the workplace that may account for the different signs and significance of unionism in the two time periods. Unions are ripped from context and treated as an exogenous, independent determinant of performance and change. Yet, as Addison and Belfield observe, the key challenge is to grasp 'the dynamic nature of workplace management' and that means studying unions as part of a wider set of influences on performance. Marrying the findings of large-scale survey evidence with longitudinal case studies of patterns of accommodation and resistance in the workplace would be a step in the right direction, but one that remains at odds with the prevailing approach (in economics, at least) that regards as ad hoc and anecdotal case-study findings on workplace changes. Similar considerations arise in respect of the emerging research literature on HRM and performance, to which we now turn.

HRM and Performance

A major concern of the new research on HRM and performance is the extent to which HRM practices have been embedded in the management systems of UK-based organizations. Do employers practise what is espoused in management theory? Interpretations of WIRS 1990, for example Sisson (1993), pointed to the limited and patchy application of HRM, and to the resulting gap in governance systems in a majority of UK workplaces following the demise of collective bargaining during the 1980s and 1990s. Reinforcing the point, Millward observed that 'there is no sign that the shrinkage in the extent of trade union representation is being offset by a growth in other methods of representing non-managerial employees' interests or views. There has been no spontaneous emergence of an alternative model of employee representation that could channel and attenuate conflicts between employers and employees' (Millward 1994: 133).

The latest evidence from WERS 1998 is in line with the earlier picture. According to Cully et al. (1999) only a small minority of UK establishments (14%) could claim to have a coherent approach to HRM. 'Direct supervision of employees was the common mode used to control and monitor the work of individual employees, and while 54 per cent of workplaces made individual employees responsible for monitoring the quality of their own work, less than 1 per cent of workplaces used this as the sole means of monitoring quality' (Cully et al. 1999: 295).

Referring to high-commitment management practices, they found that information on financial performance was rarely disclosed to employees (especially in the private sector) and little if any evidence of the devolution of authority from senior management to line managers in respect of recruitment, pay and dismissals. 'For most employers, it might be best to characterize their approach as one of retaining control and doing what they could to contain costs' (Cully et al. 1999: 295). Guest et al. (2000a) reported that only one in four UK companies had implemented 'more than half' the list of 18 'typical' HRM practices that might signify a coherent and strategic approach. Lifting the criteria to three-quarters (12 practices), they found that only one in 100 companies met the test.

Nor is it the case that HRM has been most prevalent in non-unionized establishments. The analysis of WIRS 1990 suggested that the advance of HRM in the second half of the 1980s was most significant in unionized establishments. 'The arrangements at workplace level which managements had put in place to consult, communicate with and inform employees were more widespread and highly developed in unionized workplaces than in the non-union sector' (Millward 1994: 129). Nearly a decade later, as WERS 1998 reveals, the positive association between union voice and high-commitment management practices remained intact.

The fact that the overwhelming majority of UK-based organizations do not practise HRM in a systematic way is all the more puzzling, because the research evidence points to significant performance returns to those that do. On the basis of a survey of 610 human resource managers, Guest et al. (2000a), for example, found that productivity and financial performance had been lifted by a 'high use of HRM practices'. The 'consultative climate' and level of employee involvement emerged as key determining factors. Following Huselid (1995), Guest and his colleagues link the performance gains to the application of systems of practices (HRM bundles) that are mutually reinforcing and nested in appropriate institutional support mechanisms. Enhanced training opportunities, supported by employee performance appraisals and an effective personnel department, are thus more likely to yield gains than if measures are merely implemented in a piecemeal, unco-ordinated fashion. Hoque (1999) derived similar conclusions from a study of 209 hotels in the UK with 25 or more employees.

However, in a follow-up investigation of questionnaire returns from 237 matched pairs of chief executive officers (CEOs) and HR managers, Guest et al. found that, while the HR managers highlighted the benefits of HR practices for performance, the CEOs were more circumspect. 'The analysis shows no association of any sort between the adoption of human resource practices . . . and the outcomes reported by the CEOs' (Guest et al. 2000a: 37). Interpreting these conflicting responses, Guest et al. suggest that HR managers have a more 'hands-on' knowledge of the 'implementation, value and success of HR practices, whereas the CEOs merely see the outcomes and not the processes behind them'.

As noted, the application of HRM practices has been more common in establishments in which there is also a union presence. Does the coexistence of unionism and HRM have any specific performance implications? McNabb and Whitfield (1997) examined this question using WIRS 1990 data, and found that union presence, job flexibility and teamworking together were linked to positive gains in financial performance, but that the union effect alone was negative. One possible explanation, according to Edwards and Wright, 'is that job flexibility and teams are indicative of a more consensual bargaining relationship, which promotes improved financial outcomes' (Edwards and Wright 2001: 578). Another is that the complex nature of the relationships involved cannot be interrogated with sufficient precision with the available survey data.

Ramsay et al. (2000) take a different tack. Taking as their focus three competing perspectives (high-commitment management, high-involvement management and the labour process model), their study found that all three approaches failed their empirical tests. Using WERS 1998, Ramsay et al. revealed that a composite measure of high-performance work practices (profit-related pay, employee share ownership, consultation, TQM, team autonomy and job control) delivered positive gains. Other HRM measures, including employee/union representation, consultation committees, family-friendly policies, grievance procedures, appraisals and formal training, were, however, either unrelated to performance or had a negative performance effect, as, for example, in the cases of turnover and product quality.

Against the findings of Guest et al., Ramsay and his colleagues were unable to find any evidence that the application of high-performance work systems had induced a radical shift in 'hearts and minds', thus calling into question the presumed mediating role of employee attitudes. 'This most significant finding', they argue, 'calls into question the unitarist assumption, which underlies much mainstream theory, that everyone benefits from managerial innovation' (Ramsay et al. 2000: 521). Of particular interest is their failure to derive support for the labour process model. The idea that gains for management always come at the expense of employees as a consequence of the degradation of work – surely the view of only a small minority of labour process writers? – is contradicted by their results, which show a far more complex set of relationships between, for example, increased autonomy and discretion, insecurity, intensification and job strain. There are no clear unilinear causal links.

Like other researchers on this topic, Ramsay et al. question the underlying theoretical and methodological bases for the strong assumptions and claims made in the management literature on HRM and performance. According to Wood, there is so much variation in the (theoretical and empirical) methods used that it is difficult to reach any firm conclusions (Wood 1999: 403). The above brief review of studies raises three salient issues: how is the problem of reciprocal causation to be addressed, what alternative theories and concepts might better motivate the study of the complex patterns of conflict and accommodation in the workplace, and why is the evidence of HRM in practice so limited?

On the first point, it is clear that the arrow of causality postulated by Guest et al., for example, could be reversed. Superior firm performance may allow for a more extensive application of HRM practices and the elaboration of appropriate institutional supports (Edwards and Wright 2001). Ramsay et al. address the second issue head on, and conclude that more complex theoretical models are required. They may be right in rejecting the empirical implications of a 'reduced form' labour process perspective, but more developed models embracing the contradictions inherent in any management labour control strategy may well perform better under empirical investigation. Edwards and Wright (2001) argue that HRM may be a contemporary means to ends which at other times can be secured through other means. The third point, perhaps the most crucial of all, redirects attention to the wider institutional and economic context, including the 'light touch' regulatory framework, that allows UK companies to continue to muddle along with respect to the management of people.

Conclusion

This chapter has highlighted the main critical fault-lines in the long-running debate about the impact of the management of the employment relationship on productivity and other performance measures. Several issues have emerged. Too often unions have been ripped from their social context and treated as an exogenous determinant of productivity. Too often the evidence adduced in support of the argument that unions have been a prime cause of under-performance depended on the subjective perceptions of management – scarcely a disinterested party. And too often the evidence was found to be insensitive, theoretically and empirically, to the forces of competition. How is it that isolated, decentralized, plant-based work-groups can impede the advance of management, technology, indeed the whole economy not merely over five or ten years, but, according to some writers, over the course of a century? With union coverage rarely exceeding more than 50 per cent of the workforce in the twentieth century, why did the forces of competition fail to erode the effects of unionism?

Part of the answer must lie in the exaggerated accounts of the unions' 'blocking power'. For the post-war period, it is difficult to find any persuasive evidence that supports the view that management was severely hamstrung in its attempts to modernize. The evidence suggests, on the contrary, that all too often management did not try to innovate. Even in the strike-torn car industry of the 1960s, which had a profound influence on the Donovan Commission, the evidence points to the output-restricting strategies of management (see chapter 2). Difficult to quantify and model within a regression equation maybe, but this sort of rich qualitative evidence should not be disregarded.

In the 1970s, the years in which union power and influence allegedly reached their high point, the wages of British workers continued to fall in relative terms.

International comparisons reveal that Britain became a centre for low-cost labour, and for the provision of goods and services in which labour-intensive, low-productivity methods predominated. Britain's specialized position within the international division of labour has proved remarkably difficult to dislodge (see chapter 3). Despite the heightened speculation in the 1980s that the new policy stance of governments towards industrial relations had induced a major advance in performance, the evidence failed to confirm a clear structural trend break from the past. The aggregate evidence shows that the relative position of manufacturing, a key litmus test of relative performance, continued to deteriorate.

Would the wider application of human resource management practices assist in lifting the average performance of UK-based organizations? The evidence is evidently mixed. Some studies, notably Guest et al. (2000a and 2000b), suggest that there are considerable performance benefits to be won, but 'British industry has not yet embraced human resource management with any great enthusiasm' (2000a: 4). The implication is that if more companies followed the example set by those organizations that have implemented progressive human resource practices the stubborn and widening performance differential between the UK and other leading economies could be closed. But there remain many grounds for caution. There is still no uncontested theory of HRM that clearly specifies the reasons why management innovation should produce common benefits across organizations. What are the relevant transmission mechanisms and why is the evidence so uneven, with some studies showing positive gains and others revealing no evident benefits?

The present government, as noted, has set its sights on lifting the productivity of paid employment and closing the gap between Britain and other advanced economies. The foregoing analysis has highlighted the scale of the task it is facing. It has pointed to several long-standing features of the domestic economy that continue to inhibit attempts to break out of the vicious circle of decline that characterized the second half of the twentieth century. The relatively low levels of investment in plant, people and technology, the persistence of sloppy management systems, and the limited scope and effectiveness of governance arrangements to permit workers a voice in a majority of British workplaces point to continuing difficulties ahead.

References

Addison, J., and Belfield, C. 2001: Updating the determinants of firm performance: estimation using the 1998 UK workplace employee relations survey, *British Journal of Industrial Relations*, 39 (3), 341–66.

Alford, B. W. E. 1988: *British Economic Performance 1945–1975*. London: Macmillan.

Braverman, H. 1974: *Labor and Monopoly Capital: The Degradation of Work in the Twentieth Century*. London: Monthly Review Press.

Bruno, M. 1984: Raw materials, profits and the productivity slowdown, *Quarterly Journal of Economics*, 99 (1), 1–30.

Caves, R. E. 1980: Productivity differences among industries. In R. E. Caves and L. B. Krause (eds), *Britain's Economic Performance*. Washington, DC: Brookings Institution.

Chandler, A. 1966: *Strategy and Structure*. New York: Anchor Books.

Channon, D. 1973: *The Strategy and Structure of British Enterprise*. London: Macmillan.

Clark, I. 2000: *Governance, the State, Regulation and Industrial Relations*, London: Routledge.

Clark, K. 1980a: Unionization and productivity: micro-econometric evidence, *Quarterly Journal of Economics*, 95 (4), 613–39.

Clark, K. 1980b: The impact of unionization on productivity: a case study, *Industrial and Labor Relations Review*, 33 (4), 451–69.

Clegg, H. A. 1964: Restrictive practices, *Socialist Commentary*. Cited in *Productivity Bargaining and Restrictive Labour Practices*, Research Paper 4, Royal Commission on Trade Unions and Employers' Associations. London: HMSO, 1968.

Coates, D. 1994: *The Question of UK Decline: The Economy, State and Society*. Brighton: Harvester Wheatsheaf.

Crafts, N. 1988: British economic growth over the long run, *Oxford Review of Economic Policy*, 4 (1), pp. i–xxi.

Crafts, N. 1991: Reversing relative economic decline? The 1980s in historical perspective, *Oxford Review of Economic Policy*, 7 (3), 51–98.

Cully, M., Woodland, S., O'Reilly, A. and Dix, G. 1999: *Britain at Work*. London: Routledge.

Edwards, P., and Wright, M. 2001: High-involvement work systems and performance outcomes: the strength of variable, contingent and context-bound relationships, *International Journal of Human Resource Management*, 12 (4), 568–85.

Edwards, P. K. 1983: The pattern of collective industrial action. In G. S. Bain (ed.), *Industrial Relations in Britain*. Oxford: Blackwell.

Fernie, S., and Metcalf, D. 1995: Participation, contingent pay, representation and workplace performance: evidence from Great Britain, *British Journal of Industrial Relations*, 33 (3), 379–415.

Fingleton, E. 1999: *In Praise of Hard Industries: Why Manufacturing, Not the New Economy, is the Key to Future Prosperity*. London: Buttonwood Press.

Freeman, R. B., and Medoff, J. L. 1984: *What Do Unions Do?* New York: Basic Books.

Friedman, A. 1977: *Industry and Labour: Class Struggle at Work and Monopoly Capitalism*. London: Macmillan.

Grant, W. 1991: Government and manufacturing industry. In G. Jones and M. Kirby (eds), *Competitiveness and the State*. Manchester: Manchester University Press.

Guest, D., Michie, J., Sheehan, M., Conway, N. and Metochi, M. 2000a: *Human Resource Management and Performance: First Findings from the Future Of Work Study*. Birkbeck College, University of London, School of Management and Organizational Psychology.

Guest, D., Michie, J., Sheehan, M. and Conway, N. 2000b: *Getting Inside the HRM-Performance Relationship*. ESRC Future of Work Working Paper 8. University of Leeds.

Hannah, L. 1983: *The Rise of the Corporate Economy: The British Experience*. Baltimore: Johns Hopkins University Press.

Hayek, F. 1980: *Unemployment and the Unions*. London: Institute of Economic Affairs.

Hoque, K. 1999: Human resource management and performance in the UK hotel industry, *British Journal of Industrial Relations*, 37 (3), 419–43.

Huselid, M. A. 1995: The impact of human resource management practices on turnover, productivity, and corporate financial performance, *Academy of Management Journal*, 38 (4), 635–73.

Kilpatrick, A. and Lawson, T. 1980: On the nature of industrial decline in the UK, *Cambridge Journal of Economics*, 4 (1), 85–102.

Lazonick, W. 1991: *Business Organization and the Myth of the Market Economy*. Cambridge: Cambridge University Press.

Machin, S., and Stewart, M. B. 1996: Trade unions and financial performance, *Oxford Economic Papers*, 48 (2), 213–41.

Machin, S., and Wadhwani, S. 1991: The effects of unions on organisational change and employment, *Economic Journal*, 101 (3), 835–54.

Mackay. D., Boddy, D., Brack, J., Diack, J. and Jones, N. 1971: *Labour Markets under Different Employment Conditions*. London: Allen & Unwin.

Maynard, G. 1988: *The Economy Under Mrs Thatcher*. Oxford: Blackwell.

McNabb, R., and Whitfield, K. 1997: Unions, flexibility, team working and financial performance, *Organisation Studies*, 18 (5), 821–38.

McNulty, P. J. 1980: *The Origins and Development of Labor Economics*. Cambridge, Mass.: MIT Press.

Metcalf, D. 1989a: Trade unions and economic performance: the British evidence, *LSE Quarterly*, 3, 21–42.

Metcalf, D. 1989b: Water notes dry up: the impact of the Donovan reform proposals and Thatcherism at work on labour productivity in British manufacturing industry, *British Journal of Industrial Relations*, 27 (1), 1–31.

Millward, N. 1994: *The New Industrial Relations*. London: Policy Studies Institute.

Muellbauer, J. 1986: Productivity and competitiveness in British manufacturing, *Oxford Review of Economic Policy*, 2 (3), 1–25.

Nichols, T. 1986: *The British Worker Question: A New Look at Workers and Productivity in Manufacturing*. London: Routledge & Kegan Paul.

Nickell, S., Wadhwani, S. and Wall, M. 1989: *Unions and Productivity Growth in Britain 1974–86: Evidence from Company Accounts Data*. Centre for Labour Economics Discussion Paper 353, August. London School of Economics.

Nolan, P. 1989: The productivity miracle? In F. Green (ed.), *The Restructuring of the UK Economy*. Brighton: Harvester.

Nolan, P. 1996: Industrial relations and performance since 1945. In I. Beardwell (ed.), *Contemporary Industrial Relations: A Critical Analysis*. Oxford: Oxford University Press.

Nolan, P., and Marginson, P. 1990: Skating on thin ice? David Metcalf on trade unions and productivity, *British Journal of Industrial Relations*, 28 (2), 227–47.

Oulton, N., and O'Mahoney, M. 1994: *Productivity and Growth: A Study of British Industry, 1954–86*. Cambridge: Cambridge University Press.

Palloix, C. 1976: The labour process: from Fordism to neo-Fordism. In *The Labour Process and Class Strategies*, Conference of Socialist Economists Pamphlet 1. London: Stage 1.

Prais, S. J. 1981: *Productivity and Industrial Structure*. Cambridge: Cambridge University Press.

Pratten, C. F. 1976: *Labour Productivity Differentials within International Companies*. Cambridge: Cambridge University Press.

Ramsay, H., Scholarios, D. and Harley, B. 2000: Employees and high performance work systems: testing inside the black box, *British Journal of Industrial Relations*, 38 (4), 501–31.

Scarpetta, S., Bassanoni, A., Pilat, D. and Schreyer, P. 2000: *Economic Growth in the OECD Area: Recent Trends at Aggregate and Sectoral Level*. OECD Economics Department Working Paper 248.

Sisson, K. 1993: In search of HRM, *British Journal of Industrial Relations*, 31 (2), 201–10.

Tolliday, S. n.d: High tide and after: Coventry engineering workers and shopfloor bargaining, 1945–80. In B. Lancaster and T. Mason (eds), *Life and Labour in a 20th Century City: The Experience of Coventry*. Coventry: Cryfield Press.

Tomlinson, J. 1991: A missed opportunity? Labour and the productivity problem, 1945–51. In G. Jones and M. Kirby (eds), *Competitiveness and the State*. Manchester: Manchester University Press.

Turner, H. A., Clack, G. and Roberts, G. 1967: *Labour Relations in the Motor Industry: A Study of Industrial Unrest and an International Comparison.* London: George Allen & Unwin.

Wadhwani, S. 1990: The effects of unions on productivity growth, investment and employment: a report on some recent work, *British Journal of Industrial Relations,* 28 (3), 371–85.

Wood, S. 1999: Human resource management and performance, *International Journal of Management Reviews,* 1 (4), 367–413.

Wood, S., and de Menezes, L. 1998: High commitment management in the UK: evidence from the Workplace Industrial Relations Survey and Employers' Manpower and Skills Practices Survey, *Human Relations,* 51 (4), 485–515.

20
CONCLUDING COMMENTS

PAUL EDWARDS

The purpose of these final comments is not to offer a comprehensive overview, for each chapter has indicated its own conclusions. A point running through several chapters, moreover, is that developments are open-ended and uncertain, so that any conclusion in the sense of a definitive closure would not only be presumptuous but also impose a false unity on mixed developments. Individual chapters also offer different emphases, so that what follows would not necessarily be accepted by all the contributors to this book. The purpose here is to highlight in summary form the different forces affecting British industrial relations and the different directions which might then be taken.

Running through the book is the theme of mixed approaches deriving from 'European' and 'American' models. As noted in chapter 4, for example, the British system of industrial relations has been particularly open to change, for two reasons. First, the long-standing voluntarist arrangements analysed in chapters 2 and 5 meant that Britain never had a strongly institutionalized system. Two possible bases of such a system, regulation by the state and co-ordination through multi-employer collective bargaining, were weak. Extensive deregulation and the continuing decline of multi-employer bargaining during the 1980s further weakened such structures as did exist. Second, Britain has been particularly open to influences from overseas (see also chapter 3). Yet, in this writer's view, this very openness is one reason why a single path of development cannot be discerned: there are many currents pressing in different directions. Another reason is that institutions, even those in the British environment, have historical legacies which are hard to change. This 'stickiness' is often remarked in relation to pay structures, for, as chapters 8 and 11 demonstrate, there are important elements of continuity in the private and the public sectors despite conditions that might have been expected to lead to rapid transformation. Reasons for stickiness include matters of *will* such as conscious resistance to change, but also the fact that change can be a leap in the dark, so that incremental development is sometimes preferred. Then there are issues of *ability*: organizations may lack the skills and experience to pursue developments that they might in principle welcome. Change in industrial relations is thus often more uncertain and tentative than might be expected.

If we begin with the benchmark of a European social model – embracing partnership between the institutions of capital and labour and workplace flexibility with the pursuit of new forms of work organization – we can identify some forces that promote such a model. They include broad economic and political developments around the single European market and specific mechanisms, notably the requirement to establish national-level systems for employee information and consultation (see chapter 6). At company level, partnership agendas have also developed (see chapters 9 and 10). Yet the evidence indicates that such a model is more a potential than a reality.

- Though the government offers rhetorical support to the concept of partnership, formal co-ordination at national level remains largely absent. As chapter 5 concludes, social partnership in this sense is not practised – an absence which is as true of the post-1997 governments as it was of their predecessors. Social dialogue at national or sector levels is not promoted.
- Managerial labour relations strategies in the UK are a mix of different elements in which a European social agenda remains a small part (chapter 7). Collective bargaining has certainly been shaped by the external competitive environment, but any comparative pressure has turned on unit labour costs rather than on pay rates or collective bargaining structures (chapter 8). It is argued in chapter 12 that a fundamental pressure is towards cost minimization rather than a longer-term development of skills and employee involvement.
- The evidence on the concrete practice of labour relations reinforces this picture from the level of strategy. Partnership agendas are still rare, and the extent to which they are based on genuine partnership, as opposed to a more limited bargaining of a degree of job security in return for flexibility, and are capable of surviving economic downturns, remains hotly contested (chapters 9 and 10). The take-up of high-involvement work practices is limited, as is the commitment to training and development (chapters 13 and 15). The productivity and labour cost evidence suggests that Britain has not shifted onto a path of high productivity (chapters 3 and 19).

This is not, however, to argue that nothing has changed. Change and restructuring have been central features of workplace developments, to such a degree that 'initiative overload' has become an issue in the public sector (see chapter 11) as much as in the private. What remains unclear is the degree to which such turbulence is leading to any single path of development, or a few recognizable paths. When the predecessor to this book was published in 1995, the general picture was one of promise unfulfilled. Research at the time identified Total Quality Management as 'another missed opportunity' for British firms (Wilkinson et al. 1992). It was also shown that developments such as performance-related pay were not leading to a clear pattern of individualized employment relations, if such a pattern means empowered individual employees making their own contracts with employers and being rewarded according to clear and fair stand-ards of performance (see Kessler 2000). This picture remains broadly accurate, though more recent research has been able to refine the analysis. In terms of the models laid out in chapter 12, it is possible to indicate the conditions under which workplace reforms can benefit employees as well as employers. As shown in chapter 13, the outcome of these conditions is only very rarely 'empower-ment' in any exact sense (and it may be useful for the reader to review what such an exact sense might be and why empowerment is rarely the goal and so hard to attain even when it is the goal), but employee autonomy and job commitment can increase where workplace change is managed on the basis of job security, has an affinity with previous forms of work organization, and occurs in a context where it is not undermined by short-term financial pressures and thus has the time and space to become established. Workplace change pro-grammes do not necessarily either empower workers or intensify exploitation.

Evidence available since the completion of the bulk of this book develops this picture. The Skills Survey, conducted in 2001, covers a representative sample of the workforce and it allows systematic comparison with several previous surveys back to 1986 (Felstead et al. 2002). The picture is one of a clear growth in skill, as measured by a battery of indices including formal qualifications, time taken to learn a job and self-reported skill, together with a reduction in the skills gap between men and women. Yet alongside these trends there has been a clear reduction in the autonomy enjoyed by workers. 'There has been a marked decline in task discretion' which occurred among men and women and was particularly marked in professional jobs (Felstead et al. 2002: 13). This can be explained in part by a growth in the number of measures of performance – what the survey terms 'external sources of control' – to which employees (managers and routine employees alike) are subject (see also Green 2001). Taken together with qualitative evidence, the position is one of increasing skill in the sense of technical abilities being practised under a regime of performance control and monitoring (Edwards 2001a).

What as yet remains unclear is how this balance of skill and control works through in terms of outcomes for firms and workers. The most 'optimistic' model is one of a workforce operating to agreed objectives with benefits to both parties. Less optimistically, there may be a position of resigned, pragmatic accept-ance of performance targets. Third, the targets may be resented, with morale suffering as a result. The first model might apply to those cases where change has been implemented with a degree of success, reflecting conditions discussed above. The third would characterize, for example, some parts of the public sector where, as shown in chapter 11, increasing pressures to meet new and changing targets have been common. Yet too neat a picture would be misleading. First, in any one context (a school or a hospital, for example) there are likely to be employees who have different responses to change. Second, responses can fluctuate, perhaps most obviously when the market conditions facing an organ-ization shift.

As chapter 19 shows, factors such as these undermine any straightforward view that a given set of employee relations practices has identifiable outcomes in terms of organizational performance. Core facts include the rarity of any extensive set of 'high-commitment' practices, the widespread evidence that there is no set of universal applicability (with different approaches working in different circumstances), and the difficulty, noted in many studies, of showing that there is a clear causal chain running from the practices through employee behaviour to outcomes. There is also the particularly troubling issue that influences may run in the other direction, that is, that it is 'successful' firms that can afford high-commitment practices, rather than the practices directly causing the success.

This is not, however, to conclude that industrial relations are unimportant for outcomes. Treating outcomes narrowly in terms of economic performance, it is true that particular sets of practices do not have universal effects, but it is also true that under certain circumstances such practices may be more successful. More fundamentally, though there is no formula for 'success', there are many aspects of the management of employees which can make 'failure' more likely; 'good management' may not guarantee success, but 'bad management' can make failure much more likely. This book has pointed to numerous issues which have not been handled in a coherent way, with the problem of mixed messages being a continuing one. More fundamentally still, industrial relations is about fairness and justice as much as it is about economic performance. The way in which an outcome is generated can be as important as the outcome itself.

A further element of variety emerges from the fact that several significant influences are only just beginning to be felt. Statutory trade union recognition procedures remain very recent. The impetus from legislation on national information and consultation structures is evidently a further possibility which could in principle profoundly alter the traditional voluntarist and single-channel UK system analysed in chapter 2. As shown in chapter 6, it is clear that the British system is no longer voluntarist, but the concrete implications of a more juridified system remain open to debate. As the chapter argues, the model of the employment relationship embedded in the recognition legislation is not one in which collective employee voice expressed through a trade union is taken as a core principle. Wide scope is left to employers to determine the issues on which they bargain with unions.

If a European social model is a reasonably clear benchmark, an American (i.e. United States) model is less clear than it might seem. Does it mean a *national* model of minimal legislation to control employer prerogative, in which case what can be said of a legal regime which has been in many ways more intrusive than the British (e.g. laws on union recognition since 1937 and a federal minimum wage since 1938)? The fact that Britain has laws on these matters reflects some parallels with the US, but the nature of the two countries' labour law systems means that convergence on American practice is unlikely. Or does it mean a model of *employers* who oppose unions, which model then raises issues as to the reasons for such employer behaviour and the exceptions to the model? With the decline of trade unions in the UK, an employer-led agenda has been strengthened, though without necessarily leading to specific US practices. What might comprise the American national business system is also in dispute, for some features of Britain which are held to promote a lack of competitiveness (notably 'short-termism') also characterize the US and yet have not prevented the country from maintaining its productivity lead over the UK (see chapter 19). In these respects, the US production system based on standardization remains very different from that of the UK. In terms specifically of the labour relations regime, the key characteristic of the US system is the extreme decentralization of collective bargaining, which is associated with the absence of any kind of national-level quasi-corporatist structures (see chapter 5). In this respect, the UK system can be said to be becoming Americanized (see chapter 8).

A less remarked but at least as important parallel lies in equal opportunities and diversity agendas, for in the US, as in the UK, the law has established rights to equal pay, and in some respects the American legislation was in advance of the British. In terms of outcomes, too, the two regimes have important features in common, notably a rise in income inequality which is faster than in many other countries and which is widely linked to the weakening of collective bargaining in both (see table 17.1 and related discussion). It is tempting to argue that underlying such trends is the development of individualism; in some versions of the argument, collective trade union loyalties are eroded and are replaced either by some 'post-modern' pursuit of individuality or by a much more 'modern' and calculative approach in terms of the 'psychological contract'. It would be far too extreme to suggest, however, that collective ideals have been abandoned or that they have been replaced by a coherent alternative. As discussed in chapters 12 and 14, individualism is an uncertain concept which can often be entwined with collective norms. Chapter 14 shows that the erosion of certain collective mechanisms is not synonymous with the emergence of a clear individual model, that 'individualized' labour relations differ between each other, and that some of the outcomes claimed to be associated with individualism, such as increased manager–worker trust, are often absent. Yet the language of the (individual) psychological contract is now commonplace. It is not the case that a clear-cut model is in place, and to claim that the employment relationship is now managed through such a contract is to confuse rhetoric and reality. But the prevalence of the language suggests that one set of forces, based on unitarist assumptions, is reshaping assumptions as to how to handle employment relationships. Managers may be more prone than they were to assume that managerial and employee interests can be aligned and less likely to perceive that there may be fundamentally different agendas. In the field of training, for example, employees may have views as to the most useful types of training which differ from those of managers, and may also wish to question the adequacy of existing provision and to police managerial promises. Managers who adopt the language of individualism may find it hard to grasp such points. Individualism is certainly not a coherent philosophy or practice, but its presence is one of the forces reshaping the conduct of the employment relationship.

A question about any process such as Americanization is whether the process entails the direct copying or import of parts of the model, or, rather, a convergence with the model without any direct transfer. As discussed in chapter 4, it is clear that multinational companies have played an important role in three respects: providing specific new forms of work organization in Britain; acting as exemplars for British firms; and, through coercive comparisons and investment decisions, putting pressure on British operations to meet standards of costs and quality (with the high-profile closure of plants owned by General Motors, BMW, and Corus being key cases). Yet this has not necessarily meant any straight-forward process of convergence on any one model. To take the three respects in turn, new forms of work organization have rarely been imported as a complete package of national components, with certain features only being transferred, and with the operation of these features then being subject to 'Anglicization'. In the exemplar role, it has been shown that British firms interpreted other national models in the light of their own experience. And coercive comparisons put pressure on outcomes rather than industrial relations arrangements. Borrowing has also, of course, come from Japan and Europe as well as the US, so that no one model is driving developments in the UK. As chapter 4 concludes, a picture of change without convergence may be the most appropriate.

As well as issues connected with outside influences, there are several developments in the UK itself. Chapter 4 argues that fears of a 'low-road' employment relations strategy driven by MNCs may be misplaced, for it is developments within Britain which may be more significant for such a low-road model. This was a central theme of chapter 12, while chapter 17 indicated the continuing extent of low pay in the UK.

Among other domestic trends, the 1998 WERS painted a picture of substantial decline in the institutions of collective industrial relations, notably with evidence of the very limited extent of consultation by managements with workforce representatives across a wide range of issues. As against this, some writers point to the continuation of strikes and militancy in sectors including banking, the postal services, and railways. The evidence on strikes in particular, reviewed in chapter 9, points to continuing very low levels of strike activity. It can be predicted with some confidence that the number of strikes is unlikely to approach anywhere near the numbers observed during the 1970s, for reasons made clear in the chapter. But numbers of working days 'lost' in strikes depend heavily on a few large disputes. Though unions probably lack the will and ability to organize as many large strikes as occurred up to the mid-1980s, the possibility of the occurrence of some such strikes remains present. Strikes are, in any event, not synonymous with militancy, still less with some kind of collective opposition to managerial policies. The evidence here is far from clear-cut, not least because research aimed at uncovering such opposition is less common than it used to be. But it can be suggested that overt expressions of militancy are becoming less likely as a result of forces including the changing structure of the economy and the decay of a tradition of working-class mobilization, that some instances of militancy are restricted to sectors where workers retain a trade-union-based solidarity and a sense of common identity (and hence that these are to a significant extent special cases), but also that there are sufficient sources of discontent (including long hours, high workloads and pay inequalities) that wider militancy could be resurrected.

The upshot of such reflections is that it is reasonably straightforward to say what the main *issues* facing industrial relations actors are, but much harder to identify the *specific policies and practices* that may emerge as the result of wrestling with the issues. According to Sisson and Storey (2000: 241–53) the issues are three.

- *Balancing flexibility and security*. This means achieving a balance between employers' needs for flexibility and workers' needs for security. Security is taken to embrace employment security, training, and access to information and consultation, with the last being seen as an important right that employees should enjoy. This book has addressed all these themes. In addition, it has identified, notably in relation to equal opportunities, possible tensions between employer flexibility and the flexibility that employees seek in terms of balancing work and other obligations. The work–life balance is likely to be of major significance in the future.
- *Managing individually and collectively*. Sisson and Storey go out of their way to urge companies to use partnership arrangements to strengthen their arrangements for information and consultation, arguing that there is a strong business case for better systems; the intended introduction of legislation on this topic is a further stimulus (Sisson 2002). We have seen that managing individually and collectively are not necessarily opposing methods (chapter 12) and, as noted above, this book has addressed the tensions and uncertainties around a partnership agenda. Chapter 2 highlighted several other opportunities for reform in the past which ultimately failed. The feasibility of developing a new model based on strengthened systems for information and consultation is evidently a strongly contested matter. Yet to underline the problems may be to contribute to making the model less effective. It offers some distinctive merits which could underpin a new British approach which replaces voluntarism and is neither American nor European but an amalgam that fits British histories and traditions.
- *'Integration, integration, integration'*: the linking of various aspects of the management of employees into a coherent whole, and establishing 'fit' with the strategy of the business. In addressing managers, Sisson and Storey place particular emphasis on this theme. But from a broader industrial relations point of view they should not be taken as saying that 'industrial relations strategy' follows business strategy directly, or as implying that a business driven by highly competitive market conditions is thereby condemned to an industrial relations policy of hire and fire and unrelenting discipline. First, business strategy sets the context but does not determine behaviour, and different policies can and do operate in similar conditions. Second, it can reasonably be argued that, whatever the conditions, there are basic standards of fairness which should prevail. Third, business conditions are not static, so that what 'fits' at one time may not fit at another. All that said, however, it is the case (as, for example, the discussion of equal pay issues and the management of industrial relations in small firms has shown) that there are powerful pressures making it hard for firms to sustain a model based on skills and commitment. The key issue is just how hard this will be and the strength of countervailing influences.

If we reconsider the parties to industrial relations identified in figure 1.1, we can suggest the following. The stronger the degree of articulation between the parties, the more sense it makes to identify certain models of development. But, as several chapters have stressed, the parties each follow policies containing inherent tensions, for example the tensions in government policy between market-led and regulatory approaches. And the ties between each set of parties are similarly in tension (e.g. business complaints at excessive regulation from government but also its ability to shape government agendas significantly). Add to this the pressures from an external environment, and it can be said that how the parties will address the three sets of issues given above is bound to be unclear. Yet the fact that they have to face up to them indicates the kinds of concerns that will have to be addressed, and the outcome of the process will determine the future path of industrial relations.

Finally, chapter 1 laid out the value of an 'industrial relations' approach to the study of the employment relationship. The strength of this approach has been illustrated by the substantive chapters in this book, in particular, perhaps, by those chapters which address issues (such as individualism, equal opportunities, work experience, and small firms) which are not part of a conventional industrial relations agenda. The theoretical underpinnings of this approach have also been specified elsewhere (Edwards 2001b). A key feature of this approach is that it gives analytical grounding to discussion, as in these concluding comments, that stresses uncertainty and negotiation. We have seen that there are trends towards centralization *and* decentralization, and towards autonomy *and* control. These trends reflect the inherent tensions in the employment relationship, with antinomies such as individualism and collectivism, and discretion and control, being equally important sides of the relationship, not opposite ends of continua of approaches. The new set of challenges to the conduct of the relationship calls for the continued development of the industrial relations approach. These challenges include a broadening of substantive areas of research (notably, new forms of employment lacking traditional industrial relations structures) and of issues (such as diversity). The challenges are considerable, but the approach has been flexible and innovative in the past, and it has the potential to grow further.

References

Edwards, P. 2001a: *The Puzzles of Work*. ESRC Centre for Skills, Knowledge and Organizational Performance Discussion Paper 16.

Edwards, P. 2001b: 'Industrial relations': from apparently anachronistic to analeptic and anaclastic condition. Paper to workshop on 'Industrial Relations: An Anachronism?' University of Tübingen, June. Available at <http://users.wbs.Warwick.ac.uk/IRRU/publications/conference_papers.htm>.

Green, F. 2001: It's been a hard day's night: the concentration and intensification of work in late twentieth century Britain, *British Journal of Industrial Relations*, 39 (1), 53–80.

Felstead, A., Gallie, D. and Green, F. 2002: *Work Skills in Britain 1986–2001*. Nottingham: DfES Publications.

Kessler, I. 2000: Remuneration systems. In S. Bach and K. Sisson (eds), *Personnel Management*. Oxford: Blackwell.

Sisson, K. 2002: Information and consultation in the UK: unnecessary regulation or a push to partnership? First Pat Lowry Memorial Lecture, University of Warwick, March.

Sisson, K., and Storey, J. 2000: *The Realities of Human Resource Management*. Buckingham: Open University Press.

Wilkinson, A., Marchington, M., Goodman, J. and Ackers, P. 1992: Total Quality Management and employee involvement, *Human Resource Management Journal*, 2 (4), 1–20.

INDEX

References to figures and tables are in **bold**.